READER IN BUREAUCRACY

Reader in
BUREAUCRACY

EDITED BY

ROBERT K. MERTON
AILSA P. GRAY
BARBARA HOCKEY
HANAN C. SELVIN

COLUMBIA UNIVERSITY

THE FREE PRESS, New York
COLLIER-MACMILLAN LIMITED, London

Collier-Macmillan Canada, Ltd., Toronto, Ontario

Second printing July 1967

CONTENTS

Status Systems and Gradations of Prestige

Conflicts of Authority

5. RECRUITMENT AND ADVANCEMENT

INTRODUCTION

The growth of bureaucracy, both public and private, is widely recognized as one of the major social trends of our time. Long before bureaucratization became so pronounced as to be evident to many, it had become a focus of interest to social scientists, who have produced a large literature on the subject. In part, they have been concerned with the sources of bureaucratization, and with its consequences for the life of men in bureaucratized society. In part, and particularly when stimulated by firsthand experience, they have been concerned with the internal workings of bureaucratic organization. There is also, of course, an abundant literature by critics of "bureaucracy," typically conceived by them as a despotic autocracy of civil servants, but since this is notable chiefly for its richness of invective rather than for its contributions to a social science of organization, it needs only passing reference here.

Intended for the convenience of students of organization, this Reader assembles, in easily accessible form, various types of analysis of bureaucracy presently scattered in the literature of social science. It lays no claim to completeness. A "complete" Reader would run to numerous volumes, each of considerable length. It would have to take systematic account of bureaucracy in various times and places during a large fraction of recorded history—from the ancient bureaucracies of China, Egypt and Rome, to the principal varieties of our own day. It would have to treat political, religious, economic, military and educational bureaucracies within each of these historical contexts. And finally, since the study of bureaucracy, like the study of other major forms of social organization, is not the exclusive province of the historian, economist or political scientist, the sociologist or social psychologist, this hypothetically complete Reader would have to include selections on each type of bureaucracy within each historical context from the special standpoint of each of the social sciences.

This Reader has a more limited and more nearly realizable objective. Its scope has been delimited in five respects. First of all, it emphasizes the sociological study of bureaucracy, although it includes examples of the modes of analysis utilized by political scientists and by students of organization in related disciplines. This emphasis has characteristic difficulties, one of which deserves notice here. The student trained in any one of the social sciences finds that the language of the others often seems strange at best, and, at worst, unintelligible. It requires an effort to transcend the limits of one's own specialized vocabulary, an effort not without value in the study of a subject that is variously the concern of practically all the social sciences.

Second, the selections dealing with particular bureaucracies have been limited to American and to West European bureaucracies of the relatively recent past. This is manifestly at the expense of providing material suitable for the comparative study of bureaucracy. But numerous selections in the Reader keep the need for such study before the student, and the appended bibliography affords supplementary references for students who wish to embark upon the cross-cultural analysis of bureaucracy.

Third, it seemed essential that the readings be in depth rather than thinly dispersed over the wide range of bureaucracies in the various institutional sectors of society. Accordingly, the greatest single share of attention is given over to political bureaucracy, with somewhat less attention to economic bureaucracy, and less still to military and religious bureaucracy. However, these are not discussed in isolation; a substantial number of the readings deal with the interrelations between them. And after noting the characteristic routines of organized behavior in bureaucracy, several selections dwell upon the variability of bureaucratic structure so that the student will not assume, too soon and without foundation, that what is found to be true of certain types of bureaucracy is true of them all.

Fourth, it was recognized from the start that both descriptive and analytical materials have their distinctive value, the one being only a prelude to the other. It was not ordinarily practicable, if only because of their length, to include detailed descriptive accounts of particular bureaucracies. As a general rule, therefore, such descriptive materials are only cited in the bibliography, rather than reproduced in full.

Fifth, no effort was made to impose a unity of outlook by selecting only those extracts which are mutually consistent in their definition of problems for analysis and in their interpretations of bureaucratically organized behavior. The study of bureaucracy has not hardened into categories of analysis beyond dispute, nor has it developed a single body of theory that supersedes all others. The diversity of outlook in these readings is believed to reflect the current state of a developing field of inquiry which is beginning to consolidate its findings.

Each section of this volume is prefaced by a brief statement, directing attention to the problems of chief concern in that section. Many papers which we would have wished to include, had space allowed, are cited in the bibliography, which provides a basis for the more intensive study of selected problems. The bibliography attests the rapidly mounting interest of social scientists in bureaucracy and the slower accumulation of empirical researches in this field. Since we must assume that the study of bureaucracy has a future as well as a past, there can be little doubt that, in a few years, new collections of readings on the subject will be needed to draw upon the cumulating empirical researches and theoretical developments that will have appeared in the interval.

In the successive drafts of organization and in the selection of materials, we have been greatly helped by the panel of advisory editors who do not, of course, share responsibility for the deficiencies that remain. We are indebted also to Jeremiah Kaplan, editor of the Free Press, for his encouragement in the preparation of this volume. We are grateful to Miss Mary Woods for her unfailing secretarial help. And as must be true of any compilation of readings, our greatest debt is to the authors and publishers who have granted permission to reproduce their materials, and to those scholars who have contributed articles written specifically for this volume.

R.K.M.   H.C.S.

B.H.   A.P.G.

READER IN BUREAUCRACY

BUREAUCRACY:
THEORETICAL CONCEPTIONS

It would be premature to refer to "the theory of bureaucracy," as though there existed a single, well-defined conceptual scheme adequate for understanding this form of organization. Nevertheless, categories for description and analysis, and empirical generalizations connecting these categories have been developed, and these prove helpful in analyzing the structure of bureaucracy, the conditions of its growth and decline, the sources of intra-bureaucratic conflict, the relations of bureaucracy with its social and political environment, and the connections between bureaucratic structure and the social and personal characteristics of the bureaucrat. Each of these special problems is treated theoretically and empirically in a later section of this volume. This first section is somewhat more comprehensive in scope, consisting of a general theoretical formulation of the nature of bureaucracy, three sharply focussed commentaries on one or another part of this formulation, and a critical review of bureaucratic theory current among students of administration.

Beyond all others, Max Weber may be regarded as the founder of the systematic study of bureaucracy. Certainly, as many of the papers in later sections make evident, his formulations have been the fountainhead for much theoretical and empirical inquiry into bureaucracy. The opening selection from his work is a compact statement of his theoretic framework for the study of the components, structure and functions of bureaucracy. This discussion locates the "purely bureaucratic type of administrative organization," as distinct from other types such as the "patrimonial bureaucracy," within the broader setting of a theory of legal authority, and emphasizes the basic similarity of structure and process found in bureaucratic organization in the otherwise disparate spheres of church and state, army, political party and economic enterprise—in short, in a wide range of public and private administrative organizations.

The three papers following are focussed on one or another of Weber's formulations. Weber's application of the concept of "ideal type" to his analysis of bureaucracy is subjected to a critical appraisal by Friedrich.

Among the best-known of Weber's generalizations is that which holds that the bureaucratic machine will ordinarily continue to operate essentially unchanged even in the face of revolutionary changes in the society. On the basis of case materials dealing with the transformation of bureaucracies during the National Socialist regime, Burin demonstrates that Weber's hypothesis involved an over-estimate of the political importance of the technical knowledge possessed by the bureaucratic expert. And Gouldner draws upon recent studies of industrial organization to re-examine Weber's characterization of bureaucracy, particularly the "norm of impersonality."

Supplementing these discussions of Weberian theory is Simon's critical review of bureaucratic theory current among students of administration, designed to clarify some of the major concepts presently employed in the study of bureaucracy.

THE ESSENTIALS OF BUREAUCRATIC ORGANIZATION: AN IDEAL-TYPE CONSTRUCTION

Max Weber

The effectiveness of legal authority rests on the acceptance of the validity of the following mutually inter-dependent ideas.

1. That any given legal norm may be established by agreement or by imposition, on grounds of expediency or rational values or both, with a claim to obedience at least on the part of the members of the corporate group. This is, however, usually extended to include all persons within the sphere of authority or of power in question—which in the case of territorial bodies is the territorial area—who stand in certain social relationships or carry out forms of social action which in the order governing the corporate group have been declared to be relevant.

2. That every body of law consists essentially in a consistent system of abstract rules which have normally been intentionally established. Furthermore, administration of law is held to consist in the application of these rules to particular cases; the administrative process is the rational pursuit of the interests which are specified in the order governing the corporate group within the limits laid down by legal precepts and following principles which

Reprinted from *The Theory of Social and Economic Organization* (Trans. A. M. Henderson and Talcott Parsons, ed. Talcott Parsons), pp. 329-340, by permission of the publisher. (Copyright, 1947, by the Oxford University Press.)

are capable of generalized formulation and are approved in the order governing the group, or at least not disapproved in it.

3. That thus the typical person in authority occupies an "office." In the action associated with his status, including the commands he issues to others, he is subject to an impersonal order to which his actions are oriented. This is true not only for persons exercising legal authority who are in the usual sense "officials," but, for instance, for the elected president of a state.

4. That the person who obeys authority does so, as it is usually stated, only in his capacity as a "member" of the corporate group and what he obeys is only "the law." He may in this connexion be the member of an association, of a territorial commune, of a church, or a citizen of a state.

5. In conformity with point 3, it is held that the members of the corporate group, in so far as they obey a person in authority, do not owe this obedience to him as an individual, but to the impersonal order. Hence, it follows that there is an obligation to obedience only within the sphere of the rationally delimited authority which, in terms of the order, has been conferred upon him.

The following may thus be said to be the fundamental categories of rational legal authority:—

(1) A continuous organization of official functions bound by rules.

(2) A specified sphere of competence. This involves (a) a sphere of obligations to perform functions which has been marked off as part of a systematic division of labour. (b) The provision of the incumbent with the necessary authority to carry out these functions. (c) That the necessary means of compulsion are clearly defined and their use is subject to definite conditions. A unit exercising authority which is organized in this way will be called an "administrative organ."

There are administrative organs in this sense in large-scale private organizations, in parties and armies, as well as in the state and the church. An elected president, a cabinet of ministers, or a body of elected representatives also in this sense constitute administrative organs. This is not, however, the place to discuss these concepts. Not every administrative organ is provided with compulsory powers. But this distinction is not important for present purposes.

(3) The organization of offices follows the principle of hierarchy; that is, each lower office is under the control and supervision of a higher one. There is a right of appeal and of statement of grievances from the lower to the higher. Hierarchies differ in respect to whether and in what cases complaints can lead to a ruling from an authority at various points higher in the scale, and as to whether changes are imposed from higher up or the responsibility for such changes is left to the lower office, the conduct of which was the subject of complaint.

(4) The rules which regulate the conduct of an office may be technical

rules or norms.[1] In both cases, if their application is to be fully rational, specialized training is necessary. It is thus normally true that only a person who has demonstrated an adequate technical training is qualified to be a member of the administrative staff of such an organized group, and hence only such persons are eligible for appointment to official positions. The administrative staff of a rational corporate group thus typically consists of "officials," whether the organization be devoted to political, religious, economic—in particular, capitalistic—or other ends.

(5) In the rational type it is a matter of principle that the members of the administrative staff should be completely separated from ownership of the means of production or administration. Officials, employees, and workers attached to the administrative staff do not themselves own the non-human means of production and administration. These are rather provided for their use in kind or in money, and the official is obligated to render an accounting of their use. There exists, furthermore, in principle complete separation of the property belonging to the organization, which is controlled within the sphere of office, and the personal property of the official, which is available for his own private uses. There is a corresponding separation of the place in which official functions are carried out, the "office" in the sense of premises, from living quarters.

(6) In the rational type case, there is also a complete absence of appropriation of his official position by the incumbent. Where "rights" to an office exist, as in the case of judges, and recently of an increasing proportion of officials and even of workers, they do not normally serve the purpose of appropriation by the official, but of securing the purely objective and independent character of the conduct of the office so that it is oriented only to the relevant norms.

(7) Administrative acts, decisions, and rules are formulated and recorded in writing, even in cases where oral discussion is the rule or is even mandatory. This applies at least to preliminary discussions and proposals, to final decisions, and to all sorts of orders and rules. The combination of written documents and a continuous organization of official functions constitutes the "office" [2] which is the central focus of all types of modern corporate action.

1. Weber does not explain this distinction. By a "technical rule" he probably means a prescribed course of action which is dictated primarily on grounds touching efficiency of the performance of the immediate functions, while by "norms" he probably means rules which limit conduct on grounds other than those of efficiency. Of course, in one sense all rules are norms in that they are prescriptions for conduct, conformity with which is problematical.—Ed. [Parsons.]

2. *Bureau.* It has seemed necessary to use the English word "office" in three different meanings, which are distinguished in Weber's discussion by at least two terms. The first is *Amt,* which means "office" in the sense of the institutionally defined status of a person. The second is the "work premises" as in the expression "he spent the afternoon in his office." For this Weber uses *Bureau* as also for the third meaning which he has just defined, the "organized work process of a group." In this last sense an office is a particular type of "organization," or *Betrieb* in Weber's sense. This use is established in English

(8) Legal authority can be exercised in a wide variety of different forms which will be distinguished and discussed later. The following analysis will be deliberately confined for the most part to the aspect of imperative co-ordination in the structure of the administrative staff. It will consist in an analysis in terms of ideal types of officialdom or "bureaucracy."

In the above outline no mention has been made of the kind of supreme head appropriate to a system of legal authority. This is a consequence of certain considerations which can only be made entirely understandable at a later stage in the analysis. There are very important types of rational imperative co-ordination which, with respect to the ultimate source of authority, belong to other categories. This is true of the hereditary charismatic type, as illustrated by hereditary monarchy and of the pure charismatic type of a president chosen by plebiscite. Other cases involve rational elements at important points, but are made up of a combination of bureaucratic and charismatic components, as is true of the cabinet form of government. Still others are subject to the authority of the chief of other corporate groups, whether their character be charismatic or bureaucratic; thus the formal head of a government department under a parliamentary regime may be a minister who occupies his position because of his authority in a party. The type of rational, legal administrative staff is capable of application in all kinds of situations and contexts. It is the most important mechanism for the administration of everyday profane affairs. For in that sphere, the exercise of authority and, more broadly, imperative co-ordination, consists precisely in administration.

The purest type of exercise of legal authority is that which employs a bureaucratic administrative staff. Only the supreme chief of the organization occupies his position of authority by virtue of appropriation, of election, or of having been designated for the succession. But even *his* authority consists in a sphere of legal "competence." The whole administrative staff under the supreme authority then consists, in the purest type, of individual officials who are appointed and function according to the following criteria: [3]

(1) They are personally free and subject to authority only with respect to their impersonal official obligations.

(2) They are organized in a clearly defined hierarchy of offices.

(3) Each office has a clearly defined sphere of competence in the legal sense.

(4) The office is filled by a free contractual relationship. Thus, in principle, there is free selection.

(5) Candidates are selected on the basis of technical qualifications. In

in such expressions as "the District Attorney's Office has such and such functions." Which of the three meanings is involved in a given case will generally be clear from the context.—Ed. [Parsons.]

3. This characterization applies to the "monocratic" as opposed to the "collegial" type, which will be discussed below.

the most rational case, this is tested by examination or guaranteed by diplomas certifying technical training, or both. They are *appointed*, not elected.

(6) They are remunerated by fixed salaries in money, for the most part with a right to pensions. Only under certain circumstances does the employing authority, especially in private organizations, have a right to terminate the appointment, but the official is always free to resign. The salary scale is primarily graded according to rank in the hierarchy; but in addition to this criterion, the responsibility of the position and the requirements of the incumbent's social status may be taken into account.

(7) The office is treated as the sole, or at least the primary, occupation of the incumbent.

(8) It constitutes a career. There is a system of "promotion" according to seniority or to achievement, or both. Promotion is dependent on the judgment of superiors.

(9) The official works entirely separated from ownership of the means of administration and without appropriation of his position.

(10) He is subject to strict and systematic discipline and control in the conduct of the office.

This type of organization is in principle applicable with equal facility to a wide variety of different fields. It may be applied in profit-making business or in charitable organizations, or in any number of other types of private enterprises serving ideal or material ends. It is equally applicable to political and to religious organizations. With varying degrees of approximation to a pure type, its historical existence can be demonstrated in all these fields.

1. For example, this type of bureaucracy is found in private clinics, as well as in endowed hospitals or the hospitals maintained by religious orders. Bureaucratic organization has played a major role in the Catholic Church. It is well illustrated by the administrative role of the priesthood in the modern church, which has expropriated almost all of the old church benefices, which were in former days to a large extent subject to private appropriation. It is also illustrated by the conception of the universal Episcopate, which is thought of as formally constituting a universal legal competence in religious matters. Similarly, the doctrine of Papal infallibility is thought of as in fact involving a universal competence, but only one which functions "ex cathedra" in the sphere of the office, thus implying the typical distinction between the sphere of office and that of the private affairs of the incumbent. The same phenomena are found in the large-scale capitalistic enterprise; and the larger it is, the greater their role. And this is not less true of political parties, which will be discussed separately. Finally, the modern army is essentially a bureaucratic organization administered by that peculiar type of military functionary, the "officer."

2. Bureaucratic authority is carried out in its purest form where it is most clearly dominated by the principle of appointment. There is no such

thing as a hierarchy of elected officials in the same sense as there is a hier-archical organization of appointed officials. In the first place, election makes it impossible to attain a stringency of discipline even approaching that in the appointed type. For it is open to a subordinate official to compete for elective honours on the same terms as his superiors, and his prospects are not dependent on the superior's judgment.

3. Appointment by free contract, which makes free selection possible, is essential to modern bureaucracy. Where there is a hierarchical organiza-tion with impersonal spheres of competence, but occupied by unfree officials —like slaves or dependents, who, however, function in a formally bureau-cratic manner—the term "patrimonial bureaucracy" will be used.

4. The role of technical qualifications in bureaucratic organizations is continually increasing. Even an official in a party or a trade-union organiza-tion is in need of specialized knowledge, though it is usually of an empirical character, developed by experience, rather than by formal training. In the modern state, the only "offices" for which no technical qualifications are required are those of ministers and presidents. This only goes to prove that they are "officials" only in a formal sense, and not substantively, as is true of the managing director or president of a large business corporation. There is no question but that the "position" of the capitalistic entrepreneur is as definitely appropriated as is that of a monarch. Thus at the top of a bureau-cratic organization, there is necessarily an element which is at least not purely bureaucratic. The category of bureaucracy is one applying only to the exer-cise of control by means of a particular kind of administrative staff.

5. The bureaucratic official normally receives a fixed salary. By contrast, sources of income which are privately appropriated will be called "benefices." Bureaucratic salaries are also normally paid in money. Though this is not essential to the concept of bureaucracy, it is the arrangement which best fits the pure type. Payments in kind are apt to have the character of benefices, and the receipt of a benefice normally implies the appropriation of oppor-tunities for earnings and of positions. There are, however, gradual transi-tions in this field with many intermediate types. Appropriation by virtue of leasing or sale of offices or the pledge of income from office are phenomena foreign to the pure type of bureaucracy.

6. "Offices" which do not constitute the incumbent's principal occupa-tion, in particular "honorary" offices, belong in other categories. . . . The typical "bureaucratic" official occupies the office as his principal occupation.

7. With respect to the separation of the official from ownership of the means of administration, the situation is essentially the same in the field of public administration and in private bureaucratic organizations, such as the large-scale capitalistic enterprise.

8. . . . At the present time [collegial bodies] are rapidly decreasing in importance in favour of types of organization which are in fact, and for the

most part formally as well, subject to the authority of a single head. For instance, the collegial "governments" in Prussia have long since given way to the monocratic "district president." The decisive factor in this development has been the need for rapid, clear decisions, free of the necessity of compromise between different opinions and also free of shifting majorities.

9. The modern army officer is a type of appointed official who is clearly marked off by certain class distinctions . . . In this respect such officers differ radically from elected military leaders, from charismatic condottieri, from the type of officers who recruit and lead mercenary armies as a capitalistic enterprise, and, finally, from the incumbents of commissions which have been purchased. There may be gradual transitions between these types. The patrimonial "retainer," who is separated from the means of carrying out his function, and the proprietor of a mercenary army for capitalistic purposes have, along with the private capitalistic entrepreneur, been pioneers in the organization of the modern type of bureaucracy. . . .

THE MONOCRATIC TYPE OF BUREAUCRATIC ADMINISTRATION. Experience tends universally to show that the purely bureaucratic type of administrative organization—that is, the monocratic variety of bureaucracy—is, from a purely technical point of view, capable of attaining the highest degree of efficiency and is in this sense formally the most rational known means of carrying out imperative control over human beings. It is superior to any other form in precision, in stability, in the stringency of its discipline, and in its reliability. It thus makes possible a particularly high degree of calculability of results for the heads of the organization and for those acting in relation to it. It is finally superior both in intensive efficiency and in the scope of its operations, and is formally capable of application to all kinds of administrative tasks.

The development of the modern form of the organization of corporate groups in all fields is nothing less than identical with the development and continual spread of bureaucratic administration. This is true of church and state, of armies, political parties, economic enterprises, organizations to promote all kinds of causes, private associations, clubs, and many others. Its development is, to take the most striking case, the most crucial phenomenon of the modern Western state. However many forms there may be which do not appear to fit this pattern, such as collegial representative bodies, parliamentary committees, soviets, honorary officers, lay judges, and what not, and however much people may complain about the "evils of bureaucracy," it would be sheer illusion to think for a moment that continuous administrative work can be carried out in any field except by means of officials working in offices. The whole pattern of everyday life is cut to fit this framework. For bureaucratic administration is, other things being equal, always, from a formal, technical point of view, the most rational type. For the needs of mass administration to-day, it is completely indispensable. The choice is only that between bureaucracy and dilettantism in the field of administration.

The primary source of the superiority of bureaucratic administration lies in the role of technical knowledge which, through the development of modern technology and business methods in the production of goods, has become completely indispensable. In this respect, it makes no difference whether the economic system is organized on a capitalistic or a socialistic basis. Indeed, if in the latter case a comparable level of technical efficiency were to be achieved, it would mean a tremendous increase in the importance of specialized bureaucracy.

When those subject to bureaucratic control seek to escape the influence of the existing bureaucratic apparatus, this is normally possible only by creating an organization of their own which is equally subject to the process of bureaucratization. Similarly the existing bureaucratic apparatus is driven to continue functioning by the most powerful interests which are material and objective, but also ideal in character. Without it, a society like our own— with a separation of officials, employees, and workers from ownership of the means of administration, dependent on discipline and on technical training—could no longer function. The only exception would be those groups, such as the peasantry, who are still in possession of their own means of subsistence. Even in case of revolution by force or of occupation by an enemy, the bureaucratic machinery will normally continue to function just as it has for the previous legal government.

The question is always who controls the existing bureaucratic machinery. And such control is possible only in a very limited degree to persons who are not technical specialists. Generally speaking, the trained permanent official is more likely to get his way in the long run than his nominal superior, the Cabinet minister, who is not a specialist.

Though by no means alone, the capitalistic system has undeniably played a major role in the development of bureaucracy. Indeed, without it capitalistic production could not continue and any rational type of socialism would have simply to take it over and increase its importance. Its development, largely under capitalistic auspices, has created an urgent need for stable, strict, intensive, and calculable administration. It is this need which gives bureaucracy a crucial role in our society as the central element in any kind of large-scale administration. Only by reversion in every field—political, religious, economic, etc.—to small-scale organization would it be possible to any considerable extent to escape its influence. On the one hand, capitalism in its modern stages of development strongly tends to foster the development of bureaucracy, though both capitalism and bureaucracy have arisen from many different historical sources. Conversely, capitalism is the most rational economic basis for bureaucratic administration and enables it to develop in the most rational form, especially because, from a fiscal point of view, it supplies the necessary money resources.

Along with these fiscal conditions of efficient bureaucratic administration, there are certain extremely important conditions in the fields of communication and transportation. The precision of its functioning requires the services of the railway, the telegraph, and the telephone, and becomes increasingly dependent on them. A socialistic form of organization would not alter this fact. It would be a question whether in a socialistic system it would be possible to provide conditions for carrying out as stringent bureaucratic organization as has been possible in a capitalistic order. For socialism would, in fact, require a still higher degree of formal bureaucratization than capitalism. If this should prove not to be possible, it would demonstrate the existence of another of those fundamental elements of irrationality in social systems—a conflict between formal and substantive rationality of the sort which sociology so often encounters.

Bureaucratic administration means fundamentally the exercise of control on the basis of knowledge. This is the feature of it which makes it specifically rational. This consists on the one hand in technical knowledge which, by itself, is sufficient to ensure it a position of extraordinary power. But in addition to this, bureaucratic organizations, or the holders of power who make use of them, have the tendency to increase their power still further by the knowledge growing out of experience in the service. For they acquire through the conduct of office a special knowledge of facts and have available a store of documentary material peculiar to themselves. While not peculiar to bureaucratic organizations, the concept of "official secrets" is certainly typical of them. It stands in relation to technical knowledge in somewhat the same position as commercial secrets do to technological training. It is a product of the striving for power.

Bureaucracy is superior in knowledge, including both technical knowledge and knowledge of the concrete fact within its own sphere of interest, which is usually confined to the interests of a private business—a capitalistic enterprise. The capitalistic entrepreneur is, in our society, the only type who has been able to maintain at least relative immunity from subjection to the control of rational bureaucratic knowledge. All the rest of the population have tended to be organized in large-scale corporate groups which are inevitably subject to bureaucratic control. This is as inevitable as the dominance of precision machinery in the mass production of goods.

The following are the principal more general social consequences of bureaucratic control:—

(1) The tendency to "levelling" in the interest of the broadest possible basis of recruitment in terms of technical competence.

(2) The tendency to plutocracy growing out of the interest in the great-

est possible length of technical training. To-day this often lasts up to the age of thirty.

(3) The dominance of a spirit of formalistic impersonality, "*Sine ira et studio*," without hatred or passion, and hence without affection or enthusiasm. The dominant norms are concepts of straightforward duty without regard to personal considerations. Everyone is subject to formal equality of treatment; that is, everyone in the same empirical situation. This is the spirit in which the ideal official conducts his office.

SOME OBSERVATIONS ON WEBER'S ANALYSIS OF BUREAUCRACY

Carl J. Friedrich

Max Weber's analysis of bureaucracy is one of the central points in his general sociology. His key concept of rationalization as a distinctive feature of modern society, especially as linked to his notion of a de-mystification of the world (*Entzauberung der Welt*), finds one of its concrete manifestations in bureaucracy and bureaucratization. Here lies one of the important limits of his analysis; for this notion of a progressive rationalization and de-mystification, while more sophisticated, is linked to the earlier and more grandiloquent sociological system of a Comte with its universal progress toward an intellectually conceived goal.

Rationalization and de-mystification are in turn linked to Weber's emphasis on power (*Macht*) in all social relationships, and receive their methodological patterning from his concept of an "ideal type." To deal with the second aspect first, this methodological concept of "ideal types" has aroused a good deal of speculation and controversy. Neither the careful analysis of von Schelting [1] nor the thoughtful commentary by Parsons [2]

This paper was written especially for this volume. The critical assistance of Theodore S. Baer is gratefully acknowledged.

1. A. von Schelting, "Die logische Theorie der historischen Kulturwissenschaften von Max Weber," *Archiv für Sozialwissenschaft und Sozialpolitik*, Vol. 49, and Max Weber, *Gesammelte Aufsätze zur Wissenschaftslehre*, pp. 329 ff.

2. Talcott Parsons, *The Structure of Social Action* (1937), pp. 601 ff. Limitations of space prevent a detailed analysis of this discussion, but it might be well to remark that Parsons, after outlining what an ideal type is *not*, namely (1) an hypothesis, (2) a thing or process, (3) a *Gattungsbegriff* as an average, nor (4) a *Gattungsbegriff* as a collection of common traits, agrees with von Schelting that there are two kinds of ideal types, (a) generalizing and (b) individualizing concepts. Leaving aside the latter, of which "modern capitalism" may be considered an illustration, and turning to the generalizing type of which "bureaucracy" is presumably a case, Parsons suggests that "a general ideal

has been successful in dispelling the mist which surrounds this tool. The term "ideal type" is unfortunate in that the entities to which it is applied are certainly not "ideal" even in a Platonic "ideal" sense; there is, more particularly, nothing "ideal" about bureaucracy. Furthermore, if they were "ideal" they would not be "types," since "types" derive their significance from the empirical reality which they typify. If, on the other hand, they are types,—and there seems little doubt that Weber intended such expressions as "bureaucracy" to delineate "types" in the sense just specified,— then they should be derived by carefully abstracting from empirical givens through the method of concomitant variations.[3] This method ordinarily starts with an exact appraisal (description) of one given complex or configuration of phenomena, events, or processes; then another; and then another. These in turn are subjected to comparison in terms of specific aspects, either through actual or mental experimentation.[4] But Weber, instead of thus proceeding by empirical observation and analysis of the ascertainable givens of such experience, sets forth his "ideal types" as mental constructs which are neither derived by a process of deductive ratiocination from higher concepts, nor built up from empirical data by relevant inference, nor demonstrably developed as working hypotheses from such data.[5] The profound methodological confusion associated with the notion of "ideal type" seriously affects Weber's discussion of "bureaucracy," since bureaucracy is supposed to be one of these nebulous entities.

Rationalization and de-mystification are likewise supposed to be "ideal types"; but they belong to the second category of such types, the individualizing ones. At this point, a passing comment on the neo-Kantian origin of the sharp distinction between "individualizing" and "generalizing" concepts may be in order. Rickert, among others, had sought to make this distinction the basis of his differentiation between the sciences of culture and of nature,[6] with special emphasis upon the historical studies. While no

type is such a construction of a hypothetical course of events with two other characteristics: (1) abstract generality and (2) the ideal-type exaggeration of empirical reality." (p. 605) Quite apart from a series of logical objections, this statement (and admittedly it is as good as Weber's confused thought on the subject permits) clearly shows that Weber's concept of "ideal types" contravenes the standards of empirical science and implies some kind of intuitional ground which appears beyond rational analysis. But Weber does not face this philosophical aspect, continuing to use the concept as if it were the outcome of empirical inquiry, whereas "intuition" would raise entirely different methodological problems.

3. See John Stuart Mill, *Logic*. Parsons' discussion, *op. cit.*, 610 ff. "The logic of empirical proof" proves rather that Weber's is not an empirical procedure.

4. The concept of method involved in "mental experimentation" will be more fully developed in a forthcoming study by the writer on "experience" in the fields of the social sciences (and more especially political science).

5. Note Parsons' insistence (Footnote 2) that the "ideal types" are not hypotheses.

6. Heinrich Rickert, *Kulturwissenschaft und Naturwissenschaft* (5th ed., 1921). Rickert's work is closely linked to that of Dilthey, especially to Dilthey's *Einleitung in die Geisteswissenschaften* (new ed., 1922).

one would deny the stimulating effect of this distinction upon the latter, which it freed from the more tedious objections of "scientism" (meaning the exaggerated emphasis upon the methodology of certain natural sciences), this distinction is of limited logical value due to the inherent difficulties of calling any simple concept "individualizing." And yet, Weber's notion of ideal types is oriented toward precisely this contradictory implication of individualization. Since he uses the notion of "ideal type" at the same time in a "generalizing" manner, however, a medley of transitional patterns of analysis is the result. The student accustomed to logical precision in facing "facts" cannot but be disturbed by the resulting confusion of meta-rational intuitions.[7] Rationalization and de-mystification are not simple developmental trends. Cycles of contrary trends are part of the historical past as we know it. Nor is "bureaucracy" necessarily related to either of these processes.

The preceding comments really are linked to the significance of historical research as the only basis for empirical data on the social phenomena abstractly described as bureaucracy. Whatever aspects or criteria a working concept of bureaucracy should stress is a question which should be settled, not by an intuitional typology, but by comparison of relevant historical documents.

My dissatisfaction with the "ideal-typical" approach to bureaucracy led me to make such an empirical and comparative inquiry. In *Constitutional Government and Democracy* [8] I showed that the documents pertaining to the development of central administrative bodies in England, France, Brandenburg-Prussia, the American colonies, and the United States revealed a recurrent pattern (which would presumably also be found in other modern societies). Six elements or aspects recur in a developing bureaucracy in demonstrable institutionalization: centralization of control and supervision (hierarchical aspects), differentiation of functions, qualification for office, objectivity, precision and continuity, and secrecy (discretion). The first three of these aspects are organizational, the latter three behavioral. Such topics as discipline and morale can be shown to be sub-aspects of this general pattern.[9]

These aspects (or criteria, when considered as measuring rods for de-

7. This aspect of the matter was undoubtedly the main source of Eduard Meyer's methodological objections: See his *Geschichte des Altertums*. It is interesting that the criticism to which Weber's *Protestant Ethic* has been subjected by a variety of historians carries an implied critique of his methodology. However, Parsons has suggested that Weber's methodological views are only partially reflected in his work. See his *The Structure of Social Action, passim*.

8. The first edition, entitled *Constitutional Government and Politics*, appeared in 1937; the most recent edition in 1950. We quote from the latter. The analysis is built upon the work of scholars like Schmoller and Hintze; Weber's propositions are treated as "hypotheses."

9. *Op. cit.*, pp. 38 ff.

termining the degree of bureaucratization) are quasi-quantitative: they allow the judgment of "more" and "less." But the conceivable end-points of e.g., "complete centralization" are not "ideal types"; for they are neither "ideal" nor "types." The logical nature of these "concepts" is not that of working hypotheses, either; although I would be willing to accept the proposition that the concept of bureaucracy which is based upon their six-fold combination is "hypothetical." It is hypothetical in the sense that further research and analysis may disclose (a) that more factors should be added, or (b) that the number of factors can be reduced. In that sense, one could even say that the aspects severally are "hypothetical." But it is more important to insist that they represent "unreal limits" of a developmental trend. However, these unreal limits have no teleological or normative significance. In fact, there are indications that each of these aspects engenders counter-trends which are the result of the inherent disadvantages of excessive centralization, differentiation of functions and so forth. Presumably, the cause of this must be sought in the relationship between these several aspects and the corresponding organizational needs.

The preceding remarks imply another important deviation from the analysis which Weber offered with his intuitional ideal type of bureaucracy: the rejection of the normative element. One of the striking contradictions in Weber's work is the stress he put on the need for a *wertfreie Wissenschaft,*— a social science free of value judgments,[10]—while at the same time the implications of his ideal-type analysis led him to introduce value judgments into the discussion of such issues as bureaucracy. The normative element is here represented by the qualifying expression "fully developed," [11] or again in the qualifying expression of "effectiveness of legal authority" and "acceptance of validity." [12] This definitional manifold in turn depends upon his highly normative basic concept of "legitimacy," the analysis of which can not be undertaken here.[13] Suffice it to say that the normative non-empirical

10. See, *e.g.,* "Der Sinn der 'Wertfreiheit' der soziologischen und oekonomischen Wissenschaften," written in 1917, reprinted in *Gesammelte Aufsätze zur Wissenschaftslehre* (1922), pp. 451 ff., and translated as "The Meaning of 'Ethical Neutrality' in Sociology and Economics" in Edward A. Shils and Henry A. Finch, *Max Weber on the Methodology of the Social Sciences* (Glencoe, Illinois: The Free Press, 1949), pp. 1-47. Weber himself defines *Wertungen* as "praktische Bewertungen einer durch unser Handeln beeinflussbaren Erscheinung als verwerklich oder billigenswert."

11. See *Wirtschaft und Gesellschaft,* Part III, ch. 6; translated by Gerth and Mills and included in *From Max Weber: Essays in Sociology* (1946), pp. 196 ff. "Bureaucracy thus understood (in terms of three ideal-typical 'elements') is fully developed in political and ecclesiastical communities only in the modern state, and, in the private economy, only in the most advanced institutions of capitalism." (p. 196)

12. See *Wirtschaft und Gesellschaft,* Parts I; III; II, 3 as translated by Talcott Parsons, *Theory of Social and Economic Organization* (1947), pp. 329 ff.

13. See Parsons, *op. cit.,* pp. 124 ff. and 324 ff. The author hopes to offer a critical analysis of Weber's discussion of legitimacy before long. Parsons' ingenious interpretation does not deal with the underlying problems of political theory and philosophy

aspect of Weber's approach seems to lie in the assumption that such situational givens as "validity," "acceptance," "authority," and "legal" are taken to be (a) evident in their phenomenal implications when, as a matter of fact, they constitute the real tasks of empirical inquiry, and (b) static absolutes ("ideal types"?) when, as a matter of fact, they are dynamic, highly fluid aspects of a variety of institutional manifolds, among them bureaucracy.

This range of problems is highlighted in such issues as the responsibility of a bureaucracy. In Weber's analysis of a "fully developed" bureaucracy, it is hard to escape the conclusion that a bureaucracy is the more fully developed the less responsible it is in its operation. This can be seen in the discussion Weber offers of the conditions of maximum formal rationality of capital accounting [14] as well as in that of legal authority with a bureaucratic administrative staff: "imperative coordination (control?) in the structure of the administrative staff." The most significant indication is his insistence on appointment, as contrasted with election, but his delineation of the hierarchical aspect, as well as of discipline and control are also symptomatic. The very words vibrate with something of the Prussian enthusiasm for the military type of organization, and the way seems barred to any kind of consultative, let alone cooperative, pattern. That the latter kind of pattern may be a higher type, that it may represent a "more fully developed" form of administrative organization, not only in terms of humanitarian values, but also in terms of "results," is all but excluded as a possibility.

It may be an exaggeration to hold that highly authoritarian "norms" have been embodied in this Weberian terminology. It seems to the author nevertheless striking that Weber's fully developed bureaucracy is most nearly represented by three modern organizations: (1) an army, (2) a business concern without any sort of employee or labor participation in management, (3) a totalitarian party and its bureaucratic administration. Is it not revealing that, at the outset of his discussion of the basis of "legitimacy," Weber defines "imperative control" as the probability that certain commands from a given source will be obeyed by a given group of persons? [15] Is it not equally revealing that discipline is defined as the probability that a command will receive "prompt and automatic obedience in stereotyped

which "explain" these confusions as those of a particular metaphysical position, not far removed from Spinoza's sanctification of power.

14. Parsons, *op. cit.*, pp. 275 ff.

15. See Parsons, *op. cit.*, pp. 324 and 152. I am accepting Parsons' translation of *Herrschaft* for the present purpose, and *pari passu* agree with him that the problems of translating are well-nigh insuperable. Language, in this as in so many cases, reveals behavioral (and hence cultural) predispositions, and thus carries normative implications derived from such cultural components. I am not clear why Parsons translates it as "coordination" rather than "control" in the second passage, since it is "Herrschaft" in both places in the German original, and Weber refers to the first in the second one. Difficult methodological problems are connected with Parsons' rendering of *Chance* (chance) as probability; he enhances the inherent objections by this translation.

forms" as a result of habituation? Or that, contrariwise, the vital aspect of "morale" is omitted from the discussion of an administrative staff (bureaucracy)?

The particular normative implications of Weber's terminology, linking an administrative staff one-sidedly to imperative control (*Herrschaft*) and to power (*Macht*) make it well-nigh impossible for Weber even to adumbrate the range of problems suggested by the expression "responsible bureaucracy." The conjunction of the concept of "responsibility" with that of an administrative staff is inherent, however, in the empirical data on bureaucracy afforded by Western historical experience. This is true to the extent that a history of Western bureaucracy is inconceivable without this conjunction being assigned a central place.[16]

It is well-known that Weber sought to escape the dilemma posed by the valuational aspect of social data, and more especially of political data, by introducing the category of "Verstehen." [17] We "understand," so Weber holds, because we share as human beings the valuational potential of other human beings, even when we decidedly reject the values involved. Thus Hitler's persecution of the Jews would be understandable, presumably, because we can find in ourselves comparable motivations. Weber's thought is purposely put in oversharp focus in this illustration, in order to bring out the *tout comprendre* to which the *tout pardonner* of the well-known French saying corresponds. This comprehending of other human beings from inside, as it were, undoubtedly constitutes an advantage of the studies concerned with man. But to this advantage corresponds a disadvantage not properly analyzed by Weber which results from the "Missverstehen" or misunderstanding of other human beings. Hence the most difficult methodological problems arise; to determine when we understand and when we misunderstand is one of the crucial tasks of any critical study concerned with historical data. In Weber's treatment, such misunderstanding receives scant attention. As a result, what appears to be an elimination of the valuational problems in the social sciences turns out to be the characteristic positivistic suppression of these problems under a new disguise. Rationalization, de-mystification, and bureaucracy are striking instances of this inadequacy of the Weberian *wertfreie Soziologie*.

To clinch the argument, one may turn to Weber's discussion of responsibility itself.[18] It is a simple classificatory statement, without any depth of analysis and unsupported by empirical data of any kind. He links responsibility to solidarity, distinguishes active and passive solidarity, and then

16. Cf. *Constitutional Government and Democracy*, Ch. XIX and the literature cited there.

17. Cf. the thoughtful observations of Parsons on this score in *The Theory of Social Action*, pp. 634 ff. Cf. also Shils, *op. cit.*, pp. 40 ff.

18. Max Weber, *The Theory of Social and Economic Organization*, pp. 143-145.

states that "all the participants may be held responsible for the action . . ." By his employment of the word "may" which deprives many of his statements of scientific exactitude, Weber avoids any specific analysis of the conditions under which responsibility functions, what determines its operation or limits its scope.[19] The crucial problems of policy formation, therefore, receive hardly any attention at all. The discussion of institutional manifolds such as bureaucracy, without reference to a pattern of objectives toward which their operation is directed, is like discussing plant growth without taking the sun into account.

The foregoing is not intended to suggest that Weber's analysis of bureaucracy is without value. In this, as in so many other areas, he opened important lines of inquiry. His genius overshot the mark by proliferating what would seem to us working hypotheses in the form of "ideal types" which he did not pause to test against empirical data; yet he himself would have been the first to concede the importance of doing so. It is more doubtful whether he would have been willing to yield on the broader issues of political theory and philosophy which his terminology implies. *Politica res dura* runs a Latin adage, and the emphasis upon power and imperative control in dealing with politics, to the point of indifference toward other objectives "objectified" in political institutions, may be disastrous. For theory guides policy, and so central an entity as bureaucracy must be rightly understood if policy is to be sound.

19. Cf. "Public Policy and the Nature of Administrative Responsibility," *Public Policy* (ed. Friedrich and Mason), Vol. I, pp. 1 ff.

BUREAUCRACY AND NATIONAL SOCIALISM: A RECONSIDERATION OF WEBERIAN THEORY

Frederic S. Burin

THE RULE OF BUREAUCRATIC STABILITY. Max Weber's statements about the resilience of public bureaucracies in the face of constitutional and political change [1] require reexamination. With regard to France, for instance, we must qualify his conclusion that the administrative system has remained almost unchanged since Napoleon I.[2] Correct as to the social composition of the bureaucracy and its territorial and organizational structure, Weber's thesis ignores the important changes brought about in the operation of the bureaucracy by the rise of the doctrines of public liability and account-

This article was written especially for this volume.
1. Max Weber, *Wirtschaft und Gesellschaft*, Tuebingen, 1925, pp. 669-70.
2. *Ibid.*, p. 670.

ability and their enforcement by the Council of State. Admittedly, the metamorphosis of the Council of State from an organ of executive domination into one restraining the public services in the interest of the citizen, resulted from political changes which left the formal structure of administration virtually untouched; yet, beneath that structure the effects on bureaucratic processes and behavior patterns of the change from authoritarian to responsible administration were too substantial to permit of Weber's generalization.[3] The post-war "revival" of authoritarian tendencies in Western Germany is correctly related to Allied failure to democratize the civil service. But the re-emergence of pre-Nazi institutions—in this as in other sectors of German society—should not lead us to apply Weber's rule of bureaucratic stability too rigidly, and to view today's bureaucracy, or at least its upper, academic stratum, as essentially that of the Empire. The record of what happened to the traditional bureaucracies during the Nazi era is available to dispel such a misconception.

Is there really no essential difference between the former Nazi officials now staffing the government departments of Bavaria [4] and their predecessors whom the Weimar Republic took over from the Empire? It is notorious, for instance, that, under Hitler, prosecutors and criminal judges were transformed into practitioners of violence.[5] Does that fact influence the work of the "denazified" present occupants of those positions? In order to deal with such questions we must know to what extent the Nazis succeeded in reshaping the bureaucracies they inherited from the absolute state (*Polizeistaat*) and the constitutional state (*Rechtsstaat*). This subject is important not only for our understanding of contemporary Germany. The Hitler regime is of great significance to a general understanding of the dynamics and practice of modern bureaucracy. The political and social changes brought about by the Nazis entailed extensive modifications of the composition, standards of conduct, and mental climate of the state bureaucracy, judiciary and army.[6] These modifications reflected the rise to power of

3. See Léon Duguit, *Law in the Modern State* (transl. by H. J. Laski), New York, 1918, passim; I do not intend to imply that shifts in the political balance of power during the Third Republic were accurately reflected in the French bureaucracy. After 1877 the upper strata of the civil service were at all times more conservative than the political branches of the government, and this is undoubtedly true today. But the bureaucracy's ability to thwart social and economic change was less the result of its own strength than of that instability peculiar to the French political executive. Nor was it the only extraparliamentary force successfully active in that respect.

4. See, for instance, Drew Middleton, "Hitler Aides Rule Bavaria—Germans Cool to Democracy" and the chart "Ex-Nazis in Government" in *The New York Times*, November 30, 1949.

5. Franz L. Neumann, *Behemoth*, New York, 1944, p. 458.

6. The collapse under Nazi pressure of the traditional code of conduct of the German officers' corps has received insufficient attention. To order troops to murder civilians *en masse* and to turn prisoners of war over to the security police for liquidation,

new bureaucratic organizations whose ethos and social composition expressed the essence of the Nazi system. The short duration of the "Thousand Year Reich" facilitates the study of Nazi institutions, as does the fact that the pattern of change was hardly one of shifting gradations and barely perceptible nuances: its contours stand out starkly, rich in crudities and cataclysmic events.[7]

COUNTER-REVOLUTION, PROPAGANDA, AND TERROR. Unlike the Bolshevik revolution of 1917, the Nazi advent was not a violent break with the past, wiping out all existing political institutions. For all their talk of revolution in 1933, the Nazis' assumption of power was counter-revolutionary. It took place not against, but with the help of some elements of the old governing classes and the benevolent neutrality of others. Fourteen years of Weimar democracy had left no significant imprint on the officers' corps of the army, the judiciary, and the academic civil service. With few exceptions, these groups were sympathetic to Hitler in the spring of 1933. They expected him to destroy parliamentarism, to eliminate the danger of social democracy, and to reimpose the traditional authoritarian order suited to their taste. Nazi "dynamism" as revealed in *Mein Kampf*, was "regrettably necessary" for mass consumption, but not to be taken seriously by "respectable" people. A complacent and archaic political outlook prevented these true counter-revolutionaries from understanding that Hitler's plans could not fully coincide with their own, and in fact included entirely unpalatable items.[8] Their sympathetic attitude therefore combined with their social

was no less a break with the vaunted tradition of Frederick the Great than it was a violation of the laws of war. Pre-occupation with the SS (Nazi Elite Guard) has tended to obscure the complicity of the military caste in such atrocities. See the case against Generals Keitel and Jodl in *Trial of the Major War Criminals before the International Military Tribunal*, Nüremberg, 1947 (also in State Department series "Nazi Conspiracy and Aggression"): see also *U. S. v. Wilhelm von Leeb et al.*, and *U. S. v. Wilhelm List et al.*, vols. X and XI, and *U. S. v. Ohlendorf et al.*, vol. IV of Trials of War Criminals before the Nüremberg Military Tribunals under Control Council Law No. 10, U. S. Government Printing Office, 1950.

7. The voluminous records of the Nüremberg trials are a unique goldmine of information on all sectors of the Nazi power structure. They abound in important documents from the secret files and archives of the regime. Such materials can become available only following the obliteration of a defeated government and total occupation of its territory.

8. By the time it had become clear how much the Nazi vision deviated from conservative ideals, many conservatives had become Nazis, even to the extent of discovering their "social conscience" and love of "racial community." Whatever conservative awakening there was, came much too late, and the eye-opener in many cases was not the gangsterism of the Nazis but the effectiveness of Allied arms. The putsch of July 20, 1944 was an explosion of conservative discontent that had ripened in the knowledge of impending defeat, not a sudden sprouting of democratic ideals. The posthumously published diary of Ulrich von Hassell, until 1937 German Ambassador to Rome and one of the chief conspirators, is full of passages that reveal the psychology of the "putschists." (*The Von Hassel Diaries*, New York, 1947.) Although the author expresses a revulsion at Nazi atrocities which is genuine beyond doubt, the book is studded with plaintive and often naive comments on the Nazis' vulgarity, their "demagogic attacks on the

and political strength (of which democracy had hardly begun to sap the
foundations) to insure them a low priority rating on the Nazis' schedule
for piecemeal "synchronization" of social institutions. (The elimination of
trade unions, communists, "Marxists," and liberals was both more urgent
and easier to accomplish.) Equally important was the fact that Hitler and
his aides could not dispense with the technical expertness of the existing
bureaucracies. Impairment of the efficient functioning of the military and
administrative machines would have invited domestic chaos, and would
have vitiated the Fuehrer's plans for an aggressive foreign policy.[9]

The ideal of many of Hitler's conservative supporters was the absolute
monarchy of Frederick the Great; and a close approximation to it was their
fondest expectation from the "national revolution" of 1933. In 1933 and
1934, the Nazi leaders, to the delight of the senile Field Marshal von Hindenburg, aped this tradition and sought to invoke it in their favor. Their
pronouncements on that subject were never more than fraudulent tactical
maneuvers designed to deceive the conservative groups. The state of Frederick and Bismarck, of Hegel and Stahl, with its rigidly stratified social
structure, was repugnant to the Austrian corporal and his lower middle
class henchmen. Nor was their social background unconnected with their
ability to perceive from the beginning what most conservatives were
incapable of realizing, but what 80 years earlier Napoleon III had understood: that "one can only govern with, not against the masses."[10] In the
era of mass industrialism and articulated social organization, absolute rule
cannot be maintained by "administering" the people, as the politically quiescent "lower orders" were "administered" by the mercantilist-eudemonistic
police state of the eighteenth century. The masses of the twentieth century
would not *consciously* submit to the role of "subjects" of an absolute ruler
sustained by privileged, hereditary governing elites. Yet absolute rule (plus
imperialist war) was what Hitler sought and achieved. He succeeded only
because he and his fellow conspirators appreciated the importance of con-
cealing this reality from the people, but also because they knew that in
this secular, industrial century the masses can only be dominated by being
kept in a constant state of psychological tension favorable to the ruling
group. The people must therefore be infused with the *illusion* of democracy,
of their active participation in the political process, of the subordination

entire upper class" (p. 1), "the red course upon which he (Hitler) has embarked" (p.
161), and the like.

9. For an interestingly frank Nazi formulation of these considerations, see the statement of Reich Minister Dr. Hans Frank (since hanged at Nüremberg) in *Mitteilungs-
blatt des Bundes Nationalsozialistischer Deutscher Juristen und des Reichsrechtsamtes
der NSDAP*, No. 2 (1935), p. 37, quoted in F. M. Marx, *Government in the Third
Reich*, New York, 1937, p. 127.

10. Compare Karl Mannheim's concept of "fundamental democratization," *Man and
Society in An Age of Reconstruction*, New York, 1940, p. 44 ff.

of the rulers to the will of the ruled. In this sense, it is true to say that under Hitler the German masses were "led" rather than "administered."

The function of National Socialist ideology and of its arsenal of national symbolism was to conceal the reality of absolutism and to create the illusion of democracy. The *Weltanschauung* was a gigantic smokescreen: the tenets of charismatic leadership, community, race, "blood and soil," the whole stock of mysticism, served as stratagems for hiding from the public the reality of authoritarian domination exercised by an absolute ruler and an alliance of governing elites.[11]

National Socialist rule over the German people required both the suppression of the social antagonisms of a pluralistic society and the destruction of social cohesions. Deprived of their traditional affiliations, atomized into an amorphous mass, the population was subjected to control by a number of bureaucratic organizations stretching into every sphere of human activity, and having their common apex and ultimate source of direction in the Fuehrer himself. The word "control," as here used, stands for a number of complementary techniques of manipulating the "human material."[12] The all-important task of what we may call "ideology enforcement"[13] was assigned to the National Socialist "movement," i.e., the monopolistic political "party" and its subsidiaries.[14] To the extent that to us, "propaganda" connotes an *appeal*, the term does not adequately explain the task of the movement. To the Nazis, politics and propaganda were one and the same: each meant indoctrination practised in a climate of controlled rather than competitive thought. The indoctrination of the people with Nazi irrationalism was a form of "violence to the mind" requiring, as a condition of success, the elimination of all non-conformist, i.e., non-directed, ideas. The Party's apparatus of surveillance and control was geared to that mission. Through its "block leaders" it reached into every home; its functional, "supervised," and "corporative" organizations covered every mode of earn-

11. See F. L. Neumann, *op. cit.*, pp. 438-9, 464-5. The above statement is not invalidated by: (1) the fact that the Nazi ideology was not in all respects invented by Hitler & Co., but skilfully drew upon familiar currents of nineteenth century German social thought; (2) the endowment of the Fuehrer with attributes of a "charismatic" personality, in the sense of Weber's use of the term. (See Weber, *The Theory of Social and Economic Organization*, T. Parsons, ed., pp. 329-30; compare H. R. Trevor-Roper, *The Last Days of Hitler*, New York, 1947, p. 71); (3) the probability that Hitler himself, and the certainty (in my judgment) that Himmler and many other top Nazi leaders genuinely believed what they were preaching. On the contrary, the sincerity of their belief in it enhanced the value of the ideology as a technique of domination.

12. One of Himmler's favorite terms, but "for internal use only."

13. "Weltanschauliche Ausrichtung" in Nazi jargon.

14. For a list of the "formations" and affiliated organizations of the Party, showing the extent of its reach, see "Civil Affairs Handbook—Germany—The National Socialist Party," *U.S. Army Service Forces Manual M 356-2A Suppl.*, p. 22 ff; also A. V. Boerner, "The Position of the NSDAP in the German Constitutional Order," *American Political Science Review*, XXXII (1938), pp. 1068-9.

ing a livelihood and acquiring an education, while by enforcing membership in the Hitler Youth it held the pliable, growing generation in its grasp. Yet, notwithstanding these "educational" techniques, the Hitler movement could not have succeeded without the *ultima ratio* of modern totalitarian rule: the scientific application of terror, the "technique of control by fear," the threat of unpredictable, yet imminent, physical violence. The movement gave birth to an organization supremely qualified for that assignment, the SS and political police system under Heinrich Himmler. Before the *Goetter-daemmerung* set in, the child by far dwarfed the parent.[15]

THE OLD AND THE NEW BUREAUCRACY. Where civil service and army had been the pillars of Prussian absolutism, Nazi totalitarianism was sustained by its propaganda-and-terror bureaucracies. They were the *sine qua non* of a system of domination depending on the manufacture of mass irrationality and the practice of violence. To achieve the maximum integration of the traditional administrative institutions into that system with a minimum loss of efficiency and technical skills was a major challenge facing the Nazi planners. On the whole, it was met with success.

The German ministerial bureaucracy was a rational bureaucracy.[16] It was rational in both the "functional" and the "substantive" sense of Karl Mannheim's well-known distinction.[17] It is true that the political and social values of many of the academic bureaucrats hardly rose above a technocratic interest in serving the state. What we may subsume under "substantive rationality" were their habits of regularity, legality, formalism, neutrality and their objective, non-arbitrary application ("sine ira ac studio" —Weber) of calculable legal norms, regardless of content, equally to all persons and situations.[18] Such features of traditional bureaucratic conduct were utterly incompatible with the Nazi spirit of charismatic leadership, ideological mysticism ("we think with our blood"), and arbitrary decisionism. In theory and in practice the Nazis rejected calculable rules (other than operating procedures) in favor of discretionary measures geared in every instance to the expediencies of the moment. Their denunciation, permeation, and increasing domination of the state bureaucracy and judiciary "expressed a real need of the system to do away with the rule of rational law."[19]

Though differentiated from the rational bureaucracy by their substan-

15. The best and most penetrating study of the structure, creed, and practice of the SS and Gestapo is E. Kohn-Bramstedt, *Dictatorship and Political Police*, London, 1945.

16. See Neumann, *op. cit.*, pp. 77-80, "The Rational Bureaucracy"; Weber, *Essays in Sociology*, Gerth and Mills transl., pp. 215-16.

17. Mannheim, *Man and Society in an Age of Reconstruction*, New York, 1940, p. 51 ff; the former is the capacity to devise and use operational techniques to arrive at any end, the latter the capacity to think and act rationally, above the manipulative level, with reference to ends, or at least to fixed, concrete standards.

18. See Weber, *op. cit.*, Tuebingen, 1925, vol. II, pp. 661-2, 666; Weber, *op. cit.*, T. Parsons ed., p. 361; Neumann, *op. cit.*, p. 80.

19. Neumann, *op. cit.*, p. 80.

tive irrationality, the Nazi machines vied with the older administrative bodies in their stress on functional rationality. In the Party and its "formations"—above all in the SS and political police system—symmetrical, hierarchic structure and characteristically "bureaucratic" procedures combined with ideological fanaticism and the charismatic legitimation of authority. In order to point up the similarities and differences between the traditional state machinery and these organizations, it may be appropriate to call the latter the "ideological bureaucracies."[20]

THE DEMISE OF CONSERVATISM AND THE DEBASEMENT OF THE "STATE." Because of the strong position of army, bureaucracy, and other conservative elements, and because of the official idealization of the Frederician tradition, the initial period of Hitler's rule has been referred to as that of the "totalitarian state."[21] During that period Hitler eliminated political opposition, consolidated dictatorial power, began the "synchronization" of all spheres of German life, and, finally, stamped out "left-wing sectarianism" and other forms of dissent within his own movement. The blood purge of June 30, 1934, was the great turning point. Though Generals Schleicher and Bredow and other conservatives were included in the mass liquidations, the purge was widely interpreted as the Fuehrer's defense of the forces of tradition and order against the radicals of the Nazi movement pressing for the consummation of the "revolution." This was the case in a limited sense only, for the conservative victory was a pyrrhic one. Gradually it turned into a rout, although Hitler, who alone determined its speed and direction, allowed the defeated forces to salvage much more than Roehm and his SA (storm troops, purged on June 30th) would have left them. For at that moment the Fuehrer became Germany's absolute ruler and, by his own proclamation, "supreme law lord," and Himmler his chief executioner. The general staff failed to defend law, order, and its own reputation against SS violence because, apart from settling some old accounts, the Fuehrer had struck only at the "revolutionary" wing of the Nazi movement, hardly an object for the generals' compassion. But by ignoring these old accounts, the generals traded the lives of their comrades, Schleicher and Bredow, for safety from a merger of army and SA which they could easily have prevented by force had they not lacked courage. Hitler was able to show that he alone was master over life and death in Germany. The army had not dared to raise a finger against him. The purged movement was now solidly behind him, overcome with awe and admiration. The period of dependence on the conservative forces was over. The army and traditional bureaucracy —strong, independent power factors under Weimar pluralism—were inte-

20. Compare H. Gerth's characterization of the Nazi Party as "charismatic and bureaucratic," "The Nazi Party; Its Leadership and Composition," *American Journal of Sociology*, XLV (1940), pp. 517-541, reprinted in part in this volume.
21. See Neumann, *op. cit.*, pp. 47-51.

grated into Hitler's monolithic structure. They had abdicated the substance of power in the state,[22] but for their continued and gladly rendered services they were richly rewarded by the forms and trimmings of power: marshals' batons, titles, social status, and other prizes at the disposal of a great conqueror. This satisfied most of them well enough.

With the subjugation of its exponents, an end was put to the propagation of the ideal of the totalitarian *state*—long a heresy to advanced Nazis, implying, as it does, the subordination of Party to state. It yielded to the concept of the "totality of the movement" and to the reality of totalitarian *rule* by the Fuehrer, his "court," and his ideological bureaucracies. Nazi politicians and theorists ceased to glorify the state and began, instead, to debase it. The word "state," in this connection, assumed a specific, restricted meaning: administration and judiciary, i.e., the rational bureaucracy.[23] At the 1934 Party Congress Hitler himself led the way by repeating what he had already said in *Mein Kampf*:[24] "the state is not our master, we are the masters of the state."[25] Lesser lights hastened to contribute their casuistry to explain the inferiority of the state. The favorite device was the distinction between leadership (Fuehrung) and administration (Verwaltung): the former the province of the movement, the latter that of the state. According to this doctrine, the state (i.e., in its narrow meaning, the rational bureaucracy) is a lifeless "Apparat" administering things, but incapable of leading men. Only the movement (ideological bureaucracy) is capable of the leadership of men, of generating political ideas and national policy. It alone is creative and dynamic, not bureaucratic.[26] From the Party

22. Weber probably overestimated the civil service as a political power factor. The case of Nazi Germany supports his thesis that "such a machine (bureaucracy) makes 'revolution' in the sense of forceful creation of entirely new formations of authority technically more and more impossible . . ." (*Essays in Sociology*, Gerth & Mills transl., p. 230.) only to the extent that the meaning of "revolution" is limited to a revolutionary seizure of power and violent overthrow of the established order. The type of "revolution" he does not seem to have envisaged was a revolutionary transformation of society which did entail the "creation of entirely new formations of authority" and the *gradual* subjugation of the traditional bureaucratic machine.

23. In view of its crucial importance in Hitler's schemes, the officers' corps was spared this doctrinal degradation; the army was simply severed from the "state" in its new, narrow definition and promoted to "people's army" (Volksheer), the *Volk* enjoying a high status in the Nazi hierarchy of values. It should be noted that there was no consistency in the use of the word "state" in Nazi legal and political literature. Whether, in a given case, the traditional or the narrow meaning is intended, is easily determined from the context.

24. See Neumann, *op. cit.*, pp. 63-4 and citations.

25. *Voelkischer Beobachter*, Munich edition, Sept. 8, 1934 (No. 251) cited by Neumann, *op. cit.*, p. 482. Alfred Rosenberg, chief Nazi ideologist, had opened fire against the state some months earlier, and the constitutional lawyer, Carl Schmitt, had already anticipated the trend in his book, *Staat, Bewegung, Volk*, published in 1933.

26. This distinction is, of course, spurious. As an organization and a mechanism of control, the movement was no less bureaucratic than the state. For the differences, see above.

the passive state receives its impetus and direction. In Hitler's own formulation, "The task of leadership and, in effect, that of legislation is in the hands of the party. The state is the administration and its function is that of execution."[27] Professor Theodor Maunz, whose writings reflect the endeavor to combine conformist zeal with what is sometimes perilously close to objective analysis, has rung an even more revealing variation on the theme, ". . . one must realize that the administration is demoted to a mere 'Apparat' . . . This theory necessitated the strongest rejection of authoritarian [28] concepts of administration, a rejection arising from the fact that the bureaucracy no longer constitutes a political class with a closed internal structure and no longer is the politically leading order of the *Volk*."[29]

THE NAZIFICATION OF THE CIVIL SERVICE. Such casuistic doctrinal barrages moved ahead of the growing power of movement and police and of the "synchronization" of the rational bureaucracy. The Nazis aimed at eradicating the patterns of conduct we have subsumed under "substantive rationality," and at transforming civil servants and judges into "corps of political soldiers" fully assimilated to the ideological bureaucracies of the regime.[30] Although that goal was never reached, the collaboration of "nonpolitical" experts with Nazi activists in every government bureau assured both technically effective administration and subservience to the political leadership.

There is no dearth of accounts of the "nazification" of civil service, judiciary, and army that cite statutes, decrees, and individual examples.[31] The following list covers only the methods employed in the nazification of the civil service:

(1) *Transfer of state functions to the ideological bureaucracies.* At the Party Congress of 1935, Hitler declared: "Problems which the formal bureaucracy proves unfit to solve, the German nation will assign to its *living* organization in order to fulfill the necessities of its life."[32] The SS

27. Speech at Weimar, July 4, 1936, *Voelkischer Beobachter*, Berlin edition, July 5, 1936 (No. 187).

28. I.e., in the undisguised rational sense of the *Polizeistaat;* see above.

29. In H. Frank (ed.), *Deutsches Verwaltungsrecht*, Munich, 1937, pp. 30-31.

30. Had this ever been accomplished, the stock of the old bureaucracies would undoubtedly have been boosted by official doctrine. The campaign of glorification of the police (as police) after its submersion in the SS is a case in point.

31. Consult Neumann, *op. cit.*, pp. 369-73, 378-85, 447-58, 629-32; E. Fraenkel, *The Dual State*, New York, 1941, pp. 14-64; "Civil Affairs Handbook—Germany—Government and Administration" and "The National Socialist Party," *U.S. Army Service Forces Manuals M 356-2A and Suppl.;* J. H. Herz, "German Administration under the Nazi Regime," *American Political Science Review*, XL (1946), pp. 682-702; A. V. Boerner, *loc. cit.*, pp. 1059-81; to extract information from "raw material" sources, examine the Nuremberg cases cited above. In addition: *U.S. v. Josef Altstoetter et al.*, vol. III, and *U.S. v. Ernst von Weizsaecker et al.*, vols. XII, XIII and XIV of the above cited series on the trials under Control Council Law No. 10.

32. Quoted by R. Hoehn in H. Frank (ed.), *op. cit.*, p. 75. Italics mine.

Professor of Public Law, Reinhard Hoehn, supplements that statement by noting that "the movement has the function of observing whether the state can perform certain tasks" and, if it arrives at a negative decision, "the power to take their solution into its own hands." He then paraphrases the Fuehrer to the effect that the state is by its very nature ("seinem Wesen nach") totally unqualified for the solution of certain problems.[33] These transparent phrases contain interesting implications. The rational state machinery was indeed "unfit" for the task of practising terror. The outstanding examples of the transfer of functions from the "formal bureaucracy" to the "living organization" were the police and the agencies of political justice, the dreaded "people's courts."[34]

(2) *"Personal Union."* Appointment of Party office holders to state positions. Apart from the cases of Hitler, Hess, Bormann, etc., the dual role of the Party district leaders (Gauleiter) as Reich Governors or Prussian provincial presidents, and later as defense commissars, was perhaps of the greatest significance.

(3) *Parallelism.* Establishment in the Party bureaucracy of offices with the same subject-matter jurisdiction for the exertion of pressure on government departments and, probably, in the expectation of eventual merger.

(4) *Nazification at the top.* Appointment of Party leaders and prominent members as ministers, secretaries of state, etc. Well-known is the case of Wilhelm Frick, early Party stalwart and Minister of the Interior from the beginning until 1943.

(5) *Permeation.* (a) Injection of Nazi activists into key positions in the Ministries. (b) Reservation of new career appointments to Nazi-indoctrinated personnel, based on Party control of professional training facilities (civil service academies, law schools, etc.). (c) Preferential treatment of active Party men with respect to promotions.

(6) *Conversion* to National Socialism, accomplished through a variety of channels for indoctrination and pressure.

(7) *Dismissal* of undesirable personnel. Used sparingly, except for "non-aryans" and democrats, but an important weapon for securing compliance.

(8) *Transfer* of unreliable personnel. Often "non-political" officials had to make room for Nazi activists. "Soft" penal judges were transferred to civil courts.

(9) *Enforced compliance.* The Civil Service Act of 1937 required personal loyalty to the Fuehrer of every public employee. Supervision by superiors, enforced membership in professional organizations affiliated with the Party (NS Civil Servants League, NS Lawyers League, etc.), surveil-

33. *Ibid.*, p. 75. See also Fraenkel, *op. cit.*, p. 57.
34. "Transfer of functions" must here be understood in a formal and equivocal sense. In their substance these functions were without precedent.

lance by colleagues who were sometimes SD (Intelligence Service of the SS and police) informers, served as effective media of control.

(10) *Replacement of law by discretion.* Constant pressure from the top forcing the substitution of arbitrariness for "norm consciousness" in administrative behaviour,[35] with the result that the bureaucratic sense of security was undermined. Deprived of the sense of obedience to, and protection by, impersonal law which characterizes rational bureaucracy, many bureaucrats succumbed to the Hitler myth. Their loyalty, in turn, facilitated the Nazi chiefs' conduct of public administration by individual measures ("from case to case"—Weber) instead of rational norms. All this was most pronounced at the policy-making level. The lower civil servant who only executes orders from above, is not so aware of the elimination of calculable norms. Insofar as he is, he may strive to preserve his sense of security by the more anxious observance of procedural rules. It would be worth-while to enquire into the probably inverse relationship between the amount of red tape and the degree of substantive rationality in bureaucratic organizations. The lower echelons of the Gestapo, and the administrative procedures in German concentration camps throw some interesting light on the subject.

TERROR OVER LAW: THE NAZI POLICE STATE. The supplanting of law by ideological mysticism and arbitrary discretion was the essence of National Socialist rule. The legal state was submerged in a chaos of irrationality and violence: a new type of police state arose. Institutionally, the change-over expressed itself in the ideological bureaucracies' encroachment on and permeation (in the three-fold sense of personnel, mentality and practice) of the traditional state machinery. Although it is true that most of that machinery retained its outward identity until the end, the acceleration and intensification of these encroachments and permeations after 1942 preclude the application of Weber's rule of bureaucratic stability to Nazi Germany.

Weber's position rested essentially on his exaggerated estimate of the *political* importance of technical expertness. "The 'political master,'" he said, "finds himself in the position of the 'dilettante' who stands opposite the expert." [36] And with an eye on none other than Frederick the Great, he added that "the absolute monarch is powerless opposite the superior knowledge of the bureaucratic expert." [37] Applied to 18th century absolutism such a statement may be debatable. Applied to the dilettante Hitler, whose contempt for experts as men was only matched by the success with which he used them as his tools, it becomes absurd. Weber's generalizations about bureaucratic tenacity must be modified at least to the extent that they fail to take into account the central theme of this article: the impact on the "rational-legal" type of bureaucracy of a political system of charismatic

35. Compare Gerth, *loc. cit.*, p. 538.
36. *Op. cit.*, Gerth and Mills transl., p. 232.
37. *Ibid.*, p. 234.

leadership, mass irrationality, and terrorism—and of the new, irrational types of bureaucracy peculiar to such a system. When Weber formulated his statements he doubtless thought of the resilience of the bureaucracy in the face of political changes not incompatible with the rational bureaucratic ethos he so brilliantly analyzed. Whatever the validity of these statements for cases such as republican France, they cannot apply where that ethos itself is antithetic to the new system of political domination.

In its most extreme form, the trend toward the submersion of the traditional institutions expressed itself in the rise to autonomy and omnipotence of the most fanatical and ruthless organization of the regime, the Himmler SS-and-Police Empire.[38] We can not here do justice to that story, but a list of the offices held by Himmler in the autumn of 1944 illustrates the position of the SS in the final months of Nazi rule: Reich leader of the SS and chief of all German police forces, and, as such, of all concentration camps and domestic and foreign intelligence services (including, since the 1944 generals' putsch, the military counter-intelligence); commander-in-chief of his private army, the *Waffen-SS;* commander of the German reserve armies and of the home front; Minister of the Interior; Commissioner for the Strengthening of German Folkdom—entrusted, in this capacity, with eugenics, race, and colonization measures in the occupied East, including the projected extermination of 30 million Slavs.

A corresponding aspect of the change from legal state to police state was the decline of the traditional judiciary. The bureaucracy in the Ministry of Justice, the public prosecutors, even the criminal courts were ultimately transformed into obedient tools in the practice of violence, although not without a good deal of passive resistance on the part of some judges. Before Hitler, judges had been independent, "bound" only to the law, secure against dismissal or transfer. These safeguards were abolished and the bench was turned into a rigidly disciplined administrative machine. Adjudication of criminal and, to some extent, of civil cases was not governed by statute law alone, but, above all else, by "sound racial feelings." [39] In their search for these "feelings," judges were directed to the National Socialist ideology as expounded by Hitler and his various sub-leaders. Law was, in other words, replaced by the application of political directives. Maunz, writing in 1943, again supplies some frank observations: "In the field of crime *prevention* the judge no longer merely administers justice. His . . . activity

38. "The aim of safeguarding the security of people and state is the only standard for the National Socialist political police . . . it is unlimited in the choice of its measures." H. Schlierbach, *Die Politische Polizei in Preussen*, vol. 96, Universitas Archiv, Emsdetten, 1938. Himmler's own personality apotheosized the ethos of that group: to an extraordinary degree he combined technical efficiency with the zeal of a true religious fanatic. See Trevor-Roper, *op. cit.*, pp. 17-25; for a sample of Himmler's speeches, see Kohn-Bramstedt, *op. cit.*, pp. 241-47.

39. "Law to Change the Penal Code," June 28, 1935, *Reichsgesetzblatt*, I, p. 839.

approaches that of an administrative official. He no longer looks for justice alone, but also acts in accordance with expediency. Judge and administrator, judiciary and police, often meet . . . in the pursuit of identical objectives. This change in the character of some judicial activity has led to a decline of the judiciary." [40] In the words of U. S. Military Tribunal III in *U. S. v. Josef Altstoetter et al.* (case against the judiciary), "The function of the Nazi courts was judicial only in a limited sense. They more closely resembled administrative tribunals acting under orders from above in a quasi-judicial manner.[41]

The history of the relations of police and judiciary is indispensable to the study of what the Nazis did to the organs of public power in the German state. It takes us from the early emancipation of the political police from the control of the administrative courts to the time when Himmler's men held much of the judicial machinery in their grip. The "crisis of the judiciary" in 1942, provoked by Hitler's fury at the inadequate sentences pronounced by certain courts, led to a flood of disciplinary measures against judges failing to respond to "the necessities of life of the German people," and to the appointment of the violent Nazi Thierack as Minister of Justice. These events increased the incidence of SS personnel and SS mentality in the Ministry and the courts.

The Nazis' way of thinking and acting cannot be explained in words more expressive than their own. A few selections from the remarkable judgment of U. S. Military Tribunal III in *U. S. v. Altstoetter et al.* will illustrate the permeation of administrative institutions by Nazi activists, and the mental climate it was designed to universalize. The court described the SS and administrative career of one of the defendants as follows:

The professional career of the defendant, Guenther Joel in the Third Reich proceeded at the same pace as his career as a Party man; in fact even before the war years his professional career merged with his career in Nazi organizations, and to be more precise, in the SS and the SD (Himmler's Security Service)—the organization which the IMT judgment has declared to be criminal.

He became a member of the NSDAP on 1 May 1933 and entered the Ministry of Justice as a junior public prosecutor on 7 August 1933. In quick succession he became assistant public prosecutor (1 Sept. 1933), public prosecutor (1 January 1934), senior public prosecutor (1 Feb. 1935), and chief public prosecutor (1 November 1936).

Between August 1935 and October 1937, Joel was the chief of a newly created sub-department of the Reich Ministry of Justice, the Central Public Prosecution (Zentralstaatsanwaltschaft). In October 1937 this sub-department was dissolved, but the Reich Minister of Justice, Guertner, reserved the right to assign Joel as "referent" for special cases and subsequently made use of this right. After the

40. T. Maunz, *Gestalt und Recht der Polizei*, Hamburg, 1943, pp. 51-2; italics inserted.
41. Opinion of the court, p. 10703 of the unpublished transcript of proceedings.

dissolution of the Central Public Prosecution, Joel worked as "referent" in the Ministry's penal department No. III (later renumbered IV).

By a formal letter of appointment, dated 19 December 1937 and signed by Minister Guertner, Joel was, in addition to his other duties, appointed liaison officer between the Reich Ministry of Justice and the SS, including the SD, as well as the Gestapo. A few months later, namely in a letter of 2 May 1938, signed by Heydrich, Joel was, effective 30 January 1938 admitted to the SS and, effective the same day, promoted to the rank of SS Untersturmfuehrer (2nd Lieut.) and given the position of leader (Fuehrer) in the SD Main Office.

His SS personnel record shows how quickly he climbed to high positions in the SS and the SD: on 11 Sept. 1938 he became SS Obersturmfuehrer (1st Lieut.); on 30 January 1939, SS Hauptsturmfuehrer (Capt.); on 26 September 1940, SS Sturmbannfuehrer (Major)—holding all these ranks as leader in the SD Main Office . . .

On 1 May 1941 Joel was promoted to Ministerial Counsellor. He remained with the Reich Ministry of Justice until 12 May 1943.

The reason for his leaving the Ministry was that on 7 May 1943 he was appointed Attorney General to the Supreme Provincial Court of Appeals in Hamm (Westphalia). By letter dated "Fuehrer Headquarters, 12 May 1943," Bormann, Chief of the Party Chancellery, personally confirmed his appointment . . .

Shortly after this new appointment, namely as of 9 November 1943, Joel was promoted to the high rank of SS Obersturmbannfuehrer (Lt. Col.), which appointment was approved by Himmler. His political and Party career went hand in hand with his professional career, and his promotions were made by or approved by such high ranking Nazi officials as Himmler, Bormann, Heydrich, Thierack, and Freisler . . .[42]

The next document is a sample of the mentality of Nazi administrators: "As a crowning example of fanatical imbecility," says the court, "we cite the following document issued in April 1943, which was sent to the desk of the defendant Rothenberger (Secretary of State in the Ministry of Justice) for his attention, and was initialed by him.

The Reich Minister of Justice
Information for the Fuehrer
1943 No.

After the birth of her child a full-blooded Jewess sold her mother's milk to a pediatrician and concealed that she was a Jewess. With this milk babies of German blood were fed in a nursing home for children. The accused will be charged with deception. The buyers of the milk have suffered damage, for mother's milk from a Jewess cannot be regarded as food for German children. The impudent behavior of the accused is an insult as well. Relevant charges, however, have not been applied for so that the parents, who are unaware of the true facts, need not subsequently be worried.

I shall discuss with the Reich Health Leader the racial hygienic aspects of the case.

Berlin, April 1943.[43]

42. Pp. 10868-70 of transcript of proceedings.
43. P. 10776 of transcript of proceedings.

These theories were implemented in administrative practice. The following letter shows the Nazi concept of the role of criminal justice: "On 13 October 1942 the Reich Minister of Justice Thierack wrote to Reichsleiter Bormann (Deputy Leader of the Party), in part as follows:

With a view to freeing the German people of Poles, Russians, Jews, and gypsies and with a view to making the Eastern territories which have been incorporated into the Reich available for German nationals, I intend to turn over criminal proceedings against Poles, Russians, Jews, and gypsies to the Reichsfuehrer SS. In so doing, I base myself on the principle that the administration of justice can only make a small contribution to the extermination of members of these peoples. The Justice Administration undoubtedly pronounces very severe sentences on such persons, but that that is not enough to constitute any material contribution towards the realization of the above-mentioned aim.[44]

The Nuremberg trials have revealed to the world the true nature of Hitlerism. Despite its counter-revolutionary origins, it was a profoundly revolutionary upheaval. In twelve years the Nazis succeeded not only in destroying a shaky democracy, but also in casting overboard the whole value system of western civilization. That conclusion emerges also from the study of what happened to German bureaucratic institutions.

The army abandoned standards of conduct observed by the military men of the Occident since Grotius. Bureaucracy and judiciary more than cast off the "liberal shackles" of the *Rechtsstaat;* they broke with the reason and order of the Prussian absolutist tradition. That is why Franz L. Neumann has called National Socialism "a non-state, a chaos, a rule of lawlessness." [45] That lawlessness faced millions of Nazi victims in the black uniform of the SS and political police. The boundlessness of terroristic rule inflated the power of the SS and whetted its appetite for more. Fortified by its elite status and its wealth in resources and slaves, the Himmler Moloch set out to swallow government, army, Party, and even industrial enterprise. That trend stands out most clearly from the confused history of the final years of the Third Reich. The new Dark Age which Allied arms averted would have been made in the image of that bureaucracy for which men were to be bred rather than recruited: the SS.

44. P. 10763 of transcript of proceedings.
45. *Op. cit.,* prefatory page.

ON WEBER'S ANALYSIS
OF BUREAUCRATIC RULES

Alvin W. Gouldner

It sometimes appears that Weber's theory of Bureaucracy is used as a finished tool rather than as a set of hypotheses which, while suggestive as guides to research, must be subordinated to actual findings.[1]

The Weberian ideal-type of bureaucracy is, it must be emphasized, a theory relatively innocent of spatio-temporal cautions. Weber finds "Bureaucracy" as far back as Egypt, the later Roman Principate, and China from the time of Shi Hwangti.[2] Weber's thesis maintains that Bureaucracy has existed in an essentially similar form, regardless of great differences in the social structure in which it was enmeshed. Stated differently, Weber has constructed his type of bureaucratic organization out of elements which may be constant, regardless of varying social structures.

His analysis is, therefore, pitched to the clarification of the allegedly common elements which bureaucratic organizational forms may manifest, regardless of era or region. In consequence, his work is somewhat indifferent to (a) variations in bureaucratic forms, and (b) the manner in which the common characteristics designated as bureaucratic are interrelated with historically specific social structures.[3]

In part, Weber characterizes the ideal-type bureaucracy as possessing hierarchically arranged, continuously operating offices, the behavior of whose occupants is channeled and circumscribed by general rules. Bureaucratic authority is said to reside in the office, not in the occupant, while official activity is separated from private life. The existence of general, learnable rules of procedure structuring behavior in the office is considered nuclear to the type.

Reprinted with minor modifications from "Discussion of Industrial Sociology," *The American Sociological Review*, Vol. XIII (1948), pp. 396-400, by permission of the author and the publisher. (Copyright, 1948, by the American Sociological Society.)

1. Weber himself showed greater awareness of the hypothetical character of his findings than do some of his followers.

2. H. H. Gerth and C. Wright Mills (Editors), *From Max Weber: Essays in Sociology* (Oxford University Press, 1946), p. 204.

3. Weber's treatment of this problem is not unambiguous, for while emphasizing the multiple historical sources and manifestations of bureaucracy, he does state that, ". . . the capitalistic system has undeniably played a major role in the development of bureaucracy . . . capitalism is the most rational economic basis for bureaucratic administration and enables it to develop in the most rational form. . . ." Max Weber, *The Theory of Social and Economic Organization*, translated by A. M. Henderson and Talcott Parsons, Edited by Talcott Parsons (Oxford University Press, 1947), p. 338.

It would seem doubtful that large doses of Weber, taken at regular intervals, provided an adequate antidote to the formal approach employed by students of industrial management and experts in public administration. For Weber's analysis of Bureaucracy premises, to an interesting extent, the official postulates of contemporary formal organization.[4] An example of this is Weber's functional analysis of bureaucratic rules as securing predictability of performance and eliminating "friction." That this is a formal and incomplete description of their functions may be seen if the following question is raised: Just *what* do the general rules make predictable, and *for whom* is this being made predictable?

For example, regarding factory workers' promotional opportunities and conditions of dismissal, there is *relatively* little that is predictable.[5] In short, *certain* things are *not* made predictable by the rules. In the absence of unions, certain types of rules, usually defining obligations, are apparently more fully developed for the lower industrial strata, the area of discretion being narrowed at the base.[6] Conversely, relaxation of certain rules (*e.g.*, sick-leave, lateness, holidays, etc.) increases as one goes up the hierarchy. In this respect, Weber appears to be making the same error as did Durkheim, when the latter conceived of the "collective conscience" as operating apart from the intervention of interested and differentially powerful groups.

Such variations in the rule structure find their reflection among many workers who feel that the factory is a realm of arbitrariness devoid of security.[7] Such feelings, of course, do not indicate the absence of general rules guiding their behavior—far from it! They suggest, however, that in matters of *most concern to the workers* the rules are such as to *minimize their* ability to predict. In this sense, then, the union contract may be seen as an effort on the part of workers to establish a basis of prediction relevant to *their own goals*.

Bureaucratic rules fulfill typically different functions for different ranks in the industrial bureaucracy. It would seem, in fact, that under certain con-

4. Perhaps for this reason Weber focuses on the functional, and de-emphasizes the dysfunctional, aspects of bureaucracy. *Cf.*, Robert K. Merton, "Bureaucratic Structure and Personality," in this volume.

5. The workers' "channels of advancement are not clear, the how and the when of getting ahead are not defined. When they ask their boss how they can get ahead, he can only say that if they work hard, do a good job, behave themselves, and try to learn about the work, eventually they will be given a chance at better jobs. He cannot say if they do this and this and this and this, they will be promoted at the end of so many months. . . ." Burleigh B. Gardner, *Human Relations in Industry* (Richard D. Irwin, Inc., 1946), p. 174.

6. W. Lloyd Warner and J. O. Low, *The Social System of the Modern Factory* (Yale University Press, 1947), p. 111.

7. It is interesting that this sentiment is expressed even by workers in newly industrialized China. One is reported as saying, "We the workers toil everyday. *We do not know what is coming tomorrow.* There is no light ahead for us" (our emphasis, A.W.G.). Ta Chen, "Basic Problems of the Chinese Working Classes," *American Journal of Sociology*, LIII (November, 1947), p. 188.

ditions, it is necessary and normal for the rules to be such as to make prediction difficult or impossible for lower strata personnel. For, given the
implicit but common assumption that anxiety and insecurity are effective
motivators, then employers will tend to leave undeveloped these rules which
would structure the aspirational horizon of workers. It is, perhaps, in part
for this reason that employers are loath to grant trade unions contractual
arrangements providing for conditions of promotion and, in particular, establish seniority rules.

Factories, or other bureaucracies, may not be spoken of as having ends.
It is instead necessary to specify the ends of different people, or the typical
ends of different strata within the organization. Such a refocusing suggests
that these vary, are not necessarily identical and, may in fact, be contradictory.

It may be useful to indicate the manner in which the Weberian theory
of Bureaucracy may be applied to certain problems all too manifest in the
industrial bureaucracy. One of the most important of these is the problem
of the impersonalization of human relations within the factory. This involves
behavior in which the individual uniqueness of people or their problems is
ignored and they are treated as "cases," "problems," or "things."

Though more recently developed,[8] Weber's explanation of this problem
makes explicit that "the dominance of a spirit of formalistic impersonality"
is to be understood as one of "the principal more general consequences of
bureaucratic control."[9] That is, impersonalization is a consequence of bureaucratic forms, relatively indifferent to the specific function of the bureaucracy, or the social structure of which it is a part.

It should be noted first that this analysis does not account for at least one
empirical generalization which may be made about impersonalized behavior.
Namely, that not all members of an industrial bureaucracy—or of the public
with whom the bureaucracy comes into contact—are treated with equal
degrees of impersonality. Impersonal behavior evidently tends to be strongest between status levels, while studies of informal group structure among
operatives indicate that, at least on the lowest levels, impersonalized behavior
is minimal among formal equals.

As between the industrial bureaucracy and its public, it is obvious that
an applicant for a job receives considerably greater impersonal treatment
(the "brush-off") than the customer, who, instead, receives the "glad-hand."
Nor are these variations in themselves constant, for, given a labor and material shortage, it may be the customer who receives the "brush-off" and
the job-applicant, the "glad-hand." It seems clear that a constant norm of
impersonality is an inadequate explanation for such variant and variable
behavior. Factors such as increasing monopoly, declining social mobility,

8. See Robert K. Merton, "Bureaucratic Structure and Personality," in this volume.
9. Weber, *Theory of Social and Economic Organization*, p. 340.

growing overhead costs, absentee ownership—all conceptually irrelevant to bureaucratic forms—do much to diminish intra-factory identification and make impersonalization functional. An adequate analysis of impersonalization will involve these factors.

SOME FURTHER REQUIREMENTS
OF BUREAUCRATIC THEORY

Herbert A. Simon

Administration is ordinarily discussed as the art of "getting things done." Emphasis is placed upon processes and methods for insuring incisive action. Principles are set forth for securing concerted action from groups of men. In all this discussion, however, not very much attention is paid to the choice which prefaces all action—to the determining of what is to be done rather than to the actual doing. . . .

Although any practical activity involves both "deciding" and "doing," it has not commonly been recognized that a theory of administration should be concerned with the processes of decision as well as with the processes of action.[1] This neglect perhaps stems from the notion that decision-making is confined to the formulation of over-all policy. On the contrary, the process of decision does not come to an end when the general purpose of an organization has been determined. The task of "deciding" pervades the entire administrative organization quite as much as does the task of "doing"—indeed, it is integrally tied up with the latter. A general theory of administration must include principles of organization that will insure correct decision-making, just as it must include principles that will insure effective action. . . .

It is a fatal defect of the current principles of administration that, like proverbs, they occur in pairs. For almost every principle one can find an equally plausible and acceptable contradictory principle. Although the two principles of the pair will lead to exactly opposite organizational recommendations, there is nothing in the theory to indicate which is the proper one to apply. . . .

Administrative efficiency is supposed to increase with an increase in spe-

Reprinted in part from *Administrative Behavior*, pp. 1, 20-22, 37-44, 69-70. (Copyright, 1945, by Herbert A. Simon and used with the permission of The Macmillan Company.)
    1. For two notable exceptions to the general neglect of decision-making see C. I. Barnard, *The Functions of the Executive* (Cambridge: Harvard University Press, 1938), and Edwin O. Stene, "An Approach to a Science of Administration," *American Political Science Review*, 34:1124-1137 (Dec., 1940).

cialization. But is this intended to mean that *any* increase in specialization will increase efficiency? If so, which of the following alternatives is the correct application of the principle?

(A) A plan of nursing should be put into effect by which nurses will be assigned to districts and do all nursing within that district, including school examinations, visits to homes of school children, and tuberculosis nursing.

(B) A functional plan of nursing should be put into effect by which different nurses will be assigned to school examinations, visits to homes of school children and tuberculosis nursing. The present method of generalized nursing by districts impedes the development of specialized skills in the three very diverse programs.

Both of these administrative arrangements satisfy the requirement of specialization: the first provides specialization by place; the second, specialization by function. The principle of specialization is of no help at all in choosing between the two alternatives.

It appears that the simplicity of the principle of specialization is a deceptive simplicity—a simplicity that conceals fundamental ambiguities. For "specialization" is not a condition of efficient administration: it is an inevitable characteristic of all group effort, however efficient or inefficient that effort may be. Specialization merely means that different persons are doing different things—and since it is physically impossible for two persons to be doing the same thing in the same place at the same time two persons are always doing different things.

The real problem of administration, then, is not to "specialize," but to specialize in that particular manner, and along those particular lines, which will lead to administrative efficiency. But, in thus rephrasing this "principle" of administration, there has been brought clearly into the open its fundamental ambiguity: "Administrative efficiency is increased by a specialization of the task among the group in the direction that will lead to greater efficiency.". . .

THE DESCRIPTION OF ADMINISTRATIVE SITUATIONS. Before a science can develop principles, it must possess concepts. Before a law of gravitation could be formulated, it was necessary to have the notions of "acceleration" and "weight." The first task of administrative theory is to develop a set of concepts that will permit the description, in terms relevant to the theory, of administrative situations. These concepts, to be scientifically useful, must be operational; that is, their meanings must correspond to empirically observable facts or situations. . . .

What is a scientifically relevant description of an organization? It is a description that, so far as possible, designates for each person in the organization what decisions that person makes, and the influences to which he is subject in making each of these decisions. Current descriptions of administrative organizations fall far short of this standard. For the most part, they confine themselves to the allocation of *functions*, and the formal structure of *authority*. They give little attention to the other types of organizational influence or to the system of communication.

What does it mean, for example to say: "The Department is made up of three Bureaus. The first has the function of ————, the second the function of ————, and the third the function of ————?" What can be learned from such a description about the workability of the organizational arrangement? Very little, indeed. For, from the description, there is obtained no idea of the degree to which decisions are centralized at the bureau level or at the departmental level. No notion is given of the extent to which the (presumably unlimited) authority of the department over the bureau is actually exercised, nor by what mechanisms. There is no indication of the extent to which systems of communication assist the coordination of the three bureaus, nor, for that matter, to what extent coordination is required by the nature of their work. There is no description of the kinds of training the members of the bureau have undergone, nor the extent to which this training permits decentralization at the bureau level. In sum, a description of administrative organizations in terms almost exclusively of functions and lines of authority is completely inadequate for purposes of administrative analysis. . . .

Consider the term "centralization." How is it determined whether the operations of a particular organization are "centralized" or "decentralized"? Does the fact that field offices exist prove anything about decentralization? Might not the same decentralization take place in the bureaus of a centrally located office? A realistic analysis of centralization must include a study of the allocation of decisions in the organization, and the methods of influence that are employed by the higher levels to affect the decisions at the lower levels. Such an analysis would reveal a much more complex picture of the decision-making process than any enumeration of the geographical locations of organizational units at the different levels.

Administrative description suffers currently from superficiality, oversimplification, lack of realism. It has confined itself too closely to the mechanism of authority, and has failed to bring within its orbit the other, equally important, modes of influence on organizational behavior. It has refused to undertake the tiresome task of studying the actual allocations of decision-making functions. It has been satisfied to speak of "authority," "centralization," "span of control," "function," without seeking operational definitions of these terms. Until administrative description reaches a higher level of sophistication, there is little reason to hope that rapid progress will be made toward the identification and verification of valid administrative principles.

THE DIAGNOSIS OF ADMINISTRATIVE SITUATIONS. Before any positive suggestions can be made, it is necessary to digress a bit, and to consider more closely the exact nature of the propositions of administrative theory. The theory of administration is concerned with how an organization should be constructed and operated in order to accomplish its work efficiently. A fundamental principle of administration, which follows almost immediately from the rational character of "good" administration, is that among several alternatives involving the same expenditure the one should always be selected which leads to the greatest accomplishment of administrative objectives; and among several alternatives that lead to the same accomplishment the one should be selected which involves the least expenditure. Since this "principle of efficiency" is characteristic of any activity that attempts rationally to maximize the attainment of certain ends with the use of scarce means, it is as characteristic of economic theory as it is of administrative theory. The "administrative man" takes his place alongside the classical "economic man." [2]

Actually, the "principle" of efficiency should be considered as a definition rather than a principle: it is a definition of what is meant by "good" or "correct" administrative behavior. It does not tell *how* accomplishments are to be maximized, but merely states that this maximization is the aim of administrative activity, and that administrative theory must disclose under what conditions the maximization takes place.

Now what are the factors that determine the level of efficiency which is achieved by an administrative organization? It is not possible to make an exhaustive list of these, but the principal categories can be enumerated. Perhaps the simplest method of approach is to consider the single member of the administrative organization, and ask what the limits are to the quantity and quality of his output. These limits include (a) limits on his ability to *perform*, and (b) limits on his ability to *make correct decisions*. To the extent that these limits are removed, the administrative organization approaches its goal of high efficiency. Two persons, given the same skills, the same objectives and values, the same knowledge and information, can rationally decide only upon the same course of action. Hence, administrative theory must be interested in the factors that will determine with what skills, values, and knowledge the organization member undertakes his work. These are the "limits" to rationality with which the principles of administration must deal.

On one side, the individual is limited by those skills, habits, and reflexes which are no longer in the realm of the conscious. His performance, for example, may be limited by his manual dexterity or his reaction time or his strength. His decision-making processes may be limited by the speed of his mental processes, his skill in elementary arithmetic, and so forth. In this area,

2. For an elaboration of the principle of efficiency and its place in administrative theory see Clarence E. Ridley and Herbert A. Simon, *Measuring Municipal Activities* (Chicago: International City Managers' Assn., 2nd ed., 1943), particularly chap. 1 and the preface to the second edition.

the principles of administration must be concerned with the physiology of the human body, the laws of skill-training, and of habit. This is the field that has been most successfully cultivated by the followers of Taylor, and in which has been developed time-and-motion study and the therblig.

On a second side, the individual is limited by his values and those conceptions of purpose which influence him in making his decisions. If his loyalty to the organization is high, his decisions may evidence sincere acceptance of the objectives set for the organization; if that loyalty is lacking, personal motives may interfere with his administrative efficiency. If his loyalties are attached to the bureau by which he is employed, he may sometimes make decisions that are inimical to the larger unit of which the bureau is a part. In this area the principles of administration must be concerned with the determinants of loyalty and morale, with leadership and initiative, and with the influences that determine where the individual's organizational loyalties will be attached.

On a third side, the individual is limited by the extent of his knowledge of things relevant to his job. This applies both to the basic knowledge required in decision-making—a bridge designer must know the fundamentals of mechanics—and to the information that is required to make his decisions appropriate to the given situation. In this area, administrative theory is concerned with such fundamental questions as these: what the limits are on the mass of knowledge that human minds can accumulate and apply; how rapidly knowledge can be assimilated; how specialization in the administrative organization is to be related to the specializations of knowledge that are prevalent in the community's occupational structure; how the system of communication is to channel knowledge and information to the appropriate decision-points; what types of knowledge can, and what types cannot, be easily transmitted; how the need for intercommunication of information is affected by the modes of specialization in the organization? This is perhaps the *terra incognita* of administrative theory, and undoubtedly its careful exploration will cast great light on the proper application of the proverbs of administration.

Perhaps this triangle of limits does not completely bound the area of rationality, and other sides need to be added to the figure. In any case, the enumeration will serve to indicate the kinds of considerations that must go into the construction of valid and noncontradictory principles of administration.

An important fact to be kept in mind is that the limits of rationality are variable limits. Most important of all, consciousness of the limits may in itself alter them. Suppose it were discovered in a particular organization, for example, that organizational loyalties attached to small units had frequently led to a harmful degree of intra-organizational competition. Then, a program which trained members of the organization to be conscious of their loyalties, and to subordinate loyalties toward the smaller group to those toward the larger, might lead to a very considerable alteration of the limits in that organization.[3]

A related point is that the term "rational behavior," as employed here, refers to rationality when that behavior is evaluated in terms of the objectives of the larger organization; for, as it has just been pointed out, the difference in direction of the individual's aims from those of the larger organization is just one of those elements of nonrationality with which the theory must deal.

ASSIGNING WEIGHTS TO THE CRITERIA. A first step, then, in the overhauling of the proverbs of administration is to develop a vocabulary, along the lines just suggested, for the description of administrative organization. A second step, which has also been outlined, is to study the limits of rationality in order to develop a complete and comprehensive enumeration of the criteria that must be weighed in evaluating an administrative organization. The current proverbs represent only a fragmentary and unsystematized portion of these criteria.

When these two tasks have been carried out, it remains to assign weights to the criteria. Since the criteria, or "proverbs," are often mutually competitive or contradictory, it is not sufficient merely to identify them. Merely to know, for example, that a specified change in organization will reduce the span of control is not enough to justify the change. This gain must be balanced against the possible resulting loss of contact between the higher and lower ranks of the hierarchy.

Hence, administrative theory must also be concerned with the question of the weights that are to be applied to these criteria—to the problems of their relative importance in any concrete situation. This question is an empirical one, and its solution cannot even be attempted in a volume like this one. What is needed is empirical research and experimentation to determine the relative desirability of alternative administrative arrangements. The methodological framework for this research is already at hand in the principle of efficiency. If an administrative organization whose activities are susceptible to objective evaluation be studied, then the actual change in accomplishment that results from modifying administrative arrangements in these organizations can be observed and analyzed.

There are two indispensable conditions to successful research along these lines. First, it is necessary that the objectives of the administrative organization under study be defined in concrete terms so that results, expressed in terms of these objectives, may be accurately measured. Second, it is necessary that sufficient experimental control be exercised to make possible the

3. For an example of the use of such training, see Herbert A. Simon and William Divine, "Controlling Human Factors in an Administrative Experiment," *Public Administration Review*, 1:487-492 (Autumn, 1941).

isolation of the particular effect under study from other disturbing factors that might be operating on the organization at the same time.

These two conditions have seldom been even partially fulfilled in so-called "administrative experiments." The mere fact that a legislature passes a law creating an administrative agency, that the agency operates for five years, that it is finally abolished, and that an historical study is then made of its operations is not sufficient to make of that agency's history an "administrative experiment." Modern American legislation is full of such "experiments" which furnish orators in neighboring states with abundant ammunition when similar issues arise in their bailiwicks, but which provide the scientific investigator with little or nothing in the way of objective evidence, one way or the other.

In the literature of administration, only a handful of research studies satisfy these fundamental conditions of methodology—and they are, for the most part, on the periphery of the problem of organization. There are, first of all, the studies of the Taylor group which sought to determine the technological conditions of efficiency. Perhaps none of these is a better example of the painstaking methods of science than Taylor's own studies of the cutting of metals.[4]

Studies dealing with the human and social aspects of administration are even rarer than the technological studies. Among the more important are the whole series of studies on fatigue, starting in Great Britain during the First World War, and culminating in the Western Electric experiments.[5]

In the field of public administration, almost the sole example of such experimentation is the series of studies that have been conducted in the public welfare field to determine the proper case loads for social workers.[6]

Because, apart from these scattered examples, studies of administrative agencies have been carried out without benefit of control or objective measurements of results, they have had to depend for their recommendations and conclusions upon *a priori* reasoning proceeding from "principles of administration." The reasons have already been stated in this chapter why the "principles" derived in this way cannot be more than "proverbs." . . .

4. F. W. Taylor, *On the Art of Cutting Metals* (New York: American Society of Mechanical Engineers, 1907).

5. Great Britain, Ministry of Munitions, Health of Munitions Workers Committee, *Final Report* (London: H.M. Stationery Office, 1918); F. J. Roethlisberger and William J. Dickson, *Management and the Worker* (Cambridge: Harvard University Press, 1939).

6. Ellery F. Reed, *An Experiment in Reducing the Cost of Relief* (Chicago: American Public Welfare Assn., 1937); Rebecca Staman, "What Is the Most Economical Case Load in Public Relief Administration?" *Social Work Technique*, 4:117-121 (May-June, 1938); Chicago Relief Administration, *Adequate Staff Brings Economy* (Chicago: American Public Welfare Assn., 1939); Constance Hastings and Saya S. Schwartz, *Size of Vistors' Caseload as a Factor in Efficient Administration of Public Assistance* (Philadelphia; Philadelphia County Board of Assistance, 1939); H. A. Simon *et al.*, *Determining Work Loads for Professional Staff in a Public Welfare Agency* (Berkeley: University of California, Bureau of Public Administration, 1941).

In one respect the decision problem in private organizations is much simpler than in public agencies. The private organization is expected to take into consideration only those consequences of the decision which affect *it*, while the public agency must weigh the decision in terms of some comprehensive system of public or community values. For example, when the president of a private corporation decides to give his son a position in the firm, he has to take into consideration the effect the appointment will have upon the efficiency of the enterprise; but a man in the same relative position in the public service has to be concerned equally about the effect of this step upon "equality of opportunity in the public service." This distinction between private and public management is hardly one of black and white, for an increasing number of private businesses are becoming "affected with a public interest," and an increasing number of private executives are concerning themselves with their responsibilities of trusteeship toward the community, even beyond the limits that the law imposes on them.

2

BASES FOR THE GROWTH
OF BUREAUCRACY

Numerous historical studies have traced the multiple and interdependent conditions disposing to the emergence and growth of bureaucracy. These bear directly on the doctrine of the current and, allegedly, irreversible trend of bureaucratization. The selections in this section are variously concerned with identifying the social, economic and political contexts making for the growth of bureaucratic organization. Weber discusses, in some detail, the organizational consequences of marked increases in the number and variety of administrative tasks, and analyzes the elements of a money economy that are preconditions for the emergence of a stable bureaucracy. His theoretical analysis is in part illustrated by Tout's account of the development of a governmental bureaucracy from the King's household staff in medieval England.

Further sources of bureaucratization in various spheres of social organization are taken up in the remaining selections. In his analysis of the "church-type" and "sect-type," Troeltsch links belief-systems to distinctive types of religious organization. By comparative analysis of English and German social structures, Veblen identifies the conditions making for the rapid industrial bureaucratization of Germany in the nineteenth century. The "Iron Law of Oligarchy," as set forth in the selection from Michels, holds the consolidation of power by a professionalized leadership to be an essential feature of the growth of bureaucratic organization.

The second selection from Weber presents his theory of the processes through which the essentially unstable pattern of charismatic leadership (rule based on the "extraordinary" qualities of a "leader") becomes transformed into a stable system of organization, and indicates the conditions under which this takes bureaucratic form. Locating his case-study within this theoretic framework, Gerth shows in detail how the initial charismatic domination of the Nazi party became fused with, and progressively subordinated to, bureaucratic domination.

THE PRESUPPOSITIONS AND CAUSES
OF BUREAUCRACY

Max Weber

The social and economic presuppositions of the modern structure of the office are as follows:

The development of the *money economy*, in so far as a pecuniary compensation of the officials is concerned, is a presupposition of bureaucracy. Today it not only prevails but is predominant. This fact is of very great importance for the whole bearing of bureaucracy, yet by itself it is by no means decisive for the existence of bureaucracy.

Historical examples of rather distinctly developed and quantitatively large bureaucracies are: (a) Egypt, during the period of the new Empire which, however, contained strong patrimonial elements; (b) the later Roman Principate, and especially the Diocletian monarchy and the Byzantine polity which developed out of it and yet retained strong feudal and patrimonial elements; (c) the Roman Catholic Church, increasingly so since the end of the thirteenth century; (d) China, from the time of Shi Hwangti until the present, but with strong patrimonial and prebendal elements; (e) in ever purer forms, the modern European states and, increasingly, all public corporations since the time of princely absolutism; (f) the large modern capitalist enterprise, the more so as it becomes greater and more complicated.

To a very great extent, partly even predominantly, cases (a) to (d) have rested upon compensation of the officials in kind. Yet they have displayed many other traits and effects characteristic of bureaucracy. The historical model of all later bureaucracies—the new Empire of Egypt—is at the same time one of the most grandiose examples of an organized subsistence economy. Yet this coincidence of bureaucracy and subsistence economy is understandable in view of the quite unique conditions that existed in Egypt. And the reservations—and they are quite considerable—which one must make in classifying this Egyptian structure as a bureaucracy are conditioned by the subsistence economy. A certain measure of a developed money economy is the normal precondition for the unchanged and continued existence, if not for the establishment, of pure bureaucratic administrations.

According to historical experience, without a money economy the bu-

Reprinted from *From Max Weber: Essays in Sociology* (Ed. Hans H. Gerth and C. Wright Mills), pp. 204-214, by permission of the publisher. (Copyright, 1946, by the Oxford University Press.)

reaucratic structure can hardly avoid undergoing substantial internal changes, or indeed, turning into another type of structure. The allocation of fixed income in kind, from the magazines of the lord or from his current intake, to the officials easily means a first step toward appropriation of the sources of taxation and their exploitation as private property. This kind of allocation has been the rule in Egypt and China for thousands of years and played an important part in the later Roman monarchy as well as elsewhere. The income in kind has protected the official against the often sharp fluctuations in the purchasing power of money. Whenever the lord's prerogatives have relaxed, the taxes in kind, as a rule, have been irregular. In this case, the official has direct recourse to the tributaries of his bailiwick, whether or not he is authorized. Close at hand is the idea of securing the official against such oscillations by mortgaging or transferring the levies and therewith the power to tax, or by leasing profitable lands of the lord to the official for his own use. Every central authority which is not strictly organized is tempted to take this course either voluntarily or because the officials compel it to do so. The official may satisfy himself with the use of these levies or loans up to the level of his salary claim and then hand over the surplus. This implies strong temptation and therefore yields results chiefly unsatisfactory to the lord. Another process involves fixing the official's salary: This often occurred in the early history of German officialdom; and it happened on the largest scale in all Eastern Satrap administrations: the official hands over a stipulated amount and retains the surplus.

In such cases the official is economically in a position rather similar to that of the entrepreneurial tax-farmer. Indeed, office-farming including even the leasing of offices to the highest bidder is regularly found. On the soil of a private economy, the transformation of the statutes of villenage into tenancy relations is one of the most important among numerous examples. By tenancy arrangements the lord can tranfer the trouble of changing his income-in-kind into money-income to the office tenant or to the official who is to be given a fixed sum. This was plainly the case with some Oriental regents in Antiquity. And above all, the farming out of public collection of taxes in lieu of the lord's own management of taxgathering served this purpose. From this procedure there develops the possibility for the lord to progress in the ordering of his finances into a systematic budget. This is a very important advance, for it means that a fixed estimate of the income, and correspondingly of the expenses, can take the place of a hand-to-mouth living from incalculable incomes in kind, a condition typical of all the early stages of public households. On the other hand, in systematizing his budget in this way, the lord renounces the control and full exploitation of his capacity to tax for his own use. According to the measure of freedom left to the official, to the office, or to the tax-farmer, the lasting capacity to pay taxes is endangered by inconsiderate exploitation. For, unlike the political overlord, the capitalist is not in the same way permanently interested in the subject's ability to pay.

The lord seeks to safeguard himself against this loss of control by regulations. The mode of tax-farming or the transfer of taxes can thus vary widely, according to the distribution of power between the lord and the tenant. Either the tenant's interest in the free exploitation of capacity to pay taxes or the lord's interest in the permanence of this capacity prevails. The nature of the tax-farming system rests essentially upon the joint or the opposing influence of these motives: the elimination of oscillations in the yields, the possibility of a budget, the safeguarding of the subjects' capacity to pay by protecting them against uneconomical exploitation, and a state control of the tax-farmer's yields for the sake of appropriating the maximum possible. In the Ptolemaic empire, as in Hellas and in Rome, the tax-farmer was still a private capitalist. The raising of taxes, however, was bureaucratically executed and controlled by the Ptolemaic state. The tenant's profit consisted in only a share of the respective surplus over and above the tax-farmer's fee, which was, in fact, only a guarantee. The tax-farmer's risk consisted in the possibility of yields that were lower than this sum.

The purely economic conception of the office as a source of the official's private income can also lead to the direct purchase of offices. This occurs when the lord finds himself in a position in which he requires not only a current income but money capital—for instance, for warfare or for debt payments. The purchase of office as a regular institution has existed in modern states, in the church state as well as in that of France and England; it has existed in the cases of sinecures as well as of very serious offices; and, in the case of officers' commissions, it lagged over until the early nineteenth century. In individual cases, the economic meaning of such a purchase of office can be altered so that the purchasing sum is partly or wholly in the nature of bail deposited for faithful service, but this has not been the rule.

Every sort of assignment of usufructs, tributes and services which are due to the lord himself or to the official for personal exploitation, always means a surrender of the pure type of bureaucratic organization. The official in such positions has a personal right to the possession of his office. This is the case to a still higher degree when official duty and compensation are interrelated in such a way that the official does not transfer to the lord any yields gained from the objects left to him, but handles these objects for his private ends and in turn renders to the lord services of a personal or a military, political, or ecclesiastical character.

We wish to speak of "*prebends*" and of a "prebendal" organization of office, wherever the lord assigns to the official rent payments for life, payments which are somehow fixed to objects or which are essentially *economic* usufruct from lands or other sources. They must be compensations for the fulfilment of actual or fictitious office duties; they are goods permanently set aside for the economic assurance of the office.

The transition from such prebendal organization of office to salaried officialdom is quite fluid. Very often the economic endowment of priesthoods has been "prebendal," as in Antiquity and the Middle Ages, and even up to the modern period. But in almost all periods the same form has been found in other areas. In Chinese sacerdotal law, the prebendal character of all offices forced the mourning official to resign his office. For during the ritual mourning period for the father or other household authorities abstention from the enjoyment of possessions was prescribed. Originally this prescription was aimed at avoiding the ill-will of the deceased master of the house, for the house belonged to this master and the office was considered purely as a prebend, a source for rent.

When not only economic rights but also lordly prerogatives are leased for personal execution with the stipulation of *personal* services to the lord, a further step away from salaried bureaucracy is taken. These leased prerogatives vary; for instance, with the political official, they may be in the nature of landlordism or in the nature of office authority. In both instances, and certainly in the latter, the specific nature of bureaucratic organization is completely destroyed and we enter the organizational realm of *feudal* dominion. All kinds of assignments of services and usufructs in kind as endowments for officials tend to loosen the bureaucratic mechanism, and especially to weaken hierarchic subordination. This subordination is most strictly developed in the discipline of modern officialdom. A precision similar to the precision of the contractually employed official of the modern Occident can only be attained—at least under very energetic leadership— where the subjection of the officials to the lord is personally absolute, where slaves, or employees treated like slaves, are used for administration.

The Egyptian officials were slaves of the Pharaoh, if not legally, at least in fact. The Roman latifundia owners liked to commission slaves with the direct management of money matters, because of the possibility of subjecting them to torture. In China, similar results have been sought by the prodigal use of the bamboo as a disciplinary instrument. The chances, however, for such direct means of coercion to function with *steadiness* are extremely unfavorable. According to experience, the relative optimum for the success and maintenance of a strict mechanization of the bureaucratic apparatus is offered by a secured money salary connected with the opportunity of a career that is not dependent upon mere accident and arbitrariness. Strict discipline and control, which at the same time has consideration for the official's sense of honor, and the development of prestige sentiments of the status group, as well as the possibility of public criticism, work in the direction of strict mechanization. With all this, the bureaucratic apparatus functions more assuredly than does any legal enslavement of functionaries.

A strong status sentiment among officials not only agrees with the official's readiness to subordinate himself to the chief without any will of his own, but—just as is the case with the officer—status sentiments are the consequence of such subordination, for internally they balance the official's self-feeling. The purely impersonal character of office work, with its principal separation of the private sphere of the official from that of the office, facilitates the official's integration into the given functional conditions of a fixed mechanism based upon discipline.

Even though the full development of a money economy is not an indispensable precondition for bureaucratization, bureaucracy as a permanent structure is knit to the one presupposition of a constant income for maintaining it. Where such an income cannot be derived from private profits, as is the case with the bureaucratic organization of large modern enterprises, or from fixed land rents, as with the manor, a stable system of *taxation* is the precondition for the permanent existence of bureaucratic administration. For well-known and general reasons, only a fully developed money economy offers a secure basis for such a taxation system. The degree of administrative bureaucratization in urban communities with fully developed money economies has not infrequently been relatively greater in the contemporary far larger states of plains. Yet as soon as these plain states have been able to develop orderly systems of tribute, bureaucracy has developed more comprehensively than in city states. Whenever the size of the city states has remained confined to moderate limits, the tendency for a plutocratic and collegial administration by notables has corresponded most adequately to their structure.

THE QUANTITATIVE DEVELOPMENT OF ADMINISTRATIVE TASKS. The proper soil for the bureaucratization of an administration has always been the specific developments of administrative tasks. We shall first discuss the quantitative extension of such tasks. In the field of politics, the great state and the mass party are the classic soil for bureaucratization.

This does not mean that every historically known and genuine formation of great states has brought about a bureaucratic administration. The permanence of a once-existing great state, or the homogeneity of a culture borne by such a state, has not always been attached to a bureaucratic structure of state. However, both of these features have held to a great extent, for instance, in the Chinese empire. The numerous great Negro empires, and similar formations, have had only an ephemeral existence primarily because they have lacked an apparatus of officials. And the unity of the Carolingian empire disintegrated when its organization of officials disintegrated. This organization, however, was predominantly patrimonial rather than bureaucratic in nature. From a purely temporal view, however, the empire of the Caliphs and its predecessors on Asiatic soil have lasted for considerable periods of time, and their organization of office was essentially patrimonial and prebendal. Also, the Holy Roman Empire lasted for a long time in spite of the almost complete absence of bureaucracy. All these realms have represented a cultural unity of at least approximately the same strength as is usually created by bureaucratic politics.

The ancient Roman Empire disintegrated internally in spite of increasing bureaucratization and even during its very execution. This was because of the way the tax burdens were distributed by the bureaucratic state, which favored the subsistence economy. Viewed with regard to the intensity of their purely *political* unities, the temporal existences of the empires of the Caliphs, Carolingian and other medieval emperors were essentially unstable, nominal, and cohesive conglomerates. On the whole, the capacity for political action steadily diminished, and the relatively great unity of *culture* flowed from ecclesiastic structures that were in part strictly unified and, in the Occidental Middle Ages, increasingly bureaucratic in character. The unity of their cultures resulted partly from the far-going homogeneity of their social structures, which in turn was the aftermath and transformation of their former political unity. Both are phenomena of the traditional stereotyping of culture, which favors an unstable equilibrium. Both of these factors proved so strong a foundation that even grandiose attempts at expansion, such as the Crusades, could be undertaken in spite of the lack of intensive political unity; they were, one might say, performed as "private undertakings." The failure of the Crusades and their often irrational political course, however, is associated with the absence of a unified and intensive state power to back them up. And there is no doubt that the nuclei of intensive "modern" states in the Middle Ages developed concomitantly with bureaucratic structures. Furthermore, in the end these quite bureaucratic political structures undoubtedly shattered the social conglomerates, which rested essentially upon unstable equilibriums.

The disintegration of the Roman Empire was partly conditioned by the very bureaucratization of its army and official apparatus. This bureaucratization could only be realized by carrying through at the same time a method of taxation which by its distribution of burdens was bound to lead to relative increase in the importance of a subsistence economy. Individual factors of this sort always enter the picture. Also the "intensity" of the external and the internal state activities play their part. Quite apart from the relation between the state influence upon culture and the degree of bureaucratization, it may be said that "normally"—though not without exception—the vigor to expand is directly related to the degree of bureaucratization. For two of the most expansive polities, the Roman Empire and the British world empire, during their most expansive periods, rested upon bureaucratic foundations only to a small extent. The Norman state in England carried through a strict organization on the basis of a feudal hierarchy. To a large extent, it received its unity and its push through the bureaucratization of the royal exchequer, which, in comparison to other political structures of the feudal period, was extremely strict. Later on, the English state did not share in the continental development towards bureaucratization, but remained an administration of notables. Just as in the republican administration of Rome, this English rule by notables was a result of the relative absence of a continental character, as well as of absolutely unique preconditions, which at the present time are disappearing. The dispensability of the large standing armies, which a continental state with equally expansive tendencies requires for its land frontiers, is among these special preconditions. In Rome, bureaucratization advanced with the transition from a coastal to a continental ring of frontiers. For the rest, in the domination structure of Rome, the strictly military character of the magistrate authorities—in the Roman manner unknown to any other people—made up for the lack of a bureaucratic apparatus with its technical efficiency, its precision and unity of administrative functions, especially outside the city limits. The continuity of administration was safeguarded by the unique position of the Senate. In Rome, as in England, one presupposition for this dispensability of bureaucracy which should not be forgotten was that the state authorities increasingly "minimized" the scope of their functions at home. They restricted their functions to what was absolutely demanded for direct "reasons of state."

At the beginning of the modern period, all the prerogatives of the continental states accumulated in the hands of those princes who most relentlessly took the course of administrative bureaucratization. It is obvious that technically the great modern state is absolutely dependent upon a bureaucratic basis. The larger the state, and the more it is or the more it becomes a great power state, the more unconditionally is this the case.

The United States still bears the character of a polity which, at least in the technical sense, is not fully bureaucratized. But the greater the zones of friction with the outside and the more urgent the needs for administrative unity at home become, the more this character is inevitably and gradually giving way formally to the bureaucratic structure. Moreover, the partly unbureaucratic form of the state structure of the United States is materially balanced by the more strictly bureaucratic structures of those formations which, in truth, dominate politically, namely, the parties under the leadership of professionals or experts in organization and election tactics. The increasingly bureaucratic organization of all genuine mass parties offers the most striking example of the role of sheer quantity as a leverage for the bureaucratization of a social structure. In Germany, above all, the Social Democratic party and abroad both of the "historical" American parties are bureaucratic in the greatest possible degree.

QUALITATIVE CHANGES OF ADMINISTRATIVE TASKS. Bureaucratization is occasioned more by intensive and qualitative enlargement and internal deployment of the scope of administrative tasks than by their extensive and quantitative increase. But the direction bureaucratization takes and the reasons that occasion it vary widely.

In Egypt, the oldest country of bureaucratic state administration, the public and collective regulation of waterways for the whole country and from the top could not be avoided because of technical economic factors. This regulation created the mechanism of scribes and officials. Once established, this mechanism, even in early times, found its second realm of business in the extraordinary construction activities which were organized militarily. As mentioned before, the bureaucratic tendency has chiefly been influenced by needs arising from the creation of standing armies as determined by power politics and by the development of public finance connected with the military establishment. In the modern state, the increasing demands for administration rest on the increasing complexity of civilization and push towards bureaucratization.

Very considerable expansions, especially overseas, have, of course, been managed by states ruled by notables (Rome, England, Venice), as will become evident in the appropriate context. Yet the "intensity" of the administration, that is, the transfer of as many tasks as possible to the organization of the state proper for continuous management and discharge, has been only slightly developed among the great states ruled by notables, especially Rome and England, if we compare them with bureaucratic polities.

Both in notable and bureaucratic administrations the *structure* of state power has influenced culture very strongly. But it has done so relatively slightly in the form of management and control by the state. This holds from justice down to education. The growing demands on culture, in turn, are determined, though to a varying extent, by the growing wealth of the most influential strata in the state. To this extent increasing bureaucratization is a function of the increasing possession of goods used for consumption, and of an increasingly sophisticated technique of fashioning external life—a technique which corresponds to the opportunities provided by such wealth. This reacts upon the standard of living and makes for an increasing subjective indispensability of organized, collective, inter-local, and thus bureaucratic, provision for the most varied wants, which previously were either unknown, or were satisfied locally or by a private economy.

Among purely political factors, the increasing demand of a society, accustomed to absolute pacification, for order and protection ("police") in all fields exerts an especially persevering influence in the direction of bureaucratization. A steady road leads from modifications of the blood feud, sacerdotally, or by means of arbitration, to the present position of the policeman as the "representative of God on earth." The former means placed the guarantees for the individual's rights and security squarely upon the members of his sib, who are obligated to assist him with oath and vengeance. Among other factors, primarily the manifold tasks of the so-called "policy of social welfare" operate in the direction of bureaucratization, for these tasks are, in part, saddled upon the state by interest groups and, in part, the state usurps them, either for reasons of power policy or for ideological motives. Of course, these tasks are to a large extent economically determined.

Among essentially technical factors, the specifically modern means of communication enter the picture as pacemakers of bureaucratization. Public land and water-ways, railroads, the telegraph, et cetera—they must, in part, necessarily be administered in a public and collective way; in part, such administration is technically expedient. In this respect, the contemporary means of communication frequently play a role similar to that of the canals of Mesopotamia and the regulation of the Nile in the ancient Orient. The degree to which the means of communication have been developed is a condition of decisive importance for the possibility of bureaucratic administration, although it is not the only decisive condition. Certainly in Egypt, bureaucratic centralization, on the basis of an almost pure subsistence economy, could never have reached the actual degree which it did without the natural trade route of the Nile. In order to promote bureaucratic centralization in modern Persia, the telegraph officials were officially commissioned with reporting all occurrences in the provinces to the Shah, over the heads of the local authorities. In addition, everyone received the right to remonstrate directly by telegraph. The modern Occidental state can be administered the way it actually is only because the state controls the telegraph network and has the mails and railroads at its disposal.

Railroads, in turn, are intimately connected with the development of an inter-local traffic of mass goods. This traffic is among the causal factors in the formation of the modern state. As we have already seen, this does not hold unconditionally for the past.

THE EMERGENCE OF A BUREAUCRACY

T. F. Tout

We are sometimes told that the elaboration of the political machinery of the state, which involves the existence of a bureaucratic class, is the work of quite modern times. No doubt many of the refinements of permanent officialism are modern enough. The very words, civil service, civil servant,

Reprinted in part from *The English Civil Service in the Fourteenth Century*, Vol. III, pp. 192-213, by permission of the publisher. (Copyright, 1916, by the University Press, Manchester, England.)

which we familiarly use to describe the permanent public official, are things of yesterday . . .

Whether or not we have the name, we have the thing, hundreds of years earlier. The public servants of the crown, whose special sphere was administration and finance, and who were professional administrators, not professional soldiers, go back to the earliest ages of the English state. They existed, but barely existed, in the later days of the Anglo-Saxon monarchy. They first became numerous, powerful, and conspicuous when the Norman kings gave England a centralized administration and a trained body of administrators. Their influence rose to a high level in the reigns of Henry II and his sons, when England, thanks to their work, was the best governed and most orderly state in all Western Europe. By this time another process was beginning. The early civil servants, like all early public officials, were simply members of the king's household. The king's clerks, accountants, and administrators belonged to the same category as the king's cooks, scullions, grooms, and valets. The public service of the state then was hopelessly confused with the domestic service of the court. Bit by bit, however, we get to the first stages of the long process by which the national administrative machine was slowly disentangled from the machinery which regulated the domestic establishment of the monarch. The time was still far distant when the modern distinction was made between the king in his private and public capacities, between the royal officers who ruled the king's household, and those who carried on the government of the country. Our mediæval ancestors were moved even less than ourselves by theoretical considerations. But for very practical reasons the kings found it impossible not to draw some sort of line between the men who helped them to govern the country and the men who waited on the monarch or strove to keep in order his vast and disorderly household. For one thing the king was always on the move. A Norman or Angevin monarch had no fixed "residence" and still less a fixed "capital." Business and inclination united to make him live a wandering life from one royal estate to another. Economic necessity alone kept him plodding through his continued journeys. So great was the dearth of means of communication, and so difficult was the transport of bulky commodities, that it was much easier to take men and horses to their food than to bring their food to them.

The whole administrative machine of our early kings was a part of the court. Accordingly it followed the king on his constant wanderings. It was not the least of the troubles of those, who wished to transact business with the government, that they had to find out where the king was and to attend him in his restless movements from place to place. So long as the magnates of each district ruled each one over his own estate, so long as the freemen of shire, hundred, or borough were mainly governed in their local courts, these inconveniences occurred so seldom that they counted for very little.

But by Henry II's reign the English king had centralized so much authority under his immediate direction that all men of substance had frequent occasion to seek justice or request favours at the court. Moreover, as the administrative machine grew more complex, it became a constantly harder task to carry about with the court the ever-increasing tribe of officials, to say nothing of the records, registers, and rolls that they found necessary for business or for reference. The remedy was found in establishing a headquarters for each administrative department at some fixed spot, where permanent business was transacted and where the records of the office were preserved. It was for this practical reason that the civil service slowly differentiated itself from the domestic environment of the king. For similar practical reasons London, or rather Westminster, was found the most convenient fixed spot for each permanent central bureau.

The financial administration was the first to acquire a separate life of its own. In the days when government meant exploitation, the highest aim of the ruler was to get as much out of his subjects as he could. The good king of those days promoted his people's welfare because he had the wit to see that a prosperous community could afford to pay more taxes and was likely to yield them up with less friction or rebellion. It was natural then that finance should loom largest in the royal scheme of the universe, and that the greatest attention should be devoted to the collection and administration of the royal revenue. Accordingly the good old days when Edward the Confessor kept his treasure in a box in his bedroom passed away. Under Henry I the first of modern government offices arose in the king's exchequer, and under Henry II the king's exchequer had a permanent home of its own at Westminster. If the title of chamberlain, borne by some of the king's exchequer officials, shows its origin in the king's bedroom or chamber, the exchequer was before the end of the twelfth century in all essentials an independent office of state. Its staff was quite separate from the service of the court. It was in modern phrase a branch—for the time being the only branch —of the king's civil service.

I have spoken of the exchequer as a financial office, and I have done so because its main concern was with finance. But we must not expect meticulous distinctions in those days between various branches of the royal service. The business of government was still so primitive, the number of skilled officers so small, their resources so limited, that every servant of the king had, like the modern country workman or the present Indian civilian in a remote district, to turn his hand to any job that came in his way. If he did not do it, there was no one else who could, and the job remained undone. Accordingly the exchequer officer is often found trying lawsuits, going on missions, and transacting all sorts of business that had no close relation with finance. As time went on, this proved inconvenient, and just as the twelfth century saw the creation of the financial department, so did the thirteenth century witness the slow separation from the court of a second office of state, whose main business was administration. This administrative department grew out of the little office where the chaplains of the court occupied themselves in writing out the king's letters between the hours of divine service. One of these chaplains, called the chancellor, was entrusted with the custody of the king's seal. Now in an age when writing was a rare art with laymen, and when all writing looked much alike, a great man did not authenticate his letters by signing them but by affixing his seal to them. The keeping of the king's seal then involved responsibility for the composition of the king's correspondence. Now the confidential clerk, who writes a man's letters, may generally more or less suggest the policy these letters involve. It resulted that, as the king's general secretary, the chancellor became the most trusted of all the king's ministers, his secretary of state for all departments, as Stubbs has rightly called him. He was, in effect, prime minister, and to do his work he had to gather round him a staff of skilled officials. The result was the complete separation of the king's scribes from the king's chaplains, the growth of a class of clerks of the chancery who by the fourteenth century were the ablest, most powerful, and most energetic of all officers of state. The chancery, however, long remained a part of the court, mainly because it was to the king's interest to have his chief minister always by his side. But as the office became larger, and as its prudent habit of enrolling all its acts swelled its official records to an enormous size, the same reason, which separated the exchequer from the court, began to apply also to the chancery. The process was made more imperative when the barons put in their claim to control the government of the country equally or almost equally with the king. At last a sort of compromise was arrived at by which the chancery, though still partly following the court, wandered less freely and in smaller circles. It now had headquarters of its own in London, where the clerks lived a sort of collegiate life in common. It kept there its ever-increasing mass of records, and kept them in the very same place where the Public Record Office now preserves the accumulated archives of every great department of state. By the days of Edward III the chancery, like the exchequer since Henry II, had become a government office, self-contained, self-sufficing, with its own staff, traditions, and methods, and plainly separated from the court.

The exchequer and the chancery, the office of finance and the office of administration, were the two first government departments in the modern sense. A third and lesser office separated itself from the court in the reign of Edward III. This was the office of the privy seal, whose keeper and clerks gradually drifted out of court in the generation succeeding the differentiation of the chancery from the household. The king's privy seal originated about the reign of John when the great seal, and its keeper the chancellor, became so much a public instrument and a public officer that they were no longer always at hand when their lord wished to write a letter. Moreover, the chancellor was a great man, who, though the king's servant, often had a will of his own and sometimes agreed with the barons rather than with his royal master. The result was that, as chancery and chancellor drifted out of court, there still remained, as closely attendant as of old on the monarch in all his wanderings, the ancient writing and administrative department, which continued to do for the king's household the work originally done by the chancellor. It was soon natural for the king to set up his domestic chancery against the public chancery, the privy seal against the great seal. The barons tried to stop this by claiming the control of the household office as well as the public one. Neither king nor barons could get all their way, and in the long run a sort of compromise was again arrived at. The privy seal went "out of court." It became a minor administrative office, sometimes perhaps relieving the chancery, more often, I suspect, clogging the wheels of the administration. The result was a third type of fourteenth century civil servant in the clerks of the privy seal . . .

So much for the offices: and now for the men who filled them. My apology for troubling you so much with the growth of the administrative departments is that some knowledge of them is indispensable for the appreciation of the work and position of the official class with whom we are primarily concerned. It will be my business now to try and suggest what manner of man was the civil servant who filled these offices of state.

The bare sketch of the growth of the offices will suffice to dissipate the illusion that the middle ages had no civil servants. In some ways the bureaucrat was as active and vigorous in the fourteenth century as he is in the twentieth. But we should be rash to think that he closely resembled the civil servant of the modern state. Mediæval society was always on a small scale even in great kingdoms. Mediæval resources were miserably feeble as compared with those of modern times. Men were as clever then as they are now; they were almost as "civilized." But they were overwhelmingly inferior to moderns in the command of material resources, and but a fraction of the meagre material forces at the disposal of society was under the control of the mediæval state. Hence the very slight extent to which the division of labour could be pushed. When the principle of differentiation had gone so far as to make a civil service possible, its members were but imperfectly specialized. The offices of state were few; nevertheless they overlapped hopelessly; everything was in a state of flux; and the mediæval civilian, like the modern blue-jacket, was compelled to be a "handy man" by the situation in which his lot was cast. Even in our own highly organized society it is possible, especially in times like this, for clerks to be shifted from one office to another, or for outsiders to be called in to discharge temporary war work. Under mediæval conditions the same end was attained by everybody doing everybody else's job, sometimes to the neglect of his own. The mediæval civil servant then was much less specialized than his modern counterpart.

Another striking point of dissimilarity between the modern and the mediæval civilian is that the great majority of the latter were clergymen. We still call the civil servant a clerk, just as we speak of the clerks of a bank or a merchant's office. If we ever ask ourselves what "clerk" means, we should probably say that it involves a life devoted to the mechanical task of writing, book-keeping, accounting, and copying. But historically a clerk means simply a clergyman, a member of the broad class of actual or potential ministers of the church. In the early Middle Ages it was a matter of course to regard all men of education as clerks. Writing and accounting were rare gifts for a layman, the more so since all letters were written and all accounts kept in Latin. It was because they knew how to write and keep accounts in Latin that clerks alone were trusted to man the primitive offices of state. Now these clerks were not necessarily "clerks in holy orders"; they were not even necessarily "clerks in minor orders." You could enter the clerical profession as soon as you had induced some prelate to give you the "first tonsure." With the shaven crown went the clerical dress and the important privilege of benefit of clergy, that is the right of being judged for all offences by members of your own order, and in practice the useful privilege of committing your first crime with comparative impunity. The tonsured clerk might, if he would, afterwards proceed to "orders," minor or holy; but in numerous cases he did not even enter minor orders, and it was quite common for him not to take holy orders, that is, he never became a subdeacon, deacon, or priest. Very often he passed through these stages, hastily and perfunctorily, when his service to the state received its crowning reward in a bishopric. There were few instances of mediæval civil servants declining the office of bishop, the highest stage of holy orders. Now for the majority of clerks in government offices there was little need to assume more clerical responsibility than prudence required. For holy orders were permanent and indelible; the tonsure by itself gave benefit of clergy, and the worldly clerk only needed orders to qualify him for a benefice. Thus the clerical class was very elastic and very large. In fact it comprehended all educated men, most lawyers, most physicians, all scholars, graduates, and students of universities, and most boys in grammar schools. And the clerk, when a clerk, had the disabilities as well as the advantages of his profession. All professional men then were compulsory celibates; by abandoning the clerical status they lost all prospect of worldly advancement in the one profession that had great prizes to offer.

By the fourteenth century this state of things was already passing away. There was an ever-increasing number of educated laymen, and a new lucrative profession was fully open to lay enterprise. This was that of the pleaders and exponents of English law. The schools of the "common lawyers" in

London were the first schools in England where men could study for a profession without becoming clerks. But we have not got to the time when to
be a barrister was to possess the master key to politics. The lawyers had,
then as now, more than their share of good things; but the common lawyer
at least was rarely a civil servant, though he might sometimes become a
minister. It was the civil and canon laws, the law of Rome and the law of
the church, not the common law, that were most pursued by those who as-
pired to the public service. The civil and canon laws were the only laws
studied in the universities: their students then were all necessarily clerks.

There were some advantages in the clerical official. He was better educated on the average; often a graduate, sometimes a distinguished doctor, or
master, of Paris or Oxford. He was generally a man with a career to make,
and likely therefore to be more devoted and less scrupulous in the service
of his master. Moreover, clerks could easily be rewarded without expense to
the king. They could be enriched by livings, dignities, prebends, bishoprics;
while the laymen could only be satisfied by grants of land that belonged to
the royal domain or by the custody of royal wards or by the hand of heiresses in the king's guardianship. At the worst, the clerk could be quietly got
rid of by being given some job that kept him away from his office. Moreover, a strong practical disadvantage that told against lay officials was the
fact that in the early Middle Ages all lay offices tended to become hereditary. For instance in the exchequer, the oldest of the offices of state, there
had been from the beginning a considerable lay element. Originally the layman did the rough work, while the clerks wrote, directed, and kept accounts. But by the fourteenth century laymen were often as competent as
clerks for these delicate operations. Long before that, however, the original
lay offices of the exchequer had become "hereditary serjeantries," and had
fallen into the hands of families so swelled by the profits of royal service
that their representatives were too dignified to do their work. Accordingly,
they were allowed to appoint some person of inferior social status who was
not too much of a gentleman to be afraid of soiling his hands with labour.
The result was that many actual working members of the exchequer staff
were appointed not by the king but by some nobleman, and that nobleman
was often a bitter enemy of the royal policy . . .

This state of things was beginning to pass away by the fourteenth century, but the warning of the exchequer serjeantries had not been lost. In the
exchequer clerks did, under the Edwards, the work which, under Henry II,
was performed by laymen, holding office from father to son. Moreover,
exchequer business was now largely in the hands of personages called
"barons of the exchequer." It was perhaps for reasons like this that the exchequer clerical staff was larger in the fourteenth than in the twelfth century. For instance, the barons could be, and were, indifferently clerks or
laymen. But the head of the office, the treasurer, was always a clerk and

generally was, or became, a bishop. The most rigidly clerical office was that of chancellor of the exchequer, an officer who had the pay and status of a baron. This post remained clerical because the chancellor kept the exchequer seal, and seal keeping was still looked upon as essentially clerical work . . .

As contrasted with the exchequer the newer offices of state, one and all, opened up few chances to the layman. The chancery, for instance, was entirely staffed with clerks . . .

Let us next speak of methods of appointment. In the beginnings of the public service under the Normans, the Crown sold offices of state to the highest bidders, who recouped themselves for their capital outlay, not only by the legitimate profits of office but still more by the unlawful but customary peculations and extortions in which the early mediæval functionary delighted. By the fourteenth century this primitive method had been partly outgrown; though we had a modern recrudescence of it in the sale of commissions in the army, only abolished in 1871. I have already spoken of the prevalence and of the inconvenience of the hereditary transmission of office. There was only one alternative way to it, for the modern method of recruiting the civil service by open competition was inconceivable in an age when the cult of the examination was a novelty. This other way was the method of nomination, sometimes perhaps by conscientious selection, more often I fear by jobbery, local, family, or personal . . .

It was one of the happy results of the clerical element in the mediæval service that our celibate clerical officials had not, or ought not to have had, so many opportunities of jobbery for their sons as are vouchsafed to the sages of the law in modern democratic Britain. Here again the layman had a better chance than the cleric, though the cleric's family feeling could find plenty of scope in promoting the interests of his numerous nephews. But there are other forms of jobbery besides hereditary jobbery; and although family influence was very strong in the Middle Ages, the commonest of all sorts of mediæval jobbery seems to have been "feudal" and local, rather than personal. The official that had "got on" planted not only his kinsfolk but his tenants and retainers and their families, in humbler cases the youth of his own village or district, in any posts of which he had the patronage. In the same way the king, as the ultimate fountain of office, always bestowed special favour on men sprung from manors on the royal domain. It is astonishing how large a proportion of mediæval officials showed by their surnames —surnames of the local type—that they traced their origin to some royal estate. Nor was this method of selection merely the result of favouritism. The close personal tie of lord and vassal was, under fourteenth-century conditions, the strongest possible guarantee of faithful service. Another of the distinctions between mediæval and modern political conditions is the fact that there was no clear line of division between the politicians in high office and the permanent public officials. A few great earls and barons might have an hereditary right to take a leading share in the king's councils without the preliminary training of the public service. But the greater lay magnates ruled by influence rather than as officials, for the highest dignitaries in the administration, the chancellor and the treasurer, were ecclesiastics, and in many cases had worked themselves up to these posts and to the bishoprics, which were the material reward of their political services, as public servants in the chancery, the exchequer, and, still more often, in the wardrobe and household. In fact the minister of state was as likely as not to be a promoted civil servant. Mediæval England, down to and including Tudor times, was ruled, like the modern German Empire, by ministers who had made their mark in the civil service of the Crown.

Under these conditions the English civil servant was almost as "non-political" and a good deal more "permanent" than were the mighty ministers of state who so largely emerged from the official class. This is seen when, among other foreshadowings of modern conditions, we find in the reign of Edward III something like the beginnings of parties and two ministerial crises, those of 1340 and 1371, in which one party drove its rivals from the king's favour and therefore from office. In both these years the whole ministry was turned out, really because the king disliked their policy, nominally because they were clergymen. Let us not, however, look upon even this as a clearly marked party triumph. To one of the shrewdest of contemporary chroniclers it was a struggle not between parties but between the king's confidential advisers and the ministers holding the great offices of state.[1] But when in 1340 the clerical treasurer and chancellor gave way to the first laymen appointed to these offices, the chief clerks of the chancery and exchequer, numerous judges, sheriffs, and other minor officials shared their fate. The underlings went into the wilderness along with the heads of the departments, just as in the United States every petty office is vacated when the swing of the political pendulum replaces a Democratic by a Republican president. The doctrine, sacred to Tammany and the machine politician, that to the victor belongs the spoils was one which might well have appealed to the politician of the fourteenth century.

Such general changes as those in 1340 were extremely rare. They were the more infrequent since the mediæval placeman—high and low, and especially the low—was as a rule very much of the vicar of Bray's way of thinking. Whatever king or policy reigned, he regarded it to be the very root of the matter that he should cling tightly to the emoluments of office. And his easygoing masters seldom disturbed him as long as he did his daily task decently and did not criticize the higher powers. Nor need we blame the mediæval placeman for his apparent want of principle. High affairs of state were no more his business than they were the concern of the man in the street. He was a paid functionary, not always a well-paid functionary,

1. Robert of Avesbury, *De Gestis Edwardi Tertii* (Rolls series), p. 323.

whose duty was obedience to his masters. He trusted his masters to do his thinking for him and to understand what it was no business of his to study. Obedience, loyalty, discipline were the ideals before him. Thinking out the rights and wrongs of policy was outside his job. Inspired by these conceptions, the rank and file of the civil service grew grey in their offices, vacating them only by reason of promotion, death, or incapacity to discharge the daily task. Even if they moved from office to office, they remained functionaries for the whole of their working lives.

Let us turn from the principles, or the want of them, of the mediæval placeman to the payments given for his services, to his professional prospects, as we should say. His direct pay was inconsiderable and irregular, and it was only after his particular office got separated from the household that the mediæval civil servant had the advantage of pay at all . . .

If the pay of the mediæval public servant was scanty and irregular, the indirect advantages of serving the state were open, gross, and palpable. Here the clerical official had the same pull over his lay colleagues that the clerical schoolmaster—another curious survival of the one-profession period—still has over the lay instructor of youth. Besides the chances of his immediate career, the prizes, small and large, of a great profession were open to him. Clerical preferment increased the scanty wages of his post, while he held it; clerical preferment enabled him to retire betimes and enjoy a comfortable old age on his living, his prebend, his deanery or even his bishopric. . . .

Besides ecclesiastical preferment, the worn-out civilian could look for pensions from the Crown, transference to less laborious or nominal service, or, at the worst, to what was called a "corrody," that is authority to take up his quarters in some monastery and be fed, clothed, and lodged at the expense of the monks. These latter resources were particularly welcome to laymen or to those clerics who had disqualified themselves for advancement in the church by matrimony. A still better refuge was a pension from the exchequer. But there was one drawback to the enjoyment of this most satisfactory of direct sources of support, a royal pension. It was that it was not always regularly paid. In those days the dependents on the state were always the first to suffer when war or some other exceptional cause of expenditure restricted the royal bounty, or when a careless or extravagant king neither wished to nor could keep his plighted word. Lastly, we must not neglect among these supplementary sources of income the perquisites, lawful and unlawful, of office. Mediæval propriety was not outraged by public officers receiving gratifications in money or kind from all who came to transact business with them. It was natural that the receiver of a favour should pay a fee to the source of his satisfaction. The preparation of a writ was immensely expedited when a suitable *douceur* from the applicant quickened the activity of the chancery or privy seal clerk responsible for its issue. We find that religious houses regularly entered in their accounts the sums they had given to ministers to obtain their good will. On a much lower plane was the direct bribe to do something known to be wrong; yet that also was by no means rare. Mediæval man used the discreet term "curialitas" (courtesy) to indicate transactions that varied between perfectly permissible presents and open and shameful corruption. And there were few public servants who did not take advantage of their position to do a good deal of business on their own account, such as administering or managing estates, lending money, acting as sureties, as attorneys or proxies, and the like.

Taking everything into account, the mediæval civilian's prosperity was not to be reckoned merely in wages. Besides money payments, there were also wages in kind. In the old days, when the public servant was attached to the court, he had, as we have seen, no salary, or a very small one. But he made up for this by receiving lodging, clothing, food, drink and fire-wood at the king's expense. He had, therefore, as little need of money as a soldier in the trenches or a monk in a convent. . . .

One question still remains. How did the mediæval civil servant do his work? How far was he efficient, and, if he were remiss, how far could the peccant official be controlled or punished? On the whole I am inclined to think that a respectably high level of general competence was attained. Our best evidence for this is that afforded by the wonderfully complete and well-kept series of our mediæval archives still surviving in the public record office. The mediæval public servant had plenty of disadvantages as compared with his modern successor. All the devices by which book-keeping, letter-writing, account-keeping and the like are made easy were unknown to him. His works of reference were unpractical rolls that had to be unrolled in all their length before he could verify a single entry. His material for writing on was parchment so expensive that abbreviation of his matter was necessary and to waste by a slip something of an offence. The exchequer clerk had to keep books and do sums of extraordinary complexity. The very addition of roman numerals was painful enough in itself. It was made more laborious by reckonings by scores and by hundreds, by sums, calculated indifferently in marks and in pounds, shillings and pence, being all mixed up together in the same columns of figures. Yet you will very rarely find mistakes in arithmetic even in the most complicated of accounts; and if you take the trouble, which some of our modern historians have not done, to understand the accountant's system before you make use of his figures, you will not often catch him committing many serious errors. No one can turn over mediæval official records without admiration for the neatness of the caligraphy, the immense pains taken to facilitate reference and eliminate blunders, the careful correction of erroneous entries, and the other innumerable evidences of good honest workmanship on the part of the ordinary rank and file of official scribes. It is the same with the innumerable writs and letters, all neatly drafted in common form, and duly authenticated by the appropriate seals and by the signatures of the responsible clerks. The system of enrolment of the accounts passed and the letters written, in every office, leaves nothing to be desired in completeness and precision. Anyhow, the mediæval official took plenty of pains to discharge his daily task, and his labour was all the more praiseworthy since mediæval casualness and mediæval indifference to labour-saving contrivances exacted the maximum of effort and trouble in every case. Similarly, if we turn to the collections of examples, precedents and forms, which were from time to time written for the guidance of the various offices, we strengthen our impression of sound business traditions, laboriously developed and meticulously maintained. A reforming bureaucracy too is generally an efficient bureaucracy, and a long series of reforming edicts, inspired by the chiefs of various departments, bears high testimony to the useful activity of the fourteenth century civil service. Thus the last years of the dreary reign of Edward II witnessed an immense amount of administrative reform, notably the reform of the exchequer by the treasurer Stapeldon. Yet, despite all this, constant control and watchfulness were needed to keep clean the administrative machine and there was no control so effective as the personal oversight of the sovereign. In the monarch's absence the executive always tended to get out of gear. Both the return of Edward I in 1289 after his three years' sojourn on the Continent, and the return of Edward III in 1340 after his long preoccupation with war and diplomacy in the Low Countries, were immediately followed by the two greatest sweepings out of the Augean stables of administrative incompetence that mediæval history witnessed.

THE EMERGENCE OF TYPES
OF RELIGIOUS ORGANIZATION

Ernst Troeltsch

The Church is that type of organization which is overwhelmingly conservative, which to a certain extent accepts the secular order, and dominates the mases; in principle, therefore, it is universal, i.e., it desires to cover the whole life of humanity. The sects, on the other hand, are comparatively small groups; they aspire after personal inward perfection, and they aim at a direct

Reprinted in part from *The Social Teaching of the Christian Churches*, Vol. I, pp. 331-341, by permission of the publisher. (Copyright, 1949, by The Free Press, Glencoe, Illinois.)

personal fellowship between the members of each group. From the very beginning, therefore, they are forced to organize themselves in small groups, and to renounce the idea of dominating the world. Their attitude towards the world, the State, and Society may be indifferent, tolerant, or hostile, since they have no desire to control and incorporate these forms of social life; on the contrary, they tend to avoid them; their aim is usually either to tolerate their presence alongside of their own body, or even to replace these social institutions by their own society.

Further, both types are in close connection with the actual situation and with the development of Society. The fully developed Church, however, utilizes the State and the ruling classes, and weaves these elements into her own life; she then becomes an integral part of the existing social order; from this standpoint, then, the Church both stabilizes and determines the social order; in so doing, however, she becomes dependent upon the upper classes, and upon their development. The sects, on the other hand, are connected with the lower classes, or at least with those elements in Society which are opposed to the State and to Society; they work upwards from below, and not downwards from above . . .

The word "sect," however, gives an erroneous impression. Originally the word was used in a polemical and apologetic sense, and it was used to describe groups which separated themselves from the official Church, while they retained certain fundamental elements of Christian thought; by the very fact, however, that they were outside the corporate life of the ecclesiastical tradition—a position, moreover, which was usually forced upon them —they were regarded as inferior side-issues, one-sided phenomena, exaggerations or abbreviations of ecclesiastical Christianity. That is, naturally, solely the viewpoint of the dominant churches, based on the belief that the ecclesiastical type alone has any right to exist. Ecclesiastical law within the modern State definitely denotes as "sects" those religious groups which exist alongside of the official privileged State Churches, by law established, groups which the State either does not recognize at all, or, if it does recognize them, grants them fewer rights and privileges than the official State Churches. Such a conception, however, confuses the actual issue. Very often in the so-called "sects" it is precisely the essential elements of the Gospel which are fully expressed; they themselves always appeal to the Gospel and to Primitive Christianity, and accuse the Church of having fallen away from its ideal; these impulses are always those which have been either suppressed or undeveloped in the official churches, of course for good and characteristic reasons, which again are not taken into account by the passionate party polemics of the sects. There can, however, be no doubt about the actual fact: the sects, with their greater independence of the world, and their continual emphasis upon the original ideals of Christianity, often represent in a very direct and characteristic way the essential fundamental ideas of Christianity; to a very great extent they are a most important factor in the study of the development of the sociological consequences of Christian thought . . .

The main stream of Christian development, however, flows along the channel prepared by the Church-type. The reason for this is clear: the Church-type represents the longing for a universal all-embracing ideal, the desire to control great masses of men, and therefore the urge to dominate the world and civilization in general. Paulinism, in spite of its strongly individualistic and "enthusiastic" features, had already led the way along this line: it desired to conquer the world for Christ; it came to terms with the order of the State by interpreting it as an institution ordained and permitted by God; it accepted the existing order with its professions and its habits and customs. The only union it desired was that which arose out of a common share in the energy of grace which the Body of Christ contained; out of this union the new life ought to spring up naturally from within through the power of the Holy Spirit, thus preparing the way for the speedy coming of the Kingdom of God, as the real universal end of all things. The more that Christendom renounced the life of this supernatural and eschatological fulfilment of its universal ideal, and tried to achieve this end by missionary effort and organization, the more was it forced to make its Divine and Christian character independent of the subjective character and service of believers; henceforth it sought to concentrate all its emphasis upon the objective possession of religious truth and religious power, which were contained in the tradition of Christ, and in the Divine guidance of the Church which fills and penetrates the whole Body. From this objective basis subjective energies could ever flow forth afresh, exerting a renewing influence, but the objective basis did not coincide with these results. Only thus was it possible to have a popular Church at all, and it was only thus that the relative acceptance of the world, the State, of Society, and of the existing culture, which this required, did no harm to the objective foundation. . . .

Under these circumstances, however, the Church found it impossible to avoid making a compromise with the State, with the social order, and with economic conditions, and the Thomist doctrine worked this out in a very able, comprehensive theory, which vigorously maintained the ultimate supernatural orientation of life. In all this it is claimed that the whole is derived, quite logically, from the Gospel; it is clear that this point of view became possible as soon as the Gospel was conceived as a universal way of life, offering redemption to all, whose influence radiates from the knowledge given by the Gospel, coupled with the assurance of salvation given by the Church. It was precisely the development of an objective sociological point of reference, its establishment on a stable basis, and its endeavour to go forward from that point to organize the conquest of the world, which led to this development. It is, however, equally obvious that in so doing the radical individualism of the Gospel, with its urge towards the utmost personal achievement, its radical fellowship of love, uniting all in the most personal centre of life, with its heroic indifference towards the world, the State and civilization, with its mistrust of the spiritual danger of distraction and error inherent in the possession of or the desire for great possessions, has been given a secondary place, or even given up altogether; these features now appear as mere factors within the system; they are no longer ruling principles.

It was precisely this aspect of the Gospel, however, which the sects developed still farther, or, rather, it was this aspect which they were continually re-emphasizing and bringing into fresh prominence. In general, the following are their characteristic features: lay Christianity, personal achievement in ethics and in religion, the radical fellowship of love, religious equality and brotherly love, indifference towards the authority of the State and the ruling classes, dislike of technical law and of the oath, the separation of the religious life from the economic struggle by means of the ideal of poverty and frugality, or occasionally in a charity which becomes communism, the directness of the personal religious relationship, criticism of official spiritual guides and theologians, the appeal to the New Testament and to the Primitive Church. . . .

It is this point of view, however, which makes the sects incapable of forming large mass organizations, and limits their development to small groups, united on a basis of personal intimacy; it is also responsible for the necessity for a constant renewal of the ideal, their lack of continuity, their pronounced individualism, and their affinity with all the oppressed and idealistic groups within the lower classes. These also are the groups in which an ardent desire for the improvement of their lot goes hand in hand with a complete ignorance of the complicated conditions of life, in which therefore an idealistic orthodoxy finds no difficulty in expecting to see the world transformed by the purely moral principles of love. In this way the sects gained on the side of intensity in Christian life, but they lost in the spirit of universalism, since they felt obliged to consider the Church as degenerate, and they did not believe that the world could be conquered by human power and effort; that is why they were always forced to adopt eschatological views. . . .

Although this description of the sect-type represents in the main its prevailing sociological characteristics, the distinctive significance of the sect-type contrasted with the Church-type still has a good concrete basis. (There is no need to consider here the particular groups which were founded purely upon dogma; they were indeed rare, and the pantheistic philosophical sects of the Middle Ages merge almost imperceptibly into sects of the practical religious kind.) In reality, the sects are essentially different from the Church and the churches. The word "sect," however, does not mean that these movements are undeveloped expressions of the Church-type; it stands for an independent sociological type of Christian thought.

The essence of the Church is its objective institutional character. The individual is born into it, and through infant baptism he comes under its miraculous influence. The priesthood and the hierarchy, which hold the keys to the tradition of the Church, to sacramental grace and ecclesiastical jurisdiction, represent the objective treasury of grace, even when the individual priest may happen to be unworthy; this Divine treasure only needs to be set always upon the lampstand and made effective through the sacraments, and it will inevitably do its work by virtue of the miraculous power which the Church contains. . . . From this point of view compromise with the world, and the connection with the preparatory stages and dispositions which it contained, was possible; for in spite of all individual inadequacy the institution remains holy and Divine, and it contains the promise of its capacity to overcome the world by means of the miraculous power which dwells within it. Universalism, however, also only becomes possible on the basis of this compromise; it means an actual domination of the institutions as such, and a believing confidence in its invincible power of inward influence. Personal effort and service, however fully they may be emphasized, even when they go to the limits of extreme legalism, are still only secondary; the main thing is the objective possession of grace and its universally recognized dominion; to everything else these words apply: *et cetera adjicientur vobis.* The one vitally important thing is that every individual should come within the range of the influence of these saving energies of grace; hence the Church is forced to dominate Society, compelling all the members of Society to come under its sphere and influence; but, on the other hand, her stability is entirely unaffected by the fact of the extent to which her influence over all individuals is actually attained. The Church is the great educator of the nations, and like all educators she knows how to allow for various degrees of capacity and maturity, and how to attain her end only by a process of adaptation and compromise.

Compared with this institutional principle of an objective organism, however, the sect is a voluntary community whose members join it of their own free will. The very life of the sect, therefore, depends on actual personal service and co-operation; as an independent member each individual has his part within the fellowship; the bond of union has not been indirectly imparted through the common possession of Divine grace, but it is directly realized in the personal relationships of life. An individual is not born into a sect; he enters it on the basis of conscious conversion; infant baptism, which, indeed, was only introduced at a later date, is almost always a stumbling-block. In the sect spiritual progress does not depend upon the objective impartation of Grace through the Sacrament, but upon individual personal effort; sooner or later, therefore, the sect always criticizes the sacramental idea. This does not mean that the spirit of fellowship is weakened by individualism; indeed, it is strengthened, since each individual proves that he is entitled to membership by the very fact of his services to the fellowship. It is, however, naturally a somewhat limited form of fellowship, and the expenditure of so much effort in the maintenance and exercise of this particular kind of fellowship produces a certain indifference towards other forms of fellowship which are based upon secular interests; on the other hand, all secular interests are drawn into the narrow framework of the sect and tested by its standards, in so far as the sect is able to assimilate these interests at all. Whatever cannot be related to the group of interests controlled by the sect, and by the Scriptural ideal, is rejected and avoided. The sect, therefore, does not educate nations in the mass, but it gathers a select group of the elect, and places it in sharp opposition to the world. . . .

Thus, in reality we are faced with two different sociological types. This is true in spite of the fact (which is quite immaterial) that incidentally in actual practice they may often impinge upon one another. If objections are raised to the terms "Church" and "Sect," and if all sociological groups which are based on and inspired by monotheistic, universalized, religious motives are described (in a terminology which is in itself quite appropriate) as "Churches," we would then have to make the distinction between institutional churches and voluntary churches. It does not really matter which expression is used. The all-important point is this: that both types are a logical result of the Gospel, and only conjointly do they exhaust the whole range of its sociological influence, and thus also indirectly of its social results, which are always connected with the religious organization.

In reality, the Church does not represent a mere deterioration of the Gospel, however much that may appear to be the case when we contrast its hierarchical organization and its sacramental system with the teaching of Jesus. For wherever the Gospel is conceived as primarily a free gift, as pure grace, and wherever it is offered to us in the picture which faith creates of Christ as a Divine institution, wherever the inner freedom of the Spirit, contrasted with all human effort and organization, is felt to be the spirit of Jesus, and wherever His splendid indifference towards secular matters is felt, in the sense of a spiritual and inner independence, while these secular things are used outwardly, there the institution of the Church may be regarded as a natural continuation and transformation of the Gospel. At the same time, with its unlimited universalism, it still contains the fundamental impulse of the evangelic message; the only difference is that whereas the Gospel had left all questions of possible realization to the miraculous coming of the Kingdom of God, a Church which had to work in a world which was not going to pass away had to organize and arrange matters for itself, and in so doing it was forced into a position of compromise.

On the other hand, the essence of the sect does not consist merely in a one-sided emphasis upon certain vital elements of the Church-type, but it is itself a direct continuation of the idea of the Gospel. Only within it is there a full recognition of the value of radical individualism and of the idea of love; it is the sect alone which instinctively builds up its ideal of fellowship from this point of view, and this is the very reason why it attains such a strong subjective and inward unity, instead of merely external membership in an institution. For the same reason the sect also maintains the original radicalism of the Christian ideal and its hostility towards the world, and it retains the fundamental demand for personal service, which indeed it is also able to regard as a work of grace: in the idea of grace, however, the sect emphasizes the subjective realization and the effects of grace, and not the objective assurance of its presence. The sect does not live on the miracles of the past, nor on the miraculous nature of the institution, but on the constantly renewed miracle of the Presence of Christ, and on the subjective reality of the individual mastery of life.

THE RISE OF GERMAN INDUSTRIAL ORGANIZATION

Thorstein Veblen

The German people, by native gift, were endowed with the kind and degree of intelligence required, being in this respect on identically the same footing with those British, and other, communities which had worked out this modern state of the industrial arts. They had at the same time, in their educated classes, all the intellectual habituation necessary to its ready acquisition, and in their working classes a sufficiently well-instructed force of operative workmen. So that the rate at which they could attain proficiency in the new industry was little else than a question of how fast and far their circumstances would admit its use. The rate of its introduction and expansion, therefore, became largely a question of the enterprise of those who had the discretion in matters of business and industry, which resolves itself into a question of the pecuniary inducement and of their insight into the opportunities offered by this new industry.

In these matters the German community was peculiarly well placed. The classes who were in a position to profit from these new ventures were accus-

Reprinted from *Imperial Germany and the Industrial Revolution*, pp. 192-197. (Copyright, 1915, by The Macmillan Company, 1943, by Ann B. Sims.) Reprinted by permission of the Viking Press, Inc., New York.

tomed by tradition to a relatively low return on similar industrial enterprises under the earlier régime, and so a given rate of remuneration would appeal more strongly to them than to a business community accustomed to larger returns; the natural resources to be made use of, having been lying relatively idle, were to be had at relatively slight cost; a supply of competent workmen could be had at very reasonable wages; and last but by no means least, the break with an earlier and traditional situation in trade and industry left German enterprise hampered with fewer conventional restrictions and less obsolescent equipment and organisation on its hands than the corresponding agencies of retardation in any of the contemporary English-speaking countries. This last count in the schedule of German advantages should be sufficiently evident as against the moss-grown situation of trade and industry in contemporary England,—as has already been indicated in an earlier passage. It may be less evident, perhaps less applicable, and may even be questioned, as concerns the American community,—which stands as the foremost of the outlying English-speaking countries. Americans whose vision is in any degree blurred with patriotic sentiment will, of course, repudiate such an aspersion on their vaunted spirit of business enterprise, but a dispassionate view of the relevant facts may be relied on to allow the claim as made.

The German captains of industry who came to take the discretionary management in the new era were fortunate enough not to have matriculated from the training school of a country town based on a retail business in speculative real estate and political jobbery managed under the rule of "prehension, division and silence." They came under the selective test for fitness in the aggressive conduct of industrial enterprise, not under that of making good as prehensile conservatives in a distribution of pecuniary flotsam. The country being at the same time in the main—indeed, with only negligible local exceptions—not committed to antiquated sites and routes for its industrial plant; the men who exercised the discretion were free to choose, with an eye single to the mechanical expediency of locations for the pursuit of industry. Having no obsolescent equipment and no out-of-date trade connections to cloud the issue, they were also free to take over the process of the new industry at their best and highest efficiency, rather than content themselves with compromises between the best equipment known and what used to be the best a few years or a few decades ago. So also in the financiering of the new ventures, since the aim was not so much to get something for nothing by a financial shuffle as to find the pecuniary means necessary for equipment and working capital for the production of merchantable goods and services, the road was relatively plain, with virtually no necessary recourse to the recondite and devious ways of the impecunious company-promoter who aims to produce merchantable corporation securities. Not that the company-promoter was out of sight in the German community in the days when the French milliards were in sight; but there remains after all relatively little waste or dissipation of means to be written off the German account for astute financiering designed to divert funds from industry to the strategists of conservative chicane.

These German adventurers in the field of business, being captains of industry rather than of finance, were also free to choose their associates and staff with a view to their industrial insight and capacity rather than their astuteness in ambushing the community's loose change. And of suitable men to choose from, men with a capacity for work, not gone to seed in street-corner politics, and with sufficient educational qualifications and an interest in the new industrial perspective,—of such there was also no lack, for the German community was well supplied with educated men glad to find employment in some conventionally blameless occupation.

For want of means suitable to more drastic forms of dissipation, learning had long been a chief resort of young men with time and energy to spend; and since commonplace mercantile pursuits were conventionally somewhat beneath the dignity of a gentleman, as was also commonplace manual labor, and since the respectable callings of the civil service, clergy and university instruction were already crowded to the point of the subsistence minimum, this supply of scholarly young men flowed readily into the new channel so opened to them, in which a relatively lucrative, visibly serviceable, and not positively disreputable chance of work was offered. So soon as this drift of young men into the industrial field had once set in, it directly served as its own legitimation; it gave a degree of pecuniary authentication to those who successfully followed the new pursuit, and its popularity served of itself to make it fashionable. The responsible staff and corps in these industries, being men who had come through the schools instead of through the country store and the pettifogger's law office, were not incapable of appreciating that range of theoretical and technical knowledge that is indispensable to the efficient conduct of modern industry; and so the German industrial community was as surely and unresistingly drawn in under the rule of the technological expert as the American at about the same period was drawn in under the rule of the financial strategist.

These subalterns, as well as the discretionary heads of the several industrial ventures, had been accustomed to a relatively frugal way of living and a relatively parsimonious income, for the whole German community was by tradition in consistently impecunious circumstances and in a parsimonious frame of mind. The deductions from gross earnings on account of salaries and current perquisites of management were consequently small, as compared with what was current practice in the older industrial communities, or even with what has gradually come to be the practice in the Fatherland in the course of prosperous years.

So also as regards the disposable labor supply, which was of abundant quantity and of good quality, both physically and intellectually, and which had moreover the merit of a ready pliability under authority and was well trained to an impecuniously frugal standard of living,—cheap, capable and abundant. This labor supply was also not in any appreciable degree made up of a "depauperate" population of that congenitally ineffectual kind—undersized, anæmic, shriveled and wry-grown—that bulks so large in the English industrial towns, as the outcome of that country's first hundred years of competitive business enterprise under the régime of the machine process.

This, too, has changed perceptibly in some respects since the beginning; the standard of living has advanced, though not to equal that of the English-speaking countries; and the workmen have at the same time grown difficult and discontented in some degree, but not after the refractory fashion in which they have tried the patience and narrowed the gains of their capitalist-employers in these other countries.

Working-class traditions, and indeed middle-class traditions, too, have rather favored the useful employment of women in manual occupations in the German past, and this tradition of usage stands over still in good preservation; though here again there are symptoms at least of a drift into the same general attitude of a conventionally reputable exemption or exclusion of women from manual employment, particularly from manual labor in the open. Not much loss has yet been sustained by the German community from this source of impairment; the German women, *e.g.*, still continue to work in the fields and have not yet acquired much of a putatively inferior physical capacity, nor do they, apparently, suffer in a correspondingly increased degree from the diseases of idleness. It is perhaps unnecessary to remark that all this, of course, does not apply to the women of the well-to-do, who appear to be nearly as infirm (conventionally) as the best usage would dictate.

THE BUREAUCRATIC TENDENCY
OF POLITICAL PARTIES

Robert Michels

The technical specialization that inevitably results from all extensive organization renders necessary what is called expert leadership. Consequently the power of determination comes to be considered one of the specific

Reprinted in part from *Political Parties*, pp. 31-37 (Glencoe, Ill.: The Free Press, 1949), by permission of the publisher.

attributes of leadership, and is gradually withdrawn from the masses to be concentrated in the hands of the leaders alone.[1] Thus the leaders, who were at first no more than the executive organs of the collective will, soon emancipate themselves from the mass and become independent of its control.

Organization implies the tendency to oligarchy. In every organization, whether it be a political party, a professional union, or any other association of the kind, the aristocratic tendency manifests itself very clearly. The mechanism of the organization, while conferring a solidity of structure, induces serious changes in the organized mass, completely inverting the respective position of the leaders and the led. As a result of organization, every party or professional union becomes divided into a minority of directors and a majority of directed.

It has been remarked that in the lower stages of civilization tyranny is dominant. Democracy cannot come into existence until there is attained a subsequent and more highly developed stage of social life. Freedoms and privileges, and among these latter the privilege of taking part in the direction of public affairs, are at first restricted to the few. Recent times have been characterized by the gradual extension of these privileges to a widening circle. This is what we know as the era of democracy. But if we pass from the sphere of the state to the sphere of party, we may observe that as democracy continues to develop, a backwash sets in. With the advance of organization, democracy tends to decline. Democratic evolution has a parabolic course. At the present time, at any rate as far as party life is concerned, democracy is in the descending phase. It may be enunciated as a general rule that the increase in the power of the leaders is directly proportional with the extension of the organization. In the various parties and labour organizations of different countries the influence of the leaders is mainly determined (apart from racial and individual grounds) by the varying development of organization. Where organization is stronger, we find that there is a lesser degree of applied democracy.

Every solidly constructed organization, whether it be a democratic state, a political party, or a league of proletarians for the resistance of economic oppression, presents a soil eminently favourable for the differentiation of

---

1. "In intimate connection with these theoretical tendencies, there results a change in the relationship between the leaders and the mass. For the comradely leadership of local committees with all its undeniable defects there is substituted the professional leadership of the trade-union officials. Initiative and capacity for decision thus become what may be called a professional specialty, whilst for the rank and file is left the passive virtue of discipline. There can be no doubt that this seamy side of officialism involves serious dangers for the party. The latest innovation in this direction, in the German social democratic party, is the appointment of salaried secretaries to the local branches. Unless the rank and file of the party keep very much on the alert, unless they are careful that these secretaries shall be restricted to purely executive functions, the secretaries will come to be regarded as the natural and sole depositaries of all power of initiative, and as the exclusive leaders of local party life. . . . (Rosa Luxemburg, *Massenstreik, Partei u. Gewerkschaften*, Erdmann Dubber, Hamburg, 1906, p. 61).

organs and of functions. The more extended and the more ramified the official apparatus of the organization, the greater the number of its members, the fuller its treasury, and the more widely circulated its press, the less efficient becomes the direct control exercised by the rank and file, and the more is this control replaced by the increasing power of committees. Into all parties there insinuates itself that indirect electoral system which in public life the democratic parties fight against with all possible vigour. Yet in party life the influence of this system must be more disastrous than in the far more extensive life of the state. Even in the party congresses, which represent the party-life seven times sifted, we find that it becomes more and more general to refer all important questions to committees which debate in camera.

As organization develops, not only do the tasks of the administration become more difficult and more complicated, but, further, its duties become enlarged and specialized to such a degree that it is no longer possible to take them all in at a single glance. In a rapidly progressive movement, it is not only the growth in the number of duties, but also the higher quality of these, which imposes a more extensive differentiation of function. Nominally, and according to the letter of the rules, all the acts of the leaders are subject to the ever vigilant criticism of the rank and file. In theory the leader is merely an employee bound by the instructions he receives. He has to carry out the orders of the mass, of which he is no more than the executive organ. But in actual fact, as the organization increases in size, this control becomes purely fictitious. The members have to give up the idea of themselves conducting or even supervising the whole administration, and are compelled to hand these tasks over to trustworthy persons specially nominated for the purpose, to salaried officials. The rank and file must content themselves with summary reports, and with the appointment of occasional special committees of inquiry. Yet this does not derive from any special change in the rules of the organization. It is by very necessity that a simple employee gradually becomes a "leader," acquiring a freedom of action which he ought not to possess. The chief then becomes accustomed to despatch important business on his own responsibility, and to decide various questions relating to the life of the party without any attempt to consult the rank and file. It is obvious that democratic control thus undergoes a progressive diminution, and is ultimately reduced to an infinitesimal minimum. In all the socialist parties there is a continual increase in the number of functions withdrawn from the electoral assemblies and transferred to the executive committees. In this way there is constructed a powerful and complicated edifice. The principle of division of labour coming more and more into operation, executive authority undergoes division and subdivision. There is thus constituted a rigorously defined and hierarchical bureaucracy. In the catechism of party duties, the strict observance of hierarchical rules becomes the first article. This hierarchy comes into existence as the outcome of technical conditions, and its constitution is an essential postulate of the regular functioning of the party machine.

It is indisputable that the oligarchical and bureaucratic tendency of party organization is a matter of technical and practical necessity. It is the inevitable product of the very principle of organization. Not even the most radical wing of the various socialist parties raises any objection to this retrogressive evolution, the contention being that democracy is only a form of organization and that where it ceases to be possible to harmonize democracy with organization, it is better to abandon the former than the latter. Organization, since it is the only means of attaining the ends of socialism, is considered to comprise within itself the revolutionary content of the party, and this essential content must never be sacrificed for the sake of form.

In all times, in all phases of development, in all branches of human activity, there have been leaders. It is true that certain socialists, above all the orthodox Marxists of Germany, seek to convince us that socialism knows nothing of "leaders," that the party has "employees" merely, being a democratic party, and the existence of leaders being incompatible with democracy. But a false assertion such as this cannot override a sociological law. Its only result is, in fact, to strengthen the rule of the leaders, for it serves to conceal from the mass a danger which really threatens democracy.

For technical and administrative reasons, no less than for tactical reasons, a strong organization needs an equally strong leadership. As long as an organization is loosely constructed and vague in its outlines, no professional leadership can arise. The anarchists, who have a horror of all fixed organization, have no regular leaders. In the early days of German socialism, the *Vertrauensmann* (homme de confiance) continued to exercise his ordinary occupation. If he received any pay for his work for the party, the remuneration was on an extremely modest scale, and was no more than a temporary grant. His function could never be regarded by him as a regular source of income. The employee of the organization was still a simple workmate, sharing the mode of life and the social condition of his fellows. To-day he has been replaced for the most part by the professional politician, *Berzirksleiter* (U.S. ward-boss), etc. The more solid the structure of an organization becomes in the course of the evolution of the modern political party, the more marked becomes the tendency to replace the emergency leader by the professional leader. Every party organization which has attained to a considerable degree of complication demands that there should be a certain number of persons who devote all their activities to the work of the party. The mass provides these by delegation, and the delegates, regularly appointed, become permanent representatives of the mass for the direction of its affairs.

For democracy, however, the first appearance of professional leadership marks the beginning of the end, and this, above all, on account of the logical impossibility of the "representative" system, whether in parliamentary life or in party delegation. Jean Jacques Rousseau may be considered as the founder of this aspect of the criticism of democracy. . . . A mass which delegates its sovereignty, that is to say transfers its sovereignty to the hands of a few individuals, abdicates its sovereign functions. For the will of the people is not transferable, nor even the will of the single individual.

THE ROUTINIZATION OF CHARISMA

Max Weber

In its pure form charismatic authority has a character specifically foreign to everyday routine structures. The social relationships directly involved are strictly personal, based on the validity and practice of charismatic personal qualities. If this is not to remain a purely transitory phenomenon, but to take on the character of a permanent relationship forming a stable community of disciples or a band of followers or a party organization or any sort of political or hierocratic organization, it is necessary for the character of charismatic authority to become radically changed. Indeed, in its pure form charismatic authority may be said to exist only in the process of originating. It cannot remain stable, but becomes either traditionalized or rationalized, or a combination of both.

The following are the principal motives underlying this transformation: (a) The ideal and also the material interests of the followers in the continuation and the continual reactivation of the community, (b) the still stronger ideal and also stronger material interests of the members of the administrative staff, the disciples or other followers of the charismatic leader in continuing their relationship. Not only this, but they have an interest in continuing it in such a way that both from an ideal and a material point of view, their own status is put on a stable everyday basis. This means, above all, making it possible to participate in normal family relationships or at least to enjoy a secure social position in place of the kind of discipleship which is cut off from ordinary worldly connexions, notably in the family and in economic relationships.

Reprinted from *The Theory of Social and Economic Organization* (Trans. A. M. Henderson and Talcott Parsons, ed. Talcott Parsons), pp. 364-373, by permission of the publisher. (Copyright, 1947, by the Oxford University Press.)

These interests generally become conspicuously evident with the disappearance of the personal charismatic leader and with the problem of succession, which inevitably arises. The way in which this problem is met—if it is met at all and the charismatic group continues to exist—is of crucial importance for the character of the subsequent social relationships. The following are the principal possible types of solution:—

(a) The search for a new charismatic leader on the basis of criteria of the qualities which will fit him for the position of authority. This is to be found in a relatively pure type in the process of choice of a new Dalai Lama. It consists in the search for a child with characteristics which are interpreted to mean that he is a reincarnation of the Buddha. This is very similar to the choice of the new Bull of Apis.

In this case the legitimacy of the new charismatic leader is bound to certain distinguishing characteristics; thus, to rules with respect to which a tradition arises. The result is a process of traditionalization in favour of which the purely personal character of leadership is eliminated.

(b) By revelation manifested in oracles, lots, divine judgments, or other techniques of selection. In this case the legitimacy of the new leader is dependent on the legitimacy of the technique of his selection. This involves a form of legalization. It is said that at times the *Schofetim* of Israel had this character. Saul is said to have been chosen by the old war oracle.

(c) By the designation on the part of the original charismatic leader of his own successor and his recognition on the part of the followers. This is a very common form. Originally, the Roman magistracies were filled entirely in this way. The system survived most clearly into later times in the appointment of "dictators" and in the institution of the "interrex." In this case legitimacy is acquired through the act of designation.

(d) Designation of a successor by the charismatically qualified administrative staff and his recognition by the community. In its typical form this process should quite definitely not be interpreted as "election" or "nomination" or anything of the sort. It is not a matter of free selection, but of one which is strictly bound to objective duty. It is not to be determined merely by majority vote, but it is a question of arriving at the correct designation, the designation of the right person who is truly endowed with charisma. It is quite possible that the minority and not the majority should be right in such a case. Unanimity is often required. It is obligatory to acknowledge a mistake and persistence in error is a serious offence. Making a wrong choice is a genuine wrong requiring expiation. Originally it was a magical offence.

Nevertheless, in such a case it is easy for legitimacy to take on the character of an acquired right which is justified by standards of the correctness of the process by which the position was acquired, for the most part, by its having been acquired in accordance with certain formalities, such as coronation. This was the original meaning of the coronation of bishops and kings in the Western World by the clergy or the nobility with the "consent" of the community. There are numerous analogous phenomena all over the world. The fact that this is the origin of the modern conception of "election" raises problems which will have to be gone into later.

(e) By the conception that charisma is a quality transmitted by heredity; thus that it is participated in by the kinsmen of its bearer, particularly by his closest relatives. This is the case of hereditary charisma. The order of hereditary succession in such a case need not be the same as that which is in force for appropriated rights, but may differ from it. It is also sometimes necessary to select the proper heir within the kinship group by some of the methods just spoken of; thus in certain Negro states brothers have had to fight for the succession. In China, succession had to take place in such a way that the relation of the living group to the ancestral spirits was not disturbed. The rule either of seniority or of designation by the followers has been very common in the Orient. Hence, in the house of Osman, it has been obligatory to eliminate all other possible candidates.

Only in Medieval Europe and in Japan universally, elsewhere only sporadically, has the principle of primogeniture, as governing the inheritance of authority, become clearly established. This has greatly facilitated the consolidation of political groups in that it has eliminated struggle between a plurality of candidates from the same charismatic family.

In the case of hereditary charisma, recognition is no longer paid to the charismatic qualities of the individual, but to the legitimacy of the position he has acquired by hereditary succession. This may lead in the direction either of traditionalization or of legalization. The concept of "divine right" is fundamentally altered and now comes to mean authority by virtue of a personal right which is not dependent on the recognition of those subject to authority. Personal charisma may be totally absent. Hereditary monarchy is a conspicuous illustration. In Asia there have been very numerous hereditary priesthoods; also, frequently, the hereditary charisma of kinship groups has been treated as a criterion of social rank and of eligibility for fiefs and benefices.

(f) The concept that charisma may be transmitted by ritual means from one bearer to another or may be created in a new person. The concept was originally magical. It involves a dissociation of charisma from a particular individual, making it an objective, transferable entity. In particular, it may become the charisma of office. In this case the belief in legitimacy is no longer directed to the individual, but to the acquired qualities and to the effectiveness of the ritual acts. The most important example is the transmission of priestly charisma by anointing, consecration, or the laying on of hands; and of royal authority, by anointing and by coronation. The *caracter indelibilis* thus acquired means that the charismatic qualities and powers of the office are emancipated from the personal qualities of the priest. For precisely this reason, this has, from the Donatist and the Montanist heresies down to the Puritan revolution, been the subject of continual conflicts. The "hireling" of the Quakers is the preacher endowed with the charisma of office.

Concomitant with the routinization of charisma with a view to insuring adequate succession, go the interests in its routinization on the part of the administrative staff. It is only in the initial stages and so long as the charismatic leader acts in a way which is completely outside everyday social organization, that it is possible for his followers to live communistically in a community of faith and enthusiasm, on gifts, "booty," or sporadic acquisition. Only the members of the small group of enthusiastic disciples and followers are prepared to devote their lives purely idealistically to their call. The great majority of disciples and followers will in the long run "make their living" out of their "calling" in a material sense as well. Indeed, this must be the case if the movement is not to disintegrate.

Hence, the routinization of charisma also takes the form of the appropriation of powers of control and of economic advantages by the followers or disciples, and of regulation of the recruitment of these groups. This process of traditionalization or of legalization, according to whether rational legislation is involved or not, may take any one of a number of typical forms.

1. The original basis of recruitment is personal charisma. With routinization, the followers or disciples may set up norms for recruitment, in particular involving training or tests of eligibility. Charisma can only be "awakened" and "tested"; it cannot be "learned" or "taught." All types of magical asceticism, as practiced by magicians and heroes, and all novitiates, belong in this category. These are means of closing the group which constitutes the administrative staff.

Only the proved novice is allowed to exercise authority. A genuine charismatic leader is in a position to oppose this type of prerequisite for membership. His successor is not, at least if he is chosen by the administrative staff. This type is illustrated by the magical and warrior asceticism of the "men's house" with initiation ceremonies and age groups. An individual who has not successfully gone through the initiation, remains a "woman"; that is, is excluded from the charismatic group.

2. It is easy for charismatic norms to be transformed into those defining a traditional social status on a hereditary charismatic basis. If the leader is chosen on a hereditary basis, it is very easy for hereditary charisma to govern the selection of the administrative staff and even, perhaps, those followers without any position of authority. The term "familistic state" [1] will be applied when a political body is organized strictly and completely in terms of this principle of hereditary charisma. In such a case, all appropriation of governing powers, of fiefs, benefices, and all sorts of economic advantages

1. *Geschlechterstaat.*

follow the same pattern. The result is that all powers and advantages of all sorts become traditionalized. The heads of families, who are traditional gerontocrats or patriarchs without personal charismatic legitimacy, regulate the exercise of these powers which cannot be taken away from their family. It is not the type of position he occupies which determines the rank of a man or of his family, but rather the hereditary charismatic rank of his family determines the position he will occupy. Japan, before the development of bureaucracy, was organized in this way. The same was undoubtedly true of China as well where, before the rationalization which took place in the territorial states, authority was in the hands of the "old families." Other types of examples are furnished by the caste system in India, and by Russia before the *Mjestnitschestvo* was introduced. Indeed, all hereditary social classes with established privileges belong in the same category.

3. The administrative staff may seek and achieve the creation and appropriation of individual positions and the corresponding economic advantages for its members. In that case, according to whether the tendency is to traditionalization or legalization, there will develop (a) benefices, (b) offices, or (c) fiefs. In the first case a praebendal organization will result; in the second, patrimonialism or bureaucracy; in the third, feudalism. These become appropriated in the place of the type of provision from gifts or booty without settled relation to the everyday economic structure.

Case (a), benefices, may consist in rights to the proceeds of begging, to payments in kind, or to the proceeds of money taxes, or finally, to the proceeds of fees. Any one of these may result from the regulation of provision by free gifts or by "booty" in terms of a rational organization of finance. Regularized begging is found in Buddhism; benefices in kind, in the Chinese and Japanese "rice rents"; support by money taxation has been the rule in all the rationalized conquering states. The last case is common everywhere, especially on the part of priests and judges and, in India, even the military authorities.

Case (b), the transformation of the charismatic mission into an office, may have more of a patrimonial or more of a bureaucratic character. The former is much the more common; the latter is found principally in Mediterranean Antiquity and in the modern Western World. Elsewhere it is exceptional.

In case (c), only land may be appropriated as a fief, whereas the position as such retains its originally charismatic character. On the other hand, powers and authority may be fully appropriated as fiefs. It is difficult to distinguish the two cases. It is, however, rare that orientation to the charismatic character of the position disappears entirely; it did not do so in the Middle Ages.

For charisma to be transformed into a permanent routine structure, it is necessary that its anti-economic character should be altered. It must be adapted to some form of fiscal organization to provide for the needs of the group and hence to the economic conditions necessary for raising taxes and contributions. When a charismatic movement develops in the direction of praebendal provision, the "laity" become differentiated from the "clergy"; [2] that is, the participating members of the charismatic administrative staff which has now become routinized. These are the priests of the developing "church." Correspondingly, in a developing political body the vassals, the holders of benefices, or officials are differentiated from the "tax payers." The former, instead of being the "followers" of the leader, become state officials or appointed party officials. This process is very conspicuous in Buddhism and in the Hindu sects. The same is true in all the states resulting from conquest which have become rationalized to form permanent structures; also of parties and other movements which have originally had a purely charismatic character. With the process of routinization the charismatic group tends to develop into one of the forms of everyday authority, particularly the patrimonial form in its decentralized variant or the bureaucratic. Its original peculiarities are apt to be retained in the charismatic standards of honour attendant on the social status acquired by heredity or the holding of office. This applies to all who participate in the process of appropriation, the chief himself and the members of his staff. It is thus a matter of the type of prestige enjoyed by ruling groups. A hereditary monarch by "divine right" is not a simple patrimonial chief, patriarch, or sheik; a vassal is not a mere household retainer or official. Further details must be deferred to the analysis of social stratification.

As a rule the process of routinization is not free of conflict. In the early stages personal claims on the charisma of the chief are not easily forgotten and the conflict between the charisma of office or of hereditary status with personal charisma is a typical process in many historical situations.

1. The power of absolution—that is, the power to absolve from mortal sins—was held originally only by personal charismatic martyrs or ascetics, but became transformed into a power of the office of bishop or priest. This process was much slower in the Orient than in the Occident because in the latter case it was influenced by the Roman conception of office. Revolutions under a charismatic leader, directed against hereditary charismatic powers or the powers of office, are to be found in all types of corporate groups, from states to trade unions.[3] The more highly developed the interdependence of different economic units in a monetary economy, the greater the pressure of the everyday needs of the followers of the charismatic movement becomes. The effect of this is to strengthen the tendency to routinization, which is everywhere operative, and as a rule has rapidly won out. Charisma is a phenomenon typical of prophetic religious movements or of

2. Derived from κλῆρος, meaning a "share." See the Sociology of Religion.
3. This last is particularly conspicuous at the present time (1920).

expansive political movements in their early stages. But as soon as the position of authority is well established, and above all as soon as control over large masses of people exists, it gives way to the forces of everyday routine.

2. One of the decisive motives underlying all cases of the routinization of charisma is naturally the striving for security. This means legitimatization, on the one hand, of positions of authority and social prestige, on the other hand, of the economic advantages enjoyed by the followers and sympathizers of the leader. Another important motive, however, lies in the objective necessity of adaptation of the patterns of order and of the organization of the administrative staff to the normal, everyday needs and conditions of carrying on administration. In this connexion, in particular, there are always points at which traditions of administrative practice and of judicial decision can take hold; since these are needed both by the normal administrative staff and by those subject to its authority. It is further necessary that there should be some definite order introduced into the organization of the administrative staff itself. Finally, as will be discussed in detail below, it is necessary for the administrative staff and all its administrative practices to be adapted to everyday economic conditions. It is not possible for the costs of permanent, routine administration to be met by "booty," contributions, gifts, and hospitality, as is typical of the pure type of military and prophetic charisma.

3. The process of routinization is thus not by any means confined to the problem of succession and does not stop when this has been solved. On the contrary, the most fundamental problem is that of making a transition from a charismatic administrative staff, and the corresponding principles of administration, to one which is adapted to everyday conditions. The problem of succession, however, is crucial because through it occurs the routinization of the charismatic focus of the structure. In it, the character of the leader himself and of his claim to legitimacy is altered. This process involves peculiar and characteristic conceptions which are understandable only in this context and do not apply to the problem of transition to traditional or legal patterns of order and types of administrative organization. The most important of the modes of meeting the problem of succession are the charismatic designation of a successor and hereditary charisma.

4. As has already been noted, the most important historical example of designation by the charismatic leader of his own successor is Rome. For the *rex*, this arrangement is attested by tradition; while for the appointment of the "dictator" and of the co-emperor and successor in the principate, it has existed in historical times. The way in which all the higher magistrates were invested with the *imperium* shows clearly that they also were designated as successors by the military commander, subject to recognition by the citizen army. The fact that candidates were examined by the magistrate in office

and that originally they could be excluded on what were obviously arbitrary grounds shows clearly what was the nature of the development.

5. The most important examples of designation of a successor by the charismatic followers of the leader are to be found in the election of bishops, and particularly of the Pope, by the original system of designation by the clergy and recognition by the lay community. The investigations of U. Stutz have made it probable that, though it was later altered, the election of the German emperor was modelled on that of the bishops. He was designated by a group of qualified princes and recognized by the "people," that is, those bearing arms. Similar arrangements are very common.

6. The classical case of the development of hereditary charisma is that of caste in India. All occupational qualifications, and in particular all the qualifications for positions of authority and power, have there come to be regarded as strictly bound to the inheritance of charisma. Eligibility for fiefs, involving governing powers, was limited to members of the royal kinship group, the fiefs being granted by the eldest of the group. All types of religious office, including the extraordinarily important and influential position of *guru*, the *directeur de l'âme*, were treated as bound to hereditary charismatic qualities. The same is true of all sorts of relations to traditional customers and of all positions in the village organization, such as priest, barber, laundryman, watchman, etc. The foundation of a sect always meant the development of a hereditary hierarchy, as was true also of Taoism in China. Also in the Japanese "feudal" state, before the introduction of a patrimonial officialdom on the Chinese model, which then led to praebends and a new foundation, social organization was based purely on hereditary charisma.

This kind of hereditary charismatic right to positions of authority has been developed in similar ways all over the world. Qualification by virtue of individual achievement has been replaced by qualification by birth. This is everywhere the basis of the development of hereditary aristocracies, in the Roman nobility, in the concept of the *stirps regia*, which Tacitus describes among the Germans, in the rules of eligibility to tournaments and monasteries in the late Middle Ages, and even in the genealogical research carried on on behalf of the parvenu aristocracy of the United States. Indeed, this is to be found everywhere where a differentiation of hereditary social classes has become established.

The following is the principal relation to economic conditions: The process of routinization of charisma is in very important respects identical with adaptation to the conditions of economic life, since this is one of the principal continually-operating forces in everyday life. Economic conditions in this connexion play a leading role and do not constitute merely a dependent variable. To a very large extent the transition to hereditary charisma or the charisma of office serves in this connexion as a means of legitimizing existing or recently acquired powers of control over economic goods. Along with the ideology of loyalty, which is certainly by no means unimportant, allegiance to hereditary monarchy in particular is very strongly influenced by the consideration that all inherited property and all that which is legitimately acquired would be endangered if subjective recognition of the sanctity of succession to the throne were eliminated. It is hence by no means fortuitous that hereditary monarchy is more acceptable to the propertied classes than, for instance, to the proletariat.

Beyond this, it is not possible to say anything in general terms, which would at the same time be substantial and valuable, on the relations of the various possible modes of adaptation to the economic order. This must be reserved to a special investigation. The development of a praebendal structure, of feudalism and the appropriation of all sorts of advantages on a hereditary charismatic basis, may in all cases have the same stereotyping effect on the economic order if they develop from charismatic starting points as if they developed from patrimonial or bureaucratic origins. The immediate effect of charisma in economic as in other connexions is usually strongly revolutionary; indeed, often destructive, because it means new modes of orientation. But in case the process of routinization leads in the direction of traditionalism, its ultimate effect may be exactly the reverse.[4]

4. The economics of charismatic revolutions will have to be discussed separately. It is by no means the same in all cases.

THE NAZI PARTY: ITS LEADERSHIP AND COMPOSITION[1]

Hans H. Gerth

CHARISMATIC LEADERSHIP. The National Socialist party in Germany can be adequately described only as a fusion of two types of domination, namely, the charismatic and the bureaucratic types.[2] The charismatic aspect of National Socialism is represented in the position of the "Leader" in relation

Reprinted with slight abridgments from *The American Journal of Sociology*, Vol. XLV (1940), pp. 517-541, by permission of the author and the publisher. (Copyright, 1940, by *The American Journal of Sociology*.)
    1. The author is greatly indebted to Mr. Edward Shils, of the University of Chicago, for many valuable suggestions and the complete revision of the article.
    2. Cf. H. H. Gerth and C. Wright Mills (translators and editors), *From Max Weber: Essays in Sociology* (New York: Oxford University Press, 1946), pp. 245-252 and A. M. Henderson and Talcott Parsons (translators and editors), *Max Weber: The Theory of Social and Economic Organization* (New York: Oxford University Press, 1947), pp. 358-392, parts of which are included in this volume. By charisma we refer to a personality characteristic which is regarded as extraordinary. In consequence of this,

to the faithful believers in the leader's God-given gifts, in his infallibility and in his sanctity.[3] In his own eyes and in the eyes of his followers the "Leader" does not follow man-made rules or laws, nor is he bound by any hitherto valid customs, conventions, or laws.[4] In this respect he is similar to the great prophets who have protested against orthodoxy in ecclesiastical organization and in theological doctrines. He does not follow already existing rules; he creates new ones. He is a revolutionary who does not accept the existing order but sets up instead an order of his own. His authority is not a delegated authority but one residing in himself. Hence formulas like "I decided. . . ." are the final word.[5] His decisions are not justified by their consistency with standards other than those which he himself asserts.

There are situations, however, such as crises in international relations, in which a democratic legitimation is occasionally necessary. In such cases the dictator boasts of being the "son of the people," the "unknown soldier," who articulates and expresses the will of the party. The party in its turn performs the same functions for the people as a whole, by representing their "true" preferences and racial "instincts" in a way which they themselves are not capable of doing.

It is not our task to decide whether the leader really has charismatic qualities. It is relevant only that the leader find sufficient followers who believe that he has those qualities and who acknowledge his claim for recognition. Charismatic domination exists as long as and in so far as the leader can successfully claim such acknowledgment by his followers.

This is the type of claim which is raised by Hitler in practically all spheres of life. Persons who according to conventional standards are "authorities" in music, painting, and military strategy carry no special weight alongside of him since they are in the last analysis "mere" specialists. He is *the* genius of every field of activity. . . . The charismatic claim to leadership the person who possesses it is thought to have either divinely instilled or "exemplary leadership" powers or at least extraordinary qualities which most persons cannot acquire. It is entirely irrelevant conceptually whether the characteristic in question is "objectively" true from an ethical, aesthetic, or any other viewpoint. It is important rather that it should be so regarded by those who are charismatically dominated, i.e., the disciples.

3. ". . . . We National Socialists believe . . . . that for us the Leader is . . . . simply infallible" (Hermann Göring, *Germany Reborn* [London, 1934], p 79).

4. "At such time, if anyone feels it his duty to take upon himself to be a leader of a *Volk*, such a man is not bound to follow the regulations of parliamentary customs, or to accept the obligation to act according to a particular democratic conception, but exclusively to carry out the mission intrusted to him" (Reichstag speech, February 20, 1938, *Der Angriff*, February 21, 1938).

5. Policies are not the result of majority votes of political councils. Neither the 16 members of the Cabinet nor the council of the 18 *Reichsleiter*, nor the 9 members of the Secret Cabinet council take votes. Hitler proclaims his decision after the discussions. The frequency of formulas like "I resolved . . . ." and "I decided . . . ." is symptomatic of the charismatic legitimation of his domination. . . .

It is difficult to determine how far such "decisions" are substantially personal decisions of Hitler's and how far the formula represents the legitimation of the decisions of experts and officials. . . .

which is totalitarian in nature means that no status on the basis of specialized and technical achievement can be accorded unless it has the approval of the leader or those to whom he delegates his power. . . .

A central element in the definition of the charismatic group is that during its revolutionary, or genuinely charismatic, phase it despises routine pursuits—especially the uninspiring drudgery of institutionalized and stereotyped economic activities. As a charismatic party, the Nazis have used extraordinary means for financing their political activities. These range from house-to-house begging expeditions, anonymous street collections, and the solicitation of contributions and gifts from "friends of the party," to overt bribes and confiscations. When the party came into power, it was deeply in debt.

THE "INNER CIRCLE." The charismatic leader delegates power to faithful followers whom he trusts. He does not primarily "appoint" them for specific offices which carry with them specific powers. Rather, he gives special commissions and tasks to the follower, leaving it to the latter's discretion to determine what range of authority is required for execution of the task. Territorial limits, the personal charisma of the follower, and the ability to secure the confidence and favor of the leader alone determine how much power he can wield through his administration. Göring's commission as chief forester of Germany or as head of the Four Year Plan and the unification of the Reich through eleven regents (*Statthalter*) are examples of this type of delegation of power. Party members who are commissioned personally by the leader constitute "members of the inner circle."

As the confidence and favor of the leader alone determine who belongs to the inner circle, each member competing for such appointments is in constant fear of the loss of the leader's confidence. But the members of the inner circle must act. Therefore, ever suspicious and ever watchful, they feel compelled continually to demonstrate their unswerving belief in the leader's charisma. Even though they might not actually believe in Hitler's abilities, this necessity makes for the exuberant praise and eulogy of the leader's actual or imputed virtues and qualities. This situation has given use to a great body of religious, aesthetic, mythological, poetical, and historical verbiage. It was Hermann Esser who first used the term "leader"; it was allegedly Dr. Ley who employed the possessive formula "my leader"—to mention only two incidents in this process. The spread and enforcement of the "Heil Hitler" salute in physical and written form in the nation at large falls under the same heading.

No objective criteria are utilized in the selection of members for specific tasks. They are intrusted with all sorts of tasks irrespective of their age, training, or social origin. Particular achievements in a "career" are not regarded as relevant in determining a member's eligibility for a given position. The composition of the inner circle, therefore, does not seem to be subject to any rule other than to the changing personality preferences of the leader and to the power which the individual member may secure through institutional entrenchment and factional support by powerful "friends." He is supposed to be worthy of being commissioned through his participation in the leader's charisma, through personal propinquity, long-standing friendship, and comradeship during the struggle for power. Hess's designation as "deputy leader" is the most conspicuous example. However, the past exercises no irresistible claims over the present, and the oldest friends may lose the leader's confidence, e.g., the Strassers, Röhm, Hanfstängl, and Gottfried Feder (the author of the party program). The "purge" is the form in which such differences of opinion tend to be settled. The deviation of the defeated faction is defined as indicative of a lack of faith in the leader. It was against such a charge that Karl Ernst, the commander of the Berlin Storm Troopers, shouted "Heil Hitler" when he faced the firing squad of the Elite Guard during the Röhm purge of June 30, 1934.

The charismatic leader refuses to be identified with any specific "office" no matter how many bodies of functionaries he may create. Hitler did not assume the title of "President" when he usurped the supreme command over the army and navy and proclaimed himself to be "Leader and Reichs-Chancellor" after von Hindenburg's death. The subsequent plebiscitarian acclamation of the nation has nothing to do with "democratic elections." In June, 1939, Hitler reduced his title to "Der Führer." The designation of "Aggrandizer of the Reich" is an official *epiteton ornans*, not a transferable title. It stresses the *personal* achievement and does not indicate a legally defined and delimited rank or position. Just as Cromwell refused to accept the title of "King," Hitler is unlikely to accept the title of "Kaiser"—titles which connote the hereditary character of institutionalized political charisma.

THE PARTY AT LARGE. As each member of the inner circle can only legitimate his power by invoking the favor of the leader, his exclusion from the inner circle can only be interpreted by the party at large as a consequence of disobedience and unfaithfulness. The weaker his position actually becomes, the more ardently will he emphasize his belief in the righteousness of the leader. This is true of all positions in the party hierarchy: for the 33 *Gauleitern*, the 760 subdistrict leaders, the 21,354 leaders of local groups, about 70,000 leaders of party cells, and 400,000 leaders of party blocks. (Since the reorganization of the party in 1937, every German, whether party member or not, falls under the *Hoheitsgebiet* or legal control of the party official.) [6]

The derivation of all authority from the leader excludes any party-democracy. No local leader is elected; every leader is appointed by his

6. For a discussion of monocratic rulership see Kurt H. Wolff (translator and editor), *The Sociology of Georg Simmel* (Glencoe, Illinois: The Free Press, 1950), pp. 181-303; Henderson and Parsons, *op. cit.*, pp. 337-341.

superior, and he alone is responsible to his superior for whatever action he takes, for whatever happens in his district. He alone and not vote-taking deliberative bodies decides on policies. The rapid growth of the party in numbers and power made a rapid organization of a bureaucratic staff necessary. The centralization of power secured the swift execution of undisputable commands from above, minimized the spread of clashes of opinion and disputes through the hierarchy, and allowed for quick changes of slogans and policies (e.g., the sudden co-operation with the Communist party during the Berlin transport strike in 1932 and the National Socialist faction in many parliamentary battles). However flagrantly actions may have contradicted words, nothing could disrupt the firmly disciplined organization. It is here that the charismatic aspect of the Hitler movement is fused with the bureaucratic organization in its most rationalized form into the monocratic administration. . . .

For the National Socialist, increasing power at home and abroad is a primary obligation. Every thought and action furthering that end is correct, while to miss an opportunity in the fight is unforgivable. This simple code reduces scruples. It can easily be followed by individuals of the most diversified backgrounds. The less rigid the moral, intellectual, and conduct patterns of the party member are, the less his personality is channelized by confined occupational, regional, and diversified social conventions the greater are his chances to pursue the ends of the party with a minimum of inhibitions. Hence the ascent into so many leading positions of the party of those types who have been failures in other spheres of life. Hence the contempt for bourgeois respectability.

The charismatic character of the conquest of power and the legitimation of "heroic" actions in the name of the leader appeal to such personalities. They succeeded in the efficient diffusion of faith in the leader. The monocratic structure of the party minimizes the personal responsibility of the subleader, while it gives him the support of the organization. In critical situations he has the comforting assurance that he is merely executing "commands from above." In passing, it might be remarked that it is only in such situations, and especially when the leader stresses continuously his formal adherence to "legality," that the middle-class German seems to be able to act in a revolutionary way.

THE SOCIAL COMPOSITION OF THE PARTY. The bureaucratic aspect of the party appeals greatly to those potential recruits with a bureaucratic background. It attracts especially the teaching profession, the more so as the unpolitical hero-worship and moralistic character of the propaganda allows for an interpretation which presents the conquest of power as the education of a misguided nation.[7]

The teachers—mostly elementary-school teachers—are the best repre-

7. Svend Ranulf, *Moral Indignation and Middle Class Psychology* (Copenhagen, 1937).

sented of all professional groups composing the Nazi party—97 per cent of all German teachers are members of the party or its affiliates. Among the leading former schoolteachers are Reichsminister Bernhard Rust; the Jew-baiter, Julius Streicher; the leader of the Sudeten Germans, Konrad Henlein; the head of the secret police and the Elite Guard, Heinrich Himmler; the late district leader, Hans Schemm; state minister and district leader, Adolf Wagner; and the governor of the two Silesian provinces and district leader of Silesia and South Westphalia, Joseph Wagner. Seven district leaders or vice-district leaders out of the total of 33 are former teachers, 78 out of 760 subdistrict leaders are former teachers, and about 3,000 teachers are local leaders. Altogether there are 160,000 political functionaries, leaders, and subleaders recruited from the ranks of the teachers, mainly the elementary-school teachers. They constituted 32.66 per cent of the total of 489,583 political leaders as reported in a party census of May, 1935, or 22.9 per cent of the total of 700,000 political leaders reported after the reorganization of the party in 1936–37.[8]

Persons whose career expectations are frustrated or who suffer losses in status or income in the intensive vocational competition of modern capitalism should be especially likely to accept the belief in the charismatic leader. Those placed on the disadvantaged side of life always tend to be interested in some sort of salvation which breaks through the routines associated with their deprivation.[9] Such "unsuccessful" persons were to be found in every stratum of German society. Princes without thrones, indebted and subsidized landlords, indebted farmers, virtually bankrupt industrialists, impoverished shopkeepers and artisans, doctors without patients, lawyers without clients, writers without readers, unemployed teachers, and unemployed manual and white-collar workers joined the movement. National Socialism as a salvationary movement exercised an especially strong attraction on the "old" and "new" middle classes, especially in those strata where substantive rationality [10] is least developed, and will be the most highly

8. The strength of the teachers within the party leadership may partly explain the relentlessness of the fight between the party and the church. The teacher—especially the elementary-school teacher in the rural regions—had long resented the supervision of the Protestant ministers who were usually conservative politically, orthodox theologically, and connected socially with the Prussian *Junkers*, who were their church patrons, and with the Hohenzollern monarch, the head of their church. The schoolteachers, being recruited from a somewhat lower stratum than the clergy ever since the end of the eighteenth century, inclined more to a secularized "enlightened" or "historical" philosophy of life but were tied to the church which they had to serve as organists and preceptors. This duality of school and church office was fought by the teachers from the eighteenth century onward. Intricate fiscal and property claims of state and church were connected with this setup, and the political upheavals of 1848 and 1919 and their legislative aftermaths attempted to deal with this issue but stopped short of reaching a definitive solution. . . .

9. Cf. Henderson and Parsons, *loc. cit.*, E. Beynon, "The Voodoo Cult among Negro Migrants in Detroit," *American Journal of Sociology*, XLIII (1938), 894-907. . . .

10. Karl Mannheim, *Man and Society in an Age of Reconstruction* (New York: Harcourt, Brace and Company, 1949), chap. 1.

represented among those seeking salvation by quasi-miraculous means—or
at least by methods which break through the routines which account for
their deprivation.

**TABLE I—Percentage Occupational Distribution of Nazi Party Membership,
1933 and 1935**

Occupational Classification	Party Membership		Total Gainfully Employed *	
	1933 (1)	1935 (2)	1933 (3)	1933 (4)
Manual workers	31.5	32.1	46.3	38.5
White-collar employees	21.1	20.6	12.5	12.5
Independents †	17.6	20.2	9.6	9.6
Officials	6.7	13.0	4.6	4.6
Peasants	12.6	10.7	21.1	28.9
Others ‡	10.5	3.4	5.9	5.9
Total	100.0	100.0	100.0	100.0

* Column 4 is added as decisive evidence of the National Socialist failure to win the same following
among the urban proletariat as they won among the middle classes. In column 4 the agricultural wage-
workers who were included with "manual workers" in column 3 are classified with "peasants," leaving as
manual workers only those employed in nonagricultural pursuits and therefore predominantly urban. Even
if all those "manual workers" whom the Nazis had won as party members were entirely nonagricultural,
which was undoubtedly not the case, the nonagricultural proletariat would still be considerably underrepresented in the Nazi party both in 1933 and in 1935 as compared with employers and independents.
    † Skilled artisans, professional persons, merchants, etc., excluding independent peasants.
    ‡ Domestic servants and nonagricultural family helpers.

According to official party statistics in 1935, the occupational composition of the party membership before the conquest of power as compared with its composition in 1935 was as shown in Table I. The relatively
heavy representation of the middle classes (58 per cent of the total) becomes even more evident if we compare the composition of the party with
the composition of the total gainfully occupied. The manual workers were
underrepresented in the party by 14.8 per cent, the white-collar employees
overrepresented by 8.6 per cent, and the peasants underrepresented by 8.5
per cent. The party membership amounted at that time (January 1, 1933)
to 849,009.

The common element in the situations of all these different strata was
their despair and lack of social and economic security, the wide differential
between self-esteem and actual status, between ambition and accomplishment, between subjective claims for social status and the objective possibility of attaining these goals through competitive orientation toward
"market chances," or opportunities for social ascent through bureaucratic
careers. Through the transformation of the Republic into a totalitarian sub-
sidy state, political power seemed to be the decisive instrument for the
distribution of market chances and bureaucratic careers. It became possible
to hold those in power responsible for every deprivation. The blackmailing
of the "system" was a point on which all agreed. All interests converged
in this supreme interest; hence the slogan: "Community interest ranks
higher than self-interest," in which "self-interest" refers to a system characterized by the following features: individual or collectively organized
orientation toward market chances, the stratification of society along class

lines, and competition for pecuniary rewards and social status. The preference for "community interest" involves the devaluation of competitive
modes of orientation and the subordination of all other aims to the one
supreme aim—conquest of political power by concerted party action.

As all German parliamentary parties of the twenties (with the exception
of the Catholic Center party) were recognized both by themselves and by
others as organizations for the instrumentation of class interests, National
Socialism in principle opposed them all, especially the proletarian parties,
which, as the largest and most powerful mass organizations, represented most
conspicuously the orientation toward market chances, and whose ascent implied the degradation of the lower middle classes from which the National
Socialists drew so many of their followers. Neither its patriotism during the
war, its fight against communism, its merits in maintaining the unity of the
Reich, nor its vote for naval rearmament made the Social Democratic party
acceptable to the National Socialists. All the efforts of the party to eliminate
Marxist concepts and slogans from its vocabulary, to substitute "national
comrade" (*Volksgenosse*) and "working people" (*Werktätige*) for "class
comrade" (*Klassengenosse*) and "wage-worker" (*Lohnarbeiter*), proved to
be futile. The party remained unmistakably a class party, and for this among
other reasons the Nazis opposed it.

AGE COMPOSITION. A major factor facilitating affiliation with a charismatic movement in its revolutionary phase is youthfulness; and it is instructive, therefore, in this connection to examine the age structure of the
National Socialist party. The percentage of party members between eighteen and thirty years of age rose from 37.6 of the party membership in
1931 to 42.2 just before the party came into power. But, after the conquest
of power and the consequent stabilization and bureaucratization, youth no
longer played the same role in the party; the percentage decreased to 35.4
in 1935, when "experienced" men in their forties and fifties began to join
the party in great numbers. The decoration of Hjalmar Schacht, then the
minister of economics, with the badge and title "Old Fighter of the Party"
may be cited as an illustration. For the Social Democratic party only 19.3
per cent of the total membership was in the eighteen-to-thirty-year age
group in 1931. In the population at large, according to the census of 1933,
this age group amounted to 31.1 per cent. The National Socialist party
could truthfully boast of being a "young party." Table II strikingly shows
the differential representation of the various age groups.

The leader-follower relationship with its spontaneity is particularly conspicuous in the gang-formation process of the first terroristic groups (e.g.,
the spontaneous emergence of the terroristic techniques at the first mass
meeting of the party in 1921 at Munich and the coercion of the audience
by violence). These techniques of violence appeal to youth, especially to
those who had been members of the private post-war armies. As long as the
Hitler movement consisted of relatively spontaneous and dispersed groups

*TABLE II *—Age Composition of the National Socialist Party in Percentages
of the Total in the Years 1931, 1932, and 1935 as Compared
with Age Composition of the Social Democratic Party in 1931
and of the Total Population over Eighteen Years of Age in 1933
(Excluding the Saar, Austria, and Sudetenland)*

| | National Socialist Party | | | Social Democratic Party | Total Population |
Years	1931	1932	1935	1931	1933
18-30	37.6	42.2	35.4	19.3	31.1
31-40	27.9	27.8	27.9	27.4	22.0
41-50	19.6	17.1	20.8	26.5	17.1
Over 50	14.9	12.9	15.9	26.8	29.8
Total	100.0	100.0	100.0	100.0	100.0

* Data for the National Socialist party and for the population are from *Der Schulungsbrief*, 8. und 9. Folge, 1938, p. 315; data for the Social Democratic party, from *Berliner Tageblatt*, No. 27, January 16, 1937.

in various regions of Germany, the hierarchical and bureaucratic aspect of these private armies was not overt. The hierarchical ranks which articulated career lines and channelized ambitions were easily forgotten in the years after the war, and what remained was a memory of heroism and comradeship under the most dangerous conditions. A yearning for the comradeship of the trenches and the commonly experienced dangers of the war and of post-war battles of the private armies prompted many former soldiers and those who sought the soldierly life to join the National Socialist party as long as that party made itself the chief proponent of such values on the German political scene. This contention is supported by the following data: 48.6 per cent of all political leaders of the National Socialist party took active part in warfare during the period 1914–21. About 25 per cent of all party members who took part in the fighting which marked the war and post-war periods are in the leadership, while, of those party members who did not participate, only 20.2 per cent are leaders. In an environment where military experience is highly esteemed as well as widespread, such a movement will gain many members.

Youth and war experience both constitute a basis for a rigid distinction between in-group and out-group. This division is accompanied and strengthened by the development of a dual morality, i.e., one standard for the in-group and another standard (or minimum standard) for actions toward the out-group relationships. The refusal of loyalty to the leader and indifference toward his mission are in themselves sins.[11] Members of charismatic groups must seek to extirpate such sins and bring the sinners into the fold. . . .

11. ". . . . Anyone who tries to interfere with this [the leader's] mission is an enemy of the *Volk*, whether he seeks to do this as Bolshevik, as Democrat, as revolutionary terrorist, or as a reactionary dreamer. In such a time of stress any German who only uses his time in carrying the teachings of the Bible through the country or spends his days in doing nothing, or in criticizing the actions that others carry out, does not act in God's name, but those do who give their prayers the highest form which unites humanity with God: that is work!" (Reichstag speech, February 20, 1938, *Der Angriff*, February 21, 1938).

The decisive means of achieving the submissiveness of the nonparty population—and of preserving it once it is obtained—is the interplay between propaganda and systematic terror. This mechanism achieves not only the submissiveness of the nonparty people but it guarantees the conformity of the party membership to the leader's demands whenever deviation is threatened. The more zealous elements in the party concentrate their attention on a particular situation, single out a particular enemy or a particular area, and do not yield until they dominate the situation. The "conquering" of Koburg through the massed Storm Troopers in the early twenties merely systematized the experience of the first Munich mass meeting. The technique was then developed on a nation-wide scale and it was successful. In 1932—before the great purge of the party—Hitler wrote: "Everyone who became unfaithful or broke discipline and obedience was a dead man politically."

The outside masses were forced into conformity with the party's demands by a variety of pressure mechanisms. The Germans under National Socialism have become afraid of being stamped as "Jewish-influenced liberal intellectuals," as "hidden Marxists," or as "grumbling philistines who prefer butter to cannons and world-politics." Through fear of possible legal or other disadvantages, they are induced to evince an extreme loyalty to the largest single group—the group in power. Three weapons of propaganda are of central importance in this process, namely, extortion, anonymous denunciation, and anonymous rumors. These result in boycott, isolation, and, ultimately, disrepute. And, if the case is an extreme one, direct means of physical force are brought into play, ranging from "house arrest" or concentration camp to secret trial and eventual execution.

National Socialism has had a standardizing and unifying effect on the numerous "styles of life" of the various class and regional groups. Every plebiscitary dictatorship tends to level all groups into a common mass of subjects, and in doing this National Socialism has often claimed to be "democratic." It is indeed democratic in so far as the externals of a socially stratified society such as fashion, titles, and other means making social status and class position perceivable are devalued, minimized, and occasionally suppressed.[12]

12. The irrepressibility of the urge for ostentation of the parvenu is, however, well known, and its expression among the new élite is attested to by things like Göring's opulence in general and the setting of his wedding in the Berlin Opera in particular, Goebbels' style of life, Hitler's unforgettable decree against the lavish festivities and luxury of the Berlin Storm Troop commanders after the Röhm purge and his craving for immortalization through lavish and ostentatious buildings. . . . The undemocratic aspect of the effort to suppress the ostentation of social position lies in the fact that those who have actually increased their economic and political power and social status indulge themselves less visibly. In consequence of their greater invisibility, however, they are able to do so more freely than would be possible in the limelight of publicity.

MONOPOLY OF POWER AND BUREAUCRATIZATION. When the party came into power, it had to deal with the still existing governmental bureaucracies, on the one hand, and the party and trade-union bureaucracies, on the other hand. The liquidation of the latter assured the Nazi party of its monopoly, and the masses who were thereby atomized provided an enormous field for the organizational zeal of the inner circle. Since in any highly bureaucratized society, the administrative skill and the jurisdiction of bureaucratic bodies largely determine the amount of control at the disposal of the commissioned subleaders, a competitive and unplanned race for organizing bureaucracies set in among the members of the inner circle.

The zeal to control as many spheres as possible made for a duplication of organizations immediately upon the accession to political power. Von Ribbentrop, Rosenberg, and Göring all tried to direct Germany's foreign affairs while von Neurath was still in office. Göring as Reichsforstmeister dines at hunting parties with the Prussian *Junkers*, opens the annual agricultural exposition, and has a strong hand in agricultural politics. Ley, as the head of the Labor Front, succeeded in incorporating the Reich Agricultural Estate and therewith encroached on Darré, the minister of agriculture, at the same time that he made Seldte, the minister of labor, almost superfluous.

The party archives at Munich and the Institute for the History of Modern Germany under Frank compete with the *Reichsarchiv*—they collect largely the same historical and contemporary material for the rewriting of history along the line of Hitler's *Mein Kampf* and Rosenberg's *Mythos*. Amann, who controls the enormous holdings of the Eher publishing house, and Dr. Dietrich, the Reich's press chief, encroach on the propaganda ministry. When Göring was commissioned to carry out the Four Year Plan he quickly set up a public relations office of his own and monopolized the news-coverage of economic life. It is due only to the lack of journalistic skill that the army's press bureau has no greater stake in propaganda management. . . .

Thus in every field of politics and all spheres of life an unchecked struggle for power is being waged among the members of the inner circle who immediately tend to fortify their positions through bureaucratic organizations, duplicating and encroaching on one another's functions. Behind the precisely organized façades the cliquish struggle for power remains relatively invisible to the public at large. The motives of those who join the party range from ardent belief and more or less rationalized conviction to an opportunistic adjustment to new "facts," acquiescence, grumbling concession, and, finally, mute adaptation for fear of legal and other disadvantages.

These numerous organizations with their ill-defined and overlapping functions and jurisdictions make the process of "co-ordination" very difficult for the traditional state bureaucracies. It was under the pretext that this difficulty would be eliminated that the fusion of the party and the state bureaucracies was carried out.

The extent of the replacement of civil servants by party members invalidates Max Weber's statement about the relationship between revolution and the stability of the personnel of governmental bureaucracies in modern society. Weber thought that the officials at the very top would be replaced, the bureaucratic machine with its necessity for special training and knowledge remaining intact and serving the new political master as it had the old.[13] National Socialism, however, replaced officials of all ranks and stations from top to bottom.[14]

The policy of selection has two aspects. It is not merely oriented toward those who are in office and may or may not be replaced, but at the same time it confers differential privileges upon different types of office-seekers. From 1933 to 1936, out of the 300 *Referendare* (graduates in law serving their first probationary period in the civil service), 99 per cent belonged to the party, SA or SS (Storm Troop or Elite Guard). Of these new civil servants, 66 per cent were party members before 1932. No candidate can enter the civil service without the consent of the party district leader. This policy of selection may partly be responsible for the decreasing percentage of military officers' sons studying law. Out of the total of 821 military officers' sons studying at German universities in 1928, 51 per cent were enrolled in the faculty of law. Out of the total 900 during the winter semester, 1934–35, only 21.1 per cent were enrolled in that field.

It is clear that the fusion of the party with the bureaucracy had its effect on the social structure of the party. We saw that before the conquest of power the percentage of officials amounted to 6.7 of the total membership. By 1935 they represented more than 13 per cent. According to Ministerialrat Sommer, their percentage had risen to 28 per cent by April, 1937. What this means in absolute figures is obvious when one takes into account the striking growth of the party to the total of 2,493,890 members in 1935, when it was closed to new applicants, and the youth organizations were declared the only channel for entry into the party.

Whereas the party became a cumbersome bureaucracy, the govern-

13. Henderson and Parsons, *op. cit.*, p. 385.
14. By March, 1937, in Prussia the 12 heads of the provincial administration were replaced by party members, 11 of whom belonged to the party before 1933. Out of 34 *Regierungspräsidenten*, only 3 were left in office, all the newcomers being members of the party; 19 of them were members of the party before 1933. Out of 361 *Landräte*, the key position in rural administration, 97 were left in office. With the exception of 17, all *Landräte* are members of the party; 171, or more than 50 per cent, were party members before 1933. Out of 438 so-called "political positions" in the administration of Prussia, 356 are held by National Socialists. Eighty-one per cent are in the hands of Nazi men and 48 per cent are filled by "old fighters." In other parts of the Reich the same procedure was followed. . . .

mental bureaucracies through the influx of party members lost much of the formal rigidity of the classical Prussian civil service. Arbitrary actions in all administrations increased. The arbitrary conduct of the police, judicial, and economic departments provide the more conspicuous cases. The general achievement level for the trained expert was lowered, which the party officialdom interpreted as necessitating special training sessions in camps for officials. The element of arbitrary judgment attained predominance over what the National Socialist resents in the formal, rational, and therewith predictable conduct of affairs in the bureaucratic office.

That it is the circumscribed authority of any given office within the jurisdiction of rank and department rather than the "red tape" of bureaucratic administrations which the National Socialists resent is only too obvious when one considers the charismatic efforts of party organizers in building up machines.

There is more elaborate control of visitors in party buildings than there is in ordinary government offices. The stratification of the party according to seniority of membership is carefully documented and filed. Other things being equal, the "old fighter" successfully claims legal privileges and social honors which are inaccessible to younger party members, to say nothing of nonparty members. The stormtroopers indicate seniority status by special silver stripes, while the party badge of the "old fighter" is a golden circle. The designation of rank and membership in the many party affiliations through innumerable symbols of the uniformed staffs fills many pages of the *Handbook of Party Organization*, the manual edited for the exclusive use of the party bureaucracies. Every organizer has available comprehensive membership files with personal records of ancestry, educational, vocational, and political background.

It is through magical and awe-inspiring performances that social distance against the outside world is secured. All the various organizations compete in creating "traditions." The Nazi salute is declared to be of "Teutonic" derivation. A conspicuous example are the guards, keeping "eternal watch" before all the major party buildings, where they stand immobile, with spread legs, perpetually at attention, with the stiff aimless look of the drilled soldier—the symbol of depersonalized bureaucratized force.

ULTIMA RATIO. We have seen how the charismatic movement with its spontaneity and flexibility has been compelled, in the course of its conflict with its bureaucratized political rivals and the state bureaucracies, to yield to the necessities of far-reaching bureaucratization. The structure of the "inner circle" and the rapidity of the conquest of power made for the unplanned and substantially irrational character of the cumbersome bodies engulfing all phases of life. Competitive frictions among the inner circle are likely to turn into clashes between powerful organizations. In an autocratic regime negotiated compromises and ballots are impossible. Commands of

leaders and obedience of followers determine the problems of social interaction. Co-ordination has to be secured by ultimate decisions, i.e., the
commands of the leader, backed by force. Hitler, like every other dictator,
has been compelled to organize special forces for this purpose. Whereas
during the first period of the movement terroristic actions had the spontaneous character of gang initiative, after the conquest of power the use
of force was rationalized. The spying services and the terror campaigns
were systematized, and the "irresponsible actions of subordinate organs"
were controlled.[15] This process made for the rapid ascent of the secret
police (Gestapo) and the Elite Guard, under the command of Heinrich
Himmler, chief of all police forces.

The spontaneous denunciations of former or present alleged or actual
enemies of the party and state, of "critics and grumblers," has been replaced
by systematic spy organizations. The secretary of the Reich's press chamber
in 1936 fixed a large notice on his office door: "Denouncers will be smacked
in the face!" ("Denunzianten erhalten Ohrfeigen!") The formerly officially
encouraged wave of private denunciations has been replaced by more efficient control patterns. The inaccuracy and unreliability of denunciations
emerging from the rumors which always thrive under dictatorships and
the competition for favors of officials had by then become a public
nuisance. . . .

In the preparation of such large-scale enterprises secrecy can be secured
through the broadening of the definition of the "official secret" and the
totalitarian control of all communication processes. The trend of this process of bureaucratization is ultimately determined by the necessity of the
totalitarian preparation for war—especially in its economic aspect. The
direction of its expansion depends rather on considerations of economic
and military strategy than on the Nazi ideology. The fusion of charismatic
domination and totalitarian bureaucratization allows for surprise moves
which are either enthusiastically hailed or grumblingly accepted as *faits
accomplis* by the unaware inside and outside Germany. It has allowed for
the peaceful conquest of Austria, the Sudetenland, Bohemia-Moravia, and
Memelland. As long as the leader is successful, the belief of broad masses of
followers in his charisma is not likely to be shattered. They will continue
to act in accordance with the slogan: "Leader, command; we follow."

15. "I have 100,000 eyes in my territory to see that everything goes alright. I have
100,000 ears close to the bosom of the people. They report in the shortest time where
disturbances and economic difficulties emerge, where food prices are unjust, where
there is a shortage of food—in short where the people feel thwarted. With such an
excellently functioning news service I am as *Gauleiter* in a position to provide for immediate adjustments" (Alfred Meyer, one of the eleven regents, on April 15, 1937,
before the diplomatic corps and Rosenberg's foreign political club, *Nationalsozialistische
Monatshefte*, May, 1937, p. 450).

3

BUREAUCRACY AND POWER RELATIONS

The Power Environment of Bureaucracy

Discussions of power in connection with bureaucracy have centered on two major problems: the first of these, concerning conditions for the exercise of power within bureaucracy, is considered primarily in the next part of this section; the second, concerning the relation of bureaucracy to the distribution of power in the society at large, is the focus of the present part.

In the first selection, Bendix critically reviews several current conceptions of the relation of the modern state bureaucracy to other sources of political and economic power. Coöptation, involving the actual or ostensible sharing of power, is analyzed by Selznick as a mechanism utilized by a bureaucracy for coming to terms with power groups in its immediate environment. This mechanism is found to operate variously according to whether the bureaucracy confronts organized centers of power or confronts more diffuse elements in the society. Michels discusses the conditions under which state bureaucracies have found their staunch supporters among "discontented" members of the middle classes who look to the bureaucracy for jobs appropriate to their status: he sees this essentially as a process of "siphoning off" hostility. A second selection from Michels analyzes the increasingly conservative orientation of radical political parties as a response to entrenched state power, leading the party bureaucracy to become concerned more with self-maintenance than with its initial opposition to the government. And Neumann indicates the different significance of bureaucratization for the individual in democratic and in totalitarian society.

BUREAUCRACY
AND THE PROBLEM OF POWER

Reinhard Bendix

It is part of our folklore to identify the development of bureaucracy with the diminution of individual freedom. This identification has given rise to

Reprinted from *Public Administration Review*, Vol. V (1945), pp. 194-209, by permission of the author and the publisher. The American Society for Public Administration.

a series of popular denunciations of bureaucracy, ranging from the fear of an undue usurpation of power and of vested interest of officials to complaints about the waste of public funds, unnecessary red tape, and the lack of practical judgment on the part of government officials.[1]

Scholars in the field of public administration have frequently tended to select their topics in response to such sentiments. By focusing attention on such problems as judicial review, administrative discretion, the separation of powers, quasi-judicial procedures, and administrative efficiency, these studies have in effect been meeting specific allegations against an administration (and against any administration) with specific disclaimers or suggestions for improvement. Yet these disclaimers and suggestions have, in a sense, avoided the real issues underlying the complaints. Thus, experts have attempted to formulate for the ICC or the FCC quasi-judicial procedures which would meet the standards of impartial adjudication, although the clamor for judicial review by the critics of these agencies was prompted by a desire to curb their powers, not to improve their procedures.

This is, of course, not to deny the value of such studies in public administration, but to call attention to certain neglected problems in this field. Clearly, studies concerned with the improvement of the governmental service must make some prior assumption about the desirability of such improvement. But in making this assumption they inevitably sidestep the problem of the distribution of political power, since the idea of improving the governmental service takes the given distribution of power for granted.[2]

The popular identification of bureaucracy with oppression cannot, however, be taken lightly, since the extension of governmental functions has frequently curbed and sometimes obliterated the freedom of the individual.[3] Yet, there is also much evidence to show that it has furthered the cause of human freedom; and the great critics of "governmental interference" have often overlooked the latter point. Thus, the classical critics of mercantilism tended to forget that the emergence of absolute monarchy had been a

The author wishes to acknowledge his debt to Professor Leonard D. White of the University of Chicago and to Professor Arthur Schweitzer of the University of Wyoming for their helpful criticisms and suggestions.

1. For an analysis of the historical background of this ideology see the recent statement by Gunnar Myrdal, *An American Dilemma* (Harper & Bros., 1944), I, 432 ff.

2. This corollary is not altered, but rather confirmed, if the administrative process is conceived of in terms of an arbitration of conflicting interests. In a sense all studies concerned with the improvement of the governmental service conceive of administration in these terms. Cf. Avery Leiserson, *Administrative Regulation* (University of Chicago Press, 1942), p. 14.

3. There is another aspect of the problem of bureaucracy and individual freedom which is not touched upon here. Both Karl Marx and Max Weber have emphasized with great persuasiveness that the division of labor under modern capitalism involves the separation of the worker in any field from his instruments of operation and generally the lack of meaningful participation of the individual in the processes of production and administration. From Marx, Tocqueville, and Weber to Veblen and Mannheim this has been a recurrent theme, which has an important bearing on the problem of bureaucracy and freedom.

powerful factor in the development of business enterprise, which certainly at the time was regarded as assuring the merchants greater freedom than they had hitherto enjoyed. Likewise, the modern critics of the "service state" tend to forget that governmental "interference" has increased individual freedom by promoting social security, just as the earlier governmental aid in the development of corporate enterprise and western expansion increased the freedom of the business man.

Nevertheless, the anxieties expressed in the popular distrust of modern governmental bureaucracy have a basis in fact. Today, a revolutionary overthrow of government has become infinitely more difficult than it was before the development of modern technology, and consequently the democratic right of revolution, of which Lincoln spoke, is now a right in name only. Moreover, bureaucracy in a democratic society should be a neutral agency executing policies which the people ultimately determine. Modern government does not live up to this ideal.

The following discussion takes as a point of departure Weber's characterization of modern bureaucracy against the background of historical development. This is followed by a brief analysis of the tendencies, just mentioned, which indicate how modern bureaucracy (in western Europe and North America) actually differs from this ideal type. If this bureaucracy constitutes a threat to human freedom, it is clearly important to ascertain the historical factors responsible for its development and to discern the forces affecting the exercise of governmental power. The analysis of these factors has, however, resulted in two mutually contradictory explanations. Some students maintain that bureaucracy in government is the inevitable result of the tendency toward industrial concentration and monopolization inherent in the capitalist economy. Others state that economic concentration is just as inevitably the result of government bureaucracy and its interference with economic life. An attempt to resolve this dilemma leads to a restatement of the basic issues which a study of bureaucracy should confront.

MODERN BUREAUCRACY AND THE PROBLEM OF POWER. We have witnessed a growth of governmental apparatus of the modern type ever since the rise of absolute monarchy in Europe. From the time of the Tudors on, it came to be recognized that the head of the state held an effective monopoly of power, in distinction from the feudal system, in which the power of government was delegated to semi-autonomous lords. Thus, only the king could legitimately exercise physical coercion (within the bounds of certain customary rules and legal regulations).[4] The powers of the king were exercised by officials, whose duties became increasingly technical in character with the increasing complexity of governmental affairs. These officials,

4. Cf. Franklin Le Van Baumer, *The Early Tudor Theory of Kingship* (Yale University Press, 1940).

remunerated at first by favors from the king, came to receive regular salaries, which required in turn a system of centralized taxation. Thus, remuneration for governmental service was no longer identical with what the incumbent could get out of the office. Instead, salaries were paid by the treasury and as a result remuneration became separated from the office. The struggle ever since the 16th century has been over the questions (1) whether and how much both the policies and the financing of the government would be subject to the deliberation of some representative body; and (2) how representative of the people this lawgiving body would be. It is against this background that modern bureaucracy arose.

What determines how bureaucracy in the modern state will exercise its power? In attempting to answer this question we must realize that today the problem of power in a bureaucratic government differs a great deal from what it was in the centuries prior to the rise of the modern state. Throughout the period preceding the advent of the supervisory and welfare functions of modern government, a revolutionary disruption of the administrative machinery, while extremely inconvenient and destructive, did not entail the discontinuance of "essential" services. And the technology of warfare and communication did not constitute an insurmountable barrier to an overthrow of government by force. In other words, governments did not have the technical facilities necessary for the abolition of privacy in personal life (totalitarianism). Moreover, governments then were not so dependent as they are today on specially trained administrative personnel. Since the end of World War I these factors have changed the increased role of government, its dependence on a professionally trained corps of civil servants, and the vastly improved technology of policing and defense have in fact changed the nature of modern revolutions. It may be that today a revolutionary change (other than the fascist type of revolution) is only possible after a destructive war. And with the increasing devastation caused by modern warfare the nature of these postwar revolutions may be changing as well. At any rate, it is clear that these changes are so significant in their implications for the exercise of power by government that studies of bureaucracy in the traditional sense do not suffice. We must search instead for the underlying transformations in society that have prompted these developments. We must seek to interpret the technical and social changes which affect governmental bureaucracy, not only in order to improve the civil service, but in order to understand more fully the problems of power which it involves.

The conclusions which may be drawn from the preceding ideal-typical characterization of bureaucracy and its relation to the problem of power are threefold:

1. Bureaucracy in the modern state tends to operate like an "automaton," i.e., a body of officials whose performance of duty is professionalized and

has consequently become independent of their personal sentiments and opinions.

2. As a result, policy is determined at the top (ideally, outside the executive branch), relayed to the bureaucratic apparatus, and at every step of the hierarchy executed in optimum conformity with the original policy decision.

3. Thus, while administrative power is the lifeblood of bureaucracy, the direction of its exercise lies ideally outside its jurisdiction.

Obviously, no bureaucracy ever conforms to this model, but the ideal type of modern bureaucracy, particularly in western Europe and North America, has two other specific traits:

1. Modern bureaucracy is characterized by the development of administrative autonomy due to the importance of technical skills. In the sense that these skills make the higher administrative personnel irreplaceable, a modern governmental bureaucracy holds a *monopoly of skill*.

2. Revolution against a modern governmental bureaucracy has become technically very difficult, if not impossible. A complete overhauling of such a government is very nearly out of the question, since it would involve the interruption of public services essential to the community. Modern governmental bureaucracy holds, therefore, a *monopoly of power*.

Any realistic analysis must, consequently, see its task in ascertaining the various ways in which a specific bureaucracy approximates or deviates from this model.

GOVERNMENTAL BUREAUCRACY AND MONOPOLISTIC INDUSTRY. The two most prominent theories of bureaucracy have taken as a point of departure one of these characteristics of modern bureaucracy (its "monopoly of power") and have attempted to account for it historically. Both theories assume that modern bureaucracy has in fact a monopoly of power, although they differ in their evaluation of how this power is exercised and in their historical analysis of its development; neither theory recognizes the tendency toward administrative autonomy. Both the laissez faire and the "economic" theory of bureaucracy agree further that the extension of governmental control is synonymous with the diminution of individual freedom, although for the latter theory this is of secondary, while for the former it is of primary significance. It is necessary to present these theories here, before a restatement of the problem of modern bureaucracy can be attempted.

Bureaucracy as the Result of Monopolization.[5] In recent years the con-

---

5. Bureaucracy is indispensable both in industry and in government, but it does not always present the same problems in both areas. Compare in this respect the view of Ludwig von Mises, who holds that business is democratic and government dictatorial (*Bureaucracy*, Yale University Press, 1944) with the view of Beardsley Ruml, who finds that business is dictatorial and government democratic (*Tomorrow's Business*, Farrar & Rinehart, Inc., 1945).

centration of economic power has again been described as jeopardizing democracy.

In this connection the separation of ownership and control in large corporations has been developed into a theory of the "managerial revolution." According to this theory, we are now in a period of transition, in which the central political and economic controls are passing from the hands of the old to those of a new "ruling class." The dominance of individual capitalists, who were both owners and managers of their enterprises, has passed irretrievably under the impact of the growing corporate system. The control over economic power has been concentrated in the hands of "managers"— i.e., all those who determine the policies of business enterprise and governmental agencies. According to this theory, all distinctions (other than those of degree) between different political systems (such as fascism, communism, state capitalism) become obliterated by this world-wide revolution common to all. Burnham's theory is relevant in this context because it sees in the growing bureaucratization in industry and government the reason for the concentration of power in the hands of the "managers." And since these "managers" are held to constitute one cohesive group, it follows that a new social system has emerged or is emerging.

This theory seems little more than question-begging. Burnham constructs a "new social class" by designating as "managers" all those who handle the "controls." In this way, a new class is found to control industry and government, and consequently the managerial revolution is found to be in progress in all industrialized countries.[6] But the concentration of controls in the hands of men who control but do not own does not mean that the "managers" are of one mind. The rising importance of managerial functions is undisputed. But the incidence of economic power is not changed merely because the men who exercise these functions control an enterprise without owning it.[7] The real question is, as Burnham's critics [8] have been quick to point out, whether (1) men who control the policies of industry, government, labor

6. Burnham's thesis is reminiscent of the technocratic argument of fifteen years ago, which attributed strategic control to production engineers. It is also comparable to the still older argument that contended the same for the proletariat in the old union slogan of the German labor movement: "Alle Raeder stehen still, wann dein starker Arm es will." In all these cases, the conclusion is drawn that certain people in the production system constitute a separate social group because they serve similar functions and that they are powerful because they are indispensable.

7. In fact, Joseph A. Schumpeter has argued that the managers are less likely to fight for their enterprise, since they are only employees, hired by anonymous owners. That means that they do not constitute a new social class, but only represent an old one, which is dying. See his *Capitalism, Socialism and Democracy* (Harper & Bros., 1942).

8. Cf. Franz Neumann, *Behemoth* (Oxford University Press, 1942) and Robert A. Brady, *Business as a System of Power* (Columbia University Press, 1943). Both authors are strongly at variance with Burnham, but share with him certain basic premises discussed below.

unions, farm groups, etc., constitute a cohesive group owing to this common characteristic; or (2) the ideas and policies of the so-called managerial group differ in any respect from those of the older type of entrepreneur. The problem of power which bureaucratization poses is not illuminated by the assertion that all "capitalist" countries are more or less in the hands of those who control their respective industrial and governmental bureaucracies.

Another interpretation of the changing relation between governmental bureaucracy and "business" expresses the belief that the development of trade associations by big business (so-called "peak associations") is more or less synonymous with the development of modern totalitarianism. Through these trade associations big business influences the government politically and economically, and with their help it furthers in addition the monopolization of industry. These associations have acquired national scope; they are no longer confined to the organization of competing firms in one branch of production but comprise today whole systems of industrial enterprise. In all fascist countries, the trade associations existing before the dictatorship can be shown to have been the antecedents of the trade associations under the dictatorship. Consequently, according to Brady and others, the trade associations influential in Britain and America today are simply the antecedents of the trade associations ruling the fascist Britain and the fascist America of tomorrow. In support of this thesis a wealth of evidence on the activities of trade associations has been adduced. The inference is drawn that "Business" is ready to take over the strategic controls of governmental bureaucracy. It is in these terms that Brady has interpreted the rise of fascism in the Axis countries and has forecasted similar tendencies in England and the United States.

Obviously, the tendency toward concentration of economic power is real enough. But it is still necessary to inquire why differences between fascism, communism, and democratic capitalism continue to exist. Why is it that the concentration of power in the hands of the peak associations has so far failed to bring fascism to this country—especially since, as Mr. Laski has pointed out, the feelings of fear and the inclination toward appeasement of fascist movements are rampant among the modern industrialists (or "managers").[9] Apparently, the emergence of fascism is not simply a matter of the concentration of economic power; such concentration existed in Germany, for instance, under the Kaiser during the Weimar Republic, *and* under Hitler. Such concentration has existed at the same time (if not to the same degree) in Britain. Nor can it be taken for granted that the peak associations will be able to take over the controls of government by simply continuing their "customary" activities. Moreover, these associations are not of one

9. Cf. Harold J. Laski, *Reflections on the Revolution of our Time* (Viking Press, 1943), chap. i.

mind. To what extent can they afford to see their influence on administrative arbitration and governmental assistance obliterated through the usurpation of all governmental power in the hands of a dictator? Do they not
require, in fact, a certain independence of government, which is yet subject
to their influence, in order to have an agency which can guarantee the legal
and administrative prerequisites of monopolistic practices, which industry
itself could not provide? To what extent is their propaganda against labor
unions a smoke-screen which hides a collusion of interests between industry
and labor? To what extent has this traditional antilabor attitude itself
changed? Such questions have a bearing on the relations between government and the concentration of economic power; they should, therefore, be
a part of a comprehensive study of bureaucracy in modern society.

Burnham, Neumann, Brady, and others have in common the idea that
the concentration of economic power (and the bureaucratization of industry) has encroached upon and will finally take over the control of the governmental bureaucracy. As a result, authority will be exercised to the
detriment of the individual and of the people as a whole. In this interpretation all the signs point to the ascendance of the "business system of power"
over the "governmental system of power." This tendency is the outcome
of capitalistic development, in which competition and technical innovations
have led to a greater and greater division of labor. Improved technology and
the economic advantage of large-scale production have, on the other hand,
prompted the development of industrial amalgamations, which in turn have
necessitated increased governmental controls. Large combinations of industrial enterprise are established partly for the purpose of safeguarding investments and preventing what their spokesmen regard as unfair or cut-throat
competition. They require certain governmental regulations for the same
purpose. Thus bureaucracy results from the tendencies of industrial monopolization.[10] It may be difficult to determine where regulation ends and subsidization begins, but it seems clear that such requests for governmental action
are prompted by an understandable anxiety to safeguard the huge investments which large industrial combinations represent. Thus, monopolization
and governmental regulation are employed to reduce the hazards of economic enterprise.

Up to this point there is at least superficial agreement among the writers
who regard monopolization and bureaucratization as inherent tendencies of

10. Cf. in this respect Joseph A. Schumpeter, *op. cit.*, pp. 87-106, who maintains
that the economic advances of the last century could not have been made without
monopolistic practices in industry. He criticizes those liberals who deplore these
practices and at the same time blame technological advance for grave social dislocations.
According to Schumpeter, monopolistic practices are the devices by which the capitalist
system mitigates the social effects of rapid economic expansion. For a theoretical discussion of risk-taking and its relation to monopolization see Frank H. Knight, *Risk,
Uncertainty, and Profit* (Houghton Mifflin Co., 1921).

of "society" against the encroachments of monopoly business.[11] Others capitalism. However, the role which government is called upon to play receives various interpretations. Some think of government as the protector think of governmental bureaucracy as a concomitant development of business monopolization and of both as the result of the technological trends of capitalism. Still others think of bureaucracy as the necessary result of the opposing pressures of capital and labor; both are organized to press for the realization of their demands and are held together as a political unit by governmental arbitration, conciliation, and reform. In this way, the chaotic tendencies of society are transformed into organized political existence.[12] Thus, the reasons which are given to account for the development of bureaucracy vary. But these divergent interpretations share the idea that bureaucratization in government has resulted from the "objective" development of capitalism, not from particular policies or from specific ideas about economic life.

Monopolization as the Result of Bureaucratic Interference. This latter, radically different interpretation is today advanced by the so-called liberal economists. In their opinion the history of the last two or three generations shows an increase in the functions of government and consequently an increase of the bureaucracy necessary to administer these functions. Measured against the standard of an ideally competitive economy, the increase in governmental functions and the consequent proliferation of its bureaucratic apparatus appear essentially as the result of constant, wilful "interferences" with economic life. Accordingly the history of the last hundred years is by and large explained by asserting that both bureaucracy and monopolizations in industry have resulted from bureaucratization in government, which in turn is the outcome of faulty economic policies. The first "mistake" is sometimes seen in the legal enactment of corporation charters, which promoted the growth of economic concentration.[13] A second "mistake" is seen in the fact that the government has assumed various social, economic, and regulative functions, which are decried as so many interferences with the competitive system. The resulting bureaucratization of government is interpreted as an outcome of cumulative (and sometimes or frequently, inadvertent) aggravation of initial "mistakes." Others regard it as emanating

11. This is by and large the basic idea of the investigations of the Temporary National Economic Committee concerning the concentration of economic power. See also Thurman Arnold, *The Bottlenecks of Business* (Reynal & Hitchcock, 1940).

12. The older interpretation to this effect by Lorenz von Stein, *System der Staatswissenschaft*, Vol. II; *Die Gesellschaftslehre* (Stuttgart: J. G. Cotta, 1856). Along similar lines see the recent reinterpretation of English economic history in Karl Polanyi, *The Great Transformation* (Farrar & Rinehart, 1944).

13. This leaves out of consideration that, at the time, such incorporation was advocated as the simple right of individuals to dispose of their property as they saw fit. Cf. Walter Lippmann, *An Inquiry into the Principles of the Good Society* (Little, Brown & Co., 1937).

from a more or less sinister conspiracy on the part of some people (socialists, intellectuals, crackpots, etc.), who either do not know any better or actually desire to undermine the competitive system.[14]

This interpretation of the liberal economists is obviously the reverse of the one previously mentioned. Government "interference" is spreading to many spheres especially of economic life, which were hitherto free from regulation. Increasing bureaucratization is the result. Consequently, the "governmental system of power" is in the ascendance and will eventually encroach upon all aspects of individual enterprise so that in the end a complete regulation of economic life may be anticipated. All other (non-economic) spheres of life will eventually come under government regulation, since the latter has an inherent tendency to expand. Individual freedom is, however, maintained only in a free enterprise system. Every vestige of individual freedom will, therefore, be obliterated with the disappearance of free competition.

This approach to the problems of bureaucracy starts out with an analytical account of a completely competitive economy in order to show how governmental bureaucracy has interfered with this economy instead of securing the institutional framework necessary for its unhampered operation. Thus, liberal economists account for the rise of bureaucracy historically by referring to the "mistakes" of past economic policies. It was a mistake for the government to issue charters of incorporation; it was a mistake to raise tariff barriers; it was a mistake to legalize trade unions. Responsibility for these mistakes is attributed to people who are not familiar with economics or who are wilfully undermining the free enterprise system. It is to be noted that in accounting for the historical development of bureaucracy most liberal economists begin by showing why a competitive economy is desirable and then proceed to demonstrate in what ways governments have "interfered" with it.[15] The reasons for this preference of a

14. Cf. L. von Mises, *op. cit.*, and, by the same author, *Omnipotent Government* (Yale University Press, 1944). Also Friedrich von Hayek, *The Road to Serfdom* (Univ. of Chicago Press, 1944) and his interesting articles, "Scientism and the Study of Society," *Economica*, Vols. IX-XI (1942–44). For a more temperate discussion along similar lines see Lionel Robbins, "The 'Inevitability' of Monopoly," in *The Economic Basis of Class Conflict* (London: Macmillan & Co., Ltd., 1939), 45-80.

15. The more sophisticated writers do not assert that government has interfered with an ideally competitive economy. But all assume either that at one time the approximation to a competitive economy (emerging out of the dismantling of mercantilism) was close enough to realize this economy, provided no interference would thwart this development, or that any reference to trends, tendencies, developments, etc., is purely fictitious, and consequently economic affairs change in conformity to the analytic scheme of free competition (forever maximizing production and improving technology) or as a result of political actions that interfere with the system. Only the second assumption is consistent. It rests on a strictly nominalist interpretation of society and history: all changes occur as the result of the interaction of individuals, and the actions of all individuals, taken separately or additively, are the ultimate social facts. A reduction of individual actions to any kind of collective determinant is rejected as

competitive economy vary. Some, like von Mises, insist that economic rationality can be obtained only under free competition, since no other system provides the possibility of calculating assets against liabilities. All other economic systems are, therefore, economically irrational (i.e., inefficient), since in them the allocation of resources must be arbitrary. Other writers base their preference on the value of individual initiative, which is thwarted in any economic system other than free enterprise. Still others stress primarily the historical concomitance of the competitive economy with the emergence of individual freedom, either by pointing to the history of freedom, since the industrial revolution, or by emphasizing the (absolutely) unique concatenation of historical circumstances which has given us this one chance of personal freedom and which will never recur.[16] But apart from such differences in emphasis, there is a consensus that the competitive economy has been vitiated by deliberate government action.

Preliminary Conclusion. The foregoing account of the two divergent interpretations of the historical origin of governmental bureaucracy presents us with a curious impasse. In one explanation the role of the concentration of economic power is explained in terms of inherent tendencies of capitalism, which have also entailed an increasing bureaucratization in government. In the other explanation, the increase in governmental bureaucracy is attributed to the deliberate adoption of faulty economic policies (advocated by naive or malicious radicals and intellectuals), and the concentration of economic power is, as it were, a minor offshoot of this bureaucratization. In view of this dilemma it seems reasonable to presume that each approach emphasizes what the other neglects. Clearly, those who regard the concentration of economic power as the primary cause tend to lose sight of the self-perpetuating and expansive tendencies of bureaucracy, which are in part independent of this influence of economic power. It is equally obvious, on the other hand, that the liberal view tends to lose sight of the monopolistic tendencies of industrial enterprise, which are in part independent of governmental policies which aid them. In both interpretations we find a curious naivete with regard to the separability of the economic and the political realms, either in terms of the belief that the economic causes are basic and the political phenomena are in fact epiphenomena, or

untenable. Cf. Hayek, "Scientism and the Study of Society," *op. cit.*, or Ludwig von Mises, *Nationalökonomie* (1940). See also F. A. Hayek, "The Facts of the Social Sciences," 54 *International Journal of Ethics*, 1-13 (October, 1943), and the important discussion of this article by Allan G. Gruchy, "Facts and Reality in the Social Sciences," *ibid.*, 216-22 (April, 1944). The most systematic statement of the opposite view is perhaps Emile Durkheim, *The Rules of Sociological Method* (University of Chicago Press, 1938), chap. i.

16. An impressive case is made for this point of view by Max Weber, "Zur Lage der burgerlichen Demokratie in Russland," 22 *Archiv fur Sozialwissenschaft und Sozialpolitik* 346 ff. See also, by the same author, "Der Sozialismus," in *Gesammelte Aufsätze zur Soziologie und Sozialpolitik* (Tubingen, 1924).

in terms of the belief that the competitive economy would work out if only it were not interfered with politically. Thus, each view implies a theory of social change. But the one regards the political actions leading to the formation of modern governmental bureaucracy as the dependent variable of economic changes inherent in capitalism, while the other regards these political actions as the independent cause, which leads to an interference with the (ideally) competitive economy and thereby encourages the development of bureaucracy.[17]

Thus, the principal difference in interpretation does not rest, I submit, in the instances cited to support either view. There can be little doubt that in so far as the "facts" tell us anything, they tell us both that bureaucratization is the "result" of economic concentration and that economic concentration is the "result" of governmental policies.[18] Additional historical evidence for both positions is, therefore, not likely to resolve this dispute, unless the problem itself is reformulated. In this connection it is useful to take note of Gunnar Myrdal's theory of cumulative causation, according to which the ramified effects of any institutionalized social action are so far-reaching that questions of a particular historical origin frequently lose much of their significance.[19] Accordingly, studies in the growth of bureaucratization will be illuminating only in so far as they can show in what manner the historical conditions of capitalism in the various countries of the western world were such that any piecemeal "facilitation" of the economic development by the government tended to proliferate into a growth of industrial concentration and administrative apparatus (regardless of who demanded or initiated such governmental action). Thus, the history of the corporation begins with the legalization of incorporation and especially of limited liability, without which the investment of large funds necessary to large-scale enterprise would have been very much retarded. Modern production technology as we know it today would have developed at a much slower rate, and the absence of the tremendous investment uncertainties which are involved would certainly have mitigated the tendency towards monopolization. But the historical development has now reached a point at which these original advantages of incorporation have been superseded in importance by the economic dangers of monopolization and by the political dangers of an unprecedented concentration of economic power. The question remains: What was it in the structure of this economic system which led from this

17. This divergence in historical interpretation rests in turn on a basic disagreement as to the nature of social facts.

18. See for instance, Thomas C. Cochran and William Miller, *The Age of Enterprise* (Macmillan Co., 1942) for the history of the corporation as contrasted with H. L. Childs, *Labor and Capital in National Politics* (Ohio State University Press, 1930) on the origin of the United States Chamber of Commerce.

19. Cf. Gunnar Myrdal, *op. cit.*, I, 75-78 and II, Appendix 3.

beginning to this result? And that question is not answered by repeated references to the historical origins of these latter-day developments.

This approach to the historical development of governmental bureaucracy leads in turn to a different conception of the relation between modern government and the major interest groups (such as "business" and "labor"). *By playing the role of arbitrator government helps to consolidate these groups; and governmental bureaucracy in turn grows inasmuch as these groups are compelled to assign new functions to it.* This relation between government and interest groups induces an ambivalence on both sides, a study of which would provide important insights into the emerging trends of bureaucracy. To illustrate: from the point of view of industry, monopolistic practices may be characterized as so many devices for reducing the risks of investment, for cushioning the effects of business fluctuations, etc.[20] In the opinion of business men, government must play an important role in safeguarding a smooth working of these devices; as a result, the "calculability" which has been said to characterize the legal system under capitalism has been applied to the economic sphere. That is to say, industrialists help government in shaping those policies which will make the "administration of corporate enterprise" more calculable—i.e., reasonably assured against losses. But business is just as much interested in keeping government out of the policies governing investments and the monopolistic reduction of risk and uncertainty, whenever in the judgment of business men government goes beyond the provision of safeguards or the maintenance of the rules of the game. It is difficult to see where the line between these two aspects of governmental regulation is to be drawn. Yet it is clear that the various business groups must continuously seek to draw and redraw it, notwithstanding the basic ambivalence of their whole position in its economic and psychological aspects. Thus, what appeared before as the more or less unanimous voice of "business" in its opposition to governmental interference may then turn out to be a struggle among the different groups of business and industry—with, in, and against the government, with as well as against other interest groups—over the incidence of political power and economic policies.[21]

20. Cf. Schumpeter, *op. cit.*, pp. 87-106 and Cochran and Miller, *op. cit.*, ch. iv, vii.

21. The same ambivalence of a need for government aid and a rejection of governmental interference characterizes (although in different ways) the relation between bureaucracy and other interest groups, especially labor. This more complex picture of the relation between business and bureaucracy may also help us to clarify our conception of the secular trend. *By itself* it does not lead to fascism. Fascism requires in addition that the representatives of concentrated economic power despair of the possibility to attain what they regard as "necessary for their continued dominance." Then they resort to the use of *condottieri* leaders of a mass movement (partly built upon their support, partly dependent on other developments in the labor field particularly), in order to create a social order in their own image. Fascism is attained through the use of a mass movement, over which business has at best imperfect control. It entails for business greater security of profits at the most of a sharply reduced freedom of deci-

A study of the relation between government and interest groups so conceived would seem more rewarding than the dogmatic dispute emanating from conflicting philosophies of history which has been described and criticized above. Moreover, it may then appear that governmental administration can and must function in part independently of the "pressures"—to the extent, at any rate, that the conflicting "pressures" of various groups inadvertently entail the possibility of disregarding them. But while this reorientation may help us to understand the interrelation between government and interest groups, it does not by itself enhance our understanding of present-day bureaucracy. For this purpose it is important to go back again to the two interpretations of the development of bureaucracy under capitalism which have been discussed above, since both interpretations imply a theory of bureaucracy. The idea that governmental bureaucracy has arisen from the concentration of economic power rests on the following assumptions:

1. Bureaucracy is the administrative instrument in the hands of the ruling class.

2. The recruitment of administrative personnel and the policies which it executes are both part of the political struggle, whose outcome is determined by the secular changes in the capitalist system of production.

3. The executive branch of government has, therefore, as much power as the ruling class delegates to it; since bureaucracy is the "administrative arm of the ruling class," it is a body of officials so organized as to obey the policy directives which are handed down. Bureaucracy has, therefore, no autonomous power of its own; it has a monopoly of power only in the sense in which this monopoly is derived from the power of the ruling class.[22]

As over against this view of bureaucracy, the laissez faire theory contains a number of theoretical assumptions about the nature of bureaucracy that are equally sweeping but in some respects reversed:

1. Governmental bureaucracy is the administrative instrument of its directing officials.

2. The recruitment of administrative personnel and the policies which it executes are both part of the political process; this process is the sum total of individual and group actions, concerned with the political promotion of their self-interest. While the parallel process in the economic sphere

sion. It would be important to reconsider the rise of fascism in the light of the preceding discussion—which should, however, be clearly distinguished from an analysis of its structure after the conquest of power.

22. These assumptions do not apply to Burnham's theory. He has modified the Marxian concept of the ruling class; to him the managers who control the industrial and administrative apparatus constitute the ruling class. Yet Burnham believes also that their power to control is derived from the transformations of the capitalist economy.

should be left to itself (within an appropriate legal and political framework), in the political sphere it cannot be expected to operate in a similar fashion, since no "pricing-mechanism of power" exists. It is necessary, therefore, to convince the individuals in power that it is politically and economically imperative (for the preservation of freedom) to adopt such political measures as will safeguard free competition.

3. Such policies can be made effective as soon as the directing heads of governments are convinced. (This has so far not been successful because misled intellectuals and radicals have been more influential.) Bureaucracy is the "administrative arm of these directing heads," and as such it has no power of its own.

Thus we see that both views are in agreement as to the nature of bureaucracy on a number of points. They hold that the power of government in modern society is derived, although they differ as to the origin of power.[23] Both views treat bureaucracy consequently as the "executive branch" of government with no power of its own. And both are finally agreed that the extension of governmental bureaucracy entails the diminution of individual freedom, although here again they differ radically with regard to the causes of this development.

THE PROBLEM OF BUREAUCRACY RESTATED. The preceding statement of the assumptions concerning bureaucracy which underlie the controversy over its historical origin shows—surprisingly enough—that neither view (again with the exception of Burnham) attributes any independent power to the administrative apparatus. It is more or less taken for granted by the authors discussed above (1) that bureaucracy is a pliable tool in the hands of some sinister minority (e.g. radicals, monopolists, etc.), (2) that the absolute power attributed to bureaucracy is actually derived from forces outside the government itself, and (3) that the "monopoly of power" characteristic of government is bound to be used for the diminution of individual freedom. Not one of these assumptions has been empirically verified, although much incidental evidence is cited in support of them.

It is important to restate the problem of modern bureaucracy and its exercise of power in the light of the foregoing discussion in order to outline the principal problem areas. In this respect Weber's construction of the ideal type of bureaucracy may again serve as a point of departure, since it presents us with a curious dilemma. Weber noted that modern administration has become steadily more specialized. The importance of the skill element in modern administration is such, in his opinion, that power in the

23. The pluralist doctrine conceives governmental power to be derived from the interaction of diverse voluntary groups—in analogy to the market in which interacting individuals determine price. Cf. in this respect John Stuart Mill's statement that the "antagonism of influences is the only real security for continued progress." See his "Representative Government," in *Utilitarianism, Liberty and Representative Government* (E. P. Dutton & Co., 1910), p. 201.

modern state cannot be exercised without a professionally trained bureaucratic apparatus, whatever the system of production. But he noted at the same time that modern bureaucracy has become professionalized—i.e., subject to a code of professional ethics according to which the official will faithfully execute the duties attending his office regardless of personal sentiments and disagreements with the policies involved. As a result, modern bureaucracy is ready to serve whatever party is in power, and in fact the security (calculability) of commercial transactions in a competitive economy depends upon this professional neutrality of the civil service.[24] *Thus, the indispensability of skilled administrators makes modern bureaucracy autonomous, but professionalization makes it a subservient tool.*

On the other hand, Weber observed that modern administration also implies a monopoly of power (monopoly of legitimate physical coercion). Although it depends on the circumstances in what way and to what extent this power will be used, it can at any rate not be effectively challenged. Weber noted that control over this bureaucratic apparatus by an insurgent group cannot be attained through its destruction, since under modern conditions the group would need a bureaucracy of its own to put the new policies into effect.[25] Consequently only shifts in the control over modern bureaucracy can, according to Weber, be obtained, either through the democratic machinery of representation or through a coup d'etat (substitution of one group controlling the bureaucracy by another). Thus, whatever group is in power, the unchallengeable position of the bureaucratic apparatus, by which it rules, gives the government a monopoly of power. Yet, the concern with administrative efficiency puts all policy considerations (affecting the use of power) outside the pale of bureaucratic competence. (The paradox is even greater when it is remembered that all administrative experts are agreed on the necessity of policy considerations within the administration for the purpose of making it efficient.) *Bureaucracy is, therefore, all-powerful and at the same time incapable of determining how its power should be used.*

It is important to recognize that these mutually contradictory tendencies are, indeed, to be found in modern bureaucracy. There is a growth of ad-

24. Cf. Max Weber, *op. cit.*, for his analogy between governmental and judicial bureaucracy. In both cases laws or policies are "fed" into the apparatus, which in turn issues decisions or executive acts in exact conformity with the directives. Modern economic theory speaks in this context of the "elasticity of expectations." See J. R. Hicks, *Value and Capital* (Oxford: Clarendon Press, 1939), pp. 205, 254-55.

25. Lenin maintained that the people would "take over" the government, and that the existing state needed to be destroyed. He did not think this would result in chaos; the people themselves would exercise the functions of government, since these had become sufficiently simplified in the meantime. Weber holds, on the other hand, that administration in the modern state has become more and more specialized—a tendency which would only be enhanced by the advent of socialism. Administration by the people is, therefore, impossible, and destruction of the state would only result in chaos.

ministrative autonomy (discretion) and of professionalism in the civil service. Likewise, the administrative branch of government has acquired greater powers (with the increase in its functions), and, finally, the legislature and the people have become wary over the maintenance of their right to determine policy. But if these tendencies are combined into an ideal-typical construction, it becomes more difficult to discern the factors which account for the actual relations between administrative skills and the degree of bureaucratic autonomy. In order to examine these relations, it will be helpful to outline the principal variables, especially those factors which have a bearing on the degree to which modern bureaucracy can exercise its powers independently.

In modern bureaucracy certain high administrative officials have (1) a monopoly of skill—i.e., they are irreplaceable because of the high technical qualifications which their positions require.[26] In so far as these managerial experts are irreplaceable, they are said to have a monopoly of power, which they may or may not exercise. That is to say, they have (2) a potential monopoly of power (a) to sabotage policy directives, or (b) to effect such directives on their own, in so far as these are at odds with official policy. Whether they use this potential monopoly of power will depend in turn on their (3) exercise of independent power or the degree of their administrative autonomy.[27] This is indicated by some or all of the following factors: (a) actual indispensability—a criterion which alone involves a host of variables, such as irreplaceability of certain experiences or skills, which would ordinarily be a matter of time; urgency of the demand for the continuation of a specific public service; urgency of the demand for its continuation along lines peculiarly associated with the incumbent administrator (a condition in direct contravention to the ideal of an efficient service, in which the personal equation is at a minimum—so they say);[28] ability of the incumbent to use personal influence and connections in support of his continued service; (b) the degree to which a code of professional ethics of civil servants has been developed; (c) the ease of alternative employments in other fields than government; (d) the unanimity of purpose in the managerial ranks in the sabotage of opposed policies and the independent execution of desired policies; (e) remoteness of administrative procedure

26. Typically, this does not apply to government employees who are technical experts in the scientific and industrial fields. For them substitutes can be found with relative ease, and they have a characteristically low prestige in the civil service.

27. Some of the factors under this heading are discussed by Otto Kirchheimer, "The Historical and Comparative Background of the Hatch Law," in *Public Policy: A Yearbook of the Graduate School of Public Administration, Harvard University*, II (1941), 341-73.

28. For illustrations see Ernst Fraenkel, *Military Occupation and the Rule of Law* (Oxford University Press, 1944), pp. 25-37, and the experience of our present military government in Italy and Germany with similar problems.

from the individuals and groups who are affected; and (f) technical complexity of the matters which come thereby under administrative discretion.

All these intrabureaucratic factors which help to determine the degree of administrative autonomy are in turn conditioned by forces which affect the executive branch without being fundamentally affected by it. These "external" factors pose the problem of (4) administrative autonomy as determined by the socio-economic organization of a society. Autonomy is in this sense determined (a) by the degree to which the education and recruitment of the top-flight personnel has resulted in a group of administrators of similar social derivation and social philosophy (that is to say, administrative autonomy may be extensive under conditions where the recruitment of the managerial personnel gives assurance against what powerful groups in society regard as a misuse of executive power); [29] (b) by the urgency of the demand for the continuation of public services; (c) by the implicit or explicit demand for administrative autonomy by various interest groups, either for the furtherance of their own interests (e.g. labor's demands for more discretionary action on the part of the WLB); for the "socialization of risks," which requires discretionary action on the part of administrative agencies; [30] for the pursuit of a common enterprise (e.g. war); for the promotion of cartelization or, conversely, for the freezing of given relationships among monopolistic enterprises (e.g., the case of the rate-differentials between different railroads before the ICC). Such demands always involve at least the risk that the governmental agency will go farther than desired, and in fact the fulfilment of these demands frequently makes such extension of administrative autonomy necessary. And, ultimately, the actual monopoly of power in the hands of the governmental bureaucracy may be tested (d) by the changed character of modern revolutions, which makes the military apparatus at the disposal of the government practically insuperable, if the government is disposed to use it. [31]

These specifications may serve to indicate the type of questions which would have to be answered before any conclusions can be drawn about the relation between the "monopoly of skill" and the "monopoly of power", toward which modern bureaucracy is frequently said to develop. The "variables" briefly enumerated above raise doubts about the meaning of both terms. It is difficult to conceive of a strictly irreplaceable group of sellers of managerial skill. It appears that the men of managerial skill are powerful not because their skill makes them irreplaceable but rather be-

29. Cf. the recent controversy over the dismissal of Jesse Jones and the appointment of Henry Wallace as Secretary of Commerce. Cf. J. Donald Kingsley, *Representative Bureaucracy* (Antioch Press, 1944), pp. 261-283, for an analysis of the importance of this factor in English administration. (Part of this section is included in this volume.)

30. For illustrations cf. the recent article by Fritz Karl Mann, "The Socialization of Risks," 7 *Review of Politics*, 43-57 (January, 1945).

31. Cf. an early analysis of this change in Frederick Engels' Introduction to Karl Marx, *The Class Struggles in France* (International Publishers, 1934), pp. 1-30.

cause, and to the degree that, their education and social derivation induces in them a common social philosophy. Thus, administrative autonomy is a matter not of skill but of "derived power"—i.e., of the power delegated to the administration through the organized representation of social groups. This point is further emphasized by a correct interpretation of the idea of "administrative impartiality." This impartiality means that administrative officials will faithfully execute policies of which they personally disapprove. Yet, if government is to continue, such impartiality presupposes a similarity of outlook between administrators and the forces framing public policy. Without this basic agreement administrative discretion would result in sabotage rather than in impartiality; without it, occasional or even frequent disagreements on policies would become politically and administratively unfeasible. It is, therefore, not true that the administration would serve everybody equally well.

These reservations with regard to the criterion of "monopoly of skill" are, on the other hand, not intended to detract from the growth of administrative autonomy which has developed in modern government. But it is an "autonomy of degree" which has developed, not a "monopoly of power." The true measure of this autonomy may be taken by discerning the extent to which government is in a position to remain uninfluenced by changes in class structure, by the shifting weight of social conflict groups, by long-run changes in public opinion, and, ultimately, by its ability to avert or withstand revolutionary upheaval. Consequently, it is quite possible to agree that modern bureaucracy requires skilled personnel and yet to hold that no skill-monopoly exists. Likewise, it is consistent to hold that administrative autonomy has increased but to deny that it constitutes a "monopoly of power."

From the preceding discussion it would appear that the popular identification of bureaucracy with an abuse of governmental power is at any rate misleading, since it is not the bureaucracy which abuses power; or, to put it differently, since the governmental "monopoly of power" (in so far as it exists) is derived. This opens up the whole problem of sovereignty, which cannot be discussed here except to say that recent theories either have conceived law or the state as all-embracing metaphysical entities or have explained sovereignty away by some theory of pluralism. It should be noted that most of these theories are little more than reflections of more basic postulates. Thus those who regard the modern capitalist society as moving inevitably in the direction of fascism will be inclined to state that sovereign authority is quickly disappearing,[32] and some writers end up with the belief that under fascism the state has vanished altogether.[33] Others, who are more

32. Cf. Otto Kirchheimer, "In Quest of Sovereignty," 6 *Journal of Politics,* 139-76 (May, 1944).
33. See Franz Neumann, *op. cit.,* pp. 459-76.

sanguine in their views of the prospects of the modern service state (who regard the conflicting group interests as ultimately reconcilable and who view bureaucracy as the arbitrating agent), conceive sovereign authority to be derived in various ways from the organized expression of the "popular will." Finally, there are those who regard the basic documents of American government as the source of power and who consequently have no truck with any sociological or economic interpretation.[34]

In alluding here to these large theoretical problems I am primarily concerned with showing that in all cases a theory of bureaucracy implies a larger philosophy of history [35] to which the theory must inevitably lead back. I contend, moreover, that all these theories and philosophies can be interpreted as different estimates of the specific range between the two extremes of completely decentralized anarchism and completely centralized totalitarianism which a given bureaucracy in a given country occupies. That is to say, all government lies somewhere between these extremes, and the various theories of bureaucracy are so many attempts at explaining on the basis of different philosophies of history why modern government in Britain or the United States struck its particular balance between the extremes. These remarks are, indeed, self-evident; but by calling attention to the enduring aspects of the problem of government we may perhaps throw some light on the modern problem of bureaucratic government.

It may lead to such a restatement of the problem if we deliberately go outside the usual frame of reference and inquire whether a comparative social psychology of bureaucracy may perhaps guide us where the over-all philosophies of history fail. Again, it must suffice to enumerate some significant problem areas. One important aspect of bureaucracy is the accessibility of public employment. Max Weber thought that professionalization of the public service had democratic implications, since it based government service on qualification rather than birth. Yet the implications may just as easily be non-democratic, if such professionalization of the civil service is coupled with an authoritarian prestige which government employment may have in the eyes of the public. How much social prestige does the official possess, and/or how much is public employment desired for the security of tenure, the prospects of regular advancement, and the eventual pension? And, conversely, how much is the public service in disrepute precisely because of these attributes of employment in it? [36] Markedly different answers are likely to be given to these questions, even if countries are

34. Cf. Hyman Ezra Cohen, *Recent Theories of Sovereignty* (University of Chicago Press, 1937), for a convenient summary.

35. In speaking of philosophy of history I do not have in mind that these theories of bureaucracy are without empirical foundation, but that they go beyond it.

36. Cf. L. D. White, *The Prestige Value of Public Employment in Chicago* (University of Chicago Press, 1929).

compared whose economic structures are as closely similar as those of
Germany, Britain, and the United States. Moreover, comparative research
in this respect is likely to reveal different patterns of obedience to authority
or, conversely, of spontaneous public cooperation. These patterns may in
part be traceable to the role of authority in family life which is characteristic of different cultures, since the attitudes toward the authority of the
father seem to be relevant for the formation of adult attitudes toward governmental authority.[37]

These psychological considerations lead us back to our main theme.
How has it come about historically that such different attitudes toward
governmental authority have developed, and what light do these differences
of the historical development throw on the emergence of modern bureaucracy: Little headway has so far been made in giving an answer to this question, partly because of the antigovernmental bias which has motivated many
studies of bureaucracy. Moreover, the idea of a "monopoly of power"
which was derived from studies of the *emergence* of the modern state, has
been used to characterize bureaucracy in general.[38] Students have been
primarily interested in what all bureaucracies of western Europe and
America have in common, and, apart from Veblen's work on Germany
(and Japan), no attempt has been made to show the sociopsychological and
institutional differences in the process of bureaucratization, in so far as
these can be attributed to a retarded breakdown of feudal institutions
and traditions.[39] As a result, little attention has been given to the effect of
the noncontemporaneous industrialization of different countries on the rise
of their respective bureaucracies. It would be very important to investigate
the effect of such factors on the pattern of obedience to authority and of
the degree of spontaneous public cooperation which characterizes the
different "bureaucratic cultures" of the western world.

37. Actually, the relevant psychological aspect of the problem is twofold: adult
attitudes toward governmental authority are strongly influenced by (1) the father's
authority in the family and (2) the father's own attitude toward governmental authority. The bearing of such psychocultural patterns on bureaucracy is illustrated by
such studies as Gerald Brenan's *The Spanish Labyrinth* (Macmillan Co., 1943) or
Gunnar Myrdal's analysis of the American attitude towards government in *An American Dilemma*. See also the article by Sol Tax, "The Problem of Democracy in Middle
America," 20 *American Sociological Review*, 192-99 (April, 1945). The same questions
are again relevant for the attitude toward governmental authority among the officials
themselves and for their own use of authority.

38. This tendency signifies the German influence on studies in this field. In Germany the modern state did not emerge until the 19th century. Consequently, particular
attention was paid to the "monopolization of power," which was in fact identified with
the state, although it signified only the process by which it originated from the feudal
system.

39. Cf. Thorstein Veblen, *Imperial Germany and the Industrial Revolution* (new
ed.; Viking Press, 1942) and the "Opportunity of Japan," in *Essays in our Changing
Order* (Viking Press, 1943), pp. 248-66. Retardation refers to any "lag" as contrasted
with comparable developments in England.

It seems to me that such considerations should have preceded the question whether bureaucratic tendencies have been encouraged by social forces inherent in the capitalistic economy. But it is, of course, this last problem which has given rise to so much controversy, which—as we have seen—led ultimately back to a dispute over different philosophies of history. In so far as the development of governmental bureaucracy is a question of fact, it can be resolved. But in so far as the instances of bureaucratization in government (owing to "big business" or "misguided intellectuals") are cited not to diagnose past trends but to predict future contingencies, the controversy over the causes of bureaucratization is actually concerned with the extrapolation of historical trends. Will monopoly business lead to fascism? Or will governmental regulation of labor relations lead to the eventual elimination of individual freedom? The important study of the potentialities and dangers of bureaucracy will make progress only if the underlying philosophical assumptions, which alone make answers to these questions possible, are made explicit.

COÖPTATION: A MECHANISM
FOR ORGANIZATIONAL STABILITY

Philip Selznick

The frame of reference [adopted here] includes the directive that organizational behavior be analyzed in terms of organizational response to organizational need. One such need is specified as "the security of the organization as a whole in relation to social forces in its environment." Responses, moreover, are themselves repetitive—may be thought of as mechanisms, following the terminology of analytical psychology in its analysis of the ego and its mechanisms of defense. One such organizational mechanism is ideology; another, which has been the primary focus of this study, we have termed coöptation. . . . We have previously defined this concept as "the process of absorbing new elements into the leadership or policy-determining structure of an organization as a means of averting threats to its stability or existence." Further, this general mechanism assumes two basic forms: Formal coöptation, when there is a need to establish the

Reprinted in part from *TVA and the Grassroots*, pp. 259-264; University of California Publications in Culture and Society, Vol. III, by permission of the author and the publisher. (Copyright, 1949, by the University of California Press.)

legitimacy of authority or the administrative accessibility of the relevant public; and informal coöptation, when there is a need of adjustment to the pressure of specific centers of power within the community.

Coöptation in administration is a process whereby either power or the burdens of power, or both, are shared. On the one hand, the actual center of authority and decision may be shifted or made more inclusive, with or without any public recognition of the change; on the other hand, public responsibility for and participation in the exercise of authority may be shared with new elements, with or without the actual redistribution of power itself. The organizational imperatives which define the need for coöptation arise out of a situation in which formal authority is actually or potentially in a state of imbalance with respect to its institutional environment. On the one hand, the formal authority may fail to reflect the true balance of power within the community; on the other hand, it may lack a sense of historical legitimacy, or be unable to mobilize the community for action. Failure to reflect the true balance of power will necessitate a realistic adjustment to those centers of institutional strength which are in a position to strike organized blows and thus to enforce concrete demands. This issue may be met by the kind of coöptation which results in an actual sharing of power. However, the need for a sense of legitimacy may require an adjustment to the people in their undifferentiated aspect, in order that a feeling of general acceptance may be developed. For this purpose, it may not be necessary actually to share power: the creation of a "front" or the open incorporation of accepted elements into the structure of the organization may suffice. In this way, an aura of respectability will be gradually transferred from the coöpted elements to the organization as a whole, and at the same time a vehicle of administrative accessibility may be established.

We may suggest the hypothesis: Coöptation which results in an actual sharing of power will tend to operate informally, and correlatively, coöptation oriented toward legitimization or accessibility will tend to be effected through formal devices. Thus, an opposition party may be formally coöpted into a political administration through such a device as the appointment of opposition leaders to ministerial posts. This device may be utilized when an actual sharing of power is envisioned, but it is especially useful when its object is the creation of public solidarity, the legitimization of the representativeness of the government. In such circumstances, the opposition leaders may become the prisoners of the government, exchanging the hope of future power (through achieving public credit for holding office in a time of crisis) for the present function of sharing responsibility for the acts of the administration. The formal, public character of the coöptation is essential to the end in view. On the other hand, when coöptation is to fulfill the function of an adjustment to organized centers of institutional power within the community, it may be necessary to maintain relationships which, however consequential, are informal and covert. If adjustment to specific nucleuses of power becomes public, then the legitimacy of the formal authority, as representative of a theoretically undifferentiated community (the "people as a whole"), may be undermined. It therefore becomes useful and often essential for such coöptation to remain in the shadowland of informal interaction.

The informal coöptation of existing nucleuses of power into the total (formal plus informal) policy-determining structure of an organization, symptomatic of an underlying stress, is a mechanism of adjustment to concrete forces. On this level, interaction occurs among those who are in a position to muster forces and make them count, which means that the stake is a substantive reallocation of authority, rather than any purely verbal readjustment. Formal coöptation, however, is rather more ambiguous in relation to *de facto* reallocations of power. The sense of insecurity which is interpreted by a leadership as indicating a need for an increased sense of legitimacy in the community is a response to something generalized and diffuse. There is no hard-headed demand for a sharing of power coming from self-conscious institutions which are in a position to challenge the formal authority itself. The way things seem becomes, in this context, more important than the way they are, with the result that verbal formulas (degenerating readily into propaganda), and formal organizational devices, appear to be adequate to fill the need. The problem becomes one of manipulating public opinion, something which is necessarily beside the point when dealing with an organized interest group having an established and self-conscious leadership.

Formal coöptation ostensibly shares authority, but in doing so is involved in a dilemma. The real point is the sharing of the public symbols or administrative burdens of authority, and consequently public responsibility, without the transfer of substantive power; it therefore becomes necessary to insure that the coöpted elements do not get out of hand, do not take advantage of their formal position to encroach upon the actual arena of decision. Consequently, formal coöptation requires informal control over the coöpted elements lest the unity of command and decision be imperiled. This paradox is one of the sources of persistent tension between theory and practice in organizational behavior. The leadership, by the very nature of its position, is committed to two conflicting goals: if it ignores the need for participation, the goal of coöperation may be jeopardized; if participation is allowed to go too far, the continuity of leadership and policy may be threatened.

THE EMPIRICAL ARGUMENT RESTATED. Apart from the interest of analytical theory, the statement above explains the special focus of this inquiry and the basis for its obviously selective approach to the TVA experience. That frame of reference has guided the empirical analysis, of which the following is a brief recapitulation.

1. *The grass-roots theory became a protective ideology.*—An attempt has been made to explain the high self-consciousness of the TVA, as expressed in the grass-roots doctrine, on the basis of the function of that doctrine in facilitating acceptance of the Authority in its area of operation and in fulfilling the need for some general justification of its existence as a unique type of governmental agency. The TVA was revolutionary both to the attitudes of local people and institutions and to the federal governmental system. By adopting the grass-roots doctrine the Authority was able to stand as the champion of local institutions and at the same time to devise a point of view which could be utilized in general justification of its managerial autonomy within the federal system. However, allegiance to this doctrine, and translation of it into policy commitments, have created serious disaffection between TVA and other branches of the federal government, including the Department of Agriculture and the Department of the Interior. As a result, on the basis of the TVA experience, these departments have been moved to oppose the extension of the TVA form of organization to other areas, a fact which is consequential for the future of the Authority itself.

2. *The agricultural program was delegated* [1] *to an organized administrative constituency.*—In the major example within TVA of grass-roots procedure—the Authority's fertilizer distribution program—there was constructed a strong constituency-relation involving the land-grant college system on the one hand and the Agricultural Relations Department of TVA on the other. This constituency relation may be viewed as a case of informal coöptation, wherein strong centers of influence in the Valley were absorbed covertly into the policy-determining structure of the TVA. The TVA's Agricultural Relations Department assumed a definite character, including a set of sentiments valuing the land-grant college system as such and accepting the mission of defending that system within the Authority. In effecting this representation, the TVA agriculturists have been able to take advantage of the special prerogatives accruing to them from their formal status as an integral part of the Authority, including the exercise of discretion within their own assigned jurisdiction and the exertion of pressure upon the evolution of general policy within the Authority as a whole. The special role and character of the TVA agricultural group limited its outlook with respect to the participation of Negro institutions as grass-roots resources and created a special relation to the American Farm Bureau Federation. Yet the operation of this coöptative process probably did much to enhance the stability

1. Some TVA official would question the use of "delegated" here. However, this seems to be the most significant summary word to use, in terms of its implications. Moreover in his own summation of TVA policy upon the occasion of his leaving the TVA chairmanship, David E. Lilienthal said: "The TVA has by persistent effort delegated and thereby decentralized its functions. . . ." *New York Times*, November 13, 1946, p. 56.

of the TVA within its area and especially to make possible the mobilization of support in an hour of need. In this sense, one cannot speak of the decisions which led to this situation as mistakes.

3. *In a context of controversy, the TVA's commitments to its agricultural constituency resulted in a factional alignment involving unanticipated consequences for its role on the national scene.*—In the exercise of discretion in agriculture, the TVA entered a situation charged with organizational and political conflict. The New Deal agricultural agencies, such as Farm Security Administration and Soil Conservation Service, came under attack of the powerful American Farm Bureau Federation, which thought of them as threats to its special avenue of access to the farm population, the extension services of the land-grant colleges. Under the pressure of its agriculturists, the Authority did not recognize Farm Security Administration and sought to exclude Soil Conservation Service from operation within the Valley area. This resulted in the politically paradoxical situation that the eminently New Deal TVA failed to support agencies with which it shared a political communion, and aligned itself with the enemies of those agencies.

4. *Under the pressure of its agriculturists, the TVA gradually altered a significant aspect of its character as a conservation agency.*—The TVA agricultural group, reflecting local attitudes and interests, fought against the policy of utilizing public ownership of land as a conservation measure and thus effectively contributed to the alteration of the initial policy of the Authority in this respect. The issue of public ownership is taken as character-defining in the sense that it is a focus of controversy and division, and it was such within the TVA for an extended period. The single-minded pursuit of its ideological and constituency interests led the agricultural group to involve the Authority in a controversy with the U. S. Department of the Interior over the management of TVA-owned lands. . . .

5. *The grass-roots utilization of voluntary associations represents a sharing of the burdens of and responsibility for power, rather than of power itself.*—. . . The voluntary association device—especially, but not exclusively, in the agricultural program—is interpreted as a case of formal coöptation, primarily for promoting organized access to the public but also as a means of supporting the legitimacy of the TVA program. Typically, this has meant that actual authority, and to a large extent the organizational machinery, has been retained in the hands of the administering agency. After nine years of operation, the county soil associations handling TVA fertilizer were found to be still tools of the county agent system, to which the TVA test-demonstration program was delegated. In connection with this analysis, an operational test for locating control over coöpted citizens' groups is described, as suggested in the question: Is approach to the association by outside elements channeled through officials of the coöpting agency?

ASSIMILATION OF THE DISCONTENTED
INTO THE STATE BUREAUCRACY

Robert Michels

The organization of the state needs a numerous and complicated bureaucracy. This is an important factor in the complex of forces of which the politically dominant classes avail themselves to secure their dominion and to enable themselves to keep their hands upon the rudder.

The instinct of self-preservation leads the modern state to assemble and to attach to itself the greatest possible number of interests. This need of the organism of the state increases *pari passu* with an increase among the multitude, of the conviction that the contemporary social order is defective and even irrational—in a word, with the increase of what the authorities are accustomed to term discontent. The state best fulfils the need for securing a large number of defenders by constituting a numerous caste of officials, of persons directly dependent upon the state. This tendency is powerfully reinforced by the tendencies of modern political economy. On the one hand, from the side of the state, there is an enormous supply of official positions. On the other hand, among the citizens, there is an even more extensive demand. This demand is stimulated by the ever-increasing precariousness in the position of the middle classes (the smaller manufacturers and traders, independent artizans, farmers, etc.) since there have come into existence expropriative capitalism on the grand scale, on the one hand, and the organized working classes on the other—for both these movements, whether they wish it or not, combine to injure the middle classes. All those whose material existence is thus threatened by modern economic developments endeavour to find safe situations for their sons, to secure for these a social position which shall shelter them from the play of economic forces. Employment under the state, with the important right to a pension which attaches to such employment, seems created expressly for their needs. The immeasurable demand for situations which results from these conditions, a demand which is always greater than the supply, creates the so-called "intellectual proletariat." The numbers of this body are subject to great fluctuations. From time to time the state, embarrassed by the increasing demand for positions in its service, is forced to open the sluices of its bureaucratic canals in order to admit thousands of new postulants and thus to transform these from dangerous adversaries into zealous defenders and partisans. There are two classes of intel-

Reprinted in part from *Political Parties*, pp. 185-189 (Glencoe, Ill.: The Free Press, 1949), by permission of the publisher.

lectuals. One consists of those who have succeeded in securing a post at the manger of the state, whilst the other consists of those who, as Scipio Sighele puts it, have assaulted the fortress without being able to force their way in. The former may be compared to an army of slaves who are always ready, in part from class egoism, in part for personal motives (the fear of losing their own situations), to undertake the defence of the state which provides them with bread. They do this whatever may be the question concerning which the state has been attacked and must therefore be regarded as the most faithful of its supporters. The latter, on the other hand, are sworn enemies of the state. They are those eternally restless spirits who lead the bourgeois opposition and in part also assume the leadership of the revolutionary parties of the proletariat. It is true that the state bureaucracy does not in general expand as rapidly as do the discontented elements of the middle class. None the less, the bureaucracy continually increases. It comes to assume the form of an endless screw. It grows ever less and less compatible with the general welfare. And yet this bureaucratic machinery remains essential. Through it alone can be satisfied the claim of the educated members of the population for secure positions. It is further a means of self-defence for the state. As the late Amilcare Puviani of the University of Perugia, the political economist to whom we are indebted for an important work upon the legend of the state, expresses it, the mechanism of bureaucracy is the outcome of a protective reaction of a right of property whose legal basis is weak, and is an antidote to the awakening of the public conscience.

The political party possesses many of these traits in common with the state. Thus the party in which the circle of the *élite* is unduly restricted, or in which, in other words, the oligarchy is composed of too small a number of individuals, runs the risk of being swept away by the masses in a moment of democratic effervescence. Hence the modern party, like the modern state, endeavours to give to its own organization the widest possible base, and to attach to itself in financial bonds the largest possible number of individuals. Thus arises the need for a strong bureaucracy, and these tendencies are reinforced by the increase in the tasks imposed by modern organization.

As the party bureaucracy increases, two elements which constitute the essential pillars of every socialist conception undergo an inevitable weakening: an understanding of the wider and more ideal cultural aims of socialism, and an understanding of the international multiplicity of its manifestations. Mechanism becomes an end in itself. The capacity for an accurate grasp of the peculiarities and the conditions of existence of the labour movement in other countries diminishes in proportion as the individual national organizations are fully developed. This is plain from a study of the mutual international criticisms of the socialist press. In the days of the so-called "socialism of the émigrés," the socialists devoted themselves to an elevated policy of principles, inspired by the classical criteria of internationalism. Almost every one of them was, if the term may be used, a specialist in this more general and comprehensive domain. The whole course of their lives, the brisk exchange of ideas on unoccupied evenings, the continued rubbing of shoulders between men of the most different tongues, the enforced isolation from the bourgeois world of their respective countries, and the utter impossibility of any "practical" action, all contributed to this result. But in proportion as, in their own country, paths of activity were opened for the socialists, at first for agitation and soon afterwards for positive and constructive work, the more did a recognition of the demands of the everyday life of the party divert their attention from immortal principles. Their vision gained in precision but lost in extent. The more cotton-spinners, boot and shoe operatives, or brush-makers the labor leader could gain each month for his union, the better versed he was in the tedious subtleties of insurance against accident and illness, the greater the industry he could display in the specialized questions of factory inspection and of arbitration in trade disputes, the better acquainted he might be with the system of checking the amount of individual purchases in co-operative stores and with the methods for the control of the consumption of municipal gas, the more difficult was it for him to retain a general interest in the labor movement, even in the narrowest sense of this term. As the outcome of inevitable psychophysiological laws, he could find little time and was likely to have little inclination for the study of the great problems of the philosophy of history, and all the more falsified consequently would become his judgment of international questions. At the same time he would incline more and more to regard every one as an "incompetent," an "outsider," an "unprofessional," who might wish to judge questions from some higher outlook than the purely technical; he would incline to deny the good sense and even the socialism of all who might desire to fight upon another ground and by other means than those familiar to him within his narrow sphere as a specialist. This tendency towards an exclusive and all-absorbing specialization, towards the renunciation of all far-reaching outlooks, is a general characteristic of modern evolution. With the continuous increase in the acquirements of scientific research, the polyhistor is becoming extinct. His place is taken by the writer of monographs. The universal zoologist no longer exists, and we have instead ornithologists and entomologists; and indeed the last become further subdivided into lepidopterists, coleopterists, myrmecologists.

To some of the "non-commissioned officers" who occupy the inferior grades of the party bureaucracy may be aptly applied what Alfred Weber said of bureaucracy in general at the congress of the *Verein für Sozialpolitik* held at Vienna in 1909. Bureaucracy is the sworn enemy of individual liberty, and of all bold initiative in matters of internal policy. The dependence upon superior authorities characteristic of the average employee suppresses individuality and gives to the society in which employees predominate a narrow petty-bourgeois and philistine stamp. The bureaucratic spirit corrupts character and engenders moral poverty. In every bureaucracy we may observe place-hunting, a mania for promotion, and obsequiousness towards those upon whom promotion depends; there is arrogance towards inferiors and servility towards superiors. Wolfgang Heine, who in the German Socialist party is one of the boldest defenders of the personal and intellectual liberty of the members, who is always in the breach to denounce "the tendency to bureaucracy and the suppression of individuality," goes so far, in his struggle against the socialist bureaucracy, as to refer to the awful example of the Prussian state. It is true, he says, that Prussia is governed in accordance with homogeneous principles and by a bureaucracy which must be considered as a model of its kind; but it is no less true that the Prussian state, precisely because of its bureaucratic characteristics, and notwithstanding its external successes, is essentially retrogressive. If Prussia does produce any distinguished personalities, it is unable to tolerate their existence, so that Prussian politics tend more and more to degenerate into a spiritless and mechanical regime, displaying a lively hostility to all true progress. We may even say that the more conspicuously a bureaucracy is distinguished by its zeal, by its sense of duty, and by its devotion, the more also will it show itself to be petty, narrow, rigid, and illiberal.

THE CONSERVATIVE BASIS
OF ORGANIZATION

Robert Michels

. . . Is it impossible for a democratic party to practise a democratic policy, for a revolutionary party to pursue a revolutionary policy? Must we say that not *socialism* alone, but even a socialistic *policy*, is utopian? The present chapter will attempt a brief answer to this inquiry.

Within certain narrow limits, the democratic party, even when subjected to oligarchical control, can doubtless act upon the state in the democratic sense.[1] The old political caste of society, and above all the "state" itself, are

Reprinted in part from *Political Parties*, pp. 365-376 (Glencoe, Ill.: The Free Press, 1949), by permission of the publisher.

1. Especially where there exists universal, equal, and direct suffrage, and where the working-class is strongly organized and is awake to its own interests. . . . In this case the leaders have every interest in exercising upon the state all the pressure they can to render it more democratic.

forced to undertake the revaluation of a considerable number of values—a revaluation both ideal and practical. The importance attributed to the masses increases, even when the leaders are demagogues. The legislature and the executive become accustomed to yield, not only to claims proceeding from above, but also to those proceeding from below. This may give rise, in practice, to great inconveniences, such as we recognize in the recent history of all the states under a parliamentary regime; in theory, however, this new order of things signifies an incalculable progress in respect of public rights, which thus come to conform better with the principles of social justice. This evolution will, however, be arrested from the moment when the governing classes succeed in attracting within the governmental orbit their enemies of the extreme left, in order to convert them into collaborators. Political organization leads to power. But power is always conservative. In any case, the influence exercised upon the governmental machine by an energetic opposition party is necessarily slow, is subject to frequent interruptions, and is always restricted by the nature of oligarchy.

The recognition of this consideration does not exhaust our problems, for we have further to examine whether the oligarchical nature of organization be not responsible for the creation of the external manifestations of oligarchical activity, whether it be not responsible for the production of an oligarchical policy. The analysis here made shows clearly that the internal policy of the party organizations is to-day absolutely conservative, or is on the way to become such. Yet it might happen that the external policy of these conservative organisms would be bold and revolutionary; that the antidemocratic centralization of power in the hands of a few leaders is no more than a tactical method adopted to effect the speedier overthrow of the adversary; that the oligarchs fulfil the purely provisional function of educating the masses for the revolution, and that organization is after all no more than a means employed in the service of an amplified Blanquist conception.

This development would conflict with the nature of party, with the endeavour to organize the masses upon the vastest scale imaginable. As the organization increases in size, the struggle for great principles becomes impossible. It may be noticed that in the democratic parties of to-day the great conflicts of view are fought out to an ever-diminishing extent in the field of ideas and with the weapons of pure theory, that they therefore degenerate more and more into personal struggles and invectives, to be settled finally upon considerations of a purely superficial character. The efforts made to cover internal dissensions with a pious veil are the inevitable outcome of organization based upon bureaucratic principles, for, since the chief aim of such an organization is to enrol the greatest possible number of members, every struggle on behalf of ideas within the limits of the organization is necessarily regarded as an obstacle to the realization of its ends, an obstacle, therefore, which must be avoided in every possible way. This tendency is reinforced by the parliamentary character of the political party. "Party organization" signifies the aspiration for the greatest number of members. "Parliamentarism" signifies the aspirations for the greatest number of votes. The principal fields of party activity are electoral agitation and direct agitation to secure new members. What, in fact, is the modern political party? It is the methodical organization of the electoral masses. The socialist party, as a political aggregate endeavouring simultaneously to recruit members and to recruit votes, finds here its vital interests, for every decline in membership and every loss in voting strength diminishes its political prestige. Consequently great respect must be paid, not only to new members, but also to possible adherents, to those who in Germany are termed *mitläufer*, in Italy *simpatizzanti*, in Holland *geestverwanten*, and in England *sympathizers*. To avoid alarming these individuals, who are still outside the ideal worlds of socialism or democracy, the pursuit of a policy based on strict principle is shunned, while the consideration is ignored whether the numerical increase of the organization thus effected is not likely to be gained at the expense of its quality.

The last link in the long chain of phenomena which confer a profoundly conservative character upon the intimate essence of the political party (even upon that party which boasts itself revolutionary) is found in the relationships between party and state. Generated to overthrow the centralized power of the state, starting from the idea that the working class need merely secure a sufficiently vast and solid organization in order to triumph over the organization of the state, the party of the workers has ended by acquiring a vigorous centralization of its own, based upon the same cardinal principles of authority and discipline which characterize the organization of the state. It thus becomes a governmental party, that is to say, a party which, organized itself like a government on the small scale, hopes some day to assume the reins of government upon the large scale. The revolutionary political party is a state within the state, pursuing the avowed aim of destroying the existing state in order to substitute for it a social order of a fundamentally different character. To attain this essentially political end, the party avails itself of the socialist organization, whose sole justification is found precisely in its patient but systematic preparation for the destruction of the organization of the state in its existing form. The subversive party organizes the *framework* of the social revolution. For this reason it continually endeavours to strengthen its positions, to extend its bureaucratic mechanism, to store up its energies and its funds.

Every new official, every new secretary, engaged by the party is in theory a new agent of the revolution; in the same way every new section is a new battalion; and every additional thousand francs furnished by the members' subscriptions, by the profits of the socialist press, or by the generous donations of sympathetic benefactors, constitute fresh additions to the war-chest for the struggle against the enemy. In the long run, however, the directors of this revolutionary body existing within the authoritarian state, sustained by the same means as that state and inspired by the like spirit of discipline, cannot fail to perceive that the party organization, whatever advances it may make in the future, will never succeed in becoming more than an ineffective and miniature copy of the state organization. For this reason, in all ordinary circumstances, and as far as prevision is humanly possible, every attempt of the party to measure its forces with those of its antagonists is foredoomed to disastrous failure. The logical consequence of these considerations is in direct conflict with the hopes entertained by the founders of the party. Instead of gaining revolutionary energy as the force and solidity of its structure has increased, the precise opposite has occurred; there has resulted, *pari passu* with its growth, a continued increase in the prudence, the timidity even, which inspires its policy. The party, continually threatened by the state upon which its existence depends, carefully avoids (once it has attained to maturity) everything which might irritate the state to excess. The party doctrines are, whenever requisite, attenuated and deformed in accordance with the external needs of the organization. Organization becomes the vital essence of the party. During the first years of its existence, the party did not fail to make a parade of its revolutionary character, not only in respect of its ultimate ends, but also in respect of the means employed for their attainment—although not always in love with these means. But as soon as it attained to political maturity, the party did not hesitate to modify its original profession of faith and to affirm itself revolutionary only "in the best sense of the word," that is to say, no longer on lines which interest the police, but only in theory and on paper. This same party, which at one time did not hesitate, when the triumphant guns of the bourgeois governors of Paris were still smoking, to proclaim with enthusiasm its solidarity with the communards, now announces to the whole world that it repudiates anti-militarist propaganda in any form which may bring its adherents into conflict with the penal code, and that it will not assume any responsibility for the consequences that may result from such a conflict. A sense of responsibility is suddenly becoming active in the socialist party. Consequently it reacts with all the authority at its disposal against the revolutionary currents which exist within its own organization, and which it has hitherto regarded with an indulgent eye. In the name of the grave responsibilities attaching to its position it now disavows anti-militarism, repudiates the general strike, and denies all the logical audacities of its past.

The history of the international labor movement furnishes innumerable examples of the manner in which the party becomes increasingly inert as the strength of its organization grows; it loses its revolutionary impetus, becomes sluggish, not in respect of action alone, but also in the sphere of thought. More and more tenaciously does the party cling to what it calls the "ancient and glorious tactics," the tactics which have led to a continued increase in membership. More and more invincible becomes its aversion to all aggressive action.

The dread of the reaction by which the socialist party is haunted paralyses all its activities, renders impossible all manifestation of force, and deprives it of all energy for the daily struggle. It attempts to justify its misoneism by the false pretence that it must reserve its strength for the final struggle. Thus we find that the conservative tendencies inherent in all forms of possession manifest themselves also in the socialist party. For half a century the socialists have been working in the sweat of their brow to create a model organization. Now, when three million workers have been organized—a greater number than was supposed necessary to secure complete victory over the enemy—the party is endowed with a bureaucracy which, in respect of its consciousness of its duties, its zeal, and its submission to the hierarchy, rivals that of the state itself; the treasuries are full; a complex ramification of financial and moral interests extends all over the country. A bold and enterprising tactic would endanger all this: the work of many decades, the social existence of thousands of leaders and sub-leaders, the entire party, would be compromised. For these reasons the idea of such a tactic becomes more and more distasteful. It conflicts equally with an unjustified sentimentalism and a justified egoism. It is opposed by the artist's love of the work he has created with so much labour, and also by the personal interest of thousands of honest bread-winners whose economic life is so intimately associated with the life of the party and who tremble at the thought of losing their employment and the consequences they would have to endure if the government should proceed to dissolve the party, as might readily happen in case of war.

Thus, from a means, organization becomes an end. To the institutions and qualities which at the outset were destined simply to ensure the good working of the party machine (subordination, the harmonious cooperation of individual members, hierarchical relationships, discretion, propriety of conduct), a greater importance comes ultimately to be attached than to the productivity of the machine. Henceforward the sole preoccupation is to avoid anything which may clog the machinery. Should the party be attacked, it will abandon valuable positions previously conquered, and will renounce ancient rights rather than reply to the enemy's offensive by methods which might "compromise" its position. Naumann writes sarcastically: "The warcry 'Proletarians of all countries unite!' has had its due effect. The forces of the organized proletariat have gained a strength which no one believed possible when that war-cry was first sounded. There is money in the treasuries. Is the signal for the final assault never to be given? . . . Is the work of preliminary organization to go on for ever?" [2] As the party's need for tran-

2. Friedrich Naumann, *Das Schicksal des Marxismus,* "Hilfe," October 11, 1908, p. 657.

quillity increases, its revolutionary talons atrophy. We have now a finely conservative party which (since the effect survives the cause) continues to employ revolutionary terminology, but which in actual practice fulfils no other function than that of a constitutional opposition.

All this has deviated far from the ideas of Karl Marx, who, were he still alive, ought to be the first to revolt against such a degeneration of Marxism. Yet it is quite possible that, carried away by the spectacle of an army of three million men acting in his name, swearing on solemn occasions *in verba magistri,* he also would find nothing to say in reprobation of so grave a betrayal of his own principles. There were incidents in Marx's life which render such a view possible. He certainly knew how to close his eyes, in public at any rate, to the serious faults committed by the German social democracy in 1876.

In our own day, which may be termed the age of the epigones of Marx, the character of the party as an organization ever greedy for new members, ever seeking to obtain an absolute majority, cooperates with the condition of weakness in which it finds itself vis-à-vis the state, to effect a gradual replacement of the old aim, to demolish the existing state by the new aim, to permeate the state with the men and the ideas of the party. The struggle carried on by the socialists against the parties of the dominant classes is no longer one of principle, but simply one of competition. The revolutionary party has become a rival of the bourgeois parties for the conquest of power. It therefore opens its doors to all those persons who may assist in the attainment of this end, or who may simply swell its battalions for the struggle in which it is engaged.

Thus the hatred of the party is directed, not in the first place against the opponents of its own view of the world order, but against the dreaded rivals in the political field, against those who are competing for the same end—power. It is above all in the electoral agitation carried on by the socialist parties when they have attained what is termed "political maturity" that this characteristic is most plainly manifest. The party no longer seeks to fight its opponents, but simply to outbid them. For this reason we observe a continual recurrence in socialist speeches of a claim which harmonizes ill with socialist principles, and which is often untrue in fact. Not the nationalists, they say, but we, are the best patriots; not the men of the government, but we, are the best friends of the minor civil servants [in Italy] or of the peasants [in Germany]; and so on. Evidently among the trade unions of diverse political coloring, whose primary aim it is to gain the greatest possible number of new members, the note of competition will be emphasized yet more. This applies especially to the so-called "free unions" of Germany, neutrally tinted bodies which on principle hold in horror all definiteness in respect of political views or conceptions of the world order, and which are therefore distinguishable in name only (a few trifing terminological differences apart) from the Christian unions. If we study the speeches and polemic writings directed by the leaders of the free unions against the leaders of the Christian unions, we find that these speeches and writings contain no declarations of principle and no theoretical expositions, but merely personal criticisms and accusations, and above all accusations of treachery to the cause of labour. Now it is obvious that these are no more than the means vulgarly employed by competitors who wish to steal one another's customers.

By such methods, not merely does the party sacrifice its political virginity, by entering into promiscuous relationships with the most heterogeneous political elements, relationships which in many cases have disastrous and enduring consequences, but it exposes itself in addition to the risk of losing its essential character as a party. The term "party" presupposes that among the individual components of the party there should exist a harmonious direction of wills towards identical objective and practical aims. Where this is lacking, the party becomes a mere "organization."

TOTAL BUREAUCRATIZATION
AND THE POWERLESS INDIVIDUAL

Franz Neumann

If one believes that Germany's economy is no longer capitalistic under National Socialism, it is easy to believe further that her society has become classless. This is the thesis of the late Emil Lederer.[1] A brief analysis of his book will serve to introduce our discussion of the new German society.

Lederer rejects attempts to define National Socialism as the last line of defense of capitalism, as the rule of the strong man, as the revolt of the middle classes, as domination by the army, or as the ascendency of the untalented. For him, it is a "modern political system which rests on amorphous masses." It is the masses "which sweep the dictator into power and keep him there." The masses are therefore the actors, not the tools of a ruling class.

But who are the masses? They are the opposite of classes. They can be united solely by emotions; they tend to "burst into sudden action," and being amorphous, they must be integrated by a leader who can articulate their emotions. As the very opposite of classes, the masses make up a classless society. The policy of National Socialism is to transfer a class-stratified

Reprinted from *Behemoth*, pp. 365-369, by permission of the author and the publisher. (Copyright, 1944, by the Oxford University Press.)

1. *State of the Masses; The Threat of the Classless Society*, New York, 1940.

society into masses by keeping the latter in a state of perpetual tension. Since the regime must also satisfy the material demands of the masses, it goes in for large-scale public spending and thus achieves full employment. National Socialism realizes that "people are filled with envy, with hatred for the rich and successful." The emotions can best be kept alive in the field of foreign affairs; for an aggressive foreign policy and preparation for foreign war prevent "the reawakening of thinking and of articulation into social groups."

National Socialist society is thus composed of the ruling part and the amorphous masses. All other distinctions are removed. "It is on this psychological basis that the Fascist party has been built up. With their success they attract active mass-men who then are kept in a state of emotion and cannot return to their former ways of life. Even family cohesion is broken, the pulverization of society is complete. Masses make dictators, and dictators make masses the continuing basis of the state." That is why the social stratification of society is of the utmost importance and why the Marxist theory of a classless society becomes so dangerous. National Socialism has completely destroyed the power of social groups and has established a classless society.

Were Lederer's analysis correct, our earlier discussion would be completely wrong. Social imperialism would then be not a device to ensnare the masses but an articulation of the spontaneous longing of the masses. Racism would not be the concern of small groups alone but would be deeply imbedded in the masses. Leadership adoration would be a genuine semi-religious phenomenon and not merely a device to prevent insight into the operation of the social-economic mechanism. Capitalism, finally, would be dead, since all particular groups have been destroyed and only leaders and masses remain.

Lederer is wrong, however, though a little of the truth sifts into some of his formulations. Occasionally one feels that even he realizes that the so-called spontaneity of the masses and their active participation in National Socialism are a sham and that the role of the people is merely to serve as an instrument of the ruling group. The problem is perhaps the most difficult of all in an analysis of National Socialism. The difficulties lie not only in the paucity of information and the inadequacy of the sociological categories but also in the extraordinarily complicated character of the social relations themselves. Class structure and social differentiation are not identical—failure to recognize this point is the basic error underlying Lederer's analysis. A society may be divided into classes and yet not be socially differentiated in any other way. On the other hand, a classless society may have sharp differentiations.[2]

2. This has been pointed out by Goetz Briefs in his criticism of Lederer's book: see his 'Intellectual Tragedy,' in the *Commonweal*, 25 October 1940.

The essence of National Socialist social policy consists in the acceptance and strengthening of the prevailing class character of German society, in the attempted consolidation of its ruling class, in the atomization of the subordinate strata through the destruction of every autonomous group mediating between them and the state, in the creation of a system of autocratic bureaucracies interfering in all human relations. The process of atomization extends even to the ruling class in part. It goes hand in hand with a process of differentiation within the mass party and within society that creates reliable élites in every sector. Through these élites, the regime plays off one group against the other and enables a minority to terrorize the majority.[3]

National Socialism did not create the mass-men; it has completed the process, however, and destroyed every institution that might interfere. Basically, the transformation of men into mass-men is the outcome of modern industrial capitalism and of mass democracy. More than a century ago the French counter-revolutionaries, de Maistre and Bonald, and the Spaniard Donoso Cortes, asserted that liberalism, Protestantism, and democracy, which they hated, bore the seeds of the emotionally motivated mass-man and would eventually give birth to the dictatorship of the sword. Mass democracy and monopoly capitalism have brought the seeds to fruition. They have imprisoned man in a network of semi-authoritarian organizations controlling his life from birth to death, and they have begun to transform culture into propaganda and salable commodities.

National Socialism claims to have stopped this trend and to have created a society differentiated not by classes but according to occupation and training. That is absolutely untrue. In fact, National Socialism has carried to its highest perfection the very development it pretends to attack. It has annihilated every institution that under democratic conditions still preserves remnants of human spontaneity: the privacy of the individual and of the family, the trade union, the political party, the church, the free leisure organization. By atomizing the subject population (and to some extent the rulers as well), National Socialism has not eliminated class relations; on the contrary, it has deepened and solidified the antagonisms.

National Socialism must necessarily carry to an extreme the one process that characterizes the structure of modern society, bureaucratization. In modern anti-bureaucratic literature, this term means little more than the numerical growth of public servants, and especially of civil servants. Society is pictured as composed of free men and autonomous organizations on the one hand and of a bureaucratic caste, on the other hand, which takes over more and more political power. The picture is inaccurate, for society is

3. Franz Neumann, *European Trade Unionism and Politics* (Preface by H. J. Laski), New York, 1936 (British edition, London, 1935).

not wholly free and unbureaucratic nor is the public bureaucracy the sole bearer of political and social power.

Bureaucratization, correctly understood, is a process operating in both public and private spheres, in the state as well as in society. It means that human relations lose their directness and become mediated relations in which third parties, public or private functionaries seated more or less securely in power, authoritatively prescribe the behavior of man. It is a highly ambivalent process, progressive as well as reactionary. The growth of bureaucracy in public life is not necessarily incompatible with democracy if the aims of the democracy are not limited to the preservation of individual rights, but also include the furtherance of certain social goals. Even in the social sphere the growth of private organizations is not entirely retrogressive. It brings some kind of order into an anarchic society and thereby rationalizes human relations that would otherwise be irrational and accidental.

If members of a trade union decide to change their labor conditions, they do so by accepting the recommendation of their officials, in whose hands the decision is left. When a political party formulates some policy, it is the party hierarchy that does so. In athletic organizations, the machinery of presidents, vice-presidents, secretaries, and treasurers goes into operation in arranging matches and carrying on the other activities of the group. This process of mediation and depersonalization extends to culture as well. Music becomes organized in the hands of professional secretaries who need not be musicians. The radio prescribes the exact amount of culture to be digested by the public, how much classical and how much light music, how much talk and how much news. The powers extend to the most intimate relations of man, to the family. There are organizations for large families and for bachelors, birth-control associations, advisory councils for the promotion of family happiness, consumers' co-operatives, giant food chain stores making a farce of the consumers' supposedly free choice.

There is, in short, a huge network of organizations covering almost every aspect of human life, each run by presidents and vice-presidents and secretaries and treasurers, each employing advertising agencies and publicity men, each out to interfere with, and to act as the mediator in, the relations between man and man. Civil liberties lose many of the functions they had in a liberal society. Even the exercise of civil rights tends more and more to be mediated by private organizations. Whether it is a problem of defense in a political trial or protection of the rights of labor or the fight against unjust taxation, the average man, lacking sufficient means, has no other choice but to entrust his rights to some organization. Under democratic conditions, such mediation does not destroy his rights, as a rule, since the individual still has a choice between competing organizations. In a totalitarian society, however, even if his rights are still recognized on paper, they are completely at the mercy of private bureaucrats.

What National Socialism has done is to transform into authoritarian bodies the private organizations that in a democracy still give the individual an opportunity for spontaneous activity. Bureaucratization is the complete depersonalization of human relations. They become abstract and anonymous. On this structure of society, National Socialism imposes two ideologies that are completely antagonistic to it: the ideology of the community and the leadership principle.

Ownership, Management and Power

The growth of private bureaucracy has elicited the thesis of a shift in the locus of control and power from owners to managers. At the least, this holds that control of corporate business enterprises has progressively passed into the hands of professional management; at the extreme, that the managers are well on the road to becoming the new ruling class (for example, in the judgment of "managerial theorists" such as James Burnham).

Berle and Means indicate that the absentee ownership of large corporations makes for a partial separation of ownership and control (though not of ultimate power) such that managers can on occasion operate the corporate business in their own interests. This theme is further developed in the selection from Gordon, who maintains that the organizational environment of professional managers often leads them to types of decisions differing from those made by owner-managers. The consequences of bureaucratization for the distribution of power extend beyond the locus of control within an organization. In a critical review of managerial theories of social power, Gerth and Mills conclude that the institutions of property, the limited tenure of managers and the rise of competing bureaucracies effectively limit the exercise of economic and political power by the managerial group.

THE CONTROL OF THE MODERN CORPORATION

Adolf A. Berle, Jr. and Gardiner C. Means

In discussing problems of enterprise it is possible to distinguish between three functions: that of having interests in an enterprise, that of having

Reprinted from *The Modern Corporation and Private Property*, pp. 119-125. (Copyright, 1932, by The Macmillan Company and used with their permission.)

power over it, and that of acting with respect to it. A single individual may fulfill, in varying degrees, any one or more of these functions.

Before the industrial revolution the owner-worker performed all three, as do most farmers today. But during the nineteenth century the bulk of industrial production came to be carried on by enterprises in which a division had occurred, the owner fulfilling the first two functions while the latter was in large measure performed by a separate group, the hired managers. Under such a system of production, the owners were distinguished primarily by the fact that they were *in a position* both to manage an enterprise or delegate its management and to receive any profits or benefits which might accrue. The managers on the other hand were distinguished primarily by the fact that they operated an enterprise, presumably in the interests of the owners. The difference between ownership and management was thus in part one between position and action. An owner who remained completely quiescent towards his enterprise would nevertheless remain an owner. His title was not applied because he acted or was expected to act. Indeed, when the owner acted, as for instance in hiring a manager or giving him directions, to that extent the owner managed his own enterprise. On the other hand, it is difficult to think of applying the title "manager" to an individual who had been entirely quiescent.

Under the corporate system, the second function, that of having power over an enterprise, has become separated from the first. The position of the owner has been reduced to that of having a set of legal and factual interests in the enterprise while the group which we have called control, are in the position of having legal and factual powers over it.

In distinguishing between the interests of ownership and the powers of control, it is necessary to keep in mind the fact that, as there are many individuals having interests in an enterprise who are not customarily thought of as owners, so there may be many individuals having a measure of power over it who should not be thought of as in control. In the present study we have treated the stockholders of a corporation as its owners. When speaking of the ownership of all corporations, the bondholders are often included with the stockholders as part owners. The economist does not hesitate for certain purposes to class an employee with wages due him as temporarily a part owner. All of these groups have interests in the enterprise. Yet a laborer who has a very real interest in a business in so far as it can continue to give him employment is not regarded as part owner. Nor is a customer so included though he has a very real interest in a store to the extent that it can continue to give him good services. Of the whole complex of individuals having interests in an enterprise, only those are called owners who have major interests and, before the law, only those who hold legal title. Similarly, the term control must be limited for practical purposes to those who hold the major elements of power over an enterprise, keeping in mind, however, that a multitude of individuals may exercise a degree of power over the activities of an enterprise without holding sufficient power to warrant their inclusion in "control."

Turning then to the two new groups created out of a former single group,—the owners without appreciable control and the control without appreciable ownership, we must ask what are the relations between them and how may these be expected to affect the conduct of enterprise. When the owner was also in control of his enterprise he could operate it in his own interest and the philosophy surrounding the institution of private property has assumed that he would do so. This assumption has been carried over to present conditions and it is still expected that enterprise will be operated in the interests of the owners. But have we any justification for assuming that those in control of a modern corporation will also choose to operate it in the interests of the owners? The answer to this question will depend on the degree to which the self-interest of those in control may run parallel to the interests of ownership and, insofar as they differ, on the checks on the use of power which may be established by political, economic, or social conditions.

The corporate stockholder has certain well-defined interests in the operation of the company, in the distribution of income, and in the public security markets. In general, it is to his interest, first that the company should be made to earn the maximum profit compatible with a reasonable degree of risk; second, that as large a proportion of these profits should be distributed as the best interests of the business permit, and that nothing should happen to impair his right to receive his equitable share of those profits which are distributed; and finally, that his stock should remain freely marketable at a fair price. In addition to these the stockholder has other but less important interests such as redemption rights, conversion privileges, corporate publicity, etc. However, the three mentioned above usually so far overshadow his other interests as alone to require consideration here.

The interests of control are not so easily discovered. Is control likely to want to run the corporation to produce the maximum profit at the minimum risk; is it likely to want to distribute those profits generously and equitably among the owners; and is it likely to want to maintain market conditions favorable to the investor? An attempt to answer these questions would raise the whole question of the nature of the phenomenon of "control." We must know the controlling individual's aims before we can analyze his desires. Are we to assume for him what has been assumed in the past with regard to the owner of enterprise, that his major aim is *personal profits?* Or must we expect him to seek some other end—prestige, power, or the gratification of professional zeal?

If we are to assume that the desire for *personal profit* is the prime force motivating control, we must conclude that the interests of control are different from and often radically opposed to those of ownership; that the owners most emphatically will not be served by a profit-seeking controlling group. In the operation of the corporation, the controlling group even if they own a large block of stock, can serve their own pockets better by profiting at the expense of the company than by making profits for it. If such persons can make a profit of a million dollars from a sale of property to the corporation, they can afford to suffer a loss of $600,000 through the ownership of 60 per cent of the stock, since the transaction will still net them $400,000 and the remaining stockholders will shoulder the corresponding loss. As their proportion of the holdings decrease, and both profits and losses of the company accrue less and less to them, the opportunities of profiting at the expense of the corporation appear more directly to their benefit. When their holdings amount to only such fractional per cents as the holdings of the management in management-controlled corporations, profits at the expense of the corporation become practically clear gain to the persons in control and the interests of a profit-seeking control run directly counter to the interests of the owners.

In the past, this adverse interest appears sometimes to have taken the extreme form of wrecking a corporation for the profit of those in control. Between 1900 and 1915 various railroads were brought into the hands of receivers as a result of financial mismanagement, apparently designed largely for the benefit of the controlling group, while heavy losses were sustained by the security holders.[1]

Such direct profits at the expense of a corporation are made difficult under present laws and judicial interpretations, but there are numerous less direct ways in which at least part of the profits of a corporation can be diverted for the benefit of those in control. Profits may be shifted from a parent corporation to a subsidiary in which the controlling group have a large interest. Particularly profitable business may be diverted to a second corporation largely owned by the controlling group. In many other ways it is possible to divert profits which would otherwise be made by the corporation into the hands of a group in control. When it comes to the questions of distributing such profits as are made, self-seeking control may strive to divert profits from one class of stock to another, if, as frequently occurs, it holds interests in the latter issue. In market operations, such control may use "inside information" to buy low from present stockholders and sell high to future stockholders. It may have slight interest in maintaining conditions in which a reasonable market price is established. On the contrary it may

1. See Chicago & Alton Railway Co., 12 I.C.C., 295—1907
   Pere Marquette Railroad Co., 44 I.C.C., 1—1914
   Chicago, Rock Island & Pacific, 36 I.C.C., 43—1915
   New York, New Haven & Hartford, 31 I.C.C., 32—1914
   St. Louis & San Francisco Rd. Co., 29 I.C.C., 29—1914

All of these roads went into receivership or were in financial difficulties as a direct or indirect result of financial management of highly questionable sort.

issue financial statements of a misleading character or distribute informal news items which further its own market manipulations. We must conclude, therefore, that the interests of ownership and control are in large measure opposed *if* the interests of the latter grow primarily out of the desire for personal monetary gain.

Into the other motives which might inspire action on the part of control it will not profit us to go, though speculation in that sphere is tempting. If those in control of a corporation reinvested its profits in an effort to enlarge their own power, their interests might run directly counter to those of the "owners." Such an opposition of interest would also arise if, out of professional pride, the control should maintain labor standards above those required by competitive conditions and business foresight or should improve quality above the point which, over a period, is likely to yield optimum returns to the stockholders. The fact that both of these actions would benefit other groups which are essential to the existence of corporate enterprise and which for some purposes should be regarded as part of the enterprise, does not change their character of opposition to the interests of ownership. Under other motives the interests of owner and control may run parallel, as when control seeks the prestige of "success" and profits for the controlled enterprise is the current measure of success. Suffice it here to realize that where the bulk of the profits of enterprise are scheduled to go to owners who are individuals other than those in control, the interests of the latter are as likely as not to be at variance with those of ownership and that the controlling group is in a position to serve its own interests.

In examining the break up of the old concept that was property and the old unity that was private enterprise, it is therefore evident that we are dealing not only with distinct but often with opposing groups, ownership on the one side, control on the other—a control which tends to move further and further away from ownership and ultimately to lie in the hands of the management itself, a management capable of perpetuating its own position. The concentration of economic power separate from ownership has, in fact, created economic empires, and has delivered these empires into the hands of a new form of absolutism, relegating "owners" to the position of those who supply the means whereby the new princes may exercise their power.

The recognition that industry has come to be dominated by these economic autocrats must bring with it a realization of the hollowness of the familiar statement that economic enterprise in America is a matter of individual initiative. To the dozen or so men in control, there is room for such initiative. For the tens and even hundreds of thousands of workers and of owners in a single enterprise, individual initiative no longer exists. Their activity is group activity on a scale so large that the individual, except he be in a position of control, has dropped into relative insignificance. At the same time the problems of control have become problems in economic government.

THE EXECUTIVE AND THE
OWNER-ENTREPRENEUR

Robert A. Gordon

In the very large corporation of today, the main elements of business leadership are exercised by the executive group. This general conclusion is subject to some, but essentially only minor, modifications as a result of our study of the power, influence, and activities of directors, minority stockholders, bankers, and . . . other groups. . . .

When we speak of the "executive group," the second of these two words needs to be stressed. The chief executive is the most important single figure in the large corporation, but he is only one of a sizable body of professional managers who individually and collectively make the decisions and provide the co-ordination that give unity and direction to the firm's activities.

The primary responsibility for business leadership in the large corporation has devolved upon a group of men who are professional managers. Their position is not achieved through ownership. They are salaried experts, trained by education and experience in the field of management. Though only salaried managers, they find themselves responsible for making the decisions which affect not merely the dividends their stockholders receive but also the prices consumers pay, the wages their workers earn, and the level of output and employment in their own firms and in the economy as a whole.

As far as the facts are concerned, there is nothing startlingly new about these conclusions. They have been sensed by the man in the street, and they are part of the everyday experience of those closely associated with big business. The detailed picture, however, has not been presented before in systematic form, and it has been obscured by loose generalizations about the "control" exercised by influential banking and stockholding groups. It is probably safe to say that the full extent to which professional executives have assumed the mantle of business leadership has not been adequately appreciated, either by economists or by the public generally. . . .

FACTORS AFFECTING DECISION-MAKING BY PROFESSIONAL EXECUTIVES. Our reasoning about the working of a private enterprise system has long been predicated on the assumption that the business decisions entering into the leadership function are made by owner-entrepreneurs seeking to maximize

Reprinted in part from *Business Leadership in the Large Corporation*, pp. 317-328, by permission of the publisher. (Copyright, 1945, by The Brookings Institution, Washington, D.C.)

profits for their firms and thus for themselves—or at least, if concerns are not managed by their owners, that business leaders will make exactly the same decisions as profits-maximizing owner-entrepreneurs would have made in similar circumstances. While not an unreasonable assumption to make regarding business behavior in a profit system, this is clearly only an approximation of the facts, when we come to deal with the sort of leadership conditions prevailing in the modern large corporation.

Professional executives do not necessarily react to business situations in the same way as owner-managers. The personal attributes, background, and training of the salaried manager are likely to differ from those of the owner-entrepreneur of an earlier day or of most owner-managers operating in the modern industrial scene. The incentive systems to which the two types of business leaders react differ in significant respects. Institutional pressures are by no means the same in the two cases. Finally, the transition from personal to professional management tends to invite more formal and ultimately more bureaucratic patterns of organization. These tend to grow in complexity with the size of the firm. It is in the giant corporation with which we are dealing that professional management is likely to depart to the greatest degree from the pattern of owner-leadership in the small business concern that has been the basis of much of our economic reasoning.[1] In the pages that follow we shall be concerned with this contrast—in which size, as well as professionalization . . . plays a part . . .

Decision-making has been specialized and diffused through the various layers of management in the large corporation. In particular, a great deal of the initiation of decisions must come from the lower levels. Are lower-ranking executives as willing and able to pioneer and break from the beaten path as the individual owner-entrepreneur?[2] What are the effects of internal financial controls and other checks and balances, especially those inherent in large-scale organization, as plans are initiated at one level and thread their way upward for approval? Can functional and other departmental executives be expected always to give full consideration to the consequences of particular decisions on the enterprise as a whole? It would be surprising if organizational conditions such as these did not frequently result in decisions significantly different from those which an owner-entrepreneur would make in response to a given set of underlying forces.

1. Of course, the larger the concern the less likely are we to encounter cases of owner-management. Indeed, bigness requires that some entrepreneurial decision-making be delegated to salaried managers. Large size inevitably professionalizes business leadership for two reasons. First, ownership tends to become diffused with increase in size of the firm, requiring a transfer of leadership from stockholders to salaried managers. Secondly, even if ownership is concentrated in one or a few persons, such owners of a very large concern would find it a sheer impossibility to make all the entrepreneurial decisions necessary—hence the need for some delegation to professional managers.

2. Assuming that the owner of the business himself were able to make the decisions at these lower levels.

There are also important differences between the responses and leadership activities of the chief executive and those of the owner-entrepreneur. We have noted the fact that the chief executive must stress the co-ordinating aspects of this job. This co-ordinating function, however, is of minor importance to the ordinary owner-entrepreneur who, just in proportion as his business is small and personal, can make the important decisions himself, thus reducing the co-ordinating function to a minimum. As a matter of fact, part of the co-ordinating job imposed upon the chief executive of the large concern is for the small business performed by the external forces of the market.

The professional chief executive in the large corporation must attempt to co-ordinate the decisions of many lesser executives. The larger the firm, the more must original decision-making be delegated. What the chief executive approves depends in good part on what filters up to him for approval. And in exercising his approval function he is likely to apply very broad, particularly financial, criteria. Standards of solvency and liquidity not infrequently take precedence over those of profitability and efficiency. In the very large corporation, the size of the stakes often impels the professional manager to emphasize financial caution at the expense of imaginative and creative leadership.[3] The owner-enterpriser may be more willing to gamble his own money than the chief executive of a great corporation may be to jeopardize the financial empire of which he is trustee. The daring of the owner-entrepreneur may be checked by the investment or commercial banker, but the chief executive of the large corporation is more likely to feel the responsibilities of the financier upon his own shoulders.

In general, the bureaucratic tendencies inherent in large-scale organization lessen the ability of professional executives to perform their functions effectively, even if they conscientiously seek to serve the best interests of the firm. Big business, like large-scale government, tends to suffer from a bureaucratic stiffening of the joints.[4] The result is to impair management efficiency, to create inflexibility of operation and some resistance to change, and to increase the strain placed on the personal and leadership qualities of the chief executive.

On the other hand, the professional manager's emphasis on organization and the organizational techniques permitted by the size of the large corporation have contributed to management's efficiency and have permitted constructive programs to be carried through that would have been impossible otherwise. The management structure within the large corporation has its positive as well as its negative side, so far as its effects upon business leadership are concerned.

3. These considerations are likely to hold even more for the board of directors, in so far as it is active, than for the chief executive.

4. See TNEC Monograph No. 11, *Bureaucracy and Trusteeship in Large Corporations*, Pts. 2 and 3.

In addition to problems of internal organization, top management in the large corporation must also deal with directors and with important outside interest groups. The "institutional environment" of the salaried executive, therefore, differs from that of the owner-entrepreneur, particularly of the small concern. In many companies, of course, the role of the non-officer director is a nominal one. But where the influence or leadership of directors is important, the resulting business decisions may well reflect an undue degree of financial caution. On occasion, they may reflect interests, outside the business, which particular directors wish to further.

From his stockholders and perhaps from powerful banking interests associated with the firm, the chief executive of the large corporation is subject to pressures which the owner-entrepreneur avoids, although on occasion the latter may also have his problems with (chiefly commercial) banks.[5] The large firm with outstanding securities is subject to more government regulation than the small owner-managed concern; its legal problems are more varied, hence the influence of the legal profession is greater; and its management must ordinarily be more sensitive to public opinion. The results on decision-making are two-fold. These influences create additional data which management must take into account in making its decisions. Equally important, the character of the chief executive's job is affected. He must spend a substantial part of his time handling these and other external relations of the firm. For this reason, as well as because of the complexities of internal management organization, he must stress the co-ordinating aspects of his job and leave largely to subordinates the initiation and to some extent even the approval of important operating decisions.[6]

No two business executives are exactly alike. Nonetheless, there are certain characteristics which we can attribute to professional managers as a group, and these attributes condition the business thinking and decision-making of the professional business leader.

The modern corporation executive is better educated and in many respects better trained than the owner-entrepreneur of an earlier or even the present day.[7] With this education and training has gone a marked development of a scientific approach to business problems, as evident in the increasing emphasis on careful planning, the use of advisory and research staffs, the development of accounting techniques and budget procedures, the attention

5. The owner-entrepreneur may also have occasional difficulties with partners or minority stockholders—as, for example, did Henry Ford.

6. These considerations regarding the importance of external pressures hold not only for the giant concerns we have studied but also for many corporations in the smaller size brackets.

7. The educational backgrounds of the presidents of 100 large corporations are summarized in *Fortune*, February 1940, p. 61. See also F. W. Taussig and C. J. Joslyn, *American Business Leaders* (1932), Chap. 17, for further data on the backgrounds of corporation executives.

being paid to problems of internal organization and executive personnel, and so on.[8]

Among some professional executives, scientific caution may degenerate into a tendency to play safe. They do not receive the profits which may result from taking a chance, while their position in the firm may be jeopardized in the event of serious loss.[9] This is an aspect of the bureaucratic tendencies mentioned previously making for inflexibility and some resistance to change.

In spite of the better education and training of the professional executive, his general business background may not be as wide as that of the man running his own business. In the lower executive ranks, it is particularly likely to be narrow, while the chief executive himself is apt to have come up through the ranks and to have devoted most of his career to one or a few functions. Even at the top, the latter may continue to be primarily a specialist in his decision-making; hence the dependence on influential directors and bankers for advice, the development of advisory staffs, and the great reliance on management committees and group decision-making.[10]

Of course, the greatest contrast between the professional manager and the owner-entrepreneur lies in the character of their respective stakes in the business. A considerable literature has developed concerning the implications, especially from the point of view of the stockholder, of the separation of management and "control" from ownership. . . .

Management's small stockholdings have significantly diminished the strength of the profits incentive among professional business leaders, and this has been accompanied by a strengthening of the various non-financial attractions which the large corporation has to offer. For example, satisfaction of the creative urge and professional interest in the job compete with profit-making as a guide to action, although profits for the firm remain the primary criterion. Power and prestige for the individual executive are not dependent on the personal receipts of profits, and they are only loosely correlated with profits for the firm.

8. Many large and small concerns, including those managed by their owners, acquire a good deal of specialized managerial services from accounting, management, sales promotion, and similar service companies, and also through trade association channels. Thus many untrained businessmen can benefit in some degree from the knowledge of trained experts without needing to hire them full time. Nonetheless, it is generally true that the scientific approach to management problems is most marked among the larger firms well staffed with trained professional executives.

9. For further discussion of the tendency among salaried managers to play safe, see P. S. Florence, *The Logic of Industrial Organization*, pp. 197, 219, 224-25. For an overdrawn statement of the same sort of tendency, see Miriam Beard, *A History of the Business Man*, p. 727. The tendency to play safe is, as has been noted, also found among directors.

10. For further discussion of the limited backgrounds and experience of professional executives, see the section of Dimock and Hyde, *TNEC Monograph No. 11*, included in this volume.

These considerations regarding incentives raise important questions. Do professional managements seek always to maximize profits for their firms, and is their distribution of earnings always equitable to stockholders and such as to facilitate the smooth functioning of the economic system? [11] Equally important is the broader question as to what role profits may play in a private enterprise system if they are not the reward for active business leadership. . . .

SOME POSSIBLE ECONOMIC EFFECTS OF PROFESSIONALIZING BUSINESS LEADERSHIP. Basically, the characteristics of large-scale professionalized business leadership outlined in the preceding section may affect entrepreneurial decision-making, and hence the functioning of the economy, in either of two ways. As we have already suggested, there may not be the same emphasis on maximizing profits for the firm and the stockholders, as we should expect from a proprietor running his own business.[12] If this is the case, not only is the stockholder affected but, more important, the economic system does not behave entirely in accordance with the profit rules under which it is supposed to function. Secondly, even if we assume for the moment that professional managers do seek always to maximize profits, the leadership conditions under which they operate may still result in decisions significantly different from those which would have been reached under a different set of leadership conditions. For example, complexities of internal organization may prevent management from exploiting fully every profit opportunity; or the more scientific approach of professional managers may uncover investment opportunities that might have escaped the old-fashioned type of owner-entrepreneur using hit-and-miss methods.

We run into difficulties when we try to evaluate in greater detail the effects on decision-making of the leadership conditions in the large corporations. What can be said lies almost entirely in the field of conjecture; factual evidence is largely lacking; and the tendencies which seem to be at work do not all point in the same direction.

We have already stated our opinion that the goal of profit-making, while still paramount, has been weakened in the large corporation. In view of management's small ownership and the [existing] incentive system . . . it would be surprising if this were not the case. The delegation of much decision-making to specialists in the lower executive ranks, professional characteristics emphasizing security of tenure and interest in the job for its own sake, and possible pressures from non-management groups put further obstacles in

11. See, for example, N. S. Buchanan, *The Economics of Corporate Enterprise* (1940), pp. 448-49. Buchanan concludes that, on the whole, the economic effects of the separation of ownership and management are not particularly significant.

12. Actually, two issues are involved here. Management may not seek to maximize profits for the firm. Secondly, given total profits, it may divert some part of them away from stockholders. We are interested chiefly in the first of these problems.

the way of complete adherence to the goal of profits-maximization for the firm as a whole.

The profits criterion can never be disregarded by salaried executives. As a minimum, it is necessary to keep directors and stockholders passive.[13] Beyond this, however, the executive group may or may not seek, with every decision to be made, to enlarge profits still further. There is considerable opportunity to follow other goals. Today, executives are not likely to use extensively the criterion of maximum financial gain for themselves.[14] But they may very well adopt, at least in part, such criteria as personal position and power, the desire to see the firm larger, or even more socially desirable goals such as the welfare of workers, consumers, or other broad groups. Perhaps more important, they may seek to some extent to play safe and to avoid some of the change and uncertainty which result from assiduous pursuit of every possible opportunity to increase profits further.

To the extent that salaried executives do not take advantage of every change in profit opportunities, an additional element of inflexibility is introduced into the large corporation's responses to changing conditions—over and above the inertias normally inherent in large-scale organization. In short, such managements are likely not to be as sensitive as they might to short-period changes, which are continually occurring in market conditions and profit expectations—price behavior and other economic variables being affected accordingly.[15] In this connection, large-scale business leadership has shown a marked tendency to concentrate upon long-term strategic considerations, particularly on maintaining the competitive and financial position of the firm. Prices may be maintained or changed, for example, not so much with the specific aim of maximizing profits over some period as to protect a competitive position over the very long run, or investment decisions may be based on a variety of financial and strategic considerations, not all of them concerned with a precise balancing of expected returns against cost.[16]

13. [Most stockholders are relatively impotent.] But directors and large minority stockholders can and on occasion do intervene when profits results are particularly unsatisfactory.

14. Today executives are prevented by law from trading in and out of their own stock on the basis of "inside" information. A minority, however, exploit their positions to secure the largest possible salary and bonus for themselves. Other opportunities for maximizing personal income also exist. In general, however, executives are much more restrained in this respect than they were before the thirties.

15. In so far as directors are active, they are likely to add little if anything to making the large firm more sensitive to short-period changes in profit opportunities.

16. Owner-managers also use such criteria where the size of their firms or other advantages give them the opportunity to do so. However, they are more likely than professional executives to link their strategy directly to some concept of maximum profits for the firm, and they are also likely to pay more attention to short-period market changes.

A MARX FOR THE MANAGERS

Hans H. Gerth and C. Wright Mills

There is a tendency to interpret modern history, and particularly the twentieth century, in terms of an increasing bureaucratization. In whatever domain of thought the question has arisen there have been able presentations of the facts of the centralization of industrial and administrative organization. But it is not only in statistical curves that such phenomena receive notice. They make up the stuff of several philosophies of history.

It is no accident that Max Weber is more and more frequently quoted for his thesis that the historical drift may be seen as a bureaucratization of industrial societies, irrespective of their constitutional governments. It is this *form* of organization which is taken to be the substance of history, the more so as it is identified with a growing rationality of modern society.

It is clear that the application of occidental science is an indispensable element in the development of large-scale and planned administrations. For Thorstein Veblen, as well as for Weber, the advent of science is a phenomenon unique and central to Western civilization. Veblen focused more directly upon "the sequence of accumulative technology" and drew inferences directly from the fact of its dominance. Apart from the opaque line of technological relationality, social life is drift and habituation. The irrational institutions, particularly pecuniary ones, are in the main only permissive; all they do is occasionally hinder the spread of mechanical rationality into all areas of life. It is the men who nurse the big machines, the industrial population, who implement that which makes history.

For Weber, impersonal rationality stands as polar opposite to personal charisma, the extraordinary gift of leaders. For Veblen, technology, widely construed, stands opposite irrational institutions. And for both, in whatever other respects they may differ, the rational, the technical pole of history will come through; it will increase to dominate the social life of the West.

In this kind of philosophy of history, warfare and revolutions, crises and class struggles, are not the central objects to be explained. They are part of modern man's destiny, and as subsidiary processes they further implement the big drift toward rationality. The irrational is identified with charismatic leaders (Weber) or with "a democracy of emotions" (Scheler) or "institutionalized masses" (E. Lederer) or with "pecuniary institutions" (Veblen). Authors who follow Pareto and place emphasis upon revolutionary changes

Reprinted from *Ethics*, Vol. LII (1941–1942), pp. 200–215, by permission of the authors and the publisher, the University of Chicago Press.

and historical discontinuities at the price of structures are likely to see reality under the emblems of oscillating elites. Occasionally "Youth" serves as the shibboleth of tacit hopes to escape the inevitable routinized structures of modern societies, and it is also used as an explanation of sudden crises.

One of the latest formulations which popularizes such interpretations is provided in James Burnham's book.[1] His thesis is that what is happening in the world will eventuate neither in socialism nor in capitalism; rather that through revolutions and wars we move toward "a managerial society." The alternatives of capitalism or socialism, of nationalism or internationalism, are displaced by a formula which absorbs a number of problems into the explanation of one phrase. Strangely enough, such apparently diverse structures as the New Deal, Russian communism, and naziism are taken to be phases on similar roads to this ultimate ending in "a managerial society."

In common with Spengler, the temper of Burnham's diction embodies a pervasive cultural pessimism, and from Marx it borrows the Draconian inevitableness of iron necessity. With Lawrence Dennis, Burnham shares a technical admiration of the efficient machines now prowling out from Germany and irresistibly attracting half of Russia.

The "managerial world current" is Burnham's demiurge of history, for just as a rather petty species of executive manager in the Peloponnesian states became for Plato the World-builder, so Burnham Platonizes and imputes an irresistible movement toward power to the production expert and administrative executive.

This philosophy of history is typically anchored, whether explicitly or not, in two different spheres: (1) in the changing class structure of the corporate capitalism of the twentieth century and (2) in the shifting relationship between the executive and legislative branches of parliamentary governments and administrative growth of the former. Only by understanding what has been happening in these two spheres can we locate Burnham's views. The significance of the trends evidenced in these spheres must be assessed, and their import for the rise to power of various personnels and structures must be drawn. What do they mean for the distribution of political power and the methods of holding it? How do they affect the chances of power of various strata and types of persons in modern societies?

There are several facts concerning the shift of class composition and function in twentieth-century capitalism upon which there is agreement. Occupationally, the most striking characteristic is the rise of the "new middle class." Since the first great war of this century it has gained great social weight. It is composed of white-collar groups and of various professions; it makes up the bulk of clerical and technical staffs. It contains the salaried administrator and the expert civil servant, the trained manager and the pri-

1. *The Managerial Revolution: What is Happening in the World* (New York: John Day Co., Inc., 1941).

vate engineer. It is the chief repository of those skills necessary to run administrative and industrial machinery, and its members have assumed many of the functions requisite to a capitalist society.

Recognizing the rise to economic and industrial functioning of this class, many writers have set forth lines of social action leading from it. It is precisely around the crucial facts concerning this new middle class that social interpretations have hovered, and in them are anchored disappointed socialist views and not a few prophecies and hopes.

In taking cognizance of the new middle class, G. D. H. Cole stated in 1937 that it has

acted politically, as well as economically, as the faithful servant of large-scale capitalism. . . . . . It has the power to organize and carry on industry itself, without the aid of the grande bourgeoisie, if it can insure the cooperation or the subservience of the proletariat, (and) if the proletariat could be reenforced by the adhesion of even a minority of the technicians, administrators, and professional men and women who form the active section of the new petite bourgeoisie it could be strong enough . . . . . to build socialism against the united hostility of the grande bourgeoisie and the more reactionary petite bourgeois groups.

As over against Continental Socialists, English Socialists tend to discount the state with its armed forces.

In *The Engineers and the Price System* Veblen set forth the industrial and economic situation out of which an association and group consciousness of technicians, presumably recruited from this middle class, might arise. For him the realities of the case lie within the range of industrial and technological fact. The modern technological system is indispensable to modern populations, and only the engineers can run it. In the technical planning and execution of work, "The technicians necessarily take the initiative and exercise the necessary surveillance and direction." Given the centralized and intricately connected technological system, "the wholehearted cooperation of the technicians would be . . . indispensable to any effectual movement of overturn." They are essential for any successful line of revolutionary action. But Veblen does not detail the means by which an association of engineers might come about. He does not examine political and class situations, and the differential chances of powerholding and power-grabbing do not come within his explicit purview. On this crucial point he is ambiguous by irony, and behind this guise he states that, although they are indispensable to any overthrow, the technicians will not engage in such a line of action. In so far as workers are organized, it is in organizations "for bargaining, not production," which are "of the vested interests." Yet, in order to be successful, the engineers' revolution involves "inquiry and publicity" directed at "the underlying population" and the working-out of a "common understanding and a solidarity of sentiment between the technicians and the working force engaged in . . . the greater underlying industries of the system."

There are those among the technocrats who, being less competent than Veblen, were also less cautious. For these the apocalyptic day of seized power follows quickly the night of economic and technical shifts in function.

In 1935 Alfred Bingham stated: "If . . . the original Marxist concept of a class rising from functional supremacy to political supremacy be followed, it leads today to the conclusion that *the technical and managerial middle classes are slated to be next in the sequence of ruling classes*." In assessing the chances at power of the new middle class, Cole seeks programmatically to draw their weight into the big push of the workers. Veblen seeks to draw the workers' support to the engineers among the new class. Bingham fears their support of fascism. But Burnham is not so cautious as all these. It is his thesis that the managers, who, although he does not say so, are drawn from the middle class, *are* increasingly the rulers of modern nations and that we are moving into a society over which they will be absolute lords. The heart of Burnham's thesis and the chief assumption underlying it are contained in the 1935 quotation from Bingham.

One error which pervades this interpretation of the chances at power of managerial elements of the new middle class is the assumption that the technical indispensability of certain functions in a social structure are taken *ipso facto* as a prospective claim for political power. This error is not confined to the view that technical managers and production engineers are going to usher in a society dominated by themselves; it also feeds the widespread notion that in modern Germany the middle class has attained power. If facts are brought to bear upon these points, they will disclose the infeasibility of the basic assumption which underlies them. It is our view that such interpretations unduly short-cut the road from technical indispensability to a grab and hold of power. The short cut establishes too automatic an agreement between the social-economic order and political movements.

It is only by confining the term "capitalism" to production for free markets, to a laissez faire economy under a parliamentary government, that Burnham is able to view imperialist Germany as non-capitalistic. However, there is a type of capitalism that produces for the state rather than for an open market. As a system such production has always been most profitable. Nineteenth-century capitalism may have preferred peaceful penetration, the open door, and economic pacifism. Imperialist capitalism of the twentieth century increasingly trades at the point of a gun, but it is no less capitalism.

In evaluating the class situation in Germany, we must consider that the group of big industrialists and Junkers have not lost power. If occasional members are plucked out for individual discipline, it does not mean that as a stratum they have been deprived of power but merely that what Mr. Thyssen loses becomes Baron von Schroeder's commission. Frequently the inference is made that the governmental regulations of the German war economy, the political allocation of investment capital, raw materials, labor, and the subsidization of chances to export act to the detriment of the capitalist class. To some factions they do. In general, those suffer whose products and establishments are not considered vital for the war economy. The shift from a peacetime to a wartime economy affects this class as does any such crisis. Likewise, the political guidance of investment policies deprives many establishments of profits which under a free market would have been available for reinvestment. However, the funds which are losses to some capitalists are gains for other capitalists. In the political capitalism of Germany the state acts as a co-ordinating and transferring agency. The German army is a big business, and to the extent that its acquisitions allow for the incorporation of other nations' businesses, it pays in "plant expansions." Why should munition-makers such as Henschel and Krupp, and airplane manufacturers such as Junker and Messerschmitt, feel thwarted by plant expansions because they are financed from funds that are larger than those that would have been available in an open market and which consist of taxes and governmentally compelled loans? The political control of the total economy secures an investment to the big capitalists and their subcontractors who are considered essential to the war economy. Mr. Funk is no less divorced from the capitalist group than was Mr. Schacht: the latter came out of a bank, while the former emerged from the commercial pages of the Berlin *Boersen-Zeitung*. The war economy makes the estates of the Junkers as necessary and safe as under the Kaiser or the Social Democratic regime when they faced the blockade. There is no evidence that the traditional ruling class of big industrialists and Junkers in Germany fare worse economically under Hitler than they did under the Kaiser. The Junkers' estates have been buttressed by a class of hereditarily entailed peasants. The National Socialist party domesticates labor and the middle class for the owners better than did the Democratic Socialists. Control of prices works primarily for them and only secondarily for the peasant; as part of the consumers and as a labor reserve, the middle class helps carry the load.

The fact that numerous individuals of middle-class extraction have had opportunities and have risen in the social scale does not mean that "the middle class rose to power." On the contrary, the Nazi war economy has violated all material election promises to the middle class. The middle class was politically important in the ascent of the Nazi party to power, but it is a power which they do not share. "Tax-Bolshevism" was not decimated; it was augmented. Wholesale distributions through co-operatives and department stores did not decline under Nazi control. At least half a million independent middle-class retailers closed down. And many independent enterprisers have become factory hands. In the light of such facts, it would be strange to assume that a class gets into power only to curtail its own opportunities and its own interests. Totalitarian regimentation has superseded *Burgfrieden*.

Those individuals of middle-class extraction who have become officers in the army and Gestapo agents, by virtue of their party membership, fill occupations which make them part of the state organization. From this state organization and not from their class extraction they derive such power as they have. In monarchical Germany many bureaucrats were recruited from among the *petite bourgeoisie*, but this did not mean that the imperial policy benefited the *petite bourgeoisie*. Nor does the fact that Hitler was a house-painter and Goebbels' father a blacksmith benefit the house-painters and the blacksmiths. The question is: Where is the power? And the answer is: It is the structure of domination, which is the state with its monopoly of physical force, and fused within it the industrialists and their agrarian colleagues. Neither the proclamation nor the social extraction of the political actor is the deciding factor in the use of power. Deeds answer the question *cui bono?* Discrete opportunities for individual jobs is one thing; access to the positions controlling the big business of Europe is quite another. The ascent of certain members of the middle class is more than counterbalanced by the compulsory descent of other members of this class, by the decline of their· standard of living, and by the war losses of their youth.

The role of the German lower middle class in the ascent to power of the Nazi party is well known; the meagerness of their political harvest should by now be equally evident. The rise of a few Nazi parvenus into industrial robber barons, booty capitalists of imperialist dimensions, is paid for dearly by the nonowners and by displaced owners. The spoils of the war and levies on Jewry, municipalities, political protectorates, and subjected nations accrue to the propertied class. It is a peculiarity of modern warfare irrespective of nations and constitutions, that the middle class has nothing material to gain from it. Political capitalism as it now dominates Germany does not benefit middle-class businesses, nor does it lend power to the middle class. Such psychic income of patriotic glory as they receive may compensate for social and economic deterioration. It is, however, *ersatz*.

This middle class contains the managerial professionals with whom Burnham is concerned: he speaks of their grasp of and high chance at further power. The crucial fact in Germany concerning these skilled personnels in their relation to power is that their very indispensability and scarcity value for a war economy insures their loss of income and personal freedom, and provides a decade of overwork. The close supervision over them partakes of army discipline. Not power but subjugation to martial law is their lot. They are as enslaved as any wage-worker. That skill is at a premium does not in itself mean that the skilled have an opportunity for positions entailing power decisions. They are attached to plants as mere serfs to feudal manors . . . unless their income exceeds 12,000 Reichsmarks (about $4,000) a year. A slight minority of them have salaries above this figure. As experts they give advice, but they receive orders.

Occupational skill is not identical with class position. Some engineers are hired men; other engineers do the hiring. A consultant engineer may have his own office, work for his own account, and, economically speaking, be an independent enterpriser. Or an individual with the same type and amount of trained skill may be a production engineer with a fixed salary and fixed stages in his career within an organization. The possession of a skill may well mean quite heterogeneous interests, class positions, and political loyalties. In a democracy, apart from common technical knowledge, technicians may be found on all political sides of many social fences. The technical knowledge of managers and their relation to production is one thing; their class position, political loyalties, and their stake in the current system is quite another. There is no intrinsic connection between the two.

Those who control the experts are not the "political colleagues" of managers but their powerful masters. From a managerial standpoint they may be amateurs, but perhaps it is always the experts in power-grabbing and wielding who, although not specialists in handling implements of production or destruction, master whole nations and purge experts.

Modern industry does require specifically trained staffs. But such occupational roles will be filled irrespective of the type of political system in which this modern industry is situated. The chances at political power for those filling technically indispensable roles is not a function of their technical roles but of their class position and political affiliations, whatever they may be.

Precisely because of their specialization and knowledge the scientist and technician are among the most easily used and co-ordinated of groups in modern society. This is proved in the German experience. The very rigor of their training typically makes them the easy dupes of men wise in political ways. In the face of Burnham's depiction of the sinister motives of dissatisfied managers and in defense of the trustworthiness, reliability, and loyalty of America's technical managers to owners and to our society as it is now duly constituted, it is pertinent to recall the resolution passed by the representative American Engineering Council. Their stand on the technocracy question was well to the middle right, and they thought it "appropriate at this time to record its unqualified admiration of Herbert Hoover . . . (who is) one of the world's greatest leaders and benefactors of our time."

All factual reports of the organizations of American scientists and industrial technicians disprove completely speculations about the singular class position and political stand of such groups. An American "Soviet" of technically trained persons would be as politically and socially conservative as any businessmen's service club.

One prop which is used to support belief in the shift of the Managers' *de facto* control of industry to dominance in the political order is the fact of absentee ownership. Absentee ownership is one of the problems of modern industrial society which certain thinkers, among them Burnham, solve in favor of the absentee owner's functioning agent. Where Marx had the coupon-clipping parasites expropriated by the exploited proletariat, Burnham has them expropriated by their junior partners and social colleagues, the managers. The Marxist class struggle has shifted its stage from the barricades to the Social Club. The expropriation of capitalists becomes automatic, intimate, and silent. Despite Mr. Krassin, an odd engineer whom Burnham cites, the Russian Revolution does not quite confirm this view.

Burnham notes with satisfaction for his thesis that, while the absentee owners have been absent, their functioning managers have been gaining power. But what have the owners been doing while absent from their businesses? Veblen did not tell the whole tale in his depiction of the activities of the leisure class. Absentee owners have continuously devoted themselves to politics. Mr. Chamberlain did not lose power because he substituted a premiership for the management of his private steel corporation, and it is said that the contract for the Anderson bomb shelter, instead of a large-scale investment in underground shelters, in London was, among other reasons, not entirely irrelevant to the steel industry. If they are successful, the lords now taking over the guidance of the British Empire's destiny will not lessen the prestige and luster of their class.

Tenants have not become owners because they have had disposition over houses and farms and estates; they have not, during the last three hundred years, automatically dethroned the absentee owning British aristocrats. Nor will the production engineers and administrative experts displace the economic royalists whose confidence they now enjoy.

Burnham's definition of private property significantly omits one aspect of "disposition over goods": the disposition to the next generation. It is pertinent that the sons of the managers do not inherit the managed property but rather the relatives of the absentee owners. It is not usual for managers to sell out the plants which they manage. Socialism begins where a legal order does not provide for succession of property holdings in terms of blood relationships nor for private transfers of property. Hence, in this respect, naziism stands quite remote from communism. In Germany, as far as shifts in property holding are concerned, what has occurred makes for the happiness of owners and their heirs. Only in so far as they may become owners will the managers share in such happiness. It is by overlooking the problem of inheritance of property that naziism and communism appear as two phases of the same movement. Those who hate the Nazi but fear Russian communism know why.

In treating Russian communism and German naziism as basically similar trends, Burnham confounds the regulatory power of the state with ownership. The ideal model of thought of economic theory may for certain purposes disregard the regulatory power of the state, but in reality there has never been economic conduct which has not been subject to political and legal regulations. Every tariff and industrial code, even if totalitarian, distributes differential opportunities among economic agents, and those who regulate do not thereby own. There is in Russian no private ownership of the means of production. Nobody owns them. Burnham's assumption that someone must, even if it be managers, because someone "controls" them, is a lag from capitalistic ways of thinking. His definition of property as actual disposition means an eternalization of notions of private property. No commander of a battleship owns it or transfers it at will. Nor do the heiresses to industrial properties in the United States, Germany, and England lose ownership of machines and offices which their late fathers' production engineers and executives efficiently and faithfully run for them. The belief in private and hereditary property, and the maintenance of a society stratified in terms of property, is not a technical or a "managerial" problem. It is quite evidently a political and legal problem. And it is precisely in the sphere of politics that managers do not significantly differ from owners in their beliefs and loyalties. Mr. Krassin and Friedrich Engels became communists not because they were engineers and manufacturers but despite it.

So far we have considered managers as the members of the new middle class who are technically and industrially "concerned directly in production." Burnham, however, does not restrict the term "manager" to such production and industrial functions. For him, it apparently includes a type of governmental bureaucrat. This duality of meaning, which pervades his argument, enables him to lend to its cogency in various contexts by making references to powerful groups in each of these contexts. Either by violating the principle of identity or by taking the term "manager" as an emblematic slogan to mean those in power, Burnham exploits the facts concerning the growth of bureaucratic structures for his own thesis. Sometimes the "managers" are the "European managerial politician" and frequently they are referred to as "managers, in and out of government, along with their bureaucratic and military colleagues," and "the bureaucrats (for which we may read 'managers')." Yet later it is not "the bureaucracy but the managing group which is becoming the ruling class." Again, when discussing those who attain power in the United States, Burnham says, "The bureaucrats in charge of popular mass organizations . . . take their places among the managers." He means the C. I. O. "Who are the managers?" is a real question for those who wish to understand Burnham's argument. They seem to be, as we have said, those in power in whatever context Burnham discusses. They have one trait in common: all the groups mentioned as managers are more or less associated with personnels holding offices in bureaucracies. Thus, much of the cogency that Burnham's thesis has is due to the simple fact that the form of organization all over the world is, perhaps increasingly, bureaucratic. But the ends for which these structures will be used, who will be at their tops, how they might be overthrown, and what movements will grow up into such structures . . . these are not considered; they are swallowed in the consideration of the *form* of organization, the demiurge of history, the "managerial world current."

Since the late 1920's it has been often observed that the executive branch of parliamentary government has been assuming more weight and functions at the expense of the legislative organs. Wars implement this shift. The legislature may be reduced to an interrogative, occasionally criticizing, and, after executive successes, applauding function. All modern states are bureaucratic. But bureaucracies do not operate without definite social settings.

There are several views of the power relations of a growing bureaucracy. Hegel and his followers, down to Sombart and Burnham, hold that a bureaucracy becomes an autonomous structure with ultimate and supreme power over all classes. Others have not emphasized so much the technical aspect of the machinery of power but its direction and ends. The question *cui bono?* and the question of recruitment of those who dominate in the power decisions of a bureaucracy lead to questions which cannot be answered by confining one's self to the consideration of the *formal* pattern of modern states, whether they be czarist, monarchical, democratic, or totalitarian. It opens the question as to the power relations of the bureaucracy to various classes.

If classes are ultimately defined according to their relations to the means of production, or in terms or property, a bureaucracy is certainly not a class. Typically, the official of a bureaucracy is not allowed to become an economic enterpriser. In so far Hegel is correct, they remain removed from specific economic interests. But if, as in the political capitalism of modern Germany, a ruling group uses political power for building up private economic power, for acquiring industrial properties (Goring, for example), it is probable that for once Marx may be correct in calling the state the executive committee of the ruling class. In parliamentary systems the group of owners may find its representation in the ruling party. In Germany the amassing of fortunes by Nazi chieftains does not curb but rather consolidates the power of the owning group. A new composition for an owning group does not destroy it. The robber barons fuse with the older industrialists by sharing their wealth, their interests, and their worries. In some contexts he who hesitates and does not grab is himself an object to be grabbed. Adventurous imperialism under Nazi aegis has no use for the individual brilliance of a Cecil Rhodes; they organize a disciplined advance comparable only to the older corporate adventures of such companies as the East Indian, but in a world already grabbed they must be even better armed, and they must mobilize an entire nation for their advance.

For Burnham, the import of the growth of executive bureaucracies is the ousting of the capitalist owners. But there is no evidence for this. It is true that in America the corporations have been anti-Roosevelt and that the tension between the owners and the New Deal is due to the increasing of the regulatory power of the state. But this state control has by no means aimed at dislocating ownership. It has, in fact, been security against such dislocation. The New Deal has protected the perpetuation of the system of ownership against the dangers which seem to be inherent in it. It is not property which has been "managed" but the defaults of the property system. And in this respect, naturally, the corporate owners have not resented governmental expansion. They have resented that protection has been extended to small owners, farmers and bank depositors, and to nonowning groups, as trade-unions and the unemployed. The corporate owners have sought to restrict the scope of such protection or "welfare regulation" by the government. The objection is that Roosevelt has "unduly" extended such control to the defaults of the system as it touches propertyless sectors of the population.

What is the role and relation to power decisions of the expert in government? Experts do not make decisions but influence them, and, fortunately for the wielders of power, by virtue of their specialization they are likely to draw different conclusions from the same observations. The turnover of experts within structures of power, military, industrial, and governmental, does not conduce to their steady influence upon ultimate decisions. Witness the army purges and the shuffling of "the self-confident, young men" of the New Deal. It is not irrelevant to contrast the insecurity of tenure of the expert with the legally guaranteed inheritance of private owners. In totalitarian regimes the personal insecurity of experts increases proportionately to the influence of their advice. In democracies experts may retire and grumble; in totalitarianism they are liquidated.

But is it true that the state bureaucracies that have grown up are tending to become the repository of power decisions? If not, for what class or social sector are they the instruments?

Harold Laski has pointed out that the assumptions of the British civil servant are "the same as those of the men who own the instruments of production." The general strike of 1926 showed that British bureaucrats will stand socially and politically with the ruling class. Neither their alleged neutrality nor their independence from the class in power has ever been tested by their having to administer policies counter to the loyalties of their class.

It is true that the larger a bureaucracy becomes, the more restricted its head becomes in giving orders. The means built up restrict the ends for which they can be used. But the top knocks off the "managers" before they get to be the depository of *decisional* power. The purges in Germany serve the owners, certainly not the managers. In Russia the centralization of bureaucratic agencies involved the purging of any sector of it which was gaining too much weight and threatening the absolutism of Stalin and his ruling circle. The history of brain-trusters does not bespeak the power of the "managers" in the New Deal.

The task of understanding what is happening in the world today involves a comprehension of such basic issues as the retention or abolition of private property, the structure of classes, possible political and social movements, and of war. For it is from such matters and not in the all-pervasive drift to some *general form* of organization that one may obtain a view which implements an intelligent and prepared expectation. To swallow such crucial items and possibilities into a form of organization is to be engulfed within the demiurge of history. The questions of events that require answering and which may well be weighty determinants of the course of history are not merely incidental to some unilinear tendency toward great organizations. They may well constitute the pivots of history; they may be points around which managed structures swing in new and unforeseen directions.

Nothing has been more surprising during recent decades than the disruption of large-scale bureaucratic regimes and the quick dissolution of armies. And nothing is more astounding than the speed with which new and rival social machineries may be built up. The czarist police and Communist G. P. U. may be equally harsh and brutal in their techniques of persecution; but this formal sameness should not obscure the fact that they are directed against different strata. Nothing is known of wholesale purges of production executives and army officers under czarism which would be comparable to the Communist purges of the middle 1930's. It is such facts as these which make fruitless a lumping of all executive agencies under one rubric "the managers."

We must not only consider the formal structures of history; we must also consider the various uses which are made of them. For the class pivots of such use are also a part of history . . . and an important part. Marx believed that state bureaucracies would remain fairly stable throughout bourgeois revolutionary shifts in power at the top, and Max Weber generalized this view for all revolutions. But this does not seem to be true of twentieth-century bureaucracies. Their very size and complexity make it possible for small alert groups with political loyalties to other machines to become "cells" in them and crucially to snarl and entangle their functioning. Little cells may be formed in bureaucracies which externally carry on their proper work but take commands from political groups on the outside. Such activities do not contribute to continuous bureaucratization.

It is not convincing that a book subtitled "What is Happening in the World" should be without an explanation of the drive to war. Wars seem to Burnham "natural to society"; they only further the drift toward a form of organization. In seeing capitalism's displacement by a managerial society, Burnham obviates an explanation of war. He vindicates naziism because it succeeded in eliminating unemployment. He has, however, to expand the concept of employment far beyond economic functions. The endowment of unemployed masses not with relief but with barracks and weapons may constitute a "solution," may lead out of unemployment crises, but it is no new precept to solve economic crises by plunging into imperialist warfare. The Nazi drive to war is not nihilism, but imperialism, an old phenomenon in a streamlined form. Factors which are not a part of the hypothetical managerial society but are intrinsic to the structure and power grouping of the real world are needed to explain war. Of particular importance today is the political bolstering and implementation of capitalist crises. "Germany," says Hitler, "must export or die." In shrinking world-markets German capitalism can conquer outlets for commodities and capital and raw materials only by violence. It is no longer possible by peaceful trade. *Lebensraum* for Central European capitalism means raw materials and chances to export. Socialism in one country may be possible; National Socialism is not.

Burnham suffers from too much Marx: for economic determinism control over the implements of production is the only route to power. But as E. A. Ross stated during the first World War such a view needs to be rounded out with a doctrine of martial determinism. Among wars there are revolutionary wars which may be capitalized and guided by self-elected elites but not always. No manager pushes a button to be immediately and efficiently equipped with a spontaneous mass-grasp at power. To overlook the stress of war on loyalty and morale and to count for naught the deprivations of masses may be helpful contributions to the cogency of a unilinear and formal construction of history, but it does not make for a readiness to expect the unexpected. To be grounded in history is to expect of the future that which does not follow mechanically but flows from large decisions not yet made. The belief in the stability of German totalitarianism and of the self-split and doom of the Soviet Union is a prognosis of Burnham's which does not become less a wishful thought by his dressing it in admiration of the technically efficient. The loyalties of potential revolutionary strata are not wholly determined by who has the best parachutes: workers are not necessarily loyal because their employers have shiny machines; soldiers are not necessarily loyal because their weapons are the latest.

On the other hand, Dr. Goebbels has correctly remarked that revolutionary organizations and their animi do not disappear while underground. They become dangerous in so far as they succeed by cell techniques in winning the loyalties of men within the bureaucratic structures. In France the army was defeated but the generals remained. The very extension of these bureaucratic structures brings with it the extension of chaos should they fall during their supreme test which is defeat in war. It is during such crises that not the specialist managers but revolutionary leaders may take over. The Russian and the German revolutions of 1917 and 1918 started in their navies, not with but against officers. We are not so convinced of the stability and finality of naziism in Europe. American rearmament may solve the problem of unemployment, and warfare is no Nazi patent. The military breakdown and the eventual breakdown of the Nazi war machine may well release forces which may be primarily apt in engineering revolutions and later in managing staffs of engineers. Their goal will not be to curb masses but to mobilize them. A prognosis of what is happening in the world today which reduces masses to the mere object of the mythologizing of engineers may well be surprised at the potentialities of the possible opponents of the present managers. If the present ruling owners fall, so may their managers.

Burnham's theory of historical change does not take adequately into account the *de facto* functioning of class structures. For him the constituents of society are masses and elites. History is now a struggle between managers and weak, because functionally "superfluous," capitalists; later it will be between different managers who will curb the masses with myths. In order to become dominant, all the managers must do is control the functional economy, really run the productive apparatus, silently knock over the remaining capitalists and curb the masses. That is all they have to do!

Modern revolutions are not watched by masses as they occur within the palace of elites. Revolutions are less dependent upon managerial personnels and their myths than upon those who bring to focus and legitimate the revolutionary activity of struggling classes. The Russian revolutionaries may have been slight in number, but the peasants who wanted the land were many, and it is they who make revolutionary leaders successful. The French Revolution was not dissimilar. In Central Europe in 1918 the urban proletariat was the class that pushed the socialist leaders into power. In modern history always behind the elites and parties there are revolutionary masses. Without such masses, parties may shout revolution, but (no matter how expert they may be) they cannot make it.

So far such revolutionary masses, landless peasants, striking workers, and defeated armies have ousted owners and their managers. The productive process is not always and necessarily continuous and ongoing but may well exhibit major breakdowns and discontinuities; from the standpoint of the technologist, it seems to be the dilettantes and amateurs who, coming into power, build up a new staff of expert managers. Such radical shifts in the distribution of power and in the composition of personnels are not illuminated by being covered with the all-over phrase, "the managerial revolution."

4

THE STRUCTURE OF BUREAUCRACY

Authority and Decision-Making

The calculability of behavior in bureaucracy rests on the premise that official policy will be faithfully carried out by subordinates. But as research has indicated, this policy is often modified or nullified in its passage through the administrative hierarchy.

In the opening selection, Barnard presents a theoretical analysis of the organizational and psychological factors that make for conformity and nonconformity in bureaucracy. This is further elaborated by Simon who considers also the multiple pressures on specific decisions in bureaucracy. The selection from Selznick analyzes the processes shaping the formation of bureaucratic policy with special reference to the organizational commitments which generate unanticipated modifications of policy. In his "notes on a theory of advice," Bryson analyzes the role of the expert adviser in relation to decision-making in different kinds of bureaucratic structure.

Certain of these theoretical considerations are exemplified in the remaining selections in this section. Bureaucratic constraints upon the execution of policy are examined by Kingsley, who suggests that official policy is effectively put into practice when the bureaucratic staff and the policy-setting executives identify themselves with the same social class and share a common outlook. This situation is markedly changed with the advent of a new administration with social goals differing from those of the entrenched officials, as the selection from Lipset shows in some detail. Finally, the structural pressures on decisions involving two bureaucracies are examined in Dubin's account of collective bargaining between corporations and trade unions.

A DEFINITION OF AUTHORITY

Chester I. Barnard

Authority is the character of a communication (order) in a formal organization by virtue of which it is accepted by a contributor to or "member" of the organization as governing the action he contributes; that is, as governing or determining what he does or is not to do so far as the organization is concerned . . .

If a directive communication is accepted by one to whom it is addressed, its authority for him is confirmed or established. It is admitted as the basis of action. Disobedience of such a communication is a denial of its authority for him. Therefore, under this definition the decision as to whether an order has authority or not lies with the persons to whom it is addressed, and does not reside in "persons of authority" or those who issue these orders.

This is so contrary to the view widely held by informed persons of many ranks and professions, and so contradictory to legalistic conceptions, and will seem to many so opposed to common experience, that it will be well at the outset to quote two opinions of persons in a position to merit respectful attention. It is not the intention to "argue from authorities"; but before attacking the subject it is desirable at least to recognize that prevalent notions are not universally held. Says Roberto Michels in the monograph "Authority" in the *Encyclopaedia of the Social Sciences*,[1] "Whether authority is of personal or institutional origin it is created and maintained by public opinion, which in its turn is conditioned by sentiment, affection, reverence or fatalism. Even when authority rests on mere physical coercion it is *accepted*[2] by those ruled, although the acceptance may be due to a fear of force."

Again, Major-General James G. Harbord, of long and distinguished military experience, and since his retirement from the Army a notable business executive, says on page 259 of his *The American Army in France:*[3]

A democratic President had forgotten that the greatest of all democracies is an Army. Discipline and morale influence the inarticulate vote that is instantly taken by the masses of men when the order comes to move forward—a variant of the crowd psychology that inclines it to follow a leader, but the Army does not move forward until the motion has "carried." "Unanimous consent" only follows cooperation between the *individual* men in the ranks.

Reprinted in part, by permission of the publisher, from *The Functions of the Executive* (Cambridge, Mass.: Harvard University Press, 1938), pp. 163-171.
    1. New York: Macmillan.
    2. Italics mine.
    3. Boston: Little, Brown and Co., 1936.

These opinions are to the effect that even though physical force is involved, and even under the extreme condition of battle, when the regime is nearly absolute, authority nevertheless rests upon the acceptance or consent of individuals. Evidently such conceptions, if justified, deeply affect an appropriate understanding of organization and especially of the character of the executive functions.

Our definition of authority, like General Harbord's democracy in an army, no doubt will appear to many whose eyes are fixed only on enduring organizations to be a platform of chaos. And so it is—exactly so in the preponderance of attempted organizations. They fail because they can maintain no authority, that is, they cannot secure sufficient contributions of personal efforts to be effective or cannot induce them on terms that are efficient. In the last analysis the authority fails because the individuals in sufficient numbers regard the burden involved in accepting necessary orders as changing the balance of advantage against their interest, and they withdraw or withhold the indispensable contributions.

We must not rest our definition, however, on general opinion. The necessity of the assent of the individual to establish authority *for him* is inescapable. A person can and will accept a communication as authoritative only when four conditions simultaneously obtain: (*a*) he can and does understand the communication; (*b*) *at the time of his decision* he believes that it is not inconsistent with the purpose of the organization; (*c*) *at the time of his decision*, he believes it to be compatible with his personal interest as a whole; and (*d*) he is able mentally and physically to comply with it.

(*a*) A communication that cannot be understood *can* have no authority. An order issued, for example, in a language not intelligible to the recipient is no order at all—no one would so regard it. Now, many orders are exceedingly difficult to understand. They are often necessarily stated in general terms, and the persons who issued them could not themselves apply them under many conditions. Until interpreted they have no meaning. The recipient either must disregard them or merely do anything in the hope that that is compliance.

Hence, a considerable part of administrative work consists in the interpretation and reinterpretation of orders in their application to concrete circumstances that were not or could not be taken into account initially.

(*b*) A communication believed by the recipient to be incompatible with the purpose of the organization, as he understands it, could not be accepted. Action would be frustrated by cross purposes. The most common practical example is that involved in conflicts of orders. They are not rare. An intelligent person will deny the authority of that one which contradicts the purpose of the effort as *he* understands it. In extreme cases many individuals would be virtually paralyzed by conflicting orders. They would be literally unable to comply—for example, an employee of a water system ordered to blow up an essential pump, or soldiers ordered to shoot their own comrades. I suppose all experienced executives know that when it is necessary to issue orders that will appear to the recipients to be contrary to the main purpose, especially as exemplified in prior habitual practice, it is usually necessary and always advisable, if practicable, to explain or demonstrate why the appearance of conflict is an illusion. Otherwise the orders are likely not to be executed, or to be executed inadequately.

(c) If a communication is believed to involve a burden that destroys the net advantage of connection with the organization, there no longer would remain a net inducement to the individual to contribute to it. The existence of a net inducement is the only reason for accepting *any* order as having authority. Hence, if such an order is received it must be disobeyed (evaded in the more usual cases) as utterly inconsistent with personal motives that are the basis of accepting any orders at all. Cases of voluntary resignation from all sorts of organizations are common for this sole reason. Malingering and intentional lack of dependability are the more usual methods.

(d) If a person is unable to comply with an order, obviously it must be disobeyed, or better, disregarded. To order a man who cannot swim to swim a river is a sufficient case. Such extreme cases are not frequent; but they occur. The more usual case is to order a man to do things only a little beyond his capacity; but a little impossible is still impossible.

Naturally the reader will ask: How is it possible to secure such important and enduring coöperation as we observe if in principle and in fact the determination of authority lies with the subordinate individual? It is possible because the decisions of individuals occur under the following conditions: (a) orders that are deliberately issued in enduring organizations usually comply with the four conditions mentioned above; (b) there exists a "zone of indifference" in each individual within which orders are acceptable without conscious questioning of their authority; (c) the interests of the persons who contribute to an organization as a group result in the exercise of an influence on the subject, or on the attitude of the individual, that maintains a certain stability of this zone of indifference.

(a) There is no principle of executive conduct better established in good organization than that orders will not be issued that cannot or will not be obeyed. Executives and most persons of experience who have thought about it know that to do so destroys authority, discipline, and morale.[4] For

4. Barring relatively few individual cases, when the attitude of the individual indicates in advance likelihood of disobedience (either before or after connection with the organization), the connection is terminated or refused before the formal question arises.

It seems advisable to add a caution here against interpreting the exposition in terms of "democracy," whether in governmental, religious, or industrial organizations. The dogmatic assertion that "democracy" or "democratic methods" are (or are not) in accordance with the principles here discussed is not tenable. As will be more evident after the consideration of objective authority, the issues involved are much too complex

reasons to be stated shortly, this principle cannot ordinarily be formally admitted, or at least cannot be professed. When it appears necessary to issue orders which are initially or apparently unacceptable, either careful preliminary education, or persuasive efforts, or the prior offering of effective inducements will be made, so that the issue will not be raised, the denial of authority will not occur, and orders will be obeyed. It is generally recognized that those who least understand this fact—newly appointed minor or "first line" executives—are often guilty of "disorganizing" their groups for this reason, as do experienced executives who lose self-control or become unbalanced by a delusion of power or for some other reason. Inexperienced persons take literally the current notions of authority and are then said "not to know how to use authority" or "to abuse authority." Their superiors often profess the same beliefs about authority in the abstract, but their successful practice is easily observed to be inconsistent with their professions.

(b) The phrase "zone of indifference" may be explained as follows: If all the orders for actions reasonably practicable be arranged in the order of their acceptability to the person affected, it may be conceived that there are a number which are clearly unacceptable, that is, which certainly will not be obeyed; there is another group somewhat more or less on the neutral line, that is, either barely acceptable or barely unacceptable; and a third group unquestionably acceptable. This last group lies within the "zone of indifference." The person affected will accept orders lying within this zone and is relatively indifferent as to what the order is so far as the question of authority is concerned. Such an order lies within the range that in a general way was anticipated at time of undertaking the connection with the organization. For example, if a soldier enlists, whether voluntarily or not, in an army in which the men are ordinarily moved about within a certain broad region, it is a matter of indifference whether the order be to go to A or B,

and subtle to be taken into account in *any* formal scheme. Under many conditions in the political, religious, and industrial fields democratic processes create artificial questions of more or less logical character, in place of the real questions, which are matters of feeling and appropriateness and of informal organization. By oversimplification of issues this may destroy objective authority. No doubt in many situations formal democratic processes may be an important element in the maintenance of authority, *i.e.*, of organization cohesion, but may in other situations be disruptive, and probably never could be, in themselves, sufficient. On the other hand the solidarity of some coöperative systems (General Harbord's army, for example) under many conditions may be unexcelled, though requiring formally autocratic processes.

Moreover, it should never be forgotten that authority in the aggregate arises from *all* the contributors to a coöperative system, and that the weighting to be attributed to the attitude of individuals varies. It is often forgotten that in industrial (or political) organizations measures which are acceptable at the bottom may be quite unacceptable to the substantial proportion of contributors who are executives, and who will no more perform their essential functions than will others, if the conditions are, to them, impossible. The point to be emphasized is that the maintenance of the contributions necessary to the endurance of an organization requires the authority of *all* essential contributors.

C or D, and so on; and goings to A, B, C, D, etc., are in the zone of indifference.

The zone of indifference will be wider or narrower depending upon the degree to which the inducements exceed the burdens and sacrifices which determine the individual's adhesion to the organization. It follows that the range of orders that will be accepted will be very limited among those who are barely induced to contribute to the system.

(c) Since the efficiency of organization is affected by the degree to which individuals assent to orders, denying the authority of an organization communication is a threat to the interests of all individuals who derive a net advantage from their connection with the organization, unless the orders are unacceptable to them also. Accordingly, at any given time there is among most of the contributors an active personal interest in the maintenance of the authority of all orders which to them are within the zone of indifference. The maintenance of this interest is largely a function of informal organization. Its expression goes under the names of "public opinion," "organization opinion," "feeling in the ranks," "group attitude," etc. Thus the common sense of the community informally arrived at affects the attitude of individuals, and makes them, as individuals, loath to question authority that is within or near the zone of indifference. The formal statement of this common sense is the fiction that authority comes down from above, from the general to the particular. This fiction merely establishes a presumption among individuals in favor of the acceptability of orders from superiors, enabling them to avoid making issues of such orders without incurring a sense of personal subserviency or a loss of personal or individual status with their fellows.

Thus the contributors are willing to maintain the authority of communications because, where care is taken to see that only acceptable communications in general are issued, most of them fall within the zone of personal indifference; and because communal sense influences the motives of most contributors most of the time. The practical instrument of this sense is the fiction of superior authority, which makes it possible normally to treat a personal question impersonally.

The fiction [5] of superior authority is necessary for two main reasons:

(1) It is the process by which the individual delegates upward, or to the organization, responsibility for what is an organization decision—an action which is depersonalized by the fact of its coördinate character. This means that if an instruction is disregarded, an executive's risk of being wrong must be accepted, a risk that the individual cannot and usually will not take unless in fact his position is at least as good as that of another with respect to cor-

---

5. The word "fiction" is used because from the standpoint of logical construction it merely explains overt acts. Either as a superior officer or as a subordinate, however, I know nothing that I actually regard as more "real" than "authority."

rect appraisal of the relevant situation. Most persons are disposed to grant authority because they dislike the personal responsibility which they otherwise accept, especially when they are not in a good position to accept it. The practical difficulties in the operation of organization seldom lie in the excessive desire of individuals to assume responsibility for the organization action of themselves or others, but rather lie in the reluctance to take responsibility for their own actions in organization.

(2) The fiction gives impersonal notice that what is at stake is the good of the organization. If objective authority is flouted for arbitrary or merely temperamental reasons, if, in other words, there is deliberate attempt to twist an organization requirement to personal advantage, rather than properly to safeguard a substantial personal interest, then there is a deliberate attack on the organization itself. To remain outside an organization is not necessarily to be more than not friendly or not interested. To fail in an obligation intentionally is an act of hostility. This no organization can permit; and it must respond with punitive action if it can, even to the point of incarcerating or executing the culprit. This is rather generally the case where a person has agreed in advance in general what he will do. Leaving an organization in the lurch is not often tolerable.

DECISION-MAKING AND ADMINISTRATIVE ORGANIZATION

Herbert A. Simon

It is clear that the actual physical task of carrying out an organization's objectives falls to the persons at the lowest level of the administrative hierarchy. The automobile, as a physical object, is built not by the engineer or the executive, but by the mechanic on the assembly line. The fire is extinguished, not by the fire chief or the captain, but by the team of firemen who play a hose on the blaze.

It is equally clear that the persons above this lowest or operative level in the administrative hierarchy are not mere surplus baggage, and that they too must have an essential role to play in the accomplishment of the agency's objectives. Even though, as far as physical cause and effect are concerned, it is the machine-gunner, and not the major, who fights battles, the major will

Reprinted in part from *Public Administration Review*, Vol. 4 (1944), pp. 16-25, by permission of the author and the publisher, The American Society for Public Administration.

likely have a greater influence upon the outcome of a battle than will any single machine-gunner . . .

THE RANGE OF DISCRETION. The term "influence" covers a wide range, both in the degree to which one person affects the behavior of another and in the method whereby that influence is exercised. Without an analysis of these differences of degree and kind no realistic picture can be drawn of an administrative organization. It is because of its failure to account for variations in influence that the usual organization chart, with its over-simplified representation of the "lines of authority," fails to record the complexity of actual organizations. The organization chart does not reveal the fact that the actual exercise of authority may, and often does, cut across formal organizational lines, and that forms of influence other than authority—information, training, identification—may be far more important than the former in securing coordination throughout the organization.

Influence is exercised in its most complete form when a decision promulgated by one person governs every aspect of the behavior of another. On the parade ground, the marching soldier is permitted no discretion whatsoever. His every step, his bearing, the length of his pace are all governed by authority. Frederick the Great is reported to have found the parade-ground deportment of his Guards perfect—with one flaw. "They breathe," he complained. Few examples could be cited, however, from any other realm of practical affairs where influence is exercised in such complete and unlimited form.

Most often, organizational influences place only partial limits upon the exercise of discretion. A subordinate may be told what to do, but given considerable leeway as to how he will carry out the task. The "what" is, of course, a matter of degree also and may be specified within narrower or broader limits. The commands of a captain at the scene of a fire place much narrower limits on the discretion of the firemen than those placed on a fire chief by the city charter which states in general terms the function of the fire department.

Since influence can be exercised with all degrees of specificity, in order to determine the scope of influence or authority which is exercised in any concrete case, it is necessary to dissect the decisions of the subordinate into their component parts and then determine which of these parts are controlled by the superior and which are left to the subordinate's discretion.

Influence over Value and Fact. Any rational decision may be viewed as a conclusion reached from certain premises. These premises are of two different kinds: value premises and factual premises—roughly equivalent to ends and means, respectively. Given a complete set of value and factual premises, there remains only one unique decision which is consistent with rationality. That is, with a given system of values and a specified set of possible alternatives, there is one alternative of the set which is preferable to the others.

The behavior of a rational person can be controlled, therefore, if the value and factual premises upon which he bases his decisions are specified for him. This control can be complete or partial—all the premises can be specified, or some can be left to his discretion. The scope of influence, and conversely the scope of discretion, are determined by the number and importance of the premises which are specified and the number and importance of those which are left unspecified.

There is one important difference between permitting a subordinate discretion over value premises and permitting him discretion over factual premises. The latter can always be evaluated as correct or incorrect in an objective, empirical sense (of course, we do not always have the evidence we would need to decide whether a premise is correct or incorrect, but at least the terms "correct" and "incorrect" are applicable to a factual premise). To a value premise, on the other hand, the terms "correct" and "incorrect" do not apply. To say that a means is correct is to say that it is appropriate to its end; but to say that an end is correct is meaningless unless we redefine the end as a means to some more final end—in which case its correctness as means ceases to be a value question and becomes a factual question.

Hence, if only factual premises are left to the subordinate's discretion, there is, under the given circumstances, only one decision which he can correctly reach. On the other hand, if value premises are left to the subordinate's discretion, the "correctness" of his decision will depend upon the value premises he selects, and there is no universally accepted criterion of right or wrong which can be applied to his selection.[1]

This distinction between factual and value premises has an obvious bearing on the question of how discretion is to be reconciled with responsibility and accountability, and what the line of division is to be between "policy" and "administration." To pursue this subject further would take us beyond the bounds of the present analysis, and we leave it with a reference to two recent contributions to the problem.[2]

Implications for Unity of Command. When it is admitted that influence need extend to only a few of the premises of decision, it follows that more than one order can govern a given decision, provided that no two orders extend to the same premise. An analysis of almost any decision of a member of a formal organization would reveal that the decision was responsive to a very complex structure of influences.

1. In a sense, the discretion over factual questions which is left the operative is illusory, for he will be held accountable for reaching correct conclusions even with respect to those premises which are not specified in his orders. But it is a question of salient importance for the organization whether the subordinate is guided by orders *in making his decision* or whether he makes it on his own responsibility, subject to subsequent review. Hence, by "discretion" we mean only that standing orders and "on-the-spot" orders do not completely determine the decision.

2. Wayne A. R. Leys, "Ethics and Administrative Discretion," 3 *Public Administration Review* 10-23 (Winter, 1943); and Herman Finer, "Administrative Responsibility in Democratic Government," 1 *Public Administration Review* 335-50 (Summer, 1941).

Military organization affords an excellent illustration of this. In ancient warfare, the battlefield was not unlike the parade ground. An entire army was often commanded by a single man, and his authority extended in a very complete and direct form to the lowest man in the ranks. This was possible because the entire battlefield was within range of a man's voice and vision and because tactics were for the most part executed by the entire army in unison.

The modern battlefield presents a very different picture. Authority is exercised through a complex hierarchy of command. Each level of the hierarchy leaves an extensive area of discretion to the level below, and even the private soldier, under combat conditions, exercises a considerable measure of discretion.

Under these circumstances, how does the authority of the commander extend to the soldiers in the ranks? How does he limit and guide their behavior? He does this by specifying the general mission and objective of each unit on the next level below and by determining such elements of time and place as will assure a proper coordination among the units. The colonel assigns to each battalion in his regiment its task; the lieutenant colonel to each company; the captain to each platoon. Beyond this the officer ordinarily does not go. The internal deployment of each unit is left to the officer in command of that unit. The United States Army Field Service Regulations specify that "an order should not trespass upon the province of a subordinate. It should contain everything that the subordinate must know to carry out his mission, but nothing more." [3]

So far as field orders go, then, the discretion of a subordinate officer is limited only by the specification of the objective of his unit and its general schedule. He proceeds to narrow further the discretion of his own subordinates so far as is necessary to specify what part each sub-unit is to play in accomplishing the task of the whole.

Does this mean that the decision of the officer is limited only by his objective or mission? Not at all. To be sure, the field order does not go beyond this point, for it specifies only the "what" of his action. But the officer is also governed by the tactical doctrine and general orders of the army which specify in some detail the "how." When the captain receives field orders to deploy his company for an attack, he is expected to carry out the deployment in accordance with the accepted tactical principles in the army. In leading his unit, he will be held accountable for the "how" as well as the "what."

The same kind of analysis could be carried out for the man who actually does the army's "work"—the private soldier; and we would see that the mass of influences that bear upon his decisions include both direct commands and tactical training and indoctrination.

We find, then, that to understand the process of decision in an organi-

3. U. S. *Army Field Service Regulations* (1941), p. 31.

zation it is necessary to go far beyond the on-the-spot orders which are given by superior to subordinate. It is necessary to discover how the subordinate is influenced by standing orders, by training, and by review of his actions. It is necessary to study the channels of communication in the organization in order to determine what information reaches him which may be relevant to his decisions. The broader the sphere of discretion left to the subordinate by the orders given him, the more important become those types of influence which do not depend upon the exercise of formal authority.

Once this complex network of decisional influences comes into view it becomes difficult to defend either the sufficiency or the necessity of the doctrine of "unity of command." Its sufficiency must be questioned on the same grounds that the sufficiency of the organization chart is questioned: at best it tells only a half-truth, for formal authority is only one aspect—and that probably not the most important—of organizational structure.

The necessity of "unity of command" must be questioned because there do not appear to be any *a priori* grounds why a decision should not be subject to several organizational influences. Indeed, a number of serious students of administration have advocated this very thing—we have already mentioned Taylor's theory of functional supervision—and their arguments cannot be waved aside with the biblical quotation that "no man can serve two masters." [4] It remains to be demonstrated that "unity of command" rather than "plurality of command" either is, or should be, the prevalent form of administrative structure.

ORGANIZATIONAL INFLUENCES ON THE SUBORDINATE. Thus far we have been talking about the extent of the organization's influence over its employees. Next we must consider the ways in which this influence is exerted. The subordinate is influenced not only by command but also by his organizational loyalties, by his strivings toward "efficient" courses of action, by the information and advice which is transmitted to him through the organization's lines of communication, and by his training. Each of these items deserves brief discussion.

Authority. The concept of authority has been analyzed at length by students of administration. We shall employ here a definition substantially equivalent to that put forth by C. I. Barnard.[5] A subordinate is said to accept authority whenever he permits his behavior to be guided by a decision reached by another, without independently examining the merits of that decision. When exercising authority, the superior does not seek to convince

4. For a recent advocacy of plural supervision, see Macmahon, Millet, and Ogden, *The Administration of Federal Work Relief* (Chicago: Public Administration Service, 1941), pp. 265-68.

5. Chester I. Barnard, *The Functions of the Executive* (Cambridge: Harvard University Press, 1940), pp. 163 ff., reprinted in part in this section.

the subordinate, but only to obtain his acquiescence. In actual practice, of course, authority is usually liberally admixed with suggestion and persuasion.

An important function of authority is to permit a decision to be made and carried out even when agreement cannot be reached, but perhaps this arbitrary aspect of authority has been overemphasized. In any event, if it is attempted to carry authority beyond a certain point, which may be described as the subordinate's "zone of acquiescence," disobedience will follow.[6] The magnitude of the zone of acquiescence depends upon the sanctions which authority has available to enforce its commands. The term "sanctions" must be interpreted broadly in this connection, for positive and neutral stimuli—such as community of purpose, habit, and leadership—are at least as important in securing acceptance of authority as are the threat of physical or economic punishment.

It follows that authority, in the sense here defined, can operate "upward" and "sidewise" as well as "downward" in the organization. If an executive delegates to his secretary a decision about file cabinets and accepts her recommendation without re-examination of its merits, he is accepting her authority. The "lines of authority" represented on organization charts do have a special significance, however, for they are commonly resorted to in order to terminate debate when it proves impossible to reach a consensus on a particular decision. Since this appellate use of authority generally requires sanctions to be effective, the structure of formal authority in an organization usually is related to the appointment, disciplining, and dismissal of personnel. These formal lines of authority are commonly supplemented by informal authority relations in the day-to-day work of the organization, while the formal hierarchy is largely reserved for the settlement of disputes.

Organizational Loyalties. It is a prevalent characteristic of human behavior that members of an organized group tend to identify with that group. In making decisions their organizational loyalty leads them to evaluate alternative courses of action in terms of the consequences of their action for the group. . . .

The psychological bases of identification are obscure, but seem to involve at least three elements. First, personal success often depends upon organizational success—the administrator who can build up his unit expects (with good reason) promotion and salary increases. Second, loyalty seems based partly on a transfer to the field of public management of the spirit of competition which is characteristic of private enterprise. Third, the human mind is limited in the number of diverse considerations which can occupy the area of attention at one time, and there is a consequent tendency to overemphasize the importance of those elements which happen to be

6. Barnard calls this the "zone of indifference" (*op. cit.*, p. 169), but I prefer the term "acquiescence."

within that area. To the fireman, fires are the most serious human problem; to the health officer, disease, and so forth.

This phenomenon of identification, or institutional loyalty, performs one very important function in administration. If an administrator, each time he is faced with a decision, must perforce evaluate that decision in terms of the whole range of human values, rationality in administration is impossible. If he need consider the decision only in the light of limited organizational aims, his task is more nearly within the range of human powers. The fireman can concentrate on the problem of fires, the health officer on problems of disease, without irrelevant considerations entering in.

Furthermore, this concentration on a limited range of values is almost essential if the administrator is to be held accountable for his decisions. When the organization's objectives are specified by some higher authority, the major value-premise of the administrator's decisions is thereby given him, leaving to him only the implementation of these objectives. If the fire chief were permitted to roam over the whole field of human values—to decide that parks were more important than fire trucks, and consequently to re-make his fire department into a recreation department—chaos would displace organization, and responsibility would disappear.

Organizational loyalties lead also, however, to certain difficulties which should not be underestimated. The principal undesirable effect of identification is that it prevents the institutionalized individual from making correct decisions in cases where the restricted area of values with which he identifies must be weighed against other values outside that area. This is a principal cause of the interbureau competition and wrangling which characterizes any large administrative organization. The organization members, identifying with the bureau instead of with the over-all organization, believe the bureau's welfare more important than the general welfare when the two conflict. This problem is frequently evident in the case of "housekeeping" agencies, where the facilitative and auxiliary nature of the agency is lost sight of in the effort to force the line agencies to follow standard procedures . . .

The Criterion of Efficiency. We have seen that the exercise of authority and the development of organizational identifications are two principal means whereby the individual's value premises are influenced by the organization. What about the issues of fact which underly his decisions? These are largely determined by a principle which underlies all rational behavior: the criterion of efficiency. In its broadest sense, to be efficient simply means to take the shortest path, the cheapest means, toward the attainment of the desired goals. The efficiency criterion is completely neutral as to what goals are to be attained.

The concept of efficiency has been discussed at length by economists and writers on administration, and there is little that can be added to that discussion within the scope of the present paper. Suffice it to say that the commandment: "Be efficient!" is a major organizational influence over the decisions of the members of any administrative agency; and a determination whether this commandment has been obeyed is a major function of the review process.[7]

Advice and Information. Many of the influences the organization exercises over its members are of a less formal nature than those we have been discussing. These influences are perhaps most realistically viewed as a form of internal public relations, for there is nothing to guarantee that advice produced at one point in an organization will have any effect at another point in the organization unless the lines of communication are adequate to its transmission and unless it is transmitted in such form as to be persuasive. It is a prevalent misconception in headquarters offices that the internal advisory function consists in preparing precisely-worded explanatory bulletins and making certain that the proper number of these are prepared and that they are placed in the proper compartment of the "router." No plague has produced a rate of mortality higher than the rate which customarily afflicts central-office communications between the time they leave the issuing office and the moment when they are assumed to be effected in the revised practice of the operative employees.

These difficulties of communication apply, of course, to commands as well as to advice and information. As a matter of fact, the administrator who is serving in an advisory capacity is apt to be at some advantage in solving problems of communication, because he is likely to be conscious of the necessity of transmitting and "selling" his ideas, while the administrator who possesses authority may be oblivious of his public-relations function.

Information and advice flow in all directions through the organization—not merely from the top downward. Many of the facts which are relevant to decision are of a rapidly changing nature, ascertainable only at the moment of decision, and often ascertainable only by operative employees. For instance, in military operations knowledge of the disposition of the enemy's forces is of crucial importance, and military organization has developed elaborate procedures for transmitting to a person who is to make a decision all relevant facts which he is not in a position to ascertain personally.

Information and advice may be used as alternatives to the actual exercise of authority, and vice versa. Where promptness and discipline are not primary considerations, the former have several very impressive advantages. Chief among these is that they preserve morale and initiative on the part of the subordinate—qualities which may disappear if excessively harassed by authority. Again, when the influences are advisory in nature, the formal

7. For further discussion of the efficiency concept, see Clarence E. Ridley and Herbert A. Simon, *Measuring Municipal Activities* (Chicago: International City Managers' Association, 1943).

organization structure loses its unique position as the sole channel of influence. The relation between the adviser and the person advised is essentially no different when they are members of the same organization than when the adviser is outside the organization. The extent of the influence of the adviser will depend on the desire of the decision-maker for advice and on the persuasiveness with which it is offered.

Training. Like institutional loyalties, and unlike the other modes of influence we have been discussing, training influences decisions "from the inside out." That is, training prepares the organization member to reach satisfactory decisions himself, without the need for the constant exercise of authority or advice. In this sense, training procedures are alternatives to the exercise of authority or advice as means of control over the subordinate's decisions . . .

Training is applicable to the process of decision whenever the same elements are involved in a large number of decisions. Training may supply the trainee with the facts necessary in dealing with these decisions, it may provide him a frame of reference for his thinking, it may teach him "approved" solutions, or it may indoctrinate him with the values in terms of which his decisions are to be made.

Training, as a mode of influence upon decisions, has its greatest value in those situations where the exercise of formal authority through commands proves difficult. The difficulty may lie in the need for prompt action, in the spatial dispersion of the organization, or in the complexity of the subject matter of decision which defies summarization in rules and regulations. Training permits a higher degree of decentralization of the decision-making process by bringing the necessary competence into the very lowest levels of the organizational hierarchy.

Implications for Organization. It can be seen that there are at least five distinct ways in which the decisions of operative employees may be influenced: authority, identification, the efficiency criterion, advice, and training. It is the fundamental problem of organization to determine the extent and the manner in which each of these forms of influence is to be employed. To a very great extent, these various forms are interchangeable—a fact which is far more often appreciated in small than in large organizations . . .

Administrators have increasingly recognized in recent years that authority, unless buttressed by other forms of influence, is relatively impotent to control decision in any but a negative way. The elements entering into all but the most routine decisions are so numerous and so complex that it is impossible to control positively more than a few. Unless the subordinate is himself able to supply most of the premises of decision, and to synthesize them adequately, the task of supervision becomes hopelessly burdensome. To cite an extreme illustration: no amount of supervision or direction, and no quantity of orders, directives, or commands, would be sufficient to enable a completely untrained person to prepare a legal brief for a law suit. In such a case, the problem is definitely not one of direction, but one of education or training.

Viewed from this standpoint, the problem of organization becomes inextricably interwoven with the problem of recruitment. For the system of influence which can effectively be used in the organization will depend directly upon the training and competence of employees at the various levels of the hierarchy.

A THEORY OF ORGANIZATIONAL COMMITMENTS

Philip Selznick

This volume has been subtitled "A Study in the Sociology of Formal Organization." This means that the inquiry which it reports was shaped by sociological directives, more especially by a frame of reference for the theory of organization.[1] These directives are operationally relevant without, however, functioning as surrogates for inductive theory itself. That is, while they provide criteria of significance, they do not tell us what is significant; while they provide tools for discrimination, they do not demand any special conclusions about the materials under investigation.[2] The fundamental elements of this frame of reference are these:

1. All formal organizations are molded by forces tangential to their rationally ordered structures and stated goals. Every formal organization—trade union, political party, army, corporation, etc.—attempts to mobilize human and technical resources as means for the achievement of its ends. However, the individuals within the system tend to resist being treated as means. They interact as wholes, bringing to bear their own special problems and purposes; moreover, the organization is imbedded in an institutional

Reprinted in part from *TVA and the Grass Roots*, pp. 250-259; University of California Publications in Culture and Society, Vol. III, by permission of the author and the publisher. (Copyright, 1949, by the University of California Press.)

1. For a fuller statement than the summary which follows see Philip Selznick, "Foundations of the Theory of Organization," *American Sociological Review*, XIII (February, 1948).

2. Thus, while approaching his materials within a guiding frame of reference, the author was not committed by this framework to any special hypothesis about the actual events. Indeed, he began his work with the hypothesis that informally the grass-roots policy would mean domination by TVA, because of its resources, energy, and program. After the first two months in the field, however, this hypothesis was abandoned as a major illuminating notion.

matrix and is therefore subject to pressures upon it from its environment, to which some general adjustment must be made. As a result, the organization may be significantly viewed as an adaptive social structure, facing problems which arise simply because it exists as an organization in an institutional environment, independently of the special (economic, military, political) goals which called it into being.

2. It follows that there will develop an informal structure within the organization which will reflect the spontaneous efforts of individuals and subgroups to control the conditions of their existence. There will also develop informal lines of communication and control to and from other organizations within the environment. It is to these informal relations and structures that the attention of the sociologist will be primarily directed. He will look upon the formal structure, e.g., the official chain of command, as the special environment within and in relation to which the informal structure is built. He will search out the evolution of formal relations out of the informal ones.[3]

3. The informal structure will be at once indispensable to and consequential for the formal system of delegation and control itself. Wherever command over the responses of individuals is desired, some approach in terms of the spontaneous organization of loyalty and interest will be necessary. In practice this means that the informal structure will be useful to the leadership and effective as a means of communication and persuasion. At the same time, it can be anticipated that some price will be paid in the shape of a distribution of power or adjustment of policy.

4. Adaptive social structures are to be analyzed in structural-functional terms.[4] This means that contemporary and variable behavior is related to a presumptively stable system of needs [5] and mechanisms. Every such structure has a set of basic needs and develops systematic means of self-defense. Observable organizational behavior is deemed explained within this frame of reference when it may be interpreted (and the interpretation confirmed) as a response to specified needs. Where significant, the adaptation is dynamic

3. For discussion of informal organization, see F. J. Roethlisberger and W. J. Dickson, *Management and the Worker* (Cambridge: Harvard University Press, 1941), pp. 524 ff.; also Chester I. Barnard, *The Functions of the Executive* (Cambridge: Harvard University Press, 1938), chap. ix; Wilbert E. Moore, *Industrial Relations and the Social Order* (New York: The Macmillan Co., 1946), chap. xv.

4. See Talcott Parsons, "The Present Position and Prospects of Systematic Theory in Sociology," in George Gurvitch and Wilbert E. Moore (eds.), *Twentieth Century Sociology* (New York: Philosophical Library, 1945).

5. As Robert K. Merton has pointed out to the author, the concept of "basic needs" in organizational analysis may be open to objections similar to those against the concept of instinct. To be sure, the needs require independent demonstration; they should be theoretically grounded independently of imputations from observed responses. However, we may use the notion of "organizational need" if we understand that it refers to stable systems of variables which, with respect to many changes in organizational structure and behavior, are independent.

in the sense that the utilization of self-defensive mechanisms results in structural transformations of the organization itself. The needs in question are organizational, not individual, and include: the security of the organization as a whole in relation to social forces in its environment; the stability of the lines of authority and communication; the stability of informal relations within the organization; the continuity of policy and of the sources of its determination; a homogeneity of outlook with respect to the meaning and role of the organization.

5. Analysis is directed to the internal relevance of organizational behavior. The execution of policy is viewed in terms of its effect upon the organization itself and its relations with others. This will tend to make the analysis inadequate as a report of program achievement, since that will be de-emphasized in the interests of the purely organizational consequences of choice among alternatives in discretionary action.

6. Attention being focused on the structural conditions which influence behavior, we are directed to emphasize constraints, the limitation of alternatives imposed by the system upon its participants. This will tend to give pessimistic overtones to the analysis, since such factors as good will and intelligence will be de-emphasized.

7. As a consequence of the central status of constraint, tensions and dilemmas will be highlighted. Perhaps the most general source of tension and paradox in this context may be expressed as the recalcitrance of the tools of action. Social action is always mediated by human structures, which generate new centers of need and power and interpose themselves between the actor and his goal. Commitments to others are indispensable in action: at the same time, the process of commitment results in tensions which have always to be overcome.

These principles define a frame of reference, a set of guiding ideas which at once justify and explain the kind of selection which the sociologist will make in approaching organizational data. As we review some of the key concepts utilized in this study, the operational relevance of this frame of reference will be apparent.

UNANTICIPATED CONSEQUENCES IN ORGANIZED ACTION. The foregoing review of leading ideas directs our attention to the meaning of events. This leads us away from the problem of origins.[6] For the meaning of an act may

6. In terms of origins, the TVA's policy—though not the grass-roots doctrine *qua doctrine*—of channeling its agricultural program through the land-grant colleges of the Valley states may be adequately referred to such factors as the nature of the formal agricultural program, the resources available for its implementation, and the administrative rationale which seemed conclusive to leading participants. Moreover, these factors may sustain the continued existence of the policy, and it may therefore seem superfluous when extraneous factors are brought in and somewhat tangential explanations are offered. But when we direct our attention to the meaning of the policy in terms of certain indirect but internally relevant consequences—as for the role of TVA in the agricultural controversy,—we have begun to recast our observation of the policy (taken

be spelled out in its consequences, and these are not the same as the factors which called it into being. The meaning of any given administrative policy will thus require an excursion into the realm of its effects. These effects ramify widely, and those we select for study may not always seem relevant to the formal goals in terms of which the policy was established. Hence the search for meanings may seem to go rather far afield, from the viewpoint of those concerned only with the formal program. Any given event, such as the establishment of a large army cantonment, may have a multitude of effects in different directions: upon the economy of the area, upon the morals of its inhabitants, upon the pace of life, and so on. The free-lance theorist may seek out the significance of the event in almost any set of consequences. But in accordance with the principle stated above, we may distinguish the random search for meanings—which can be, at one extreme, an aesthetic interest—from the inquiry of the organizational analyst. The latter likewise selects consequences, but his frame of reference constrains his view: it is his task to trace such consequences as redound upon the organization in question; that is, such effects as have an internal relevance. Thus, only those consequences of the establishment of the army cantonment in a given area which result in adjustments of policy or structure in the administration of the cantonment will be relevant.

There is an obvious and familiar sense in which consequences are related to action: the articulation of means and ends demands that we weigh the consequences of alternative courses of action. Here consequences are anticipated. But it is a primary function of sociological inquiry to uncover systematically the sources of unanticipated consequence in purposive action.[7] This follows from the initial proposition in our frame of reference: "All formal organizations are molded by forces tangential to their rationally ordered structures and stated goals." Hence the notion of unanticipated consequence is a key analytical tool: where unintended effects occur, there is a presumption, though no assurance,[8] that sociologically identifiable forces are at work.

as a set of events) itself. We are then concerned not with the question, "how did the grass-roots policy come into being?" but with the question, "what are the implications of the grass-roots policy for the organizational position and character of TVA?"

7. Consequences unanticipated from the viewpoint of the formal structure are not necessarily undesired. On the contrary, the result may be a satisfactory adjustment to internal and external circumstances, upon which the leadership may find it convenient to declare that the results were actually intended, though close analysis might show that this is actually a rationalization. In this type of unintended consequence, some need is fulfilled. The same unintended consequence may fulfill a need for a part of the organization and at the same time cause difficulties for the whole, and conversely. Many unintended consequences are, of course, sociologically irrelevant. For an early statement of this general problem, see Robert K. Merton, "The Unanticipated Consequences of Purposive Social Action," *American Sociological Review*, Vol. I (December, 1936).

8. Where unintended consequences occur due to error, or to individual idiosyncrasy, they are sociologically irrelevant. However, there is often, though not always, a

There are two logically fundamental sources of unanticipated consequence in social action, that is, two conditions which define the inherent predisposition for unanticipated consequences to occur:

1. *The limiting function of the end-in-view.*—A logically important but sociologically insignificant source of unanticipated consequence exists because the aim of action limits the perception of its ramified consequences.[9] This is legitimate and necessary, for not all consequences are relevant to the aim. But here there arises a persistent dilemma. This very necessity to "keep your eye on the ball"—which demands the construction of a rational system explicitly relating means and ends—will restrain the actor from taking account of those consequences which indirectly shape the means and ends of policy. Because of the necessarily abstract and selective character of the formal criteria of judgment, there will always be a minimum residue of unanticipated consequence.[10]

2. *Commitment as a basic mechanism in the generation of unanticipated consequences.*—The sociologically significant source of unanticipated consequences inherent in the organizational process may be summed up in the concept of "commitment." This term has been used throughout this study to focus attention upon the structural conditions which shape organizational behavior. This is in line with the sociological directive, stated above, that constraints imposed by the system will be emphasized. A commitment in social action is an enforced line of action; it refers to decisions dictated by the force of circumstance with the result that the free or scientific adjustment of means and ends is effectively limited. The commitment may be to goals, as where the existence of an organization in relation to a client public depends on the fulfillment of certain objectives;[11] or, less obviously, to means, derived from the recalcitrant nature of the tools at hand. The com-

systematically nonrational factor at work whose presence is manifested by mistakes and personality problems.

9. This follows, of course, from the hypothetical, and therefore discriminating and ordering, status of the end-in-view. See John Dewey, *Logic: The Theory of Inquiry* (New York: Henry Holt, 1938), pp. 496–497.

10. The use of the terms "end-in-view" and "anticipated" may easily lead to the fallacy of formulating this problem as one of the subjective awareness of the participants. This is a serious error. What is really involved is that which is anticipated or unanticipated by the system of discrimination and judgment which is applied to the means at hand. This may, and very often does, involve subjective anticipation or its want, but need not do so. Moreover, the system may be adjusted so as to be able to take account of factors previously unpredicted and uncontrolled. This addition of systematically formulated criteria of relevance occurs continuously, as in the recognition of morale factors in industry. . . . However, the tendency to ignore factors not considered by the formal system—not so much subjectively as in regard to the competence of the system to control them—is inherent in the necessities of action and can never be eliminated.

11. As in the TVA's commitment to become a successful electric power business; this type of commitment was much milder in the distribution of fertilizer, permitting adaptation in this field which would contribute to the fulfillment of the prior commitment to electricity.

mitments generated by the use of self-activating and recalcitrant tools are expressed in the proliferation of unintended consequences.[12]

The types of commitment in organizational behavior identify the conditions under which a high frequency of unanticipated consequences may be expected to occur:

i) *Commitments enforced by uniquely organizational imperatives.* An organizational system, whatever the need or intent which called it into being, generates imperatives derived from the need to maintain the system. We can say that once having taken the organizational road we are committed to action which will fulfill the requirements of order, discipline, unity, defense, and consent. These imperatives may demand measures of adaptation unforeseen by the initiators of the action, and may, indeed, result in a deflection of their original goals. Thus the tendency to work toward organizational unity will commit the organization as a whole to a policy originally relevant to only a part of the program. This becomes especially true where a unifying doctrine is given definite content by one subgroup: in order to preserve its special interpretation the subgroup presses for the extension of that interpretation to the entire organization so that the special content may be institutionalized.[13]

ii) *Commitments enforced by the social character of the personnel.* The human tools of action come to an organization shaped in special but systematic ways. Levels of aspiration and training, social ideals, class interest—these and similar factors will have molded the character of the personnel. This will make staff members resistant to demands which are inconsistent with their accustomed views and habits; the freedom of choice of the employer will be restricted, and he will find it necessary in some measure to conform to the received views and habits of the personnel. Thus, in recruiting, failure to take into account initial commitments induced by special social origins will create a situation favorable to the generation of unanticipated consequences. The TVA's agricultural leadership brought with it ideological and organizational commitments which influenced over-all policy. This was a basically uncontrolled element in the organization. It is noteworthy that where the character of any organization is self-consciously controlled, re-

12. Our use of the notion of unanticipated consequence assumes that the functional significance of such consequences is traceable within a specific field of influence and interaction. Thus price decisions made by a small enterprise affect the market (cumulatively with others), with ultimate unanticipated and uncontrolled consequence for future pricing decision. This is not an organizational process. When, however, the retailer builds up good will or makes decisions which will enforce his dependence upon some manufacturer, these are organizational acts within a theoretically controllable field, and are analyzable within the frame of reference set forth above.

13. In the TVA, the agriculturists made vigorous efforts to extend their interpretation of the grass-roots policy to the Authority as a whole; in respect to the federal government, the TVA attempts to have its special interpretation of administrative decentralization become general public policy.

cruitment is rigidly qualified by the criterion of social (class, familial, racial) origin.

iii) *Commitments enforced by institutionalization.* Because organizations are social systems, goals or procedures tend to achieve an established, value-impregnated status. We say that they become institutionalized. Commitment to established patterns is generated, thus again restricting choice and enforcing special lines of conduct. The attempt to commit an organization to some course of action utilizes this principle when it emphasizes the creation of an established policy, or other forms of precedent. Further, the tendency of established relations and procedures to persist and extend themselves, will create the unintended consequence of committing the organization to greater involvement than provided for in the initial decision to act. Where policy becomes institutionalized as doctrine, unanalyzed elements will persist, and effective behavior will be framed in terms of immediate necessities. An official doctrine whose terms are not operationally relevant will be given content in action, but this content will be informed by the special interests and problems of those to whom delegation is made. Hence doctrinal formulations will tend to reinforce the inherent hazard of delegation. A variation of this situation occurs when the role of participants comes to overshadow in importance the achievement of formal goals. Action then becomes irresponsible, with respect to the formal goals. . . .

iv) *Commitments enforced by the social and cultural environment.* Any attempt to intervene in history will, if it is to do more than comment upon events, find it necessary to conform to some general restraints imposed from without. The organizers of this attempt are committed to using forms of intervention consistent with the going social structure and cultural patterns. Those who ascend to power must face a host of received problems; shifts in public opinion will demand the reformulation of doctrine; the rise of competing organizations will have to be faced; and so on. The institutional context of organizational decision, when not taken into account, will result in unanticipated consequences. Thus intervention in a situation charged with conflict will mean that contending forces will weigh the consequences of that intervention for their own battle lines. The intervening organization must therefore qualify decision in terms of an outside controversy into which it is drawn despite itself. More obviously, the existence of centers of power and interest in the social environment will set up resistances to, or accept and shape to some degree, the program of the organization.

v) *Commitments enforced by the centers of interest generated in the course of action.* The organizational process continuously generates subordinate and allied groupings whose leaderships come to have a stake in the organizational status quo. This generation of centers of interest is inherent in the act of delegation. The latter derives its precarious quality from the necessity to permit discretion in the execution of function or command. But in the exercise of discretion there is a tendency for decisions to be qualified by the special goals and problems of those to whom delegation is made. Moreover, in the discretionary behavior of a section of the apparatus, action is taken in the name of the organization as a whole; the latter may then be committed to a policy or course of action which was not anticipated by its formal program. In other words, the lack of effective control over the tangential informal goals of individuals and subgroups within an organization tends to divert it from its initial path. This holds true whether delegation is to members and parts of a single organization, or to other organizations, as in the TVA's relation to the land-grant colleges.

These types of commitment create persistent tensions or dilemmas. In a sense, they set the problems of decision and control, for we have identified here the key points at which organizational control breaks down. Operationally, a breakdown of control is evidenced in the generation of observable unanticipated consequences. This is the same as to say that significant possibilities inherent in the situation have not been taken into account. The extension of control, with concomitant minimization of unintended consequence, is achieved as and if the frame of reference for theory and action points the way to the significant forces at work.

The problems indicated here are perennial because they reflect the interplay of more or less irreconcilable commitments: to the goals and needs of the organization and at the same time to the special demands of the tools or means at hand. Commitment to the tools of action is indispensable; it is of the nature of these tools to be dynamic and self-activating; yet the pursuit of the goals which initiated action demands continuous effort to control the instruments it has generated. This is a general source of tension in all action mediated by human, and especially organizational, tools.

The systematized commitments of an organization define its character. Day-to-day decision, relevant to the actual problems met in the translation of policy into action, create precedents, alliances, effective symbols, and personal loyalties which transform the organization from a profane, manipulable instrument into something having a sacred status and thus resistant to treatment simply as a means to some external goal. That is why organizations are often cast aside when new goals are sought.

The analysis of commitment is thus an effective tool for making explicit the structural factors relevant to decision in organized action. Attention is directed to the concrete process of choice, selecting those factors in the environment of decision which limit alternatives and enforce uniformities of behavior. When we ask, "To what are we committed?" we are speaking of the logic of action, not of contractual obligations freely assumed. So long as goals are given, and the impulse to act persists, there will be a series of enforced lines of action demanded by the nature of the tools at hand. These commitments may lead to unanticipated consequences resulting in a deflection of original goals.[14]

14. The British Labor Party, when it assumed power in 1945, had to accept a large number of commitments which followed simply from the effort to govern in those circumstances, independently of its special program. "Meeting a crisis," in a women's club as well as in a cabinet, is a precondition for the institution of special measures. To assume leadership is to accept these conditions.

NOTES ON A THEORY OF ADVICE

Lyman Bryson

This tentative and fragmentary analysis of advice is offered to indicate what might be worked out as the basis of a guide for the scholars, scientists and experts who move into the world of affairs on invitation. By reason of training and intellectual habit, they are capable of seeing clearly the abtract or schematic picture of what goes on and should be helped to do so. They should be able, if called on, to describe the behavior of policy makers, and their assistants, to the policy makers themselves, since administrators are not often given to the self-indulgence of abstract thought. One sure mark of the man of action is to use intuitions in place of abstractions and this is true even in a society like ours, where skills are so generally explicit and "know-how" is so much discussed. The man of thought is very different; he will make a small cosmos out of the smallest experience.

The expert who accepts an invitation from a policy maker is entering a situation in which he can expect to observe the working of four or more distinguishable functions in the six or more stages of the decision-making process. We can take the functions first, understanding, of course, that one person may act at different times in different functions and that functions may occasionally be merged.

First is the making of the policy decision which we shall call the function of administration. It is final for the unit of action being examined. It includes the right, as will be explained later, to appeal to a free constituency, which is another way of saying that even the administrator who makes the final decision in any unit of action has the right and the responsibility of being judged by somebody. Swift remarked, "a flea hath smaller fleas that on him prey," and what was expressed as lyric annoyance is a true descrip-

Reprinted from *Political Science Quarterly*, LXVI (1951), pp. 321-339, by permission of the author and the publisher. (Copyright, 1951, by the Editors of the *Political Science Quarterly*).

tion of sober fact. Every decision, in any kind of organization, must please somebody who has a right to be displeased, no matter how final it may be for all subordinates. For the immediate purpose, however, we think of the policy-making decision as a terminal point in a process. The expert is called in to help eventually in giving that decision as much prescience and caution as is possible. The expert is not responsible, however, for making it; if he does, he is fulfilling the function of administration, not of advice.

The second function can be called execution. It is performed, if the unit is small, by the administrator himself; in larger organizations, there are executive assistants. It must be clearly understood that execution is here considered part of the policy-making process; it is not a merely mechanical performance in which the intentions of the policy maker are automatically realized. Execution always involves a series of subsidiary decisions which arise in carrying out the powers that have been delegated to the executive by the policy maker. Opposition, treachery, political manipulations or useful inventiveness may make or mar the policy as it is realized. The adage, "If you want something well done, do it yourself," is an admonition to an administrator not to trust his executives. The other adage, "A man who is his own lawyer has a fool for a client," may incidentally express the other side of the case. Or we might find it in the Chinese maxim of political administration which states that the good administrator does nothing; he does nothing, in order to give his executives the opportunity to do their best. This ambivalence in popular folklore shows that the decision as to how much he shall personally intervene in the execution of his own policies is one of an administrator's most sticky problems.

The third function is advice. Here the expert enters the situation; his work is almost wholly the giving of advice. How the location and content of his advice are to be determined will be discussed in connection with the stages of the decision-making sequence. At this point, while we are considering the functions, we can note that the function of advising is performed by all the members of an organization in some contexts and that this advice giving is almost never politically innocent. It is only the outsider, the expert who is paid primarily for his advice and listened to for his special professional knowledge, who can expect his opinions to have entirely objective standing.

If the invited expert is an academic person, whose experience of controversy has been scientific or scholarly, he is very likely to misunderstand much of what goes on around him because he thinks of proffered opinions as opinions only. He weighs them in the same scales of objective valuation he expects his own opinions to be weighed in; he tries to examine them courteously but "impersonally." By living up to the ascetic ideals of his own intellectual discipline he heightens the value of his own work, of course, but keeps himself alien to the other elements in the decision-making process. We believe that he will be more useful in performing his special function if he knows the differences between his own behavior and that of his temporary colleagues, and this analysis is a suggestion of the kind of work that ought to be done to help him.

There is also a fourth function which we can call interpretation. It is not often the job of a designated person; either an executive assistant or an expert can perform it and is likely to do so without thinking that he is, widening his own special task. The function is not clearly conceived, and is assumed by different persons thoughtlessly. This partly accounts for the fact that it is in this area of what we call interpretation that experts and executives most frequently fall afoul of each other without knowing why. The unspecified function is the cause of the trouble, as can be better understood when we examine the stages in the decision-making and decision-realizing process.

The decision-action process is a series of decisions whose nature and scope must be studied if we are ever to conceptualize fully, and arrange logically, the coöperation between the elements of knowledge and power that make the world go round. What is said in these notes is at least sufficiently abstract to apply to any kind of business, whether government, industry or the management of organizations. Power hunger shows itself openly in government and business; it may be disguised in a church hierarchy or a philanthropic society. Whether or not ambition is less potent in the competition of service, where money and material success are less obvious stakes, is a question we need not try to answer. But we need not put a cheap Machiavellian color on the matter; we can take each group of persons at their own valuation and make no moral judgments. The factors are about as we describe them in any single situation and any one factor may be more or less present, according to pressures in the situation and the characters of the persons.

The first stage in decision-action is to describe the problem. In practice, most problems are partially formulated by the executive assistants in the regular administration of the enterprise. They note failures in the working out of previously initiated policies, report unexpected obstacles, complain of lack of tools, which may be in machines, money or personnel; or, much more rarely, they may think of possible new objectives. The active administrator, for reasons to be suggested later, is not very likely to have much time for the discovery or the invention of problems. His primary function in all aspects of his job is to choose among suggestions received from his staff and from outside; the problems come to him in that form. Much of this flow of problems in the formulations of the executives is taken care of by routine decisions. When it is too difficult for that kind of "staff meeting" treatment, the expert may be called in.

A vague realization that the problem as now described is too difficult for staff routine decision is not enough, however, to determine the choice, the rôle or the problem of the expert. In fact, there is often a period when some of the executive assistants may resist the suggestion of bringing in a consultant since they have more or less routine suggestions of their own that they want to have favorably considered. The suggestion that only an expert can solve a problem is itself a suggestion, an "idea," and is immediately subject to all the kinds of scrutiny and resistance that meet every other idea. If the administrator accepts the idea in general, he is then open to new suggestions and may add a few of his own, leading to such a precise description of the problem as will make it possible to decide what kind of expert to call in.

Among executive assistants there is always competition. The energy of this conflict is one of the things with which an administrator works; it is also one of the factors that complicate the life and work of the outside specialist.

If the first decision by the administrator is that a consultant of specified knowledge shall be invited into the organization for the purpose of giving advice on a problem, that decision indicates that the problem is at least partly described in the administrator's mind. If he has not seen the problem clearly, he is merely indulging, for political or personal reasons, some member of his staff who offers a suggestion. The degree to which the problem actually is described before the advisory relation is established is of the greatest importance to the expert. There may be a later phase of the situation in which the expert can perform his own function only by stating that the problem has been wrongly described and that some other formulation, or indeed some other problem as yet undisclosed, must be tackled ahead of, or instead of, the one he has been assigned to.

Before this problem can arise for any expert, however, and before one is chosen, there is a choice to be made among the suggestions from executives as to the nature of the expert knowledge needed and as to the best available exponent of that kind of knowledge. The executive assistants will act as experts on experts and on expert knowledge. From among their suggestions, or on his own, the administrator chooses a person.

After being invited, and after accepting the assignment or agreeing to negotiate, the expert adviser is given a description of the problem. The first contact between him and his employers may be the locus of profound conflict or misunderstanding. If he accepts without question the problem, and the description of the problem which is given him by the administrator or by the designated subordinate, he is bound in his function as adviser to serve all the purposes of the administrator that are implied in it, or to make a clear rejection.

The question is raised at once, What right has an adviser to reformulate or to change the problem? The answer is still obscure but it is evident from experience that each member of the relation between expert and executive, or expert and administrator, is likely to take it for granted that he has the privilege of naming and describing the problem. The expert, if not well trained by relevant experience in such affairs, coming probably from an academic situation in which it is the chief part of his work to rank problems in their respective importance and to formulate them for study, will try to go beyond the immediate presentation offered him to what he thinks is an understanding of ulterior policy considerations so that he can (if still willing to associate himself with those purposes) help to achieve them. The administrator and executives have much more complicated and less innocent ideas about those ulterior policy matters and may not believe that it is necessary to disclose them. They may, of course, listen watchfully to the expert's queries and suggestions regarding the nature of the "real" problem, and accept what can be used, provided it involves for them no embarrassment in their relations with each other.

Even at this early point in the process, the inexperienced adviser should begin to learn a few lessons about the competitive factors in decision making. He may overlook them or fail to see them. In fact, men of academic background can often be seen trying to act as administrators in institutional leadership for which their expert knowledge fits them, without knowing or being willing to believe that what goes on around them is in any way different from scholarly or scientific discussion. Their expert knowledge fits them to understand the problems of the institution which may be school, library, business research department, or government bureau. They may have had an extensive knowledge of men in intellectual rather than power competitions. They may have a good second-hand knowledge of practical affairs from reading and acquaintance. They may even have detected rudimentary power impulses in some of their academic colleagues, especially as manifested in malicious gossip. But they feel shamed by the suspicion that men of affairs are not always wholly objective in what they say, as if, indeed, the morals of the seminar and the laboratory were the only morals extant.

The fact is observable and inescapable, whatever moral judgment one may insist on passing on it, that the decision-making process is a field of personal ambition and sharp competition in all practical situations, whether business, government or institutional. It might be argued that this is necessary and useful, that a scientific objectivity in the expression of opinions, the interpretation of facts, and the communication of ideas, among practical men would lead to worse, not better, results. We are not prepared to argue in that fashion any more than we are prepared to be shocked. The analyst has no moral obligation beyond stating the ascertainable facts in such a way as will be useful to other men of knowledge who mix in action and hope to serve a good purpose.

The administrator and his executives, generally through one person as a delegated intermediary, interpret to the expert a complex of administrative judgments as to the nature of the problem. The expert, after agreement as to the nature, or locus and formulation, of the problem, does his work by suggesting alternative courses of action and predicting the consequences to be expected from them. He is giving new dimensions of freedom to the thinking of the administrative group because he is describing for them, and enabling them to entertain in their imaginations, a range of choices they would not otherwise have considered.

It is evident that prediction of the consequences of a set of alternatives is a very difficult task which should always be performed with caution. The records would seem to indicate that the gifted man of action prefers to initiate a maneuver and invent most of his planning as he goes. This has a number of psychological implications into which we cannot go at this point, related to the fact that men of action generally maintain their own morale by frequent rearrangement of goals so that neither defeat nor victory can be too demoralizing. But when the expert, by definition not a man of action and therefore assumed to be more concrete in his expectations, is asked to describe alternative choices, he is expected also to tell the advantages and disadvantages of each choice. This is the same as asking him to predict, in spite of unpredictable circumstance, what will happen in any course of action. He is lucky if he can present plans in such a way as to indicate that future events will make new choices necessary, and the road ahead is full of forks, each of which must be negotiated in the light of experience which cannot even be imagined until after arrrival at that particular fork. He is not lucky if the administrator demands of him an absolute map of the future; some administrators think they are entitled to that kind of prophecy.

However, the expert is still caught in the process of decision making, after he has described alternative courses of action, because he will probably discover that his ideas are subject to interpretation by the executive assistants before they are finally accepted or discarded. He may find that the executive who gives him the greatest degree of general approval and support interprets his suggestions in such a way as to produce results the expert did not intend. The expert can protest and argue; he may find himself silenced by the claim that his expertness goes only to the general idea and that translating it into action requires another kind of knowledge which he does not possess, that is, knowledge special to the time and occasion and occupational in character.

After a decision is made by the administrator and a policy is explicitly chosen, then further interpretation in terms of action ensues and the next decision will be as to which of the proposed practical lines of action will best achieve the policy's goal. The expert may be consulted on the alterna-

tives here but most of the suggestions will be offered by the various executive assistants; the administrator or one of his staff with delegated powers
will choose. Subordinate decisions in a long series of budget making, personnel selection and concurrent commands will follow from this point
forward.

We go back now to the essential character of decision making in practical affairs and the understanding of it that will be most useful to the
visiting consultant. A more or less conscious desire to dominate and get
ahead in the administrative hierarchy pervades the behavior of all members
of the staff. As we indicated before, this apparently cynical observation is
subject to correction or reduction in any particular case. It can be observed,
however, in the world of affairs, that the devoted and impersonal staff members who think only of the organization, never of themselves, seldom rise
very high. And this may be better for the organization.

There are whole ranges of human endeavor in which competition in this
sense does not enter; where the desire to excel is only a race for personal
usefulness or service. It is also true, as I have insisted in many other places,
that the goods that can be acquired by struggles for material power in
business or politics are not of the highest order. We could even go so far
as to say that the deepest satisfactions for men who constantly struggle for
power and advancement in practical affairs seldom develop out of material
success. All these statements are true and important; but the expert consultant who goes into the decision-making process, expecting to rely upon
these reassuring facts, is immorally stupid. He is not exercising the ordinary prudence expected of any man of goodwill who has a practical purpose. If he discovers what ought to surprise him, namely that the hierarchically ranged members of the staff achieve an objectivity in opinion
which he is himself striving for, he has lost nothing but anxiety. If any of
them turn out to be more basely human and he is surprised, he may have
found out the truth too late. A kindly skepticism regarding the motives of
all men in practical affairs is the usual attitude of experienced men of action; it becomes the expert quite as well if he can attain it.

The competitive modifications of opinion which we are accusing the
members of the staff of making are, of course, partly unconscious, sometimes entirely so. The first to be looked at are the power ambitions of the
executives. The difficulties of the administrator, the final arbiter, can be
spoken of later. The executives, who are, by our definition, all the members of the staff who have access to the administrator for purposes of policy
discussion, will generally become quick advocates of some one of the
various alternatives that are open in making the decisions listed above.
They will have honest convictions about these alternatives and will in most
cases be expressing those honest convictions. The administrator who cannot count on getting such honest opinions, either because he demands timid

caution and "yessing," or because he has put men on his staff who are so completely political that they merely intrigue, deserves what he gets and is almost certain to fail in the long run. The administrator who is just and honest in his own opinions can expect a fair return in honesty. The executives, however, will almost certainly have something in their minds beyond the intrinsic worth of the opinions they back. They will also have more or less conscious mind-sets that have organized in complicated fashion their desires to raise their own prestige and to make it likely that they will be allowed to help in further decisions and in decisions on other matters.

In scientific and scholarly disputes, or in consultative debates, it is more likely to be one opinion against another; one opinion wins if the question gets settled. In practical matters, the question almost always gets settled but it is a man and not an opinion that wins. Every member of the staff wants to be that man, or to be associated with him. The description sounds more dramatic, of course, than the event generally seems to those who take part in it, but smiling friendliness and general acquiescence should not deceive the outsider.

The ambitions of the members of the staff, moreover, are not confined to motives of power. In many situations, the decision to call in an expert has followed deliberations in which members of the staff offered their own quasi-expert opinions and suggested courses of action. These suggestions were turned down, either by administrative fiat or by consensus; in any case, the executives are always inclined to resist the appeal to an outsider. His expertness is itself something of a criticism of their competence. Of course, situations may develop in which the adviser and his advice become a stake in the power game itself. At this point, the ambitious executive will affirm or deny the expert's competence without completely responsible regard for his real value. Academic veterans will probably have become indurated against the melancholy fact that some of their own colleagues on the campus will occasionally deride some other scholar's claim to eminence because of motives not strictly scholastic; that is, they may deny a man's scholarly attainments in order to express their dislike or envy or fear of the man. The partisanships of executives are also colored by this kind of irrelevant feeling, but it is not so likely to sway them as are more clearly competitive motives. The expert, then, may have allies and opponents, to both of whom he has become a stake in the power game, but it would not be wise for him to count on simple friendships. His mere existence is a mild slur on the competence of the men he is dealing with, and to whom he is giving the supposed benefit of his superior knowledge. Even the administrator, the decision maker, may not be above claiming expert knowledge which helps to bolster up his ascendancy over his executives and lessens his obligations to the outside adviser. What the administrator says is not likely to be listened to with complete objectivity by anybody.

There is a story that tells of the conversations which used to be held on the palace hill in Rome to entertain the Emperor Hadrian. He loved disputes about grammar and usage and word origins; professors were invited to dine with him and argue for his pleasure. Sometimes, he ventured an opinion of his own and on one occasion one of his experts rejected the emperor's theory summarily. The argument waxed hot and the emperor shouted. The deipnosophist shouted less and less as the exchanges went on, until at last the administrator, Hadrian, pronounced a final truth and his challenger was silent. "Aha," cried Hadrian, "my arguments have left you nothing to say." "Sire," replied the visiting expert, "who am I to disagree with the master of thirty legions?"

In the court at Rome, it would have been suicidal for the expert to have power ambitions of his own to match the knowledge ambitions of the emperor. In less deadly arguments, without his being well aware of it, his own pride in making decisions instead of merely outlining alternatives may lead him into actions which are appropriate only if he is prepared to enter fully into the power contest. If he does so, his sense of objectivity and his reputation for disinterested knowledge are both likely to be damaged.

The problems of the administrator, the one who makes the final policy decisions, are one aspect of what has already been said. One of his most difficult procedural decisions, made generally by accident or intuition, is to choose the moment at which he will become a working member of the group that is examining the possible alternative lines of action. As long as he keeps out of it, he is only a useful future umpire. As soon as he joins the discussions, all ambitions are heightened because the dispenser of promotion and prestige is on hand to be impressed. If he makes choices at that time among alternatives, he is inescapably choosing among advocates as well as among plans.

On the other hand, if the administrator holds aloof too long, he is at the mercy of his executive assistants since he must accept, as his range of choices, whatever they bring to him in the report of deliberations. This is one of the most acute of the phases of the general administrative problem: How much should a manager be immersed in the actual diurnal round of his business in order to manage it? There is not likely to be any handy rule that will settle all cases. The principle needs far more thorough working out than it has received.

The special problems of the administrator can only be mentioned; they require much more elaborate treatment in other contexts. But it is useful, when we are plotting the difficulties of the outside expert in the swiftly changing patterns of an organizational process, to recall that the administrator has a primary task in keeping his own power as against rivals both inside and outside his own organization. It is a romantic notion of power, which ought to be blown out of an academician's imagination in his first experience as a committee chairman, that a man who struggles to get power can, having gained it, loll back and think about the good of his enterprise. He has, in fact, moved himself not to a seat of thoughtful leisure but to the center of a popular target. And to some extent, the greater the emoluments and the prestige of his position, the less he can think about anything but keeping it. All proposals for the single-term occupancy of the White House are based on this fact, usually described in a more gingerly fashion. Exercising power is drastically interfered with by the need to hold it, unless you have agreed to get out on a fixed day. In politics, this is always a preoccupation of all but the innocent statesmen. In business, it is closely entangled with other motives and problems because a business administrator's power may be diminished as much by the loss of his company's competitive position as by his own loss of position in the company. The two problems are often faced in the same decision. In any case, these things absorb time and attention that might otherwise go into thinking about function as well as purpose.

In dealing with his executive assistants and the whole staff attached to him through them, the administrator has to give the example and the general direction of morale, as well as to make final choices among suggested alternatives. Sometimes he shakes morale by the seeming caprice of his choice, or by disagreeing with too many of his subordinates. As he listens to arguments, after he enters the deliberations, he is kept busy in settling the power disputes among his assistants in order to get the best ideas, to promote the fittest men and to keep the appearance as well as the fact of justice. He must be alert to disentangle the knowledge values from the power bids of his advisers, whether they are executives or consulted experts.

He has also to think up ideas of his own. For this task, he has little time. His fitness to be the administrator, the man who makes the last decision and determines policy, is not determined by his fecundity in ideas. His ability to see the intrinsic as well as the situational value of an idea suggested to him is obviously far more important; other qualities which lie outside the scope of a theory of advice may count still more. It is evident enough that men of action, in business and politics, are often gifted with high intellectual powers, even beyond the needs of their work. They are not likely to exercise them for fun, as is the privilege of philosophers, artists and teachers. But success in practical affairs is not commanded by sheer intellectual ability; other qualities of mind and character are also needed. Inventiveness does not seem to be one of them, and there is more inventiveness for sale in the market than there is of first-rate administrative capacity.

The adviser, coming in *ad hoc*, has also some special problems of his own, for which he needs to be prepared. One is his responsibility to protect himself against being used to justify decisions already made. Just as some manager will, with naïve dishonesty, call in workmen to "discuss" decisions already finally taken, so some administrators will ask advice when what they want is help. If the expert accepts the rôle of rationalizer, he may destroy his own integrity; he can often detect the hidden invitation to serve as mere helper in the formulation of the question he is asked to advise on. The first battle between adviser and staff, as we have already indicated, may be at that point, where the problem is described. Dr. John Gardner, of the Carnegie Corporation, has pointed out in a privately circulated memorandum that the expert is often challenged at the very outset of his work by the question of who has the right to say what the problem is. As a responsible practical manager, the administrator will usually assume that he has a right to tell a hired man what he is hired to do. On the other hand, as master of a field of knowledge, the consultant may well assume that he alone, and no other person of less knowledge, can understand the implications and history of a problem. Most men who have been consulted by business executives have discovered that much of what they think is pertinent is considered "theoretical" by business men and that an attempt to extend the span of time of either hindsight or foresight is resented. No rule will suffice to guide the consultant here; he is the keeper of his own conscience.

There are limits on the criticism of one expert by another and the consultant has to decide what is appropriate for him to do in the competitive aspect of the world of knowledge. A more difficult question is what he will do in service to the public relations of the company he is temporarily working for. He may be asked by his own employer to issue a statement which, while technically truthful, is clearly planned to be a sales appeal. He may be asked by a newspaper or broadcasting station to comment on the general area in which he is working, as when physicians who are advising pharmaceutical manufacturers are asked to tell the public all about cures for the common cold. The problem is to keep honest. For the salesman or the advertiser to push his own product is honest; that is his economic function. But to what extent can the expert permit the use of his name and his personal prestige for the same purpose? He expects his findings, accurately reported, to be used. What about his professional standing? The old rule, that doctors and lawyers do not advertise, does not help very much since that has to do with whether or not they should advertise themselves. To what degree can a physician who has helped, as expert, to make a drug useful allow his name to be used to increase public use of it? The answer is not suggested; the purpose here is only to mark the crossroads, with full stop signs.

Another aspect of the policy-making process which involves theoretical problems of freedom and authority, as well as practical problems of the relation between knowledge and power, is the definition of constituencies. Every person in a policy-making situation has his constituency, which may be free or captive. He has a group of people to whom he can appeal, in his own terms, for support and they can or cannot defy his administrative superiors. The analysis of this structural aspect of decision making, when adequately done, will greatly help to solve the difficulties arising from the fact that our governments must deal more and more with technical questions, wherein legislators, voters, administrative officers and elected executive officers have different kinds of competence, different degrees of freedom, and different private purposes. The same sort of complex relations on a smaller scale can be seen in industrial and other kinds of private organizations.

The concepts can be explained in terms of an ordinary hierarchy of authority in a political situation, and the operation of constituencies will be understood as the mechanism by which democratic institutions restrain power. It is the criterion of freedom for any person in an administrative complex to discover whether or not he has a group to which he can appeal for help which is not itself subject to the same superior pressures that he is subject to. For example, the head of a bureau in the state government of New York has a lesser degree of freedom than a member of the state legislature. The legislator can appeal to the voters of his district, who owe nothing but a reasonable hearing to the administrative officers of the state, whereas the bureau head, if he quarrels with his superiors, has no such independent group to appeal to. An appeal to an unorganized "public opinion" is of slight avail for the bureau head since he has no special relation to any part or organ of the general body politic.

At the same time, the bureau head does have another kind of a constituency, which we can call "captive." It is made up of his fellow administrative officials, both above and below him in the hierarchy. They are not a free constituency because, although they may with more or less effect and safety take his side in a dispute against his superiors, they are subject to the same kinds of pressure that affect him. If they are his subordinates in a direct line they are somewhat bound to him; if in an indirect way, they are bound by their own superior's action whatever it may be. If they are his coördinate or superior officials, they will be influenced by all the lines of authority and the inner struggle for power and will more or less consciously have to calculate the effects of their own overt opinions on their own ambitions.

The term "free," as applied to the voters in a legislator's district, does not mean that these persons are free of self-interest, prejudice, psychological pressures and all the rest of the circumstances that bedevil the political thinking of all populations. They are a free constituency only in the sense that they have an established relation to the legislator which enables them, if they are persuaded, to exert pressures in his behalf, and they are not in any way affected by the administrative hierarchy in which he works. The bureau chief can organize support for himself inside the administrative system of the state, but his colleagues are not free to act as are the voters. To put it crudely, the governor, as administrator, can give orders to a bureau chief but not to a legislator.

One chief difference between a representative democracy and a totalitarian government, in purely technical terms, without regard to purposes or ideology, is here. In Russia, for example, in the present operational development of administration, no official of any kind, appointed or elected, can be said to have a "free" constituency. The only free constituency is the people as a whole to whom in some measure the supreme government is responsible. No one has any legal machinery by which he can appeal to the country, or to any part of the country, as against his superiors or colleagues. It is the essence of a totalitarianism that all constituencies are captive. Anyone to whom any official might appeal for support in a dispute is himself a member of the administrative hierarchy and thus handicapped in his opinions, still more in his action. In a completely totalitarian country, a legislator cannot appeal to the voters as against administrative officials or against his legislative colleagues because he is named to his post by the party; and only the party, through its regular graded channels, can express opinions. In a country with a more open system, like the United States, the tradition of allowing appeals to a free constituency is so deep rooted, and so close to our moral convictions regarding fair play, that an astute politician like President Truman will allow General MacArthur to dispute in public the administration's policies, although MacArthur has no legal constituency, and is actually under strict orders which could include an order not to discuss political or military matters in public. The fact that a rebellious and disgruntled military hero would not have been given open triumphs in Russia, but would have disappeared, is simple evidence of the causal fact that Russian political machinery offers no method by which MacArthur could have appealed to public opinion except by armed revolution. Caesar brought his legions with him when he crossed the Rubicon; MacArthur got his biggest triumph in a city controlled by the administration with Democratic party officials leading the cheers. The tradition is powerful and the machinery offers no obstacle; one could scarcely work without the other.

In more regular situations, the member of the cabinet who disagrees with the president has no free constituency to which he can appeal; he has to rely upon arguments with his chief and whatever support he can get from his captive constituency which is made up of the president's other advisers and the subordinate ranks of the government staff. The member of Congress has the ideal type of free constituency in the voters of his district who will, without any obligation or deference toward other members of the government, give him their judgment on what he does, in so far as they know about it and can understand it.

This is a concept of broader use, moreover, than can be seen in these commonplace political examples. Take, for example, the administrative hierarchy of a broadcasting network which is a profit system of the most modern kind. A vice president in charge of programs who has been reasonably successful in his past judgments will be listened to thoughtfully by the administrator above him. But if there is disagreement, the vice president has only a captive constituency, of the same sort as the one that can give limited help to a cabinet officer in the federal government. In the case of a performer on the air, however, even though he may be bound by contracts and have no administrative rights, there is always a free constituency to appeal to; it comprises his fans. He can appeal to this audience as against his editor, and the same kind of relations gives freedom to a novelist or a magazine writer. The principle can be extended. The meaning in larger terms is that any system which does not give to some members of the administrative or ruling group the chance to appeal to another free group for support must necessarily be authoritarian and monolithic.

The principle applies with special force to the function of the expert, the adviser, whom we were discussing previously. His free constituency is the company of scholars and scientists of which he claims to be a member. The administrator of a private organization is not bound to take the adviser's opinion, but the adviser can walk out of the assignment. In a free country, the adviser who is working for the government can appeal to his scholarly colleagues and they can reply not only as specialists but also as part of the general public, which in a free country is the locus of free constituencies. In a totalitarian country, there are no fully private organizations, and the expert has no way of escaping the pressures of power. If he submits to these pressures, as he almost certainly will, the scientific and technological progress of the state is retarded. The administrator, whether in business or in government, is sure to profit in the long run by the amount of honest information he can get out of his advisers.

In this paper only two aspects of the function of advice have been touched on: the relation of the adviser to the inner hierarchy of power, and and the relation of any member of a decision-making process to his possible support. It will be noted that nothing has been said about communication, although the difficulties of communication enhance every kind of difficulty mentioned. Such omissions of factors are justified only if the isolation of other factors makes for clarity. This is an area of human behavior which has been cluttered with generalizations, but is seldom subjected to analysis; there is not even a taxonomic basis for discussion.

The function of advice is one of the oldest in human affairs and certain abstract generalizations about it that could have been made in palaeolithic times are still true. Most of those generalizations, however, have not been made and, as far as can be discovered, no standard treatise in this field has ever been written. There are mountain piles of books on salesmanship, which is not disinterested advice, and a molehill of books on leadership, but nothing on the techniques and difficulties of trying to put knowledge at the service of power. The right relation of knowledge and power is, however, one of the key problems of our age. We need to give the closest scrutiny to the processes whereby decisions are made, and the effect on those decisions of rational information, if we are to master the difficulties of freedom in a time when power is so developed and knowledge is so dispersed. The function of advice is one of the crucial points in that relation and on that account may well be studied first.

THE EXECUTION OF POLICY

J. Donald Kingsley

"As trifles make the sum of human things," Sir Henry Taylor once observed, "so details make the substance of public affairs." Here, in a single sentence, is the explanation of the increasing importance of the bureaucracy. With the development of technology and the growing complexity of social relations, both the number and the variety of those details which form the warp and woof of policy have multiplied, until today they are as varied and numerous as the shells of the sea. Even seventy-five or a hundred years ago, Ministers of the Crown and the more conscientious Members of Parliament could master the trifles from which policy is fashioned. Great politicians like Gladstone and Lord John Russell were intimate with the minutiae of the problems confronting them, and Gladstone frequently drafted clauses in the bills he sponsored. Sir James Graham could be personally aware of everything that happened at the Admiralty, and Palmerston was practically a one man Foreign Office, conducting the important correspondence of his Department in his own hand, and sometimes pursuing a policy all his own. Even in more recent times, Lord Salisbury, who never trusted his officials, could disregard them with more or less impunity.

Under these circumstances, the famous dictum of Lord Welby is under-

Reprinted in part from *Representative Bureaucracy*, pp. 264-265, 270-278, by permission of the author and the publisher, The Antioch Press. (Copyright, 1944, by J. Donald Kingsley.)

standable. "The business of a Civil Servant," he often said, "is to do what he is told." But that could be an accurate description of the relations between a Minister and his permanent officials only so long as the Minister's grip upon details was firm. It could not be correct once the duties of the Minister became so complex and the functions of his Department so involved, that he could not personally be acquainted with all their aspects. Even when the observation was made it was not wholly true, for it was about this time that a rule is said to have obtained in one of the great Departments that all documents must be so drawn "as to be intelligible to the stupidest Cabinet Minister." The Peels, Palmerstons, Russells and Gladstones were exceptional, even in the nineteenth century.

Today, the business of a Civil Servant is much more difficult and important than in Lord Welby's day; for the higher Civil Servants alone are the masters of those details which "make the substance of public affairs." The scope of governmental activities has expanded to a point where only those persons who deal with them from day to day over a long period of time can be familiar with their manifold ramifications; and this fact has altered the balance of the Constitution. It has led, in the first place, to an increasing dependence of the House upon the Government, and in the second, to an increasing dependence of the Government upon the higher Civil Service. Yet this has occurred, as I hope to show, without seriously threatening the democratic basis of the State. . . .

It is sometimes suggested that the higher Civil Servants have assumed their central position by a process of usurpation. This is not the case. Their power, which is undoubtedly considerable, depends upon their influence; and they have become influential because they have been competent. They do not, for the most part, possess power in their own right, but wield it only as they can persuade. Yet the distinction here may be more apparent than real, for their strategic position in relation to the details from which policies are built may render persuasion less than difficult. How true this is will appear from a closer scrutiny of the governing process.

Let us take first the function of amassing information. An Under Secretary of State in the War Office once described his position as largely that of "Remembrancer"; and while this was too modest a view of the duties of the permanent officials, there was more than a little truth in the characterization. The Civil Service embodies the accumulated experience of government. Ministers come and go; they constitute, in Sir William Harcourt's phrase, the "evanescent items" in the administration. But the permanent officials remain and the bulk of their files constantly increases. Day after day the Departments accumulate and collate information dealing with the area of work in which they are engaged.

This congealed experience enters into the determination of policy in many ways, of which two are of principal importance. It may lead in the first place to the development of new policies and programs by the Department itself,—and usually does. It is in the day to day application of a law that its inadequacies are to be perceived and in the daily rub of the administrative mill that ideas for reform are burnished. Thus, the experience of officials in the Ministry of Health with the problems of local government will lead them over a period of time to reach conclusions regarding desirable new policies in this area. They will then attempt to persuade a Minister to sponsor such policies before the Cabinet, or will wait until a Government decides to introduce a new local government bill and then urge the inclusion of their ideas. This was, in fact, what occurred in the case of the Local Government Act of 1929. At the hands of the political chiefs that measure started out as a simple one to provide financial relief to certain property holders; but before it reached the House of Commons it had become a comprehensive measure, incorporating the local government reforms desired by the permanent officials.

This illustration suggests the second major way in which departmental experience impinges upon policy. A Minister or a Cabinet committee decide that action should be taken in respect to a particular problem. The Minister consults his permanent officials as to possible lines of procedure and as to the probable effects of alternative approaches. Such consultation may take many shapes. In its preliminary stages it is likely to be informal: a conversation with the Permanent Secretary at lunch, or an informal conference with the higher departmental officials. But eventually it will begin to take the form of memoranda. If the problem is one involving technical considerations, there will be memoranda from the technical officers involved. If it affects other Departments, like the Treasury, there will be memoranda from them and an interdepartmental committee may even be set up to work out details. Junior and senior officers will add facts and express opinions as the growing file moves through the departmental hierarchy. In the process the relevant facts will be brought to light and the accumulated wisdom of the officials will be focussed on the problem. The result will usually be a clear recommendation that a particular line be followed; and that recommendation will be heavily buttressed with supporting data. Under such circumstances, only the bravest or the most foolhardy of Ministers will undertake to pursue another course. In the normal progress of events, the outlines of policy will have been determined by the departmental memoranda. It is this which explains the persistence of "departmental policies."

This is not to say that a strong Minister may not still follow his own line. He may decide, as Sir William Harcourt did in the matter of an all-sea penny postage, that the departmental conclusions are "unmitigated nonsense and feeble twaddle." Sir William's marginal notes on the Post Office memorandum in this instance provide a classic example of the reactions of a strong Minister when confronted with official opposition: "Nonsense." "Still greater nonsense." "Oh! sagacious administration." . . .

Under different circumstances, the undoubted dependence of the Minister upon his officials might be a matter of grave constitutional importance,— as it was, for example, in Weimar Germany. There, an attempt was made to impose parliamentary control upon a Civil Service but partially committed to the ends the Republic sought to pursue; and the attempt failed disastrously. In France, too, reactionary officials successfully sabotaged the efforts of the Blum Government in finance and foreign affairs; and the Roosevelt Administration was forced to assemble almost a whole new set of officials to carry out the New Deal reforms. No comparable situation has arisen recently in England; but that is clearly because the bureaucracy in its upper ranges has been representative of the ruling class as a whole and because its aspirations have been those to which successive Governments were committed.

The point that I wish to emphasize, and to which I shall presently return, is that the essence of bureaucratic responsibility in the modern State is to be sought, not in the presumed and largely fictitious impartiality of the officials, but in the strength of their commitment to the purposes that State is undertaking to serve. Able men,—and Government commands such men,—will be impartial only in respect to trifles; they will not remain indifferent when confronted with matters of real importance. The view of the Civil Servant as a disinterested assembler of facts simply will not stand examination. . . .

But if Civil Servants are likely to be men of strong views, and if even Ministers wish them so, what is the meaning of the convention of impartiality? It certainly does not mean, as we have seen, that officials are indifferent to the ends a Government undertakes to serve. It does not mean that they will refrain from pressing upon Ministers their own conceptions of high policy, nor that they will be coldly objective in indicating alternatives. It does not mean that they are merely the registrars of facts. What the doctrine does mean has been stated authoritatively on several occasions, although its probable limits have never been officially explored. Thus, the authors of the famous Dardanelles Report were of the opinion that in cases of disagreement between an official and a Minister,

It is the duty of the official not to resign but to state fully to the head of his department, and should any proper occasion arise, to other members of the Ministry, what is the nature of his views. Then, if after due consideration, those views are overruled, he should do his best to carry out the policy of the government, even although he may not be in personal agreement with it.

And Sir Warren Fisher, then Head of the Civil Service, informed the Tomlin Commission that in his view,

Determination of policy is the function of Ministers, and once a policy is determined it is the unquestioned and unquestionable business of the Civil Servant to strive to carry out that policy with precisely the same energy and precisely the same good will whether he agrees with it or not. That is axiomatic and will never be in dispute . . .

These statements are both clear enough, yet they do not by any means settle the question. Are there no limits to the extent to which an able and honest man will make himself the instrument of policies with which he disagrees? Suppose that he is convinced, as Sir Thomas Legge apparently was, that it is criminal for a Government to permit the use of white lead in paint. Will he associate himself with the execution of a policy which does violence to that conviction? Sir Thomas refused to do so and resigned when his views were disregarded. Suppose that he is convinced, as Sir Evelyn Murray is alleged to have been, that the administrative reforms proposed by a Minister will wreak havoc with a Department. Will he enthusiastically put them into operation? Sir Evelyn was transferred to the Board of Customs and Excise in 1934 presumably because his views of Post Office administration ran counter to the reforms Sir Kingsley Wood was determined to carry out. Suppose that he believes that the pursuit of a particular foreign policy will be disastrous for the country. Will his administration of that policy be as vigorous as might otherwise be the case? Or will it seem advisable to promote him out of an administrative position, as was done with Sir Robert Vansittart?

These are not academic questions. Under conceivably different circumstances they might become of pressing constitutional importance. For while only a few individual instances can now be cited in which the limits of impartiality appear to have been reached, that is in large measure a reflection of the representativeness of the bureaucracy. There are obviously points beyond which a man cannot go in carrying out the will of another; and the fact that those limits have seldom been approached in the conduct of the Civil Service since 1870 bears witness to the unity of the middle class State. . . . There is no good reason to suppose that the doctrine of impartiality, and the permanence of tenure with which it is associated, could survive a political struggle in which the foundations of the State were in play. Men can hardly be expected to remain loyal to institutions whose purposes they suspect or disapprove; and it is scarcely likely that the British Communist Party would find the present Service as useful to them as it has undoubtedly been to the Liberal and Conservative parties. Even a few Labour Party leaders have expressed grave doubts that their program could be carried through without changes in the key personnel of the Service, although former Labour Ministers like Arthur Henderson and Sidney Webb have testified to the whole-hearted cooperation they received during their brief periods in office.

This is a point, however, upon which one can do no more than speculate at present. It is possible to argue, as Mr. W. I. Jennings has recently done, that the distinction between the programs of the Labour and Conservative parties is only one of degree, and that there would therefore be little likelihood of a breach in the convention of impartiality in the event of Labour's rise to power. Or one may take the view that the Labour Party is essentially a proletarian party which would be as seriously handicapped in office by a middle class Civil Service as the middle classes were by an aristocratic Civil Service. Neither position can be maintained with full certainty. What can be said, with little fear of contradiction, is that the Civil Service as now constituted would be much less representative of a State in which Labour wielded power than it has been of a State in which that prerogative belonged to the upper middle classes. . . .

As a matter of fact, of course, the essence of responsibility is psychological rather than mechanical. It is to be sought in an identity of aim and point of view, in a common background of social prejudice, which leads the agent to act as though he were the principal. In the first instance, it is a matter of sentiment and understanding, rather than of institutional forms. . . .

BUREAUCRACY AND SOCIAL CHANGE

Seymour Martin Lipset

The political problem of the power and influence of a permanent civil service with its own goals and traditions was not important so long as the social and economic values of the bureaucracy and the governing politicians did not seriously conflict. The problem becomes crucial, however, when a new political movement takes office and proposes to enact reforms that go beyond the traditional frame of reference of previous governmental activity or which upset the existing set of relations within the bureaucracy. It is especially important today, when the explicit formal goals of many democratic states are changing from the laissez-faire police regulation of society to those of a social-welfare planning state.[1]

The tradition and concept of a merit nonpatronage civil service was related in many countries to the needs of the dominant business groups, who demanded cheap and efficient service from the state. J. Donald Kingsley has

Reprinted in part from *Agrarian Socialism*, pp. 255-275, by permission of the author and the publisher. (Copyright, 1950, by the University of California Press.)

1. J. Donald Kingsley, *Representative Bureaucracy* (Yellow Springs, Ohio: Antioch Press, 1944), pp. 287-305, part of which is included in this volume.

shown how in England the policy of a merit civil service grew with the increase in political power of the business class.[2] The business groups desired an efficient state that would facilitate and protect the development of commerce. Permanent, nonpolitical officials insured continuity of government regulations and practices, and made for stable relations with the state, regardless of shifts in party fortunes. This idea of a merit civil service was not challenged as long as party politics remained contests between groups who accepted the basic orientation and activities of the state and the society. The establishment of reform and socialist governments, which propose radical changes in the functions of the state, raises the problem of whether such reforms can be successfully initiated and administered by a bureaucratic structure that is organized to regulate different norms, and whose members possess values that do not correspond with those of the "radical" politicians.

Since the days of Karl Marx, some socialists have maintained that a successful socialist state must destroy the old state apparatus and erect a new administrative organization.[3] In recent times, persons who have served in, or studied, socialist governments have suggested that one crucial reason for their failure to proceed more vigorously toward the attainment of their goals has been the "bureaucratic conservatism" of old civil servants.

In Weimar, Germany, the Social Democratic Party, which held majority power from 1918 to 1920, was not able to make fundamental changes in the power and economic structures. Participants in that government report that the bureaucracy played a major role in obstructing changes. . . . George Lansbury, who was a member of the second Labor government in Great Britain, and subsequently became leader of the Party, unequivocally declared, "All through the life of the late [1929–1931 Labor] Government, Treasury officials obstructed and hindered the Ministers in their work. No one can deny this."[4]

Saskatchewan is the latest in the series of examples of radical governments attempting to make drastic changes in the direction and functions

2. *Ibid.,* pp. 42-77.

3. Marx characteristically expressed this idea in a letter to Kugelmann: "If you look at the last chapter of my *Eighteenth Brumaire* you will find that I say that the next attempt of the French Revolution will be no longer, as before, to transfer the bureaucratic-military machine from one hand to another, but to smash it." Karl Marx and Friedrich Engels, *Correspondence, 1846–1895* (New York, International Publishers, 1936), p. 309. See also Marx, "The Civil War in France," *Selected Works* (Moscow, Publishing Society of Foreign Workers in the U.S.S.R., 1936), Vol. 2, pp. 498-505.

"To destroy officialism immediately, everywhere, completely—of this there can be no question. That is a utopia. But to *break* up at once the old bureaucratic machine and to start immediately the construction of a new one . . . this is not a utopia . . . it is the direct and necessary task of the revolutionary proletariat." V. I. Lenin, *The State and Revolution* (New York, Vanguard Press, 1926), p. 155.

4. London *Daily Herald,* October 23, 1933; quoted in Edgar Lansbury, *George Lansbury, My Father* (London, S. Low, Marston and Co., Ltd., n.d.), p. 197.

of government while retaining permanent civil servants in key administrative policy-making posts. There are, however, major differences between Saskatchewan and most other countries in which radical parties have come to power. Civil-service traditions are very different from those prevailing in England and other British Commonwealth countries; they are, in fact, more similar to those of nineteenth-century United States than to those of England. Party loyalty and obligations determine the choice of civil servants, as the following report makes clear.

It is possible to find four main corrupt features in the Saskatchewan Liberal organization, features which are common to most party organizations in Canada, whether Liberal or Conservative: the use of the civil servants as party workers; the patronage system by which party supporters were appointed to the civil service; the use of public works appropriations, particularly the road money, for pork barrel purposes; and the granting of contracts, especially in public works and printing, in return for financial or press support. . . .

The dislike of the blatant excesses of patronage government led the party, while in opposition, to oppose partisan appointments; but the recognition that the civil service was honeycombed with Liberal politicians made C.C.F. [Cooperative Commonwealth Federation] leaders specifically exempt deputy ministers and other major policy posts from civil-service protection. Unlike socialist parties in Europe and Great Britain, which were prevented from advocating changes in the civil service because of the popular acceptance of a politically neutral bureaucracy, the C.C.F. was free, in terms of the political values of Saskatchewan, to advocate the replacement of top-ranking conservative civil servants by C.C.F. experts, and did so in its 1944 program. . . .

Once in office, however, the new C.C.F. cabinet ministers changed their views. Instead of the expected housecleaning, most of the key civil servants were retained. Few changes in the top administration were made during the first two years of the C.C.F. government. Men who had served under the Liberals were promoted to fill vacancies in the upper levels of the civil service.

Every group of responsible C.C.F. leaders except the cabinet ministers, however, continued to believe that extensive changes in the top-level personnel of the government were necessary if the movement was to carry out its objectives of social reform. . . .

The difference between the cabinet and the rest of the party hierarchy lay in the fact that the new ministers were exposed to unanticipated pressures. They were faced with the immediate problem of assuming responsibility for departments that had to deal with a multitude of day-to-day problems. No department could stop operating until the new administration rebuilt its working apparatus. The new ministers, like most politicians, were amateurs in their respective departments. None of them had ever had administrative experience in a large organization.

The members of the cabinet were under pressure to implement the legislative and administrative reforms promised by the party platform. This platform, like that of most political parties, was necessarily general, lacking concrete steps to be taken after election. Beside drawing up new legislation, changing administrative regulations of their departments, and taking part in cabinet meetings, the ministers had to continue being active politicians, making speeches and caring for the needs of their constituents.

In any government, such pressures force the cabinet ministers to lean heavily on their civil service. In Saskatchewan, however, many of the cabinet ministers had anticipated deliberate "sabotage" or resistance to their plans by the Liberal civil service. They entered office ready to remove the deputy ministers as soon as they showed signs of opposition to government plans. The key civil servants, on the other hand, expected to be discharged soon after the C.C.F. took office. They knew that the C.C.F. was aware of the partisan nature of their appointments. Some of them had begun to look for other jobs, or planned to retire. The majority, however, in the hope of maintaining their positions, tried to ingratiate themselves with their ministers. . . .

The leading civil servants did their utmost to convince the cabinet that they were cooperative. In many departments, during the early period of the C.C.F. government, the best "socialists" in Saskatchewan were in the top ranks of the governmental bureaucracy. The administratively insecure cabinet ministers were overjoyed at the friendly response they obtained from the civil servants. To avoid making administrative blunders that would injure them in the eyes of the public and the party, the ministers began to depend on the civil servants. As one cabinet minister stated in an interview, "I would have been lost if not for the old members of my staff. I'm only a beginner in this work. B__ has been at it for twenty years. If I couldn't go to him for advice, I couldn't have done a thing. Why, now [after two years in office] I am only beginning to find my legs and make my own decisions . . . I have not done a thing for two years without advice."

The failure to change key members of the civil service had important consequences for the future work of the government. Some of the civil servants interpreted it as revealing personal weakness on the part of their ministers and political weakness on the part of the C.C.F. The deputy ministers, realizing that there was no danger of being discharged, fell back into the traditional bureaucratic pattern. A number of civil servants were able to convince their ministers that certain changes were not administratively feasible or that they would incur too much opposition. Some deputy ministers exchanged information with other deputies on their technique of controlling their ministers. It is difficult to demonstrate concretely

—without certain breaches of confidence—which policies were drastically affected by civil-service action, but it is a fact that some key officials boasted of "running my department completely," and of "stopping harebrained radical schemes."

The resistance of top-line civil servants to C.C.F. measures was not necessarily a result of conscious opposition to the party. The most important bureaucratic conservative influence on the government does not seem to be a result of attempts to injure the government in the eyes of the electorate. Many top-ranking civil servants, even though appointed as political partisans, appeared to be honestly concerned with doing their jobs. Their objections to C.C.F. proposals were based on a desire to maintain the stability of their departments and their own positions. These civil servants would probably have attempted to modify Liberal or Conservative schemes which they considered to be unworkable. The bureaucracy, however, had become institutionalized under old party governments. It had a set pattern of reacting to problems. New methods of administration were often designated "difficult" or "impossible" because they had never been tried before or would require revamping the work of a department. In opposing such changes, the civil servant was only taking the easy way out of preserving the *status, quo* of his own area of working and living. . . .

Civil-service modification of C.C.F. goals took three major forms: (1) the continuation of traditional and, from the C.C.F. point of view, reactionary procedure in government departments; (2) changes in the intent of new laws and regulations through administrative practices; (3) influence on cabinet ministers to adopt policies advocated by top-level civil servants. Information on the role of the civil service in modifying government activities was difficult to obtain, but, in discussing the work of the government, C.C.F. leaders, cabinet ministers, and civil servants provided significant glimpses into the operation of government policy.

Many local C.C.F. leaders expressed public resentment against the continuation of undesirable practices by local representatives of the government. Informants reported that before the C.C.F. was elected it was common practice in two departments to discriminate against non-Anglo-Saxon groups. These practices continued after the C.C.F. took office, for no one gave explicit orders to the contrary. The ministers were not aware of the fact that discrimination was the informal policy of the department. One cabinet minister changed the procedures in his department when he learned about these practices from local C.C.F. leaders, who had received complaints from people who had been discriminated against. The discrimination practiced by the second department was known only to persons within the department; as no public complaint was ever made, no changes occurred.

Similar charges about the continuation of "reactionary" practices were reported about the work of local field men in government departments.

These men had built up a local network of informants over a period of years. Many of the informants were active Liberals or local businessmen. The civil servants continued to rely on them for information after the C.C.F. took office. This sometimes resulted in government actions favoring the preservation of the partisan *status quo* in local administration. One cabinet minister, who has since discharged a large part of his field staff, found as a result of complaints from local members of the C.C.F. that members of his staff continued to grant leases and farming privileges to well-to-do persons who had secured them under previous governments, though it was now government policy to give them to poorer farmers and landless veterans. . . .

Civil-service activities that ran counter to over-all government policy could be checked only when the portion of the public served by the departments could observe what was being done. The permanent civil servant at the top of the administrative hierarchy was too deeply involved in the structure of mutual informal obligations and personal relations that exist in any long-established institution to call to his minister's attention practices that were contrary to C.C.F. objectives. The older civil servants did not realize that many of the practices of previous governments were repugnant to people who believed in the social reform philosophy of the C.C.F. movement, and thus were often not aware of any conflict between practices and objectives.

Cabinet ministers can hope to control the activities of their bureaucracy through reports from clients of government departments or sympathetic party followers. The minister, however, is at the mercy of his subordinates in situations in which the public at large is not aware of government activity. In such situations, civil servants who do not agree with, or do not understand the purposes of, the government are able to modify policy without much fear of detection. Max Weber has pointed out that the absolute dictator is often completely in the power of his bureaucracy, since, unlike the democratic ruler, he has no means of discovering whether his policies are being enforced.[5] Weber suggested that the bureaucracy is less powerful in a democracy, for the governing politicians will be kept informed by the public. This suggestion is only a half-truth, however, for the public can be aware of only a part of the government's activities. The areas of government work that are hidden from the eyes of the public are often closed to the cabinet minister as well. When the clients and the civil servants of a government department both disagree with the minister's policies, there is a great possibility that government policies will not be enforced. Both the clients and the bureaucracy will attempt to convince the minister that his policy is wrong, or they may simply ignore it.

5. H. H. Gerth and C. Wright Mills (translators and editors), *From Max Weber: Essays in Sociology* (New York: Oxford University Press, 1946), p. 234.

One cabinet minister decided that certain government work that had previously been contracted out to private concerns should be done by government employees whenever possible. His deputy minister, however, continued sending the work out to private concerns. This deputy told confidants that he considered government employees less competent than employees of private firms. Jobs were sometimes done twice, first by civil servants and later by private firms.

It is much more difficult to gather evidence about practices that take place behind closed doors. Members of the civil service have reported numerous examples of the modification of policies by civil servants—in confidence, however, which indicates that those coming to public or ministerial attention are only a small part of the actual efforts to change government policy at the administrative or enforcement level.

The modification of goals through administrative decisions represents only one aspect of the power of the civil service "House" to influence policy. Direct influence over the making of final policy, however, constitutes an aspect of the power of the permanent civil service which is as important as its ability to modify accepted policy through administrative procedure. An outsider cannot scientifically analyze the component elements entering into the decisions of a government department. Both permanent civil servants and new appointees of the C.C.F. report, however, that a number of top-ranking civil servants were able to convince cabinet members that some aspects of the C.C.F. program were impractical to administer. It is impossible to demonstrate that these civil servants were objectively wrong or insincere in opposing specific changes. Their objections to C.C.F. policy were usually based on the honest belief that the changes would not work.

Civil servants, of course, do not operate in a social vacuum. Their opinions about relative "right" and "wrong" are determined, like those of all persons, by pressures existing in their social milieu. A department official is interested not only in whether a minister's proposals can be put into practice, but with the effect of such policies on the traditional practices of the department and on its long-term relations with other groups. A reform which may be socially desirable, but which disrupts the continuity of practices and interpersonal relations within the department, will often be resisted by a top-ranking civil servant. He is obligated to protect those beneath him in the administrative hierarchy from the consequences of a change in policy.

Second, and equally important, the opinion of government officials on the feasibility of any proposal is necessarily colored by their political outlook and by the climate of opinion in their social group. Many top-ranking civil servants in Saskatchewan are members of the upper social class of Regina. Most of their social contacts are with people who believe that they will be adversely affected by many C.C.F. policies. Government officials who belong to professional or economic groups whose position or privileges are threatened by government policies tend to accept the opinion of their own group that reforms which adversely affect the group are wrong and will not work. Cabinet ministers who desire to make social reforms may therefore be dependent for advice on permanent civil servants who, in part, are members of the special-interest group which the ministers oppose. In Saskatchewan, as in other places, civil servants have been known to reduce the significance of reforms directed against their own group. They could hardly have been expected to draw up effective safeguards against "evils" the very existence of which they denied. . . .

An unplanned consequence of the struggle in the C.C.F. over civil-service reform has been an experimental test of the theories of those who urge that a radical reform government must have a sympathetic bureaucracy to carry out its program successfully. The Saskatchewan civil service today is a compromise between two approaches to the problem of bureaucracy; the larger part of it is a carry-over from previous governments, but a large minority of top-level positions are held by socialist experts. Many of the older civil servants had resisted changes which the C.C.F. ministers wanted. Some refused to serve on top-level committees where they would be personally responsible for government policies.

Many of the new C.C.F. civil servants, on the other hand, have suggested new policies that would probably never have been proposed if policy formation had been left to the cabinet and the permanent civil service. The ministers did not have the technical knowledge to suggest needed changes, and the old civil servants were not imbued with the C.C.F. values of finding means to reduce the wealth and power of private-interest groups and of using every agency of government to raise living standards. In at least two departments, the differences in orientation of the new and the old civil service resulted in a covert struggle to determine department policy. The permanent civil servants in two departments repeatedly brought their ministers in contact with representatives of the more conservative groups, while the C.C.F. civil servants encouraged supporters of reform to visit the ministers and impress them with the widespread public support for changes.

To specify the innovations initiated as a result of the activities of party experts would compromise the position of informants now working for the government. It is apparent, however, that there is a direct relation between the extent and vigor of reform and the degree to which key administrative positions are staffed by persons who believe in the formal goals of the C.C.F. If the government had followed its original intention of completely separating the civil service from politics, many of the changes that have been accomplished, both on the administrative and the legislative level, would not, in all probability, have taken place.

In recent years many have become concerned with the problem of bureaucracy in a large-scale society. The sheer size and complexity of social organizations, whether private or public, have created the need for a new "class" of administrators or bureaucrats to operate them efficiently. This new administrative group, necessarily, has been given a large amount of discretionary power. Once entrenched in corporations, trade-unions, political parties, and governments, the administrators develop "vested interests" of their own which may conflict with the interests of those who placed them in office. It seems to be universally true in social organization that men in power seek to maintain and extend their power, status, and privileges. Modern democratic society, therefore, faces the dilemma of making extensive grants of power without at the same time abdicating the right of the democratic constituency to change the policies and the personnel of the bureaucracy.

The justified concern with the dangers of oligarchic or bureaucratic domination has, however, led many persons to ignore the fact that it does make a difference to society which set of bureaucrats controls its destiny. There are bureaucracies and bureaucracies. To suggest, as many social scientists have done, that trade-unions, cooperatives, corporations, political parties, and states must develop a bureaucratic social structure in order to operate efficiently still leaves a large area of indeterminate social action for a bureaucratically organized society. Bureaucrats are human beings, not automatons. The desire to maintain a given bureaucratic organization is only one of the complex series of factors determining their actions. In a given situation, each group acts somewhat differently, according to its background. The reactions of the Russian "socialist" bureaucrats to problems of power were very different from those of the English socialist bureaucrats. A deterministic theory of bureaucratic behavior, such as that advanced by Robert Michels or James Burnham, neglects the implications of an alternative pattern of bureaucratic response.[6]

The focus on a single theory of bureaucracy has been encouraged by the lack of a sociological approach among political scientists. For the most part they have not raised questions about the social origins and values of government administrators and the relationship of such factors to government policy.[7] It is possible that the political scientists' blindness to the

6. See the excerpts from Michels included in this volume and James Burnham, *The Managerial Revolution* (New York, John Day Co., Inc., 1941).

7. Bendix's study of the origin of American federal administrators is the first such study in the United States. He reports that only one similar study was made in Europe. Reinhard Bendix, *Higher Civil Servants in American Society* (University of Colorado Press, 1949). See also Philip Selznick, *T.V.A. and the Grass Roots* (University of California Press, 1949), parts of which are included in this volume.

sources of civil-service "biases" may be related to their own identification with the government administrator, and their disinclination to accept the fact that the behavior of their own group is determined by personal "prejudice-creating" factors. Political scientists accepted the value of an unbiased civil servant who makes his decisions after analyzing the facts, presents the data to his minister, carries out the policy of the government in power, and then reverses his policy when a new government comes into office. Political history has been analyzed mainly in terms of struggles among interest groups and political parties. The civil service, like the political scientists, was simply a passive, neutral factor.

In recent years, however, political scientists have become aware of the fact that the government bureaucracy does play a significant role in determining policy. They still, however, leave the bureaucrat in a social vacuum. They now recognize that he plays an active role, but the determinants of that role are analyzed purely on the bureaucratic level. The bureaucrat's actions are analyzed on the basis of the goals of the civil service—self-preservation and efficiency. These interests may be defined in terms of prestige and privilege, preservation of patterns of organization or relationships within a department, or maintenance of department traditions and policies. There is little recognition that the behavior of government bureaucrats varies with the nongovernmental social background and interest of those controlling the bureaucratic structure. Members of a civil service are also members of other nongovernmental social groups and classes. Social pressures from many different group affiliations and loyalties determine individual behavior in most situations. The behavior of an individual or group in a given situation cannot be considered as if the individual or group members had no other life outside the given situation one is analyzing.

The direct relationship between class affiliations of members of a bureaucracy and the policies of the government has been demonstrated in the English civil service. J. Donald Kingsley has shown that as England changed from an aristocratically controlled nation to a capitalist state its civil service changed correspondingly.[8] The aristocrats who once dominated the British civil service gradually gave way to members of the middle class.

The experiences in Saskatchewan also indicate the relationship between the background and the actions of the civil service. Trained in the traditions of a laissez-faire government and belonging to conservative social groups, the civil service contributes significantly to the social inertia which blunts the changes a new radical government can make. Delay in initiating reforms means that the new government becomes absorbed in the process of operating the old institutions. The longer a new government delays in making changes, the more responsible it becomes for the old practices and the harder it is to make the changes it originally desired to institute. The prob-

8. Kingsley, *op. cit.*, pp. 42-77.

lem has not been crucial in Saskatchewan because of the small size of the government and its fairly limited powers. On a larger scale, however, as in Great Britain today, dependence on a conservative bureaucracy may prove to be significant in the success or failure of the Labor Government.

The suggestion that shake-ups in the civil service on the expert policy-making level may be necessary at times for the adequate functioning of democratic government has rarely been considered by North American political scientists. On this continent, the problem of the civil service has traditionally been that of patronage appointment with its resultant inefficiency and malpractice. European social theorists, on the contrary, have been concerned with the implications for social change of a permanent governmental bureaucracy with its own vested interests and social values.

The necessity to face up to the problem of bureaucratic resistance to change becomes urgent only when a "radical" party comes to office. The theory of civil-service neutrality breaks down when the total goals of the state change. A change from the Liberal to the Conservative Party or from the Democratic to the Republican Party does not usually require a civil servant to make any major adjustments.[9] The functions of the department and of the government as a whole remain fairly constant.

The socialist state, however, which has as its goal a reintegration of societal values, giving priority of government services to groups that had been neglected and securing a large measure of government control, may fail in its objectives if it leaves administrative power in the hands of men whose social background and previous training prevent a sympathetic appreciation of the objectives of the new government. "The planning state . . . will require men wholly committed to the purpose the State is undertaking to serve . . . men of 'push and go,' energetic innovators and harddriving managers." [10]

In American history, the two most significant departures from a merit civil service came during administrations which proposed shifts from the values and purposes of the previous government. Andrew Jackson felt it necessary, as the spokesman of the eastern workers and the western farmers, to break up the old permanent staff of the government in order to effect his program. His actions were based in part on a reasoned criticism of the actions of the civil service of his day, expressed in his Message to Congress in December, 1829.

There are, perhaps, few men who can for any great length of time enjoy office and power without being more or less under the influence of feelings un-

9. In defending a merit civil service, Leonard D. White and T. V. Smith suggest that it is possible to have a neutral bureaucracy in the United States because "the battles between Democrats and Republicans are fought on a narrow stage, with far greater areas of agreement between them than of disagreement." White and Smith, *Politics and Public Service* (New York, Harper and Brothers, 1939), pp. 132-133.

10. Kingsley, *op. cit.,* pp. 304-305.

favorable to the faithful discharge of their public duties. Their integrity may be proof against improper considerations immediately addressed to themselves, but they are apt to acquire a habit of looking with indifference upon the public interests and of tolerating conduct from which an unpracticed man would revolt.[11]

During the period of the American New Deal in the 1930's, "leaders of the Roosevelt administration privately complained of the difficulty of deflecting the bureaucracy from its ancient ways. The public service machine tended to continue in a straight line in disregard of the deviating influences of different public policy." [12] According to James A. Farley, "Some of the greatest troubles the President had were caused by subordinate officials who were in sharp disagreement with his policies and, rightly or wrongly, were sabotaging the job he was trying to accomplish." [13]

"The Roosevelt Administration was forced to assemble almost a whole new set of officials to carry out the New Deal reforms." [14]

There is no simple solution to the dilemma of keeping government administration efficient as well as responsive to the will of the electorate. The increase in the power, functions, and sheer size of modern government necessitates the search for some means of controlling the bureaucracy. It is utopian to think that the electorate's dismissal of the inexpert politician, who formally heads the bureaucracy, will by itself change the course of bureaucratic activities. As Max Weber stated: "The question is always who controls the existing bureaucratic machinery. And such control is possible only in a very limited degree to persons who are not technical specialists. Generally speaking, the trained permanent official is more likely to get his way in the long run than his nominal supervisor, the Cabinet Minister, who is not a specialist." [15]

Government today is a large-scale administrative job requiring experts to operate it. Unless the electorate is given the opportunity to change the key experts as well as the politicians, elections will lose much of their significance. This problem will become more and more significant as efforts are made to increase the economic and social welfare role of the state.

11. Quoted in White and Smith, *op. cit.*, p. 44.
12. *Ibid.*, p. 57.
13. *Ibid.*, p. 92.
14. Kingsley, *op. cit.*, p. 274.
15. Max Weber, *The Theory of Social and Economic Organization* (trans. by Talcott Parsons and A. M. Henderson; New York, Oxford University Press, 1947), p. 128.

DECISION-MAKING BY MANAGEMENT IN INDUSTRIAL RELATIONS

Robert Dubin

Collective bargaining is bargaining. It is the active interplay of demands and counterproposals. It results from a series of immediate and long-range decisions marked by extremely sensitive responses between bargainers. Understandings and disagreements are made explicit. Little if anything is left to gentlemen's agreements. Union-management relations are characterized by highly developed, self-conscious interaction between the parties whose moves are dictated by a continual stream of decisions made in adjusting to each other and the bargaining situation. Hence, the importance of examining some of the factors influencing management decision-making in industrial relations.

There are important imperatives arising out of the organization of business itself which affect decisions concerning industrial relations. These organizational imperatives deserve serious study. They profoundly influence the kind and timing of decisions made in collective bargaining by business managers.

Immediate expediencies and the compromises of collective power relations determine much of what happens in union-management relations. Yet, within the context of this rapidly shifting relationship, it is possible to detect repeating uniformities, some of which are directly attributable to the requirements of business organizations.

GOVERNING BY RULES. In a large company with multiple plant operations the most obvious single consideration affecting labor relations decisions is the need for standardization and uniformity. Unquestionably, the administration of a work force of several hundred thousand, or fifty thousand, or even five thousand is a staggering job. It would be totally impracticable to attempt individualized treatment of so many workers. The almost nostalgic plea for the "clinical" approach,[1] that is, for the setting-forth of "all the facts" in every employee problem, is hardly possible in the large-scale enterprise.[2] This is not to say that it would not be desirable or humane to treat

Reprinted from *The American Journal of Sociology*, LIV (1949), pp. 292-297, by permission of the author and the publisher. (Copyright, 1949, by *The American Journal of Sociology*.)

1. Cf. B. M. Selekman, *Labor Relations and Human Relations* (New York: McGraw-Hill Book Co., 1947), chap. v.

2. See, *e.g.*, P. Pigors and C. A. Meyers, *Personnel Administration* (New York: McGraw-Hill Book Co., 1947), chap. v.

each worker as an individual. The emphasis is rather on the fact that administration in the big firm necessitates standardization through rules and uniform procedures as a basis for prediction of future events. Management must be in a position to predict what will be the outcome, granting a given personnel situation. Similarly, employees are provided with a basis for predicting the effect of their own action or that of management representatives in the light of the rules governing their relationship to each other.

The "reign of rules" is the administrative answer to the problems of governing in large-scale organizations. This rule-making habit is all-pervading. It takes its most obvious form in shop rules governing personal conduct and in the union agreement which sets forth the mutual rights and obligations of the contracting parties and their constituents. But job descriptions, production standards, standard procedures, wage-rate structures, and policy manuals are rule-making, too. Even a casual examination of the manuals of procedures, operating codes, standards, and specifications to be found in most any industrial or commercial firm should be convincing evidence that rule-making and enforcing for the class rather than decision-making in the individual case plays an increasing role in the functions of the executive.

There is an interesting paradox involved in the growth of governing by rule in large businesses. The goal of standardization and hence of predictability is certainly achieved. But making the rule for the class rather than the individual does two things to the individual worker. He becomes aware of his personal inability to make an individual "deal" for himself outside the company rules and procedures, except under the circumstances of a "lucky break." He tends also to view himself as part of a group of similarly situated fellow-employees who are defined by the rules as being like each other. In addition, uniform rule-making and administration of the rules makes unionism easier and, in a sense, inevitable. It should be reasonably clear that collective bargaining is joint rule-making. It is no great step to the joint determination by union and management of rules governing employment from the determination of them by management alone. Both proceed from the basic assumption that generally applicable rules are necessary to govern the relations between men in the plant. Once a worker accepts the need for general rules covering his own conduct, he is equally likely to consider the possibility of modifying the existing ones in his favor rather than to seek their total abolishment.

The paradox stands out clearly. Governing men by general rules in a business makes for administrative efficiency. At the same time it is likely to assist the growth of unionism, if not make it inevitable. The question is then raised as to how much efficiency in decision-making is lost though collective bargaining as over against decision-making solely through the management structure.

This paradox is not the sole result of governing by rules. In a company which bargains with a single union for many plants, as General Motors does with the U.A.W.-C.I.O., company-wide bargaining reinforces the existing tendencies toward standardization. From the union standpoint a gain or loss made in the contract is shared by all members of the bargaining unit in all plants of the company. From the company standpoint a master-contract is necessary lest bargaining in the individual plant should result in local gains which would then be pressed by the union for application throughout the company. The company seeks to protect itself from such whipsaw tactics with a master-contract, standardized for all company bargaining units.

A second result of governing by rules is centralization in decision-making on industrial relations problems. It is clear that high-level decisions are required for broadly applicable rules. Personnel and collective bargaining policies tend to be applied generally throughout the organization. The decisions affecting them gravitate to a central point, less and less discretion being permitted to the local or department management. Thus, General Motors, with a highly developed theory of decentralized management, has perfected centralized control in the industrial relations field—even individual job rates negotiated locally must be reviewed and approved in Detroit before becoming effective.

What, then, are the organization imperatives affecting industrial relations decisions which can be related to size of firm? We can expect unco-ordinated decisions dealing, case by case, with individual workers to be replaced by rules which apply impartially to classes of employees. The real decision-making power and skill are involved in establishing the rules. Their administration tends to be reduced to mechanical formula or may even be permitted to go completely outside the company structure by the settlement of disputes by umpires or arbitrators. In addition, centralized decision-making is generally associated with standardized rules. Unionism is both an effective means for worker intervention in company rule-making as well as a force amplifying the tendency for centralized management decision-making.

What the union regards as the "buck-passing" sometimes displayed by lower-level supervisors and executives is, in reality, logical behavior in a system of centralized decision-making. In addition, the slowness with which systems of rules are permitted to change through collective bargaining or administrative decision is a product of the cohesion of the rule systems and the internal logic which binds the rules into systems. The personal relations between company and union officials will tend to have diminishing influence upon decisions affecting their relationship. The criterion of sound decisions is then conformity with a pre-existing set of rules; the character and integrity of the bargainer on the other side of the table hardly matter. There is no cordiality in the relations that exist between John L. Lewis and the coal-industry spokesmen with whom he bargains on an industry-wide basis. Yet the two parties are able to establish elaborate rules through collective bargaining as a basis for continuing relations.

THE RULE-MAKING PROCESSES. A business is characterized by a high degree of organization. This is exemplified in the formal organization chart and the minute functional divisions of work. A consequence of the complicated structure of a firm is its sensitivity to changes in operations; indeed, the very existence of an individual business may depend upon its ability to adjust to changing conditions affecting operations.

It is typical for a business to operate on a crisis basis. There are always problems, either internal or external, whose solution requires constant choices among several courses of action. Conscious and explicit decisions are repeatedly being made throughout the company which solve immediate problems. Such problems arise constantly in all phases of the business. Generally minimized in a business are the areas in which common understandings and traditional solutions to problems are prevalent. The "new" and "novel," the "better" way of doing it, "bigger" and "better" products, are commonly used adjectives reflecting the premium placed upon change. But change resulting from meeting crises in the business is not given unlimited range.

Decisions affecting the firm are made in the light of a body of policy and practice already in existence. This provides a practical limit on the extent to which innovations can be incorporated into the operating creed of the business. Moreover, decision-making areas have different degrees of susceptibility to change. In the fields of production processes and methods engineering, changes which produce greater efficiency or lower costs are constantly being sought. The highest premium on change is probably in those areas. The same is true of the sales field and advertising. In the area of industrial relations or personnel management changes may be accepted much more reluctantly. In fact, the objective of management policy may be stability rather than change.

Within particular areas of decision there is a tendency toward consistency in policy. This consistency may be seen in two ways: (1) decisions making changes from established policy or practice are tested and generally brought into alignment with (or necessitate a change in) the existing body of procedure and policy; and (2) in putting the change into practice organizational realignments may be necessary. In any event, the very segregation of areas of decision from each other creates an imperative only for consistency within rather than between areas. Sometimes one of the most difficult functions of the key management decision-makers is to resolve conflicts in policy or practice between areas of business operations. For example, the sales department may insist on a particular design of the product because of its consumer appeal. The production people argue against the design on grounds of difficulty or expense of manufacture. Both groups are right and consistent within their respective areas of operation. When the choice is finally made, it will represent a tactical defeat and not a defeat in principle to the losing group. The loser would urge the same course under similar circumstances in the future.

This point has an important bearing on decision-making in industrial relations. Observers have often been struck by what appears to be an abandonment of strict business thinking in certain decisions about labor relations. For example, very severe financial risks may be accepted in pursuit of a labor policy—witness the year-long strike at the J. I. Case Company after the war which practically halted production and sales during most of the period of the strike. A decision to risk such a lengthy interruption in sales, if based upon considerations of production or raw materials or design, would certainly be viewed with skepticism. But a decision leading to the same result in labor relations was judged on quite other grounds than its influence on profit and loss. What such an instance illustrates is that policy formation on labor issues can readily proceed from premises unlike those behind other business decisions. Management decisions in the field of industrial relations are not always characterized by the logic of the market.

The characteristic of specialized areas of decision following the functional division of labor is common to all organization. It represents a feature of bureaucracy in which the job-holder succeeds in making his job self-contained and as independent as possible of all other jobs. The "let George do it" attitude, when found in a firm, is an excellent index that George operates in a separate compartment of business action and decision, recognized as discrete by both himself and his fellow-workers. Contrariwise, emphasis on "co-ordination" or "integration" or "rationalization" in the business firm is another evidence of concern with over-specialization of action and decision.

The officials responsible for accounting or production or personnel come to think in terms of their professional specialization within a framework peculiar to their own line of work. As the ideas unique to a specialty become more specialized, associates in other departments of the firm are more inclined to stay out of the area of the specialist, partly because they are no longer familiar with his frame of reference or comfortable with his jargon. The specialist follows the logic of his specialty and tends to bring his actions and decisions into conformity with it. The segregation of industrial relations as a separate field of business activity has resulted in the designation of distinct functionaries and the rise of outside paid consultants. The specialization, however, does not insure a broad consensus regarding a frame of reference for industrial relations men. What, then, is the basis for the logical system within which the individual industrial relations executive operates?

An industrial relations specialist typically does not have firsthand knowledge of production processes and plant operations. His knowledge is about people and the operations of hiring, placement, training, promotion, layoff, discharge, retirement, etc. All these processing operations are standardized and of general application. They are most easily controlled through general rules. Again we come back to the question of rule-making, but this time in terms of specific policy problems rather than as previously considered in terms of the broad movement toward governing by rules. It is one of the important advisory functions of the industrial relations specialist to emphasize to line officials the need for hewing to the line of shop rules, company policy, and the union agreement.

Most of the issues dealt with by personnel and labor relations men can be handled with little reference to the details of production processes.[3] This has led to an almost universal plagiarism in the field. Industrial relations specialists have an insatiable hunger to know what is being done in other companies. Any policy, technique, or gadget which might be used in the home company is quickly copied. In fact, many of the paid consultants in the field have as their main stock-in-trade a set of gadgets or a "system" which is extolled for universal application.

The logic of the industrial relations specialists can then best be characterized as a preoccupation with the internal consistency of rules, procedures, and operations concerning the processing of groups of people within a company. Increasing separation from production and operations has tended to divorce many of the decisions of policy in industrial relations from production decisions, whether the labor decisions are made directly by the industrial relations specialist or by top executives on his advice.

COLLECTIVE BARGAINING. We will examine three of the several aspects of collective bargaining which relate directly to the decision-making processes in a company.

When union and company bargain, the relative flexibility of each side to compromise is a significant condition. Structurally, management is in a more favored position in this regard. Management has centralized and absolute control at the top levels over its own policy formation. It does not need ratification of its policy except within its own ranks, and then only at the top. The union is a political organization, and its officials owe an accounting to membership for official action in collective bargaining. Union leadership is constantly confronted with the need for bringing the outcome of its bargaining into accord with the initial promises made.

In actual contract negotiations unions often appear to be more flexible than management. An explanation is not hard to find. Management policy is generally more firmly fixed and explicitly expressed in company rules and policy. Furthermore, management has a central core of resistance to union invasion of management's decision-making authority. Jointly determined

3. The current emphasis in the labor relations literature on "bringing the foremen in on pre-bargaining sessions to help formulate company policy" is a reflection of the extent to which company labor relations specialists have lost contact with the production end of the business. The general approval with which it is urged to bring line officers into closer contact with labor relations policy formation indicates the self-conscious recognition by some labor specialists that they may have overspecialized their role.

policies always invade what were formerly exclusive management decisions. Management was there first. It had sole power within the limits of government regulation to set the conditions for employment in the business. The union is always making the demands. The company seeks to defend itself against the "inch-worm" tactics of the union to gain a point here and there in an apparently unco-ordinated drive against aspects of company policy. Any management concession is a potential threat to the entire labor policy because it is likely to unstabilize a more or less consistent structure. The result can be either a slow change and the gradual evolving of a new pattern of management-labor policy through long-time collective bargaining or a dramatic conversion and reorientation. Industry generally was shocked and surprised when the Taylor-Lewis agreement opened the door to the organization of the steel industry in 1937 and the eventual organization of most mass-production industries as well.[4]

A second point related to the question of flexibility in decision-making has to do with the extent of a break from past policy. It must be recognized that each individual union-management relationship does not recapitulate the historical development of collective bargaining in general. A union seeks to incorporate all its latest gains in the labor contract at the newly or recently organized company. This means that on the employer's side, in addition to giving up or modifying the powers of sole decision in labor matters, there is little opportunity for a gradual union encroachment on management decision-making prerogatives. One need only to talk to a typical open-shop foreman faced with living under his first union contract to realize the impact of this situation within the entire management structure. The same type of crisis is faced by a management which has developed a feeling of security because of a stable relationship with its union. Suddenly a new pattern is set in a key union contract. The local union wants the concession gained in the pattern-setting company. The local management is forced to readjust, or at least consider readjusting, its entire policy structure to the new conditions.

The extent, then, to which the new body of policy proposed to management departs from the existing structure of policy may be crucial in determining the ease of transition. At the same time, of course, a temporary alternative is to go along with the proposed change, however radical. Management may view compliance with the pattern as expedient until the day when matters will be restored to an older balance. Management usually has very strong incentives for taking advantage of every opportunity to hasten the

---

4. The "conversion" character of management reaction to the initial thrust of unionism is not untypical. It can be taken as further evidence of a major reorientation of management-labor policy on the concession of only one point—in this case, recognition. Ford, it will be recalled, far exceeded the other motorcar companies in meeting union demands after he recognized the union. This came after the bitterest sort of opposition to unionism continuing long after union recognition had been gained at General Motors and had made headway generally throughout the industry.

return to the older balance. Thus, the imperative of relative consistency in labor policy may provide the basis, not only for management defense against current union demands, but also for the framework of a positive formulation of management demands. There is some considerable evidence at present, for example, that individual firms are succeeding in bargaining successfully for a return to previous positions in relations with the union.

The third general point with respect to collective bargaining is the development of formalism as distinct from a more pragmatic approach. There has been an almost universal growth in the length and complexity of union contracts. This is in part because they now cover more subjects. It is primarily due, however, to the compulsion to expand, qualify, and define rules and their application and limitation. The very rule-making process leads to formalism and a legalistic outlook. This is no better illustrated than in the briefs often submitted to impartial umpires and arbitrators. They are written in courtroom jargon, with appropriate reference to the rule or rules violated, precedent decisions and interpretations of the rules, and the evidence supporting the actions of the parties to the controversy. One of the results of formalism and the reign of rules is to deal with symptoms of worker dissatisfaction and industrial unrest rather than their causes. For example, in one of our very largest corporations, a union official was discharged for leadership in organized defiance of management in violation of the contract. Workers objected to a work schedule and the arrangement of time clocks in relation to place of work. Yet, the umpire ultimately had to rule on the merits of the union official's discharge and was never even asked to consider—and, in fact, would have been prohibited according to the contract from considering—the issues which created worker unrest.

Emphasis has been centered in this discussion on some of the considerations affecting management decision-making in industrial relations. In particular, attention has been focused on some of the influences which are traceable to the character of business organization and generally not within the scope of personal control. This is by no means a complete coverage of management decision-making in the labor field. Nevertheless, these notes may suggest an approach to the study of industrial relations by seeking the underlying uniformities which characterize a highly mercurial social relationship.[5]

5. *Cf.* Herbert Blumer, "Sociological Theory in Industrial Relations," *American Sociological Review*, XII (June, 1947), 271-78.

Status Systems and Gradations of Prestige

In recent years, empirical studies of industrial, political and military bureaucracies have rediscovered the importance of the small groups and interpersonal relations which form, typically not according to plan, at many points in these large organizations. The newfound emphasis of social research on these informal groups has contributed greatly and promises to contribute further to our understanding of the ways in which bureaucracies operate. But as it gathers force, this emphasis threatens to obscure the basic fact that the main lines of authority and control are not merely the resultants of these informal relations, however much they may be affected by them. The importance of small groups, emerging spontaneously from interactions within the bureaucracy, may for a time have been lost to view; it would be a disservice to have renewed interest in these groups crowd out systematic concern with the formal structure. The selections in this chapter avoid any such tendency, being variously concerned with the linkages between the two. Among other things, they show how there develop two systems of status which are not always in accord: the individual's formal position in the bureaucracy need not coincide with the informal ranking assigned him by associates.

Barnard traces out the sources of status systems within bureaucracy and their implications for the adaptability of the organization. In their brief summary of the formal and informal organization of an industrial plant, Roethlisberger and Dickson emphasize the interdependence of the two and their distinctive social functions. The selection by Dreyfuss goes on to suggest that recognition of the importance of prestige gradations can lead employers to substitute wholly symbolic distinctions for other forms of reward.

Status systems generate their own sustaining beliefs and myths. The selection by Stouffer and his collaborators presents systematic data of a kind not often utilized in the study of bureaucracy to show how status barriers in the American army impeded communication and led officers to develop distorted images of sentiments prevailing among enlisted men. And the article by Myers illustrates the status-preserving function of myths for various occupational groups in industry.

THE FUNCTIONS OF STATUS SYSTEMS

Chester I. Barnard

The analysis to be presented herein is based upon experience and observation of the kind commonly understood by those who have organizing and executive experience, but it does not purport to express a consensus of opinion. It sets forth that systems of status in formal organizations are necessary as a matter of need of individuals, and as imposed by the characteristics of cooperative systems, especially with respect to the techniques of communication essential to coordination. But it also appears that systems of status generate uncontrolled and even uncontrollable tendencies to rigidity, hypertrophy, and unbalance that often lead to destruction of organization.

The scheme of presentation is as follows: the·nature and technical apparatus of status systems; the functions of status systems with respect to individuals; the functions of status in cooperative systems; and the destructive tendencies of systems of status.

THE NATURE AND TECHNICAL APPARATUS OF SYSTEMS OF STATUS IN FORMAL ORGANIZATIONS. By "status" of an individual in an organization we mean in the present text that condition of the individual that is defined by a statement of his rights, privileges, immunities, duties, and obligations in the organization and, obversely, by a statement of the restrictions, limitations, and prohibitions governing his behavior, both determining the expectations of others in reference thereto. Status becomes systematic in an organization when appropriate recognition of assigned status becomes the duty and the practice of all participating, and when the conditions of the status of all individuals are published by means of differentiating designations, titles, appellations, insignia, or overt patterns of behavior.

Two kinds of systems of status may be discriminated, both being simultaneously observed in nearly all organizations and being partly overlapping and interdependent. The first kind, which we shall call *functional* systems of status, is that in which status does not depend upon authority and jurisdiction but upon function. The ranks are vertically divided into lateral groups of different callings, trades, crafts, métiers, divisions of labor, specializations, and professions. One common characteristic of them all is that authority of command of one over another is lacking, or is irrelevant at least to the functional status. But this does not mean that functional statuses are equally

Reprinted in part from "Functions and Pathology of Status Systems in Formal Organizations," pp. 207-243, in *Industry and Society*, edited by William F. Whyte. (Copyright, 1946. Courtesy of McGraw-Hill Book Company, New York.)

valued. On the contrary, the variation is wide, from the "low" of common, unskilled, and casual labor, intermittently attached to organizations, to the "high," *e.g.*, of the expert accountant, lawyer, architect, physician, and clergyman. Though lateral differentiation of status is not confined to formal organizations, it is a characteristic of such organizations generally and especially of the larger organizations conspicuous for their elaborate divisions of labor.

Functional status is a general attribute. For example, merely performing carpentering at a given place, which would determine specific status varying for each individual from time to time and from place to place, is not what we mean by functional status. The "carpenter" is presumed by all to have certain capacities regardless of who he is or what he is doing and conversely is presumed to have limitations, *e.g.*, he is not authorized to give medical advice. It is the presumption of capacities and limitations without necessary regard to the immediate concrete activities of the individual that is the essential feature of systematic status. The emphasis is upon the potentialities of behavior, not necessarily upon the immediately observable behavior.

In the second kind of status system, which we shall call the *scalar*, status is determined by (1) the relationship of superiority or subordination in a chain of command or formal authority and (2) by jurisdiction. In this kind of status system the primary relationships are customarily conceived as being along vertical lines, of above and below, of superior and subordinate. Status is distinguished by horizontal levels, and integration is by vertical groups, several such groups exemplifying a "pyramid of authority." It should be noted that status is a general attribute of an individual associated with the occupation of a usually rather narrowly restricted position. For example, a naval captain possesses certain prerogatives not enjoyed by those of inferior rank and is deemed qualified for positions for which those of inferior rank will not ordinarily be acceptable; but the position of command actually occupied at a given time will be confined to a particular ship or shore station or staff position, and the immediate authority and responsibility will be correspondingly restricted.

Although the status systems of general societies will not be treated in this paper, the close interrelation of general social status and status in organizations should be noted. Where in a general society a low status is assigned, based, *e.g.*, on race, nationality, sex, age, education, ownership of property, or family, it is difficult in general to acquire high status in formal organizations in that society; and where there is high social status it tends to facilitate attainment of high organization status, though less so in democratic than in aristocratic societies. Conversely, those having low status in a formal organization are not likely to have high social status, though there are many exceptions; and those having high status, especially in important organizations, tend thereby to acquire higher general social status. The bearing of this is that if status systems are necessary in formal organizations, it is probable that they will extend into general social relationships, in greater or less degree, depending upon the society.[1]

Nearly all members of formal organizations may be observed to be much preoccupied with matters of status; and the leaders or managers of such organizations are almost constantly concerned with problems of status for reasons that will be treated in some detail later. But to fix more clearly what we mean by status, it seems desirable to present briefly here the organization apparatus by which status is established and maintained. This apparatus may be described as of the following categories: (1) ceremonies of induction and appointment; (2) insignia and other public indicia of status; (3) titles and appellations of office and calling; (4) emoluments and perquisites of position and office; (5) limitations and restrictions of calling and office. . . .

THE FUNCTIONS OF SYSTEMS OF STATUS WITH RESPECT TO INDIVIDUALS. Systems of status of different kinds and of various degrees of elaborateness and complexity are found in most if not all formal organizations. The establishing of a nucleus of such a system is one of the very first steps in creating an organization.[2] Are these facts merely reflections of habitual attitudes and needs transferred from general society and coming down from antiquity? The view to be developed here is that systems of status, though they may be affected in degrees and in details by habitual attitudes and needs projected from the customary beliefs of people, are fundamentally determined by the necessities associated with the needs and interests of individuals as biological and social units, and upon the requirements arising from the physical and social limitations inherent in systems of cooperation. . . .

It may be asserted first of all that systems of status arise from the differential needs, interests, and capacities of individuals. I shall discuss these in five topical divisions, as follows:

  I. The differences in the *abilities* of individuals.
  II. The differences in the *difficulties* of doing various kinds of work.
  III. The differences in the *importance* of various kinds of work.
  IV. The desire for formal status as a social or organizational tool.
  V. The need for protection of the integrity of the person . . .

  1. Differences of ability with respect to any kind of effort in which

1. During the last several generations, when scalar organizations were developing rapidly in Germany, organization status was carried over widely into generalized status in German society, formally, *i.e.*, by title. See Talcott Parsons, "Democracy and Social Structure in Pre-Nazi Germany," *Journal of Legal and Political Sociology*, November, 1942.

2. In the case of corporations, corporation law provides . . . often for both boards of directors and for two or more general officers. Bylaws almost always provide for additional general officers. In the case of individually owned businesses and partnerships, the nucleus of the status system rests initially directly upon property ownership. Similarly with noncommercial organizations, the first steps in organizing are likely to be to create an initial governing board and a set of officers.

there is social interest obviously lead to a recognition of difference of status of individuals in respect to that kind of effort. This does not necessarily imply superiority or inferiority in general, although, in fact, usually the lack of capacity of individuals for most kinds of effort or even for any valued effort whatsoever does inescapably establish for them a general position of at least technical or productive inferiority. . . .

II. The second base for status is, as contrasted with personal ability, the relative difficulty of things to be done. The difficulties will usually be appraised on judgment based on general experience and observation; or, more objectively, on the basis of the numbers or proportions of individuals who can or cannot do well the various tasks. . . .

III. Superiority in formal organizations depends upon exceptional ability for exceptionally difficult work of exceptional *importance*. "Importance" in this context includes more than economic importance. High status is not accorded to superior ability to do unusually difficult things of trivial character, except perhaps in very restricted circles. On the contrary, if an activity is regarded as exceptionally important, even though not very difficult, superior status is nevertheless likely to be accorded to superior ability with respect to it. . . .

IV. Generally, the possession of title and of other indicia of rank certifies that those in the best position to have responsible judgment acknowledge and publish the status indicated, which all whom it may concern may accept at least tentatively. The convenience and efficiency of the status system is such that men seek status as a necessary tool in their work; and for the same reasons it is imposed upon them by those responsible for their work. It is to be noted that this applies as much to functional status as it does to scalar status.

V. In so far as systems of status are imposed "from the top" they are expressions of the requirements of coordination rather than of the ambitions of the most able and powerful acting on the basis of personal motives. The personal motivation of most profound effect, applying equally to those of superior and to those of inferior status, is the need for protecting the integrity of the person in a social environment. This leads some to seek superior formal status, but it also leads others to refuse superior status and even to seek inferior status, depending upon the individual and the circumstances. This may be demonstrated sufficiently by presenting four modes in which the need for status is expressed: (1) the need of integrating personal history by the conferring of status; (2) the need of imputing superior status to those from whom commands are to be received; (3) the need of imputing superior status as a means of symbolizing possession of personal value in participating in an organization; and (4) the need of status as a protection against excessive claims against the individual . . .

THE FUNCTIONS OF STATUS IN COOPERATIVE SYSTEMS. Up to this point the approach to systems of status has been in terms of the characteristics of human beings and their bearing on behavior and fundamental relationships in formal systems of cooperation. . . . Much of the theory stated above appears to be sensed by executives, though not necessarily comprehended intellectually and not made explicit. . . .

Proceeding, then, on this level of discourse it appears necessary to the executive to recognize by some formal means differences in the ability of individuals and differences in the importance of their work or of their contribution to cooperative effort. However, executives are probably much more conscious of the necessity of systems of status as (I) a function of the system of organization communication, the fundamental process in cooperation; (II) as an important part of the system of incentives; and (III) as an essential means of inculcating and developing a sense of responsibility and of imposing and fixing responsibility.

I. A system of organization communication, in order that it may operate with sufficient accuracy and rapidity, has to be so designed that it may easily and quickly be assured that particular communications are (1) authentic, (2) authoritative, and (3) intelligible.

(1) Under ordinary circumstances, and especially with respect to routine matters, explicit authentication of communications is not required. Personal acquaintance with or knowledge of the communicator together with the relevance of the communication to the general context and to previous communications are sufficient. The status system is not of great importance in this connection. But in times of emergency and great danger or in respect to important matters, explicit authentication of communications often becomes necessary. Witnessed written communications or letterheads indicating the name, position, and title of the communicator and personal introductions by mutually known third parties are among the means used. There is no doubt that here the status system greatly facilitates authentication—it is one of the practical uses of insignia of office.

(2) It is in respect to the authoritativeness of a communication, however, that we find the basic need for systems of status. The primary question of the recipient of a communication, assuming that it is authentic, i.e., comes from whom it purports to come, is whether the contents of the communication may be relied upon as a basis for action. This is what we mean by authoritativeness. Authoritativeness in this context is of two kinds: functional authoritativeness; and scalar or command authoritativeness.

Whether a communication reflects the facts and needs of the situation depends upon whether the individual (or body) that emits it has the general qualifications for understanding what he (or it) communicates about and whether he is *in a position* to have the essential concrete knowledge.

A report from a carpenter about the condition of a generator in a power house is initially not credible; that of the electrician in charge is credible, though not conclusive; that of an electric power engineer is more credible and *may* be accepted as final. The authoritativeness of the report depends in part upon the qualifications of those reporting, and these are presumptively established by formal status. . . .

The functional status system is so extraordinarily convenient in providing prima-facie evidence of the authoritativeness of communications that we depend upon it almost exclusively in the conduct of daily affairs generally as well as in all organizations. It does not imply any generalized superiority or inferiority of status in this aspect. It does not exclude discrimination as between individuals having the same status, nor does it assume errors may not occur in relying upon the prima-facie evidence granted by status. . . .

(3) The special system of status associated with chains of command or hierarchy of authority depends upon each position being a "communication center," the inferior command being associated with restricted areas or fields, the higher command being more comprehensive. Outside the technical competence special to each field of organization, the general functions common to all hierarchies of command are: to evaluate the meaning of communications received in the form of advices and reports, largely affected by the status of the transmitter; to know to whom communications should be relayed (*i.e.*, to know the relevant status system or "the organization"); to select that which needs to be relayed; and to translate communications, before relaying, into language appropriate to the receiver.

The system of command communication cannot effectively work except on the basis of a status system. For very small organizations communication may effectively be addressed to persons, but for larger systems status becomes primary. Contrast saying to the new office boy, "Take this order to Bill Jones in building K" (in which there are two Bill Joneses) and "Take this order to the foreman of section 12 in the Y Department in building K." . . .

Although both functional and scalar systems of status are essential to establishing in a practicable degree the authoritativeness of communications, authoritativeness is not sufficient. Unless communications are intelligible, they cannot be acted upon correctly or effectively. Now, it is apparent that the intelligibility of a communication depends not merely upon the capacity of the communicator but also upon that of the receiver. Thus communications of the same content will differ very greatly, depending upon the status of those to whom they are addressed. Whether a communication is intelligible depends upon the use of language having the same meaning to the originator and to the receiver of the communication. This requires a selection of language, depending upon from whom and to whom the communication is made. Systems of status are an indispensable guide to the selection of appropriate language. . . .

II. Systems of status are also important because maintenance of status and improvement of status are among the essential incentives to cooperation. The scarcity of effective incentives calls for use of many kinds of incentives; and their wise use requires, especially in larger organizations, their systematic use.

Status as an incentive has two aspects suggested earlier. The first is that of prestige for its own sake, as a reinforcement of the ego, as security for the integrity of the person. This is an important need of many individuals. They will work hard to satisfy it and forego much to attain it. The second aspect is that of prestige as a valuable or indispensable means to other ends. Thus some men endure publicity or accept conspicuous positions of onerous character as a means of supporting organizations or of eliciting the support of others because they like philanthropic, or scientific, or cultural work, which is their fundamental incentive.

The importance of status as an incentive is shown by the immense amount of work and sacrifice made by innumerable volunteer heads of social, philanthropic, religious, political, and scientific organizations. For some the motive is directly personal. For others it is the "good of the cause" and the personal incentive is satisfaction in the promotion of that cause . . .

III. The system of status is a strong and probably an indispensable developer of the sense of responsibility and therefore of stability and reliability. Loss of status is more than loss of its emoluments; it is more than loss of prestige. It is a serious injury to the personality. Thus while improvement of status is important, especially to the more able, and desirable to many, loss of status is much more generally resisted. It is difficult to accept, or to be accepted in, a reduced status. Indeed, the fear of losing status is what leads some to refuse advancement of status. The desire for improvement of status and especially the desire to protect status appear to be the basis of the sense of general responsibility. Responsibility is established and enforced by specific penalties for specific failures and by limitation of status or by loss of a particular status for failure in general. Although both methods in conjunction are most effective, of the two it would appear that the second is much more effective than the first, especially as to those above low levels of status. In view of the extreme importance of dependable behavior, the function of status in creating and maintaining dependable behavior is probably indispensable. The extent of criminal behavior suggests that specific sanctions are not sufficient in general to establish adequate responsibility.

We have now completed an abbreviated presentation of a rationale of status systems universally found in scalar organizations. What has been set forth may well be summarized before we proceed to consider the disruptive tendencies inherent in them.

Status systems have their origins in differences in the biological and socially acquired characteristics of individuals, in differences in the difficulties of the various kinds of activities, and in differences in the valuation of these activities. Systems of status are a means of protecting the integrity of the person, especially of those of inferior ability. Superior status is often necessary to the effectiveness of the work of those of superior ability. All this is on the level of biology and social psychology. Additional observations on the level of sociology and the technique of organization show that systems of status are necessary to specialization of function; that they are essential to the system of organization communications for purposes of coordination; that they are important and sometimes indispensable as affording incentives; and that they are important in promoting the sense of responsibility and, therefore, the dependability and stability essential to cooperation. These inductions from experience and observation and from history are not scientific proof of the theory outlined; but they are believed to present a fair basis, of considerable probability of correctness, for the assertion that systems of status are not the product of irrational mores, mythologies, and rationalizations, but are specific modes of adaptation of behavior to fundamental characteristics of individuals and to the fundamental physical, biological, and social properties of systems of scalar organization.

DISRUPTIVE TENDENCIES INHERENT IN STATUS SYSTEMS. The concern of executives is not only with the organizing functions of systems of status but with their disruptive tendencies; for, paradoxically, such systems operate like principles of growth, necessary to attain maturity, but without a self-regulative control that prevents disproportionate development of parts, unbalance, and maladaptation to the environment. Thus, the executive who promotes by positive means an improved system of status, however essential to immediate purposes, thereby generates disorganizing forces, the neutralizing of which is the more difficult in that the executive himself is a central part of the system of status. . . .

The pathological aspects of systems of status to which these remarks refer have not been adequately investigated. We shall focus our consideration of the subject on the following topics:

I. The status system tends in time to distorted evaluation of individuals.

II. It restricts unduly the "circulation of the elite."

III. It distorts the system of distributive justice.

IV. It exaggerates administration to the detriment of leadership and morale.

V. It exalts the symbolic function beyond the level of sustainment.

VI. It limits the adaptability of an organization.

I. As set forth hereinbefore, the system of status is founded on and made necessary by the following four factors, in addition to others, relevant to the present topic: (1) differences in the abilities of individuals, (2) differences in the difficulties of various kinds of work, (3) differences in the importance of various kinds of work, and (4) the needs of the system of communication.

The first of these factors is strictly personal and individual . . . To the extent that status depends upon individual ability and willingness to employ it, it may be said to be individual and not social. Personal status may to this extent be said to be correlative with personal merit. . . .

As we ascend to the other bases of status, more and more qualification of the conception of individual merit is required. . . . The rating of the individual by the importance of his work, a social evaluation, may be necessary to effective and efficient allocation of ability in the social system, and it may therefore be essential to the adaptation of the society as a whole to its environment. However, status so determined tends, as experience shows, to be imputed to the individual *as such* rather than to a particular socially valued *role* of the individual. When inferior status is assigned on this basis, it is transferred to the individual generally, and similarly when superior status is assigned. Thus exaggeration of personal inferiority and superiority results. The effect upon the characteristics of the individual contributors to an organization is deleterious—depressing and limiting those of inferior status, stimulating and sometimes intoxicating those of superior status. Restoring or creating morale in the one, restraining the other, then become a major problem of organization.

The system of communication by means of which coordination is secured in cooperation is a strictly social phenomenon. Being indispensable to purposeful cooperation, the necessities of the system of communication become prime, being secondary only to the prior existence of an organization whose members are willing to cooperate. Now, undoubtedly the capacity of individuals to function in a system of communications depends upon natural abilities, general knowledge and experience, facility in general and special languages, technical and other special abilities; but though often indispensable, such general capacities and potentialities are secondary to the abilities directly associated with a particular communication position and with immediate concrete knowledge. One cannot function as, or in, a communication center if one is not at that center nor, if at that center, without knowledge of the immediately available means of communication and of the immediately precedent communication materials, *i.e.*, what has just transpired, what further communication is called for, to whom and where further communication should be made, from whom and where communication should be elicited. Neither general nor special abilities suffice to meet the requirements if this local and concrete knowledge is not available.

Thus the primary specific abilities required in communication are those of *position*—of being at the place where communication may effectively be had and where immediate concrete knowledge may be obtained. The manning of posts of communication by those possessing the requisite abilities of position is so indispensable to cooperation that a system assuring such manning and hence of the acquirement of such abilities has precedence over all other considerations in an organization, for the breakdown of communication means immediate failure of coordination and disintegration of organization. . . .

The indispensability of systematic communication in organization thus leads to imputing a value to the individual that relates to the role he plays and to the exaggeration of the importance of immediate local ability in communication as against more general and more personal ability.

The dilemma involved may be brought out in terms of a practical organization problem. It will ordinarily be the experience of the general executive that there are able men available for appointment to positions occupied by men recognized to be of inferior ability, but who are immediately superior with respect to local knowledge and experience in their posts and also superior in the sense that they are accepted in their posts by others. It may be clear that in the long run, provided immediate breakdown is not involved, it would be better to replace the inferior with the superior man. Nevertheless, to do so may involve costs in terms of immediate organizational disadvantages so substantial that the net effect even for the long run might be adverse. These disadvantages are: (1) If replacement is made, there will be ineptitude of functioning for a longer or shorter period. In so far as this occurs because of lack of local knowledge, it will correct itself in time, which in general will be shorter the greater the general ability of the replacing individual. The less difference there is in ability, the more doubtful is the utility of change. (2) Communication involves mutual relationships and habitual responsive reactions. A new man, entirely aside from his intrinsic abilities in the position, is new to others in the immediate communication network. *Their* capacity to function is disturbed by change. (3) The operation of the system depends in considerable degree upon mutual confidence of the communicators. Change decreases this confidence. This is ordinarily not important as related to single changes not frequently occurring. Its importance increases at an accelerating pace as either the number or the frequency of replacements increases.

II. Thus, although systems or status are based upon individual abilities and propensities as related to tasks socially evaluated and upon the requirements of the system of communication in organizations, we find that the rating of the individual by the role he occupies and emphasis upon the importance to the organization of immediate local abilities of position lead to under- and overvaluation of individuals artificially, *i.e.*, in terms of status as an end instead of as an intermediate means.

Whatever the system or principle by which posts of communication are filled, in general, errors occur, with the result that some men of inferior abilities are placed in relatively superior positions. . . . The effects of aging, of physical, moral, and intellectual deterioration, of changing conditions and purposes, all call for continual readjustment and replacement in the status system. The process of readjustment and replacement is well known as the "circulation of the elite." Ideally the circulation of the elite should be so free that the status of all should at any given time be in accordance with their relative capacities and the importance of their functions. It is rather obvious that failure of this circulation to the extent that generally those of inferior capacity occupy positions of superior status will so reduce the efficiency of cooperation that survival of organization is doubtful, and that the dangers of rebellion and revolution will be so great that even for the short run such a stoppage of circulation may be fatal . . .

III. Without a system of status, as has already been stated, injustice results to those who are the less capable, by failure to protect them against overburden. If an adequate system of status is employed, it may involve injustice when the higher emoluments of higher status are greater than warranted in the sense that they are greater than necessary. It is not intended to discuss here the problem of distributive justice generally involved in differential emoluments. We shall assume that a differential system is necessary and just. What concerns us now is the distortions of justice arising from the restrictions upon freedom of promotion and demotion. The injustices arising are of two sorts: (1) The aggregate of emoluments of higher status are excessive in the sense that they do not secure the degree of service that the capacities ideally available make possible. The "social dividend" in the broadest sense is less than it should be, and the failure is a loss to those of inferior status generally. (2) Individuals capable of filling positions of higher status better than those occupying such positions are unjustly deprived of the emoluments that they are often encouraged to seek. I am using emoluments in a most general sense, including not only remuneration, but also recognition, prestige, the satisfaction of exercising one's abilities, and, for those of philanthropic motivation, the satisfactions of the largest service of which they are capable.

These injustices inherent in the practical operations of systems of status are not hidden. Men are aware of them in general and sometimes exaggerate them; and they are also aware of them specifically as affecting them individually in many circumstances. The effect of the sense of injustice involved depends partly upon the degree to which the status system is sluggish or congealed. When status is fixed by birth or limited by race or religion, the extreme of disorganization may follow. When the status of individuals corresponds well with their abilities, some loss of *esprit de corps* and of cooperative efficiency only may be involved.

Nevertheless, the effects of the injustices inherent in status systems are sufficiently great to require positive balancing considerations and sentiments. The consideration of most importance is that, except as to those of the lowest status (and at least in some conditions probably also to them), conservatism is protective of individuals. Even though the retention of someone in a position of higher status may be felt to be specifically unjust to one of lower status, the situation may be duplicated with respect to the latter and some-one of still lower status. In some degree, recognition of a right to retain status is therefore felt to be generally just even though in particular cases the effect may be thought not so.

The sentiments supporting conservatism with respect to status are de-veloped and maintained by rationalizations, ceremonies, and symbolism. They have for their broad purpose the inculcation of the doctrine that the pri-mary interest of the individual is dependent upon the maintenance of the whole organization and its effective operation as a whole, and that whatever is necessary to this end, even though it adversely affects the individual, is offset even to him by the larger advantage accruing from it.

iv. An effective system of communications requires not only the stable fill-ing of specific positions of different status, but also habitual practices and technical procedures. Failure to follow these procedures with routine per-sistence in general leads to confusion, lack of coordination, and inefficiency or breakdown of the system. The lines of communication, the system of status, and the associated procedures, though by no means constituting "ad-ministration," are essential tools of administration and are the most "visible" general parts of it. Being the tangible machinery of administration and in-dispensable to it, the protection both of status and of procedure comes to be viewed quite sincerely as the *sine qua non* of the organization.

The overvaluation of the apparatus of communication and administration is opposed to leadership and the development of leaders. It opposes leader-ship whose function is to promote appropriate adjustment of ends and means to new environmental conditions, because it opposes change either of status in general or of established procedures and habitual routine. This overvalu-ation also discourages the development of leaders by retarding the progress of the abler men and by putting an excessive premium on routine qualities.

v. Among the phenomena connected with the status system are symbols of office or of class of trade. . . . Much of this symbolic practice related to office in the abstract is transferred to the person of the individual filling the office, and in this way the individual himself by reason of his status becomes a symbol of the organization and of its purposes. This is so true that although it is usually not difficult to distinguish between personal and official acts *per se*, it is not acceptable in general to distinguish personal and official be-havior of officials or for them to tolerate contumelious behavior of others toward them when wearing insignia of office or otherwise publicly known to hold office. . . .

One effect of the symbolic function of office and its associated status is to retard the circulation of the elite. The removal of an official to whom symbolic attributes have become attached, whether for incompetence or for other more reprehensible causes, unless they are very grave and publicly known, is widely felt to be derogatory to the office and to be an injury to

the organization both internally and often externally as respects its prestige. . . .

Thus it comes about that the symbolism involved in office and status in
the aggregate outruns the capacities of the men who have become symbols
of organization.

vi. From what has been presented it is perhaps evident that in sum the effect
of the status system, though essential to coherence, coordination, and *esprit
de corps*, is to reduce flexibility and adaptability. When the external conditions to which an organization must be adapted are stable, the importance
of flexibility and adaptability is much less than under rapidly changing conditions, and the importance of coherence and refinement of coordination, in
terms of efficiency, is much greater. Were it possible to forecast for a long
period what the conditions will be, the problem in principle would be merely
to establish an optimum system of status, a mean between extremes minimizing disadvantages and dangers, but reasonably conserving the advantages
and certainly adequate to the minimum necessities. It would hardly be appropriate to call such a problem a dilemma. The dilemma lies in the fact that
future conditions cannot be forecast correctly. Hence for current purposes
it is necessary to employ and often to elaborate a system of status whose
inherent tendency is to become unbalanced, rigid, and unjust.

We have seen that both functional and scalar systems of status are necessary to formal organizations of scalar type, but that interests are generated
by or within them forcing them to rigidity, lack of correspondence to real
merits and real needs, and to hypertrophy, especially in their symbolic functions. As these matters are reflected on and as the technical apparatus of
organization is studied, no doubt corrective measures can be known. They
can be applied, however, only with great difficulty from within an organization, for even the chief executive is the chief of the status system and dependent on it. It therefore requires endless persistence, extraordinary ability,
and great moral courage to control the dangerous developments in them.
Probably, the principal needs can be summarized as three: to ensure that
there is correspondence between status and ability by free movement; to
prevent the systems of status from being ends or even primary means; and
to see that the emoluments of office and of trade or profession are propor-
tionate to the necessary level of incentives and morale. . . .

FORMAL AND INFORMAL STATUS

F. J. Roethlisberger and William J. Dickson

THE FORMAL ORGANIZATION OF THE PLANT. The social organization of the industrial plant is in part formally organized. It is composed of a number of strata or levels which differentiate the benchworker from the skilled mechanic, the group chief from the department chief, and so on. These levels are well defined and all the formal orders, instructions, and compensations are addressed to them. All such factors taken together make up the formal organization of the plant. It includes the systems, policies, rules, and regulations of the plant which express what the relations of one person to another are supposed to be in order to achieve effectively the task of technical production. It prescribes the relations that are supposed to obtain within the human organization and between the human organization and the technical organization. In short, the patterns of human interrelations, as defined by the systems, rules, policies, and regulations of the company, constitute the formal organization.

The formal organization of an industrial plant has two purposes: it addresses itself to the economic purposes of the total enterprise; it concerns itself also with the securing of co-operative effort. The formal organization includes all the explicitly stated systems of control introduced by the company in order to achieve the economic purposes of the total enterprise and the effective contribution of the members of the organization to those economic ends.

THE INFORMAL ORGANIZATION OF THE PLANT. All the experimental studies pointed to the fact that there is something more to the social organization than what has been formally recognized. Many of the actually existing patterns of human interaction have no representation in the formal organization at all, and others are inadequately represented by the formal organization. This fact is frequently forgotten when talking or thinking about industrial situations in general. Too often it is assumed that the organization of a company corresponds to a blueprint plan or organization chart. Actually, it never does. In the formal organization of most companies little explicit recognition is given to many social distinctions residing in the social organization. The blueprint plans of a company show the functional relations between working units, but they do not express the distinctions of social distance, movement, or equilibrium previously described. The hierarchy of

Reprinted by permission of the publisher from *Management and the Worker*, pp. 558-562 (Cambridge, Mass.: Harvard University Press, 1939).

prestige values which tends to make the work of men more important than the work of women, the work of clerks more important than the work at the bench, has little representation in the formal organization; nor does a blueprint plan ordinarily show the primary groups, that is, those groups enjoying daily face-to-face relations. Logical lines of horizontal and vertical co-ordination of functions replace the actually existing patterns of interaction between people in different social places. The formal organization cannot take account of the sentiments and values residing in the social organization by means of which individuals or groups of individuals are informally differentiated, ordered, and integrated. Individuals in their associations with one another in a factory build up personal relationships. They form into informal groups, in terms of which each person achieves a certain position or status. The nature of these informal groups is very important, as has been shown in the Relay Assembly Test Room and in the Bank Wiring Observation Room.

It is well to recognize that informal organizations are not "bad," as they are sometimes assumed to be. Informal social organization exists in every plant, and can be said to be a necessary prerequisite for effective collaboration. Much collaboration exists at an informal level, and it sometimes facilitates the functioning of the formal organization. On the other hand, sometimes the informal organization develops in opposition to the formal organization. The important consideration is, therefore, the relation that exists between formal and informal organizations.

To illustrate, let us consider the Relay Assembly Test Room and the Bank Wiring Observation Room. These two studies offered an interesting contrast between two informal working groups; one situation could be characterized in almost completely opposite terms from the other. In the Relay Assembly Test Room, on the one hand, the five operators changed continuously in their rate of output up and down over the duration of the test, and yet in a curious fashion their variations in output were insensitive to many significant changes introduced during the experiment. On the other hand, in the Bank Wiring Observation Room output was being held relatively constant and there existed a hypersensitivity to change on the part of the worker—in fact, what could almost be described as an organized opposition to it.

It is interesting to note that management could draw from these studies two opposite conclusions. From the Relay Assembly Test Room experiment they could argue that the company can do almost anything it wants in the nature of technical changes without any perceptible effect on the output of the workers. From the Bank Wiring Observation Room they could argue equally convincingly that the company can introduce hardly any changes without meeting a pronounced opposition to them from the workers. To make this dilemma even more striking, it is only necessary to recall that the sensitivity to change in the one case occurred in the room where no experimental changes had been introduced whereas the insensitivity to change in the other case occurred in the room where the operators had been submitted to considerable experimentation. To settle this question by saying that in one case the situation was typical and in the other case atypical of ordinary shop conditions would be to beg the question, for the essential difference between the two situations would again be missed. It would ignore the social setting in which the changes occurred and the meaning which the workers themselves assigned to the changes.

Although in both cases there were certain informal arrangements not identical with the formal setup, the informal organization in one room was quite different from that in the other room, especially in its relation to the formal organization. In the case of the Relay Assembly Test Room there was a group, or informal organization, which could be characterized as a network of personal relations which had been developed in and through a particular way of working together; it was an organization which not only satisfied the wishes of its members but also worked in harmony with the aims of management. In the case of the Bank Wiring Observation Room there was an informal organization which could be characterized better as a set of practices and beliefs which its members had in common—practices and beliefs which at many points worked against the economic purposes of the company. In one case the relation between the formal and informal organization was one of compatibility; in the other case it was one of opposition. Or to put it in another way, collaboration in the Relay Assembly Test Room was at a much higher level than in the Bank Wiring Observation Room.

The difference between these two groups can be understood only by comparing the functions which their informal organizations performed for their members. The chief function of the informal group in the Bank Wiring Observation Room was to resist changes in their established routines of work or personal interrelations. This resistance to change, however, was not the chief function of the informal group in the Relay Assembly Test Room. It is true that at first the introduction of the planned changes in the test room, whether or not these changes were logically in the direction of improvement, was met with apprehension and feelings of uneasiness on the part of the operators. The girls in the beginning were never quite sure that they might not be victims of the changes.

In setting up the Relay Assembly Test Room with the object of studying the factors determining the efficiency of the worker, many of the methods and rules by means of which management tends to promote and maintain efficiency—the "bogey," not talking too much at work, etc.—were, in effect, abrogated. With the removal of this source of constraint and in a setting of heightened social significance (because many of the changes had differentiated the test room girls from the regular department and as a result had elevated the social status within the plant of each of the five girls) a new type of spontaneous social organization developed. Social conditions had been established which allowed the operators to develop their own values and objectives. The experimental conditions allowed the operators to develop openly social codes at work and these codes, unhampered by interference, gave a sustained meaning to their work. It was as if the experimenters had acted as a buffer for the operators and held their work situation steady while they developed a new type of social organization. With this change in the type of social organization there also developed a new attitude toward changes in their working environment. Toward many changes which constitute an unspecified threat in the regular work situation the operators became immune. What the Relay Assembly Test Room experiment showed was that when innovations are introduced carefully and with regard to the actual sentiments of the workers, the workers are likely to develop a spontaneous type of informal organization which will not only express more adequately their own values and significances but also is more likely to be in harmony with the aims of management.

Although all the studies of informal organization at the Hawthorne Plant were made at the employee level, it would be incorrect to assume that this phenomenon occurs only at that level. Informal organization appears at all levels, from the very bottom to the very top of the organization.[1] Informal organization at the executive level, just as at the work level, may either facilitate or impede purposive co-operation and communication. In either case, at all levels of the organization informal organizations exist as a necessary condition for collaboration. Without them formal organization could not survive for long. Formal and informal organizations are interdependent aspects of social interaction.

1. Barnard, C. I., *The Functions of the Executive*, Harvard University Press, 1938, pp. 223-4.

PRESTIGE GRADING:
A MECHANISM OF CONTROL

Carl Dreyfuss

My discussion of the social relations among the employees in the commercial department will have as its basis the rank order of the organization.

Reprinted in part from *Occupation and Ideology of the Salaried Employee*, Vol. I, pp. 1-18 (trans. Eva Abramovitch), Works Progress Administration and Department of Social Science, Columbia University, New York, 1938.

This gradation furnishes the main principles of division for my observations; social influences, relations, and reflexes are due to and shaped by this setup.

In the enterprise, the line of demarcation between management and employees is by no means distinctly drawn. The hierarchy is a highly differentiated structure. Its rank gradations are marked by various characteristics: first, by the individual's actual or usurped power to issue orders and to demand obedience; second, by the responsibility which an individual has or believes himself to have—in other words, by his independence, or the degree of his dependence on a superior; third, by his real or fictitious participation in the management of the enterprise or the department; fourth, by his representation of the firm in public, either in purchases or sales or by signing the firm's papers or letters.

A broad power to command and issue orders always carries with it a wide responsibility; conversely, it is possible for an employee to occupy a responsible (that is, a confidential) position which gives him no authority to issue orders yet makes him feel that he participates in the management.

Briefs, in his description of the hierarchy of an enterprise, mentions but two of the foregoing items, the first and the third: "The gradation is made according to the power to issue orders, to expect and to demand discipline. The extent of the power to issue orders and the distance of that power from the central management of the enterprise are the principles of the hierarchic structure." [1] Exception must be taken to this definition. First, it is incomplete; second, it fails to indicate that, as a mark of distinction, not only the actual power to issue orders is of importance, but also the unauthorized exercise of this power, and likewise not only the real, but also the illusory closeness to the central management. Neither is it permissible to call these marks of distinction the "principles of the hierarchic structure." They are only the marks of gradation, not the principles. In the following pages I shall explain the factors that brought the rank order into existence . . .

THE INTERESTS OF THE EMPLOYER. The employer is fundamentally interested in preventing the employees of his enterprise from confronting him as a homogeneous group. He attempts to undermine and split their strength through minute subdivision and differentiation. Furthermore, the employee's intense yearning "to be somebody" in the enterprise is not to be underestimated; it has its effect upon the shaping of the rank order. Not only is the outer form of the organization greatly influenced by this motive, but also the formation of its inner structure; a multitude of departments and gradations strengthen the self-respect of the employer and his ambition to be the head of an important organization. The gradation, however, extended far beyond the technical necessities and requirements of the organization, effects a social and psychic equalization within the rank order for the eco-

1. Goetz Briefs, "Betriebssoziologie," in *Handwörterbuch der Soziologie* (Stuttgart, 1931), p. 39.

nomic exploitation of the employees. Exaggerated differentiation causes the employees to forget their dependence and stimulates the illusion of the possibilities of promotion. The small power in the hands of some of the employees in the system, even though it is illusory, makes them tolerate their many hardships. Thus the system of gradation, as shown in subsequent discussions, becomes of great ideological importance.

THE INTERESTS OF THE EMPLOYEES. The rank order gives the employee his definite and fixed position within the organization. This position confers upon him rights and duties and determines his technical function. It also decides whether or not the employee, in his occupational activity, can satisfy his urge for social recognition and such impulses as in the ordinary course of his life remain unsatisfied. This opportunity, however, exists to a far greater degree under the system of "artificial" differentiation than under one in which "artificial" influences are eliminated and the gradation is made according to the strict requirements of the organization. (By "artificial" differentiation we mean the gradations of the hierarchy caused by social and psychic factors, in contrast to the "real" differentiation which is determined by the technical requirements of the work.)

If he holds a position which at least affords him the illusion of superiority to some of his coworkers, the employee is enabled to attain a degree of social recognition within the organization as compensation for economic need and social oppression outside it. Such a position is seemingly of higher rank, and in the detailed organism of the artificial setup it stands, in fact, somewhat apart from other positions. This has its effect upon the social circumstances of the employee outside the enterprise; conversely, the desire for such a position in the establishment is due to social differentiations existing outside the establishment.

It is, however, mainly through psychic motives that the employee consents to and collaborates in differentiations of the rank order not based upon technical necessities. The force of impulses and drives is of the greatest influence upon the gradations of the business ladder.

The sadistic inclination inherent in many individuals finds an opportunity for satisfaction in the artificial setup wherever an individual holds a position of power, either actual or apparent. This opportunity exists for almost every employee, because even the lowest rungs of the ladder always offer possibilities for the illusion that the employee has some power to issue orders, although this power may be exercised only over apprentices, office boys, or messengers. Sadistic impulses, especially when coupled with a strong craving for authority, often render an employee a very undesirable coworker or superior, as he is always anxious to exercise and to overreach his power of command and to torture and harass his coworkers.

Another powerful impulse, narcissism, helps along the recognition and formation of the artificial gradations. Narcissism is part of the make-up of every individual, although, of course, its manifestations are not of equal force. An individual holding a job in a business craves satisfaction of this impulse all the more as the work itself and the economic and social position of the employee alone do not satisfy it. Narcissistic individuals, therefore, welcome the artificial differentiation and complication of the business gradation and grasp the chance of exercising even the smallest power of command, despite the fact that the authority bestowed on them may be only fictitious. Some promotions—to manager of a sub-department, to a semi-independent post, or to representative of the firm—afford the employee deep satisfaction and flatter his pride to an extent not justified by the importance of such events from an organizational and economic standpoint. A position which enables the employee to shine in the outside world is the most desirable of all. The positions of traveling salesman, buyer, and sales-girl—as we shall see further on—are desired chiefly because they offer opportunities for the satisfaction of narcissistic urges. Often the most superficial signs of priority are sufficient to satisfy the narcissistic individual: a word of recognition from the employer, praise from a superior, or an office somewhat better equipped than others. The narcissistic desire for authority is intensified by considerable resentment in all those cases, where, through pauperization and loss of class, former independent employers, army officers, or public servants have been forced to become employees.

Jealousy and envy among employees of the same rank or among those just one step higher or lower in rank are incited and inflamed by the continuous struggle for promotion due to the employer ideologies of employees. The fear lest they lose their position and thereby all source of income aggravates the struggle. Thus arises that type of employee described by the term "scorcher" or "slave-driver." Such an employee identifies himself intensively with the executive powers that be, with the superior and the employer; and, although an individual part of the organization, he considers himself a powerful representative of the present system . . .

THE INFLUENCE OF THE EMPLOYER. The disturbance of the solidarity of the employees is intensified by the efforts of the employer to prevent, from the beginning, a too close relationship among his employees. In many establishments, for instance, there is a rule forbidding the employees, in their conversation among themselves, to use the familiar "Du" (thou) instead of the more formal "Sie" (you). A similar order states that friendly relations among the employees are to be avoided as much as possible, as they interfere with the normal conduct of business. These rules exemplify the effects made to disrupt the solidarity of the employees by a multiplication of the business gradations.

The arguments offered in defense of these regulations and wishes are not very plausible. An article on this question published by the house organ of a department store includes the following comment: "A particular reason why the too familiar form *du* should be avoided is the fact that one of the employees may be promoted and so become the superior of his former colleagues. In such case, perhaps for the very reason that formerly he was a colleague, it is imperative for him to maintain a certain distance between himself and his subordinates. To term such an attitude highhatting would by no means be justified. Now, if the new superior continues to use the informal *du* with his former co-workers he will certainly find it difficult to maintain that degree of authority which his new position requires of him. If, on the other hand, in his relations with his former colleagues he changes immediately after his promotion from the familiar *Du* to the formal *Sie* he will lose a considerable amount of sympathy, and a smooth cooperation will be made difficult . . . But, all other considerations aside, the use of *du* is offensive to many customers. The standing of the business, and consequently that of the employees, suffers. For it cannot be denied that persons of good breeding usually preserve a certain distance and use the familiar *du* only in addressing those with whom they actually have narrower bonds of sympathy." [2] Even the *Book of Etiquette* suggests that, though friendliness and courtesy should prevail among employees, too great familiarity is not to be encouraged. Especially in the office and places of work, *du* should be avoided.[3] The rules of an Austrian provincial bank contain the following: "Section 28. The management looks unfavorably upon personal social relations of its employees outside the Bank." [4]

SALARY GROUPS AMONG THE EMPLOYEES. The principles of division in the official salary schedule of employees are symptomatic of the artificial structure of the rank order. In these schedules we still find differentiation long since discarded in practical business; the so-called occupational and business groups have in part been done away with through the process of rationalization and mechanization. For these theoretical groupings the desire for manifold differentiations is also decisive, and illusions of "higher" positions and of possibilities of promotion are of far greater influence than the conditions actually existing in the establishment, in spite of the fact that in the rationalized establishment these various classifications have, as such, long ago been abolished. Just as the various functions of organization have already become specialized in the management, so the work of individual departments is thoroughly divided. In the large modern establishment we no longer find the correspondent and accountant with their wage-scale tag as described above. If the stenographer handles foreign correspondence, then she is a specialist in one particular language in which she takes dictation and transcribes on the typewriter. The accountant who, without any de-

2. *Hauszeitung Tietz*, Band 6, Heft 10.
3. Otto Andreas, *Gesellschaftlicher Wegweiser für alle Lebenslagen*, 5. Auflage (Weidlingen, 1931), p. 222.
4. Cited by Franziska Baumgarten, *Psychologie der Menschenbehandlung im Betriebe* (Halle, 1930), p. 19.

gree of independence, operates the bookkeeping machine or who performs other special work, is now tied to standardized or routine work.

It is true that in a large establishment there are more rank than salary gradations, but even the latter exceed the number of groupings actually required from a technical point of view. It is interesting to note what one of the largest German publishing houses has to say on this point: "in the case of commercial employees, the regulation of the position in the business by salary agreement has not been successful in the long run. The mere fact that the salary schedule enumerated fifty-four different categories of employee groups was proof that the situation of the employees was unsuited to a collective regulation; furthermore, these fifty-four groups did not include all groups necessary for a complete classification of the employees. This attempt to bring a large number of different individual performances within one scheme of salary schedule resulted in the injuring and restricting of a majority of employees working independently and in the permitting of a minority of subordinate employees to profit at the expense of the others." [5]

PSYCHOLOGICAL OBSERVATIONS. The psychological expert gives an interesting confirmation of artificial division in the rank order of the establishment. Psycho-technical investigations, conducted by experimental psychologists in a large Berlin office of the electrical industry, indicated that the differentiation made by the personnel staff as to the work of the employees had no justification in fact. After a close examination, the psychologists reduced to three groups the twenty-five declared by the management to be the ultimate number of technical and functional groups necessary for the proper working of the establishment. The first group comprised the large army of employees who merely performed standardized or routine services, such as shipping clerks, typists, file and office clerks, etc. At all times during the day, from morning to night, these employees perform nothing but standardized and mechanized work, whether by machine or by hand. No distinction was made between the employee who operates the Hollerith machine, the typist who day after day has to write the same stereotyped letters, and the shipping clerk who makes out, day by day, the same shipping blanks according to detailed instructions. The second group, that of bookkeepers, was established solely because, from an experimental psychologist's point of view, the bookkeeping activity is to be considered separately, since it deals continually with figures and computation of figures. The examining psychologists gave as the reason for this separate treatment the desire to make specific bookkeeping tests. Otherwise, they agreed that this group, in the general psychological sense, might just as well have been omitted and the greater part of it classified among the first and the smaller part among the third group. This third group included those employees whose work carried

5. Georg Sydow, "Die Sozialpolitik des Hauses Ullstein," *50 Jahre Ullstein* (Berlin, 1927), p. 369.

with it a limited amount of responsibility and a certain independence and discretion of action. The higher type of correspondent in the complaint department, for instance, whose duty it was to cope with the objections of customers, had to act with a certain amount of independence and responsibility. It is true, however, that this work can be called individual in a very narrow sense only, because under the system of thorough rationalization of the process of work the function of such a correspondent has, in the last analysis, also come to be purely routine work, as he acts upon a few similar cases again and again. In regard to the other employees of this group similar parallels can be drawn. This analysis of work functions and of the way in which they determine positions in the enterprise differs in many respects from our own examination, because its aim has been the preparation of psycho-technical fitness tests. Nevertheless this digression into experimental psychology can furnish certain indices for our study.

"BUREAUCRATIZATION" OF THE COMMERCIAL DEPARTMENT. The artificial complication of the rank order, which permits numerous employees to feel that they hold higher positions and are to a certain extent independent, is, with its unwarranted differentiations, telescoped positions, and ramifications, diametrically opposed to efforts of rationalization. Illusory powers and fictitious responsibilities are obstacles to a division of the work functions and to a scientific, standardized, and planned course of management. The conflict between the economic force necessitating rationalization and the social and psychic forces within the enterprise is found, to a greater or lesser degree, in every organization. The process of rationalization with its consequences, which mechanize the work of the employees and deprive it of its personal and true character, considerably undermines the hierarchic system. On the other hand, gradation based on factors which are, from a business point of view, by no means adequate frequently crosses the lines of the rationalization process. The result of these crossings is a phenomenon much resisted by scientific business circles. They give to it the name "bureaucratization." Unfortunately, the genesis of this difficult state of affairs is falsely described. The cause of "bureaucratic" rigidity, which turns to loss the very process of rationalization established for the express purpose of profit, is not the process of rationalization, the division of the work functions resulting from it, or the structure of the establishment shaped to suit the requirements of that process; the cause is rather the artificial differentiation of the rank order, which by far exceeds the gradation warranted by the technical requirements of an establishment.

BARRIERS TO UNDERSTANDING
BETWEEN OFFICERS AND ENLISTED MEN

Samuel A. Stouffer, et al.

Although the Army's social system was such that officers with the best will in the world would find it difficult to bridge the gulf which separated them from the thoughts and feelings of the men under their command, one of the surprises experienced by the observant social scientist in the Army was the number of officers who assumed, apparently quite sincerely, that they succeeded in so doing.

All comparative studies made by the Research Branch showed that officers tended to believe that their men were more favorably disposed on any given point than the men's own anonymous responses showed the men to be.

Table I presents a typical illustration of this wishful thinking on the part of officers. In each of 53 Infantry rifle companies in the United States, the company commander was asked a question like the following:

How many of your enlisted men would you say feel proud of their company?
   _____ Almost none of them
   _____ About one fourth of them
   _____ About half of them
   _____ About three fourths of them
   _____ Almost all of them

TABLE I—Accuracy of Estimates by Company Commanders of Favorable Attitudes Among Men in Their Own Company

	Number of Companies in Which the CO:			
Attitude Area	Over-estimated	Estimated Correctly	Under-estimated	Total
Pride in outfit	43	8	2	53
Desire to be a soldier	42	4	7	53
Satisfaction with job	33	18	2	53
Importance of Infantry	31	14	8	53

Data from S-121, United States, April 1944.

The men in the same company were asked:

Do you feel proud of your company?
   _____ Yes, very proud
   _____ Yes, fairly proud
   _____ No, not proud
   _____ Undecided

Reprinted from Samuel A. Stouffer, Edward A. Suchman, Leland C. DeVinney, Shirley A. Star, and Robin M. Williams, Jr., *The American Soldier*, Vol. I: Adjustment During Army Life, pp. 391-401, by permission of the authors and the publisher. (Copyright, 1949, by the Princeton University Press.)

If over 87½ per cent of the men checked either "very proud" or "fairly proud," the CO was considered correct if his answer was "almost all of the men" would say they felt proud of their company. If 62½ to 87½ per cent of the men checked "very proud" or "fairly proud," the CO was considered correct if he checked "about three fourths." Enlisted checks by 37½ to 62½ per cent were equated with officers' checks of "about half"; enlisted checks by 12½ to 37½ per cent of the unit sample were equated with officers' checks of "about a fourth," and enlisted checks by less than 12½ per cent with officers' checks of "almost none."

As Table I shows, 8 of the 53 officers estimated their men's responses correctly by the above definition. But 43 *overestimated* the proportion of their men who would say they were proud of their company, as contrasted with only 2 who *underestimated*. The same tendency is seen with respect to other items shown in Table I.[1]

The same tendency was observed in studies overseas as well as in the United States.

Psychologically, one of the elements in this habit of officers of overestimating their men's favorable attitudes was a product of the tendency to project one's own attitudes upon the men. Overseas studies of officers and men who were veterans of Infantry campaigns showed that if officers felt in rather low spirits they tended to think that enlisted men did also, while if the officers manifested high spirits they tended to think enlisted men did the same. How much this represents projection only and how much, if at all, it represents some possible causal connection (e.g., if officers have low spirits this will infect the men) or some other association (e.g., officers and the men they know best have shared very similar experiences), cannot be separately determined from the data.

In so far as the tendency to projection existed, the net effect ordinarily would be to lead officers to overestimate the favorableness of men's attitudes—for the reason that officers' own attitudes generally were more favorable than the men's.

Characteristic differences in attitudes between officers and enlisted men are evident in almost any area one could mention. With very few exceptions, officers tended to have more favorable attitudes toward all aspects of the military system than enlisted men. They were more content with Army life; they were more satisfied with their jobs; they had greater pride in

1. These items were:

"If it were up to you to choose, do you think you could do more for your country as a soldier or as a worker in a war job?" (As a soldier, as a war worker, undecided.)

"How satisfied are you about being in your present Army job instead of some other Army job?" (Very satisfied, satisfied, makes no difference, dissatisfied, very dissatisfied.)

"How important a part do you think the Infantry will play in winning the war?" (A very important part, a fairly important part, not a very important part, not important at all.)

being soldiers; they had less aggression against the Army, and so on through the whole gamut of attitudes toward the structure and functioning of military society.

In Table II are presented some of these comparisons in attitudes drawn from scattered studies in which, in each case, cross sections of officers and enlisted men in the same units were asked parallel questions. In no case can the observed differences in response be accounted for simply in terms of differences in background characteristics. It is difficult to account for such differences in attitudes except in terms of a class patterning of views.

TABLE II—Comparison of Officers' and Enlisted Men's Attitudes on Selected Subjects

	Officers	Enlisted Men
QUESTION: "How interested are you in the work you are doing in your present Army assignment?" *		
Per cent saying, "Very much interested"	82	50
QUESTION: "In general do you feel that you yourself have gotten a square deal from the Army?" *		
Per cent saying, "Yes, in most ways I have"	65	41
QUESTION: "In general, how would you say you feel most of the time, in good spirits or in low spirits?" †		
Per cent saying, "I am usually in good spirits"	53	24
QUESTION: "What do you think of military control and discipline at this post?" †		
Per cent saying, "It's about right"	62	42
QUESTION: "How many of your officers are the kind who are willing to go through anything they ask their men to go through?" ‡		
Per cent saying, "All" or "Most"	92	37
QUESTION: (On the whole do you agree or disagree with the statement) "The Army would be a lot better if officers and enlisted men were more friendly with each other" §		
Per cent saying, "Disagree"	47	15

* Cross section of 5,000 officers and 3,500 enlisted men in the United States surveyed in February 1945. (S-198-O and E.)
† Cross section of 595 officers and 808 enlisted men in the India-Burma Theater surveyed in July 1945. (S-219 and 220.)
‡ Cross section of 444 officers and 4,078 enlisted men in two Infantry divisions in the South Pacific Theater surveyed in March 1944. (S-124.)
§ Cross section of 323 officers and 954 enlisted men in the United States surveyed in November 1945. (S-234B.)

Apparent class differences in thinking between officers and enlisted men extend, as has been indicated, to many different areas. It is interesting, however, to note one bit of evidence that these differences appear to be sharpest on matters which tend to reflect on those aspects of the military system which place the enlisted class at a disadvantage relative to the officer class and for which officers are likely to feel some responsibility. In the February 1945 survey of 5,000 officers and 3,500 enlisted men in the United States, cited in Table II, the following question was asked: "Below is a list of things en-

listed men commonly gripe about. In your experience which of these do
you think enlisted men usually have good reasons to gripe about?" Table III
shows the percentages of officers and men who said they think enlisted men
usually have good reason to gripe about each item. It will be noted that the
first four gripes on the list, where the differences in attitudes are the sharpest, all relate to matters in which enlisted men are disadvantaged relative to
officers and for which officers are likely to feel some direct responsibility.
The last two gripes on the list, concerning which there are practically no
differences in attitude between officers and men, are matters for which officers are less likely to feel responsible and from which they are likely to feel
they themselves suffer almost as much as enlisted men.

From the same study on which Table III is based comes an exemplifica-
tion of the point illustrated earlier, in Table I, of the tendency for officers
to overestimate the favorableness and underestimate the unfavorableness of
enlisted men's responses. Both officers and men were asked to check the
following statement: "Most enlisted men do *not* respect their officers.—Agree
—Disagree." Only 25 per cent of the officers agreed, as contrasted with 54
per cent of the enlisted men.

While psychological interpretations in terms of projection will help explain the discrepancy between what officers thought men felt and what the
men felt, it must be recognized that the basic social system of the Army
impeded rather than facilitated a meeting of minds. Not only were the experiences of officers and men different, but also the barriers of power and
social distance were almost insurmountable.

The power relationship was an obvious barrier. A considerable difference
in perspective between officers who exercise authority and men over whom
the authority is exercised is probably inevitable, at least in an organization
operated on an authoritarian basis. And whether in the Army or elsewhere,
completely candid interchange of attitudes on all subjects does not ordinarily occur between those who wield power and those who are subject to
that power.

But in the Army this inescapable barrier was augmented by the fostering
of status differences and physical as well as social distance between officers
and men. Officers could be easily misled by the rituals of deference exacted
from all enlisted men. They were "sirred" and saluted and rarely answered
back. It is easy to understand how during the course of time they could
come to mistake these compulsory outward symbols of deference for voluntary respect and fail to perceive underlying hostilities and resentments. Officers were practically entrapped into assuming that they were symbols of
respected authority.

It is easy to understand, too, how the different treatment accorded to
officers because of their different status blurred their insight into some typical enlisted attitudes and the reasons for those attitudes. Some flavor of the

**TABLE III—Comparison of Officers' and Enlisted Men's Attitudes Toward
Enlisted Men's Complaints ***

	Per Cent Who Think Enlisted Men "Usually Have Good Reason to Gripe" About Listed Complaint		
	Among Enlisted Men (N = 2377)	Among Officers (N = 5000)	Difference
"Discipline too strict about petty things"	51	23	28
"Not enough passes and furloughs"	53	28	25
"The wrong men get the breaks"	53	28	25
"Too much 'chicken' to put up with"	71	49	22
"Work too hard or hours too long"	23	9	14
"Too much time wasted during the day" †	48	59	— 11
"Wrong job assignment"	64	59	5
"Promotions frozen or too slow"	69	68	1

Data from S-198-O, EA and EB, United States, February 1945.
* The question asked was, "Below is a list of things enlisted men commonly gripe about. In your experience which of these do you think enlisted men usually have good reasons to gripe about?"
† It is possible that officers and men interpreted this item differently. Enlisted men commonly gripe
about their time being wasted by officers requiring them to wait, a complaint epitomized in the Army
expression, "Hurry up and wait." Officers, on the other hand, are more likely to be critical of time
wasted by enlisted men through goldbricking and dilatory tactics.

status difference between officers and enlisted men and of one type of difference in treatment that went with it is revealed in the following account
written for the Research Branch by an officer commissioned directly from
the ranks. The actual episode may have been an unusual one, but it is illus-
trative of some common underlying attitudes:

After being commissioned and discharged as an enlisted man I was transferred
to station complement to be sent from camp. I had to check over some items of
clothing with the supply sergeant of the new assignment. Not wishing to put on
my uniform until I was ready to go, I was wearing the clothes of a private. As I
stepped into the supply room the Sergeant was not there, but a few privates were
waiting. Being in a hurry I started to look for him in the next room. Just as he
came into the room, leaving me and a couple of other privates a little ways in
the supply room, his opening remark, with a belligerent glare, was: "How about
over there behind that counter" and without waiting for compliance, "and
what's the matter with you getting out of there too," was directed at me, I being
a little further in the room than the other two. I moved out and said nothing.

The first man to the desk was handing in laundry. The Sergeant took the
slip. "God damn, this isn't the way to make out a laundry slip. Haven't you been
shown how to make this out right?" The man said "no." "Yes you have, by God
and don't tell me you haven't. Weren't you in that formation yesterday? Yes,
I thought so. I told everyone of you how to do this right. By Jesus, you haven't
any more brains than a frog on a railroad track. Now you take that slip and
you make it out right." Here was the noncom in perfect form and attitude. He
turned to me next. "Now what the hell do you want?" It was a little extra
strong. He remembered I had gotten in his way a moment before. I wanted to
see what would happen so I quietly told him that I had been commissioned an
officer and transferred prior to leaving camp and that I'd like to check some
clothes off. "Oh yes sir, I'll take care of that right now." He was all courtesy
and service. He wanted to fix things about himself and ended up with an apology
for treating me as he had, saying "I certainly wouldn't have if I'd known." The
fact is that he hadn't been out of form at all. I just occupied two roles which
brought out the contrast sharply.[2]

2. By William Reeder.

In view of the barriers to communication between officers and enlisted men imposed by power and status, strengthened by the psychological stresses of officer training . . . , and enforced by physical as well as social separation, it can hardly be surprising that officers were often so inadequately aware of what enlisted men were thinking. As a partial corrective to this situation, the Chief of Staff ordered the Director of the Information and Education Division to prepare for distribution to field grade officers a monthly publication called *What the Soldier Thinks*. The first issue appeared in December 1943 and the publication continued throughout the war. After the first three issues appeared, the distribution was ordered extended to company commanders throughout the world. This publication . . . was prepared in the Research Branch.

Another source of information from which officers could get a flavor, if not always a representative sampling, of enlisted men's thinking was in enlisted men's publications, like *Yank* and *Stars and Stripes*. The attitudes expressed in many cartoons and stories were unmistakably clear. The mail columns were full of letters setting forth the views of enlisted men in no uncertain terms. But such sources of information, whether in the Army or out, are of dubious reliability and easily challenged. The Army had two somewhat contradictory but widely accepted antidotes: (1) the old Army tradition that griping is a universal form of amusement among enlisted men, ordinarily harmless and without specific meaning and, hence, not to be taken seriously unless it becomes excessive, and (2) the conviction of many officers that any expression of opinions they dislike must represent only the unjustified extreme views of a small minority of disgruntled troublemakers and that such expression is likely to damage the morale of the great majority who are good soldiers and, hence, such expressions should be suppressed. In this connection it is revealing to compare the answers of cross sections of 300 officers and 2,000 enlisted men in the European theater to this question asked in October 1945: "If someone back home—not in the Army—were to read B-Bag [an enlisted men's gripe column which was frequently highly critical of officers] every day, how true a picture would he get of the problems of most soldiers in the European theater?" 58 per cent of the officers as compared with 16 per cent of the enlisted men replied "very untrue" or "fairly untrue."

From time to time, the vigorous character of enlisted criticisms drew down fire from high commanders. But at the very top the freedom of B-Bag and of cartoonists like Mauldin was vigorously protected during the war. And it is something of a tribute to the officers in the ETO study just reported, that in spite of the critical character of B-Bag, 69 per cent of them said they liked B-Bag "very well" or "fairly well," and only 19 per cent felt that articles in the *Stars and Stripes* which criticized the Army had, in general, done more harm than good.

Traditionally, the most important formal Army machinery for facilitating communication upward from enlisted men to officers was the Inspector General system. Any enlisted man had the right to talk to a representative of the Inspector General. Since this officer was outside the soldier's immediate chain of command, the soldier could, in theory, talk with him with impunity and voice any complaints he chose.

At the end of the war in 1945 a survey of a cross section of 2,908 soldiers in the United States was made to ascertain how the system worked, as viewed by the men. About half of the men said that during their Army careers they had felt the desire to bring a complaint to the attention of the Inspector General. Yet only 1 in 5 said they actually took their stories to the IG. Why did the majority not exercise their prerogative? The men were asked to tell their reasons, which fell into three groups:

1. Difficulty in getting to see the Inspector General

     Too much red tape to go through to see him.

     You have to get permission from your 1st Sgt. to see the CO. Then permission from the CO to see the IG.

     Unable to obtain information or permission as to the routine or place to take complaint.

     The day our officer found out as to my and others' going we were forced to fly eight hours and could not get to see the IG. This took place when the IG visited our field.

2. Uselessness of seeing the Inspector General

     I didn't think it would do me any good.

     Because I did not think they would act on it anyway.

     Because I spoke to him once, then nothing happened.

     It would be futile.

     I've taken complaints to them before and no action was taken whatever. So the hell with it.

3. Fear of reprisal

     For the simple reason that if my CO found out he would have made it hard for me.

     Being afraid of punishment after doing so.

     Because figuring we will get it later from the CO.

     Afraid of kickback.

     Because of being threatened by another officer not to.

     Because in almost every instance company brass finds out and you suffer more.

     Because the IG gave our names over to the officer we bitched about on a prior occasion.

Men who had taken their complaints to the IG were more likely to be critical of the IG system than men who had not. Only 33 per cent of the former said the system worked "very well" or "fairly well" as compared with 53 per cent of the latter. This may merely reflect the possibility that the kind of men who took complaints to the IG were the kind of men who were more critical of Army organization in general, a hypothesis supported by the fact that the better educated men were both more likely to see the IG and to be more critical of the IG and the Army in general. Nevertheless, such figures are hardly a testimonial to the effectiveness of the system as a method of channeling complaints upward.

The chaplain also was a repository of confidences, and Research Branch representatives, in going from post to post in the United States and overseas, met with instances in which a chaplain with a particularly effective personality played an apparently significant role as a channel of communication. No study is available as of the end of the war, but evidence from a survey made in 1942 indicates that most men were not as likely to go to their chaplain with a personal problem as to their own commanding officer. For example, among 751 soldiers with over 1 year of service, only half of the men said they had ever consulted an officer about a personal problem, 33 per cent mentioning their commanding officer and 13 per cent mentioning the chaplain as the one to whom they went, with scattering mentions of other officers. Catholics were a little more likely to mention the chaplain —17 per cent as against 11 per cent for Protestants. In some organizations, the medical officer was an important channel of communication—notably in the Air Forces with relation to flying personnel.

The problem of establishing locally a really effective means by which unit officers could be apprised of what their men were thinking was never effectively solved in the Army. A promising procedure was tried out in 1944–1945 in the Redistribution Centers in the United States. Group sessions were held at which enlisted men (all of whom were returnees from overseas) were invited to voice their complaints and discuss them with one another and with the officers. The same procedures also were tried in some other situations, where commanding officers were sensitized to the importance of better rapport.

Need for maintaining effective lines of communication upwards from men to officers at the unit level is not unique to the Army. It has its parallel in civilian industry. But in industry the organized labor movement has achieved formal recognition of rights of workers to have spokesmen, and behind the exercise of those rights stand the sanctions of the privilege of striking or of quitting one's job permanently. Since such sanctions are inadmissible in the Army, it becomes all the more important for the Army to review its methods for transmission of attitudes upward and to conduct in peacetime controlled experiments to measure the effectiveness of new procedures which might be proposed.

MYTH AND STATUS SYSTEMS
IN INDUSTRY

Richard C. Myers

Among all occupational groups, but particularly in the skilled trades possessing a craft tradition, occupational morale, i.e., the particular conception of the well being of the work group held by workers and the ego satisfactions derived therefrom, is to a certain extent dependent upon myths and fictions.[1] The mythical and fictional elements of occupational culture emerge as the selective aspects of the occupation, and the job conditions change while traditionally established conceptions of social relationships remain relatively unaltered.

Although technological change and mass production techniques have reduced many skills and have opened the way to disintegrative forces in many of the trades, yet there are substantial traditions remaining in the industrial field. Studies of specific occupations have pointed out the organizational and ideological elements of contemporary work groups which have survived despite an encroaching technology, and, in fact, in some instances have become strengthened and further elaborated.[2] Actually, in those trades which are struggling most vigorously to protect their identity, the recourse to myth is most pronounced, because, as pressures for purely logical behavior are intensified, there is a tendency to hold to those things which have the sanction of time and which have produced occupational satisfaction in the past.

Below the level of the skilled trades one finds a considerably more rudimentary tradition, particularly in the more emergent occupations of the mass production industries. Rather than myths centered in a complete occupational culture, more unitary fictions of fairly recent origin are characteristic of this level, developing across occupational lines and oriented with regard to factory derived policies and procedures.[3]

Reprinted from *Social Forces*, Vol. XXVI (1948), pp. 331-337, by permission of the publisher. (Copyright, 1948, by the Williams and Wilkins Company.)

1. The occupational myth is composed of a belief or set of beliefs which constitutes a factually untrue but socially real conception of the occupational world. The term fiction may be applied to lesser, more specific, false conceptions.

2. See W. Fred Cottrell, *The Railroader* (Palo Alto: Stanford University Press, 1939); David Rodnick, "Status Values Among Railroad Men," *Social Forces* (Oct. 1941); Richard R. Myers, "Inter-Personal Relations in the Building Industry," *Applied Anthropology* (Spring), 1946.

3. There are fictions such as the following to be found in the modern factory. A Detroit plant, manufacturing gauges for the automobile industry, regularly employs

The myth in industry is subject to examination from a number of different points of view, in addition, perhaps, to an initial determination of the degree of difference between the facts and the false conceptions which are held, or, as the case may be, persistently presented by certain groups in the industrial structure. A useful analysis of myth would seem to be directed toward discovering (a) the self-conscious quality of items in occupational culture, (b) functions performed, and (c) the relationship of myths to certain status systems in industry. Such an analysis makes it possible to distinguish important variations between myths and enables one to know the conditions under which myths persist or tend toward elimination.

From the standpoint of the self-conscious quality of mythical items in occupational culture, two general types of myths can be distinguished—the Culture-Centered, or Unconscious Myth, and the Strategic Myth.

1. The Unconscious Myth is so centrally established as a part of the occupational sub-culture that its validity is not usually questioned by those who are indoctrinated in the occupational tradition. Although the essential falsity of the postulates of the myth is perhaps known to other groups and is subject to check and validation by any who may wish to conduct the proper investigation, some occupations possess an integration in terms of which the dispensable items of culture are reduced to a minimum. Where occupational sub-cultures have been allowed to accumulate in relatively undisturbed fashion, many of the practices, beliefs, and sentiments tend to depend on and reinforce one another, e.g., the "superior" morality of craft experience automatically justifies and ensures the legitimacy of fixing "proper" production schedules. Ideologically self-contained insofar as the worker is concerned, the occupation does not admit of much self-conscious evaluation. The trades or crafts constitute the occupations in industry whose integration is such that essentially mythical beliefs are not subject to constant logical challenge and thus may be said to be unconsciously held. . . .

from fifteen to twenty girls on calibrating machines. In this process, a gauge is put in the machine and an electric impulse moves the indicator up to the appropriate point. If the indicator does not come up, the gauge is rejected. A standard electric current is used and it is impossible for the machines to vary, yet there is a well established fiction among the operators that some machines are "faster" than others. However, the girls do not agree among themselves as to which are the "fast" machines. As a result of this fiction there is considerable discontent in the reassignment of machines. As the girls are on a piece-work basis, the fiction appears to offer a necessary explanation for some personal inadequacy in a competitive situation. There are also signs of an ongoing group adjustment, as the lower output operators on the whole are not anxious to give up their machines, saying that they are accustomed to the inferior machines and "might as well" continue on, although it should be obvious to the company that they are doing harder work.

In another factory there is the fiction that the company at one time allowed an hour for lunch. As the regular period maintaining in the plant is half an hour, there is constant agitation, involving petition after petition, for a return to the "rightful" lunch period. Actually, the facts reveal that the company has never had a one hour lunch period. This particular fiction appears to offer itself as a convenient issue for the expression of general dissatisfaction about plant conditions.

An example of this type of myth is to be found in the building industry, particularly among such old-line trades as carpentry and bricklaying. Here one can identify, at least for significantly large groups in local areas, what might be termed the *myth of the boy apprentice*.

The apprenticeship type of training, emphasizing a lengthy period of systematic indoctrination during youth, has social as well as technological meaning in the trades, since it serves as a distinguishing mark separating craft workers from those "overnight" mechanics in other occupations who have acquired neither skill nor an occupational morality. Carpenters, bricklayers, and other building tradesmen place a high value upon "growing up in the trade" and rather categorically assume such a process to be true of all building craftsmen.[4] The concept of the "boy" is important as it represents to the tradesman a kind of dedication in youth to a course of action involving patience, abstinence, and the arduous acquisition of high skill. The concept of the boy also evokes strong sentiments because it tends to symbolize the linkage of familial tradition and occupation.

Building tradesmen frequently speak disparagingly of middle-aged workers from factory occupations who from time to time make tentative efforts to find building employment. In the same manner, the tradesman rejects the young man who accepts the high entering wage of factory employment and, who, presumably by doing so, indicates that he lacks the stamina and foresight to undergo the more demanding, but more ethically rewarding, sequence of apprenticeship training. On the surface, and in view of the restrictions found in the trades as to the number of apprentices who may enter training, these beliefs might seem to represent sheer hypocrisy maintained for logical ends, and, in fact, among critical groups in management and business largely outside of the building industry, they have been so interpreted. However, careful examination of these beliefs, centering around the concept of the boy apprentice, point to the conclusion that, if such beliefs are rationalizations, they are almost wholly occupationally derived rationalizations of long standing with relatively little self-consciousness.

Although rather complete, uncritical acceptance of the concept of the boy apprentice is characteristic of skilled building craftsmen, investigation indicates that for substantial groups in certain areas the facts concerning entrance into the trades do not conform to the standard conception. In 1940 and 1941, a total of 1600 occupational histories were obtained from building tradesmen working on jobs in the Michigan cities of Detroit, Jackson, and Saginaw, and in metropolitan Chicago. Data were obtained concerning age at which the trade was entered and the nature of the trade training. Of this group, 39 percent of the tradesmen indicated that they had entered their

4. All of the building unions specify minimum terms of apprenticeship. Minimum terms, specified in the constitutions are: 5 years for the Plumbers and Steamfitters; 4 years for Carpenters, Plasterers, Cement Finishers, and Sheet Metal Workers; 3 years for Bricklayers, Painters, and Paperhangers. The usual minimum age set for entrance into apprenticeship training is seventeen and the maximum usually twenty-one.

particular trade at 25 years or above and 42 percent of the tradesmen indicated that they had experienced no formal, regulated, apprentice training, but instead, had come in as "backdoor mechanics," i.e., had "picked up" some skills in an informal, unsupervised way and had been "voted in" as journeymen.[5] Private studies of construction managers and some union officials support this view. Several union officials expressed the opinion that "over half" of their union membership had never been actually apprenticed in the "legal" sense.

Although these findings are obviously limited in scope, all available evidence points in the same direction, namely, that the conditions of formal boy apprenticeship do not accurately describe the entry into the trades of substantial numbers of operating journeymen, and thus that the conception is an occupational myth, for the most part unconsciously held.

2. The Strategic Myth in industry is based upon an awareness by an official group within the formal structure of occupational organization that there is some discrepancy between the facts and traditionally held conceptions, and that there is some utility to the preservation of mythical beliefs.

In many of the occupations the final crystallization of working rules and practices is represented in the codes of the union. The union has taken over the function of systematizing and maintaining the various items of occupational culture. However, the unions of the old line trades, as well as those of the mass production occupations, are formal organizations which possess an administrative structure and a number of "legitimate" objectives which conform, at least in part, to the objectives sanctioned by business generally. Relative economic advantage, as expressed in varying wage rates and the negotiations over hours of labor, constitute the legitimate objectives as accepted by the professional negotiating and administrative classes in both management and labor. Most of the formal organizations of workers have developed relatively small but administratively powerful groups of officials, who, through extended periods in office (very frequently because others in the organization lack the desire to take on unfamiliar administrative tasks), have come to divorce themselves from their previously held work roles and occupational tradition and have come to accept values of the managerial type. There are numerous examples of the "disassociation" of trade union officials from the values of the rank and file. The almost continuous process of negotiation with management on rate questions, which reflect management's supreme preoccupation with the logical factors of production, almost inevitably pushes the professional union representative into management's "rational" value system.

Frequently, union officials are confronted by facts, such as substantial

5. It was necessary to rather insistently request exact details on this latter point, as the tradesmen interviewed were inclined to respond with a quick if rather vague affirmative answer to the question of formal apprenticeship. In many instances this was finally changed to a negative answer after a more specific consideration of early work experience.

changes in tools, materials, and manufacturing processes, which logically indicate a possible downward revision of job classifications and wage rates. Readily recognizing a threat to the economic bargaining position of the trade organizations, union officials may turn to whatever strategic weapons are at hand. Emphasizing the irreplaceable quality of certain manual skills and trade practices, union administrators frequently make the attempt to cloak fundamental changes and strive to give the job a traditional appearance. To this end, union workers are urged to maintain their claims to all old operations, as well as to take over and elevate the standards of any new work where "shoddy" or "cut-rate" practices might be introduced. This affirmation of the ethical quality of occupational experience and training makes a strong appeal to the worker who unselfconsciously accepts his own presence on the job as a guarantee of proper production practices and is relatively unaware of the possible economic inappropriateness of his classification and hourly rate.

This type of industrial myth in which there is an attempt to hide or to frustrate increasingly simplified tasks by (a) an unwillingness to recognize change, and (b) the insistence that there are no operations that do not require traditional occupational abilities, is strategic in that it is used by union officials in a rational manner to further larger purposes of economic bargaining. However, to many of the rank and file workers in the occupation the mythical aspects of the work situation are not particularly apparent. Actually, for such a myth to be a useful strategic device, it is necessary that the workers be culturally centered. When self-consciousness begins to appear, that is, when the worker begins to be keenly aware that his operations are definitely outmoded or degraded and that his pay and prestige are only artifically maintained, the strategy is no longer effective, as the myth diminishes.

At times, occupational self-consciousness among certain groups of workers may block union management's strategic purposes. If workers of some tradition become convinced that the tasks to which they are assigned involve some occupational degradation in terms of pace, skill, materials handled, individual initiative, and relationship to other work groups, they may refuse to subscribe to the economic objectives of their union officials. For example, in Detroit, the Tile Layers have rather persistently refused employment at high rates on jobs involving the use of the increasingly popular metal tile. They have argued that such a material "degrades" the skill of those that "stick it on," and, as a result of their choice, have lost much of the work to other groups. Although union leaders have consistently urged them to work with the material as if nothing in the trade had changed, such a logical argument has apparently only served to impress the tradesmen with the unsatisfactory reality of their technological position.

On one of the large war housing projects near Wayne, Michigan, the carpenters walked off the job on several occasions because the methods used in construction involved an unusually large amount of form building and "saw and hatchet" work. The carpenters charged that it was obvious to everyone on the job that they were doing work of an inferior grade although at a high rate. During this time the union officials made every effort to keep the men operating as if no changes in construction had taken place to preserve the myth of undifferentiated tasks and appropriate skills.

3. There are other industrial myths in which the factor of occupational culture is not so clearly involved, but, instead, the function of the myth for the individual in a status system which emphasizes individual achievement constitutes the dominant element. Such myths lie largely in the realm of the conceptions which supervisors and other managerial personnel have of their jobs. This myth may be called the Compensatory Myth,[6] and may be regarded as having the central function of explaining the failure of a logical system to operate to the personal satisfaction of individuals identified with it in industry. There is steady pressure upon certain persons in the plant and on the job to "get ahead." To many, this means constant concern over promotions and progress into or through the ranks of supervision, rather than the development of further occupational virtuosity. The formal, rational, "line," or "chain of command" organization of industry sets up the relatively narrow channels of "rising in the world," and the social values emphasize the importance of achieving positions of authority.

Although informal factors, such as integration in the work group, personality traits, and service to family and community are considered valuable and significantly influence the satisfactions of some persons, there are many individuals in industry who evaluate themselves, not in occupational terms, but in terms of access to the higher levels of authority.

When promotion of the "line" organization of industry is blocked, this kind of therapeutic myth which provokes an inclusive rationalization for failure of the individual to achieve advancement, may be found. The individual egoistically rejects personal responsibility for failure and is receptive to a general cultural explanation of the situation. The myth is likely to appear in terms of a common denominator of general cultural rejection and prejudice. Stereotyped religious, racial, and ethnic evaluations are held to be operative. Such beliefs are repeated again and again in the office and shop until they achieve true mythical proportions. In some instances, of course, religious and ethnic discrimination as to advancement in industrial systems does have some definite basis in fact and thus constitutes reality, not myth. However, investigation of particular industrial concerns reveals that

6. The terms Compensatory and Strategic are used in the classification of myths, not because they are entirely satisfactory in representing exclusive categories (as strategy is implied in the fabricated myth and other myths may be thought of as being compensatory in some general sense), but because the term strategic seems to lend emphasis to the self-conscious factor in occupational culture as opposed to the unselfconscious, and because the term compensatory tends to suggest a particularly characteristic function of myth in a special status system.

in numerous situations there is no evidence of systematic bias in the control of promotions, despite the fact that individuals in the organization constantly make such statements as "every one knows" that "a Catholic," "an Italian," or "a southern white" "can't get ahead around here," as the case may be.[7]

A variation of the myth occurs when a minority group in the general culture is believed to have assumed control of the personnel system in the industrial organization. In the situations where there is relatively little communication between upper level executives and the lower managerial ranks personal fears and frustrations about "getting ahead" can be eased by full adherence to the mythical belief that a clique in the organization is systematically exploiting prejudice on other than occupational grounds.

A related type of myth is one which might be termed the Folk Myth, which offers a categoric explanation of human differentials in industry in terms of qualities assigned groups and individuals in the folk culture. Such qualities are usually considered to be organic in character. Examples of this myth are found in the beliefs in industry that Negroes "love" wet work or instinctively enjoy "hot" work in the foundry or mill. The Compensatory Myth assumes a manipulation of ethnic and religious characteristics for logical ends while the Folk Myth emphasizes the inevitable outcome of certain innate human abilities and limitations.

The final myth that we may perhaps distinguish here is the Fabricated Myth. This myth may be created by management and union organizations in industry to serve rational purposes, such as achieving a favorable position in the bargaining process. The fabricated myth of management or of the unions can be directed either internally toward the labor force or toward the public.[8] Such a myth whose outlines are once agreed upon by public relations and labor relations experts can take almost any form, although to be most successful it must adhere to the most creditable objectives accorded management and the unions in the general culture. The myth is synthesized by (a) limiting and controlling access to information concerning internal policies and economic position, and (b) the use of effective

7. In a Grand Rapids furniture concern, among the furniture craftsmen where the Dutch-Americans constitute a dominant group, the myth has it that one cannot become a supervisor without a good Dutch name. However, the records show supervisors with Jewish and South European names, some of long standing and some more recent promotions. Similarly, interviews in a Detroit automotive parts manufacturing concern indicated a well developed belief among workers of Polish extraction that management regards "Hamtramck Poles" as troublemakers and undesirable as supervisory types. Careful check, however, indicated that management proportionately employed more foremen of Polish background than of any other ethnic antecedents. This myth is a reflection of the general self-consciousness and sense of persecution which many Polish-Americans have in Detroit, and represents a device for easing personal frustration in a competitive situation.

8. With regard to their own members and related workers the old line unions are frequently limited by the outlines of occupational culture and thus the myths tend necessarily to take on a more restricted strategic character.

propaganda techniques. Myths of this kind stemming from industrial sources can have far reaching effects, e.g., the myth actively sponsored during World War II that the production workers in the factories were "selling out" the men overseas.

It would seem to be of significance to relate the foregoing types of myths to the status systems found in industry, as not all groups in industry— laborers, craftsmen, managers, and union members—measure their social position in the same manner. They are, in fact, responding in some degree to separate status systems. Briefly stated, one can identify the system of *general social status*, or status based upon the factors of age, sex, race, and nationality, which extends throughout the community. Secondly, there is the *lateral* system, following the outlines of the division of labor. Further, as Barnard [9] points out, there exists what might be termed the *scalar* system, which is characteristic of formal organizations and in which status is determined by superiority or subordination in a chain of command and by jurisdiction. The essence of scalar status is a vertical ranking of authority, as in the pyramiding levels of supervision in industry.

In industry, as in the community, these status systems tend to overlap, making it at times difficult to determine the relative degree to which persons and groups respond to each. However, despite the cross-system influence of status, among certain broad groups in industry status is more consistently evaluated within one framework than another. The groups in industry and their status systems are roughly the following:

(a) *Operatives and laborers in mass production industries.* These unskilled and semi-skilled workers in the industrial cities today are frequently recent migrants from relatively isolated regions of the agricultural South. They represent folk cultures with well established beliefs centering around the family, and sentiments and rituals derived from similar experience on the land. When not fully integrated into new cultural systems, e.g., union organizations, they respond both in the factory and in the community largely on the basis of status as defined in the folk cultures. General status of this kind is assigned on the basis of physical and social characteristics which have already been interpreted by pre-industrial experience.

(b) *Skilled tradesmen.* The skilled workers in building, railroading, and other industries are identified with particular cultural traditions which have grown up around well defined occupations. Lateral status is the status which is associated with this group, as all of those who have partaken of a particular tradition and perform the same function are possessors of the same rights and privileges.

(c) *Managers and supervisory officials.* The supervisory officials in industry are principally linked to the scalar system. Those who are designated

9. For an excellent discussion of the various status systems in industry see C. I. Barnard, "Functions and Pathology of Status Systems in Formal Organizations," in *Industry and Society*, William F. Whyte, ed. (New York: McGraw-Hill, 1946), part of which is included in this volume.

to supervise the work of others, particularly outside of the craft area, tend to evaluate themselves and all others in terms of the degree of authority allowed them and the degree to which access to the next higher rung on the ladder of authority is available to them.

(d) *Mass-production unionists.* A most significant group in industry from the standpoint of possessing a separate status system is the group of unskilled workers from folk culture backgrounds who have joined the more recent, mass-production unions and have been rather completely indoctrinated with the idealized conception of worker well-being propounded in union ideology. Here, status is not based upon function, as all functions are of a rudimentary type; neither is status of the scalar type, in which the primary measurement of worth is the supervisory position and its degree of authority. Neither does the union system exactly correspond with general status, as the idealized system may be somewhat at variance with some items in the general system, such as race attitudes and behavior. Status is achieved in the union system by taking a strong union stand on all issues defined as critical by the union ideology and by vigorously opposing managerial values.

The fact of separate status systems in industry suggests the linkage of the particular types of myths outlined above with particular status systems.

The Folk Myth, and to a certain extent, the Fabricated Myth, are identified with the system of general social status, within which system the operatives and laborers in the mass production industries function. The Culture-Centered Myth and the Strategic Myth are more peculiarly myths of the skilled tradesman, where status is laterally established within the limits of the occupation. The Compensatory Myth is the myth of management, where persons measure themselves in scalar terms. At the present time it is probably true that the Fabricated Myth is the myth most characteristically found among mass production union members.

Some implications of the analysis and classification of myth presented above may be stated as follows:

1. Depending upon their status systems, persons in industry are more highly influenced by one kind of myth than another.

2. In determining the length of time that a myth is likely to persist or the speed with which it may decline and disappear, knowledge of the type of myth is of primary importance. For example, the *Strategic* type of myth is much more subject to decline than the *Culture-Centered* myth.

3. As the *Culture-Centered* myth is significant in maintaining occupational morale, the tendency of such a myth to be modified under modern industrial conditions is of importance to persons concerned with the practical aspects of industrial relations, since definite behavioral changes on the part of workers are likely to follow disturbances in the myth.

4. As the *Compensatory* myth represents a vital factor in the personality integration of individuals in the management system of industry, an understanding of its function may offer the basis of the better adjustment of the individual to formal structures.

Conflicts of Authority

*Large bureaucracies do not commonly have the unified character sug-
gested by their outward monolithic appearance. Component bureaus may
engage in acute conflict as a result of overlapping jurisdictions, competing
loyalties and incompatible objectives. Dimock provides a case-study of bureaucratic infighting which illustrates the tactics utilized by a newly-created
division to maintain itself against the opposition of rival agencies in the
larger bureaucracy. The selection from the Hoover Commission presents
another case-study analyzing the sources and consequences of continued
conflict between two Federal agencies operating in the same sphere.*

EXPANDING JURISDICTIONS:
A CASE STUDY IN BUREAUCRATIC CONFLICT

Marshall E. Dimock

The only way an executive can be certain that any failure to perform effectively is his own is to assure himself in the first place that all the elements
necessary for a unified administration are in his hands. He cannot afford,
however, to stop dead in his tracks in order to iron out the problems of a
limited jurisdiction, nor to clarify the relationships between his own organization and those which have the power to detract from its full effectiveness
and efficiency. The work must go forward. But if he has a clear idea of
what is required of him in getting his job done, if he knows precisely what
his objectives are and can identify and be on guard against the hazards to
survival that surround him, then he will have constantly on the border of
his mind those steps which are necessary to round out his jurisdiction and
protect the future of his program. It becomes a sort of sixth sense with him,
always present but scarcely ever conscious. It is this sixth sense which, when
unexpected opportunities arise, causes him unhesitatingly to move into a
position where his enterprise can avail itself of the chance to complete its
powers. Thus does the executive enter the arena of power relationships.

There is a difference between aggrandisement which merely looks to
greater financing, more employees, and increased power and prestige, and
that which is an integral part of the strategy of performing a unified and
rounded function. It is easy to rationalize the one into the other. The executive, therefore, must honestly examine his own thought and motives so as

Reprinted in part from *The Executive in Action*, pp. 53-68, by permission of the publisher. (Copyright, 1945, by Harper and Brothers.)

to make sure that his desire for a unified authority is not in reality an avid, if disguised, thirst for power. Nothing will more quickly dissipate the strength of his organization than the assumption of unnecessary and unrelated activity. Similarly, nothing is more indispensable to success than the proper juxtaposition of related parts so that his machine may operate smoothly and with no cylinders missing.

The first step in rounding out your jurisdiction is the clear determination of objectives, for you cannot make valid detailed plans for either your program or your strategy until you know just where you are going. The determination of objectives influences policy, organization, personnel, leadership, and control. . . .

In the RMO [Recruitment and Manning Organization of the War Shipping Administration—Editors] the determination of objectives entailed a good deal of paper work. Our purpose was to prevent ship delays, but in order to accomplish this we needed to do a great many things, such as keep a supply of men on hand; shift them to different parts of the country as needed; see that men in the correct ratings were placed aboard the right ship at the proper time; devise means of recruiting experienced seamen; determine how many more would have to be trained in each rating; and improve seaman health and morale through a program of repatriation, health, and welfare. Thus did our field of operation become increasingly multiple and the determination of objectives more complicated.

As a first step, our control officer had to discover how many officers and men we would need in each category over specified periods of time—by weeks, months, and a year. A careful calculation revealed that we must manage to retain most of the 70,000 men already employed by the merchant marine and at the same time add an approximately equal number to the employment lists over a twelve months' period. With this information at hand we could now consider the possible sources of supply.

We knew that there were plenty of experienced seamen in the country, the majority of whom, however, had secured lucrative and safe employment in shore industries. We decided, therefore, upon a recruitment campaign, based upon an appeal to patriotism and self-advancement because of the high wartime wages for seamen, in order to attract as many of these men as possible back to their original calling.

The only other source of manpower supply was the government training program for seamen operated by the United States Maritime Service, and here, in an important area so far as our success was concerned, we encountered our first problem of divided authority and jurisdictional overlapping. Only two months before the RMO was created, this training program had been transferred from the Maritime Commission to the Coast Guard, following an administrative survey and recommendations by the Bureau of the Budget. Thus, the Coast Guard now controlled the principal and most reliable source of new seaman recruits. This was a matter of vital concern to us, since planning forceful action requires an integration not possible under divided authority.

In addition to this hazard, we now met with competition within the WSA itself. A Director General of Shipping had been appointed to supervise the WSA Division of Operations, and had made provision for a manning operation separate from ours. It was argued that the manning of ships was part of their operation, that personnel was not a separate function in the private shipping companies, and that there was no dividing line between the supplying of men and the actual discharge of their duties on board. The operating officials of the WSA contended, therefore, that the RMO should merely recruit the men as they were needed, and that thereafter the marine superintendents, contacting the individual companies, would act as intermediary and notify the RMO of what was required.

This would have meant that the RMO would be cut off from all direct contact with its clients, the executives of the shipping companies operating WSA vessels as agents of the government. To us, this seemed clearly undesirable. We felt that the extra step, involving an intermediary, was cumbersome and unnecessary and that, furthermore, the only way we could be sure of giving satisfactory service was to deal directly with the ship operators. This question, which closely affected our survival, was clearly in the area of power relationships and would have to be settled in open combat if necessary.

Also, at this point, we were beset by difficulties from without. Chief among these were the maritime labor unions, who watched our every move with deep concern in the belief that a government manning program was a potential threat, especially during wartime, to their future welfare. The maritime industry differs from most others in the central position occupied by the union hiring hall. Some 85 per cent of those employed in the industry were organized. In the case of dry cargo operators, for example, contracts between the unions and the companies were almost 100 per cent effective, there being only one or two exceptions. This coverage had been won only after long, bitter fights, strikes, and setbacks. For many years, attempts had been made to break the union organizations, by company unions, by shipping masters (fink halls, crimps), and by competitive government hiring halls. The old Sea Service, created during the first World War and continuing for a period thereafter, was still unpleasantly remembered in union circles. For the most part now, so far as we were concerned, the union officials were more suspicious than openly hostile. They wanted to be sure of our intentions, and whether the motives of those in command would stand scrutiny. But there were others who took the position that it was better to destroy at the outset a program which, although harmless at the moment, might become the tool of persons less scrupulous.

Another difficulty from the outside stemmed from the attitude of the ship operators, many of whom became suspicious of us when they realized that we were not eager to antagonize the unions. Our attitude of co-operation in that direction meant to them, apparently, that we were automatically controlled by the unions, so that they also were lukewarm in their support of our program. Thus we worked in an atmosphere of sharp watchfulness, both from within and from without.

Clearly, therefore, we had some points of controversy to settle before we could count on a successful operation. When a jurisdictional fight is to be undertaken, you first look around you for your natural allies. Then you try to estimate the possible strength of your opponent. Finally, you outline your tactical campaign, keeping always in mind the importance of the right kind of timing. Timing is a constant factor of management and contributes more than most to the quality of individual executive achievement.

In our case, the first priority was to stabilize our own internal situation in the WSA. Accordingly, Captain Macauley and I approached Admiral Land and emphasized the necessity of a clarification of jurisdiction within the WSA. We argued that the RMO should have undivided responsibility for the recruiting of seamen, placing them in the manpower pools at the various ports, and referring them aboard ship as the requirements arose. We pointed out that, to be effective, the RMO must have an unimpeded and direct line of operation from recruitment through placement. It was our contention that not until the men crossed the gangplank did the jurisdiction of the Operating Division begin. After listening to both sides, Admiral Land agreed with our viewpoint and brought that particular controversy to an end. We were now free to proceed on other fronts.

Our next step was to define the relationships that were to exist between the RMO and the maritime unions, for we recognized that they could be a valuable ally once they understood our position and gained confidence in our motives. No question of policy could be more important. Our position was clear: we recognized the central role of the union hiring halls; we were determined not to infringe upon the agreements between operators and unions; we wanted the hiring halls to continue to meet the principal manpower requirements of the merchant marine and were content to supplement their work.

We made it clear to the union officials, therefore, that the principal responsibilities of the RMO were, first, to collect exact information on personnel supply and demand; second, to make sure that all the sources of supply were tied together in such a way that available manpower could be used as efficiently and as economically as possible; and third, through effective organization, to make sure that no ship was delayed because the right man was not available in the right place at the right time. Ours was a job of planning and co-ordinating. We were not interested in taking over functions already being satisfactorily handled by the unions.

The unions, for their part, recognized frankly that they could not supply all the personnel which would be needed under the expanded merchant marine program and in the face of increasing shortages; they acknowledged, therefore, that the RMO would have to furnish a large number of both officers and men. If the total active manpower was to be doubled in a year's time, and the only sources of additional supply were the experienced men who might be brought back to the industry through direct recruitment activities, plus new men trained in the government schools, then it seemed clear that the RMO would have to be the point of intake for both.

Here it became necessary to lay down another fundamental principle of operation. The RMO would supply officers and men to the unions when they were needed for assignment to specified vessels in carrying out collective agreements, and any such men would be sent via the hiring hall rather than directly to the ship. If an operator having a contractual agreement attempted to get men from the RMO rather than from a union, he would be politely told that they could not be supplied. On the other hand, we recognized the needs of the unorganized companies, especially the tankers, who could be expected to make heavy demands upon our manpower resources. Our agreement with the unions and the companies, therefore, was that when an unorganized company requested officers or men they would be supplied directly, since obviously here the unions had no right to be consulted.

Having reached this point in our negotiations with the unions, we took up a proposal that would do much to make or break our effectiveness from the standpoint of controlling the problem of manpower supply and demand. If a unified job was to be carried through, it was obvious that we, as the central agency, must have complete information on all sources of manpower supply. This meant that the RMO must receive daily reports on how many men each union had available, the number in each rating, and the particular ports at which they were located. If to this number were added those on call at the offices of the RMO, then this combination, plus any alien officers and seamen who might be secured in an emergency, constituted the grand total. We were fortunate in that our proposal for a steady flow of this information was readily agreed to by all the maritime unions. It was further agreed between us that when the unions were short of men they would call upon the RMO, and when we needed men they would reciprocate if possible.

These arrangements were to bear fruit when we shortly encountered a problem that had to do with the stabilization of the personnel of the shipping industry. It involved a fundamental truth of manpower utilization, namely, that with the right kind of organization and co-operative agreements a relatively few trained men are worth more than a larger group whose number is not certain and who are not immediately available.

The merchant marine industry had been one of the worst offenders—if not actually the worst—with regard to the turnover of personnel. Some

400,000 men, for example, had had sea service at one time or another in the six-year period during which the Bureau of Marine Inspection maintained records. This meant that three-fourths or more of their number were rolling stones, men who went to sea but once or who shipped out only when they felt like it. These were of no use to us. Drifters could not be tolerated in wartime; the casual worker was a burden. It was the good, hard core of those who made the sea their livelihood on whom we needed to rely, a group of some 45,000 to 60,000 men who could be counted upon to ship out regularly. The only way we could double the size of merchant marine personnel in a year's time and get men who would stick to their posts was with the help and co-operation of the unions. Accordingly, we issued instructions to our field offices, copies of which were sent to all operators and union officials, setting forth as simply and decisively as possible these principles of operation. Thus the unions were assured that their best men would be used to the best advantage, while at the same time those few operators who were inclined to chisel and had previously relied primarily upon crimps were plainly told that the government's manning organization would be run on the level.

Having now worked out a satisfactory relationship with the unions, and (incidentally) with the operators as well, we were prepared at this point for our second jurisdictional struggle. This had to do with the government seaman-training program, then located in the Coast Guard which, accordingly, controlled our most reliable source of manpower. On this question our natural allies were the maritime unions, the state maritime academies themselves, and the ship operators, all of whom might be expected to favor a civilian administration of seaman training as against the military type of supervision exercised by the Coast Guard.

In our attempt to regain control of the training program we had to work through the Bureau of the Budget. The argument that weighed most heavily with them was our contention that the seaman personnel program could not be effectively operated unless it was unified. The output of the training schools constituted one of the principal sources of new sea personnel. In order to plan and control its most economical disposition, the schools themselves needed to be tied in closely with the organization responsible for over-all planning and manning. In addition, we pointed out that the armed forces were already so busy that it was a mistake to entrust a civilian function to them. Finally, we stated our belief that advantage should be taken of the wartime situation in order to create a unified shipping administration that would place the industry in as sound a condition as possible by the end of the war, thus avoiding a setback such as it received following the first World War.

There was a further aspect of our relationship with the Coast Guard which also seemed important to us. This had to do with the control of entry into the merchant marine. Under law, the Coast Guard was responsible for the issuing of certificates to men in the entry ratings and licenses to those in the skilled ratings. These functions had likewise been transferred to that agency within recent months—this time from the Commerce Department—as part of the general reorganization scheme recommended by the Bureau of the Budget. Here, again, it seemed desirable to us that all the government controls involved should be drawn together in the interest of a unified manning operation. This would mean combining the licensing and inspection functions of the Coast Guard with the jurisdiction of the WSA.

Estimating the strength of our opponent, however, it did not seem that we could be successful in this and so, rather than fail on two fronts for lack of concentration, we worked on the transfer of the training program alone, hoping that a more favorable opportunity would later present itself so far as the licensing and inspection functions were concerned. The Bureau of the Budget proved co-operative and saw the point of our arguments, with the result that in three months, in August of 1942, the training program was retransferred to the WSA. The RMO thereafter had a full-fledged brother. Captain Macauley's title was changed from Assistant to the Administrator of the WSA, to Deputy Administrator, and now supervised two divisions to which a third, Maritime Labor Relations, was soon to be added.

We were to discover, however, that the rounding out of jurisdiction by means of this transfer did not solve the whole problem. Here, again, we faced the question of power relationship between our organization and a possible rival, even though we were now both responsible to the same superior official. To be sure, we no longer had a competitor in another agency soliciting prospective employers for the placement of seamen; but other difficulties became clear.

One of the truest of statements about institutional life is that man's psychology is created by his job. The employee of the RMO, for example, accepted as a matter of highest conviction that the most important thing in the world was to prevent a ship delay due to crew shortage. The employee of the new Training Organization, on the other hand, naturally adopted as his crowning article of faith the belief that the best man is the trained man. This was accompanied by certain corollaries, one of which was that a trained man should have preference over all others, even those with previous sea experience, and with this the RMO could not agree. Another corollary was that the merchant marine had for years been manned by untrained seamen who were not so high physical and intellectual types as those chosen by a selective process. Their conclusion was that the manpower of the merchant marine must be remolded.

This attitude was understandable but impractical. During the war period, when the manpower situation was abnormally tight, experienced men had to be given preference even though potentially they might be less qualified than those who were trained. Convinced to the contrary, however, the Training Organization proceeded to turn out as many candidates as it could, despite the occupational imbalance thus created, and resented our failure to give them placement preference on every occasion. Loyalty and family feeling were argued. The result was that at various periods during the life of the RMO there was an overproduction of trainees in the various entry ratings, which sometimes became a matter of serious embarrassment. The Training Organization then argued that there was not an overproduction of trainees so much as a deliberate failure on the part of the RMO to place them. This was the familiar game of buck-passing.

There was, however, this much merit to their charge: We did attempt to adhere to the over-all manpower policy of the country as laid down by the War Manpower Commission, which rightly insisted that experienced men should be preferred over new men brought into an industry, whether trained or not. We also argued that the emphasis of the Training Organization might better be on the upgrading of men already in the industry to meet the new needs and avoid an imbalance, rather than upon the turning out of large numbers in the entry ratings. We were finally successful in getting this recommendation accepted, but the achievement was slow and painful, due in part at least to the greater ease with which those in the entry ratings could be trained compared with the difficulty of setting up and operating upgrading schools. Moreover, the upgrading schools were only a temporary, wartime measure, whereas the regular training program could continue on a permanent basis. The sense of institutional survival and of power, although natural and universally shared, was a force in the Training Organization with which we had to reckon in a serious way.

Nor were we free of other potential competition. The Army Transport Service, for example, although it operated relatively few ships, manned them with civilian crews. For a while we dreamed of the possibility of a unified manning organization for all water transportation, but were soon awakened when the ATS made it clear that they intended to take care of their own placements. This seemed to us a duplication of time and effort and we remained alert to the possibility of collaboration. Eventually, after nearly a year, we were able to enter into an understanding with them whereby the RMO took care of most of their recruitment and manning requirements, including the sending of personnel to the various theaters of war.

And finally, hovering over us like a sword of Damocles, was the threat that the navy might take over the merchant marine. This had nearly occurred in the first World War and there were rumors that such a proposal was not yet dead. This danger had a salutary effect on the RMO, of course, because it gave us a sense of competition and tended to tone up all our operations. We realized more clearly than ever that it would not be sufficient merely to supply the quantity of manpower needed; we must also supply the right quality so that the ships might be operated efficiently and under proper discipline, thus giving the navy no grounds for saying that it could do a better job of operating the merchant marine. In addition, with our own survival in mind, we made comparative studies of the relative cost of operation under navy and civilian supervision. These revealed that, whereas the WSA was operating Liberty ships with crews of less than 45 men, the navy customarily required several times that many on the same model vessel, and that in consequence the cost of navy operation was greater despite the fact that civilian wages were higher than those of enlisted men. Our most telling point, however, was the long-standing tradition and technique of merchant ship operation which resulted in better methods of stowage, a more skillful handling of cargo, and shorter turnaround time. Navy personnel is trained to handle guns, civilians to handle cargo, and there is all the difference in the world between the two. Because of these considerations we felt confident that if we did a good job we could avoid the rocks of navy expropriation. In this, of course, we were supported by the operators and by the maritime unions. ·

These survival factors are the stuff out of which the executive must fashion his strategy, based upon timing, influence, and the right use of power. The administrator does not operate in a self-contained vacuum. His work is part of the flow of social forces. He is placed in a managerial position for a purpose, but it is not self-perpetuating. It is more than mere housekeeping. It is more than the application of textbook theories, important as these are. The executive is a tactician and a philosopher. He must live by his wits, his competitive instincts, his understanding of social forces, and his ability as a leader. He does not operate in a fixed environment. He must change his environment or adapt to it where necessary, and then try to influence it in any ways which seem indicated in the accomplishment of the ultimate purposes of his program. . . .

Power relationships are inherent in every administrative situation. The executive must be fully aware of their necessary implications and prepared to struggle openly for power and for survival lest, by false modesty, weakness or self-delusion, he lose or seriously restrict his jurisdiction and endanger his program. No job can be done satisfactorily when any important element is missing. Clashes between business and government, between business concerns in the same field, between management and labor, between related government bureaus, and between geographical and sectional interests, are the stuff from which such power conflicts are fashioned.

Thus it is that the leadership of an organization, whether in business or in government, involves a constant struggle against other wielders of power. Men with red blood and courage derive satisfaction out of fair contests fought along constructive lines. But when the pugnacious quality is too pronounced, then fighting becomes an end in itself instead of a legitimate means to program effectiveness. It requires men of considerable breadth and perspicacity, therefore, to draw the discreet line between what is socially useful and what is merely a consequence of vanity and combative instincts. Thus, if competition and infighting are not to cause more social harm than good, our future leaders must be educated broadly in the elements of statecraft, found equally in business and in government and essential to the health and welfare of both.

DUPLICATION OF FUNCTIONS:
A CASE STUDY IN BUREAUCRATIC CONFLICT

The Hoover Commission

In February, 1940, Congress received two separate reports recommending construction of a multiple-purpose reservoir on the Kings River in California—one prepared by the Corps of Engineers and the other by the Bureau of Reclamation. The reports were dissimilar in several important respects. Each report had acquired proponents and opponents among the local interests, and the two Federal agencies were put in competition with one another to obtain the support of the California beneficiaries.

Why did two Federal water development agencies plan similar multiple-purpose projects on the same river? Why were not the conflicts between the two agencies reconciled at an early stage in the planning process, and the competition between the two put to an end by the President's office? What have been the results of this uncoordinated conflict? What has been the effect on the public interest of agency competition to win the support of local groups of water users? A case history of the Kings River project offers an excellent illustration of the type of uncoordinated water resource development which calls for immediate remedial action in the public interest. Such a case history may indicate the broad outlines of necessary reform. . .

As early as 1937 both the Corps of Engineers and the Bureau of Reclamation undertook investigations of the Kings River area. The investigation of the Corps of Engineers was initiated under the Flood Control Act of 1936; that of the Bureau of Reclamation, under an allotment from an appropriation

Reprinted from report of United States Commission on Organization of the Executive Branch of the Government (Hoover Commission), *The King's River Project in the Basin of the Great Central Valley—A Case Study*. Task Force Report on Natural Resources (Appendix L to report of Commission), Appendix 7 to above appendix. (Washington: Government Printing Office, 1949). This report was prepared by Arthur A. Maass, a member of the Commission's staff.

under the National Industrial Recovery Act. Both investigations were requested originally by the same water users' association in the Kings River area. The association apparently wanted to see what each agency would propose so that they would be in a position to express a preference for that plan which would afford them, as existing water users, the greatest benefits at the least costs.

The likelihood of controversy between the two Federal agencies developed soon thereafter. Although the engineers of the Corps and Bureau effected an exchange of physical data, separate field investigations were conducted and each agency developed its conclusions and recommendations independently.

Through its drainage basin committee for the Central Valley area, the Water Resources Committee of the National Resources Planning Board was made aware of the developing agency conflict before the field reports were completed. The water committee was very much opposed to the submission of separate reports by the two agencies; they preferred that the survey organizations cooperate to deliver a single report reflecting the combined judgment of the water experts in the Executive Branch of the Government. From experience they knew that integration of investigations is effective if undertaken at the initiation and field study stages of project investigations before findings are crystallized; it is largely and necessarily perfunctory if delayed until the basic conclusions have been reached independently by those concerned.

The committee, however, was unable to effect the desired cooperation before the field reports were completed and the valley water users, having learned of the conflicting recommendations of the two agencies, had begun to take sides for the Bureau or for the Corps depending largely on which plan would provide greatest benefits at least costs to them and under fewest operating restrictions. The survey report of the district engineer was submitted to Washington in April 1939, and soon thereafter the tentative field report of the Bureau of Reclamation was transmitted to Washington headquarters.

President Roosevelt was made aware of the developing conflict in the area. Although one would not expect that the President of the United States should take time to personally concern himself with an interagency conflict over a public works project, President Roosevelt viewed the Kings River controversy with such concern, particularly as regards any precedent it might set for irrigation and flood control policy, that he instructed the two agencies to keep their reports confidential insofar as their contents had not already become known to local interests and requested a conference in his office on the problem on July 19, 1939.

At this conference the President indicated his concern over the duplication of water resource development functions in the Central Valley and similar areas and stated his firm desire and intention to eliminate similar duplication in the future. As for the Kings River project, the President agreed to an arrangement whereby the two agencies would cooperate in preparing independent reports, but these reports should contain agreement on both design and economic features of the project. As for future areas of potential conflict, the President instructed the Departments of War, Interior, and Agriculture, in cooperation with the National Resources Planning Board, to draw up a memorandum of agreement which, by insuring consultation in the early stages of project planning, would preclude the possibility of similar conflicts.

The interagency agreement, negotiated in response to this request, and known as the tripartite agreement, authorized free interchange of information between the three agencies in the field in the preparation by any one of reports on multiple-purpose projects, and joint consultation in the field and in Washington on any such reports. At the time the agreement was negotiated, many in the Executive Office of the President felt that it fell short of the requirements of the situation and of the desires of the President. Experience under the agreement confirmed these fears. Although it did contribute to some improvement in field cooperation, the agreement did not eliminate conflicts and divergencies in later reports.

The Water Resources Committee would have preferred that the arrangement on the Kings River project provide for the submission of a joint report by the two agencies rather than of separate, but reconciled, reports. However, the President requested the agencies to submit their revised reports to him, and it was the understanding of the two agencies that the reports would then be reviewed for the President by the Water Resources Committee before they were made public or submitted to the Congress. In this way some of the advantages of a joint report might be realized.

On January 23, 1940, the Secretary of the Interior submitted to the President, through the National Resources Planning Board, the revised report of the Bureau of Reclamation. Four days later the director of the Board informed the Chief of Engineers that the Secretary of the Interior had forwarded his report on the project "to the President through the Board" and stated that, "When your report on the project is received, the Board will then have an opportunity to comment upon any points of difference which may exist between the two sets of recommendations. This we will do promptly."

On January 31, the Chief of Engineers acknowledged receipt of the director's letter in writing and stated that he understood that the Reclamation report had been forwarded to the President, through the National Resources Planning Board. The Chief of Engineers, however, did not state that the report of his Department had been completed nor that it had been sent directly to the President on the preceding day. By the time the National Resources Planning Board heard that the Engineer Department report had been sent directly to the White House and communicated with the President's executive clerk to catch up with it, they found that it had been allowed to pass directly to the Congress. Thus, the recommendations of the Corps of Engineers were made public without any opportunity for review by the Water Resources Committee and before they had been fully reconciled with those of the Bureau of Reclamation.

As for the action of the White House in allowing the War Department report to pass directly to the Congress, no definite explanation is available. However, it is believed that it was a clerical error, that the White House was under the impression that the report had cleared the Planning Board. As for the action of the Chief of Engineers, it may well be that the instructions of the President at the July conference has been to submit the revised and reconciled reports to him; but the Engineers knew that the reports were not fully reconciled and they knew that the Secretary of the Interior had transmitted the Reclamation report to the President through the National Resources Planning Board where it was being held, awaiting receipt of their report.

Whether or not the urgency of competition between the two executive agencies over matters relating to the Central Valley was in any way responsible for the actions of the Engineer Department surrounding transmittal of their report to the President, this competition may very well have been responsible for a significant variation from the uniform procedure for the preparation of Engineer survey reports. The procedure, as prescribed by orders and regulations, requires that the district engineer conduct the survey in the field and that the division engineer, the Board of Engineers for Rivers and Harbors in Washington, and the Chief of Engineers, each review the survey report and state their conclusions and recommendations in an endorsement to the district engineer's report. In this case, however, the report of the district engineer which was transmitted to Washington in April 1939, was not used nor was any revision of this report which might have been made after the President's conference. Instead, the Chief of Engineers used as the basis for his report a very brief interim report of the Board of Engineers which had been prepared in Washington in June, 1939 before the original conference with the President, and which made no reference to the district engineer's survey.

To this brief interim report the Chief attached his own recommendations, containing those revisions in project design which had been agreed to jointly by the Office of the Chief of Engineers and the Commissioner of Reclamation. The play for time advantage may have dictated this procedural variation. More important, however, is the fact that thereby the President and the Congress were provided with a report which, though designed to serve as the basis for action upon a highly controversial project recommendation, was seriously lacking in basic data.

Upon learning that the Engineer report had gone to Congress, the Chairman of the National Resources Planning Board, on February 2, 1940, wrote to the President:

We understand that the Army report has already gone to the Congress. In justice to the Secretary of the Interior and the Bureau of Reclamation, it now seems desirable that the Interior Department report should also go to the Congress even though the Army and Reclamation recommendations have not yet been completely reconciled.

And so, in February 1940, the Congress received two separate reports from the Federal agencies, each recommending construction of a reservoir at Pine Flat site on the Kings River. The reports were generally reconciled on features of engineering design but were far apart on matters of water economics. The conflicting recommendations became a matter of public record. They attracted ardent proponents and opponents. The scheme for insuring integration prior to the crystallization of findings and recommendations had failed.

Future events were to confirm the conviction of many in the water field that integration which is delayed until basic conclusions have been reached and published independently by those concerned is extremely difficult, if not impossible, of effective attainment. . .

FINDINGS.

a. *Results of Central Valley Conflict.*

1. Seven years elapsed between the time the agencies first submitted their reports to the Congress on the Kings River project and the time President Truman released funds for commencing construction. Although a large part of this delay can be attributed to the intervening war years, a significant portion is due to the conflict.

2. It is still questionable whether or not the water resources of the Kings River are being developed and will be utilized in accordance with the most economical and beneficial utilization of all water and related land resources of the San Joaquin Valley and the Central Valley Basin.

3. The Kings River project will cost the Federal Government considerably more than it should. A significant portion of the irrigation benefits, as yet not subject to precise evaluation, will in all likelihood never be repaid to the Federal Treasury.

4. Some of the beneficiaries of the Kings River project may be able for all time to avoid the acreage, land speculation, and full repayment provisions of Federal law.

5. The easing of repayment and operating requirements of Federal reclamation law with respect to the Kings River project may result in considerable pressure on the Federal Government to make equivalent concessions on other existing and proposed irrigation projects. Such pressure, if it succeeds, will increase the cost to the Federal Government of water resource programs by hundreds of millions of dollars.

6. The outcome of the conflict will in all likelihood favor the owners of large tracts of land and the present users of large quantities of irrigation water. Prospective and small landowners and water users will not benefit proportionately. This finding has greater application to the Kern River and other areas to the south than to the Kings River area, where there are a number of relatively small landholders.

7. Duplication of water-planning work in the Kings River area has added an unnecessary charge to the Federal budget.

8. The conflict over the Kings River project has consumed an unreasonably large amount of the time and effort of the President of the United States.

9. The intensity of the conflict over the Kings River project has led to embarrassing and unbecoming conduct on the part of both the Corps of Engineers and the Bureau of Reclamation and a consequent loss of public confidence in both agencies.

b. *Causes of Continuing Inability to Resolve the Central Valley Conflict.*

1. The basic cause of the conflict over the Kings River lies in the fact that two Federal water-resource agencies are operating in the same river basin, each planning multiple-purpose water-control projects.

2. The basic water-use philosophies of the Corps of Engineers and the Bureau of Reclamation, as revealed by their plans for the Kings River, are in sharp contrast. The Bureau gives primary emphasis to closely integrated, multiple-purpose drainage-basin development. The social objectives are those related to the wide distribution of Federal land-improvement benefits among small independent landholders and of Federal power benefits among all ultimate consumers—rural and urban. The Corps gives primary emphasis to the cost-benefit ratio of individual water projects, measured largely in terms of the localized benefits and costs that result when each project is considered alone. The major concern is flood control, and there are few social objectives related to the wide distribution of benefits.

3. The conflict arises in part from the different laws under which the two agencies operate. Statutory inconsistencies are important, but care must be taken not to lay full blame on this cause. Disharmony, often attributed to statutory differences, "could be reduced through the conscientious effort of those engaged in the work."

4. The two agencies hold conflicting concepts of administrative responsibility. The Bureau holds itself directly responsible to the President and, through the President, responsible to the Congress. The Corps holds itself directly responsible to the congressional committees which handle its legislation and hardly responsible to the President at all. This basic difference makes effective coordination within either the legislative or executive branches extremely difficult.

5. The procedure whereby the Corps of Engineers and the Bureau of Reclamation announce to local interests the tentative recommendations, contained in field survey reports, before these recommendations are fully reconciled with those of other Federal agencies, makes effective reconciliation more difficult. The recommendations acquire partisan support and opposition among local interests who attach themselves to, and provide support for, one Federal agency or the other.

6. The dominant interest theory has failed to solve the conflict. All parties have accepted the statement of the theory, but failed to agree on its application. New questions raised by the application of the theory include: (1) Should the theory be applied to each individual project or to an entire basin-wide plan? (2) Should the dominant interest be determined solely by a comparison of prospective benefits to be derived from each purpose of a multiple project or should other factors be taken into consideration? (3) Where estimates of benefits prepared by the Corps and the Bureau differ, which figures are to be adopted?

7. Executive coordination by the Executive Office of the President has failed to solve the conflict. In addition to the reasons indicated in preceding paragraphs, the following are important:

A. Vigorous and effective efforts at coordination on policy matters were not taken at the initiation of the investigations. Integration of investigations is effective if undertaken at their initiation before findings are crystallized. It is largely and necessarily perfunctory if delayed until the basic conclusions have been reached independently by those concerned.

B. The two agencies have been allowed to submit separate reports—on both the Kings River and other individual projects and on the comprehensive basin plan—rather than a single coordinated report reflecting the combined judgment of the water experts of the executive branch of the Government.

C. Since the abolition of the National Resources Planning Board, the Executive Office of the President has taken little positive action to facilitate the reconciliation of conflicting agency recommendations. The Office has taken a stand for the President and has required agencies to inform Congress of the President's program, but it has not prevented the submission of conflicting reports to Congress and, more important, it has not taken the affirmative steps necessary to effect the development of a single coordinated basin-wide plan.

8. The Federal Inter-Agency River Basin Committee has been ineffective as a means for reconciling conflicting agency views, policies, and recommendations.

9. Lack of uniformity in legislative consideration of authorization and appropriation for projects recommended by the Corps of Engineers and the Bureau of Reclamation has abetted the conflict between the two agencies.

5

RECRUITMENT AND ADVANCEMENT

Like other forms of social organization, bureaucracies face the problem of evolving patterns for recruiting, and thereafter distributing, personnel. In some degree, the character of personnel is determined by the wider social structure constituting the environment of the bureaucracy. Changes in the cultural values or educational opportunities of social strata, for example, may lead to marked changes in the social origins of aspirants to positions in public or private bureaucracy. Within these limits, each bureaucracy can, in some measure, control the nature of its personnel. The composition of those seeking employment in a bureaucracy will presumably be affected by public images of the social status, security, financial reward and prospects of advancement it affords. Various methods of recruitment from these aspirants each pose distinctive problems of adaptation by the bureaucracy. These and related problems which have been subjected to careful study are considered in the present section.

The selection from Sharp traces historical shifts in the composition of recruits to the French civil service. The apparent decline in the status of the governmental bureaucracy and the correlative rise in the status and comparative financial rewards provided by business organizations and independent professions are linked with important changes in the social origins of functionaries. These changes, in turn, presumably affect the adequacy of public administration. Using more systematic data, Miller studies the social origins of chief executives and directors in American business bureaucracies about the turn of the century. His findings are at odds with the belief, common among some eminent American historians, that these officials were largely recruited from the lower social and economic strata. Apart from the relevance of these particular findings, this study shows the importance, in this as in other problems of bureaucracy, of supplanting casually illustrated impressions of observers with the facts of systematic research.

In their study of the recruitment of bureau chiefs in the Federal government, Macmahon and Millett find that, contrary to some current opinion, the use of formal merit systems does not lead to an increase of average age at appointment. This selection focusses throughout on the interplay between methods of recruitment and advancement, and the requirements *of effective administration. Much the same emphasis is found in the short comparative review by Dimock and Hyde of policies for recruiting chief executives in business and government. They go on to suggest criteria which must be satisfied if these officials are, in general, to be adequate to their organizational tasks.*

However much it may differ in detail, the patterning of inducements for seeking and holding employment in a bureaucracy has some underlying uniformities, and these are theoretically formulated by Simon. He analyzes the major types of motives, among which the concern with advancement is only one, for accepting participation in organizations, and outlines the relations between organizational and personal objectives in diverse kinds of bureaucracy. Though advancement in a bureaucratic career may be a motive for participation, it does not follow that the actual chances for advancement are easily or correctly evaluated by members of the organization. Through systematic surveys of the attitudes of American soldiers, Stouffer and his collaborators uncovered the fact that the lower the rate of promotion in a given branch of the Army, the more favorable the appraisal of promotion opportunity by the personnel in that branch. This seeming paradox is explained by the social contexts in which these appraisals of opportunity occur.

The promotion of individuals within a bureaucracy may, of course, also be described as the succession of individuals in bureaucratic positions. Such replacements, particularly of chief executives and managers, give rise to a series of organizational repercussions which are in part examined by Gouldner. Focussing on a case history of succession in an industrial organization, he analyzes the connections between succession, the subsequent replacement of auxiliary personnel, bureaucratization, and the need for the successor to take account of the established, though informal, networks of social relations, sentiments and expectations of personnel in the organization.

HISTORICAL CHANGES IN RECRUITMENT

Walter Rice Sharp

The transition from patronage to open competition during the last thirty years has been paralleled by an equally significant change in the sources of recruitment for public employment. As has already been suggested, the dominant urge that led most young Frenchmen to seek careers in government

Reprinted in part from *The French Civil Service: Bureaucracy in Transition*, pp. 84-90 (New York: The Macmillan Company, 1931), by permission of the author.

offices before the war was a desire for the calm bourgeois security they
seemed to offer. Stability of tenure and a sure, if modest, provision for old
age satisfied the French youth of the nineteenth century. He was not then
interested in the possibility of making, American-wise, a fortune in a few
years; rather it was his hope to live a respectable, socially esteemed life in
his own *milieu*. In those days the public service carried high prestige; no
profession or occupation enjoyed a better social rating. The fact that so
many State posts were by tradition "honorary" appointments bears eloquent
witness to the esteem in which public employment at the middle and upper-
grade levels was held. Magistrates and military officers, prefects and ambassa-
dors, inspectors of finance and state engineers, departmental directors and
bureau chiefs; even *rédacteurs* and lowly copyists—all these were valued
more highly than comparable employments in private life. French literature
is filled with tales of heart-ache over failure to pass the *concours* that would
open the magic door to the title of *fonctionnaire*, and not a little of the incessant intrigue resorted to by family and friends in their efforts to "salvage"
the defeated aspirant.

   This situation, however, was already beginning to change as the present
century opened. Formerly, the public service had been recruited almost
entirely from aristocratic and bourgeois circles. One found few sons of
shopkeepers and peasants wearing the uniform or insignia of public officials.
Most of the full-time civil servants came from families that at least touched
the *rentier* class, if they were not squarely inside it. Geographically, recruitment was heaviest from Southern France, where industrial development
lagged. It was more common than not for a young man entering upon a
government career to possess an independent income of appreciable proportions. There would usually be enough, at any rate, to supplement his official
salary so as to cause him no worries about establishing a family in the approved thrifty, "birth-controlled" French manner. But by the dawn of the
present century the cost of living had mounted so much higher than the
Third Republic's official salary range that the fonctionnaire's bourgeois
rentes frequently became inadequate to bridge the chasm between official
and private scales of remuneration. Furthermore, opportunities in the field
of business and the private professions were becoming more and more attractive to ambitious young men. The latter, too, seemed to become infected—
at any rate many of them—with the virus of commercialism. "More and
more," wrote M. Lefas in 1912, "certain advantages which formerly attracted
men to State employment are losing favor; namely, the value that used to
attach to certain honorary positions, rank, title or decoration; also, the matter of old age retirement pensions, since the practice of insurance against
old age is now general and accessible to every one."

   As early as 1910, government personnel officers were lamenting the omi-
nous falling off in the supply of candidates for posts which were formerly

in great demand. Instance after instance might be cited in proof of this alarming state of affairs. From the Foreign Office to the postal administration came the plaint that vacancies could not be filled without appreciably lowering the entrance standards traditionally set for them. The youth of France was even then showing some signs of that restlessness which was to shake the generation following the struggle of 1914–1918. The bourgeois sources from which governmental recruitment normally sprang were tending to be engulfed in the wave of "democratization" that swept over political and social institutions everywhere in western Europe in 1900. Sons of *le peuple* began to see in the public services an opportunity to push upward a social niche or two. Here and there among applicants for intermediate posts appeared young men from families whose heads belonged either to the industrial proletariat or to the peasantry. Due to the gradual spread of educational scholarships by grants from State funds, a limited number of the more talented children of factory workers and *concierges*, of small farmers and agricultural laborers, might aspire to careers calling for a secondary education as a pre-requisite. Government posts that had once been the exclusive preserve of the *upper* bourgeoisie began to be filled increasingly from the *middle* and *lower* bourgeoisie.

The war greatly accentuated this evolution. What had in 1910 been, in the French vernacular, a mild *crise*, became by 1926 a *véritable crise*. Before the war, the father might say to his son, "If you don't work hard at your studies, you will be good only for business"; to-day, he tends to reverse his admonition: "If you are not studious you will have to resign yourself to becoming a fonctionnaire!" The result has been that in recent years entrance examinations have been "deserted" by the wholesale. At least three reasons may be assigned for this extraordinary state of affairs: (1) the depreciation of the franc to one-fifth its pre-war value, together with the failure of the government to adjust salaries upward to keep pace therewith; (2) the corresponding loss of income from *rentes*, forcing thousands of civil servants to live almost entirely from their meagre official salaries; and (3) the decided post-war increase in French per capita wealth, with living standards for the commercial and industrial classes which would be relatively higher even if governmental salaries had retained their 1914 purchasing power. What has been taking place is a quasi-revolution in the internal economic and sociological texture of the French nation,—a revolution hitting worst of all the old bourgeoisie.

The new generation of students after the war found themselves completely disillusioned about the "glory and honor" of spending all one's life behind a government desk at a rate of pay which seemed to them ridiculously inadequate to the amenities of *la vie modernisée*. Returned from the trenches, they were seized with a spirit of freedom and initiative that reacted in terms of an urge to recoup the economic losses of the war over

night. Life, after all, was short. The old social categories seemed to be break-
ing up. Fortunes had been made in a few months by those behind the lines.
High taxes and currency inflation gave one cause to wonder whether anything was stable. These youth felt that they must make hay while the sun
shone, and that they must do it by their own immediate efforts. They could
not afford to wait long years for infrequent promotions which at best promised a livelihood wholly out of proportion to the levels they might hope for
in following industrial, financial, or journalistic careers. At a time when, in
1927, the maximum basic remuneration for the highest-ranking permanent
State officials was 80,000 francs, it was not uncommon for the big banks and
insurance companies to pay from 200,000 to 300,000 francs to men on their
directing staffs.

How difficult it was for the State to win against such competition from
la grande industrie may be seen from an instance related by the Secretary
of the *Syndicat des Professeurs de Lycées*. An *agrégé* (holder of the highest
pedagogical certificate in the French educational system), although without
any technical knowledge of finance, was offered an attractive position in a
large bank at the salary several times higher than the maximum for *lycée*
teachers. What the bank wanted was a man of high culture—a man with
ideas and imagination; the necessary technical knowledge he could easily
learn. The sequel was that the State lost to the banking world a teacher of
brilliant promise whose vacancy could not be filled for a long time, if at all.
Only by postponing the age of retiring the older men in secondary education has the government been able to keep its teaching staffs reasonably well
manned since the war.

Other examples of this tendency are legion. Two-thirds of the young
technicians graduating from the *Ecole Polytechnique*, the great State engineering school, are now going elsewhere than into State service. Those who
do enter the Ministry of Public Works stay hardly four or five years until
they are lured away by attractive offers from industrial concerns. Candidates for posts in the colonial service have alarmingly diminished during the
last few years: those naturally attracted to adventure overseas prefer to
attach themselves to big private exporting and importing houses. In the
Ministry of Labor, where it was customary before the war for as many as
150 applicants to take each examination given to fill four or five vacancies,
there were in 1927 only 30 candidates. During the four years immediately
preceding the war, 321 candidates tried out for clerkships in the division of
indirect taxes of the Ministry of Finance, during 1923–1926, only 121 took
the examination. In the P. T. T., the ratio of applicants to appointments fell
by one-half in thirteen years. Applicants for executive and clerical posts in
the customs service fell from 153 in 1913 for 31 vacancies, to 45 in 1926 for
37 vacancies. So the comparison might continue for numerous other branches
of the administrative services.

It is only in the *subaltern* field staffs of the postal, educational, and similar establishments that recruitment has remained easy. Here the old desire for stability of employment, with the prospect of an old age pension, is still strong among the un-ambitious who do not feel drawn toward any particular vocation. As one goes up the hierarchical scale, however, it may safely be postulated that recruits for the civil service are being drawn in steadily increasing numbers from lower social strata than a generation ago. Surprising enough, this generalization will hold even for the "gilded" ranks of French diplomacy, where emphasis upon classic culture and *savoir faire* has been traditionally notorious. More and more, according to the testimony of none other than the Director of Personnel at the Quai d'Orsay, are the sons of gendarmes and elementary school teachers presenting themselves for the foreign service. Not a few have been accepted for such posts, although the majority of successful applicants still come, of course, from *la bonne bourgeoisie*, as "toned up" by a substantial sprinkling of "aristocrats."

For the most part, then, the dominant motivation of those nowadays seeking entry into the service of the State is more strongly than ever a desire for security and steady, but not too strenuous, work. Moral considerations play to-day a less conspicuous rôle than formerly. As France moves forward in the direction of an "industrialization" of values, the prestige of serving the State tends proportionately to diminish. It is common to hear the term "fonctionnaire" treated with mild contempt. To the new leaders of the French business and professional world, it suggests small honor. Since any one—even a *marchand de beurre!*—can now maneuver so as to get an official decoration of some sort, the French weakness for personal insignia can be satisfied outside the ranks of the military and civil services. The result is that youth with ability and ambition are turning away from State employment in growing numbers.

SOCIAL BACKGROUNDS OF THE BUSINESS ELITE

William Miller

One might have supposed that historians, largely occupied as they have been with the activities of ruling classes, would have been among the first to study systematically the problem of the recruitment and tenure of elites.

Reprinted in part from "American Historians and the Business Elite," *Journal of Economic History*, Vol. IX (1949), pp. 184-208, by permission of the author and the publisher. (Copyright, 1949, by the New York University Press.)

This problem is an especially interesting one in a country such as the United States which has had no official caste systems and no legally established hereditary hierarchies. Yet most American historians have shied away from it.[1] Few of them have even raised questions about the locus and transmission of power or status in modern times. Moreover, those who have discussed in particular the ascent of nineteenth- and early twentieth-century business leaders have tended to attribute their success simply to the possession of more shrewdness or trickiness or more pluck or luck or other private qualities than competitors who failed to rise; the very few historians who have considered social determinants such as family background or work experience have, by stressing the alleged values of poverty or of starting business in boyhood, placed their emphasis, as we shall see, quite at the opposite pole from where it belongs.[2]

The present study of 190 business leaders of the first decade of the twentieth century and of 188 contemporary political leaders on whom data are presented for comparison aims to call historians' attention to the critical but neglected field of elite recruitment, to suggest a method by which data may be collected and analyzed,[3] and to present some of the results of applying this method to a particular area in which a few historians have speculated to strikingly misleading effect. The men discussed in these pages were all officeholders; many of them *never* organized a business of any kind. Yet the dull titles by which these men are called and the bureaucratic maneuvering in which they must often have engaged should not suggest that these were petty men exercising small powers in petty domains. The mere fact that they were bureaucrats should suggest the contrary, for while there are many examples of petty bureaucracies, generally speaking only large enterprises operating in large theaters need hierarchical structures. . . .

At the start of this work I had decided that two hundred men were all that an individual could study in a reasonable time and that from that num-

1. One reason for this may be that the traditional framework and the traditional assumptions of American history writing preclude serious questions about personal aspirations and the patterns of ascent. This framework is the "presidential synthesis," and one of the key assumptions is equality of opportunity. On this theme see Thomas C. Cochran, "The 'Presidential Synthesis' in American History," *American Historical Review*, LIII (1948), 748-59. See also N. W. Stephenson, "Roosevelt and the Stratification of Society," *Scripps College Papers*, No. 3 (1930), esp. pp. 71-72.

2. The role of such social factors and of others to be considered here, such as education, nationality, and faith, in the selection of men even for training for high executive posts in modern corporations is brilliantly set forth by the former president of the New Jersey Bell Telephone Company, Chester I. Barnard, in his book, *The Functions of the Executive* (Cambridge: Harvard University Press, 1938). See also "The Thirty Thousand Managers," *Fortune*, February 1940.

3. Sociologists (and a few others in special fields) were the first to adapt to the analysis of elite recruitment in social terms quantitative methods evolved by statisticians and used initially in elite studies by eugenists. For the early literature, see J. McKeen Cattell, *American Men of Science* (2d ed.; New York: The Science Press, 1910), p. 537.

ber (various contingencies reduced the final group to 190) statistically reliable results could be obtained.[4] If these men were selected from the largest companies regardless of field, the bulk of them would have come from the railroads; if, on the other hand, an equal number were taken from each major business field, representatives of small insurance companies and banks would have mingled with the elite while many from great railroads would have been excluded. This dilemma could be solved only arbitrarily.

The companies from which men were chosen were taken from the following major fields: (1) manufacturing and mining, (2) steam railroads, (3) public utilities, (4) finance (commercial banking, life insurance, investment banking).[5] Companies in the first three fields were ranked by capitalization, the commercial banks by deposits, and the life-insurance companies (no other types of insurance companies approach the life companies in size) by assets.[6] From the *Statistical Abstract of the United States* and other sources summarizing census information, I then took the capitalization of

4. For a study of business bureaucrats it seemed reasonable to select the leaders from among those who held the topmost *positions* in the largest business companies. This was done without regard to the problem of getting biographical information on the men who happened to hold these positions. As it turned out, most of the information sought (approximately thirty questions to be answered for each of these men were put on a schedule, the answers then being coded and punched on Hollerith cards) could be obtained for all but a few of these men. Only a part of this information is analyzed in this essay; I hope in later studies to present more of it.

To describe in detail the sources used for information would use up far too much of the space available here. Besides obvious sources such as individual biographies (of which only eighteen of these business leaders have been subjects), the *Dictionary of American Biography* (which has essays on only fifty-six of these men), the *National Cyclopedia of American Biography* (a much more useful source than the *DAB* and often more accurate), and other encyclopedias, state and local histories, and diverse *Who's Who's*, I consulted magazine articles, newspaper files, folders of clippings in morgues of newspapers and magazines, and carried on an extensive correspondence with business companies, historical societies, and relatives of men discussed here.

5. Of the seventy-four nonfinancial corporations represented by the men studied here, fifty-eight (under original or other names) are among Berle and Means' two hundred. Forty-five are among the two hundred (as of 1937) listed in Monograph 29, "The Distribution of Ownership in the 200 Largest Nonfinancial Corporations," of the TNEC *Investigation of Concentration of Economic Power* (Government Printing Office, 1940). See pp. 346-47.

6. Those in the first three fields were taken from Part VI of Moody's *The Truth About the Trusts*, published in 1904. Financial companies are not listed in Moody's book; hence they were taken from Moody's *Manual*, 1903. The leading investment-banking houses were named not on the basis of size but largely on that of testimony before the Pujo Committee, of which the following is a pertinent example: Samuel Untermeyer questioning George F. Baker: "Will you be good enough to name a single transaction in the last 10 years of over $10,000,000 in amount which had been financed without the participation of Messrs. *Morgan & Co.*, or the City Bank, or *Kuhn, Loeb & Co.*, or *Speyer & Co.*, or *Lee, Higginson & Co.*, or *Kidder, Peabody & Co.*, of Boston, and the First National Bank and the Illinois Trust and Savings Bank, of Chicago?" Mr. Baker could not name one. See United States Congress, Committee on Banking and Currency, *Money Trust Investigation* (Government Printing Office, 1913), II, 1540. Men from all the banks named here are included in this study; those italicized are the five investment banking houses from which nine partners were selected.

the entire manufacturing and mining, stream railroad, and public-utilities industries in the United States in or near 1910, the total deposits of the national banks, and the assets of the life-insurance companies. These I simply added together and distributed the leaders among the four fields more or less according to the proportion of the total represented by the figure used for each. . . .

The next step was to choose the topmost positions from which these men should be selected. Should directors be included, or chairmen and members of key panels such as finance or executive committees? What of executive vice-presidents, general managers, or cashiers of banks? Investigation of the locus of different types of power in large corporations has only just begun;[7] for the period of this work it may fairly be said that there are no studies. The decision to limit this work to presidents and board chairmen of corporations and some partners of unincorporated investment-banking houses permitted me to choose men from a larger group of companies that would have been possible had men from more positions been selected; it may have caused some persons of great importance to be excluded, but all of those included, at any rate, were bound to be men of first rank.[8] No one who was president or board chairman in a listed company in the decade 1901–1910 has been excluded.[9]

One hundred and seventy-four of these men (information on this score is lacking for sixteen) held approximately 2,720 business directorships. A few held more than 100 each; the average was about 16.[10] Clearly, these men were leaders not only in their own companies but in the entire business community. . . .

7. Among the leading studies in this field are those already cited, by Gordon, Barnard, and Berle and Means.

8. I plan in another place to discuss in detail the selection of the 188 political leaders for this study. It is sufficient to state here that this number includes *all* the presidents, vice-presidents, cabinet members, and United States Supreme Court judges in the decade 1901-1910, these being 44 men plus 67 United States senators and 77 representatives. Twenty-three of the senators and 31 of the representatives held *all* the chairmanships in the 57th through the 61st Congresses of "major" committees in their respective houses, the list of committees being adapted from that in George H. Haynes, *The Senate of the United States*, II, 1059, and that in DeAlva Stanwood Alexander, *History and Procedure of the House of Representatives* (Boston: Houghton Mifflin Co., 1916), pp. 399-410. The remaining 44 senators and 46 representatives held all the chairmanships of certain other committees designated "minor" but sometimes of major importance in channeling legislation. Of the total of 144 senators and representatives, only 14 were not members of some "major" committee.

9. The only exception is Bruce H. Ismay, an Englishman, who was president of the International Mercantile Marine Company beginning in 1904 and who served in this capacity abroad.

10. This information is based on listings for 85 men in the *Directory of Directors*, City of New York, 1909-1910; for 58 men, in similar directories issued during the decade 1901-1910; for 31 men, on other sources. Two thousand seven hundred and twenty directorships is a conservative figure; were the maximum number ever held by each of these men available, the total would be appreciably higher.

As stated earlier in this essay, some general American historians have made enough casual remarks about the recruitment of modern business leaders to form a rough explanatory model. I want now to point out some of the facets of this model and then to introduce some of my own findings to show how obsolete it had become by the first decade of this century, if, indeed, it ever fitted the facts.

Virtually all the generalizations that go to make up this model are based upon a few remarkable life histories from the "robber baron" period; thus in most of the books that are at all concerned with the recruitment of business leaders one finds accounts of Andrew Carnegie, John D. Rockefeller, J. Pierpont Morgan, James J. Hill, and Edward H. Harriman. In *The Growth of the American People 1865–1940*, Arthur M. Schlesinger, Sr., cites in addition such older heroes as Cornelius Vanderbilt and Gustavus F. Swift but not later ones.[11] Charles A. and Mary R. Beard, in *The Rise of American Civilization*, add to the ubiquitous five Jay Gould, William H. Vanderbilt, Collis P. Huntington, Jay Cooke, William A. Clark, and Philip D. Armour.[12] Few general historians discuss a greater number of men than do the Beards; but much more significant, practically none discusses any *later* men. . . . Arthur Schlesinger says vaguely of the latest group of business leaders he discusses that they arose "in most cases from obscure origins and unhindered by moral scruples, they were fired by a passionate will to succeed." [13] In the last discussion of business leaders in *The American Nation*, John D. Hicks says: "Typical of the railroad builders was James J. Hill," who, he points out, was an immigrant from Canada.[14] The Beards' analysis of the life histories of American business leaders ends with the eleven men named above, of whom they write:

Of the group here brought under examination only two, Morgan and Vanderbilt, built their fortunes on the solid basis of family inheritances while only one had what may be called by courtesy a higher education: Morgan spent two years in the University of Göttingen. Carnegie began life as a stationary engineer; Jay Cooke as a clerk in a general store in Sandusky; Jay Gould as a surveyor and tanner; Huntington, Armour, and Clark as husky lads on their fathers' farms; Hill as a clerk for a St. Paul steamboat company; Harriman as an office boy in a New York broker's establishment; Rockfeller as a bookkeeper in Cleveland.[15]

The Beards' inference is that these men, starting from the lowliest jobs as exemplars of the tradition, rose from the most humble origins to the very top. This may actually have been so, not only of these few men but of the large majority of business leaders whom they are taken to represent. But,

11. P. 129.
12. II, 172-73.
13. *Growth of the American People*, p. 129.
14. P. 168.
15. *Rise of American Civilization*, II, 173.

it may be asked, how many in modern times start much higher than these men did, even among the well-born, college-trained young men who, as *Fortune* put it, spend a few years in "the mummery of 'working in the plant' " before ascending to the highest executive levels? [16] Surely, of itself, an initial low-status job does not necessarily imply lowly origins.[17]

It is instructive to note that even the more perspicacious historians, when they err on the origins of business leaders, do so on the side of the tradition. Thus the Beards describe Rockefeller, the son of a "Barnumesque" itinerant entrepreneur, as "the son of a farmer"; [18] and Henry B. Parkes writes of

16. "The Thirty Thousand Managers," *Fortune,* February 1940, p. 61.

17. In fairness to the Beards it should be pointed out that they were aware of changes in the recruitment of business leaders by the turn of the century. They write: "By the end of the century the government of American railways and staple industries, with exceptions of course, had been lost by the men who had grown up in the round-houses and the mills through all the technical processes. On the whole, the high command in the empire of business was now in the hands of great banking corporations, and captains of industry were as a rule no longer evolved by natural selection; they were chosen by the dominant bankers who served as financial guardians."—*Rise of American Civilization,* II, 196-97. Two things must be said about this statement. (1) After making it, the Beards say nothing more about the leaders selected under the new conditions; they name no men and make comparisons with the older group discussed earlier in such detail. (2) Much more important, they fail to focus upon the lasting change that took place in the period of which they write. They say the new men no longer were selected from the plants. But whence, then, did they come? The Beards do not even raise this question. They do not, in fact, even establish that the older business leaders did rise from long years in "the roundhouses and the mills," and indeed it is more likely that, except for some in railroads, the older leaders started their own enterprises at early ages and rose *with* not *in* those enterprises. But whatever may be said of the older men, the majority of the *new* business leaders, along with hundreds of thousands of others who never rose out of the "ruck," did spend many years in the plant, or, in more instances, in the offices of their industries—for the problems of administration had already become complex enough to take an entire career to master. Bankers and other directors at the turn of the century did place "outsiders" at the head of the companies they financed—after all, many of these were newly organized or reorganized companies into which the introduction of outsiders early in their history probably was necessary and expedient. No one, to my knowledge, has studied the business backgrounds of these outsiders. I suggest that they were frequently experienced in the industries if not the companies into which they were placed. But the lasting change was not the importation of outsiders by the bankers; it was the tendency to select top bureaucrats from the hierarchy below. And the question of lasting social import is not whom did the bankers select from the outside but whom did the top bureaucrats select from the whole eager army of aspirants *within* the hierarchies to develop for, and finally install at, the top? Virtually all the candidates have been, in recent decades, so to speak, in business, often in *the* business. What then were the factors that differentiated the more from the less successful? If this was not the key question earlier in our history when business bureaucracies, in the main, were nonexistent, since the turn of the century it has been a question the answer to which has been of increasing social moment—a question, nevertheless, that most historians have not yet asked.

18. *Rise of American Civilization,* II, 181. The adjective "Barnumesque" is Allan Nevins'; see his *John D. Rockefeller, the Heroic Age of American Enterprise* (New York: Charles Scribner's Sons, 1940), I, 15-16. See also I, 39-40, for Nevins' discussion of the role of the business background in Rockefeller's life. See, too, John D. Rockefeller, *Random Reminiscences of Men and Events* (New York: Doubleday, Page & Co., 1909), p. 33.

F. Augustus Heinze, the copper magnate who was born in Brooklyn, New York, into a comfortable business family, as a "young German immigrant." [19]

Though most historians say little about it, there has been in the United States for well over a century a sizable and growing working class, propertyless, segregated, often remarkably apathetic to the alleged opportunities of American business and political life. Into this class most immigrants, starting with the Irish in the 1840's, have been channeled. Historians generally imply by the individuals they select as examples that this class and (for so little is said in this connection of rich men's business-bred, college-educated sons) this class alone has supplied our business leaders, that their school, to quote Carnegie himself, was "the sternest of all schools—poverty," that they were graduated from it early in life into apprenticeships as "mechanics" or "poor clerks," and that "against the boy who swept the office, or who begins as a shipping clerk at fourteen," the college graduate "has little chance, starting at twenty." [20]

Yet to read the lives of business leaders, even of those who presumably are the pillars of this tradition, is to look almost in vain for working class or foreign origins, and even poor and unschooled farm boys are not conspicuous among such leaders. Of Rockefeller and Heinze I have already spoken. The historians themselves have accounted for J. Pierpont Morgan and William H. Vanderbilt. Jay Cooke's father, Eleutheros, was "a lawyer who was sent to Congress." Harriman's father, Orlando, was an Episcopal clergyman, "the one exception of his generation in a family of several brothers" who followed the family tradition of successful "trading and commercial pursuits." Harriman himself married the daughter of a banker and railroad president who started him on his railroad career. Even a farm boy such as Elbert H. Gary, who "experienced early in life the arduous regimen of work on a pioneer farm, an experience which endowed him with excellent health and a robust physique," was raised in a settlement named after his forebears and in a house that "was a large one for the time—the largest in the settlement . . . . 'the big white house on the hill' it came to be called." [21]

Doubtless, examples can be found in the period emphasized by the historians of men whose life histories more fully substantiate the tradition. What of the men in the later period to which the historians tacitly allow their explanations of origins and ascent to apply and which is the subject of this essay?

19. Henry B. Parkes, *Recent America* (New York: Thomas Y. Crowell Co., 1945), p. 55. Heinze's father was a German immigrant.

20. Andrew Carnegie, *The Empire of Business* (New York: Doubleday, Page & Co., 1902), pp. 107-11.

21. The last quotation in this paragraph is from Ida M. Tarbell, *The Life of Elbert H. Gary* (New York: D. Appleton & Co., 1925), p. 20. The other quotations are from the *DAB*.

Had the "typical" American business leader of the first decade of the twentieth century been an immigrant? . . . Simply to ask the question is to answer it. Of the 187 businessmen studied here whose birthplaces are known, only 18, or less than 10 per cent, were born abroad.[22] Surely these men were less "typical" of the topmost business leaders of their time than the 55 per cent who were born in the eastern part of the United States, in New England and the middle Atlantic states. . . .[23] Of the eighteen business leaders who were foreign-born, moreover, scarcely two or three fit the historians' concept of the *poor* immigrant who made good, and even these men had been brought to the United States at such an early age that they may be said to have been bred if not born here. . . .

If not typically poor immigrants, were these business and political leaders the sons of foreigners? More of them were, surely, but . . . the typical leader in each field was born into an American family.

Moreover, these families themselves had, in most instances, been in America for many generations. Almost three fourths of the business and political leaders were at least of the fourth generation of their paternal lines to reside in America; many were of the seventh and even the eighth generations. Colonial families were represented by 73 per cent of the business leaders and 79 per cent of those in politics.[24] Fifty-six per cent of the former and 47 per cent of the latter were of families that had settled in America in the seventeenth century.

Even were they not of colonial ancestry, most of these leaders could point to British, and many to English, forebears.

They could claim Protestant, and often Episcopal or Presbyterian, backgrounds.

If not of recent foreign origin, was the typical American business leader of the early twentieth century a migrant from a farm? . . . The political leaders far more frequently than those in business came from rural areas, . . . almost 60 per cent of the latter were recruited from the larger towns and cities. Indeed, more than 20 per cent of them were born in cities that around the middle of the nineteenth century had populations of 100,000 or

22. The average age of the 190 business leaders in 1905 was 54 years; of the political leaders, 57 years.

23. In his study of 1,464 businessmen born between 1570 and 1879, C. Wright Mills found that 18.6 per cent had been foreign-born. He divided his men, by birth dates, into seven generations starting in the following years (in parentheses after each date is the proportion of foreign-born businessmen in the generation starting at that date): 1570 (78.4%), 1700 (28.3%) 1730 (28.1%), 1760 (22.3%), 1790 (10.2%), 1820 (17.5%), 1850 (10.9%). Thus, in each of these generations, except that born between 1790 and 1819, there was a greater percentage of foreign-born businessmen than in Mills' last generation, which is nearest to the period of the present study and in the group used in this study. [Mills, "The American Business Elite," *The Tasks of Economic History* (Supplemental Issue of *The Journal of Economic History*, V, 1945), 22].

24. Defining "colonial" families as those settled in America before 1776.

TABLE I—American Business and Political Leaders by Paternal Family's Origin *

Family Origin	Business Leaders (Per Cent of)	Political Leaders (Per Cent of)
British Empire	82	83
Germany	12	8
Other countries	6	9
Total cases (= 100 per cent)	162	162

* Or country of leader's own origin if he was the first in the family to settle in America. In either case, last country before settlement in America.

more. Upon these men rural influences even in a predominantly rural society must have been at a minimum.

Yet more significant in answering the question are the occupations of the fathers of these business leaders. Here we find that even of those born in rural areas fewer than one third (and only 12 per cent of the whole group) had fathers who were mainly farmers. Fifty-six per cent of all the business leaders, on the other hand, had fathers who had been in business— often big business—before them; eight of ten, indeed, came from business or professional families . . .

The next table shows the social status of the families of these business and political leaders. . . . A few . . . were classified as lower class. Men were classified as of the upper class when it was clear that their fathers, like those of August Belmont, Cornelius K. G. Billings, or Charles Deering, were themselves big businessmen, or where their families, like those of Robert Todd Lincoln or Winslow Shelby Pierce, were politically eminent. Generally speaking, those in between—including some businessmen with no special claims to wealth or power or professionals like the average clergyman, doctor, or lawyer—were ranked as of middle-class origins. This does not mean that their fathers were not of help to them. James B. Duke, for example, rose to wealth and power with a company founded by his father; George W. Perkins moved to a partnership in the House of Morgan—probably the acting head of the house at one stage—from a vice-presidency in the New York Life Insurance Company in which his father, a minor executive there, had given him his business start . . .

TABLE II—American Business and Political Leaders by Family Status

Status	Business Leaders (Per Cent of)	Political Leaders (Per Cent of)
Upper	50	36
Middle	45	50
Lower	5	14
Total cases (= 100 per cent)	179	180

Poor boys, as Carnegie rightly said, usually go to work early in life. Clearly, few of these business and political leaders were poor boys. And, as the following table shows, few of them went to work at an early age.

TABLE III—American Business and Political Leaders by Age on Going to Work *

Age	Business Leaders (Per Cent of)	Political Leaders (Per Cent of)
15 or under	20	13
16-18	35	10
19 and over	45	77
Total cases (= 100 per cent)	179	182

* This is age on taking first regular business, professional, or other job (except work on father's or other relative's farm) after leaving school or, in a very few instances, after leaving the Union or Confederate armies.

THE SELECTION OF BUREAU HEADS

Arthur W. Macmahon and John D. Millett

The selection of bureau chiefs by promotion—whether pursuant to requirements or as a matter of practice—is already sufficiently prevalent to sharpen a much-discussed and fundamental problem of personnel. This turns on the relation of technique to administration. Especially does it center on the question of the suitability of scientific or other technical training and experience as preparation for broad responsibilities of direction and supervision. The scope of the bureaus emphasizes the issue. Many are vast in terms of any comparison. But beyond the needs of internal control are the managerial tasks involved in the ramifications of the external relations of bureaus as instruments of public policy: to the impinging activities of other agencies; to the management of the national administration as a whole; to Congress; to the particular complexes of competing groups with which the bureau is immediately concerned; and through the spreading circles of obscure and indirect effects, to the compounded interests which are the public. Bureau leadership calls for an awareness of all these.

A pervasive problem is thus posed for consideration in reviewing the selection and tenure of bureau heads. It is emphatically not a question of the desirability of internal recruitment by promotion. Rather it is a question of the implications of the latter. . . .

Experience, when focused in terms of the mode of choice of the bureau chiefs in office at the close of 1938, is doubly revealing. In the first place, as a matter of formal requirements, the selection of the heads of slightly less than half of the sixty-two units is already subject to some variety

Reprinted in part from Arthur W. Macmahon and John D. Millett, *Federal Administrators*, A Biographical Approach to the Problem of Departmental Management (New York: Columbia University Press, 1939), by permission of the publisher. (Copyright 1939 by Columbia University Press, New York.)

of merit system, twenty-seven of the posts being in the competitive classified service and three being covered by special closed schemes of commissioned personnel. In the second place, the practice of selection by promotion has run beyond such requirements. The heads of fourteen other
bureaus were taken from within the national administration, being drawn
almost without exception from the competitive classified service. In addition, four others were brought from related state or local work by what
amounted to a sort of promotion. Of the sixty-two bureau chiefs, therefore,
forty-eight (approximately four-fifths) might be considered instances of
career tenure. Eight of the remaining fourteen bureau heads, though
recruited from outside, possessed varying degrees of related administrative
experience gained under semipublic or public auspices. Political considerations appear to have dominated in the choice of only six of the chiefs in
office at the close of 1938.

The condition summarized in the foregoing figures is not temporary.
Being of slow growth in response to long-present need, it has been the
prevailing practice for some years. This fact is shown in a comparison
of bureau leadership in 1926 and in 1938. The dates that are involved are
not only convenient [1] but are also logical in their relation to overturns of
party control in the national government. In each case approximately five
years had elapsed since a change in the political complexion of the White
House. It is hardly necessary to observe that any comparison doubles the
hazards of judgment which are involved in a realistic classification of the
modes of selection of individuals.

The twelve years after 1926, although attended by changes in the
leadership of all but nine bureaus, brought no striking alteration in the
relative prevalence of the main types of selection. The scope of the comparison, of course, is narrowed by numerous intervening modifications of
administrative structure. Of the sixty-two bureaus treated in the analysis
of leadership in 1938, only forty-seven were in existence in 1926. It is
appropriate to confine the present discussion to these units. The comparison
may be stated in tabular form, as in Table I. . . .

Despite the extent to which bureau chiefs are selected by promotion,
whether in connection with formal merit systems or otherwise, the rate
of turnover has been considerable. Nor has this varied greatly within the
last thirty years. Comparisons from period to period are embarrassed, to
be sure, by the extent to which bureaus merge, disappear altogether, or
are created. A crude indication of the survival of bureau chiefs from decade
to decade will suffice to indicate the relative rapidity of renewal at this
level of personnel.

1. Comparable material for 1926 is available in "The Selection and Tenure of
Bureau Chiefs in the National Administration of the United States," *American Political
Science Review*, Vol. XX (1926), pp. 548-82, 770-811.

TABLE I—Relative Prevalence of the Several Modes of Selection of Bureau Chiefs in Forty-Seven Comparable Bureaus

Mode of Selection		1926		1938
Subject to formal merit systems				
In the competitive classified service		19		19
Chosen by promotion	14		14	
Chosen by examination	1		3	
Chosen under Rule II, Sec. 10	4		2	
Subject to self-contained schemes of commissioned personnel		3		3
Total		22		22
Unrestricted				
Chosen by virtual promotion within the national administration		16 [a]		12
Taken from state or local service				2
Taken from long service with congressional committee		1		
Taken from the outside but with marked degrees of preparation		1		5 [b]
Taken from the outside on a patently political basis		7		6
Total		25		25

[a] Included here are two instances in which the prior national service was of slight extent and the spirit of career tenure absent.
[b] Three of these five individuals had at some time done administrative work for the national government; the other two had been very active in semipublic organizations.

It has been noted that forty-seven of the sixty-two units dealt with in 1938 existed as bureaus in 1926, a little more than a decade before. In only nine cases was the incumbent in 1938 the individual who had been in charge of the bureau in the earlier year. The heads of these units, having served as chiefs for an average of sixteen years, had attained an average age of fifty-eight years in 1938. . . .

It is especially in point to note the rate of turnover of bureau chiefs whose posts have been covered by formal merit systems. Eight of the thirty bureaus in that category had been established after 1926; these are disregarded in the present discussion. In the twenty-two that went back at least a dozen years, seven of the incumbents in 1926 were still in office at the end of 1938; five were appointed between 1926 and the beginning of the new Administration in 1933; and ten attained bureau leadership thereafter. This situation may be compared with that in the other bureaus. Expressing the matter in percentages, it is observed that sixty-eight percent of the chiefs protected by formal merit systems were appointed in the twelve-year period, 1926 to 1938; and forty-five percent within slightly less than six years after President Roosevelt's inauguration in 1933. In the case of the chiefs of all other bureaus which go back to 1926, ninety-two percent had been chosen since 1926, and eighty percent since early in 1933. These differences are important. Nevertheless, it is apparent that formal merit systems in actual operation bring a high rate of turnover at the level of bureau chief, with many opportunities for renewal. . . .

The rate of turnover found in the posts subject to formal merit systems, far from being an evil, becomes an advantage in the proper setting. It is to be regretted if it reflects a tendency to advance men to bureau leadership late in their careers, when they have only a few years to serve. The question of age may appropriately be examined, with comparisons to show the reaction of various methods of selection and to indicate trends during the last decade.

The average age at appointment as bureau head for all chiefs in office at the close of 1938 was 48 years. This was almost exactly the average age at appointment for the chiefs who were serving in 1926. The average current age in 1938 was 53.6 years; in 1926, 54 years. These negligible differences are hardly clues to a tendency. Certainly no increase of average age at appointment resulted from the operation of formal merit systems or from the practice of filling unrestricted posts by promotion. On the contrary, an analysis of age differentials refutes the notion that political recruitment freshens administration by injecting youth into positions of bureau leadership. . . .

The problem of superannuation which has been given point by the preceding remarks . . . may be stated more generally. In connection with an ingredient so baffling to analysis as administrative talent and in the presence of factors as variant as individual ability and stamina, it is impossible to dogmatize. Crude age limits must be set and these have been drawn (though not without a saving degree of upward flexibility) in the statutory provisions for superannuation and retirement. The point at which the increasing returns of tenure in executive posts may change to diminishing returns is an endlessly special problem. As things have stood in the highest ranges of the public service in the United States, general doubts could safely be resolved in favor of the value of continuity. Service at the level of bureau chief might profitably begin earlier; and in many instances it might advantageously be terminated sooner. The departments should experiment further in the discovery of roles which aging bureau chiefs not ready for full retirement could fill usefully and with honor. . . .

The comments that have just been made on the problem of succession in bureau leadership had their point of departure in the question of age in relation to mode of selection. The salient lesson in this regard should be recalled in closing, and restated in its lowest terms. Formal merit systems do not result in older chiefs, either at the time of appointment or even currently. Nor is such the outcome of virtual promotion to positions not in the competitive classified service. From the standpoint of age, the search for bureau leadership (though admitting the general problems of superannuation) can safely turn inward. To do so, however, raises the problem already anticipated in introductory remarks: the ability of existing systems of career recruitment to provide the raw materials capable of advancement to high administrative posts. The difficulties thus presented have been discussed largely in educational terms. It is timely, therefore, to pass to a consideration, illustratively, of the educational backgrounds of the bureau chiefs who were serving in 1938. . . .

Of the sixty-two bureau chiefs, only eleven did not undergo some form of so-called higher education prior to entrance into government service. In nine of the eleven cases, bureau leadership was attained by promotion (including here an instance of recruitment from related state work). The bureau heads in question had averaged seventeen years in public administration prior to appointment as chief. . . .

Formal education beyond high school was participated in by five-sixths of the bureau chiefs. Sometimes it was collegiate work in arts only; sometimes merely an undergraduate professional course; but oftener a combination of college and postgraduate or college and professional elements. In eighteen cases the training was undergraduate in the sense that it was entered upon and completed immediately after high school. This number comprised ten individuals who took general college work; six whose undergraduate study was essentially technical (four preparing thus in engineering, one in the law, and one in agricultural science); and two future bureau chiefs who attended service schools, one at the Coast Guard Academy and one at the Naval Academy. Passing now to the thirty-three individuals who pursued postgraduate work of some kind, mention may first be made of ten instances of law school training (in one of which graduate work of a more general nature was also done at other institutions, including study in Europe). Two of the future bureau heads were trained in medicine. In the case of one, the work was directly, indeed indispensably, preparatory to his official career, and related graduate study in public health was also taken; in the other case, the individual turned very early to journalism. One man went directly from college to a school of forestry; another, to a veterinary college. For each this special training was the avenue to official advancement. In addition to those mentioned, nineteen did graduate work of a somewhat less professional nature. In seven instances the training was technical in that the emphasis was upon research in the physical sciences. In nine cases the center of gravity lay in the social studies, especially economics. Three individuals did fragmentary graduate work of a less special character.

In view of the importance which many contemporary discussions of personnel have given to the question of the availability of a common core of general academic training in the United States, a word should be added, in passing, in regard to the institutions attended by the fifty-one bureau chiefs whose formal study was carried beyond high school. The most striking feature was the scattering of this attendance. The condition is shown simply in the fact that the eighteen individuals who pursued only undergraduate work took it in as many as seventeen institutions, few of them famous and some of them obscure; that the nineteen individuals who essayed graduate study did it in sixteen universities, four of them in Europe; and that even in the study of law, the ten persons so trained attended as many as seven law schools. Such is the dispersal—natural, no doubt, in a country of continental scale—which schemes for the improvement of recruitment to the national public service must continue to take into account. . . .

The larger implications of the aspect of initial education have already been suggested. The question of the human material needed in the making of administrators and of its availability for advancement raises problems in the reconstruction of the ideals and methods of recruitment to the public service which are beyond the scope of this analysis. The canvass of bureau chiefs has negative importance, at least, in indicating the extent to which promotion prevails, on the one hand, and, on the other, in showing the relatively large number of individuals, if not of types, who can be winnowed in the process. The vitality of the practice of promotion, even where there have been no formal requirements to encourage it, has in itself been a partial rebuttal of the most serious charges that have been leveled against the ability of the merit system to bring up administrators. But thoughtful supervisory officials in certain of the departments are not satisfied. Experience has taught them to be cautious in generalizing about subject matter so personal and individual. Nevertheless, from the standpoint of filling posts such as those of bureau chiefs, they are fully conscious of the difficulties that inhere in the extent to which the merit system has been geared to the recruitment of vocational expertness.

To speak of a solution would be to imply a simplicity that does not exist in a problem which in part concerns tendencies in governmental personnel as a whole and in part hinges upon the existence of departmental managements capable of flexible and far-reaching judgments in the use of the human resources at hand. The system would gain by the infusion of elements more interested in the objectives of scientific technique than in its application. Without formalizing the requirement, these new ingredients could be considered alternatively in arranging promotions that point toward administrative leadership. Meanwhile, the logic of development will engender correctives within the old methods of personnel. Technicians who show an aptitude for relationships can be encouraged in their administrative interests. They can be ripened by staff assignments at bureau or at departmental headquarters. In supplementing the broadening facilities available to them within the governmental service itself, they should be enabled, when opportunity affords (in the form of a grant or otherwise), to withdraw temporarily for purposes of travel, observation, and reading. Below all this, at the source, changes may be expected in the social reorientation of instruction in the better vocational schools.

In connection with the problem under discussion, it is at least desirable that the sole reward of scientists should not be conversion into administrators. Able men, whose genius or talent and whose real interests lie in research, should not have to look for recognition, in grade and salary, to appointment in posts that are essentially administrative. As things have happened, this has often been the situation. There have been scientists of outstanding achievement, of course, who have been content to remain with a limited group of assistants at work on special problems. Some have renounced a new administrative position after a period of trial has given them an opportunity to test their aptitudes and ambitions. Such have been exceptions. In general it would have been surprising if the association of the outward signs of success with posts of administrative command had not frequently elicited a human response. The injury has sometimes been a double one; for even where (as has often been the case) the scientist has proved a competent administrator, the diversion of his special abilities may have meant an irreparable loss. The remedy is not easy to find, for in any scheme of hierarchy prestige tends to concentrate in the managerial scale. The corrective, obviously, lies partly in the arrangement of rewards which would permit outstanding scientists to receive tangible as well as intangible recognition in their own fields. The approach to this solution is partly a matter of personnel classification. In addition, an ingenious departmental management could doubtless devise other methods of recognition less material in character.

The full admission of the underlying difficulty is not inconsistent with the further encouragement of the characteristics of stability and of internal recruitment already so marked in the selection of bureau chiefs. Far from being obstacles, these offer the indispensable basis of improvement.

Bureau chiefs are critical links in the managerial chain. Their essential permanence is a prerequisite of command through the hierarchy as a whole.[2]

2. With all respect, it is submitted that Lewis Meriam is profoundly wrong when he suggests the need for a distinction among operating bureaus in this matter. In a recent book, *Public Personnel Problems* (Washington: Brookings Institution, 1938), p. 309, Meriam writes: "Certain bureaus are political hot spots and for them a political head performing the political duties and carrying the political responsibilities would be essential. Associated with them and with respects to all political matters entirely subordinate to them would be the top civil service man with authority over the nonpolitical matters." Meriam does not name the "hot spots." He has indicated elsewhere that bureaus which are "hot" at one period may be "cool" at another time. How could a distinctive structure be provided if the basis of distinction among bureaus were changeable? But the objections to dual bureau leadership are more fundamental. First, political appointment is not an assurance of political compatibility between the department head and his junior associates. Second, dual leadership at the intermediate level would introduce an inherent confusion of responsibility in the departmental organization. If a department is to exist truly, the distinction between political and the nonpolitical elements is possible at one point only: the apex. Meriam, it seems, is talking about bureaus which would be departments in disguise. If so, it would be better to organize frankly on that basis.

Career tenure in their posts is not inconsistent with the ideal of political responsibility as the galvanizer of freshening influences. Political officers can accomplish proper ends more readily through trained administrators than through the clumsy mediation of newcomers. This has been the consensus of the judgment of thoughtful departmental heads in the past. Nor does the career principle among bureau chiefs endanger the cohesion of departments. Here, again, experience offers a paradox. It has been the transient chiefs, selected under political or semipolitical auspices, who have contributed most to the sort of bureau autonomy which is unwholesome, for they have reflected the diverse factionalism that attends the use of patronage. The conclusion is unmistakable. It is time to bring all bureau chiefs within the merit system. The practical trends of recruitment and tenure have anticipated this arrangement and confirmed its desirability.

EXECUTIVE APPOINTMENT IN PRIVATE AND PUBLIC BUREAUCRACIES

Marshall E. Dimock and Howard K. Hyde

The field of leadership as a whole is too broad a subject to be discussed here in detail. We may, however, mention briefly some of its elements as they bear on the direction of the large corporation.

The importance of leadership is universally acknowledged. With almost equal unanimity corporation officials testify to the difficulties which attend the training and promotion of leaders to fill positions where their influence is needed and where it will be effective. Although the degree to which the executives of large corporations inspire their subordinates is too subjective for extended consideration we may nevertheless mention some of the more important aspects of the matter. We have evidence, for example, that the leaders, and particularly the chief executives, set the tone of the whole enterprise. It is, therefore, important that this tone, with its direct effect on morale, be not characterized by the harmful elements of bureaucracy which we have indicated.

For our present purposes the discussion of the relation of executive leadership to bureaucracy may be confined to five general requirements. These are that the executive not be too old upon appointment; that he possess a

Reprinted in part from *Bureaucracy and Trusteeship in Large Corporations,* pp. 45-54, TNEC Monograph No. 11 (Washington: Government Printing Office, 1940).

broad outlook; that he reach office primarily on the basis of merit; that he remain in office long enough to be effective but not so long as to become senile; and that positions of leadership be attractive to potential leaders. It is recognized that these are capable of broad interpretation; we may, however, note tendencies in each of them.

A leading figure in the field of industrial management maintains: "It is hardly to be gainsaid that with the steadily increasing age at which executives reach the top rank of president or chairman of the board, they find themselves physically, as well as intellectually, less able than under former conditions of corporative simplicity to cope with the question of future progress and growth." [1] It cannot be flatly said, of course, that advanced chronological age means a corresponding loss in mental resiliency. Daniel Willard, president of the Baltimore & Ohio Railroad, and the late Justice Holmes serve amply as refuting examples. There can be no doubt, however, that there is a general tendency in this direction—that, in general, resiliency is lost with age. Because of this, summary figures on age have meaning in relation to corporate leadership.

Table I presents some biographical data on the heads of 35 of the Nation's largest companies. The size of the sample is small, but it should at least indicate some of the tendencies.

TABLE I—Executive Heads of 35 Giant Corporations, 1939 [1]

Corporate Group	Age on Appointment to Present Position	Age in 1939	Years with Company	Years in Particular Field of Business [2]	Source, in Per Cent [3]	
					Promotion from Within Company	Brought from Outside Company
Industrials	[4] 49.3 (49.6)	61.3 (60.6)	36.3 (30.7)	37.3 (34.2)	90	10
Utilities	46.3 (45.0)	55.0 (57.0)	20.0 (19.4)	30.5 (31.1)	70	30
Railroads	55.0 (55.0)	62.0 (64.2)	38.0 (34.9)	40.0 (42.1)	75	[5] 25
All	50.5 (49.9)	60.7 (60.6)	36.0 (29.3)	37.3 (35.4)	80	20

1. The group includes 19 of the 20 largest industrials (data was unavailable on 1), the 8 largest utilities, and the 8 largest railroads. . . . Data on 2 industrials and 1 utility are incomplete; averages in the affected categories are derived from the remaining number.
2. Figures are very rough because the point of entry into a particular field is difficult to define.
3. Percentages are approximate.
4. Median values used are the arithmetical averages of the central 2 or 3 items and are shown without parentheses: arithmetical means are shown in parentheses. Where 1 man was not clearly the executive head of a company the average of the combination of men which appeared to hold that position is used. The titles of the executive heads vary. Usually it is the chairman or the president or those two combined. In 1 case, however, it was the executive vice president, though he has been subsequently made president. The men are those that held the top positions when Moody's Annuals for 1939 went to press. Changes since then are not incorporated in this table.
5. The 2 heads of railroads included here were brought from the presidencies of other, smaller railroads.

For this group as a whole, the chief executives were appointed at an average age of about 50 years. By 1939 they were aproximately 61 years old, having served an average of about 11 years. As might be expected there is much variation among the companies. For example, in the cases of three of the industrials and two of the utilities, the chief executives were chosen at

1. Harry A. Hopf, in the *Georgetown Law Journal,* XXIV (1938), p. 1067.

the age of 40 or less. At the other extreme, one railroad and one industrial had heads who were more than 64 years old when appointed. Obviously the term of office for these older men must be relatively short.[2] In general, it may be said that with an average age of 50 for the group as a whole, a number of these executives were advanced to top positions when they were somewhat beyond their prime.

Age upon appointment is probably more important than that at a given date because the executive who has served for some time has the advantage of experience in the job to balance against the handicaps of his advancing years. Current age, however, is interesting. For example, the executives as a group were approximately 61 years old in 1939. Again there were rather wide variations. Only 1 was younger than 45 and 3 younger than 50; at the other extreme 4 were 70 or more. Half were 60.7 years old (the median) or more; 10 were 65 or over. Since the retirement age in many companies is 65 this indicates that a fairly large proportion had passed the point which, according to many corporation officials, should mark the cessation of active dominant executive direction, unless rather exceptional circumstances intervene.

The age tendencies are not at all alike among the 3 corporate groups which were examined. The picture for the industrials, for example, is quite similar to that of the 35 corporations considered as a whole. The averages and the dispersions are about the same for both. The utilities and the railroads, however, present a different picture. Thus, the largest utilities have chief executives who were appointed when they were 4 or 5 years younger than was usual for the 35 corporations, and their present age is likewise about 4 years below that of the group average.

The railroads, on the other hand, are run by substantially older men. The usual appointment age here is some 5 years higher than for all of the 35 corporations; the age in 1939 was 1.3 to 3.6 years above the average for the larger group, depending upon whether the median or the arithmetic mean is considered. The belief that bureaucracy in railroad management is partly due to the relatively advanced years of railroad executives seems to be substantiated by these data. The unprogressiveness of railroad management in service, pricing, and operational policies may well be due to some extent to the decreased mental and physical vigor of those at the top, although doubtless there is more than this in the picture as a whole.

A question which should be raised, however, is how the relative youth of the top executives of the utilities affects bureaucracy in those companies compared to its prevalence in the railroads. Although we are not prepared to give a complete answer, it does appear that the unprogressiveness and unaggressiveness of the utilities are more in their pricing and other market-

2. One of these was retired late in 1939 after having served for 4 years. The other was appointed more recently and is still in office.

ing policies and practices than in their operational and administrative aspects; while among the railroads the ills of bureaucracy extend to these latter activities as well as the former. . . .

Insofar as direct comparisons are possible, the following may be said in summary: the appointment age of the top officials of the Nation's largest corporations is about the same or slightly above that of the top layers of Government officials. The average current age, however, is considerably higher than that of Government officials. To the extent that the undesirable aspects of bureaucracy are due to the advanced years of some of the top executives, it is apparent that this cause exists in the large corporation to at least the same degree if not more than it does in Government.

The second aspect of executive leadership is broadness of outlook. In even a moderately large corporation the administrative problems are many and diverse. The executive must be capable of harmonizing a multitude of conflicting forces. In the giant corporation, therefore, the ability to see things broadly and in relation is correspondingly more essential. Since most of the heads of the largest companies are promoted from within, the question should be raised as to whether broad-gage executives can readily be developed in such enterprises.

A number of executives believe that the large corporation develops outstanding executives with considerable difficulty. The head of one company went so far as to say that "large corporations do not produce great executives. The men tend to become too specialized. The man in a smaller organization gets to know the business as a whole at an earlier age." Another phrases the problem in this way: "Specialization results in a dearth of top executives. You can't find men to integrate because they themselves aren't integrated. I know more good all-around business men in small concerns than I do in big corporations." Or again, "As activities become more specialized and routinized it becomes more difficult to develop ability in the ranks. . . . It may not be safe for us to rely upon securing a sufficient number from the ranks who will qualify for executive leadership." [3]

The benefits of specialization, of course, constitute one of the principal advantages of the large corporation and can ill be sacrificed. Although some top executives demonstrate that specialization is not an insuperable barrier in the development of leaders, nevertheless it remains an impediment in the process of such development and is, therefore, a contributing cause of bureaucracy in big business.

In the Federal Government the bureau chiefs are probably specialized to about the same degree as the corporation executives. Among the higher

3. James O. McKinsey, Organization Problems Under Present Conditions (New York: American Management Association, 1936), General Management Series No. 127, p. 13. The late Mr. McKinsey was chairman of the boards of Marshall Field and Co. and of the American Management Association.

political heads, however, there is a characteristically broader experience and outlook. It is the business of the politician to compose differences and to recognize the implications of particular policies over a broad realm. To the extent, then, that specialization is a cause of bureaucracy, the large corporation suffers as much as and perhaps more than Government.

The third general requirement for good leadership is that the executive shall have reached his position on the basis of merit. The degree to which merit now plays a part in appointments is difficult to determine. With the diffusion of ownership, which is characteristic of the large corporation, there is a corresponding decline in the practice of placing the chief owner or his son or some other relative in the higher executive positions. Although the propensity to "play ball" with the existing control is doubtless a factor in the selection of executives, this relative disappearance of inheritance as a selector opens the way for an emphasis on merit per se and it is possible that this will be the future trend. Inheritance is too unreliable a determinant for us to weep over its eclipse.

Although merit has doubtless played an increasingly important part in the selection of the top executives of large corporations, one nevertheless hears the complaint, from other than those who may be expected to be prejudiced, that seniority has been too much emphasized. This is particularly true, for example, among the railroads and doubtless contributes to the relatively high age at which men in this field are appointed to top positions. The idea of promotion by seniority permeates the railroads all the way down the hierarchy, where men are apt to think more in terms of the time in their records than in how effectively that time has been spent.

But promotion by seniority is not confined to the railroads. Some executives feel that the practice is generally characteristic of the large corporation. Moreover, even if it were no more common there than in the small enterprise, the process of reaching the top would take longer because of the greater number of steps in the hierarchy. In any case, it is at least certain that the big companies as a rule do not have an adequate system of executive recruitment. In regard to this lack, Edward R. Stettinius, Jr., for example, believes that a method of inventories should be developed whereby just as exact a record could be kept of executive material as now exists for other materials.[4] Some of the largest companies are now engaged in developing the first stages of rating systems and refined records to assist in uncovering executive talent and in advancing it rapidly enough to be really effective. But such methods are relatively difficult to operate and do not enjoy wide acceptance in big business. On the other hand seniority is so easy a method to apply that in the lack of a better one it is natural that it should be used. Seniority is one of the few things about an executive that can be accurately

4. Edward R. Stettinius, Jr., "The Selection of Executives," *Management Review*, XXV (November, 1936), pp. 332-333.

and objectively determined. Those who are passed over cannot complain that on the basis of selection used they should have been advanced instead. Nevertheless, length of service does not guarantee the requisite qualities of a leader. It is essential, therefore, that other methods of rewarding such devotion be discovered and used so that leadership will not be sacrificed on the altar of convenience and in a way that is of doubtful benefit to employee morale.

Seniority, of course, is also used in public administration as a basis of promotion. We do not, however, have available material to indicate the extent to which this method is employed. Nevertheless, since the average ages of the top officers at the time of appointment, both in government and in private enterprise, are not widely divergent, there is at least an indirect indication that promotion by seniority is no more prevalent in one instance than in the other. . . .

The fourth qualification for leadership is that the executive remain in office long enough to be effective. Just what this term may be is difficult to say. Some executives claim that "a creative man delivers all he has in 3 to 5 years on one job." While this may be true at some of the lower levels of the hierarchy we doubt that it accurately describes the situation at the top. A well-conceived program of action would require 3 to 5 years to be properly developed and put into operation. An even longer period would be required for it to become an integrated part of the enterprise as a whole. Continuity of office is essential to smooth continuity of policy. Our general conclusion, therefore, is that although the exact length of appointment cannot accurately be determined, 10 years is not too long for a capable man to direct an enterprise while even 3 years is too long for a poor one. The problem is to select well and then to allow a sufficient length of time for the executive leader fully to put his ideas into effect.

In general, the top executives of the largest corporations have terms of office that are satisfactorily long. Table I indicates that the present incumbents, on the average, have held office for 10 or 11 years. Since this measure is taken in the midst of their terms we may suppose that the total, on the average, will be somewhat longer. If the sample were entirely representative both as to time, in relation to say, the business cycle, and as to coverage of variation among corporations, the average term would be approximately twice that of the time already served. In spite of such imperfections as the sample undoubtedly has, we may safely suppose, therefore, that the average term is at least 5 years longer than the elapsed part of it, which would indicate a minimum average for top executives of about 15 years. The average term for the railroad executives would be something less than this because of their more advanced age. This assumption is supported by the smaller elapsed time which current railroad executives have served. These men, as shown in Table I, have been in office from 7 to 9 years while the average for utility and industrial executives is from 9 to 12 years. Thus, for the group as a whole there appears to be a healthy continuity of office,[5] although individual variations are wide, of course, and some executives remain after senility overtakes them. In general, however, the picture is favorable.

Public administration presents a somewhat different state of affairs, though again there are wide variations. The average tenure of bureau chiefs seems to be fairly constant. As we have noted, the average appointment and current ages were about the same for both 1926 and 1938. Because of this stability we are justified in doubling the average elapsed period of service in order to obtain a rough estimate of the average total term. Since the average elapsed period of service in 1938 was 5.6 years the total terms would run about 11 years. While this is not as long as the average terms of the top corporation executives, it may be considered satisfactory.

Above the bureau level, however, the holders of public office are much more volatile as to tenure. Thus, the average term for Secretaries, Under Secretaries, and Assistant Secretaries is only 3 to 5 years. The average period of service for our last eight Presidents and for all our Presidents combined has been about 5 years. Whatever the political merits of rapid turn-over, they are largely demerits when viewed from an administrative standpoint.

Walter Sharp saw in the transitoriness of the French Cabinet one of the prime causes of bureaucratic inefficiency in that nation's government.[6] We are more fortunate in the United States, for it is an unusual French Cabinet that lasts more than a year. However, we do not wholly escape the problem. Thus, in his blast against governmental bureaucracy in the United States, James Beck stated that "the heads of departments and their Assistant Secretaries hold office for comparatively short periods of time and they cannot during such short periods become familiar with all the duties of their departments—certainly not of the more technical phases of such duties. The consequence is that the heads of departments make nearly, if not all, of the decisions in name only, while the case is actually developed . . . [by] a subordinate in the department." [7] President Taft believed that the short terms of the top departmental officials had the result that "for a year and a half, at least, sometimes for a longer period, it throws the administration of the department into the complete control of minor subordinates." [8] These may be overstatements for purposes of emphasis but they indicate an actual problem. Of course, a somewhat similar difficulty exists when a new corporation

5. While some persons believe that a relatively long term of office is an undesirable attribute of bureaucracy we do not subscribe to that notion. A rapid turn-over may bring more bureaucratic chaos than it does desirable change.

6. Walter R. Sharp, *French Civil Service: Bureaucracy in Transition* (New York: Macmillan, 1931), p. 33.

7. James M. Beck, *Our Wonderland of Bureaucracy* (New York: Macmillan, 1932), p. 173.

8. Quoted in *ibid.*, p. 121.

president takes office, but his relatively longer term means that such periods of poor coordination need less frequently occur.

Thus, on the basis of turn-over of leadership, big business compares favorably with the Government. Both business executives and bureau chiefs have quite satisfactory terms of office. Above the bureau level, however, turn-over is generally more rapid—too rapid, in fact, for effective administration.

Finally we should mention briefly the ability of the two groups to attract executive talent. Three elements may be mentioned: Salary, security, and prestige. Annual salaries of over a hundred thousand dollars for the top men are common among the largest corporations, though of course there are variations. Since most top executives have risen within their companies, however, and there is little cross-over among companies, the variations do not result in a flow of executive talent to those paying the highest salaries. Remuneration schedules appear to be at least sufficient to make the top positions attractive from that angle to subordinate executives within particular concerns—which is about all that matters in practice, except perhaps in the case of the railroads where there is some transfer among them.

Judging from the length of service of the top executives of the largest corporations, security of tenure at that level at least would also seem to be adequate. Likewise the position of head of one of the large corporations carries with it a good deal of prestige in the corporate family and is therefore an inviting goal.

In comparison with business, government is generally less attractive from the standpoints of salary and security for men at the top levels. In all of government there is no salary of a hundred thousand dollars. The term of office of those above the bureau level is also considerably shorter than that which obtains in the largest corporations. In regard to the element of prestige, however, the situation is different, for identification with the public service has always appealed to men and in recent years this attraction has considerably increased due in large part to the expanding role of government in modern life.

In summary, therefore, it may be said that business leadership often contributes to bureaucracy because of defects in regard to age, narrowness of outlook, and the too frequent resort to seniority in making promotions. The rate of turn-over among the top business executives of the largest corporations is small—in fact, so small that complaints are sometimes made of stoppage at the top. In comparison with business, Government executives are no older, they probably have a broader outlook, and seniority has been less important in appointments above the bureau level, while tenure, at this point, on the other hand, has been relatively short. The prestige attached to the top governmental positions has been as great as that of the top business positions for the past decade and will probably continue to be high, though the attractiveness of salary and tenure are somewhat below the level of the major positions in big business. In short, the defects of leadership contributing to bureaucracy bulk about as large in business as they do in Government.

INDUCEMENTS AND INCENTIVES IN BUREAUCRACY

Herbert A. Simon

Individuals are willing to accept organization membership when their activity in the organization contributes, directly or indirectly, to their own personal goals. The contribution is direct if the goals set for the organization have direct personal value for the individual—church membership is a typical example of this. The contribution is indirect if the organization offers personal rewards—monetary or other—to the individual in return for his willingness to contribute his activity to the organization. Employment in a business concern is a typical example of this. Sometimes these personal rewards are directly related to the size and growth of the organization—as in the case of the stockholders of a business; sometimes, not very directly— as in the case of most wage earners. The characteristics of these three bases for participation are sufficiently distinct to make it worth while to consider them separately: personal rewards deriving directly from the accomplishment of the organization objective; personal inducements offered by the organization and closely related to its size and growth; and personal rewards derived from inducements offered by the organization but unrelated to the organization size and growth. Organizations are ordinarily made up of three groups of individuals, in each of which one of these types of motivation prevails; and it is the presence of these three groups that gives administration its specific character.

The phrase "personal goals" which is used here should be understood in a broad sense. It is by no means restricted to egoistic goals, much less to economic goals. "World peace" or "aid to the starving Chinese" may be just as much a personal goal for a particular individual as another dollar in his pay envelope. The fact that economic incentives frequently predominate in business and governmental organizations should not obscure the importance of other types of inducements. Nor should intangible egoistic values,

Reprinted from *Administrative Behavior*, pp. 110-119. (Copyright, 1945, by Herbert A. Simon and used with the permission of the author and The Macmillan Company.)

such as status, prestige, or enjoyment of organization associations, be forgotten.

. . . In business organization the "customers" are a group that has, predominantly, the first type of motivation—direct interest in organization objectives; employees, the third type; and the entrepreneur the second type. This is true, of course, only to a very rough approximation, and the necessary qualifications will be set forth later . . .

The members of an organization, then, contribute to the organization in return for inducements that the organization offers them. The contributions of one group are the source of the inducements that the organization offers others. If the sum of the contributions is sufficient, in quantity and kind, to supply the necessary quantity and kinds of inducements, the organization survives and grows; otherwise, it shrinks and ultimately disappears unless an equilibrium is reached.[1]

Types of Organization Participants. Organization members may be classified in other ways than in terms of the inducements they receive for their participation. They may be classified in terms of the types of contributions they make to the organization: specific services (a supplier of material); money or other neutral services that may be employed as incentives (customers); and time and effort (employees).

Still a third method of classification would distinguish those who control the organization—that is, have a right to fix the terms on which the others will be permitted to participate in it—from the remaining participants. The various possible combinations of inducements, contributions, and control arrangements make for a considerable variety of organizational forms, and this variety must be taken into consideration in the succeeding discussion.

Organization Goals as Inducements. Most organizations are oriented around some goal or objective which provides the purpose toward which the organization decisions and activities are directed. If the goal is relatively tangible—e.g., making shoes—it is usually not too difficult to assess the contribution of specific activities toward it, and hence to evaluate their usefulness. If the goal is less tangible—like that of a religious organization—it becomes more debatable whether a particular activity contributes to the goal; and hence there may be considerable controversy, even among those who wish to work for the goal, as to how it is to be attained. Even where the goal is tangible there may be some activities whose relation to it is so indirect, though not necessarily any less substantial for that indirectness, that the problem of evaluation is difficult. It is much easier to budget, for example, for the production line than for the advertising department or for supervision.

1. This idea of an equilibrium is due to C. I. Barnard. See in his *The Functions of the Executive* (Cambridge: Harvard University Press, 1938), pp. 56-59 and chaps. xi and xvi.

It has been fashionable in the literature of business administration to debate whether "the" purpose of a business organization is service or profit. There really is no problem to debate about. Certain individuals, primarily the customers, contribute to the organization because of the service it provides; others, the entrepreneurs, because of the profits they may derive. When the system of organization behavior itself is examined, it is found that both service and profit aims influence decisions. It is for terminological convenience that the label of "organization objective" is here applied to the service aim.

Application to Specific Organization Types. In the case of the business organization the organization goal—the output of product—is a personal goal for individuals who are ordinarily not considered members of the organization, that is, the customers.[2] In return for this product the customers are willing to offer money, which provides a principal inducement for the employees and entrepreneurs to participate in the group. The relation of customers to the organization is distinguished not only by the type of inducement they receive, but also by the fact that it is based on a contract or bargain for a specific product without, ordinarily, any assumption of permanence or continuity in the relationship.

In the case of a government agency the organization goal is a personal goal for the ultimate controlling body of the organization—the legislature—and for the citizen. The relationship here is in part the same as in a business organization, in that the legislators, viewed as "customers," furnish the agency with its funds. It is decidedly different in that, first, they retain final legal control over the organization, and second, their "personal" motivation is based, in turn, on their peculiar status as elected representatives. To examine the way in which legislators make value judgments in determining the policy of governmental agencies would lead away from the present study into a study of the whole legislative process.

In volunteer organizations the organization objective is ordinarily the direct inducement that secures the services of the organization members. The peculiar problems of administration in volunteer organizations derive from the facts that the contributions are often on a part-time basis, that the various participants may have conflicting interpretations of the organization objective, and that the organization objective may play such a modest role in the participant's system of values that it offers only a mild inducement for cooperation. In this respect, the volunteer shares many of the characteristics

2. Barnard, in *The Functions of the Executive*, was perhaps the first writer to insist that the customers must be considered as a part of the system of organization activity in any theory of administration. His views on this point have still apparently not gained wide acceptance among writers on administration. As pointed out earlier, the important question here is not how "organization membership" is to be defined but whether or not the behavior of customers is to be included in the analysis of the organization.

of the customer of a business organization, although the former contributes services to the organization instead of money.

Adaptation of the Organization Objective. The organization objective is by no means a static thing. In order to survive, the organization must have an objective that appeals to its customers,[3] so that they will make the contributions necessary to sustain it. Hence, organization objectives are constantly adapted to conform to the changing values of customers, or to secure new groups of customers in place of customers who have dropped away. The organization may also undertake special activities to induce acceptance of its objectives by customers—advertising, missionary work, and propaganda of all sorts.

Hence, although it is correct to say that organization behavior is oriented toward the organization objective, this is not the whole story; for the organization objective itself changes in response to the influence of those for whom the accomplishment of that objective secures personal values.

The modification of the organization objective usually represents a compromise of the interests of several groups of potential participants, in order to secure their joint cooperation where each group individually is unable to attain its own objectives unaided. Hence the organization objective will seldom coincide exactly with the personal objectives of even those participants whose interest in the organization lies in its attainment of its goal. The crucial issue for any such individual is whether the organization objective is sufficiently close to his personal goal to make him choose to participate in the group rather than try to attain his goal by himself or in some other group. As will be seen, this process of compromise takes place, whether the controlling group of the organization is itself directly interested in the organization objective, or whether the inducement it receives from the organization is of some other type.

Loyalty of Employees to Organization Objective. Although the organization objective is of greatest importance in relation to the behavior of those participants who have been called "customers," almost all the members of an organization become imbued, to a greater or lesser degree, with the organization aim, and are influenced by it in their behavior. This has already been pointed out in the case of volunteer organizations; it is also true, although to a lesser extent, of governmental agencies and commercial organizations. It is one component, and a very important one, of organizational loyalty. If the objective has any appearance of usefulness, the organization members, whose attention is continually directed to it by their everyday work, will acquire an appreciation of its importance and value (often an exaggerated appreciation), and the attainment of the value will come, to that

---

3. The word "customer" is used in a generic sense here to refer to any individual —customer, legislator, or volunteer—for whom the organization objective has personal value.

extent, to have personal value for them. It will be seen later that, in addition to this loyalty to the organization objective, there may also develop in employees a very different loyalty—a loyalty to the organization itself and an interest in its survival and growth.

INCENTIVES FOR EMPLOYEE PARTICIPATION. To an employee of a non-volunteer organization the most obvious personal incentive that the organization offers is a salary or wage. It is a peculiar and important characteristic of his relation with the organization that, in return for this inducement, he offers the organization not a specific service but his undifferentiated time and effort. He places this time and effort at the disposal of those directing the organization, to be used as they see fit. Thus, both the customer relation (in the commercial organization) and the employee relation originate in contract, but in contracts of very different sorts. The employment contract results in the creation of a continuing authority relation between the organization and the employee.

How can this be? Why does the employee sign a blank check, so to speak, in entering upon his employment? First, from the viewpoint of the organization, nothing would be gained by offering an inducement to the employee unless the latter's behavior could be brought into the system of organization behavior through his acceptance of its authority. Second, from the viewpoint of the employee, the precise activities with which his time of employment is occuped may, within certain limits, be a matter of relative indifference to him. If the orders transmitted to him by the organization remain within these limits of acceptance, he will permit his behavior to be guided by them.

What determines the breadth of the area of acceptance within which the employee will accept the authority of the organization? It certainly depends on the nature and magnitude of the incentives the organization offers. In addition to the salary he receives, he may value the status and prestige that his position in the organization gives him, and he may value his relations with the working group of which he is part. In setting his task, the organization must take into consideration the effect that its orders may have upon the employee's realization of these values. If the employee values white-collar status, for example, he may be completely unwilling to accept assignments that deprive him of that status even when the work he is asked to perform is not inherently unpleasant or difficult.

There is great variation among individuals in the extent to which opportunities for promotion act as incentives for participation. Promotion is, of course, both an economic and a prestige incentive. Burleigh Gardner has pointed out the importance for administrative theory of the presence in organizations of certain highly "mobile" individuals, i.e. individuals who have a strong desire for advancement. It would be a mistake (which Gardner carefully avoids) to assume that these desires provide a strong incentive in all individuals.[4]

We find, then, that those participants in organization who are called its employees are offered a variety of material and non-material incentives, generally not directly related to the attainment of the organization objective nor to the size and growth of the organization, in return for their willingness to accept organization decisions as the basis for their behavior during the time of their employment. The area within which organization authority will be accepted is not unlimited, and the boundaries will depend on the incentives that the organization is able to provide. In so far as these incentives are not directly dependent upon the organization objective, modification of that objective will not affect the willingness of employees to participate, and hence the latter group will exert little influence in the determination of the objectives.

VALUES DERIVED FROM ORGANIZATION SIZE AND GROWTH. The third type of incentive that induces individual participation in organization derives from the size and growth of the organization. These might be referred to as "conservation" values. Most prominent in the group for whom these values are important is the entrepreneur. It is true that the entrepreneur, to the extent that he is an "economic man," is interested in profits, and not in size and growth. In practice this objection is not serious: first because profits usually are, or are thought to be, closely related to size and growth; and secondly because most entrepreneurs are interested in nonmaterial values, such as prestige and power, as well as profit. This attachment to conservation objectives is even more characteristic of the professional managerial group who exercise the active control of most large business enterprises.

Conservation objectives may provide important values, also, for the other employees of the organization as well, particularly those who are mobile. An organization that is growing and prospering offers greater opportunities for prestige and advancement than one that is static or declining. Conservation values are not, therefore, completely independent in practice from values of the second type, though for purposes of analysis there is some advantage in considering them separately.

Interest in conservation of the organization provides the basis for an organizational loyalty distinct from that previously mentioned. The individual who is loyal to the *objectives* of the organization will resist modification of those objectives, and may even refuse to continue his participation if they are changed too radically. The individual who is loyal to the *organization* will support opportunistic changes in its objectives that are calculated to promote its survival and growth.

4. On this and other aspects of the problem of incentives see Burleigh B. Gardner, *Human Relations in Industry* (Chicago: Richard D. Irwin, 1945), particularly chaps. i and viii.

Loyalty to the organization itself is perhaps the type of loyalty most characteristic of commercial organizations, but both species prevail widely in both public and private administration, commercial and noncommercial. Some of the most striking manifestations of conflict between these two types of loyalty are to be found in religious and reform organizations, where there is often controversy as to the extent to which organization objectives shall be modified to insure survival. This was certainly one basis for the Stalinist-Trotskyist rivalry. As previously indicated, the motives of the opportunists in such a controversy may, of course, be tactical rather than egoistic. The opportunist, assessing unfavorably the chances of survival without adaptation, may prefer half a loaf to no bread, while the "idealist" may assess the chances of survival more optimistically, or may consider that the concession in objectives more than outweighs the improvement in survival chances. . . .

ORGANIZATION EQUILIBRIUM AND EFFICIENCY. The basic value criteria that will be employed in making decisions and choices among alternatives in an organization will be selected for the organization primarily by the controlling group—the group that has the power to set the terms of membership for all the participants. If the group that holds the legal control fails to exercise this power, then, of course, it will devolve on individuals further down the administrative hierarchy.

Whatever group exercises the power of determining the basic value criteria will attempt to secure through the organization its own personal values—whether these be identified with the organization objective, with the conservation objectives, with profits or what not. But their power of control does not in any sense imply that the control group exercises an unlimited option to direct the organization in any path it desires, for the power will continue to exist only so long as the controlling group is able to offer sufficient incentives to retain the contributions of the other participants to the organization. No matter what the personal objectives of the control group, their decisions will be heavily influenced by the fact that they can attain their objectives through the organization only if they can maintain a positive balance of contributions over inducements, or at least an equilibrium between the two.

For this reason the controlling group, regardless of its personal values, will be opportunistic—will appear to be motivated in large part at least by conservation objectives. . . .

WHO WERE THE MOST CRITICAL OF THE
ARMY'S PROMOTION OPPORTUNITIES?

Samuel A. Stouffer, et al.

Data from research surveys to be presented will show, as would be expected, that those soldiers who had advanced slowly relative to other soldiers of equal longevity in the Army were the most critical of the Army's promotion opportunities. *But relative rate of advancement can be based on different standards by different classes of the Army population.* For example, a grade school man who became a corporal after a year of service would have had a more rapid rate of promotion compared with most of his friends at the same educational level than would a college man who rose to the same grade in a year. Hence we would expect, at a given rank and a given longevity, that the better educated would be more likely than others to complain of the slowness of promotion. The facts, as we shall see, tend to bear this out. The better educated, in spite of their superior chances of promotion, were the most critical.

A similar phenomenon appeared to operate between different branches of the service. This, along with the differentials by rank and education, is illustrated in Chart I. Here the responses of Military Police to the question, "Do you think a soldier with ability has a good chance for promotion in the Army?" are compared with responses of Air Corps men, in early 1944. Longevity is held roughly constant by taking only men who had been in the Army 1 to 2 years. It will be noted that more of the less educated, among both privates and noncoms in both branches, had favorable opinions than did the better educated. For example, among privates and Pfc's in the Military Police, 33 per cent of the less educated said that a soldier with ability had a very good chance for promotion, as compared with 21 per cent of the better educated privates and Pfc's. Finally, it will be seen, among both privates and noncoms in each educational group, that the Air Corps men tended to take a dimmer view of promotion opportunities for men of ability in the Army than did the Military Police.

Without reference to the theory that such opinions by soldiers represent a relationship between their expectations and their achievements relative to others *in the same boat with them*, such a finding would be paradoxical, in-

Reprinted from Samuel A. Stouffer, Edward A. Suchman, Leland C. DeVinney, Shirley A. Star, and Robin M. Williams, Jr., *The American Soldier*, Vol. I: Adjustment During Army Life, pp. 250-257, by permission of the author and the publisher. (Copyright, 1949, by the Princeton University Press.)

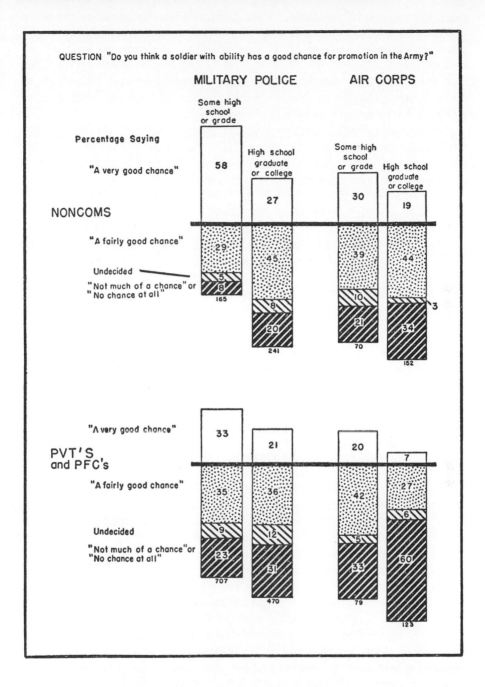

QUESTION "Do you think a soldier with ability has a good chance for promotion in the Army?"

deed. For chances of promotion in the Military Police were about the worst
in any branch of the Army—among this sample of men in the Army 1 to 2
years, only 24 per cent of MP's were noncoms as compared with 47 per
cent of the Air Corps men. The MP's felt, too, that as a *branch* the Military Police had been discriminated against in getting ratings, two thirds of
them saying in answer to another question that MP's do not have as good
a chance for promotion as men in other branches.

But consider a high school graduate or college man in the Military Police
with Army longevity of 1 to 2 years. The chances of his being a noncom
were 34 out of 100, based on the proportions of noncoms in this sample at
this time. If he earned the rating, he was one of the top third among his fellows of equal educational status. If he failed to earn the rating, he was in
the same boat with two thirds of his fellows with equal schooling. Contrast
him with the Air Corps man of the same education and longevity. The
chances of the latter's being a noncom were 56 in 100, based on the proportions in this sample at this time. If he had earned a rating, so had the majority
of his fellows in the branch, and his achievement was relatively less conspicuous than in the MP's. If he had failed to earn a rating, while the majority had succeeded, he had more reason to feel a sense of personal frustration,
which could be expressed as criticism of the promotion system, than if he
were one of two thirds in the same boat, as among the MP's.

The process would work in the same way among the less educated. In
both the Military Police Branch and the Air Corps, the promotion chances
of the less educated were inferior to the chances of others. In the MP
sample, only 17 per cent of the less educated were noncoms; in the Air
Corps sample, the corresponding figure was 47 per cent. An MP who did
not complete high school would feel unusually rewarded compared with
others in his outfit in becoming a noncom; one who remained a private had
so much company that he hardly could view discrimination against him as
a reflection on his personal competence. In the Air Corps, those with ratings had almost as much company as those who remained privates—with less
room for personal satisfaction over comparative achievement and more
room for dissatisfaction over comparative failure to climb the status ladder.

While the psychological mechanisms seem to operate as described above
in producing the pattern of opinions about promotion possibilities, we must
not lose sight of the fact that on the average those with ratings had more
favorable opinions about promotion than those without. Nor must we jump
to the conclusion that men who were critical of promotion policy were
necessarily dissatisfied with their Army jobs. True, cross tabulation, within
a particular subgroup, of opinions about promotion and expressions of job
satisfaction will almost invariably show that men who were most critical
about promotions were also least satisfied with their jobs. But that is *within*
a given subgroup. As between subgroups, the relationship may vanish or

reverse itself. In the case of the comparison of the Military Police and the Air Corps it reverses itself. Although the Air Corps men were more critical of promotion, they also were more likely than the MP's to be satisfied with their Army job. For example, 36 per cent of the Air Corps men in this sample said they would *not* change to some other Army job if given a chance, whereas only 21 per cent of the MP's gave this response. Promotion opportunity was only one of many factors in job satisfaction. . . . Other elements, such as the chance to learn something useful in civilian life, entered in, as did informal status factors such as the general prestige of the branch to which assigned. In general, Air Corps was a high prestige branch, Military Police a low prestige branch. One of the elements which contributed to making the difference in prestige was, no doubt, the difference in T/O [1] opportunities for social mobility.

The illustration presented in Chart I was based on a special cross-section survey of Military Police in March 1944 and the Air Corps segment of a cross-section survey of the Army at the nearest available date—namely, January 1944. These data were especially selected to exhibit the structure of opinion on two sharply contrasting groups with respect to promotion opportunities in the Army. It is desirable to see whether the same general pattern holds up on a broader basis, where there is less contrast between groups. . . .

In general, differences in opinion about promotion opportunities are rather small, tending in any individual case to be somewhat less striking than in the extreme illustration presented earlier, but a definite pattern is present. . . . Four findings emerge:

1. *For a given rank, the shorter the longevity the more favorable tends to be the opinion about promotion.* Compare, for example, less educated AGF privates in the Army less than 6 months with those in the Army 6 months to 1 year. The proportion of men who say that promotional opportunities are very good drops from 50 per cent to 42 per cent respectively. A total of 18 such comparisons can be made . . . and all 18 are in the same direction.

2. *For a given longevity, the higher the rank the more favorable tends to be the opinion about promotion.* For example, consider less educated AGF men in the Army a year or more. The number who say that opportunities are "very good" is 64 per cent among the top three grades, and it drops to 52 per cent among buck sergeants, and to 45 per cent among corporals. Thirty comparisons are possible between any two grades. . . . Of these, 25 show the tendency indicated, 1 shows no difference, and 4 show the reverse tendency. (It must be remembered that many of the percentages are based on a small number of cases and are thus subject to a large sampling

1. Table of Organization. This specified the number of grades authorized for the organization.

error. Moreover, the tie and reversals are all found in the Pfc-private comparisons.)

3. *For a given rank and longevity, the less the education the more favorable tends to be the opinion about promotion.* This, as are the two conclusions above reported, is in accordance with the expectation based on the analysis previously presented. Take AGF top three grades with over a year in the Army. Among the less educated, 64 per cent rated promotion opportunity "very good"; among the better educated, 56 per cent. There are 24 such comparisons possible. . . . Of these, 22 are in the direction indicated, 1 shows no difference, and 1 is a tie.[2]

4. *For a given rank, longevity, and educational level, the less the promotion opportunity afforded by a branch or combination of branches, the more favorable the opinion tends to be toward promotion opportunity.* This, again, is in accord with our previous discussion. On the average, promotion opportunity was very much better in the Air Corps than in either Service Force or Ground Force branches. It was somewhat better in Service Forces than in Ground Forces. Consider privates first class with less than high school education and less than 6 months in the Army. In Ground Forces, 51 per cent rated promotion opportunities "very good," in Service Forces 50 per cent, in Air Forces 43 per cent. Between Ground Forces and Air Forces, 16 such comparisons can be made . . . and of these 14 are in the direction indicated and 2 are reversals. Of the 16 comparisons between Air Forces and Service Forces, 13 are in the direction indicated with 1 tie and 2 reversals. Of the 16 comparisons between Ground Forces and Service Forces, the Ground Force men are more favorable in 11, the Service Force men more favorable in 4, and in 1 comparison both are the same. These patterns of difference are statistically significant,[3] but the picture tends to become less decisive if looked at from some other viewpoints. For example, we know that promotion opportunities were best in Air Forces, intermediate in Service Forces, and least in Ground Forces. But in only 10 of the 16 comparisons do

2. In view of the possibility that some of the apparent difference between the less educated and better educated conceivably could be attributable to an artifact—namely, a slightly greater tendency of the less educated than the better educated to check the first and extreme category in a list of responses—it is worth noting that when comparisons are made . . . after combining the responses of "very good chance" and "fairly good chance," the conclusion is essentially unaltered. The less educated still were more favorable than the better educated in 18 out of 24 comparisons, with 6 reversals. Because of the extremely skewed nature of the overall distribution of responses, 80 per cent of the entire sample checking either "very good" or "fairly good," comparisons on the basis of the "very good" category alone are preferable, as long as the educational response bias is not more serious. An educational response bias would not likely apply, of course, to other comparisons, for example between rank groups, as education is at least broadly controlled in these comparisons.

3. Assuming, as a null hypothesis, that a positive difference was equally as likely as a negative difference and calling ties failures, the likelihood of getting 12 or more successes by chance, in 16 comparisons, would be less than .04. The likelihood of getting 13 or more successes would be 01 (using the point binomial distribution).

the proportions "very favorable" come out in exactly the reverse order. And the results, though still in the same direction, tend also to be statistically indecisive if comparisons between any two forces are made by combining the "very favorable" and "fairly favorable" categories. To be conservative, we should limit our conclusion by saying that a force with relatively less promotion chances tended to have a larger proportion of men speaking very favorably of promotion opportunities than another force with greater promotion chances.

   As in our earlier discussion of the Military Police and the Air Corps, a caution must be sounded against assuming from these findings that a liberalization of promotion policy—which might reduce rather than raise the relative self-gratification of the successful men and increase rather than reduce the sense of defeat of the unsuccessful—would increase job satisfaction. What actually would happen we do not know, because this could be determined only from controlled experiments, which were never made. But it is relevant to point out that job satisfaction was highest in the Air Forces, intermediate in Service Forces, and lowest in Ground Forces—reversing exactly the direction seen in attitudes toward promotion.

THE PROBLEM OF SUCCESSION IN BUREAUCRACY

Alvin W. Gouldner

Classical political scientists, attuned to the vicissitudes of crowns and courts, have, in their concept of succession, left a residue of observation and analysis that bears reexamination by modern social scientists. Limiting their attention to the *highest* authorities of government, they have noted that replacement of an old by a new ruler was often attended by public crises. "Such periods have frequently been characterized by bitter conflicts occasionally developing into full-fledged wars, of which the Spanish, Polish, and Austrian wars of succession are outstanding examples." [1] Political scientists have conceived of the method of succession as "one of the principal factors determining the stability of any given form of government" [2] and have therefore used it as an attribute for the classification of types of government.

Reprinted from *Studies in Leadership: Leadership and Democratic Action* (ed. Alvin W. Gouldner), pp. 644-659, by permission of the author and the publisher. (Copyright, 1950, by Harper and Brothers.)
   1. Frederick M. Watkins, "Political Succession," *Encyclopedia of the Social Sciences.*
   2. *Ibid.*

However, modern sociologists, far from being influenced by these judgments, have almost entirely ignored the phenomenon of succession. It is possible that the political scientists' association of the concept of succession with problems of the most supreme authorities may partially account for this, for modern sociology is largely secular in outlook and, carrying the stamp of disenchantment common to our age, looks to "pedestrian" things for enlightenment.

The sociologists' neglect of the concept of succession becomes acutely problematical if account is taken of the pivotal role it acquired in the work of Max Weber. Insofar as Weber had a theory of historical change, his major analytical categories posited an alternation of charismatic and bureaucratic or traditional modes of authority. These rotations were conceived of as cyclical fluctuations within a trend which moved toward increasing rationalization of social action.[3]

Charismatic authority, involving the acceptance of a ruler because of his singular personal attributes, was held to disrupt the process of rationalization when existing routines proved inadequate. Hostile to workaday procedures, a charismatic movement is alienated from economic and familial institutions and supports itself irregularly. Charismatic authority is, then, ephemeral to the extreme. Ordinarily, its instability provokes insecurity among the charismatic leader's staff and followers, who seek to safeguard their material and ideal interests. Their anxiety, Weber states, is brought to a climax by the problem of succession.

Weber proposes that the new methods used to secure a successor result in routinizations which, depending mainly on the economic context, move in either a traditionalistic or bureaucratic direction. To Weber, then, the problem of succession is the umbilical cord which connects charisma to its heir. Succession is the key concept which in his analysis bridges the polarized modes of authority. Yet despite this concept's analytically strategic role, Weber fails to give a coherent picture of its content and its function in his system of theory. Exactly how succession leads in the one case to bureaucratic, and in the other, to traditionalistic, authority is unclear.

More recently, some of the problems attendant on succession in a bureaucracy have received comment from Arnold Brecht[4] and Marshall Dimock.[5] Both Brecht and Dimock have focused on the problem of "bu-

---

3. Cf. Introduction by H. H. Gerth and C. Wright Mills (editors), *From Max Weber: Essays in Sociology* (New York, 1947). My late colleague, Jeremiah Wolpert, suggested that continuing rationalization increasingly delimits the possibility of traditionalistic authority and also radically modifies the nature of charismatic authority, so that the latter's traits may be deliberately manipulated. This type is perhaps more accurately characterized as pseudo-charismatic, according to Wolpert.

4. Arnold Brecht, "Bureaucratic Sabotage," *Annals of the American Academy of Political and Social Science*, June, 1937.

5. Marshall E. Dimock, "Bureaucracy Self-Examined," *Public Administration Review*, Summer, 1944, partially reprinted in this volume.

reaucratic sabotage," the resistance of the "permanent" staff of a bureaucracy to the policies of their superior, especially when he is new to office. Dimock attributes this conflict to a short circuit in communication between the successor and the old staff who, over the years of their association, have developed subtly expressed understandings of which the successor is ignorant. Why the communication failure occurs, and in particular its institutional conditions, is not considered in any detail. While noting that the successor is primed for change, Dimock gives no explanation of the circumstances which engender this attitude.

In actuality, empirical studies of the process of succession and its concomitant problems are practically nonexistent. In the following discussion, observations will be drawn from a study of an absentee-owned factory near Buffalo, New York. This factory, which combines both mining and surface processing operations, is located in a rural community into which urban characteristics are only slowly seeping. These observations are offered with the following intentions: (1) To suggest and provide a warrant for certain hypotheses concerning the interrelations between succession and the development of bureaucracy. (2) To outline a theoretical context in which one commonly noted industrial phenomenon, "strategic replacements," may be usefully fitted. (3) To illustrate the potential utility of employing a "secularized" concept of succession in the study of organization. By a "secularized" concept of succession is meant the replacement (for any reason) of an individual in a strategic position in any formal or informal group, without prejudice as to whether this group is large or small, autocephalous or heterocephalous, of broad or narrow jurisdiction and composition. Such a concept of succession would, it seems, escape the Carlylean implications of that employed by political scientists.

CASE HISTORY OF A SUCCESSION.[6] At the time we began our study two things were at the center of the plant personnel's attention: first, an accelerating degree of bureaucratization and, second, a series of replacements among foremen and supervisors.

Among many evidences of growing bureaucratization [7] was an increasing separation between the company's and workers' property, the company having begun a stricter control over its machinery, raw material, and finished product, making these less accessible to workers for personal use than formerly. The old personnel manager, an informal, community-conscious man with little formal education and a "dislike of paperwork," was replaced by a rule-sensitive, company-conscious man with some college education. The number of paper reports required from supervisors

6. I should like to record my deep appreciation to Maurice Stein, Paul Mahany, Joseph Davis, John Sommers, Cornelius Vodicka, Gunnar Hanson, George Amos and Jo Ann Setel, students who assisted in the field work.
7. Max Weber's ideal-type bureaucracy has been used as a heuristic guide, and most of the variables mentioned below are stressed in his concept of bureaucracy.

was being increased; a formal, printed "warning" notice used for disciplinary purposes was introduced. The no-absenteeism rule was being strictly enforced; new modes of punching in and out were promulgated; the supervisory staff was being extended and divided into two groups—"know-how" and "do-how" foremen. The characteristic impersonalized "atmosphere" of bureaucratic structures began to pervade the plant.

These innovations, it is crucial to observe, began shortly after the arrival of a new plant manager, Vincent Keat.[8] The correlation between succession and crystallization of bureaucratic trends was striking. Shortly after his arrival, Keat began to remove some of the old supervisors and foremen and to bring in new ones. Four replacements were made with men in the plant. The new personnel manager was brought in from the plant at which Keat had formerly been manager. (It had been a smaller and less important factory.) Several new foremen's positions were opened up and promotions made to them. This rapid change of supervisory personnel following a succession is so familar in an industrial situation that it deserves a distinctive name and in this paper has been called "strategic replacement."

What is there about the role of a successor that conduces to increased bureaucratization and strategic replacement? The problem may be separated into two parts: (1) The frame of reference of the successor and the definitions of his situation to which it disposes, and (2) the objective attributes of the factory situation.

The Successor's Frame of Reference. In this case, succession involved advancement for Keat, the new plant manager. The main office personnel who determined his promotion reminded Keat of his predecessor's inadequacies and expressed the feeling that things had been slipping at the plant for some while. They suggested that the old plant manager, Godfrey, was perhaps getting overindulgent in his old age and that he, Keat, would be expected to improve production quotas. As Keat put it, "Godfrey didn't force the machine. I had to watch it. Godfrey was satisfied with a certain production. But the company gave me orders to get production up." With the pressure of renewed postwar competition things would have to start humming; traditionalized production quotas were to be rationalized.[9]

Keat, grateful for his opportunity to ascend in the company hierarchy, of course, heeded the main office counsels. It may be emphasized that a "briefing" does more than impart technical data; it also functions to struc-

8. This name, like all others used, is fictitious in order that the anonymity of the company, plant, and personnel will be preserved.

9. Roethlisberger and Dickson have emphasized the tendency of informal cliques of workers to limit their output in a traditionalistic way. This comment indicates that restriction of output, or "sabotage," as Veblen referred to it, is not manifested solely by operatives, but is found among managerial personnel as well. Veblen has, of course, long since noted this; he tended, however, to focus on the rational motives for "sabotage" among managers, neglecting the traditionalistic component.

ture attitudes toward an assignment. Keat, therefore, came to his new plant keenly sensitive to the impersonal, universalistic criteria which his superiors would use to judge his performance. He knew his progress would be watched; he desires also to express his gratitude and is, consequently, anxious to "make good." As a member of the main office administrative staff commented: "Keat is trying hard to arrive. He is paying more attention to the plant. But he lacks Godfrey's (the old plant manager's) personal touch. Keat will follow along organizational lines, while Godfrey handled things on the personal basis."

There is, however, a second and apparently conflicting element in the new plant manager's frame of reference. On his way up, he may have made friends whose loyalty and help expedited his ascent. Since the time of succession is often a time of promotion and enhanced power, it may be the moment of reckoning awaited by the friends when their past favors to the successor can be reciprocated. There seems little question, however, that this particularistic element in the new plant manager's frame of reference is a minor one. For if worse comes to worst, he may evade the old obligations, since he is now no longer among those to whom he owes them. Or, more likely perhaps, he may interpret fulfillment of old particularistic obligations as a means of securing personnel which would enable him to guarantee successful accomplishment of his new mission and of the abstract, impersonal goals to which he is mainly oriented. This need evoke no conflict of values within the successor, for one's friends are most often viewed as "competent" people, and in the case of a highly placed individual there are reasons why this is very probable.

Thus, even before setting foot into the plant, Keat had a notion of the kinds of things which needed "correction" and was tentatively shaping policies to bring about the requisite changes. He defined the situation as one calling for certain changes, changes oriented to the abstract, rational standards of efficiency. Because he is a successor, new to the plant, a stranger among strangers, as yet untied by bonds of friendship and informal solidarity with the people in his new plant, both his perceptive and executive capacities may be relatively devoid of nonrational considerations.

The Factory Situation. Oriented toward efficiency and the minimization of nonrational aspects of the factory organization which would impede it, the new plant manager entered the factory. He found that to which his frame of reference has been sensitized. Inevitably, a factory, like any other social organization, reflects a compromise between formal and informal organization, between rational and nonrational norms. Keat found that workers "borrowed" tools from the plant for their own personal use, that they have customarily helped themselves to raw materials and even finished products for use about their homes, workshops, and farms. He found that some workers preferred to "punch in" early and accumulate a little overtime, or "punch out" early on special occasions. The miners, far from eager to conform with Protestant norms of regular work, believed that a certain amount of absenteeism was one of their traditional prerogatives and a normative way of manifesting that "down here, we are our own bosses." The new plant manager's expectations were confirmed: the plant was in "evident" need of specific changes to heighten its efficiency.

Whom could Keat hold responsible for this "lax" state of affairs? Oriented to formal and individualistic diagnoses, he tended to place responsibility on the old supervisory staff, and indicated that he considered it their duty to remedy the situation along lines he suggested. At this point he encountered his first sharp resistance. "Every foreman had set ways," explained Keat. "When I wanted to make some changes the supervisors told me, Godfrey used to do this and that. . . . I didn't make many changes and I'm satisfied with the changes I've made. The foremen are getting smoothed off now. (You had some difficulty with the supervisors . . . ?—interviewer) Yes, I had some trouble in straightening out shirkers. Some of them thought they were going to get fired. I could work on these guys. But others, who didn't expect to get fired, were. Each foreman is just a little bit on edge now. They don't know whether they're doing right. . . . A new plant manager is going to make some changes—to suit my own way. I had to watch them. I made those changes."

Thus among the things the new plant manager resolves to change, when he encounters their resistance, are the old supervisory personnel. But why is it that the old supervisory staff resists the new manager's plans?

A new manager is faced with a heritage of promises and obligations that his predecessor has not had an opportunity to fulfill. These old obligations are most important when made to the old supervisory staff, or to others constituting the old plant manager's informal social circle. For, placed as they often are in powerful positions, they may be able to mobilize sentiment against him or use dilatory tactics to impede his efforts, unless he fulfills his "inherited" obligations.

An interesting illustration of this at the plant involves the present union president, Ralph Byta. Byta was a neighbor of Godfrey and had been induced by him to come to work at the plant. Godfrey had made Byta some promises which he was unable to meet, due to his sudden death. Some four months after Keat's arrival, Byta ran for and was elected president of the local union. Byta's new position was now much more invulnerable than those of the other "old lieutenants" who held supervisory positions. He could not be replaced or fired and had to be "dealt with." As Byta put it, "The good men know that a union's the best way to get ahead. You can't walk into the company and ask them for a raise for yourself. It's different, though, if you represent 150 men. Then, too, if the company sees you're a leader (and the company sees it!) well, maybe you can get yourself a raise."

Nor was Byta's expectation a fanciful one; it had solid justification in the company's previous actions. As a member of the main office administrative staff told an interviewer: "Some of our foremen are ex-union presidents. . . . The union can pick out a good man for president. If you want a good man pick the president of the union. If you have good morale, the men elect responsible people to the union leadership." At first Byta played the role of a "militant" and was characterized by management as "bitter." Months after his election, the new plant manager had a "man to man" talk with him, and Byta is now viewed by management as much more "reasonable" than when newly elected. Byta's case is an example of the problems with which a new manager is confronted through the old lieutenants and members of the old informal group.

Resistance to a new plant manager by the old group of lieutenants may be provoked for reasons other than the former's reluctance to acknowledge the old manager's obligations. The new manager, for example, may not be viewed as a legitimate successor by the old lieutenants; they may consider one of their own group as the legitimate heir. In this company, the supervisor of ——— building is customarily viewed as "next in line" for promotion to manager. It seems significant, then, that Keat was most hostile to the supervisor of ——— building, considering him to be the "least strict" of all the supervisors. On one occasion Keat had to be hospitalized during a siege of heated wage negotiations. The supervisor of ——— building became acting plant manager. From management's point of view, he played an extremely ineffectual role in the negotiations, not attempting to "handle" or "control" the situation when it headed toward a strike.

In general, the annoyance of the old lieutenants is sharpened when they find their once-favored status incompletely understood and perhaps ignored by the successor. The old lieutenants' resistance to the new manager finds its counterpart among the rank-and-file operatives when measures planned to foster efficiency are initiated. The operatives resist because they resent the infringements that these make on their established prerogatives. That an increase in efficiency often means greater work effort on their part without compensatory rewards is viewed as unjust. They may also, like the supervisors, question the legitimacy of the new manager. Whether or not this occurs depends in part on the specific yardsticks used by a particular group of workers to evaluate a manager's "right" to hold his job. The point to be underscored is that succession provides an occasion when questions about the legitimacy of a manager will be considered most permissible.

The manner in which a manager gets his position may be one of the criteria of legitimacy. For example, "coming up from the ranks" may be a criterion of legitimate authority among workers in present-day industry. The way in which the manager exercises his authority may be another measure of his legitimacy. If, for example, he recognizes workers' traditional rights and "does not act superior," the workers in this plant are likely to consider his authority legitimate. These workers also think a manager should "stand on his own feet" and not be meticulous about clearing problems through the company's main office.

Sensitized, however, as he has been by his main office briefing, the successor is quick to define some of the workers' customary rights as impediments to efficiency. Again influenced by his status as a successor, he will tend to await main office dispositions of problems, thus irking operatives who still think of a manager very much as an independent intrepreneur. As a main office staff member recognized, "A new plant manager is more prone to lean on the top administration than is a more experienced one."

An index of the degree of rank-and-file resistance to a new manager is the prevalence of what may be called the "Rebecca Myth."[10] Some years ago, Daphne DuMaurier wrote a book about a young woman who married a widower, only to be plagued by the memory of his first wife, Rebecca, whose virtues were widely extolled. The idealization of the absent is a well-known phenomenon. One may suspect that almost every former plant manager is to some extent idealized by the workers, even though he may have been disliked while present.

It was precisely such a situation that confronted Keat. Workers' reminiscences about the regime of "Old Godfrey" are scarcely less than a modern version of "Paradise Lost." The workers' comments spontaneously contrast and compare, playing the old manager off against the new. The social function of the Rebecca Myth seems plain enough. By attaching themselves to Godfrey's memory, the workers can, in his name, legitimate their resistance to changes planned or implemented by Keat.

The new manager was, therefore, faced with two interrelated problems. First, how to implement the efficiency goals he had set himself. Second, how, as a necessary condition for solution of the first problem, to eliminate the resistance to his plans by workers and supervisors. In addition, Keat was enmeshed in a problem on a totally different psychological level. This is the problem of coping with his own mounting anxiety which, aroused by the definition of his promotion as a "test," is further accentuated by the resistance he meets. He has two major tactics of solution available to him: (a) the technique of informal solidarity and/or (b) the technique of impersonal routinization or other changes in the formal organization.

10. In another connection the Lynds have commented on this phenomenon. "Middletown is wont to invoke old leaders against new leaders who threaten to leave the safe and tried middle of the road." Robert S. Lynd and Helen Merrell Lynd, *Middletown in Transition* (New York, 1937), p. 413. Cf. Chap. VIII, "Managers and Owners, Then and Now," in W. Lloyd Warner and J. O. Low, *The Social System of the Modern Factory* (New Haven, 1947) for a pithy account of the functioning of the Rebecca Myth during a strike.

BUREAUCRATIZATION AND STRATEGIC REPLACEMENT AS PROBLEM SOLUTIONS. The successor can attempt to arouse informal solidarity and group sentiment, harnessing them to his goals. Such an approach might be exemplified by the appeal: "Let's all pitch in and do a job!" The use of *gemeinschaft* or, more properly, *pseudo-gemeinschaft* [11] as a tactic for promoting his ends is employed by Keat within the limits permitted by his personality. He has, for example, taken pains to get to know the men. "I talk with them," he says, "I congratulate them about births and things like that, *if I can only get an inkling of it.* Personal touches here and there help." But *pseudo-gemeinschaft* is an inadequate means to the manager's ends because it premises two things not always available.

It requires, first, a greater consensus of ends and sentiments between management and workers than exists. As an obvious example, Keat (like most managers) was primarily concerned about meeting his production quota and keeping costs down. The workers are, however, much less interested in these. It is difficult to maintain, to say nothing of creating, informal solidarity in pursuit of ends which are differentially valued by group members.

Second, the successor wise to the ways of *pseudo-gemeinschaft* would require knowledge of the informal networks and the private sentiments they transmit, if he were to manipulate them successfully. But because he is a successor and has little "inkling" of the subtle arrangements and understandings comprising the informal structure, these are inaccessible for his purposes. As already indicated, he even has difficulty with the informal group nearest his own level, the old lieutenants. The successor is, therefore, impelled to resort to tactics more congruent with his role: impersonal techniques, formalized controls, and strategic replacements.

The problem of disposing of the old lieutenants takes time. A new manager cannot, and often will not, act too hastily for fear of precipitating a conflict for which he is not yet prepared. He does not wish to be accused of failing to give the old lieutenants a "chance," nor of seeking to install his favorites with indecent haste. He spends some time "sizing up" the situation, looking for possible allies and lining up replacements.

In the meanwhile, however, the manager has no social "connective tissue," that is, an informal group structure between himself and the lower echelons. Relatively isolated at this point, he receives mainly formal and technical communications. His anxiety is channeled into suspicion of what is happening below. One worker sized up the situation as follows: "When Godfrey was here, it was like one big happy family. Keat is all business. Why, Godfrey could get on that phone, call up the foreman, and have

11. See Robert K. Merton, with the assistance of Marjorie Fiske and Alberta Curtis, *Mass Persuasion* (New York, 1946), pp. 142-144, for a general discussion of the concept of *pseudo-gemeinschaft*.

the situation well in hand. Keat has to come around and make sure things are all right. Maybe that's why he's bringing in his own men."

In the absence of a position in the well-developed system of informal relations within the plant, and because he cannot be everywhere at once personally checking up, the new manager begins to introduce rules and emphasize adherence to them. He elaborates a system of "paper reports" which enable him to "keep his finger on things." Observing informal gatherings of workers chatting, he is somewhat upset, not merely because of what they are not doing, but also by what they may be saying and doing. He is therefore attracted to a "make work" policy and seeks to keep the men busy, perhaps acting on the Protestant precept that the "devil finds work for idle hands."

When he considers the moment judicious, he begins to make the strategic replacements, spinning out a new informal group that will conform to his needs and support his status. Through this network he can guarantee that the meaning or "spirit" of his orders will be communicated. This last point deserves emphasis, for, no matter how model a bureaucratic structure he may mold, its formal rules will be enmeshed in and in need of reinforcement by a framework of non-rational values.[12]

The technique of strategic replacements obligates the new lieutenants to the successor, establishing extra-formal ties between them, which the manager may draw upon to implement his goals. The degree to which this technique does obligate the new lieutenant to the successor was observed in an interview with a newly appointed foreman. Unlike his references to the preceding managers, this foreman called the new manager by his first name, was very reluctant to give voice to the near-universal references to Keat's strictness, and fantasied that Keat is better liked than Godfrey. Thus changes in the occupants of formal statuses, strategic replacements, have consequences for informal organization which are functional for the successor.

To summarize this discussion of the interplay of succession, bureaucratization, and strategic replacements: It should be clear that, since this was a plant with a history of some twenty-five years as part of a large, expanding company, it was far from innocent of bureaucratic intentions prior to his arrival. There was no such pure case available for study. On the contrary, the plant had experienced a degree of bureaucratization, and the new manager was oriented to values which might have led him in a bureaucratic direction, regardless of the circumstances of succession. The point, here, however, is that the role of a successor apparently involves the occupant in certain problems which, from his viewpoint, are conditions of his action. These conditions conduce to the same process of bureau-

12. Cf. Reinhard Bendix, "Bureaucracy: The Problem and Its Setting," *American Sociological Review*, October, 1947, for a discussion of this problem.

cratization as do the new manager's company-structured values. The existence of the conditions concurrent with succession make bureaucratization functional to the successor. Put in another way, it is the emergence of the problems of succession which require that the successor learn and use bureaucratic methods. The presence of these conditions exerts pressure on the successor to organize bureaucratically. *He organizes bureaucratically, not only because he wants to or because he values these above other methods, but because he is compelled to by the conditions of succession—if he wishes to maintain his status.*

In this plant there were about six managers from the time of its inception: an average of about one for every five years of its existence. This suggests that it is necessary to consider another specific dimension of succession, the rate of succession. When contrasted with comparable institutions of societies antecedent to our own, the rate of succession in the modern factory seems "high." The modern corporation, one of whose manifest functions is to enable business organizations to persist beyond the life of their founders, is an institutional condition for this high rate. Another institutional condition is, in one of its facets, absentee ownership or, more fundamentally, private ownership of large-scale means of production.

In such a situation authority becomes something of a commodity handed back and forth under certain general conditions. Like a commodity, it can then only rarely be custom-tailored, fitted to size, and it tends to be standardized to facilitate its transfer. Where authority may have to be transferred frequently, personalized loyalty to those who wield it may impede its mobility. It is therefore functional for the mobility of authority to attach workers' loyalty to the rules, not to the plant manager. Thus bureaucratization is functional for an institutionally conditioned high rate of succession, while, in turn, a high rate of succession operates as a selecting mechanism to sift out a bureaucratic mode of organization.

Reference to authority as a "commodity," while somewhat inexact in the above paragraph, nevertheless calls attention to some distinctive dynamics of certain modern forms of social control. In modern business-industrial societies, as in all their Western European predecessors back to the epoch of tribal disintegration, property is a basis for the acquisition of authority, prestige, influence, and power. In itself, "property" connotes the superiority of those who have specific rights in a valuable object as against those who do not—at least, insofar as these valuable objects are concerned. Thus the factory owner, by virtue of his ownership of a specific property form, is simultaneously endowed with authority over his employees. In current business societies, authority is a concomitant of ownership of means of production.

Insofar as production property is involved in a market and can be bought and sold for cash and credit, so too is the correlate authority. If

modern property forms are distinguished by the extent of their involvement in a market, so also are modern means of social control, including
authority.[13] The high rate of succession in the economy has, therefore,
as a further institutional condition, a market for production property. If the
problem of succession is translated into the economist's terms, "labor turn-
over" among strategic personnel, another of the institutional conditions for
a high rate of succession emerges: a free labor market. There seems reason
to believe that a high labor turnover on any level would disrupt informal
group systems, deteriorate nonrational consensus, and impede integration
of worker and job. The careful specification and delimitation of functions
and the emphasis on rule-oriented behavior—both crucial aspects of bureaucratic organization—may serve as functional equivalents for disorganized
informal patterns.

Informal organization and consensus is not, of course, disrupted solely
by succession or labor turnover. Other crucial sources of their disorganization, which cannot be developed here, would include cleavage along status
lines. Moreover, it seems uncertain whether the conclusions tentatively presented here would apply, on the same level of abstraction, to other institutional spheres such as political parties and governmental organization. It
may, however, prove fruitful to examine the differential degrees of bureaucratization manifested by the Democratic and Republican parties on the
one hand and small radical parties on the other. Despite the greater size
of the former (and this should seem crucial to those who consider size
a compelling determinant of bureaucratization), they have only recently
begun to develop in a decidedly bureaucratic way.[14]

The tiny groups of the left, however, are far more advanced in this
respect. Whether the persevering traditionalistic loyalties to the larger
parties, creating a low degree of succession and turnover, and the much-
remarked-upon high turnover among radical groups, are related to their
differential bureaucratization is a hypothesis worth investigation. In a similar
area, the history of the Russian Bolshevik party is rich with data suggestive
of the role played by rapid succession in fostering bureaucratization. Lenin's
definitive defense of his bureaucratic conception of party organization
(*What Is to Be Done?*) is largely oriented to the problem of maintaining
"continuity of organization" and the need to cope with repeated police

13. Nor, of course, is authority the only means of social control involved in market
transactions in modern society. A recent New York court decision awarded J. Moffatt
$1,150,000 from the Arabian-American Oil Co. for using his Washington "influence" to
obtain Saudi Arabian concessions for the company. "Influence isn't illegal; it's a saleable
commodity . . ." T. R. B., *The New Republic*, March 7, 1949. Similarly, the Lafollette
Committee on "Education and Labor" revealed in its study of labor spies that violence
was purchasable for use by established institutions. Prestige also is available for purchase through modern "public relations counselors" or "press agents."

14. Cf. Edward J. Flynn, *You're the Boss* (New York, 1947) on the bureaucratization of sections of the Democratic party.

arrests of "leading comrades." The history of the development of civil service in the United States (or elsewhere) would also appear to contain data for evaluating the hypothesis presented here. Two aspects of succession in this area apparently deserve close study: (1) the high rate of succession among elected or appointed departmental heads, which is institutionally conditioned by periodic elections; (2) the "spoils system" with its rapid "rotation in office," as the historical antecedent of American civil service.

It may be well to close this section with a caution: No systematic theory of bureaucracy is here intended. All that has been suggested is that a high rate of succession is one mechanism, among others, apparently functional for the development of bureaucratic organization. Deserving of more positive emphasis, however, is this: Since groups possess forms of stratification, it can not be tacitly assumed that all individuals, or all positions, in the system of stratification exert equal influence on those decisions from which bureaucratization emerges as planned or unanticipated consequence. Bureaucratic behavior must be initiated by the manager or, in any event, finally ratified by him or by his superiors. What has here been essayed is an analysis of some institutionally derived pressures that converge on certain strategic industrial positions, compelling their occupants to behave in ways which make them initiate or accept bureaucratic patterns.

6

THE BUREAUCRAT

The word "bureaucrat" is most often an invidious epithet applied to the official who is primarily concerned with concentrating administrative power in his bureau or in himself. In the neutral usage adopted here, it simply refers to an official appointed to one or another level in the administrative hierarchy, without the presumption that he must be motivated to maximize his power, if he is to qualify for the designation.

The preceding section on recruitment and advancement considered selective processes which might lead certain types of personality to seek a bureaucratic career; this section considers the ways in which the organizational role of the bureaucrat tends, in due course, to shape his personality. It thus represents a special case of the more general problem of the influence of occupational roles upon personality. There has been little empirical research on either the general or the special problem. Social theory suggests that the same position may exact varying degrees of adjustment by the incumbent, depending in part on his own personality and the extent to which this meshes with the requirements of the position. Quite apart from differences of technical competence, bureaucrats presumably differ in the ease with which they can fulfil the bureaucratic role. It would seem, therefore, that officials, not initially suited to the demands of a bureaucratic position, progressively undergo modifications of personality. Although research findings are scanty, this has been the subject of numerous speculative discussions. The present section is largely made up of selections which state theoretically derived hypotheses about the effects of bureaucratic structure on personality.

As a preliminary to further analysis, this section opens with the outline of a bureaucratic role by Dale, who describes the range of activities making up a typical day in the life of a middle-level bureaucrat. (More systematic methods for describing the routines of bureaucratic behavior are set forth in Section 8.) The short selection from Mannheim suggests the hypothesis that bureaucrats tend to convert "all problems of politics into problems of administration" and thus develop a trained incapacity to take into account the irrational factors in society. It should be noted that other observers, among them Chester Barnard, would question the presumptive *validity of any such general hypothesis, on the ground that it does not correspond to their observations in numerous public and private bureaucracies.*

The article by Merton starts with the sociological premise that the structural emphases of bureaucracy induce characteristic sentiments, orientations and affectively significant expectations among officials, these presumably varying according to the position they hold in the organization. On this basis, he develops hypotheses concerning the structural sources of the occupational personality of the bureaucrat, and of major types of conflict between bureaucrats and the clientele with whom they come into contact. The case studies by Turner and Davis of selected aspects of the Navy bureaucracy set forth anew the ways in which bureaucratic structure shapes the orientations of certain types of personnel. Turner distinguishes several types of responses to conflicting pressures upon the disbursing officer, and Davis suggests the conditions under which the discipline of the formal organization induces a displacement of goals among officers that lessens the effectiveness with which naval functions are fulfilled.

So notable is the paucity of reasonably adequate data to test hypotheses of the kind advanced in this section, that the relation between bureaucratic structure and personality easily takes its place as one of the chief problems requiring systematic empirical research.

THE DAILY LIFE OF THE CIVIL SERVANT

H. E. Dale

What happens to the official aristocracy when it disappears into its own fortresses about 10.30 a.m. every week-day morning? What do its members do? How do they spend the 8½ hours till 7 or 7.15 p.m., the time about which most of them depart to their homes and dinners on five days a week? In order to answer such questions it is necessary to state, rather crudely and not according to any logical order or division, the main forms in which the work of British government and administration presents itself in detail and hour by hour to the highly placed civil servant. From this point of view it may be classified as follows:

Reprinted from *The Higher Civil Service of Great Britain*, pp. 22-31, by permission of the publisher. (Copyright, 1941, by the Clarendon Press, Oxford.)

1. Giving written [1] instructions on matters submitted to him by his subordinates which he regards as within his own competence and therefore does not refer to higher authority.

2. Writing minutes or memoranda to indicate his own views on matters submitted to him by his subordinates which in his opinion are sufficiently important to require reference to higher authority.

3. Examining, and when he sees fit altering, the terms of letters, memoranda, etc., submitted to him by his subordinates for his signature, or submitted in draft for his approval, or sent to him for his concurrence by colleagues in other Divisions.

The discharge of this function needs constant vigilance: one unguarded phrase or careless omission in a letter which on a hasty reading appears perfectly safe may embarrass the Department for years afterwards.[2] If the document is intended to be an argued exposition and defence of the Department's attitude towards some difficult and important problem, he may quite possibly draft it himself; he will then be called on to display some of the highest qualities of the civil servant—a complete knowledge of the relevant facts, a clear and logical intellect, a simple and direct style, some feeling for shades of language, the resolution to reject arguments which however useful for the immediate purpose are dangerous because in other contexts they may be turned against the Department, and, finally, enough imagination to form some idea how the result of his efforts will impress the person or persons to whom it is addressed, as well as the House of Commons and the general public if it should ever be published.

The three kinds of work already described usually present themselves to

1. "Written" includes and generally means "dictated." Nowadays in many Departments civil servants of the rank of Assistant Secretary and upwards have or can have a "secretary-typist" at their disposal to whom they dictate their letters, minutes, and memoranda. Most high officials write with their own hands very little beyond their names or initials—a great saving of their time and labour at some expense of brevity, precision, and stationery.

2. The only official pronouncement upon human life and the universe in general of which I have ever heard arose from a momentary lapse of this kind in the Education Department long ago—when the Department was still "My Lords of the Committee of Council for Education." I have been told that the clerk to an obscure little School Board was astonished to receive one morning the following terse but weighty epistle from My Lords:

"Sir—In reply to your letter of the 5th ult: I am commanded by My Lords of the Committee of Council for Education to inform you that in Their Lordships' opinion the sexes are separate, and nothing else is clear.

I am, sir,

Your obedient servant,

A. B.,

Assistant Secretary."

This particular philosophy of life is perhaps followed in practice more often than it is openly professed.

(On looking up his letter of the 5th ult. the clerk found that it submitted the plans of a proposed alteration of school buildings.)

the high official on registered files, each of which deals with a separate matter, and is supposed to contain within a numbered jacket all the letters, memoranda, minutes, etc., bearing closely on that matter, in chronological order. But files and work upon them do not fill the whole of his life, or even occupy the greater part of it. His other activities, now to be enumerated, ordinarily take the most and best of his day.

4. Interviews with all manner of people. His own colleagues and subordinates he sees often; but there are also the Minister and the Parliamentary Secretary, who may require his presence at any time, civil servants from other Departments, deputations from and representatives of important or unimportant bodies outside the strictly official circle (local authorities, governing bodies of institutions, professional and voluntary associations, commercial firms, and so forth); and, finally, persons representing only themselves. These last will not succeed in penetrating to a high official unless they are already known to him or have some sort of introduction.

5. Committee work. It is enough here to say that a high official of any great Department is sure to be from time to time a member of committees: he may possibly be a member of two or three at once and Chairman of one or more. The amount of work falling on him personally from this cause varies enormously with the committee's terms of reference, its constitution, and the relation of his Department to its subject-matter. Much more rarely he will appear as a witness on behalf of his Department before a Royal Commission, Parliamentary Committee, or similar body. This is a serious affair if his Department is closely concerned with the subject of the inquiry. Normally he will be asked to supply beforehand a written memorandum stating the gist of the evidence he proposes to give; the preparation and thorough digestion of this memorandum may well cost him and his subordinates many hours of labour. When he appears before the Committee he will need to have all his wits about him. Though Committees are as a rule friendly to witnesses from the Civil Service, they often include at least one member to whom the sport of "baiting the bureaucrat" is congenial; nor is it easy even for a man with a full knowledge of his subject to stand up to long cross-examination on complicated matters by very different types of questioners without saying some things which he would afterwards wish to have put differently.

6. Parliamentary business. From the civil servant's point of view this may be classified, in ascending order of the time and labour required of him, under three main heads—questions, isolated debates, Bills. It takes precedence over all his other work, however urgent. Though thousands of acres may be on the point of being flooded, or the Governor of a Colony may be anxiously awaiting instructions on the line he is to take in the face of acute native disaffection, the Minister or Parliamentary Secretary must have in good time the draft reply to a question in the House of Commons or House

of Lords, the brief for his speech in a debate that night, the notes for a second or third reading speech on a Bill which the Department is promoting, or, if the Bill is in Committee, notes on each of the perhaps numerous amendments appearing on the order paper. If it is a case of a debate, the civil servant concerned with the subject may go down to the House of Commons and spend some hours, from 4 p.m. onwards, in the official gallery on the Speaker's right—a pastime as a rule neither educative nor entertaining; if it is a bill in Committee he may have several evenings of that pastime, perhaps in quick succession.

7. Closely allied with the Parliamentary business, though not precisely similar, is the production of memoranda and draft letters, usually short but sometimes not so short, on matters referred to him from his official superiors. The Parliamentary chiefs of a great Department are sure to receive many letters on the Department's affairs from correspondents whom they are bound to answer over their own signatures—colleagues in the Government, Members of the House of Commons or House of Lords, constituents, men or women known to them personally. Or points may be raised in conversation—a Member meets the Minister casually in a corridor of the House of Commons and says to him, "An influential constituent of mine, Mr. A. B. of C.D., has been much upset by a letter he has had from one of your local Inspectors: I wish you would look into it"; the Minister naturally replies, "All right: I'll look into it and let you have a note." Whether it be a letter or a conversation, the result is that in an hour or two the civil servant will receive from one of the Minister's Private Secretaries a request for a statement of the facts and reasons, and for the draft of a note which the Minister can sign and dispatch to the disturber of harmony.

8. Finally, there are some miscellaneous kinds of work not falling under any of the heads enumerated above. He may be responsible for the whole or part of an Annual Report required either by statute or custom to be laid before Parliament and published; some time or other he has to write it, or at least to revise carefully the draft of his subordinates. Occasionally he may be asked to deliver a lecture to some society or to make an after-dinner speech; he may even be expected to spend a few days at a summer conference. If his subject has extra-national interest he may be deputed to represent the Department during negotiations or at a congress in some foreign capital—probably a welcome change from Whitehall.

On this rather appalling recital of a high official's activities one general remark should be made. They are not by any means mutually exclusive; in particular, interviews and telephone conversations run through most of them. Before he writes a minute or memorandum or drafts a reply to a Parliamentary question, he will very likely have seen one or more of his own subordinates or spoken to them on the telephone, to make sure that his facts are right or that some argument which has occurred to him has not previously occurred to other people and been rejected as unsound; or he may have spoken to his "opposite number" in another Department who is interested in the affair of the moment. During the Session a high official dealing with matters of importance spends the greater part of his day in conversation of one kind or another.

Let us now see how these activities are distributed over a fairly typical day in the life of an Assistant Secretary or Principal Assistant Secretary in a busy Division of a great Department during the Session.

About 10.30 a.m. he reaches his room; it is quite comfortable, with good if not beautiful furniture, including two privileges of rank—a large armchair for his visitors and a carpet. He will find on his desk letters addressed to him personally, and he looks first at these. They are a miscellaneous lot: one or two purely private, some advertisements and circulars and booksellers' catalogues, perhaps an invitation to a dinner given by the Government or by some society or institution with which he has dealings. But most of them will be "semi-official," i.e. concerned with Government business but addressed to him personally because the writers know that a particular matter falls within his province and want to avoid the delay, trouble, and absence of privacy which are involved by a full-blown official communication. The writers will usually be civil servants of his own rank in other Departments, but sometimes friends or acquaintances outside this close circle, such as a member or official of a Local Authority, or the chairman or secretary of a society or institution, or (if the Department deals with affairs external to Great Britain) a member of an Embassy abroad or of the Colonial Civil Service.

After a preliminary glance through these communications and the consignment of some of them to the wastepaper basket on the floor at his side, he surveys the bundles of files on his desk. Some of them he left there when he departed for home the previous evening unless he is one of the few men "righteous overmuch" whose pride it is to leave a clear desk behind them every night; but some are new arrivals. The drab landscape is illumined here and there by patches of colour, from slips of red and green paper attached to the front of some bundles, to signify urgency in various degrees: a file with a cover entirely green means (at least in one Department) that it contains a Parliamentary question. This he seizes at once, and looks anxiously for the date on which it has to be answered; all other business gives way if the date is that afternoon. Usually there is at least a day or two's notice; but nevertheless an Assistant Secretary arriving innocently at his usual time may find that he has an hour and a half in which to provide facts and devise phrases to meet two or three very awkward questions—a task which will often require personal or telephonic consultation with several of his subordinates and colleagues in his own and other Departments. If he is at all late with his draft he will be interrupted by a call from one of the Minister's personal staff, come to inquire when it will be ready.

After he has disposed of questions he will look next at any notes there may be from the Private Secretaries to the Minister or Parliamentary Secretary. As explained above, such notes usually ask for his remarks, often also for draft replies, on matters raised by personal letters to Ministers from M.P.s, constituents, etc., or conversations with them. They are not as a rule very urgent; but every Minister naturally likes to give a speedy answer to his personal correspondents, and there will be trouble if there is any noticeable delay with this kind of business. Accordingly our Assistant Secretary will settle down to attend to it, and also to anything at all urgent in his own semi-official correspondence or in the files on his table—dictating to a typist replies to those letters and notes which he can answer off-hand, telephoning to the appropriate person for the information or papers required to enable him to answer others, perhaps asking some subordinate to come down to discuss a knotty point. If he wants to consult a colleague of equal rank in his own Office, or of any rank outside it, at a length beyond the possibilities of a telephone conversation, he will need to seek his colleague in the latter's own abode. The less urgent correspondence he puts aside for a more convenient season, because by this time (say noon) he will almost certainly have some one to see by appointment. Meanwhile he may quite possibly be himself called up on the telephone several times, or summoned from his room to see the Minister or the Permanent Secretary. By 1 p.m. the activities of the telephone and the demands for an interview with him will have begun to abate; either then or a little later, according to his personal habits, he goes to lunch. A few members of the Higher Civil Service lunch ordinarily in their offices, and many do so during times of stress; but most of them go to their clubs if they possibly can. Nearly all belong to one (rarely to two) of six of the great clubs within easy reach of Whitehall—the Athenaeum, the Travellers', the Reform, the Union, the United University, and the Oxford and Cambridge. A few belong to others such as Brooks's, the Savile, the National, and the National Liberal; but the six first named are the most popular, and of these the Reform and the Union in particular are loud with murmurations of lunching officials between 1.15 and 2.15 p.m. on most days of the week. Fortunately it is not usual to talk "shop"; but of course it can be done, and it does sometimes happen that A. will ask B. to lunch with him at his club or, if they are members of the same club, to arrange to meet him there for a quiet talk on some piece of business. After lunch our Assistant Secretary looks for a few minutes at a paper or book in the smoking-room, or even perhaps plays a game at snooker; or he may join himself to a small group of friends where in the strictest confidence the gossip of the Service is passed about—what the permanent Head of a Department really thinks of his Minister, what a horrible nuisance it is to have a Parliamentary Secretary who "seems to himself to be somewhat," why C. refused such and such an appointment before it was offered to and accepted by D., which Minister's stock is rising or falling in the political market. Not a great deal happens in Westminster and Whitehall of which the inner truth is not sooner or later exhaled among civil servants in their clubs.

On one or two afternoons in the week, he will probably have a committee to attend, a deputation to receive, or at least a conference of some nature at which he must be present. Such meetings, frequent during the Session, are mostly held in the afternoon, beginning either at 2.30 or 3 p.m. The morning or late afternoon is apt to be inconvenient for high officials because Ministers may be active at those times: from lunch time till at least 4 p.m. they are usually occupied by their Parliamentary duties. As I have already remarked, the amount of work and strain entailed on a civil servant by a committee or conference varies enormously with the subject of the meeting and his relation to it. It may be a matter in which he has no very direct interest and he is there with only a "watching brief": in that case the meeting will be to him a relaxation if not a refreshment. But that kind of happy chance is rare. It is more likely that he will be either Chairman, or a witness giving evidence, or a combatant at a conference of parties whose views are widely divergent; from a meeting of this kind, lasting perhaps two hours or two and a half, he will return to his own room with the feeling that he is not as young as he was. On his return he will have a cup of tea brought to him by his messenger; and then settle down, with some hope but no certainty of peace untroubled by visitors or the telephone, to deal with the remainder of his correspondence and with the files which throughout the day have been accumulating on his desk. From long practice in seizing the essential points of written documents, and from previous familiarity with most of the subjects, he can dispose of many of them in a few minutes each; but one or two are sure to require some time and concentrated attention, particularly if they contain the drafts of important letters. Unless he is summoned to the Houses of Parliament, either to see his Minister in the latter's room or to attend a debate, he will as a rule depart to his home (or club) and dinner some time between 6.30 and 7.30 p.m. He will not often leave before 6 p.m.; he is lucky if he gets away by 6.30; round about 7 p.m. is the usual hour at which the high official leaves Whitehall to charwomen, night-watchmen, and resident clerks.

ORIENTATIONS OF BUREAUCRATIC THOUGHT

Karl Mannheim

The fundamental tendency of all bureaucratic thought is to turn all problems of politics into problems of administration. As a result, the majority of books on politics in the history of German political science are *de facto* treatises on administration. If we consider the role that bureaucracy has always played, especially in the Prussian state, and to what extent the intelligentsia was largely an intelligentsia drawn from the bureaucracy, this one-sidedness of the history of political science in Germany becomes easily intelligible.

The attempt to hide all problems of politics under the cover of administration may be explained by the fact that the sphere of activity of the official exists only within the limits of laws already formulated. Hence the genesis or the development of law falls outside the scope of his activity. As a result of his socially limited horizon, the functionary fails to see that behind every law that has been made there lie the socially fashioned interests and the *Weltanschauungen* of a specific social group. He takes it for granted that the specific order prescribed by the concrete law is equivalent to order in general. He does not understand that every rationalized order is only one of many forms in which socially conflicting irrational forces are reconciled.

The administrative, legalistic mind has its own peculiar type of rationality. When faced with the play of hitherto unharnessed forces, as, for example, the eruption of collective energies in a revolution, it can conceive of them only as momentary disturbances. It is, therefore, no wonder that in every revolution the bureaucracy tries to find a remedy by means of arbitrary decrees rather than to meet the political situation on its own grounds. It regards revolution as an untoward event within an otherwise ordered system and not as the living expression of fundamental social forces on which the existence, the preservation, and the development of society depend. The juristic administrative mentality constructs only closed static systems of thought, and is always faced with the paradoxical task of having to incorporate into its system new laws, which arise out of the unsystematized interaction of living forces as if they were only a further elaboration of the original system.

A typical example of the military-bureaucratic mentality is every type of the "stab in the back" legend, *Dolchstosslegende* which interprets a revolutionary outbreak as nothing but a serious interference with its own neatly planned strategy. The exclusive concern of the military bureaucrat is military action and, if that proceeds according to plan, then all the rest of life is in order too. This mentality is reminiscent of the joke about the specialist in the medical world, who is reputed to have said: "The operation was a splendid success. Unfortunately, the patient died."

Every bureaucracy, therefore, in accord with the peculiar emphasis on its own position, tends to generalize its own experience and to overlook the fact that the realm of administration and of smoothly functioning order represents only a part of the total political reality. Bureaucratic thought does not deny the possibility of a science of politics, but regards it as identical with the science of administration. Thus irrational factors are overlooked, and when these nevertheless force themselves to the fore, they are treated as "routine matters of state." A classic expression of this standpoint is contained in a saying which originated in these circles: "A good administration is better than the best constitution." [1]

1. Obituary of Böhlau by the jurist Bekker. *Zeitschrift der Savigny-Stiftung.* Germanist. Abtlg., vol. viii, p. vi ff.

BUREAUCRATIC STRUCTURE AND PERSONALITY

Robert K. Merton

A formal, rationally organized social structure involves clearly defined patterns of activity in which, ideally, every series of actions is functionally related to the purposes of the organization.[1] In such an organization there is integrated a series of offices, of hierarchized statuses, in which inhere a number of obligations and privileges closely defined by limited and specific rules. Each of these offices contains an area of imputed competence and responsibility. Authority, the power of control which derives from an acknowledged status, inheres in the office and not in the particular person who performs the official role. Official action ordinarily occurs within the framework of preexisting rules of the organization. The system of prescribed relations between the various offices involves a considerable degree of formality and

Reprinted with minor modifications from *Social Forces*, Vol. XVII (1940), pp. 560-568, by permission of the author and the publisher. (Copyright, 1940, by the Williams and Wilkins Company.)

1. For a development of the concept of "rational organization," see Karl Mannheim, *Man and Society in an Age of Reconstruction* (New York: Harcourt, Brace, and Company, 1949), esp. pp. 51 ff.

clearly defined social distance between the occupants of these positions. Formality is manifested by means of a more or less complicated social ritual which symbolizes and supports the "pecking order" of the various offices. Such formality, which is integrated with the distribution of authority within the system, serves to minimize friction by largely restricting (official) contact to modes which are previously defined by the rules of the organization. Ready calculability of others' behavior and a stable set of mutual expectations is thus built up. Moreover, formality facilitates the interaction of the occupants of offices despite their (possibly hostile) private attitudes toward one another. In this way, the subordinate is protected from the arbitrary action of his superior, since the actions of both are constrained by a mutually recognized set of rules. Specific procedural devices foster objectivity and restrain the "quick passage of impulse into action." [2]

THE STRUCTURE OF BUREAUCRACY. The ideal type of such formal organization is bureaucracy and, in many respects, the classical analysis of bureaucracy is that by Max Weber.[3] As Weber indicates, bureaucracy involves a clear-cut division of integrated activities which are regarded as duties inherent in the office. A system of differentiated controls and sanctions is stated in the regulations. The assignment of roles occurs on the basis of technical qualifications which are ascertained through formalized, impersonal procedures (e.g. examinations). Within the structure of hierarchically arranged authority, the activities of "trained and salaried experts" are governed by general, abstract, clearly defined rules which preclude the necessity for the issuance of specific instructions for each specific case. The generality of the rules requires the constant use of *categorization*, whereby individual problems and cases are classified on the basis of designated criteria and are treated accordingly. The pure type of bureaucratic official is appointed, either by a superior or through the exercise of impersonal competition; he is not elected. A measure of flexibility in the bureaucracy is attained by electing higher functionaries who presumably express the will of the electorate (e.g. a body of citizens or a board of directors). The election of higher officials is designed to affect the purposes of the organization, but the technical procedures for attaining these ends are carried out by a continuous bureaucratic personnel.[4]

2. H. D. Lasswell, *Politics* (New York: McGraw-Hill, 1936), pp. 120-21.

3. H. H. Gerth and C. Wright Mills, translators and editors, *From Max Weber: Essays in Sociology* (New York: Oxford University Press, 1946), pp. 196-244. For a brief summary of Weber's discussion, see Talcott Parsons, *The Structure of Social Action* (Glencoe, Illinois: The Free Press, 1949), esp. pp. 506 ff. For a description, which is not a caricature, of the bureaucrat as a personality type, see C. Rabany, "Les types sociaux: le fonctionnaire," *Revue générale d'administration*, LXXXVIII (1907), 5-28.

4. Karl Mannheim, *Ideology and Utopia* (New York: Harcourt, Brace, 1936), pp. 18n., 105 ff. See also Ramsay Muir, *Peers and Bureaucrats* (London: Constable, 1910), pp. 12-13.

Most bureaucratic offices involve the expectation of life-long tenure, in the absence of disturbing factors which may decrease the size of the organization. Bureaucracy maximizes vocational security.[5] The function of security of tenure, pensions, incremental salaries and regularized procedures for promotion is to ensure the devoted performance of official duties, without regard for extraneous pressures.[6] The chief merit of bureaucracy is its technical efficiency, with a premium placed on precision, speed, expert control, continuity, discretion, and optimal returns on input. The structure is one which approaches the complete elimination of personalized relationships and nonrational considerations (hostility, anxiety, affectual involvements, etc.).

With increasing bureaucratization, it becomes plain to all who would see that man is to a very important degree controlled by his social relations to the instruments of production. This can no longer seem only a tenet of Marxism, but a stubborn fact to be acknowledged by all, quite apart from their ideological persuasion. Bureaucratization makes readily visible what was previously dim and obscure. More and more people discover that to work, they must be employed. For to work, one must have tools and equipment. And the tools and equipment are increasingly available only in bureaucracies, private or public. Consequently, one must be employed by the bureaucracies in order to have access to tools in order to work in order to live. It is in this sense that bureaucratization entails separation of individuals from the instruments of production, as in modern capitalistic enterprise or in state communistic enterprise (of the 1951 variety), just as in the post-feudal army, bureaucratization entailed complete separation from the instruments of destruction. Typically, the worker no longer owns his tools nor the soldier, his weapons. And in this special sense, more and more people become workers, either blue collar or white collar or stiff shirt. So develops, for example, the new type of the scientific worker, as the scientist is "separated" from his technical equipment—after all, the physicist does not ordinarily own his cyclotron. To work at his research, he must be employed by a bureaucracy with laboratory resources.

Bureaucracy is administration which almost completely avoids public discussion of its techniques, although there may occur public discussion of its policies.[7] This secrecy is confined neither to public nor to private bureaucracies. It is held to be necessary to keep valuable information from private economic competitors or from foreign and potentially hostile political groups. And though it is not often so called, espionage among competi-

5. E. G. Cahen-Salvador suggests that the personnel of bureaucracies is largely constituted of those who value security above all else. See his "La situation matérielle et morale des fonctionnaires," *Revue politique et parlementaire* (1926), p. 319.

6. H. J. Laski, "Bureaucracy," *Encyclopedia of the Social Sciences*. This article is written primarily from the standpoint of the political scientist rather than that of the sociologist.

7. Weber, *op. cit.*

tors is perhaps as common, if not as intricately organized, in systems of private economic enterprise as in systems of national states. Cost figures, lists of clients, new technical processes, plans for production—all these are typically regarded as essential secrets of private economic bureaucracies which might be revealed if the bases of all decisions and policies had to be publicly defended.

THE DYSFUNCTIONS OF BUREAUCRACY. In these bold outlines, the positive attainments and functions of bureaucratic organization are emphasized and the internal stresses and strains of such structures are almost wholly neglected. The community at large, however, evidently emphasizes the imperfections of bureaucracy, as is suggested by the fact that the "horrid hybrid," bureaucrat, has become an epithet, a *Schimpfwort*. The transition to a study of the negative aspects of bureaucracy is afforded by the applications of Veblen's concept of "trained incapacity," Dewey's notion of "occupational psychosis" or Warnotte's view of "professional deformation." Trained incapacity refers to that state of affairs in which one's abilities function as inadequacies or blind spots. Actions based upon training and skills which have been successfully applied in the past may result in inappropriate responses *under changed conditions*. An inadequate flexibility in the application of skills will, in a changing milieu, result in more or less serous maladjustments.[8] Thus, to adopt a barnyard illustration used in this connection by Burke, chickens may be readily conditioned to interpret the sound of a bell as a signal for food. The same bell may now be used to summon the "trained chickens" to their doom as they are assembled to suffer decapitation. In general, one adopts measures in keeping with his past training and, under new conditions which are not recognized as *significantly* different, the very soundness of this training may lead to the adoption of the wrong procedures. Again, in Burke's almost echolalic phrase, "people may be unfitted by being fit in an unfit fitness"; their training may become an incapacity.

Dewey's concept of occupational psychosis rests upon much the same observations. As a result of their day to day routines, people develop special preferences, antipathies, discriminations and emphases.[9] (The term psychosis is used by Dewey to denote a "pronounced character of the mind.") These psychoses develop through demands put upon the individual by the particular organization of his occupational role.

The concepts of both Veblen and Dewey refer to a fundamental ambivalence. Any action can be considered in terms of what it attains or what it fails to attain. "A way of seeing is also a way of not seeing—a focus upon object A involves a neglect of object B." [10] In his discussion, Weber is al-

8. For a stimulating discussion and application of these concepts, see Kenneth Burke, *Permanence and Change* (New York: New Republic, 1935), pp. 50 ff.; Daniel Warnotte, "Bureaucratie et Fonctionnarisme," *Revue de l'Institut de Sociologie*, XVII (1937), 245.
9. *Ibid.*, pp. 58-59.
10. *Ibid.*, p. 70.

most exclusively concerned with what the bureaucratic structure attains: precision, reliability, efficiency. This same structure may be examined from another perspective provided by the ambivalence. What are the limitations of the organization designed to attain these goals?

For reasons which we have already noted, the bureaucratic structure exerts a constant pressure upon the official to be "methodical, prudent, disciplined." If the bureaucracy is to operate successfully, it must attain a high degree of reliability of behavior, an unusual degree of conformity with prescribed patterns of action. Hence, the fundamental importance of discipline which may be as highly developed in a religious or economic bureaucracy as in the army. Discipline can be effective only if the ideal patterns are buttressed by strong sentiments which entail devotion to one's duties, a keen sense of the limitation of one's authority and competence, and methodical performance of routine activities. The efficacy of social structure depends ultimately upon infusing group participants with appropriate attitudes and sentiments. As we shall see, there are definite arrangements in the bureaucracy for inculcating and reinforcing these sentiments.

At the moment, it suffices to observe that in order to ensure discipline (the necessary reliability of response), these sentiments are often more intense than is technically necessary. There is a margin of safety, so to speak, in the pressure exerted by these sentiments upon the bureaucrat to conform to his patterned obligations, in much the same sense that added allowances (precautionary overestimations) are made by the engineer in designing the supports for a bridge. But this very emphasis leads to a transference of the sentiments from the *aims* of the organization onto the particular details of behavior required by the rules. Adherence to the rules, originally conceived as a means, becomes transformed into an end-in-itself; there occurs the familiar process of *displacement of goals* whereby "an instrumental value becomes a terminal value." [11] Discipline, readily interpreted as conformance with regulations, whatever the situation, is seen not as a measure designed

11. This process has often been observed in various connections. Wundt's *heterogony of ends* is a case in point; Max Weber's *Paradoxie der Folgen* is another. See also, MacIver's observations on the transformation of civilization into culture and Lasswell's remark that "the human animal distinguishes himself by his infinite capacity for making ends of his means." See R. K. Merton, "The Unanticipated Consequences of Purposive Social Action," *American Sociological Review*, I (1936), 894-904. In terms of the psychological mechanisms involved, this process has been analyzed most fully by Gordon W. Allport, in his discussion of what he calls "the functional autonomy of motives." Allport emends the earlier formulations of Woodworth, Tolman, and William Stern, and arrives at a statement of the process from the standpoint of individual motivation. He does not consider those phases of the social structure which conduce toward the "transformation of motives." The formulation adopted in this paper is thus complementary to Allport's analysis; the one stressing the psychological mechanisms involved, the other considering the constraints of the social structure. The convergence of psychology and sociology toward the central concept suggests that it may well constitute one of the conceptual bridges between the two disciplines. See Gordon W. Allport, *Personality* (New York: Henry Holt & Co., 1937), chap. 7.

for specific purposes but becomes an immediate value in the life-organization of the bureaucrat. This emphasis, resulting from the displacement of the original goals, develops into rigidities and an inability to adjust readily. Formalism, even ritualism, ensues with an unchallenged insistence upon punctilious adherence to formalized procedures.[12] This may be exaggerated to the point where primary concern with conformity to the rules interferes with the achievement of the purposes of the organization, in which case we have the familiar phenomenon of the technicism or red tape of the official. An extreme product of this process of displacement of goals is the bureaucratic virtuoso, who never forgets a single rule binding his action and hence is unable to assist many of his clients.[13] A case in point, where strict recognition of the limits of authority and literal adherence to rules produced this result, is the pathetic plight of Bernt Balchen, Admiral Byrd's pilot in the flight over the South Pole.

According to a ruling of the department of labor Bernt Balchen . . . cannot receive his citizenship papers. Balchen, a native of Norway, declared his intention in 1927. It is held that he has failed to meet the condition of five years' continuous residence in the United States. The Byrd antarctic voyage took him out of the country, although he was on a ship carrying the American flag, was an invaluable member of an American expedition, and in a region to which there is an American claim because of the exploration and occupation of it by Americans, this region being Little America.

The bureau of naturalization explains that it cannot proceed on the assumption that Little America is American soil. That would be *trespass on international questions* where it has no sanction. So far as the bureau is concerned, Balchen was out of the country and *technically* has not complied with the law of naturalization.[14]

STRUCTURAL SOURCES OF OVERCONFORMITY. Such inadequacies in orientation which involve trained incapacity clearly derive from structural sources. The process may be briefly recapitulated. (1) An effective bureaucracy demands reliability of response and strict devotion to regulations. (2) Such devotion to the rules leads to their transformation into absolutes; they are no longer conceived as relative to a given set of purposes. (3) This interferes with ready adaptation under special conditions not clearly envisaged by those who drew up the general rules. (4) Thus, the very elements which conduce toward efficiency in general produce inefficiency in specific instances. Full realization of the inadequacy is seldom attained by members of the group who have not divorced themselves from the "meanings" which

12. See E. C. Hughes, "Institutional Office and the Person," *American Journal of Sociology,* XLIII (1937), 404-413; R. K. Merton, "Social Structure and Anomie," in *Social Theory and Social Structure* (Glencoe, Illinois: The Free Press, 1949); E. T. Hiller, "Social Structure in Relation to the Person," *Social Forces,* XVI (1937), 34-44.

13. Mannheim, *Ideology and Utopia,* p. 106, reprinted in this volume.

14. Quoted from the *Chicago Tribune* (June 24, 1931, p. 10) by Thurman Arnold, *The Symbols of Government* (New Haven: Yale University Press, 1935), pp. 201-2. (My italics.)

the rules have for them. These rules in time become symbolic in cast, rather than strictly utilitarian.

Thus far, we have treated the ingrained sentiments making for rigorous discipline simply as data, as given. However, definite features of the bureaucratic structure may be seen to conduce to these sentiments. The bureaucrat's official life is planned for him in terms of a graded career, through the organizational devices of promotion by seniority, pensions, incremental salaries, *etc.*, all of which are designed to provide incentives for disciplined action and conformity to the official regulations.[15] The official is tacitly expected to and largely does adapt his thoughts, feelings, and actions to the prospect of this career. But *these very devices* which increase the probability of conformance also lead to an over-concern with strict adherence to regulations which induces timidity, conservatism, and technicism. Displacement of sentiments from goals onto means is fostered by the tremendous symbolic significance of the means (rules).

Another feature of the bureaucratic structure tends to produce much the same result. Functionaries have the sense of a common destiny for all those who work together. They share the same interests, especially since there is relatively little competition insofar as promotion is in terms of seniority. In-group aggression is thus minimized and this arrangement is therefore conceived to be positively functional for the bureaucracy. However, the esprit de corps and informal social organization which typically develops in such situations often leads the personnel to defend their entrenched interests rather than to assist their clientele and elected higher officials. As President Lowell reports, if the bureaucrats believe that their status is not adequately recognized by an incoming elected official, detailed information will be withheld from him, leading him to errors for which he is held responsible. Or, if he seeks to dominate fully, and thus violates the sentiment of self-integrity of the bureaucrats, he may have documents brought to him in such numbers that he cannot manage to sign them all, let alone read them.[16] This illustrates the defensive informal organization which tends to arise whenever there is an apparent threat to the integrity of the group.[17]

It would be much too facile and partly erroneous to attribute such resistance by bureaucrats simply to vested interests. Vested interests oppose any new order which either eliminates or at least makes uncertain their differential advantage deriving from the current arrangements. This is undoubtedly involved in part in bureaucratic resistance to change but another process is perhaps more significant. As we have seen, bureaucratic officials affec-

15. Mannheim stresses the importance of the "Lebensplan" and the "Amtskarriere." See the comments by Hughes, *op. cit.*, 413.

16. A. L. Lowell, *The Government of England* (New York, 1908), I, 189 ff.

17. For an instructive description of the development of such a defensive organization in a group of workers, see F. J. Roethlisberger and W. J. Dickson, *Management and the Worker* (Boston: Harvard School of Business Administration, 1934).

tively identify themselves with their way of life. They have a pride of craft which leads them to resist change in established routines; at least, those changes which are felt to be imposed by coworkers. This nonlogical pride of craft is a familiar pattern found even, to judge from Sutherland's *Professional Thief,* among pickpockets who, despite the risk, delight in mastering the prestige-bearing feat of "beating a left breech" (picking the left front trousers pocket).

In a stimulating paper, Hughes has applied the concepts of "secular" and "sacred" to various types of divisions of labor; "the sacredness" of caste and *Stände* prerogatives contrasts sharply with the increasing secularism of occupational differentiation in our mobile society.[18] However, as our discussion suggests, there may ensue, in particular vocations and in particular types of organization, the *process of sanctification* (viewed as the counterpart of the process of secularization). This is to say that through sentiment-formation, emotional dependence upon bureaucratic symbols and status, and affective involvement in spheres of competence and authority, there develop prerogatives involving attitudes of moral legitimacy which are established as values in their own right, and are no longer viewed as merely technical means for.expediting administration. One may note a tendency for certain bureaucratic norms, originally introduced for technical reasons, to become rigidified and sacred, although, as Durkheim would say, they are *laïque en apparence.*[19] Durkheim has touched on this general process in his description of the attitudes and values which persist in the organic solidarity of a highly differentiated society.

PRIMARY VS. SECONDARY RELATIONS. Another feature of the bureaucratic structure, the stress on depersonalization of relationships, also plays its part in the bureaucrat's trained incapacity. The personality pattern of the bureaucrat is nucleated about this norm of impersonality. Both this and the categorizing tendency, which develops from the dominant role of general, abstract rules, tend to produce conflict in the bureaucrat's contacts with the public or clientele. Since functionaries minimize personal relations and resort to categorization, the peculiarities of individual cases are often ignored. But the client who, quite understandably, is convinced of the "special features" of *his* own problem often objects to such categorical treatment. Stere-

18. E. C. Hughes, "Personality Types and the Division of Labor," *American Journal of Sociology,* XXXIII (1928), 754-768. Much the same distinction is drawn by Leopold von Wiese and Howard Becker, *Systematic Sociology* (New York: John Wiley & Sons, 1932), pp. 222-25 *et passim.*

19. Hughes recognizes one phrase of this process of sanctification when he writes that professional training "carries with it as a by-product assimilation of the candidate to a set of professional attitudes and controls, *a professional conscience and solidarity. The profession claims and aims to become a moral unit.*" Hughes, *op. cit.,* p. 762 (italics inserted). In this same connection, Sumner's concept of *pathos,* as the halo of sentiment which protects a social value from criticism, is particularly relevant, inasmuch as it affords a clue to the mechanisms involved in the process of sanctification. See his *Folkways* (Boston: Ginn & Co., 1906), pp. 180-181.

otyped behavior is not adapted to the exigencies of individual problems. The impersonal treatment of affairs which are at times of great personal significance to the client gives rise to the charge of "arrogance" and "haughtiness" of the bureaucrat. Thus, at the Greenwich Employment Exchange, the unemployed worker who is securing his insurance payment resents what he deems to be "the impersonality and, at times, the apparent abruptness and even harshness of his treatment by the clerks. . . . Some men complain of the superior attitude which the clerks have." [20]

Still another source of conflict with the public derives from the bureaucratic structure. The bureaucrat, in part irrespective of his position within the hierarchy, acts as a representative of the power and prestige of the entire structure. In his official role he is vested with definite authority. This often leads to an actually or apparently domineering attitude, which may only be exaggerated by a discrepancy between his position within the hierarchy and his position with reference to the public.[21] Protest and recourse to other officials on the part of the client are often ineffective or largely precluded by the previously mentioned esprit de corps which joins the officials into a more or less solidary in-group. This source of conflict *may* be minimized in private enterprise since the client can register an effective protest by transferring his trade to another organization within the competitive system. But with the monopolistic nature of the public organization, no such alternative is possible. Moreover, in this case, tension is increased because of a discrepancy between ideology and fact: the governmental personnel are held to be "servants of the people," but in fact they are usually superordinate, and release of tension can seldom be afforded by turning to other agencies for the necessary service.[22] This tension is in part attributable to the

20. " 'They treat you like a lump of dirt they do. I see a navvy reach across the counter and shake one of them by the collar the other day. The rest of us felt like cheering. Of course he lost his benefit over it. . . . But the clerk deserved it for his sassy way.' " (E. W. Bakke, *The Unemployed Man*, New York: Dutton, 1934, pp. 79-80). Note that the domineering attitude was *imputed* by the unemployed client who is in a state of tension due to his loss of status and self-esteem in a society where the ideology is still current that an "able man" can always find a job. That the imputation of arrogance stems largely from the client's state of mind is seen from Bakke's own observation that "the clerks were rushed, and had no time for pleasantries, but there was little sign of harshness or a superiority feeling in their treatment of the men."

21. In this connection, note the relevance of Koffka's comments on certain features of the pecking-order of birds. "If one compares the behavior of the bird at the top of the pecking list, the despot, with that of one very far down, the second or third from the last, then one finds the latter much more cruel to the few others over whom he lords it than the former in his treatment of all members. As soon as one removes from the group all members above the penultimate, his behavior becomes milder and may even become very friendly. . . . It is not difficult to find analogies to this in human societies, and therefore one side of such behavior must be primarily the effects of the social groupings, and not of individual characteristics." K. Koffka, *Principles of Gestalt Psychology* (New York: Harcourt, Brace, 1935), pp. 668-9.

22. At this point the political machine often becomes functionally significant. As Steffens and others have shown, highly personalized relations and the abrogation of formal rules (red tape) by the machine often satisfy the needs of individual "clients" more fully than the formalized mechanism of government bureaucracy.

confusion of status of bureaucrat and client; the client may consider himself socially superior to the official who is at the moment dominant.[23]

Thus, with respect to the relations between officials and clientele, one structural source of conflict is the pressure for formal and impersonal treatment when individual, personalized consideration is desired by the client. The conflict may be viewed, then, as deriving from the introduction of inappropriate attitudes and relationships. Conflict with*in* the bureaucratic structure arises from the converse situation, namely, when personalized relationships are substituted for the structurally required impersonal relationships. This type of conflict may be characterized as follows.

The bureaucracy, as we have seen, is organized as a secondary, formal group. The normal responses involved in this organized network of social expectations are supported by affective attitudes of members of the group. Since the group is oriented toward secondary norms of impersonality, any failure to conform to these norms will arouse antagonism from those who have identified themselves with the legitimacy of these rules. Hence, the substitution of personal for impersonal treatment within the structure is met with widespread disapproval and is characterized by such epithets as graft, favoritism, nepotism, apple-polishing, etc. These epithets are clearly manifestations of injured sentiments.[24] The function of such "automatic resentment" can be clearly seen in terms of the requirements of bureaucratic structure.

Bureaucracy is a secondary group structure designed to carry on certain activities which cannot be satisfactorily performed on the basis of primary group criteria.[25] Hence behavior which runs counter to these formalized norms becomes the object of emotionalized disapproval. This constitutes a functionally significant defence set up against tendencies which jeopardize the performance of socially necessary activities. To be sure, these reactions are not rationally determined practices explicitly designed for the fulfilment of this function. Rather, viewed in terms of the individual's interpretation of the situation, such resentment is simply an immediate response opposing the "dishonesty" of those who violate the rules of the game. However, this

23. As one of the unemployed men remarked about the clerks at the Greenwich Employment Exchange: " 'And the bloody blokes wouldn't have their jobs if it wasn't for us men out of a job either. That's what gets me about their holding their noses up.' " Bakke, *op. cit.*, p. 80.

24. The diagnostic significance of such linguistic indices as epithets has scarcely been explored by the sociologist. Sumner properly observes that epithets produce "summary criticisms" and definitions of social situations. Dollard also notes that "epithets frequently define the central issues in a society," and Sapir has rightly emphasized the importance of context of situations in appraising the significance of epithets. Of equal relevance is Linton's observation that "in case histories the way in which the community felt about a particular episode is, if anything, more important to our study than the actual behavior. . . ." A sociological study of "vocabularies of encomium and opprobrium" should lead to valuable findings.

25. *Cf.* Ellsworth Faris, *The Nature of Human Nature* (New York: McGraw-Hill, 1937), pp. 41 ff.

subjective frame of reference notwithstanding, these reactions serve the latent function of maintaining the essential structural elements of bureaucracy by reaffirming the necessity for formalized, secondary relations and by helping to prevent the disintegration of the bureaucratic structure which would occur should these be supplanted by personalized relations. This type of conflict may be generically described as the intrusion of primary group attitudes when secondary group attitudes are institutionally demanded, just as the bureaucrat-client conflict often derives from interaction on impersonal terms when personal treatment is individually demanded.[26]

PROBLEMS FOR RESEARCH. The trend toward increasing bureaucratization in Western society, which Weber had long since foreseen, is not the sole reason for sociologists to turn their attention to this field. Empirical studies of the interaction of bureaucracy and personality should especially increase our understanding of social structure. A large number of specific questions invite our attention. To what extent are particular personality types selected and modified by the various bureaucracies (private enterprise, public service, the quasi-legal political machine, religious orders)? Inasmuch as ascendancy and submission are held to be traits of personality, despite their variability in different stimulus-situations, do bureaucracies select personalities of particularly submissive or ascendant tendencies? And since various studies have shown that these traits can be modified, does participation in bureaucratic office tend to increase ascendant tendencies? Do various systems of recruitment (e.g. patronage, open competition involving specialized knowledge or "general mental capacity," practical experience) select different personality types? Does promotion through seniority lessen competitive anxieties and enhance administrative efficiency? A detailed examination of mechanisms for imbuing the bureaucratic codes with affect would be instructive both sociologically and psychologically. Does the general anonymity of civil service decisions tend to restrict the area of prestige-symbols to a narrowly defined inner circle? Is there a tendency for differential association to be especially marked among bureaucrats?

The range of theoretically significant and practically important questions would seem to be limited only by the accessibility of the concrete data. Studies of religious, educational, military, economic, and political bureaucracies dealing with the interdependence of social organization and personality formation should constitute an avenue for fruitful research. On that avenue, the functional analysis of concrete structures may yet build a Solomon's House for sociologists.

26. Community disapproval of many forms of behavior may be analyzed in terms of one or the other of these patterns of substitution of culturally inappropriate types of relationship. Thus, prostitution constitutes a type-case where coitus, a form of intimacy which is institutionally defined as symbolic of the most "sacred" primary group relationship, is placed within a contractual context, symbolized by the exchange of that most impersonal of all symbols, money. See Kingsley Davis, "The Sociology of Prostitution," *American Sociological Review*, II (1937), 744-55.

THE NAVY DISBURSING OFFICER
AS A BUREAUCRAT

Ralph H. Turner

Every administrative structure exists in order to achieve certain goals, which goals normally originate outside the structure and are imposed on it from the top. A bureaucratic administrative system is supposed to function as a nearly impersonal machine, individual discretion entering only when alternate procedures are compatible with the system. The ordinary official is expected to apply procedures with blind precision, irrespective of the degree to which they achieve or subvert the general goals.

Needless to say, actual administration often fails to adhere closely to the goals of the organization. Reasons for the divergence may be inadequacies of the procedural pattern and conflicting procedures, conflicting goals within the organization, inadequacies of the bureaucrats themselves, and, most important, the position of each functionary as not only a square on the organization chart but also as a focus of pressures applied by a number of informal structures not envisaged in the formal pattern.

The purpose of this paper is to describe a few of the sociologically relevant influences which bear on a certain type of bureaucratic official, namely, the Navy disbursing officer. Bureaucracy is conceived as defined by Max Weber.[1] Though certain types of influence are more clearly displayed in the position of the disbursing officer, most of what is said will also apply to any Supply Corps officer and, to a lesser degree to all naval officers. The findings are the result of participant observation by the writer, both as a disbursing officer during the war and as an observer of other officers in a similar position.

From the standpoint of the present analysis there are three characteristics which distinguish the disbursing officer in degree from the remainder of the naval organization. First, disbursing officers handle matters of immediate personal importance to their clients. Navigation, gunnery, etc., may be more vital to the lives of the men, but their problems are vague to those not directly concerned. An error in a pay account or a delay in pay day is more quickly recognized and more loudly protested by the rank and file than

Reprinted from *The American Sociological Review*, Vol. XII (1947), pp. 342-348, by permission of the author and the publisher. (Copyright, 1947, by the American Sociological Society.)

    1. *Cf.* H. H. Gerth and C. Wright Mills, translators and editors, *From Max Weber: Essays in Sociology* (New York: Oxford University Press, 1946), pp. 196-244, part of which is included in this volume.

deficiencies in most other departments aboard ship. Consequently the disbursing officer and his staff are under constant bombardment for favors and incessant criticism for their mistakes—real or imagined—or failures to grant favors.

Second, the disbursing officer is a bureaucrat serving a larger bureaucracy of which he is an integral part. Robert Merton has noted the important fact that a government servant is usually superordinate to his clients,[2] not in any formal sense, but because the client has no direct authority over him and no effective access to anyone of superior authority. Superordination and subordination are clearly defined in the Navy by the label which each man carries on his uniform. Though most of the disbursing officer's clients are enlisted men and hence subordinate, a good many will be officers of senior rank who are thereby empowered to reward or punish him in various ways. Thus in adhering to the formal patterns relating to disbursing the officer must often act counter to the larger formal pattern by defying a senior officer.

Finally, the disbursing officer, unlike most other bureaucrats, is personally accountable and financially liable for any deviation from regulations in the expenditure of government funds in spite of any contrary order from a superior officer.

Three characteristics of the social structure in which the disbursing officer finds himself which make it difficult for him to behave as the ideal bureaucrat will be discussed. First is the frequent conflict between regulations (as interpreted by the disbursing officer) and orders from superiors, both of which are supposed to be obeyed. Second is the subordination of the disbursing officer through rank to many of his clients. Third is the network of informal structures, which exert particular pressure on the disbursing officer because of the crucial services which he dispenses. The facilitating conditions for the operation of these influences include the following: the disbursing officer's incomplete command of voluminous and rapidly changing regulations; the ambiguousness or incompleteness of regulations with respect to many situations; acceptance of properly signed vouchers as proof of fact by the General Accounting Office in auditing disbursing accounts, so that certain documents can be falsified with impunity; those personality traits of the officer which resist strictly impersonal behavior.

Within the formal structure the distinctive problem of the disbursing officer is that of reconciling orders from superiors with regulations when they seem to conflict. Orders may be issued by senior officers in the supply department (of which disbursing is a part) or by the commanding and executive officers of the activity. Conflicts with superior officers in the supply department are usually reconciled fairly smoothly because the supply officer understands the problem of disbursing accountability, often from

2. "Bureaucratic Structure and Personality," in this volume.

earlier experience as a disbursing officer, and because of fairly close relationships between them. Conflicts stemming from orders by the commanding and executive officers, who have little knowledge of and little patience with disbursing regulations, and who are generally not accustomed to being asked by a subordinate to discuss the advisability of an order they have issued, present a ticklish problem. If the order seems to be at all important to the officer in question, the senior supply officer can usually be expected to add his pressure, through threats and suggested devices for "getting around" the law. The subsequent careers of disbursing and supply officers can be materially affected by notations which the commanding officer may enter in "fitness reports" submitted periodically to the Bureau of Naval Personnel.

The conflict between regulations (as interpreted) and orders from superiors is not limited to the disbursing function or even to military organizations. The conflict is incipient in every bureaucratic structure because the rational type of authority, as Weber has indicated, involves recognition both of rules and the right of officials to issue orders.[3] Though the hierarchy of officials exists only to administer the rules, which in turn express the purposes of the organization, it is patent that official behavior and commands may often counter the rules. In the small informal organization of a business hiring only a handful of employees, rules may be largely unformulated and procedures passed verbally down the hierarchy as required, thereby eliminating the conflict by making orders supreme. Or the opposite extreme in which authority is expressed solely through a code of rules, each functionary being left to apply the rules without supervision, might be imagined but hardly realized in an actual situation. Because of the inadequacy of either rules or hierarchical authority alone to serve the purposes of bureaucratic administration, both must be present. Thus the ideal type, bureaucracy, is itself a compromise between two ideal extremes, utilizing and compromising two channels of authority which may be in conflict.

Bureaucracies differ, however, in the degree to which they emphasize chain of command or rules. Business organizations tend to vest greater authority in the chain of command, minimizing numbers of rules and winking at violations if the official achieves results. "Cutting through red tape," is the popular phrase for de-emphasizing rules. Government bureaucracies stress rules more strongly because of their different aims and because of fear of abuse of authority by officials, and through civil service regulations functionaries are given more authority to defy superiors in the application and interpretation of rules. Many a former business executive serving as a naval officer in charge of civilian employees in navy yards has been startled to find his orders called into question by subordinates, and to find himself powerless to enforce his orders. As businesses get larger the emphasis on rules to insure

3. Max Weber, *Wirtschaft und Gesellschaft* (Tübingen: J. C. B. Mohr, 1925), p. 124.

uniform practice reduces the contrast with government bureaucracy. Custodians of funds in business or government are more tightly bound by rules and less subject to arbitrary orders from superiors.

In the Navy, and probably in other bureaucratic structures, the intensity of the conflict varies with different levels in the hierarchy. For the lower ranks of enlisted men the conflict hardly exists because they are explicitly denied the right to make decisions on their own.[4] At the higher levels the official is confronted with fewer and broader orders so that in the top ranks the conflict arises less frequently. Thus the conflict between orders and regulations is most acute at the intermediate levels, from ensign to lieutenant in particular.

In business and in most naval positions, this conflict is resolved in favor of the order, the functionary not being held responsible for violating a rule in compliance with an order from a superior official. As indicated previously, the personal accountability of the disbursing officer denies this way out. Consequently, the Navy, recognizing the possibility of conflict, has provided two procedures for its resolution. The disbursing officer is to point out the apparent discrepancy to the superior and, if no understanding is reached, an inquiry may be sent to the Bureau of Supplies and Accounts. Or, the matter may be referred to the commanding officer who may order the disbursing officer to make the expenditure "under protest," the commanding officer thereby assuming full financial liability. The former procedure was used often during the war for minor issues, but senior officers are often unwilling to wait several months for answers and a disbursing officer who frequently resorts to this tactic is soon in poor standing. A disbursing officer considering the second method invariably pictures himself being transferred to "amphibs" and suffering various awful fates at the hands of a wrathful commanding officer, so the method is seldom employed. However, the occasional disbursing officer who has courage enough to threaten its use usually finds the commanding officer unwilling to assume the personal risk involved in defying him.

The very training given the disbursing officer in the supply corps school teaches him that the above methods are not approved ways of handling such difficulties. The young officer is taught that he must be a "Can do paymaster," in contradistinction to the type of officer who is always ready to cite the paragraph in the *Manual* which prevents any particular action being taken. The "Can do" officer can almost always find a way to do anything he is ordered to do. This emphasis, of course, partly reflects a general deemphasis of rules fostered by the war. But it further reinforces the tendency for the disbursing officer to find "informal" ways of dealing with matters and to deviate from the ideal pattern of a bureaucrat.

4. *Cf.* United States Navy, *The Bluejackets' Manual* (Annapolis: U.S. Naval Institute, 1940), p. 32.

The second obstacle to impersonal functioning by the disbursing officer is the system of rank. As indicated by Weber, military officers are marked off by class distinction.[5] And Talcott Parsons has observed that, "there is no legitimate order without a charismatic element." [6] It is the union of class distinctions with a strong element of "charisma of office" which gives the rank structure its peculiar and powerful nature. Senior officers are expected to be treated with deference irrespective of their actions. Because of "class" levels, senior officers are usually able to punish or reward a lesser officer indirectly. However, through their charisma officers are generally held in far greater awe than their actual powers or inclinations warrant, and a lesser officer is often afraid even to suggest to a superior that his request is not in keeping with regulations. One of the problems of military organization lies in the rather widespread fear of superiors which creates extra labor and ill-feeling on the part of men who feel that they must find some way to conform to an erroneous or careless order. Rank has been too widely discussed to need further elaboration here except to note that the disbursing officer, who is at once both a functionary with specified duties and a position in a system of levels, sometimes finds that he cannot act without violating one of these roles.

A third obstacle to bureaucratic impartiality is the system of informal social groupings. Philip Selznick's three characteristics of the informal structure as found in business and labor union bureaucracies, namely, spontaneity, network of personal relations, and orientation toward control,[7] apply equally to naval situations.

These informal structures are of three sorts. Relatively enduring *friendship patterns* weigh heavily where the disbursing officer belongs to the same primary associations as do many of his clients. Particularly aboard ship where a relatively small number of officers live, eat and play poker together in a small space is this true. "Say, 'Pay,' I sure could use about twenty dollars before payday," or, "Isn't there some way I can get flight pay this month?" is the sort of appeal which comes constantly from friends. As a human being the disbursing officer wants to help his friends, and the penalty for brusque disposal of such requests is social ostracism.

A second type of *simulated friendship* or, in Navy jargon, "earbanging," relationships includes less enduring and more uncertain influences. Nevertheless, these are in many cases sufficiently persistent and organized relations among persons to justify the term "structure." They take a multitude of well-known forms: an officer treats one of lesser rank as an equal, he compliments the disbursing officer on the good reputation of his office, he jokes

5. Max Weber, *op. cit.*, p. 128.
6. *The Structure of Social Action* (New York: McGraw-Hill, 1937), p. 665.
7. "An Approach to a Theory of Bureaucracy," *American Sociological Review*, 8:47-54, 1943. Selznick uses a different definition of bureaucracy, referring to deviations from the Weber construct which become informally organized and routinized.

and attempts to appear as an old friend. The aim is always, first, to be defined as a person rather than an applicant in the disbursing officer's eyes, and second, to be defined favorably.

The third and most extensive sort of informal structure is that which may be called an *exchange system*. The officer who assigns staterooms aboard ship finds it easy to get extra food from the galley. The ship's photographer who makes some personal pictures of the supply officer gets first choice when the next shipment of fountain pens reaches "ship's store." Such exchanges are not usually verbalized as such among officers, but the officer who does another a favor has no doubt that there will be a return. However, there also exist extensive and well-verbalized systems for distribution of favors and certain types of supplies, especially at shore stations. The exchange structures extend so far that it is often difficult for a man to secure those services and equipment which are essential to his job unless he can promise some return. Aboard a large ship one attempt was made in the ship's store to sell the limited stock of watches and cigarette lighters on the basis of impartial drawings. Complaints were so many and vigorous from persons who claimed they had been promised a watch or were owed one that thereafter the "spoils" system was used, with much less complaint. Even some enlisted men in key positions, such as the mail clerk and carpenter's mates, are able to exercise influence over officers because of the services at their disposal. Needless to remark, any resort to strictly formal procedure impairs the disbursing officer's potentially exceptionally good position in the system of mutual benefits. Denunciations of these exchange structures are periodically issued by some commands, but such pronouncements are read by only a few and are seldom implemented by more than one or two courts-martial for petty thievery. Furthermore, commanding officers are frequently among the beneficiaries of such systems.

To the participants these exchange systems are widely different from bribery. Bribery is impersonal and is recognized as contrary to law and morals. Favor exchange systems are eminently personal. As long as the system functions smoothly it is just one man doing a favor for a "buddy," and only when a return favor is not forthcoming will the idea of exchange be stressed. And secondly, the exchange system incorporates its own code of behavior. The individual who puts legal technicality ahead of reciprocity is reprehensible, is spoken of with almost moral indignation. The system is not "wrong" or "crooked"; it is a moral system of its own and anyone who puts legality first is a hypocrite. However, there is an ambivalence of attitude toward the system. The official who follows it deliberately and impersonally in order to acquire too great a quantity of goods is disliked, though with a mixture of envy. The system is supposed to operate in leisurely fashion, maintaining the appearance that the goods acquired are secondary to the friendships involved.

The three sorts of systems described operate not only to grant favors to some but to withhold fair consideration from others. Since disbursing officers generally are stereotyped as acting slowly, being tied up in red tape and giving unsatisfactory assistance, prompt careful attention to the business of a client is often defined as a favor. Persons not favorably placed in the informal structures may be deprived of pay because of inadequate attention to their accounts or may suffer undue delay in the handling of their business.

The influence of these systems is felt not only directly by the disbursing officer but also through the enlisted men in his office. Because of their lack of official status, enlisted men develop especially elaborate and powerful informal structures. A new disbursing officer, in the interest of fairness, stopped the dispensing of favors by his enlisted men. A serious morale problem ensued because the disbursing office personnel, no longer able to contribute services, were simply dropped from the status-producing structures, or, as they complained, they had lost their "drag."

Under the combined impact of the informal structures and his formal office, what solutions does the disbursing officer reach? Four types of disbursing officer will be suggested on the basis of their divergent resolutions of the conflicting forces at work. These will be ideal constructs, but have sufficient empirical validity that any disbursing officer should be able to recognize them as applying to other officers he has known and also to tendencies within himself.

The *Regulation* type approximates the true bureaucrat in that he remains impervious to rank, informal structures, and orders of his superiors, but goes further in employing the narrowest possible interpretation of every regulation. For fear of the General Accounting Office his rule is, "When in doubt, don't." He is the stereotyped disbursing officer and the stereotyped bureaucrat.[8] This type is not in a majority during wartime, and consists chiefly of "green" officers who have not yet felt the full pressure of the contrary influences or have not yet learned how easily regulations may be manipulated, and of "mustangs," former enlisted men who have secured commissions.

Opposite is the type who doubts the potency of the General Accounting Office and feels that, "They can't hold me," if money is expended loosely. He will do anything for a friend or superior without debate. This type is limited to a very few reserve officers who seldom last very long, though many officers have sought escape from the anxieties of their position in the assurance that after the war Congress will pass a "relieving act."

On a different axis, and also fairly infrequent, is the *Sincere* type. He fails to recognize conflicts between regulations and orders from superiors and is unaware of the importance of the informal systems. Apparent conflicts he attributes to his own incomplete understanding of regulations, and

8. *Cf.* Ludwig Von Mises, *Bureaucracy* (New Haven: Yale University Press, 1944), p. 41.

rules are seen less as controls than as tools for the execution of orders. He is 100 per cent "sold" on the Navy, is well liked by his superiors and will be assigned positions of favor and responsibility so long as he is a junior officer. His naivete places him in less favor when he reaches higher levels.

The commonest type is the *Realist*. Regulations are seen as illogical concatenations of procedures, restrictions and interpretations, frequently ambiguous, sometimes contradictory, and often, when strictly applied, defeating the purpose for which they were constructed. Rules specify chiefly the papers which must be filed in support of expenditures, and these may be correct without the payment being correct. The most successful career men of the supply corps include many of this type. They assume the regulation facade when the client is not fortunately placed in the informal or rank structure, but know how any payment may be made "legally" if the request comes from an important enough source.

Many conscientious officials join this type when they come to recognize that strict interpretation of rules often works injustice in terms of the rules' obvious intent and that efforts at strict enforcement are frequently nullified because other people know how to prepare papers "in correct form." Such an official begins by helping a client whose claim is payable within the intent of the law but is invalidated by a technicality to give the "right" information to insure payment. Differential treatment of clients on this basis is hard to maintain, so the officer soon finds himself giving such aid without reference to justification, or more frequently, under varying pressures and moods, wavering between a regulation attitude and an opportunistic attitude.

Two general tendencies emerge among disbursing officers as the consequence of orders conflicting with regulations and the pressures of rank and informal structure. One is differential treatment of clientele. Because of the time consumed in extra-routine treatment of persons on the "in," others get summary treatment. The second tendency is for loopholes in regulations to become tools in the hand of the disbursing officer to elevate his own status. Thus he may become more concerned with his own bargaining power than with correct application of rules.

In sum, what has been shown is that during this last war powerful influences were at work on the Navy disbursing officer, diverting him from functioning as an ideal-typical bureaucrat. These influences move him, not in the direction of ultra-formalism so frequently observed for bureaucrats in other contexts,[9] but toward personal functioning within systems of power and status in which rules become of secondary importance.

9. *Cf.* Merton, *loc. cit.*

BUREAUCRATIC PATTERNS
IN THE NAVY OFFICER CORPS

Arthur K. Davis

This paper concerns the sociology of occupations. Within the general framework of the occupational system, reference is made first to Max Weber's concept of bureaucracy. The military variant of this ideal type is then outlined to set the stage for our central interest: some structural strains inherent in military bureaucracy.[1]

Our specific hypothesis is: *the effective performance of the manifest functions of a military bureaucracy requires a certain type of occupational discipline and formal organization; these in turn tend to create inherent pressures toward recession of goals, occupational ritualism, and professional insulation; which in turn may alter the actor's definition of the situation so as to impair systematically his effectiveness in carrying out the manifest functions of the bureaucracy.*

Concrete data for this paper, which in no way represents the official views of the Navy Department, are based on three years in the Naval Reserve as an Air Combat Intelligence Officer with two Fleet Air Wings. Observations are limited to four aspects of naval social organization: (1) the tendency to avoid responsibility; (2) legalism; (3) the Navy as an insulated occupation; (4) ceremonialism. These aspects are functionally related to each other and to the ideal (normative) pattern of military bureaucracy, whence they issue and upon which they profoundly react. This study relates the ideal pattern or "manifest structure" of a military bureaucracy to concrete social reality. It points to unintended "latent structures" which necessarily emerge from attempts to realize in practice an abstract ideal pattern.[2]

Reprinted from *Social Forces*, Vol. XXVII (1948), pp. 143-153, by permission of the author and the publisher. (Copyright, 1948, by the Williams and Wilkins Company.)

1. Cf. Robert K. Merton, "Bureaucratic Structure and Personality," in this volume.

2. The terms *manifest structure* and *latent structure*, credit for which belongs to Professor Marion Levy of Princeton University, resemble Merton's well known concepts of manifest and latent function. In this study latent structure is viewed as an emergent property of the manifest structure. Manifest structure is the abstract formal organization consciously taken as a model or normative ideal pattern to realize the manifest (intended) functions of a group. Latent structure is that structure, originally unintended but prone to become increasingly "manifest" over time, which results from the concrete activation of the manifest structure, by virtue of the influence of other elements in the situation not foreseen or not provided for in the manifest structure. Structure of course cannot be equated with function, since a given structure may serve several functions.

For scientific relevance, participant-observer studies like this one depend on integration with a more highly generalized theoretical system. Empirical observation can thus gain support and validity from the body of older propositions, which in turn it may confirm or refine. In this way a series of such observations may form a significant element of cumulative, systematic and therefore compelling scientific knowledge, though each investigation by itself may provide merely plausible "post factum" sociological interpretations, "proving" nothing.[3] This study is accordingly oriented to the work of Weber and Parsons on institutional structure and to the significant contributions made by Merton and Barnard in the field of large-scale organization.[4]

Our growing concern with such dynamic processes as goal-recession and the development of latent structures points up what seems to be a serious weakness of Parsons' institutional approach—its preoccupation with ideal types which are identified essentially with institutional or normative patterns.[5] On the theoretical level this approach does provide explicitly for non-normative elements in action.[6] These are called situational or conditional elements, and are treated in effect as a residual category. Whether that conception is adequate is debatable: residual categories usually indicate unfinished areas in scientific systems. On its empirical level, however, the institutional approach may be criticized for dealing almost exclusively with the normative elements of social systems and with that deviance which arises from the conflict of such elements. A considerable degree of institutional integration is clearly a functional imperative of any social system, and conflict among institutions is sometimes a source of deviance. But institutional theory is not a comprehensive theory of social systems. On its most abstract level it is at least potentially comprehensive. But as currently used it slights many functional prerequisites[7] which every social system must meet—problems of recruitment, handling frustration, socialization, etc. Action is only partly a function of ideal patterns.

Moreover preoccupation with institutional patterns, by definition the

3. Cf. Merton, "Sociological Theory," *American Journal of Sociology*, L (1945), 467-473.

4. Cf. Weber, *Theory of Social and Economic Organization*, (New York: Oxford University Press, 1947); and *Essays in Sociology* (New York: Oxford University Press, 1946), ch. 8; Parsons, *Structure of Social Action* (New York: McGraw-Hill, 1937), and miscellaneous papers (bibliography in *Psychiatry*, X, May, 1947); Merton, "Bureaucratic Structure and Personality," in this volume, and "Role of the Intellectual in Public Bureaucracy," *Social Forces*, XXIII (1945), 504-515; Barnard, *Functions of the Executive* (Cambridge: Harvard University Press, 1938), and "Functions and Pathology of Status Systems in Formal Organizations," in W. F. Whyte, ed., *Industry and Society* (New York: McGraw-Hill, 1946), 46-83, reprinted in part in this volume.

5. Cf. Parsons, "Sociological Theory," in Gurvitch and Moore, eds., *Twentieth Century Sociology* (New York: Philosophical Library, 1945), pp. 61-62.

6. *Ibid.*, pp. 60-62.

7. This concept is discussed by Albert K. Cohen, "Themes and Kindred Concepts in Social Theory," *American Anthropologist*, L (1948), 436-443, a paper highly relevant to the problem of developing a more adequate theory of social systems.

most stable normative elements in a society, may lend itself to a static and
unrealistic view of concrete social organization. It is but a short step thence
to the pitfall of ideological affirmation of the traditional social order. This
would be unfortunate, to say the least. The danger can be avoided by directing attention toward more explicit analytical formulation of non-normative
action structures and situational elements. A theoretically integrated conception of social deviation and of social change will probably depend on the
formulation of a mature theory of social systems.

THE NAVY AS A MILITARY VARIANT OF BUREAUCRACY. In terms of occupational functions the Navy corresponds to the general occupational pattern
of modern industrial economics. On an ideal-typical level, this pattern may
be conceived as large-scale organization, the upper and smaller division of
which is a steep hierarchy of executive and technical-expert functions ("line"
and "staff"), roughly equivalent to Weber's concept of bureaucracy. The
lower division is a broad mass of easily learned "labor" roles (operatives,
enlisted men), usually classified as skilled, semi-skilled, and unskilled. The
"foreman" role (army noncom, navy Chief Petty Officer) is a subsidiary
link between the two divisions. Executive, technical-expert and labor functions as used here are analytical abstractions. Any specific job usually includes elements of all three, with one predominating. The "foreman" role
alone is a fairly balanced blend.

Our present concern is with the upper division, the Navy Officer Corps,
the social structure of which is highly bureaucratized. A label and not an
epithet, bureaucracy denotes an integrated hierarchy of specialized offices
defined by systematic rules—an impersonal routinized structure wherein
legitimized authority rests in the office and not in the person of the incumbent. Founded on technical competence, the bureaucratic career begins with
successful examination or appointment to office, and it proceeds by regular
stages of promotion, often based largely on seniority, to honorable and pen-
sioned retirement. Salary is better conceived as a means of maintaining requisite social status than as a wage for irksome labor. We do not "pay" military
men to risk their lives in war. Rather, we give them high social status and
tacitly invoke extraordinary service on the principle of *noblesse oblige*. Officers are gentlemen by common consent as well as by legal fiat, as is shown
by their frequent admission to exclusive clubs regardless of their social
origins.

Achieving any high occupational status usually involves a probationary
ordeal which inculcates the requisite technical skills sometimes, and the necessary social attitudes and behavior patterns always. Examples are an Annapolis education or getting a Ph.D. Such apprenticeship devices are often
ritual rather than rational.

The key to understanding the military variant of bureaucracy probably lies in (1) its ultimate purpose of winning battles; (2) the highly "seasonal" nature of combat operations; (3) the consequently acute problem of maintaining a battle organization during long stand-by periods. Sociologically, a Navy is a bureaucratic organization designed to operate under battle conditions which rarely occur. Civilian groups can usually operate in terms of probabilities calculated from their everyday experience. But in military groups the dire consequences of defeat preclude routines based to the same degree on the weight of experience, that is, on non-combat conditions. A Navy can never exist entirely in the present. It must keep in view a future moment which rarely comes, but which must be assumed as constantly impending. Hence it builds its routines on the abnormal, its expectations on the unexpected. This procedure affords a rational technique for war and an equally necessary rationale for peacetime.

The extreme uncertainty of the battle situation directly affects the social organization of the Navy. Size alone would impose the bureaucratic pattern on Naval organization. Coördination of masses of men and material clearly requires those properties of precision, impersonality, and reliability which make bureaucracy the most efficient form of large-scale organization. The battle premise greatly intensifies the need for those same qualities. This pressure is met by an extraordinary emphasis on authority and tradition which also serves the need for peacetime self-maintenance.

The essence of any military organization is its structure of authority, the ultimate source of which is the enormous file of written regulations. Military groups carry the normal bureaucratic stress on authority to its extreme development. It is the function of a multitude of practices—drills, musters, inspections, deference to superiors—to minimize uncertainty by instilling habits of automatic response that will survive the distractions of combat and the *ennui* of peace. Reducing the jobs of officers and men to the simplest possible operations permits rapid substitution of personnel on the principle of the interchangeability of standardized parts. Uniforms and insignia, by "telegraphing" the wearer's status in the hierarchy of authority and his job in the division of labor, facilitate communication, coördination and impersonality.

Against the hazards of sea and battle, a mass of rules is designed for every possible occasion. Men must come to attention at the approach of an officer. This is partly because he may announce an emergency wherein split-second response is the only alternative to destruction. Such a consideration will be irrelevant 999 times, but navies are more prone than other groups to take the thousandth chance as their norm. The other 999 cases symbolically reaffirm and "exercise" the Navy's basic social structure—its system of authority. Both as rehearsal for battle and as a device for self-perpetuation of the organization, deference is an instrumental pattern. Yet its endless repetition tends to build up the pattern as an end in itself so that hierarchy comes to be an ultimate value far beyond its instrumental requirements.[8]

Carrying out his prime function of military command may require a line officer to order men to death. Impersonality is often a prerequisite to maximum efficiency both in issuing and obeying the order; hence the institutionalizing of the "caste line" between officers and enlisted men. Within the Officer Corps the danger from particularism is minimized partly by the secondary caste lines which exist between all commissioned ranks, especially between Ensign and Lieutenant (junior grade), between Lieutenant-Commander and Commander, and between Captain and Flag Officers. It is also restricted by the Navy's pervasive formality and ritual, both vocational and social. But even more important in reinforcing impersonality is the intensive indoctrination of the Officer Corps with the idea of duty—with such sentiments as "Don't give up the ship." The instrument of this indoctrination is the 4-year Annapolis course. On the enlisted level there is nothing corresponding to this indoctrination. Petty Officers have less need of it since they merely administer the hazardous orders which commissioned officers issue.

The military variant of bureaucracy may thus be viewed as a skewing of Weber's ideal type by the situational elements of uncertainty and standing by. Detailed description of the Navy's "blueprint" organization [9] would tell us how the Navy ought to work without always showing how it actually does work. We turn therefore to some concrete material. Clearly our analysis must be far from comprehensive. The limited empirical uniformities described below, since they are recurrent, may be conceived as structural pressures or tendencies—sometimes overt, sometimes latent—subject in any particular instance to modification by other basic tendencies, by local circumstances, and by the effect of individual personalities. Attention is focussed on the Regular Officer Corps. Although by 1945 there were more than five times as many Reserve Officers as there were Regulars, the latter defined the situation to which the others were indoctrinated to conform.[10]

SOME CHARACTERISTICS OF NAVAL ORGANIZATION. A. *Avoiding responsi-*

8. *Cf.* Merton, "Bureaucratic Structure and Personality," in this volume, on the displacement of goals; also G. W. Allport, *Personality* (New York: Henry Holt, 1937), ch. 7 on "functional autonomy" as the motivational aspect of goal-displacement. The tendency of formal organization sometimes to defeat its own ends by overemphasizing the elements most essential to its success is a recurrent theme of this paper.

9. *Cf. U. S. Navy Regulations* (Washington: Government Printing Office, 1932); A. A. Ageton, *Naval Officer's Guide* (New York: McGraw-Hill, 1943), and *Naval Leadership* (New York: McGraw-Hill, 1944); R. P. Erdmann, *Reserve Officer's Manual* (Washington: Government Printing Office, 1932); L. P. Lovette, *Naval Customs* (Annapolis: U.S. Naval Institute, 1934); *The Watch Officer's Guide* (Annapolis: U.S. Naval Institute, 1935); *The Bluejacket's Manual* (Annapolis: U.S. Naval Institute, 1940).

10. R. L. Warren, "The Naval Reserve Officer: A Study in Assimilation," *American Sociological Review*, XI (1946), 202-211; R. Lewis, "Officer-Enlisted Men's Relationships," *American Journal of Sociology*, LII (1947), 410-419.

bility: the philosophy of do-the-least. So pervasive a tendency must be explained primarily in terms of social organization and only secondarily on the basis of particular personalities and local conditions. The "buck-passing" pattern includes (a) minimizing responsibility for making decisions, especially those for which no precedent exists; (b) getting out of doing work (carrying out decisions). Responsibility tends to be passed upward; work, downward.[11] Whenever it is practiced in primary groups, whether in the context of large-scale organization or not, it is generally sanctioned by the primary group as a whole. Sentiments of solidarity together with informal sanctions like ridicule usually keep the members in line. The basic explanation of avoiding responsibility must therefore lie outside the informal organization. It must be sought in the pressures generated by the formal organization or by the situation. Five propositions are submitted.

1. Shunting responsibility upward stems partly from the universal fact that a functionary's area of responsibility invariably exceeds that of his control. No official can direct or even recognize all the complex social, personal, and technical factors operating in his department. Yet he is generally accountable for whatever befalls there, and most strictly and necessarily so in military organizations. For adequate performance and a successful career the official must rely heavily upon favorable attitudes on the part of his superiors. Consequently, he is strongly tempted to slide his problems into his superior's lap by asking advice, requesting instructions, securing approval in advance. And he will accept for decision some of his subordinates' problems to minimize uncertainty in his own sphere of accountability. Responsibility for making decisions tends to move upward. This does not apply to authority to carry out decisions. Interference by superiors in the routine execution of work is strongly resented.

The discrepancy between control and responsibility makes for avoiding responsibility particularly in the lower and middle levels of a bureaucracy. For the man at the top there is no such escape from the strains of decision except by a do-nothing policy.[12] Another pressure on top executives is to find subordinates who will get things done.[13]

11. But sometimes an officer, ignorant of his job and unable to shift responsibility upward, had to shift it downward to his Petty Officers. This was probably easier to do in the Navy, which gave more attention than the Army did to technical competence in enlisted men's assignments. Unlike the Army, Navy enlisted ratings specify technical function (gunner, radioman) as well as rank.

12. Apparently this was the course of the 1941 Hawaiian commanders with respect to proposals for improved reconnaissance around Oahu and warnings of Japanese aggression. Cf. W. B. Huie, *The Case Against the Admirals* (New York: E. P. Dutton, 1946), pp. 92-99. Accession to august rank does not change overnight the habits of a lifetime.

13. Mr. B. Barber of Harvard University has suggested that the buck-passing tendency is related to the great popularity of Hubbard's story, "A Message to Garcia," among top executives. Rowan in the Garcia story was a man to get things done. He was almost blindly obedient as well as strikingly competent. The point also illustrates the authoritarian character of bureaucracy.

2. A second incentive for buck-passing is the latent conflict between authority and specialization. When organizations involve elements as dynamic as science and technology, officials sometimes lack the specialized knowledge prerequisite to making adequate decisions. The temptation is strong to get rid of such problems as soon as possible. The rapidity of wartime technological and organizational changes made for an extraordinary circulation of these hot potatoes among military units.

The two tendencies just outlined are in some degree common to all bureaucratic hierarchies. Business corporations partly counteract these pressures by making status and rewards depend heavily on individual initiative. These incentives and sanctions are less available to the Navy, where seniority is primary and competition often operates negatively. Officer personnel are seldom dismissed, and then usually for offences against discipline rather than for incompetence. "Misfits" are often transferred to posts where they can do no harm. In military organizations the rewards for assuming responsibility and the penalties for failing to do so seem less extreme than in the business world.

Moreover, cost reduction is a constant pressure in modern capitalism. No such compulsion operates on military organizations, whose competition for income is lobbying for a larger share of the federal budget. Lobbying is confined to a few top officers, whereas the cost-consciousness of many business firms permeates their entire hierarchy.

3. Bureaucracies often develop an *esprit de corps* which congeals individual initiative. They present two conflicting goal-orientations: (a) the tangible and intangible rewards for efficient performance in the formally defined role; (b) the informal social satisfactions from harmonious in-group relations, which are prerequisite to (*a*) yet incompatible with the invidious sentiments aroused by (*a*). For the "eager beaver" often appears to his fellows as a threat to their status and self-esteem. Epithets such as "sucking around" and "brown-nosing" operate as informal sanctions.[14] The resultant *esprit* protects in-group solidarity by restraining competition and resists change by intrenching vested interests.

The "sucker philosophy" of the Armed Forces grew partly from this conflict. The widespread sentiments against volunteering for special tasks were tacitly recognized and conciliated by "compulsory volunteering" ("Three volunteers—you and you and you!"). Enlisted men seeking commissions were observed to conceal the fact from their fellows, although they discussed it freely with their officers. Trainees at the Quonset Officers In-

14. These epithets are primarily related to the violation of universalistic norms, but rationalization easily distorts others' success into unfair competition. The "sucker philosophy" is also closely linked to other aspects of naval organization such as legalism and wartime fatalism. It is not a simple function of the conflict between manifest and latent functions of formal and informal organizations.

doctrination School were invariably eager beavers until they got out on a
billet. The zeal of trainees at the Navy Air Combat Intelligence School contrasted sharply with the later indifference of the same officers back for a
refresher course. Instructors without field experience loaded graduating student officers with intelligence publications. But instructors who had seen
field duty advised the graduates to stow such paraphernalia in the nearest
furnace and to carry whisky instead. It was the writer's observation that the
latter advice was the more functional.

4. Structuralized discrepancies between individual effort and reward
in military systems restrain initiative in both war and peace, though for different reasons. The wartime Services expanded so rapidly that they could
attend only to categories and not to individuals. The imputed needs of the
organization at the moment determined the disposition of resources. Most
of the individual's vital interests—his work, friends, rewards, punishments—
were largely outside his control. Uncertainty evokes many responses, including "griping," scapegoating, magic, and religious conversion. Here we
will indicate only its relation to buck-passing.

Zeal could bring undesirable results as often as not. An "eager beaver"
might be held overseas or in rank longer than less valuable personnel. Sudden transfer to another unit could deprive a man of the fruits of prestige
hard-earned in his old outfit. Unearned rewards might fall into his lap. Everyone knew of such cases if he did not experience them himself. Many basic
needs which are major incentives in civilian occupations are furnished automatically in the Service. All this contributed to fatalism and inertia. The
individual naturally sought refuge in his primary-group relationships. If
clique behavior did not modify one's formal situation, it did at least make it
more endurable.

Competitive achievement officially counted for promotion in the Army
Officer Corps but not in the Navy, except for rare "spot" promotions and
for ranks above Lieutenant Commander. But the Army system aroused more
discontent. Its capriciousness was due to (1) the exigencies of the organization; (2) lack of standardized competitive criteria; (3) invidiousness aroused
by competition. And non-competitive criteria (e.g. seniority) drew resentment because they contradicted official ideology. Navy promotions, based
on seniority, evoked less resistance, although the fact that some incompetents
went up with everyone else was disliked because of the implied downward
levelling.

In time of peace unpredictability is minimized, but a ritualism stemming
from minute observance of routine and regulation submerges initiative more
than ever. Military organizations between wars, in terms of their wartime
raison d'etre, are relatively lacking in manifest functions. To maintain their
organization they must fall back on routine for its own sake. Security and

every possible comfort are provided, unhampered by wartime hazards and improvisations. The philosophy of Do-the-least rules unchallenged.[15]

5. The unofficial conception of a Regular Navy career often minimizes assumption of responsibility. Promotions below and to Lieutenant Commander are *en bloc,* based on seniority, examination, and quotas authorized by Congress. Higher appointments are filled by individual selection. Elaborate "fitness reports" on each officer are periodically filed with the Navy Department by his superior. During the war these examination and quota rules were suspended, and mass promotions in the junior grades became in effect automatic on completion of the specified months in rank. The ranks above Lieutenant Commander continued to be filled by individual selection. Despite the large element of seniority the naval career is competitive in important respects, and it thus conforms roughly to the basic occupational pattern of the United States. In peacetime the "up or out" principle is applied to all ranks.

But this is often a negative competition to avoid departure from precedent. If an officer makes a decision unsupported by regulation or custom he is sticking out his neck, because he is officially responsible for his acts and nothing will save him if things go wrong. Deviation from routine may pull down his fitness report and cause him to be passed over years later by the Selection Board. It is difficult indeed to escape indoctrination with a psychology of affirm-and-conform. Minimizing responsibility is simply playing it safe. This is reinforced by the inherent exaltation of authority-obedience relationships in military organizations, by the relatively greater role of seniority in the early and formative stages of the career, and by strong tendencies toward ritualism and legalism.

An apparent exception to the buck-passing philosophy was the Construction (Seabee) Branch. Its slogan, "Can Do," seems to have been a realistic index of attitudes toward work and responsibility. Instances on Okinawa were observed where Seabee outfits consistently volunteered for additional *routine* tasks—a sharp contrast to the atmosphere in the writer's own attachment, a relatively elite combat command. A partial explanation may be the fact that the Seabees were drawn from the construction industry with a minimum of occupational reorientation. They could give maximum scope to the industry's best traditions of visible achievement and ingenious improvisation.

B. *Legalism: the psychology of affirm-and-conform.* This results from the characteristic bureaucratic tendency toward displacement or recession of goals whereby instrumental patterns become ends in themselves. A Navy's hierarchy of authority is necessarily overemphasized because of (a) the primacy of authority-obedience relationships in military groups; (b) the necessity for bureaucracies to proliferate and to refine rule-systems so as to

15. Cf. E. Larrabee, "The Peacetime Army: Warriors Need Not Apply," *Harper's* (March, 1947), pp. 240-247.

minimize role-conflict; (c) the prevalence of the "play-it-safe" attitude toward the naval career. Regulation becomes a sacred cow.

Military systems do not countenance debate about orders. The severest sanctions enforce compliance because of the need for countering the proven fallibility of military commanders with the assumption and trappings of infallibility. Otherwise, the precision and coördination essential in battle would be lost.

The minimizing of role-conflicts in a complex organization requires a clear definition of jurisdictions. Because of the need for standardization, new situations bring a ceaseless flow of new regulations.[16] *Navy Regulations* specifies detailed behavior for thousands of situations. If trouble results from failure to observe these directions, responsibility can be pinned on someone. Against the pressure of authority from above, the sole defense of the individual lies in strictly observing regulations—an outcome reinforced by the endless routine in naval life.[17]

Bureaucratic personnel suffer from chronic status-anxiety. Everyone focuses his attention on his superior, whose slightest display of pleasure or displeasure is magnified and distorted downward. The mildest criticism from a superior is often viewed by the recipient as a crushing attack. Praise may bring an accusation of "brown-nosing" from one's colleagues. To counteract both these tensions is one function of the Navy's extraordinarily emphasized norm of "loyalty upward."

As examples of the disfunctional tendency of formal organizations to overemphasize their main instrumental devices, we cite two cases. For efficient coördination, official communications must travel by the chain of command. In one large air unit, even the most trivial correspondence was routed up to the Chief of Staff and often to the Admiral, then down to the appropriate department for action. Here the reply was drafted, typed, routed back to the top for approval and signature (often refused, pending minor changes) and finally routed down to the dispatching office. Mail which a clerk should have handled in and out in 24 hours was thus sent to the top and back two or three times, drawing attention from eight to twelve persons over a ten-day period.

We cite next the behavior of certain heavy-bomber crews on anti-submarine patrols. Because of their short tour of duty, the infrequency of submarine sightings, and the complexity of anti-submarine tactics, these air crews usually made several errors in the course of an attack. For this they

16. *Cf.* the development of gunnery safety precautions, 1818–1924, as a result of the lessons from fatal accidents, by W. H. P. Blandy in H. F. Cope, *Command at Sea* (New York: Norton, 1943), pp. 159-174.

17. In wartime the predominance of Reservists and the pressure of situational necessities resulted in systematic rule-breaking. This could be done safely where in-group solidarity and/or approval of superiors gave such practices a secondary or *ad hoc* institutionalization. Their contribution to winning the war was probably very great, although there were disfunctional aspects too.

would be sharply criticized by their superiors. Hence arose a serious morale problem. At least three flight crews in one squadron began going out for "quiet patrols" by their own admission. Observing the letter of their instructions legalistically, they flew their patrols exactly as charted. If a suspicious object appeared a few miles abeam, their course lay straight ahead.

Combining legalism and avoidance of unnecessary responsibility, we arrive at the golden rule for the professional military career: Follow the book or pass the buck.

C. *The navy as an insulated occupation.* (". . . this little world . . . set in the silver sea"—W. S.) To some extent every bureaucracy and occupation draws its members into common interaction, though not intensively. But in the Regular Navy Officer Corps both workaday routine and out-of-hours social life are concentrated largely within the profession. Unusual insulation is a structural feature of the naval occupation.

(1) The separation between place of work and residence characteristic of urban occupation is minimized in the Navy. At sea officers are thrown together both on and off duty. On shore stations during peacetime, senior officers with their families occupy quarters on the compound. Families living off the station have many interests aboard—the commissary sells food to naval personnel at low cost, free medical care is available, and the well appointed but inexpensive Officers' Club is the social center for everyone. Whereas Navy families spend most of their time on guarded compounds, other occupations are widely dispersed about the community, subject to a rough class-segregation, rather than a strict occupational segregation. One function of the extraordinary formality of Navy routine and social life is to maintain the requisite professional impersonality in the face of this unusually close contact.

(2) The geographic mobility of Navy families needs no emphasis here. The systematic rotation of duty afloat and ashore in different parts of the world reduces local ties, while the fund of common experience in the same places is a significant occupational bond.

(3) The non-political tradition of the American military further reduces participation in the civil community. Whatever an officer would say about professional matters is restricted to communication by the chain of command. Speaking out on nonprofessional public issues is prevented by the conception of the Forces as nonpartisan servants of the State—a device to avert praetorian tendencies.

(4) A more positive occupational tie is the heavy demand made on officers by social and ritual activities. Formal calls, the extensive use of visiting cards,[18] and similar indispensables of polite social life are legitimized obliga-

18. Even after three years of war the Quonset Indoctrination School included in its curriculum the advice to lay in a supply of these cards to take to the western Pacific beachheads.

tions. At the Naval Academy the young midshipman wisely spends much time in acquiring these estimable proficiencies, the value of which is fully proven when later with his wife he enters the exacting social competition of a peacetime shore establishment. Unlike other professional or business occupations, the Navy wife must be a "lady" with an unusual mastery of the delicate arts of status-exhibition and status-deference. A working Navy wife would be distressing less for her lack of lady-like tone than for her lack of leisure to do justice to the subtle and intricate expressions of social punctilio.

Numerous other Service customs, some of which the women of Navy families participate in or observe, also act as in-group occupational ties—commissioning ceremonies, visits to ships in port, formal receptions, the impress of training and rituals at Annapolis.[19] Above all must be stressed the wearing of uniforms and the lore and lingo of Navy life. A unique occupational vocabulary serves both utilitarian and symbolic purposes. It provides essential nomenclature, thereby setting the group apart in its specialized knowledge; and it verbalizes in-group attitudes, thus strengthening them and performing the same latent function as ritual.[20] Few other occupations are knit by such ancient traditions or by so much symbolism.

The margin of personal choice in out-of-hours social life is much smaller in the Navy than in most other occupations. In the latter one is generally free to accept or decline a relatively larger proportion of whatever social participation is accessible. In the Regular Navy there is a definite pecking order according to the husbands' dates of rank. References to a wife usually specify the husband's rank: "Mrs. X, wife of Commander X." [21] Invitations from higher ranking officers or their wives have the force and often the form of positive orders.[22] Little time is left for social ties outside Navy circles, even if such were desired.

It is possible that the sexual behavior of Naval personnel, wives, and juniors follows patterns distinctive to this occupational group. Systematic evidence on this important point is unfortunately not available.

(5) Another way to indicate the Navy's insulation is to refer to its strong *esprit de corps*, some ingredients of which have just been outlined. *Esprit* is based on common traditions, symbols, shared routines and goal-orientations—in brief, an integrated way of life. The forces segregating naval personnel contribute to their morale and their in-group cohesiveness with results both functional and disfunctional for the system. Strong *esprit* helps

19. Summarized in A. B. Pye and N. Shea, *The Navy Wife* (N. Y.: Harper's, 1942).

20. *E.g.* "all Navy" and "4.0" are approving phrases. "Lubber" and "civilian" connote contempt. Neutral words like "topside" and "scuttlebutt" are solidary influences because their knowledge and use are confined to *the* in-group. For glossaries of occupational terms, see Pye and Shea, *op. cit.*, pp. 308-325; Lovette, *op. cit.*, pp. 207-270; F. W. Cottrell, *The Railroader* (Stanford University Press, 1940), pp. 117-139.

21. See the authors' acknowledgments to various Naval personnel, Pye and Shea, *op. cit.*, pp. xi, xii.

22. *Cf.* L. H. Conarroe, "Buttering the Navy Brass," *Collier's* (June 21, 1947).

the organization to survive battle crises: it has written famous sagas in our naval history. But it also hampers adjustment to the external situation by developing parochialism. The few Regular Officers observed by the writer in two theatres knew little or nothing about the places they visited, despite their global travels. Their experience had been limited to the Officers' Clubs at Pearl, the big Shanghai hotels, the British Officers' Club on Repulse Bay.[23] The Regular Navy is probably the most travelled and least cosmopolitan of American occupational groups. This is a function of occupational ethnocentrism.

Here we may suggest that the three tendencies discussed above illuminate the Pearl Harbor disaster. That bureaucracies are often vulnerable in their external relationships seems clear. Avoiding responsibility, legalism, and insulation of officers preoccupied with professional routine and Navy social life may converge to obstruct adaptation to changing external conditions. At Pearl Harbor the reality principle forcibly reclaimed this self-sufficient little world.

D. *Ceremonialism: the conspicuous consumption of military systems.* If regulation is the sacred cow of a military system, ritual is its golden calf. An essential aid in exercising bureaucratic authority, ritual is symbolic behavior more important for its latent functions than for its manifest objectives. In time of peace military groups more than other bureaucratic types exist on routine. Ritual helps to provide the goal-orientation and motivation needed to maintain organization.

Ritual may become an end in itself at the expense of the organization's capacity to perform efficiently its manifest functions. When the crews of certain seaplane tenders were set to polishing brass after V-J Day instead of repairing seaplanes, the next fortnightly typhoon wrecked many aircraft which should have been fit to fly out of the storm track.

Ceremonialism may be viewed as the conspicuous consumption of power hierarchies. The Navy's cocked hats and swords are archaic survivals which have become functionally autonomous, significant chiefly for in-group solidarity. The 1947 Navy Department budget proposed $97,000 (deleted by Congress) for officers' silver-plated finger bowls, properly engraved for each rank. As he gains in rank, an officer acquires a larger ceremonial due, symbolizing his professional success. Though not highly paid he is a "gentleman," and must exhibit proper gentility. He learns that it is unseemly to carry bundles. Pye and Shea devote much attention to servants.[24] They

23. *Cf.* Pye and Shea, *op. cit.,* ch. 15. In this description of life on foreign naval stations, Mrs. Pye (the wife of a Vice-Admiral) devotes most of her attention to a careful exploration of the native-servant situation.

24. *Ibid.,* pp. 28-29, 33-34, 41, 58, 60, 276, 296, 299. Acknowledging that ensigns and lieutenants cannot always afford servants, they suggest that "it is not unusual" for young wives to cook dinner themselves, hiring a waiter to serve it to the guests, p. 176.

strongly advise owning a car,[25] and name the monthly amount ($30) a young officer should put aside for one. An unusually large proportion of an officer's income must go for uniforms, whereas but a minor part of a civilian family's clothing budget is spent on the head of the household.

One function of differential rewards is to provide incentives for assuming responsibility. Higher ranks receive more deference, better quarters, more money. Another function is to give officers the public status and prestige necessary to exercise authority. So essential is this instrumental pattern that it is often subject to disfunctional over-emphasis. Two cases are cited.

1. Awards and citations, theoretically given for extraordinary service beyond the call of duty, could legally be granted to many persons not morally entitled to them. Under the "strike-flight" system of aviation awards adopted late in 1944, 5 operational flights in areas where enemy action was "expected" automatically won an Air Medal, and 20 missions won a Distinguished Flying Cross. Formerly awarded very charily for heroism, these medals were now passed out profusely. Some strike-flight awards represented real hazards, but about three-quarters of the thousand-odd citations processed by the writer during a three-month period did not. Some strenuous ribbon-hunting developed. The ribbon rather than the achievement it symbolized became the conscious goal.

Among high-ranking USN officers there is a well defined pattern of awarding each other ribbons more by virtue of position than performance. Soon after D-Day Normandy, the Legion of Merit (a fairly high award) was given to a number of senior USN officers in the European theatre. Though many were in charge of rear echelons doing routine work but indirectly significant for the invasion, their citations all mentioned D-Day— the ostensible occasion of the awards. Since senior officers receive a disproportionate share of the medals, especially of the higher ones, awards may be viewed sociologically as a perquisite of high rank. A chestful of ribbons does not mean that the wearer is a super-hero.[26] It is an infallible sign of only one fact—that he is a high-ranking Regular Navy officer. Regular officers received a greater proportion of awards than Reservists did, and officers in general were favored over enlisted men.

2. The "caste system" is popularly used as an epithet to suggest excessive discrepancy between the privileges of officers and men. The epithet indicates a problem but poses it inexactly. Stratification and differential privileges are recognized even by the rank-and-file as prerequisites of any legitimized structure of authority. Hence mere stratification can hardly be the

---

25. ". . . the Navy family usually owns a fairly good one even if the home is a one-room apartment,"—*Ibid.*, 148. For the Army version of ceremonialism, see *The Officer's Guide* (Harrisburg: Military Service Publishing Co., 1942), pp. 323-344.

26. Of course it does not preclude that possibility either. It is not very likely, however, in the writer's estimation.

source of the intense antagonism felt by many GI's toward the military hierarchy.

If differential privileges are necessary to clothe high status with moral
authority, the principle of *noblesse oblige* is equally essential, at least on the
public level, to get the rank-and-file to acquiesce in differential privileges.
Noblesse oblige legitimizes the expectation that the higher the status, the
greater the obligations and the severer the punishment for failing to live up
to those obligations.[27] The rub comes in implementing this principle in practice. Violation of the norms of expected competence and self-restraint of
officers arouses moral indignation.[28] Failure to punish officer violations intensifies the sense of outrage, further reinforced by the vague American
tradition of egalitarianism. This abuse of rank rather than stratification itself
probably explains GI hostility to military hierarchy.

Differential privilege and punishment (*noblesse oblige*) are legitimized,
but differential implementation of the law is not. With minimum friction the
law can favor the powerful, as we may assume it always does, but only while
the powerful do not publicly abuse their privileges so as to make the protective ideology of *noblesse oblige* an unrealistic myth.

This may help us to understand the reluctance of military systems to
punish their officers. A public trial is a threat to the charisma of the uniform
and to the whole structure of authority, because it destroys the basic premise
that the King will do no wrong. Article 96 of *Navy Regulations* shows the
organization's concern for this functional prerequisite: "No officer shall use
language which may tend to diminish the confidence in or respect due to a
superior in command; and it is the duty of every officer who hears such
language to endeavor to check it. . . ." Apart from possible guilt-feelings,
the hierarchy is caught between the demand for justice and the need of the
system for (public) inviolability. The latter pressure is usually the stronger
because of the primacy of authority in military structures. Hence military
organizations resist admitting that an officer can commit a crime, and they
thereby compound the offense in the eyes of the rank-and-file.

CONCLUSION. We may conclude that there is considerable evidence from

27. *Cf.* the 95th Article of War: "Any officer or cadet who is convicted of conduct
unbecoming an officer and a gentleman shall be dismissed from the Service"—*United
States Code* (Washington: Government Printing Office, 1941), I, 625. Also the first
Article of the Navy: ". . . commanders are required to show in themselves a good
example of virtue, honor, patriotism, and subordination; . . . any commander who
offends against this article shall be punished as a court-martial may direct"—*Navy
Regulations, loc. cit.* No such extraordinary demands are made on enlisted men. I am
indebted here to A. K. Cohen, Differential Implementation of the Criminal Law, unpub.
Master's thesis, Indiana University, 1942.

28. Since its authoritarian hierarchy lacks checks and balances, the Navy very
strongly emphasizes norms of individual self-control, duty and honor to restrain exploitation of privilege. *Cf.* Ageton, *Naval Leadership, loc. cit.,* pp. 1-19; Erdman, *op. cit.,*
pp. 263-271.

the Navy Officer Corps affirming the hypothesis stated at the head of this paper. Avoiding responsibility, legalism, insulation, and ceremonialism can be found in all bureaucratic organizations; they are especially prominent in military bureaucracies. Other pressures may and often do counteract them.[29] This study is not a comprehensive analysis of the Navy or of any other bureaucracy.

Beginning with Weber's ideal bureaucratic type, we have discussed the military variant of bureaucracy chiefly in terms of its special emphasis on authority and tradition. These elements require such emphasis because of the situational pressures of uncertainty and organizational self-maintenance. Devices for meeting those pressures were shown to be disfunctional at times as well as functional for the organization. Significant latent structures, such as those making for legalism and avoidance of responsibility, were outlined. Points of articulation between this paper and other studies of large-scale organization, particularly those by Merton and Barnard, were indicated as part of the generalized theoretical system upon which the present observations depend for much of their scientific relevance.

This study suggests the great plasticity of individual behavior in response to occupational discipline. What was it that almost overnight made us all buckpassers? that steeped us in a psychology of affirm-and-conform? The answer—in this case, bureaucracy—may be sought in the structure of the action situation. In industrial society the occupational pattern is a primary aspect of that situation.

Further light would be shed on the problems of this paper by investigation of the following hypothesis: the effectiveness of military leaders tends to vary inversely with their exposure to a conventionally routinized military career. Some outstanding military leaders were men who (1) had had experience in non-military occupations; or (2) rose with phenomenal rapidity through the ranks; or (3) belonged to military organizations newly created or renovated—e.g. the German and Soviet armies and the several air forces. Conventional career soldiers on the other hand have frequently resisted essential innovations like automatic firearms in the nineteenth century, tanks in World War I, the modern conception of air power, the unified command.

29. O. L. Nelson, *National Security and the General Staff* (Washington: Infantry Journal, 1946), pp. 578-580, mentions the tendency of peacetime Army departments to aggrandize their authority, often under the impetus of "pride of place" and unclear lines of responsibility. Such patterns need further research.

7

SOCIAL PATHOLOGIES OF BUREAUCRACY

In a sense, the preceding sections on the fundamental requirements of bureaucratic organization and the structural arrangements for meeting these requirements have dealt obliquely with the pathologies of bureaucracy. This section on pathology centers on the stresses which impair the efficiency of the administrative apparatus, or which violate the values and defeat the objectives of those who have occasion to fall within the ambit of the bureaucracy, either as employee or as client.

These pathologies seem to be of two major types. The first type, which may be called over-organization, *involves an excessive development of those bureaucratic routines which, kept within limits, are functionally necessary to the operation of a large administrative apparatus. For example, documentary records are to a certain point indispensable to large-scale organization, but when these are so valued for their own sake as to be needlessly multiplied and elaborated, they involve a degree of over-organization that gets in the way of discharging the functions of the bureaucracy. The second type is* under-organization. *This includes those bureaucratic ills, as instanced by nepotism, favoritism, graft, corruption, and the like, which, upon analysis, are found to represent failure to live up to the requirements of bureaucratic structure.*

Some critics, adopting an attitude of anti-organization, *do not confine themselves to these pathologies, but oppose bureaucratic structure in principle. This attitude is commonly based on the values of a more simply organized society in which much of life's business could be conducted within a parochial sphere characterized by personal ties rather than by structures of impersonal relations.*

In the study of bureaucratic pathologies, the analytic task is to discern those features of bureaucratic structure, or of its social environment, which induce over- or under-organization. Earlier sections of this volume have in effect examined structural devices, not always planned for the purpose, which curb the emergence of such tendencies, or correct these developments once they have occurred. This section examines the conditions under which these devices fail to operate effectively so that tendencies toward "bureaucratic excesses" get out of hand. One of these corrective mech-

396

*anisms is presumably provided by the hostile response of publics to bureau-
cratic excesses, insofar as this leads to review and appropriate change of the
organization by its staff. A fully bureaucratized society would be one in
which bureaucracies were inadequately responsive to the attitudes and
values prevailing in the society, or were consistently managed in the interests of one social stratum at the expense of other strata.*

*For the most part, the following selections deal descriptively with
major types of over- or under-organization in bureaucracy, though some
also analyze the conditions giving rise to these difficulties. The article by
Dimock itemizes the putative sources of that bureaucratic behavior which
invites the charge that bureaucracy represents "inflexibility, unimaginativeness, uniformity, complexity, routinism, stratification, delay, dispersion,
timidity, unresponsiveness, officiousness, mediocrity, and stagnation." Sharp
describes the conditions under which organizational routines, originally designed as mere instrumentalities, become ends-in-themselves, with particular
reference to the processes making for "red-tape." Gouldner shows that a
wide variety of practices is identified as "red-tape" by the clientele of bureaucracies, and indicates the diverse values which are violated by these
practices. And finally, the selection from Sutherland's work on "white
collar crime" traces the organizational features of bureaucracy that conduce to certain types of corporate criminality.*

BUREAUCRACY SELF-EXAMINED

Marshall E. Dimock

Bureaucracy may be defined as the composite institutional manifestations
which tend toward inflexibility and depersonalization. Any institution may
prove bureaucratic, and since individuals are moulded by their environments,
they also take on bureaucratic coloration. I have purposely used the word
"composite" in my definition because there is an aura or atmosphere which
hangs over bureaucratic institutions, an atmosphere which is the sum of the
parts plus the traditions of the organization and the spirit of its employees.
Bureaucracy is simply institutionalism written large. It is not some foreign
substance which has been infused into the life-blood of an institution; it is
merely the accentuation of characteristics found in all. It is a matter of degree, of the combination of components, and of the relative emphasis given

Reprinted in part from *Public Administration Review*, Vol. IV (1944), by permission
of the author and the publisher, The American Society for Public Administration.

to them. This delimitation does not minimize the importance of bureaucracy as a reality deserving careful study and attention. On the contrary, it can be shown that most problems are brought about by differences in combinations and in degrees, not by differences in kind or by the injection of mysterious substances.

Complexity produces bureaucracy. When life is simple, when interpersonal relationships are direct and institutions small, individuals may be lazy, indifferent, or even slothful; but rarely do you find an institutional situation which may accurately be described, either in the popular sense or in the technical one we are using, as bureaucratic. In a complex environment, however, institutions become large, relationships impersonal, and organization and procedures meticulously worked out, and bureaucracy is a natural consequence. Bureaucracy cannot be eliminated unless the causes producing complexity are removed. It is universally bad only if complexity and size are inherently bad.

The term "bureaucracy" not only describes a given institutional situation but may be used to characterize a way or stage of life. It is the state of society in which institutions overshadow individuals and simple family relationships; a stage of development in which division of labor, specialization, organization, hierarchy, planning, and regimentation of large groups of individuals, either by voluntary or by involuntary methods, are the order of the day. There may be a question as to whether individuals prefer such a system or feel that their chances of success and happiness are as good under it as under some simpler system. Let us not deceive ourselves, however, as to the inevitable conjunction between complexity and bureaucracy.

Complexity is the most general underlying cause of bureaucracy, but there are also more specific institutional and administrative causes. I shall mention these and suggest briefly the corresponding characteristics which emerge therefrom.

(1) *Size.* There is likely to be a direct relationship between the size of an institution and its bureaucratic tendencies. The larger it becomes, the more pronounced is the tendency toward red tape; the smaller its size, the freer it is likely to be of inflexibilities. There are, of course, exceptions to this general hypothesis, because some small ventures are stodgy whereas some much larger ones are responsive. Where these exceptions occur, they seem to be due in large part to the presence or absence of managerial awareness and skill.

(2) *Organization.* Organization requires a hierarchical arrangement of functions and persons. Paradoxically, organization releases energies but also rigidifies them. There is in every hierarchy, therefore, the tendency toward inflexibility.

(3) *Specialization.* Specialization tends to restrict and narrow individuals just as hierarchy grooves institutions. Both are necessary and both are effi-

cient for certain social purposes, but both add to the total number of factors producing inflexibility and impersonality.

(4) *Rules and Regulations.* These, like laws, set forth commands and instructions which persons subject to them are forced to follow. The more authoritative pronouncements there are, the more the individual is bound and the greater is the degree of inflexibility. The common complaint of the exasperated citizen, like that of the irate telephone subscriber, is, "Oh, their old rules! They don't care what I think. They can't make a common-sense decision. They throw the rule book at me." Government by law is the most bureaucratic of all institutions because to a greater extent than other institutions it feels bound by its own rules.

(5) *Character of Executive Direction.* Specialization and organizational compartmentation tend toward insularity and stratification. The thing doesn't hang together; it is divided up into pieces. Only strong executive leadership can weld the parts into a unified, vital whole. But the larger and more specialized the organization, the greater become the centrifugal forces tending toward separatism and lack of integration. When this inherent tendency is unchecked, because of failure of leadership, the consequence is unresponsiveness, confusion, and delay.

(6) *Improper Staff Activity.* When staff activity is overemphasized or misdirected, there is an inevitable weakening of the unity and drive of the organization. My observation is that this situation is more likely to develop in government than in business. The larger the unit of organization, the greater the danger. When the staff function gets out of line, the chief executive devotes too little of his time to operational heads and too much to staff agencies, which proliferate and attempt to run things. We then find dispersion of effort, segmentation, and stalemating—all of them symptoms of bureaucratic malfunctioning.

(7) *Central Staff Controls.* It will be one of my chief contentions in dealing with the correctives of bureaucratic inflexibility that operating heads must be assured autonomy of management and unity of executive direction. Therefore, anything which restricts or weakens the executive's power and responsibility leads to timidity and ineffectuality. Central staff agencies, such as the United States Civil Service Commission, the General Accounting Office, and the Bureau of the Budget, run the constant danger of contributing to this result. The consequence is timidity in the prosecution of operating programs. It requires a high degree of self-restraint and finesse on the part of these central agencies to combine control and requisite freedom at the same time. When their zeal exceeds their management sense, the results are bureaucratic in the worst form.

(8) *Group Introversion.* The antithesis of dispersion is introversion, a danger to which any self-contained organization is constantly exposed. The stronger the group loyalty becomes and the more completely career people

lose themselves in pride of service, the more pronounced become their tendencies to live apart, to seek jurisdiction at the expense of others, and to lose a sense of relatedness and responsiveness. They stake out for themselves exclusive provinces within the larger empire in the manner of medieval feudal chieftains. The self-development of individuals is sublimated to the group interest. Those for whose service the organization presumably exists are looked upon as power blocs to be used rather than as customers to be served. Introversion is the consequence of deep psychological needs of individuals who have been denied other, more normal, outlets for their loyalties and interests. The problem, I fear, is omnipresent. It is by no means hopeless, however, because, like most forces in collective activity, it is merely a good instinct carried to excess for want of better balance.

(9) *Lack of Sales Motive.* The virtue of competition is that survival depends upon pleasing the customer and attracting his trade. This keeps the organization responsive and on its toes. Introversion, inflexibility, and other uncontrolled attributes of bureaucracy must be avoided if success is to be attained. Where, therefore, governmental and private programs must depend upon competition and sales incentive they possess a driving force which guards against bureaucratic excesses. To the extent that this motive is lacking, as in the case of monopolies, police functions, and authoritative programs generally, the managerial equivalents become correspondingly more difficult to provide and maintain. Officiousness, one of the public's strongest objections to bureaucracy, is the evil which must be guarded against.

(10) *Security.* When an individual or an organization feels utterly secure, the sense of struggle which produces much of the world's best effort is lost. Lassitude results. Laziness gradually translates itself into managerial slothfulness, one of bureaucracy's worst faults. The point beyond which security is transformed from a good to an evil is one of society's most difficult problems of incentive and one of management's perennial brain-teasers. The career service aspect of the civil service, leading to what British writers call civil service mentality, provides a pivotal difficulty of bureaucracy. Security means lack of struggle, which in turn produces tameness and docility. Work performed under these conditions requires more workers than where employees have verve. Moreover, the executive difficulties are incomparably more trying.

(11) *Seniority.* The head of one of America's largest business bureaucracies once said to me, "If big business ever fails it will probably be due to the deadening effect of seniority more than to anything else." I have no doubt that he did not exaggerate. An inexorable seniority system is security at its worst. It disregards individual superiorities, unusual combinations of skill, superior effort, all the springs of capacity which keep enterprise from ossifying and finally dying by inches. I realize that the managerial problems

are intricate and numerous and that the "B" men must be energized as well as the rare bird who has executive genius. But the problem must be solved. Otherwise, complexity will dull our intellects and efforts and we will be engulfed by the inert monsters of our witlessness. If bureaucracy is not to mean a dull mediocrity, management people must accept the challenge and prove their contriving capacity.

(12) *Age and Tradition.* The influence of hoary age on institutional functioning is a factor which probably ranks with complexity and size in explaining bureaucracy. The older an institution becomes, the more settled its mould and procedures are likely to be. Traditions are hallowed. Ways of doing things take on a reverence which defies successful change, even when they may have been quite accidental in the first place or when better methods have since been discovered. Institutions are conservative in the extreme. They seem to have a life of their own after they have been in existence for some time; it is as though they were the collective embodiment of all those devoted souls who have gone before. The older they are, the more unshakable are their halos. The sacred cows may be the cheapest of clay, but to the inheritors they are the purest of metal. An all-consuming smugness settles down over the landscape, like a London fog which stops traffic and penetrates every keyhole. The institution is stronger than the men. The executive must conform with becoming propriety or be politely but effectively shunted aside. Age is the quintessence of bureaucracy. Bold and capable is the man who can rebuild the ivy-covered edifice to a modern design, peel off some of its outer layers of complacency, and infuse a new life into it.

If I have adverted to some of the socially undesirable aspects of bureaucracy, it is only to call attention to the fact that with the good and necessary we must also expect some bad elements needing correction by administrative contrivance. I have also tried to show that the popular conception of bureaucracy is not unrelated to the technical analysis of the institutional problem. If the public calls attention to inflexibility, unimaginativeness, uniformity, complexity, routinism, stratification, delay, dispersion, timidity, unresponsiveness, officiousness, mediocrity, and stagnation, it is because we management people allow a good and necessary thing—the ordering of institutional life, which we call bureaucracy—to get out of hand. It would be foolish and shortsighted to dismiss the public's characterizations as merely the parroting of propaganda designed to win political wars. No, there is a direct connection between cause and complaint, between scientific analysis and public parlance. Our job as institutional management people is to see that a good thing is not run into the ground, that correctives are applied where they are needed, and that forces are rerouted where necessary into socially approved ends.

The causes of bureaucracy discussed above can be grouped in several different ways. In a former study in which I participated, a twofold classi-fication was employed—structural and personnel factors.[1] This classification is fairly inclusive, but it does not provide adequately for the socio-biological elements of age and complexity. Within the compass of this paper, there-fore, I expect to delve into this aspect of the matter, to call attention to some managerial contrivances which executives may wish to consider, not attempting to deal with the human problems except in passing reference, and to conclude with a thumbnail sketch of a positive emphasis suggested for the federal government. Until an organization settles down and people get used to working with each other, the institution cannot be expected to be efficient. . . . In order to secure smoothness and efficiency of operation, the organization must operate in a groove, but it must not be permitted to get into a rut. There is a distinction, and it is an important one. An organ-ization must have fixed and established ways of carrying on its business, but it dare not lose its flexibility and its responsiveness to human desires and expectations. Institutional inflexibility may be compared with hardening of the arteries. As a rule, it develops over a long period of time, and the pre-vention of the affliction therefore goes back to the early life of the organ-ism and is not merely a matter of controlling the ravages of old age. The executive who would prevent institutional resistances and managerial inflex-ibilities when the enterprise becomes old and established must be aware of the causes from which such difficulties develop and be on guard against them from his earliest days with the enterprise. The causes of institutional inflexibility, their early diagnosis, and the measures which must be put into effect by management to obviate them are all matters about which, unfor-tunately, we know far too little at this time. As institutions become increas-ingly larger and society becomes increasingly complex, it is only reasonable to expect that institutional morphology will become one of the most im-portant fields of knowledge.

When people work together in an organization, they come to have com-mon understandings, prejudices, appreciations, loyalties, and outlooks simi-lar to those of the members of a family. They have a feeling of identity and exceptionalness which sets them apart from others. They think in terms of "ourselves" and "others." They have an awareness that the interests of the program and the symbols which are identified with it are larger and more important than the interests of any one person connected with the organiza-tion. They tend to depersonalize their interests and affections and to con-centrate them upon symbols which represent programs of one kind or an-other—money-making, construction, education, government, welfare, reli-gion. In this group spirit which develops, subtleties exist which are not per-ceptible to the outsider. The longer the members of the enterprise work

1. *Bureaucracy and Trusteeship in Large Corporations*, Monograph No. 11. Tem-porary National Economic Committee (U.S. Government Printing Office, 1940).

together, the more complete their mutual understanding, and the more pronounced their common likes and dislikes, the more subtle become the nuances of meaning conveyed by their words and actions.

One of the reasons that institutional resistances are found characteristically in bureaucratic organizations is that the communications system among the oldtimers is so subtle and effective that newcomers who are attempting to manipulate the organization ultimately feel that they are fencing with shadow men. One of the problems of the executive who is responsible for policy is that his program must be carried out through the instrumentality of professional workers who are members of a hierarchy in which the signals are understood by everyone and the subtleties of understanding are such that the top executive finds it difficult to know what is going on in the minds of his workers. The consequence is that the workers frequently resist particular policies and programs, perhaps more or less unconsciously, and the executive finds himself powerless to cope effectively with the situation.

This subtle resistance is particularly likely to be encountered in a governmental program where the bulk of the employees are civil servants who have come up through the ranks and only the top level of the organization is brought in from the outside for policy decision and executive direction. The situation which results is one of the as yet unsolved problems of government. The policy official is theoretically the boss, but actually he is at the mercy of a permanent bureaucracy. He can accomplish only as much as it is willing that he should accomplish. I do not mean to suggest that extra amounts of energy put forth by the executive and differences of personality and appeal are without significance in determining the results which are achieved. It is quite obvious that they are influential. What I do suggest, however, is that, compared with the power of bureaucracy to determine how much will be accomplished, the influence of policy officials is quite disproportionate.

As a general rule, the policy official comes into the enterprise with a feeling that about 50 per cent of what has been the established procedure must be changed, and he proceeds to insist that these changes be made, even without adequate investigation. It is obvious that the amount of change which is necessary varies within various programs, but, generally speaking, the necessity of change in the eyes of the career officials is nearer, say, 10 per cent than 50 cent, and hence, consciously or unconsciously, there is an understanding on the part of the career officials that they will support so-called reforms up to the extent of their 10 per cent, but not beyond.

The technique of feigned acquiescence is one of the indispensable tools of the career official. If his advice is asked—and all too frequently it is not— he tries to give what he considers an honest reply which will be for the benefit of the long-range program and of the policy official then in authority. If the advice of the "organization" is not asked, then naturally there is an almost instantaneous and automatic resistance to any program that is forced upon it in this manner. Even when consultation does taken place, if it is the opinion of the career officials that the suggested reforms will have an injurious effect upon the prestige and reputation of the service, they try, consciously or unconsciously, to balk the program which to them seems to be mistaken. They do this by giving outward acquiescence and cooperation while actually slowing down the reform or killing it entirely. There are several established ways of accomplishing this result. One—perhaps the most common—is dilatory tactics. The career officials promise to do what the policy official directs, but at each stage in the hierarchy there is a progressively longer delay in actually taking the necessary steps. When the policy official becomes exasperated because of the delay, as he usually does, the career officials rely upon buck-passing or upon a variety of excuses. One standard excuse is inadequacy of personnel; another is the press of work which makes it necessary to give attention to a large variety of factors, with the result that the organization is unable to concentrate upon the one to which the policy official is determined to give priority.

If the program involves legislation, the career officials may talk confidentially with members of the legislature with whom over a period of years they have developed a close relationship and explain frankly to them the difference of viewpoint between the temporary policy official and the long-term interest of the institution, and in consequence they may get support from that quarter. As a general rule, the relationships of the higher career officials to the older members of the legislature are so much closer and more intimate than those of the policy official that they have a considerable advantage over him in this respect. Moreover, the older members of the legislature have a great deal in common with the permanent members of the bureaucracy, because in both cases they are influenced primarily by institutional considerations, and hence when the career officials of the executive departments are able to convince the members of the legislature that a proposed program would have an injurious effect upon the prestige of the service which would extend almost indefinitely, far beyond the anticipated life of the administration in power, they usually secure a sympathetic response from the career members of the legislature.

The baffling thing about institutional resistances is that they are so subtle and elusive that it is next to impossible for the policy officials to spot all the points at which the slowing-down process is occurring. Permanent bureaucracy is amorphous. It is as though each person has his finger pointed at the next person; the group as a whole is responsible, and no one individual can be pinned down. Contrariwise, when the "organization" is very much in favor of a new program and sees in it an opportunity to increase the prestige, influence, size, and importance of the program with which its life and fortunes are identified, there is the same kind of groundswell which makes it difficult to put one's finger on any one individual or on any one point in explaining why the response is so instantaneous. It is this kind of institutional behavior, sometimes manifesting itself in the form of resistance and obstructiveness and sometimes in the form of whole-hearted response, which leads one to speak of the inner life of bureaucratic organizations as being a force which is greater than the sum total of the obviously constituent elements. It is based upon long-established understandings, nuances, ways of doing things; it is based upon an appreciation of what constitutes the long-range interests of the career group.

The individual members of the bureaucracy realize that the institution is more important than any one part, that the work will go on even after they are retired, and that their individual interests are directly connected with the prestige and influence of the program as a whole. They can afford to take chances of incurring the displeasure of the policy official because the stakes are so large and they know that they will receive the support of their fellows if they make a sacrifice on behalf of what is considered the greater good of the greater number. If the career officials are skilled in these techniques, as usually they are, there is at no time any action which can be called outright disloyalty or open insubordination. The resistance is far more subtle and difficult to get at.

It is this force which almost without exception alters the attitude and the demeanor of policy officials after they have been in office for a relatively short time. The policy official soon learns that the new broom should be put in the closet. He learns that, if he is to be at all effective, he must woo and win the career officials; instead of acting superior to them, issuing peremptory orders to them, he consults them more and more. Instead of appealing to them in terms of policies and programs and the administration in power, he places the emphasis upon the long-range interests of the bureaucracy. In a word, he appeals to the self-interest of the career officials and to their pride in the program to which they have devoted their lives. So far as possible, he attempts to identify himself with their interests, assumptions, and objectives. In other words, he has learned that without their support he is powerless; that anything he accomplishes will be with their active help and not in spite of their opposition.

Because of the gulf which exists between the bureaucracy and the policy official brought in from the outside, some students of government have advocated that all the positions in an organization, including that of the policy official, should be occupied by career officials. They argue that only in this way is it possible to achieve that unity of management and program which is necessary to secure outstanding results. This argument is certainly valid so far as obtaining identity of viewpoint and of interest is concerned. However, it overlooks important social and institutional considerations which need to be taken into the reckoning. One of these is the inherent tendency of bureaucracy, if left to its own devices, to get into a groove and to grind the groove so deeply that a rut is created, to develop along a given line and to lose the ability to change direction, to lose all the flexibility and resiliency which are necessary if an institution is to adapt itself to changing forces and circumstances. The effect of routine is the same as that of the chronic use of sedatives. It makes thinking unnecessary and hence impossible. It makes the means the all-important consideration, with the result that the end is progressively lost sight of. It makes the internal life of the mechanism the predominant factor and not the interests and welfare of the outside public which, presumably, is being served. It is the institutional equivalent of introspection on the part of individuals. It leads to insensitivity and complacency. It is the path of least resistance. It has all the dulling effects of complete security, from which struggle and competition have been entirely eliminated.

Now, if one desires a society in which these characteristics are sought, then the multiplication of bureaucratic situations is a policy which will produce that result. If, on the other hand, the opposite of introspection, complacency, grooving, inflexibility, and insensitivity is what we wish to achieve in our social order, then clearly steps must be taken to discourage the inherent characteristics which produce bureaucracy. An institution tends to take on the character of its leadership. If the leadership is bureaucratic, the institution will become progressively bureaucratic also. If the leadership has a fresh viewpoint and one that is attuned to social forces and social change, then there is at least hope of carrying the bureaucracy along with it.

Pursuing this line of reasoning, therefore, we are led to the conclusion that if bureaucracy is not to have a monopoly of all positions, including policy positions, the logical alternative is to increase the influence of the policy officials vis-à-vis the career officials; and this obviously requires a larger number of them in strategic positions. The number of executive officials should be in direct ratio to the weight of the permanent career service. I am convinced that this policy is more desirable than the alternative, and that this reform is one of the most necessary in all types of institutional life, and particularly in the field of government.

PROCEDURAL VICES: LA PAPERASSERIE

Walter Rice Sharp

Every large-scale organization controlled from a single center sooner or later finds it advisable to elaborate systematic routine procedures in the interest of fiscal regularity and operational consistency. Private business corporations are no more immune to this process than are government departments. Nor do routine procedures necessarily slow up staff decisions. On the contrary, if they are properly adapted to the daily problems of the enterprise, they expedite action.

An organization conforming closely to the hierarchical principle, however, faces the constant danger that these routine operations will become sterilizing ends in themselves rather than effective means to desirable ends. When this happens the usual result is an entanglement of "red tape," or as the French are wont to call it, *la paperasserie, mere* routine thereby becoming *bad* routine. Formal instructions issued at the center overwhelm those who have to handle out on the circumference concrete situations unforeseen in their variety. Almost inevitably an adequate delegation of discretion to subordinate officials is missing in such a system and the field agent stationed on the administrative firing line stands helpless before demands for prompt decision or immediate action. The fact that every case must be "referred" somewhere means a postponement of any decision about it, the more circuitous the course of reference, the greater the delay.

In a nationally centralized bureaucracy an excess of red tape may become a notorious curse. The social pathologist would probably denominate it a veritable institutional disease. For more than a century French critics have themselves been the first to recognize this paralyzing attribute of their national administrative organism. Some of the most vivid passages in Balzac's *Les Employés* are devoted to the abominations of official *paperasserie*.[1] As one among many *litterateurs* Courteline gives us a most colorful recent satire on it. Nearly every serious commentary on French public affairs castigates it for its sterilizing effects upon the economic and social development of the country. The indictment presented by M. Henri Chardon in

Reprinted from *The French Civil Service: Bureaucracy in Transition*, pp. 446-450 (New York: The Macmillan Company, 1931), by permission of the author.

1. Here are two of Balzac's most picturesque passages:

"Dossiers, cartons, papers in support of documents without which France would be lost, the circular without which things could not move, accumulate and embellish (every office)," p. 18. "A tall man could only with difficulty walk along these tortuous pathways, or bend over, or climb up, or lose himself in the morass," p. 19.

his brilliant essay entitled, *Le Pouvoir administratif*, is devastating. All branches of the public service, says M. Chardon, are organized and staffed so as "to produce words, papers, inaction. No technical consideration directs their efforts; instead, there is an intricate network of routine mechanisms; constant dissipation of forces; chains of costly links, on which business stagnates as successive verifications pile up; men consider, then reconsider; men verify, then re-verify or counter-verify; the least discrepancy gives rise to doubt, to supplementary inquiries, to commentaries, to pointless arid discussions. Meanwhile, the interested party languishes from chagrin or hunger, happy when he is not congealed in the process."

In another essay by the same author specific counts in support of this sweeping indictment are submitted. To build a new bridge in place of one palpably unsafe, twenty distinct administrative steps were necessary, with the result that it took fifteen to eighteen months to initiate construction. The re-alignment of a highway required nineteen different steps. In the Ministry of Public Works, continues M. Chardon, the simplest matters must pass and repass three or four times through each bureau while numerous other agencies like the P. T. T., the Division of Indirect Taxes, and the artillery service usually have to be consulted, always by the "hierarchical" route. Twenty persons often collaborate in preparing a single *dossier*. "You may request authorization to plant a hedge in the spring, but it will not reach you before the first frosts of winter!" "The capable engineer in the field fights in vain against a system which dissipates his nervous force and mental energy; sooner or later, it is never long, he is broken, while all around him they continue to superimpose authorities, to erect controls, and to reveal an inexhaustible ingenuity for creating useless services which grow thereafter like mushrooms."

Or take *L'Europe nouvelle's* damaging characterization of the Division of Registrations and Stamps in the Treasury as it operated as late as 1927: [2]

". . . Centralization continues unabated, bogging the functioning of a service already heavily burdened. Responsibility is diluted and scarcely exists except for these maladroit subordinate employees who do not know how to shift it in time to their immediate superiors, the latter relieving themselves by passing it still higher until it disappears in the anonymous bureaus at division headquarters. This centralization checks initiative, which is so important, and at the same time retards, often for months, the solution of affairs that the field agent might frequently have settled in little or no time if he had had a more extended power of decision."

Or consider the post office again: Mr. Ford Madox Ford relates his adventures in trying to trace a postal money order gone astray. When this occurs, the usual course is to take the matter up through official channels, give the postman a big tip, or put the case into the hands of "an adviser of

2. In the oft-cited issue of 26 March, 1927.

public companies." On this occasion, however, Mr. Ford decided to go directly to the *Direction de la Seine des P. T. T.* on the Boulevard Montparnasse. At two o'clock he was ushered into the Director's office by a smiling charwoman. After a half hour the Director returned from lunch and scrutinized the documents with great care. Following further consultation with an official in a blue uniform, the Director announced that Ford should betake himself to the "Chief Sub-office for the Recovery of Money Orders" on the other side of Paris. There he was directed to Room V on the sixth floor. While he conversed with an attractive young woman for an hour about face powders and the like, her chief examined the papers and asked questions about Ford's war record and family, finally instructing him to return to the Boulevard Montparnasse, this time to Room XVI on the third floor. From there he was sent back to Room XI in the Chief Sub-office; thence to Room IV, Boulevard Montparnasse; next to Room III, Chief Sub-office; and finally to the "open sesame"—Room XIII, on Montparnasse. Although assured there that he would receive his money by the first delivery the following day, it actually arrived seven weeks later, only after a generous tip had been showered upon the postman.

Any foreigner who, like the writer, has undergone the vicissitudes of securing and using a French *carte d'identité* will hardly be disposed to regard Mr. Ford's story as an exaggerated or isolated episode. Every few days one hears similar tales not only from visitors unused to the idiosyncrasies of public *fonctionnaires*, but from native-born citizens accustomed from childhood to the devious modes of handling simple administrative matters. As one amusing example, a French friend of mine told me how in his native town in the Midi it was not uncommon to hear of taxpayers having to purchase government-stamped paper costing fifty centimes with which to pay a tax of ten centimes! To complain about the mysterious intricacies of official forms seems a patriotic obligation for Frenchmen. To request information from a government bureau and expect to get what one asks for within a reasonable time would be going counter to the prevalent *moeurs* of the Third Republic. The consecrated formula with which official replies to such requests are begun, *"je m'empresse de vous faire pouvenir,"* et cetera . . . would be ironical if it were not so often the concomitant of exasperation provoked by delays in receiving the answer or by the incompleteness or inaccuracy of the information it conveys.[3] While gladly recognizing the generous courtesy shown him by most high officials in his repeated requests for data on departmental personnel policies, the present

3. A new staff employee, upon going into certain ministries, has to consult fifty volumes or more of uncodified official bulletins and several shelves of green cartons in order to locate the regulations governing the department. *Cf.* Moufflet, *Revue générale d'Administration*, March-April 1930.

investigator more than once had the experience of having to follow up a simple request for an interview or some readily available document a second or third time before eliciting a response.[4] In two instances his inquiry became completely lost in the process of being transmitted from one ministerial bureau to another.[5]

4. It took, for example, ten months of courteous but persistent follow-up to obtain a reply to a simple questionnaire submitted to the *Direction de l'Enseignement supérieur* of the Ministry of Public Instruction. It is in order to point out, however, that inquiries originating with the American Embassy usually elicited a somewhat more expeditious initial response than those which were "unofficial" in character.
5. It was explained in one of these cases that the outgoing office secretary had failed to transmit my letter to his successor. In France, governmental filing often takes on a peculiarly "personal" flavor at the price of impersonal continuity!

RED TAPE AS A SOCIAL PROBLEM

Alvin W. Gouldner

"These clients came to plead with us. Instead of storming the office and knocking everything to smithereens, they came to plead."—FRANZ KAFKA

It is now something more than a century since the term "red tape" was introduced into the English language in its figurative sense. Sidney Smith (1771–1845), an Englishman who could not make up his mind whether he wished to be remembered as a clergyman or as a wit, did much to popularize the satirical connotations of the term.

In 1838, Lord Lytton averred that "the men of dazzling genius began to sneer at the red-tape minister as a mere official manager of details." The redoubtable Carlyle once described someone as "little other than a red-tape talking machine." Probably the first person to give red tape its sociological baptism was Herbert Spencer (about 1873). It was not, however, until 1889 and 1890 that the term began to appear in American newspapers and periodicals.

Present day interest in red tape on the part of sociologists largely derives from studies in bureaucratic structure. Alexander Leighton[1] and Robert Merton have analyzed it as a dysfunctional behavioral pattern which impairs the persistence or continuity of an organization.[2]

Here, and in similar approaches to the subject, red tape is interpreted as

This paper was written especially for this volume.
1. *The Governing of Men* (Princeton University Press, 1945), p. 309.
2. "Bureaucratic Structure and Personality" reprinted in this volume.

being the actual behavior engaged in by the bureaucrat, or of its consequences, interpreted in terms of the ends of the *organization*.[3]

There is, however, one set of observations which this approach to red tape was not designed to encompass. Namely, that red tape is a popular and widespread complaint which is explicitly articulated. There is, then, a second, not an alternative but an additional, context in terms of which red tape may be analyzed—i.e., as a "social problem" taken cognizance of by large numbers of laymen.

The implications of this further analysis may be clarified if two questions are asked:

(1) Why is it, for example, that not all means which have become transformed into ends are thought of as red tape, e.g., the American Constitution?

(2) Why is it, also, that the very same procedures or practices which one group may characterize as red tape may be viewed by another group as deserving no invidious label? The latter may, in fact, attach an approving (possibly, "green-tape") label to the procedure. For example, some landlords but few tenants characterize rent control procedures as red tape.[4]

Commonplace as those observations are, they, nevertheless, suggest that red tape involves phenomena of two orders: (1) the perceiving individual who, with a given frame of reference, comes into some relationship with (2) objective, perhaps bureaucratic, practices or behavior patterns.

Thus red tape as a social problem cannot be explained unless the frame of reference employed by the individual who uses this label is understood, as well as the objective attributes of the situations with which he comes into contact. Both elements are interrelated and changes in either alter the scope and formulation of the problem.

This analysis of red tape as a social problem does not seek to attach a new meaning to a familiar term. Rather, it seeks to identify the frame of reference of people who are hostile to red tape and for whom it therefore comprises a problem, as well as to describe the structural context and the social functions of red tape.

The data upon which this tentative account is partly based are of two kinds: first, secret ballot, group interviews, qualitatively analyzed; second,

---

3. We have, elsewhere, suggested the possibility of analyzing this phenomenon in theoretical contexts other than the means-end schema. Alvin W. Gouldner, "Discussion of 'Industrial Sociology: Status and Prospects.'" *American Sociological Review*, XIII (August, 1948), p. 399, reprinted in part in this volume under the title of "On Weber's Analysis of Bureaucratic Rules."

4. "When at the threshold of World War II motormaker William Knudsen assumed a post of great importance in the defense effort of the nation, he said of Washington red tape, 'In Detroit we call it system.'" John A. Vieg, "Bureaucracy—Fact and Fiction," in Fritz Morstein Marx (ed.), *Elements of Public Administration* (New York: Prentice-Hall, Inc., 1946), p. 54.

interviews with a small sample of 124 respondents stratified in terms of status and ethnic group.[5]

RED TAPE AS THE UNNECESSARY. As might be expected, the meanings ascribed by our interviewees to the term "red tape," as indicated both by their general definitions and concrete illustrations, are most often stated in the language of efficiency. For example, "going through a lot of unnecessary beating around the bush." Another: "Red tape is something which disagrees with the theory that the shortest distance between two points is a straight line." And again: "It means a lot of unnecessary rigmarole and delay in filling out forms."

The language of efficiency is not a valueless and detached judgment on the part of people in our society. "Efficiency"—the choice of those alternatives that maximize the realization of objectives, or minimize expenditures in their pursuit—is widely regarded as a good in and of itself. It is in this sense that a belief in efficiency is one critical element in the frame of reference for the perception and judgment of red tape.

Since efficiency is a widely acknowledged value in a society priding itself upon its "technique" and "know-how," it is apparently employed to mask negative judgments based on less universally accredited values or less easily articulated sentiments. It is not merely that there are other nonrational elements in the red-tape frame of reference, but that these may be implicit in seemingly rational judgments expressed in terms of efficiency.[6] This will be evident from the discussion following.

THE SEPARATION OF PUBLIC AND PRIVATE SPHERES. In describing the meaning red tape has for them, interviewees tend to emphasize presumably "unnecessary" or dispensable features. These, however, are condemned not solely because they violate the canons of efficiency, but because they transgress less easily expressed values. One of the most important of these is the sacredness of privacy, or a belief that the individual should be privileged to withhold certain information about himself from anyone. In this context, the unnecessary is that which violates privacy.

The clichés and commonplaces of complaints regarding red tape repeatedly strike this same keynote: too many people have a chance to observe something of a nature which the respondent deems private; he feels that he is being forced to divulge matters construed as intimate. For some,

---

5. Preliminary statistical analyses of these are reported in footnotes. Only suggestive at best, these are intended to indicate that further study is warranted.

6. Proportion of Respondents Using Differing Values in Defining and Illustrating Red Tape:

Value	Per Cent of Respondents *
Efficiency	74
Equality	17
The separation of private and public spheres	10
	(N = 124)

* Some, of course, use more than one value: 61 per cent of the respondents use "efficiency" alone; 17 per cent of those using "efficiency" use it in conjunction with either or both of the other values.

red tape means: "filling out forms," "going through many hands," "too many details asked," "being investigated," or "too many interviews needed."

One respondent remarks: "When I wanted to withdraw $300 from my bank account, they wouldn't let me take it out unless I first saw a vice-president. They could see that I had the money in my account from my bank book. He wanted to know what I wanted the money for, and I had to explain I was moving and buying new furniture. Why was it his business?" This theme is compactly summarized by another: "Many questions that are asked are of a personal nature and should not be the ordinary business of a stranger."

Not only is the individual's privacy invaded by the information demanded of him, but he is himself investigated, and thus placed on the defensive. One respondent, describing an experience with what he called red tape, reports:

"A commercial vehicle struck my automobile. To settle the matter, I had to give a report to my insurance company. They had to send out a man to inspect my damage to see if the estimate I had given them was correct. . . ." Another says that a "mild example" of red tape "would be in the attempt to borrow money from a finance company. All your references have to be *checked*, your source of income *checked*, your honesty, reliability, etc." A respondent describing efforts of a married couple to adopt a child says: "They must undergo *investigation* for moral and financial reasons. After they finally get a child, they must be *investigated* again before they can legally adopt the child. . . ." Finally, a respondent complains that "You are asked questions which have to be *verified* by so and so and so and so."

In these instances regarded as red tape, the individual's ego is challenged on two counts: (1) A claim which he believes legitimate is not taken "at face value." He must either supply proof or allow it to be investigated. He is, as one remarked, "treated as a criminal"—he may feel his worth is questioned, his status impugned. (2) Not only are his claims and assertions challenged, but other details of his "private life" are investigated. The individual enters the situation on "official," "technical," or "public" business, and feels that he ends up by being investigated as a person.

It seems clear that this conception of red tape would turn up only if the individual accepted the current value which insists upon the division of social activity into the spheres of the public and the private.[7] In such cases,

7. Respondents were asked: "On the whole, do you feel that: (a) Most of the red tape you came across is really necessary, (b) Some of the red tape you came across is necessary but some is not, (c) Practically none of the red tape you came across is necessary?" Respondents choosing either (a) or (b) were classified as "tolerant" toward red tape; those choosing (c), as "hostile." Among a battery of questions designed to explore their values, they were asked to indicate their agreement or disagreement with the following statement, (which was used as an index of their belief

the individual responds to the violation of the value by feeling, as some expressed it, that "he is getting involved;" that he is experiencing the fusion of spheres which should be kept separated.

THE BELIEF IN EQUALITY. The foregoing comments of interviewees may have suggested that the situation is defined as red tape when pursuit of an end is obstructed and especially so when the ends themselves are defined in a particular way—namely, as rights. One respondent mentions that veterans encounter red tape when "trying to get the V. A. to approve dental work to a veteran who is *entitled to it. . . .*" Another tells of his difficulty in obtaining an army promotion when he was "due for" it. A third speaks of his difficulty in collecting back flying pay, even though "I had papers with me verifying my *entitlement* to the flying pay. . . ."

It is not necessarily the absolute, but rather the relative complexity of demands made by an organization upon its clientele which leads these to be regarded as red tape. Ordinary routines are so regarded if there is the suspicion that special privilege exempts others from these routines. A commercial aviator thus considers the customs procedures encountered in international flights as red tape, going on to declare that if you belong to the "right organizations" you pass through customs much more quickly. A respondent speaking of banks says that they "act as if they are doing you a favor to take your money. When you first open your account, they keep you waiting until they are ready. . . . They really don't want a small account. They're interested in the big accounts."

The democratic creed with its accent on equality of rights may thus provide a value component of the red tape frame of reference,[8] one which would presumably not be common in a nondemocratic society

POWERLESSNESS. Sensitivity to disparities of power seems to be another element in the red tape frame of reference. A veteran refers to his army experiences to illustrate his conception of red tape: "If a soldier wishes to

in the value of maintaining a separation of private and public spheres) "A man's business and private life should be kept strictly separated." Cross-tabulation of answers to the first and second questions gave the following table ("no answers" and "don't knows" eliminated).

Attitude Toward Red Tape	Attitude Toward Separation of Private and Public Spheres		
	Agree	Disagree	
Tolerant	62	19	
Hostile	24	2	
Total	86	21	107

The probability of the corrected chi square for this table is between 0.10 and 0.20.

8. Responses to the following statement were used as an index for the respondent's attitude toward equality: "All people are born equal and should be treated that way."

Attitude Toward Red Tape	Attitude Toward Equality		
	Agree	Disagree	
Tolerant	61	19	
Hostile	26	3	
Total	87	22	109

Probability for the corrected chi square is about 0.02.

go on leave, first of all the G. I. must present the claim to his platoon sergeant. Then it is referred to the top sergeant who, in turn, goes over the request and gives either his approval or disapproval. He then presents this to the C. O. who will either approve or disapprove your request."

Another: "In factories, when persons have grievances, they are usually sent to many different persons before 'hitting' the particular one who will handle the case, rather than being sent directly to the person who will give you the satisfaction."

A student discussing an encounter with what he calls red tape says:

"To secure permission to use school records for the purpose of doing an attendance survey, I was first directed to an employee at the Board of Education, then to another employee, then to the deputy superintendent, the superintendent, the first employee asked, the superintendent again, then to the attendance director and, finally, permission to use the records was obtained."

These and similar statements suggest that the individual who decries red tape feels that he is unable to "get to" the people who have the power, or get to them readily enough. You first have to go before the powerless people—they seem to be saying—who though they may be able to deny your request, are often unable to approve it finally. They can say, "no," but not "yes." Power centers are felt to be out of reach and the individual experiences himself and those with whom he can have some face to face contact as powerless.[9] This feeling of powerlessness may in some cases be a character trait rather than an artifact of a social situation.

SUSPICION AND THE INABILITY TO DEFER GRATIFICATIONS. Two further character traits of clients apparently encourage them to perceive red tape where others do not. These are suspiciousness and an apparent inability to defer gratifications. The prevalence of suspicion manifests itself in the motives that respondents ascribe to those who present them with the red tape obstacles. "Apparently the only thing to be gained in making this application complicated, which resulted in many applications rejected," said one informant, "was the increase and duration of political jobs." Red tape, says another, "seems to be used in order to have only the very anxious ones receive whatever they're after and discourage those who are not too eager." These remarks, among others, seem to imply that there exists deliberate intent to frustrate the client. For some, the world of red tape is not merely

9. Agreement with the following statement (here selected from several others of like kind) was used as an index of the respondent's feeling of powerlessness: "An awful lot of people are getting stepped on these days."

Attitude Toward Red Tape	Sense of Powerlessness		
	+	−	
Tolerant	53	20	
Hostile	27	2	
Total	80	22	102

Probability for the corrected chi square is between 0.05 and 0.02.

"unnecessary," "complicated," or "meaningless"; it becomes meaningful as willful maliciousness when viewed in the context of suspicion.[10]

Those who are particularly sensitive to "waiting," when they emphasize the time it takes to comply with their requests or to get a decision on them, may include some whose capacity to defer gratification has become weakened. It would seem that suspicion and an inability to defer gratifications are closely interlocked. For, to the extent that the world is felt to be peopled with those who would do us harm and who cannot be trusted, safety lies only in the *immediate* satisfaction. The satisfaction that has to be deferred is imperiled by all manner of hostile forces that may prevent its realization.

INADEQUATE "SUBSTANTIAL RATIONALITY." One further characteristic of the red-tape-sensitive frame of reference deserves special mention: its apparent inhibition of an "intelligent insight into the interrelations of events in a given situation," what Karl Mannheim called [11] "substantial rationality." Persons complaining of red tape often say, in effect, that the things they experience are meaningless and make no sense to them. They describe red tape as "complicated," "unnecessarily complex," a "mix-up" or "befuddlement."

We need not presuppose that the demands placed upon a client, or the procedures with which he is forced to comply, are actually necessary or unnecessary. The only question of interest here is whether anything can be learned about the client and his frame of reference from his repeated references to red tape as "confused" or "mixed-up." Our data do not permit us to say whether, in some objective sense, the situation is really "befuddled." We can be reasonably certain, however, that it does "confuse" the client, and that it provides him with experiences which are meaningless in his frame of reference.

As Lundberg has indicated,[12] the degree to which a situation appears complicated or simple is not only determined by the situation itself. It is also influenced by the frame of reference through which it is viewed. Thus individuals coming upon a situation which they label "red tape" and finding it confusing are likely to have a frame of reference that cannot make sense of their experience.

10. Responses to the following statement were used as an index to the respondent's feeling of suspicion: "Lots of people seem to be friendly and sincere but many of them only pretend to be that way."

Attitude Toward Red Tape	Suspiciousness +	−	
Tolerant	11	65	
Hostile	10	19	
Total	21	84	105

Probability for the corrected chi square is about 0.05.

11. *Man and Society in an Age of Reconstruction* (Harcourt, Brace and Company, 1941), p. 53.

12. George A. Lundberg, *Foundations of Sociology* (Macmillan Company, 1938), p. 138.

What are some reasons for this eclipse of substantial rationality and for the inadequacy of the red-tape-sensitive frame of reference? Some clues may be provided by examining the kinds of organizations alleged to have the least red tape. Most respondents mention nonprofit, private associations, as having least red tape. These include churches, Y's, the American Legion, the Salvation Army, fraternities, and trade unions. In part, these groups are distinguished by their relatively personalized and informal relationships. The tendency to choose "least red tape" groups on the basis of this criterion is epitomized by one person who nominated, "the home."

A second criterion apparently used by respondents involves the effectiveness of the possible cash transactions. Thus one respondent, who declared that second-hand car dealers have little red tape, went on to say, "Here, money talks!"

The organizations listed as having least red tape in general appear to have well-developed, personalized, and informal relations or effective cash relationships. Among privately owned businesses believed to have little red tape, *small* businesses were prominent. These, providing "service with a smile," also effectively fuse informal and pecuniary ties.

Apparently, many individuals in our society expect organizations to operate on one or both of these bases. But a distinctive feature of contemporary bureaucracies is their use of relationships which are neither personalized nor pecuniary, neither informal nor contractual. Instead, they are attuned to abstract and impersonal rules. These considerations suggest that those who pronounce red tape to be a "mix-up" and "befuddlement" are utilizing a frame of reference which relies upon somewhat outmoded techniques for realizing goals. A frame of reference which depends upon market and informal arrangements as instrumentalities will be less and less effective as bureaucratic organization invades ever-widening spheres of the society.

RED TAPE AS "RESENTMENT." Other social sources of the red-tape-sensitive frame of reference are indicated in Max Scheler's concept of "resentment." According to Scheler, "resentment" is a compound of envy and suppressed aggression, a compound which sometimes bursts into the open and is directed against some diffusely defined group or object. Scheler maintains that, "The wider the gulf existing between the juridical condition of divergent social groups established by the political system or tradition, on the one side, and their actual power on the other, the more powerful will be the charge of psychological explosiveness implicit in the situation." [13]

In certain major respects the red tape frame of reference and Scheler's description of resentment converge. Both involve a belief in equality which is violated by a sense of powerlessness. Like the "man of resentment," the

13. As quoted in Gerard de Gré, *Society and Ideology* (Columbia University Bookstore, 1943), p. 11.

individual hostile to red tape also feels that there are things to which he is entitled but never receives. Essentially, however, what distinguishes the man of resentment is not his frustration, but his feeling of powerlessness. He has little hope of rectifying the situation. It would appear, therefore, that a full analysis of the social roots of the red-tape-sensitive frame of reference must link up with the phenomenon of alienation.

ALIENATION OF THE CONSERVATIVE. If this is so, it is likely that we are confronted with the alienation of a distinct ideological group, roughly characterizable as "conservatives." For it is the conservatives, rather than the "radicals," who seem most concerned with red tape as a social problem.[14] To designate this group simply as "conservative," without specifying its other attributes, especially its status properties, is clearly inadequate. Further analysis of our data is required, however, before the other characteristics of this group can be stated with confidence.

For the present, a tentative formulation might hold that red tape, as a culturally familiar epithet, has largely developed under conservative sponsorship.[15] This may explain why those indignant at red tape frequently direct their aggression against clerks at the bottom of a structure, while higher echelons escape unscathed. Their hostility is, moreover, aimed at *means*—e.g., forms and questionnaires—rather than at group *ends*. Criticisms embodied in the term "red tape" enable the individual to express aggression against powerful and prestige-laden organizations, while still permitting him to be "counted in." As such, "red tape" is a social critique readily acceptable to conservatives.

The significance of the red tape stereotype seems, however, to be even deeper. Social institutions during the last century or so have undergone profound changes partly describable as bureaucratization. The red tape stereotype gives compact but blurred expression to the resentment against the alienation, the impersonalization, and the dull routines that afflict bureaucracy. This suggests that the growth of concern with "red tape" may indicate new types of social problems.

14. The question here is: in what kind of a political orientation is red tape ascribed the *most importance*. To ascertain this we asked: "How important a problem would you say red tape is?" Respondents could check one of the following answers: (a) of great importance, (b) of some importance, (c) not very important, (d) not sure. Responses to the following statement were used as a crude index of "radicalism-conservatism": "The country would be better off if the trade unions had more power." Omitting those without a definite opinion, the following table was obtained:

	Political Orientation	
Importance Ascribed to Red Tape	"Radical"	"Conservative"
High (a, b)	19	43
Low (c)	15	8
Total	34	51

Probability for the corrected chi square is better than 0.01.

15. It is an interesting fact of intellectual history that those passages of Karl Marx's writings in which he castigates alienation, impersonalization, and dull, routine work find little echo among the present Marxian epigoni.

CRIME AND CORPORATE ORGANIZATION

Edwin H. Sutherland

The characteristics of white collar crime . . . depend to some extent on the corporate form of business organization. The statement is frequently made that big business is more legal and more honest than small business. No organized research has demonstrated the truth or falsity of this claim. Research on violations of price ceilings during World War II indicated but did not prove conclusively that no significant difference was found between large and small firms.[1] At any rate, the corporate form of organization which is generally used in big business has two advantages over other forms of organization from the point of view of violations of law: anonymity of persons so that the location of responsibility is impeded, and increased rationality in behavior.

The policies of a business which has corporate form are actions of a corporate unit. Responsibility is divided among executives, directors, subordinates, and stockholders. A director loses his personal identity in this corporate behavior and in this respect, but in no other, corporate behavior is like the behavior of a mob. Persons do not act in these situations as they would act if segregated from each other. This is true even when the corporation is essentially a dictatorship under the control of one person. The difficulty of locating responsibility and the resulting security to individuals is exemplified in the decision against the automobile companies in the six percent case, where the corporations were convicted but all of the directors and executives were acquitted: the corporation was guilty of a crime but no person directing the corporation was guilty of a crime.

The corporate form of business organization also has the advantage of increased rationality. The corporation probably comes closer to the "economic man" and to "pure reason" than any other person or any other organization. The executives and directors not only have explicit and consistent objectives of maximum pecuniary gain but also have research and accounting departments by which precise determination of results is facilitated, and have discussions of policies by directors with diverse abilities and diverse interests, so that the sentiments of one person are canceled by those of another. This general advantage does not deny the disadvantages of corporate organization. Two principal disadvantages have been pointed out in

Reprinted from *White Collar Crime*, pp. 228-233, by permission of Myrtle Sutherland and the publisher. (Copyright, 1949, by the Dryden Press.)

1. George Katona, *Price Control and Business*, Principia Press, Monog. No. 9, 1945.

the literature. First, the directors do not necessarily have their attention fixed on the balance sheet of the corporation, but often engage in log-rolling for personal advantages, just as is true in politics. Second, the corporation, like a government, tends to become bureaucratic with all of the limitations of bureaucratic organization.

In the earlier days the corporation aimed at technological efficiency; in the later days it has aimed more than previously at the manipulation of people by advertising, salesmanship, propaganda, and lobbying. With this recent development the corporation has developed a truly Machiavellian ideology and policy. It has reached the conclusion that practically anything is possible if resources, ingenuity, and strenuous efforts are used. It has appropriated the physical and biological sciences and applied them to its objectives of technological efficiency, and in the process has made significant contributions to those sciences. Similarly, it has appropriated the social and psychological sciences and applied them to the objective of manipulating people.

Three aspects of the rationality of the corporation in relation to illegal behavior may be mentioned. First, the corporation selects crimes which involve the smallest danger of detection and identification, and against which victims are least likely to fight. The crimes of corporations are similar in this respect to professional thefts: both are carefully selected and both are similar to taking candy from a baby, in that the victim is a weak antagonist. The advantage of selecting weak victims was stated explicitly by Daniel Drew in the decade of the eighties:

> I began to see that it is poor policy for big men in Wall Street to fight each other. When I am fighting a money-king, even my victories are dangerous. Take the present situation. I had scooped a fine profit out of the Erie deal and it was for the most part in solid cash. But—and here was the trouble—it had all come out of one man—Vanderbilt. Naturally it had left him very sore. And being so powerful, he was able to fight back. As has been seen, he did fight back. He had put me and my party to a lot of inconvenience. That always happens when you take money from a man on your own level. On the other hand, if I had taken these profits from outsiders, it would in the aggregate have amounted to the same sum, but the losers would have been scattered all over the country and so wouldn't have been able to get together and hit back. By making my money from people on the outside, an insider like myself could make just as much in the long run, and not raise up any one enemy powerful enough to cause him discomfort.[2]

The victims of corporate crimes are seldom in a position to fight against the management of the corporation. Consumers are scattered, unorganized, lacking in objective information as to qualities of commodities, and no one consumer suffers a loss in a particular transaction which would justify him in taking individual action. Stockholders seldom know the complex procedures of the corporation which they own, cannot attend annual meetings,

2. Bouck White, *The Book of Daniel Drew* (New York, 1910), pp. 270-271.

and receive little information regarding the policies or the financial status of the corporation. Even if stockholders suspect illegal behavior by the management, they are scattered, unorganized, and frequently cannot even secure access to the names of other stockholders. In their conflicts with labor, the corporations have the advantage of a friendly press and of news commentators whose salaries are paid by business corporations, so that their unfair labor practices can be learned generally only by consulting official reports.

The ordinary case of embezzlement is a crime by a single individual in a subordinate position against a strong corporation. It is, therefore, one of the most foolish of white collar crimes. The weakness of the embezzler, in comparison with the corporation, is illustrated in the case of J. W. Harriman. He was indicted for embezzlement in 1933 and later convicted. No criminal complaint was made against the banks which were accessory to this crime, and which were discovered in the course of the investigation. Their crimes included loans to one corporation in excess of the limit set by law, a pool formed by the officers of the bank to trade in the stock of the bank in violation of law, concealment of the embezzlement by officers of the bank and of the clearing house, and refusal by many of the banks to meet the losses of the Harriman bank which they had agreed to do on condition that the embezzlement be concealed.

A second aspect of corporate rationality in relation to crime is the selection of crimes in which proof is difficult. In this respect, also, white collar crime is similar to professional theft. The selection of crimes on this basis is illustrated by advertising: since a little puffing is regarded as justifiable, the proof of unreasonable puffing is difficult. Again, a corporation organizes a company union under its own domination because proof that this is an unfair labor practice is difficult.

Third, the rational corporation adopts a policy of "fixing" cases. This is similar to the professional thief who maintains that if he has money and good standing with the "fixer" he can fix any case anywhere, since it is always possible to find a weak link in the chain of persons necessary for a conviction. A former officer of the Federal Food and Drug Administration has described the pressures on that organization to prevent the execution of the law on particular offenders. These pressures include threats by Senators and Representatives that appropriations for the Food and Drug Administration will be cut unless charges against a constituent are withdrawn. When the Federal Trade Commission after the First World War was active in the enforcement of the law, representatives of large corporations went to the President of the United States, who replaced some of the commissioners by others more sympathetic with business practices; this resulted in the dismissal of many complaints which had been made against corporations. When minority stockholders bring suit against the management of the corporation, a customary procedure is to make a settlement with the leader of that group. This is similar to the reimbursement by the professional thief of the victim of the theft in order to stop prosecution.

The "fixing" of white collar crimes, however, is much more inclusive than the fixing of professional thefts. The corporation attempts not only to "fix" particular accusations against it, but also to develop general good will before accusations are made, and even to prevent the implementation of the law. An instance of this broader policy is provided by the fire insurance companies of Missouri, which had agreed to pay Pendergast a bribe of $750,000 to intervene in a rate case. Four of these companies which paid shares of this bribe immediately appointed as vice-president a person who had great influence in the national capital. While Pendergast was promptly convicted and committed to prison, almost ten years elapsed before the fire insurance companies were convicted and their penalties were limited to fines.

The preceding analysis justifies the conclusion that the violations of law by corporations are deliberate and organized crime. This does not mean that corporations never violate the law inadvertently and in an unorganized manner. It does mean that a substantial portion of their violations are deliberate and organized.

8

FIELD METHODS FOR THE STUDY OF BUREAUCRACY

Until recently, most studies of bureaucracy have necessarily been based on documentary materials which turn up in the ordinary course of events. Autobiographies, memoirs, diaries, journals, newspaper reports, note books, letters, and official papers of the organization (official statistics, memoranda, charters, rules, tables of organization, etc.) have chiefly comprised the raw materials for reconstructing the structure and functions of bureaucracy. Common to these materials is the fact that they were usually produced without concern for the needs of the social scientist; they already exist by the time he arrives on the scene. Indispensable as they are, therefore,— and not exclusively for the study of bureaucracies in the past—it is only to be expected that these pre-established materials will have their characteristic deficiencies for social science. Often, they do not detail daily behavior of officials variously placed in the bureaucracy, being largely confined to information about the higher echelons. Often, the representativeness of data concerning a particular official cannot be determined. Often, too, irreparable gaps in these data make it difficult to reconstruct, with any assurance, some of the salient features of the bureaucracy; for example, the linkages of informal groups with the formal structure of the organization. And useful as they may nevertheless be for historical accounts of a particular bureaucracy, these documents are often not sufficiently standardized to allow the comparative study of various bureaucracies. Historians and others have, of course, been amply aware of these and other deficiencies of documentary materials, as can be seen in some of the works cited in the bibliography, and would therefore concur in the view that these materials afford an insufficient basis for the detailed study of present-day bureaucracy.

To supplement these documentary sources, social scientists have devised procedures for the field collection of data bearing on social organization, and these are the subject of this concluding section. Methods of systematic self-observation by officials, direct observation of bureaucratic routines, interviews, and measures of attitudes, sentiments and expectations partly meet the deficiencies inherent in documentary materials prepared without the aid of the social scientist. As will be seen, these current methods of collecting data are only in their beginnings. Indeed, the authors of the following selections uniformly urge the need for their further development. But even now, their tentative findings do credit to their method.

In the opening selection on self-observation by officials, Lasswell shows that large staffs of field-workers are not required to study selected aspects of bureaucracy. He sets forth some rudimentary procedures, which lend themselves to elaboration, whereby the executive can describe essential parts of his organizational environment. However much these procedures may exclude from view, they have the merit of assuring a representative record of experience, in contrast to the essay-diary, the journal and other documents which report, in patchy and unrepresentative form, the run of experience of the executive.

These suggestions of procedures for systematic observation are taken up, elaborated and applied to several organizations by Carlson in his pilot study of the daily routines of business executives. By describing the various practical difficulties that need to be overcome, he provides a tentative guide for the further development of these systematic records of executive behavior. No one method is adequate to understand such a complex organization as bureaucracy. Whereas Carlson indicates the several points at which observational records of organizational behavior need to be supplemented by periodic interviews, Roethlisberger and Dickson indicate the points at which systematic interview materials need to be supplemented by direct observation. The latter selection presents working principles to guide the behavior of the observer, directing attention, in particular, to the difficulty, familiar to other fields of more disciplined inquiry, that the presence of the observer may change the behavior under observation from what it would normally have been in his absence.

Stogdill presents a compact review of several methods of studying administrative behavior,—among them, sociometry, rating-scales and interviews—appraising their distinctive uses and examining the interrelations between them. The interlocking of different methods of inquiry serves numerous purposes; for example, it enables the inquirer to test the validity of administrators' own reports of behavior by more objective indices of their actual behavior. Particularly germane in this selection is the brief summary of different kinds of problems which can be analyzed by use of materials gathered by different methods.

SELF-OBSERVATION: RECORDING
THE FOCUS OF ATTENTION

Harold D. Lasswell

How can a busy man keep useful records? Time, or rather, the lack of it, is the enemy—a deadlier enemy than lack of objectivity.

The inventive ability of man has not yet been adequately applied to the task of recording his own experience. There is, of course, the diary and the journal. However much we welcome the invaluable jottings of a Gideon Welles, we are always left thirsting for more. Besides, the essay-diary is highly selective and yet it chooses on the basis of no explicit principle. When we leaf through an essay-diary we learn that our diarist saw the head of a manufacturing corporation, who came to protest that he had been passed over in the awarding of government contracts. How many other manufacturers succeeded in reaching the secretary for the personal presentation of such a complaint? We scan through the diary, and sure enough we find another instance, and then a second or a third. Are these all the manufacturers who got through to him during his years in office? Or is the complaint so frequent that the secretary makes a note of it only on rare occasions?

It is the problem of representativeness that plagues anyone who relies on the essay-diary. What is the typical, not the special, appointment pattern of a given official? How much time is taken up in contact with members of the department, of other government agencies, with private persons? Among the private persons, how many are seeking favours—appointments, revisions of contract, news of government decisions? How many requests are acceded to and how many are postponed or rejected outright?

A high degree of disciplined interest in human affairs is enough to keep some busy policy-makers busy on elaborate records. We cannot, however, assume this disciplined interest on the part of all "practical" men. We do not imply that the task of obtaining better sources for political science and history must be postponed to a future in which policy is in the hands of conscientious and skilful historians and political scientists. Many active executives can be brought to understand how the keeping of certain records will yield facts that bear directly on their own efficiency.

If more "practical" men are to make better records, two requirements

Reprinted in part from *Analysis of Political Behaviour:* An Empirical Approach, pp. 279-286 by permission of the publisher. (Copyright, 1948, by the Oxford University Press.)

must be met. First, a question must be asked that seems to them worth answering. Second, a procedure must be available that does not interfere with their work.

One bureau chief in the federal government was having "budget trouble." A veteran of the public service in Washington, he commanded the destinies of a bureau devoted to the collecting, reporting and scientific processing of certain data. For several years his appropriation had remained stable, though the relative trend was downward. Although somewhat concerned about the failure of his operation to expand, he had done very little about it. We had occasion to ask him if he had ever looked objectively at his own methods of administrative management in search of a clue to the static position of his bureau.

We outlined to this bureau chief a simple method of keeping a record of his contacts. The purpose was to take note of every person who came to his focus of attention in the course of the day. He provided himself with a packet of slips (four inches by six, fitting snugly into the inner pocket of his coat). Only a slip a day was used. At the top he wrote the date. In the upper left-hand corner he wrote the letters "In," and halfway down "Ex." By the symbol "In" was meant "internal"; by "Ex," "external." The words referred to persons inside or outside his bureau. Each time the chief had a face-to-face contact, he entered a tally opposite "In" or "Ex."

The results of this extremely simple procedure were somewhat revealing to the administrator. Well over nine in every ten contacts were with members of his own bureau—this included all waking hours of the day. This bureau head was a bachelor who was interested in the scientific phases of his work and practically submerged himself among his immediate colleagues. The test period of record-making brought sharply to his focus of attention some of the facts about his ordinary focus of attention. The effect was to underline some of the factors explaining the static position of his bureau. He, as the representative of the collective life of this organization, was not impressing himself or the enterprise upon the environment upon which it depended for survival. The degree to which the chief had "internalized" his contacts was given even greater emphasis when he noted among the "Ex" entries whether the person, though outside his bureau, was inside his department, or whether he was in another executive agency, in Congress, or in private life. During the trial month the record showed not a single legislative contact and less than 10 per cent of total contacts outside his department.

The executive secretary of a trade association, who used the same procedure for a test period, was also surprised to see how exclusively his focus of attention was controlled by members of the association. Well over nine in ten contacts were intra-organizational. Although nominally serving the membership as an intermediary with the external environment, he was actually doing a different job. He decided to alter his tactics and to extend the scope of his effective impact on the environment beyond the association.

A very different pattern was revealed by a college president, who made use of the recording system. Living in a large metropolitan area, constantly drawn into civic and other activities, the president realized—when the question was raised—that he had cut down his faculty-student associations. But he was shocked to see how far this process had gone. The test run showed that over half of his contacts were external, that is, with other than faculty, students, employees, board of trustees, parents of students. Of the internal contacts, more than half were with members of the board of trustees and with one dean. Sensing the degree of alienation that had grown up between him and the campus, the president deliberately modified his pattern of contact in order to multiply his direct associations with faculty and students.

Even such a simple "home-made" procedure as the record slip calls for the solution of many small technical problems. The basic idea is so flexible that any number of adaptations can be made. Suppose two people are interviewed at the same time; a small circle can be added at the top of the tally to indicate the extra person. Suppose one person is an insider, the other an outsider; the tally can be under "In" and the small circle blacked in. If the contact is by telephone, a small circle may be drawn at the bottom of the tally. Contacts outside the office can be shown by a dotted line.

Beginning with this humble device, a never-ending set of complications can be added in order to answer questions that arise out of the material. An administrator may want to know in detail which persons or groups inside or outside of his organization occupy his attention. The superintendent of a hospital may examine his relations with trustees, medical staff, nurses, administrative and technical employees, patients and families of patients. All these constitute the "internal" environment. In addition, he may want to distinguish certain groups in the external environment—physicians, press, clergy, teachers, politicians, business men. The persons or groups selected may be shown by letters (A, B, C, . . .) put by the side of each tally mark.

The basic procedure can be extended to characterize the significance of each contact. To what extent does the administrator play an indulgent rôle by granting requests and distributing rewards? To what extent does he play a deprivational rôle by turning down requests and applying disciplinary measures? Every administrator is necessarily a source of both indulgence and deprivation; however, it is possible for him to exercise some measure of control over the balance. The objective situation may justify tipping the balance one way or the other, but even under adverse conditions, such as retrenchment, the administrator can often find ways of diluting his negative function. Occasions may be created to justify a distribution of praise and the giving of tangible reward.

With regard to technique, the administrator who gives the indulgence may enter a plus at the top of the tally; a deprivation can be registered as minus (other contacts are assumed to be zero). If in the same relationship the interviewer is simultaneously plus and minus, overlap can be shown by circling the signs.

The executive is himself a target of a stream of indulgences and deprivations from his environment. He may be the object of praise or criticism, of promotion or reprimand. If he cares to describe the impact of life on his own experience, the administrator may modify the recording procedure in order to make the appropriate entries. One convenient expedient is to put the plus and minus signs that refer to acts by the administrator above the tally and to put signs referring to acts toward the administrator below the tally. If desired, entries can be very detailed in regard to the nature of indulgence or deprivation. In the interest of reliability, the record-maker may lay down a series of instructions for his own guidance. Plus 1 or minus 1 may be defined to mean indulgence or deprivation in accordance with Standard 1, power. Standard 2 may be income. Subdivisions of these and other standards may be carried out indefinitely. The power relation, for example, may be broken down into many categories. Plus 1A may be defined to mean acceptance of proposals by others; such a notation would be used when another person accepts a suggestion. Minus 1A would mean a rejection. Plus 1B may mean approval of a past official act, minus 1B disapproval.

The simple framework of the procedure can be adapted to more and more precise observations. Each contact may be timed approximately by dividing the slip horizontally according to hours or minutes. Slips may be filled out for each half-day or hour. With slight adaptation, the basic procedure can be applied to collective situations like committee meetings. On a diagram, movements can be assigned to individual participants according to the position they occupy. A tally can be made when anyone participates. . . .

These recording methods may be used by an individual to discover many perhaps unanticipated characteristics. Categories may be used to describe the approach of the other person (or of the self). . . . The type of aggressive or passive approach may be assigned code numbers and added to the tally of a given contact.

The basic procedure can be adapted to the recording of what is said by the parties to a given contact relationship. An administrator may want a record of the frequency with which he hears criticisms of himself, his organization, his policies, or his ideas. Every symbol (key word or phrase) can be assigned a code number, to be recorded on a slip each time it occurs. These methods of content analysis are more fully described in connection with a study of what appear in the mass channels of communication.[1]

These record-making devices are not only contributory to personal insight; from a scientific point of view they improve the source materials of history and therefore of science. These methods are especially valuable in improving our knowledge of the focus of attention, the long-neglected dimension of personal and social reality. To·account for what people do it is necessary to describe their environment in two ways: as surroundings and as milieu. By *surroundings* we mean what the outside observer sees regardless of whether the people who are there see it. The surroundings of a great power include all the people and resources of all other powers in the world. The *milieu,* on the other hand, is what comes to the focus of attention of the members of a great power. The same surroundings do not always evoke the same milieu.

Since it is comparatively easy to find reliable ways to describe surroundings, the data available to political science is comparatively ample with respect to population, material resources, technical equipment, output, resource consumption and depletion. . . .

More refined methods of analysis and description will enable us to interpose two series of data between environment, in the sense of surroundings, and ideological and institutional effects of a "final" sort (e.g. trade union activity). The milieu of one group of workers may include clarifying explanations of why adjustments in wages and working conditions may be necessary to maintain the firm in production, while the milieu of a similarly situated group of workers in another plant may contain no such clarifying explanations. Unless our methods of data-gathering provide us with this type of material, we are at the very least prone to underestimate the time relations between the "final effect" and the environmental (surroundings) change. Moreover, it is by no means demonstrated without these data that the choice of "final" effect is justified.

Some of the procedures outlined here are capable of providing many of the facts needed about the focus of attention of those who occupy known positions in the social process. The ideal is to obtain more satisfactory records of the typical foci of attention (milieux) of policy-makers, advisers and members of the rank and file.

In this discussion, emphasis has been put upon self-observation as a means of describing those with whom one comes in contact and the content of what they say. This is only part of the process of self-observation. We may, in addition, take note of what we ourselves feel about the people with whom we are in contact. We may take note of our expectations

1. Cf. Lasswell, Harold D., and Associates, "The Politically Significant Content of the Press: Coding Procedures," *Journalism Quarterly* (March, 1942).

about the way in which the situation will develop. In this is included our conceptions of goal and procedure for getting what we want (when the relationship is one in which objectives are consciously defined). As a means of exploring the structure of expectation, demand and identification with which we enter any given series of contacts, we may make use of the technique of free fantasy (developed by Sigmund Freud for clinical purposes, though applicable to non-clinical situations). Records of this type do not relate to the focus of attention (milieu) of the individual but to his predispositions and response. It is important to keep these distinctions clear on both the conceptual and observational levels. Unclarity in this zone has handicapped both the writing of history and the advance of political sicence. Among political scientists, A. Lawrence Lowell and Graham Wallas have made the most valuable exploratory analysis of the function of attention in politics. It has been impossible to implement their insights, however, in the absence of more adequate methods of recording empirical data. Lowell's most significant suggestions are in *Public Opinion in War and Peace* (Cambridge, Mass., 1926). Nearly all of Wallas's remarkable essays are in point.

RECORDS OF EXECUTIVE BEHAVIOR

Sune Carlson

In the present state of knowledge our primary task has been to devise and test a method for an observational description of executive work. In so far as we have succeeded with this task, that will be our most important result. But what we want is an observational technique that will not only help us to describe the actual work of the business executive, but will also be a useful instrument for the detection of deficiencies in his work. . . .

As a frame of reference we devised a set of operational concepts rather similar to Barnard's system of specialization. . . . His first and third bases of specialization: (a) the place where work is done, and (c) the people with whom work is done, we also used. His fourth and fifth bases: (d) the things upon which work is done, and (e) the methods or process by which work is done, we formulated in a somewhat different way, distinguishing the technique of communication used in contacting people, the nature of the questions that are brought up before the managing director, and the kind

Reprinted in part from *Executive Behaviour; A Study of the Work Load and Working Methods of Managing Directors*, pp. 32-50, by permission of the publisher. (Copyright, 1951, by C. A. Stromberg Aktiebolag, Stockholm, Sweden.)

of action he takes with regard to these questions. Thus for every executive action we tried to collect data on: I. Place of work; II. Contact with persons and institutions; III. Technique of communication; IV. Nature of question handled; V. Kind of action.

Before I comment further on these bases of classification, I shall say a few words regarding Barnard's second base: (b) the time at which work is done. The element of time was brought into our study in two different ways. Firstly, we had to select a specific time period, during which the observational recording of the executive behaviour would take place. . . . Secondly, the time together with the frequency was our main unit of measurement. We tried to observe the actual time used in every contact and for every particular piece of work. By doing so we regarded time units as homogeneous units irrespective of what they were used for and when they took place. Thus, a ten-minute review of reports was regarded as one and the same operation, whether it was made in the morning, when the executive's brain was thoroughly rested, or late at night after a long and tiring working day.

Let us now return to our system of classification and see how this was applied in the observational study.

I. *Place of work*. The mere recording of the place of work gave us some idea of what the managing director was doing, or rather what he was not doing. If we found, for example, that he spent his whole day in his office, we knew that he was not on an inspection tour in the plant. If he was attending a conference outside the firm, the mere observation of where this conference was held also often gave us some notion of his duties.

II. *Contacts with persons and institutions*. Starting out with the conception that the main task of the executive is to administer his own people and to represent the firm vis-à-vis other people, the recording of the people he met in his daily work became perhaps the most important part of the whole study. It may be mentioned that the managing directors we have studied thus far spent between 65 and 90 per cent of their total working time in contact with other people. These people included not only the firms' own staff and the members of their boards of directors, but also all the persons from outside with whom they had to deal as the chief representatives of their firms.

III. *Technique of communication*. "I believe," says Elton Mayo, "that social study should begin with careful observations of what may be described as communication; that is, the capacity for an individual to communicate his feelings and ideas to another, the capacity of groups to communicate effectively and intimately to each other."[1] By technique of communication we mean here the methods used by the executive in order

1. Elton Mayo, *The Social Problems of an Industrial Civilization*, New York 1945, p. 22.

to get into contact with the people and the institutions he has to deal with. It describes how he obtains information from others and how he himself conveys ideas to other people. For the sake of simplicity we have also included under this heading the technique of getting information by direct observation, e.g. during an inspection tour in the plant.

IV. *Nature of question handled.* The concepts thus far discussed were useful also for the study of what questions the executives had to deal with in their daily work. The statistics of the distribution of their working time with respect to various places of work, of their contacts with institutions and people inside and outside the firm, of their attendance at committee meetings and of the reports they received gave us some ideas about the material contents of their work. In fact, during the first stage of our investigation this was the only data we collected. Our working hypothesis was that a mere observation of the personal contacts would also enable us to draw some conclusions regarding the nature of the questions brought up. We simply assumed that if, for example, the managing director had a talk with the sales manager, the issue discussed was a question of sales.

The limitations of such an approach are obvious. The main task of the chief executive is, of course, not to consider a problem in its "functional" but in its company-wide aspects. Thus, a question brought to him by the sales manager may very well be classified as a sales problem from the point of view of the latter, but from the point of view of the managing director it may just as well be a problem that touches manufacturing, financing or personnel, and should be classified accordingly. If the problem had no other aspect than sales, it would in most cases never have been referred to the chief executive's consideration. Furthermore, from a mere observation of his contacts we shall never find out either what the managing director does when he works by himself, or which problems he specially wants to talk to other people about. During the later stage of our study we observed that there may be some questions, e.g. personnel questions, that the chief executive wants to discuss with all his subordinates. If we were to assume in such a case that personnel problems are only discussed in the presence of the personnel manager, our conclusions would, of course, be completely wrong.

In order to avoid these shortcomings we introduced during the later stage of our investigation a series of concepts relating to the nature of the question handled. We were here forced to abandon the purely observational approach and to introduce continuous interviews as a supplement to the behavioristic study.

Firstly, we classified the questions the executive dealt with according to what might be called their material contents or field of activity. . . .

Secondly, we classified the questions dealt with as questions of development or questions of current operation. . . .

Thirdly, we classified the questions handled as questions of policy or questions of application. . . .

V. *Kind of action.* Our curiosity did not end when we had acquired a knowledge of the nature of the questions dealt with by the chief executives. We also wanted to know what they did about these questions. . . . In our observational study the kinds of actions, consequently, were classified under the following subheadings: getting information, systematizing information, taking decisions, confirming or correcting the decisions of others, giving orders, advising and explaining, inspecting and reviewing, executing, and personal development.

There are several critical comments to be made regarding this list of concepts, but before I embark on such a critique I want to review some of the problems of recording and classification.

RECORDING AND CLASSIFICATION OF DATA. It should be remembered that the main part of this study took place in firms with which I had been connected for several years, and about which I already had a great deal of information. This information was, of course, of great help both when I had to plan the collection and classification of my new data and when these data were finally analysed. The problem of collecting data was that the recording must not interfere with or influence the executives' usual behavior patterns; and I think that we were rather successful in this respect. The recording technique used varied with the nature of the data. Some data were collected by the chief executives' private secretaries or their personal assistants, by the telephone exchange operators and the porters, and one of my assistant's chief tasks in connection with the collecting of data was to train these people in the recording technique to be used. Other data were recorded immediately by the chief executives themselves, while for other parts of our study we got the necessary information through extensive interviews with the chief executives, their private secretaries, and other persons in their immediate surroundings who had an intimate knowledge of their working patterns.

Place of work and personal contacts. The recording of the time the chief executive spent in various places of work and in personal contact with people visiting him at his office was generally done by his private secretary. A special form was supplied for this purpose, of which one part was to be filled in for the morning period, and another for the afternoon period and the evening. When the secretary could not observe the relevant events herself she obtained the necessary information from the porter, the telephone exchange operator or the chief executive himself. If, for example, the managing director left his office for the day in the early afternoon in order to attend a meeting outside the firm, the secretary would ask him the next morning when the meeting ended and if he had done any other work after the meeting. A similar recording of all incoming and outgoing telephone calls was made on another form by the telephone exchange operator. Finally the private secretary prepared a list of all letters dictated and signed by the chief executive.

Although with the aid of this recording technique we got fairly complete information regarding the time distribution of the executives' work with reference to the place of work and the contacts he had with persons and institutions, there were some deficiencies in the recording which should be noticed. Thus we never succeeded in recording all the personal contacts the executive had outside his office, e.g. when he made an inspection tour in a plant or when he attended a meeting outside the firm. It was also difficult to get a complete record of the telephone calls with respect to both their frequency and their duration—particularly the latter. This was especially the case with the internal calls, and where a conference telephone was used, we could merely observe which persons could be reached by this telephone. Fortunately the conference telephone was used mostly in order to make appointments or for matters where only a quick answer was needed on a special question, and seldom for conversations of any length.

Another item which was difficult to record completely was the executives' working time outside the firm. As was mentioned above, the executive had to report this work daily to his secretary, but it was not always so easy for him to decide what activities he ought to regard as work. Was reading of memoranda and trade journals work only when it was done in his office or without disturbance at his home in the evenings, or was it also when he did it in the train going to and from his office? Was it work when he discussed the firm's affairs with a colleague or a subordinate during a Sunday walk? We never tried to formulate any rules for the judgment of these questions, but left them for the individual executives to decide for themselves. . . .

Technique of communication. The technique of communication, as I have said, is the technique used by the executive in order to obtain information from, and convey ideas to, the people he is in contact with. We may here distinguish the following subclasses:

Direct contacts:
1. Personal observations (e.g. during an inspection tour)
2. Conversations, person to person
3. Conferences—regular and *ad hoc*
4. Telephone calls
Indirect contacts:
5. Via persons (e.g. staff assistants, private secretaries, etc.)
6. Via papers (which the executive reads or writes)

A great deal of information regarding the use of these different communication techniques could be obtained from the data on the executive's contacts, mentioned above. These data told us, for example, how much time he spent on inspection tours to various parts of the firm, or in formal and *ad hoc* conferences. They also told us when he made use of letter writing, telephone calls or personal appointments. Additional information regarding the communication technique was obtained by collection of data for a full year on internal committees and conferences, on internal control reports, etc. Thus we made a systematic survey of all the committee meetings and conferences inside the firm in which the chief executive regularly took part, recording how the meetings were announced, how they were planned and run, if minutes were kept, etc. We made another survey of all the reports which were read regularly by the chief executive, recording their size, main contents, and periodicity. In addition we learned about the technique used with respect to personal appointments, telephone calls and correspondence, and private reading from interviews with the private secretary, the telephone exchange operator and the chief executive himself.

Nature of question handled and kind of action. In order to find out what questions the chief executives actually deal with in their daily work and what actions they made in relation to these questions, we had to ask the executives themselves. Our technique was as follows: We designed a standardized questionnaire, sized about 4" x 5½", which we spread all around the executive. He had copies of the questionnaire on his desk, in his pocket, at his home, etc. The headings contained on this questionnaire were the following:

1. *Date*
2. *Time*
3. *Telephone call,* with appropriate space for noting incoming and outgoing calls
4. *Place of work;* annotations were made only if the place of work was other than the executive's own office
5. *Person contacted;* in order to simplify the annotations, symbols were given for the persons with whom the executive was in contact most frequently. Otherwise it was sufficient if the executive marked the initials of the person in question, which would permit his identification . . .
6. *Nature of question handled,* with sub-headings for:
   A. The fields of activity
   B. Questions of development and current operations
   C. Questions of policy and of application
7. *Kinds of action,* with the sub-headings described above.

For every personal appointment, conference, or telephone call, and for every question the chief executive worked on for himself, he was asked to tick the appropriate headings on this questionnaire. After a short introductory training this task was done in a few seconds, and it in no way interfered with his ordinary work. (In fact, some of the directors got so used to filling in these questionnaires, that they complained when at the end of the investigation period they were not supplied with more forms!) Twice a day the questionnaires were collected by the private secretary or an assistant, who had to check them against the forms used for registering visitors and telephone calls. Naturally, the quality of the data thus obtained varied as between different individuals studied, but at least in five of the seven cases where this technique was used, the questionnaires returned to us were quite complete and very conscientiously marked.

These data regarding the nature of the questions handled and the kind of actions taken are, however, of a different kind from the data previously described. While we could register the actual behavior of the chief executive with respect to place of work and personal contacts, what we register here is not the executive's behavior but their *opinions* about their behavior. The opinions are expressed in standardized terms and they are registered almost simultaneously with the corresponding actions, which makes them very useful, but as with all opinions, they relate to particular persons at a particular instant of time. Thus, it becomes very difficult to make comparisons of the questions handled and the actions taken as between different executives. What one may hope for is merely that the individual executive will be consistent enough in his own marking for comparisons to be made as between the nature of the questions discussed with different people or the kind of actions taken for different types of questions. Since we did not expect to make any interpersonal comparisons, it was not necessary for us to define the concepts to be used in an exact way. We could leave it to the executive himself to decide within rather wide margins how he wanted to classify the particular items.

While the executives generally had no difficulty in classifying what fields of activity an individual question related to, or whether it was a question of development or current operations, they said that in many cases it was rather difficult to decide whether it was a question of policy or of application. There is no clear borderline between these concepts. One may think at the beginning of a discussion that the item brought up is merely a trifling detail, while further consideration reveals that the decision taken turns out to be a most important precedent for the future. Nevertheless, every scrap of actual information regarding this aspect of executive work is, of course, most welcome.

In the analysis of the data relating to the nature of questions handled, we got—among other things—into the following difficulty. It often happened that the chief executive classified a question under several different headings. An item discussed with a *sous-chef* could, e.g., be marked as "manufacturing" and "finance," "development" and "current operation," and "policy." Whether in such a case there were actually two different subjects that were discussed during the same visit, or one subject which had all these aspects, we never knew. At the final stage of the study we got one of the executives to make out a separate form for every separate item he worked on and not only one form for every visit, etc., but he said that it was generally very difficult to decide whether and when the conversation shifted from one item to another. This weakness in our investigation technique prevented us from drawing any but very tentative conclusions regarding the frequency of "company-wide" questions as compared with questions of a purely "functional" character, a study which, of course, would have been very interesting to make.

The study of the kind of action was, as I expected it to be, the most difficult part of our whole investigation, and neither the concepts nor the recording technique used are as yet sufficiently refined in this respect. Nevertheless the data obtained were most valuable. They clearly showed, for instance, that for the chief executive the main problems were those of "getting information" and "advising and explaining." In their own opinion, most of the directors studied did not take part in so very many decisions and it was seldom that they gave orders. It is probable, however, that if we had asked the subordinate to mark down the kind of actions taken, the picture might have been quite different. A conversation which from the point of view of the managing director merely means the getting of information may very well be regarded by the subordinates as decision-making or even the receiving of orders.

It seems to me that our knowledge of this aspect of the executive work would have been much more complete if we had classified the nature of the questions handled with respect to their time aspect also. By that I mean whether the particular question related to a coming or a past event. When, for example, the executive "gets information" regarding something which has not yet happened, this seems to have more of a directive significance than if the event has already taken place. In general, the concepts used for describing various kinds of actions only get an exact meaning when they are clearly related to the time aspect of the question on which action is taken. Unfortunately this was not done.

Complementary data. As a complement to the observational study thus far described, we carried out a fairly extensive interview program, which included not only the chief executives themselves but also their secretaries and other persons inside their organization who had first-hand knowledge of their daily behavior patterns. The interviews were generally semi-directed; there were some definite topics which we wanted to bring up, but they were complemented by a series of free conversations. We also collected data regarding the formal organization plans of the firms, the location and size of the various plants, the local amenities and the internal system of communication of the head offices, the associations, boards, and outside committees the executives were members of, the number of meetings these various institutions had had during the last twelve months, the number of days the executives had been away from their firms during the same period, etc.

GROUP OBSERVATION AND PERSONAL INTERVIEWS

F. J. Roethlisberger and William J. Dickson

THE NEED FOR A MORE SYSTEMATIC INQUIRY. The foregoing illustrations [1] of social organization among employees were derived almost entirely from interviews with the men in the different groups. The investigators had little opportunity to observe the groups at work, they knew little about their output except what could be learned from departmental records, which were kept for practical rather than research purposes, and they knew almost nothing about the overt behavior of the employees toward one another and their supervisors.

The statement that little was known about the overt behavior of the people studied implies a distinction which should be made more clear. By overt behavior is meant the manner in which the employees acted toward one another. In the interview situation the investigators obtained only statements of how the employees said they acted. The interviewers had no means of relating these statements to what actually transpired. This distinction between actions and words, or between overt and verbal behavior, is emphasized here because it led to an innovation in method which distinguished the study to be reported from all the others dealt with so far, namely, supplementing the interviewing method with direct observation. The Bank Wiring Observation Room study, then, was planned with

Reprinted by permission of the publisher from *Management and the Worker*, pp. 384-391 (Cambridge, Mass.: Harvard University Press, 1939).

1. [This excerpt was preceded in the original text by an account of interviewing procedures in the study of a large factory. The observational and interview procedures discussed here supplied the empirical basis for the excerpt entitled "Formal and Informal Status" in Section IV of the present volume.—The Editors.]

two purposes in mind: to develop the new method and to obtain more exact information about social groups within the company. It was conducted with a group of fourteen male operators who were working, as they were accustomed to work, under standard shop conditions. The study lasted from November, 1931, to May, 1932, when it had to be terminated because of lack of work. The investigators spent the period of six and one-half months in observing the situation before them. No intentional changes were made in the situation once the group was so placed that observation was possible.

One need not have an intimate acquaintance with shop departments to anticipate many of the problems which arise in studying them. There is, for example, the question of size. Many departments in the plant contained one hundred or more employees exclusive of supervisors. To study such a large group carefully would not only require a large staff of investigators and entail a great deal of expense, but it would also require an unusual amount of tolerance on the part of the supervisors and employees.

Closely connected with the question of size is that of complexity. Technical, administrative, supervisory, and personal problems are all mixed up into one interacting whole. It is practically impossible to study all of these factors in detail; some selection is essential. The selection made, of course, must be determined by the questions one has in mind. In this study, for example, the investivators were interested in the technical aspects of the work to a certain extent, but they were not interested in engineering problems as such. It was enough for them to know that the workers used certain materials and were supposed to carry through certain specified operations. Whether or not the workers' routines and the layout of the job were organized in the best possible way was a question with which they were not concerned. They were, however, very much interested in administrative and supervisory practices because these deal with the organization and motivation of the personnel.

A third problem is that of change. Most departments are exceedingly dynamic. The personnel is frequently increased or decreased, technical changes are made, and people are often shifted from one job to another. The keeping of records becomes very difficult in such a situation, especially if they are to be kept individually and with precision.

Quite apart from problems like these is one related to the sociological nature of working groups. This problem is too frequently ignored or considered unimportant by investigators in industry. A protective or defensive attitude surrounds many shop departments. It may be brought into play whenever the employees feel that their security is being threatened. Any person unknown to them who expresses more than a casual interest in their work or affairs is likely to be regarded with suspicion unless he takes pains to make clear to them just what he is doing and why. Even

then, they may not believe him and may alter their work habits and behavior in defense. This attitude has a parallel in the suspicion of the stranger
manifested by many closely knit groups in modern and primitive societies.
It was especially important to overcome such resistance as this in the
present study because the success of the study depended on establishing a
situation in which the employees would feel free to work and behave as
they were accustomed to, even though the investigators were looking on.
To illustrate the manifestation of such a protective attitude, the following
case may be cited:

One day an interviewer entered a department unobserved. There was
a buzz of conversation and the men seemed to be working at great speed.
Suddenly there was a sharp hissing sound. The conversation died away,
and there was a noticeable slowing up in the work pace. The interviewer
later discovered from an acquaintance in the department that he had been
mistaken for a rate setter. One of the workmen, who acted as a lookout,
had stepped on a valve releasing compressed air, a prearranged signal for
slowing down.

The problem of allaying the attitude of distrust had been handled exceedingly well in the interviewing program, and by continual demonstration of the company's good faith the same end had been achieved in the
Relay Assembly Test Room. It was felt, however, that the problem would
be much more difficult in studying a whole or a vertical section of a department because the entire departmental structure, including the supervisory organization, would be brought into focus. To the apprehensions
of the employees would be added those of the supervisors, from the foreman on down. One false step might ruin the relation between the investigators and the department. Accordingly, this aspect of shop situations had
to be kept constantly in mind throughout the study.

Closely related to the above problem is that of what constitutes a change
in a situation. It is one thing to overcome defensive attitudes; it is quite
another thing to do so without introducing a fundamental change in the
situation. This difficulty arises from the fact that the importance of a
change in a worker's situation, however insignificant it may appear to an
outsider, can only be judged in terms of the meaning attached to it by the
employee. Changes unwittingly made in a situation while experimenting
with rest pauses or hours of work, for example, might have more effect on
efficiency than the experimental change itself; yet the investigators might
attribute the entire result to the experimental change. The success of this
study really depended upon being able to study a situation without at the
same time introducing major changes in it. Those things which the investigators were careful not to alter will be discussed later. The foregoing discussion is intended to emphasize certain difficulties in studying shop departments which otherwise might be overlooked or considered negligible.

The importance attached to them by the investigators was such that every step they took was in some degree guided by consideration of them.

THE METHOD OF STUDY. In view of the size and complexity of the average shop department, the investigators decided that it would be better to concentrate on one small group engaged in one type of work rather than to spread their efforts over a number of groups with dissimilar jobs. Inasmuch as departmental rules, policies, and practices applied to every worker, it was believed that they could be assessed in relation to one group as well as another. The same was true of the departmental supervisory organization. Accordingly, the investigators decided to study a vertical section of a department. It was assumed that one vertical section was essentially the same as another and that any vertical section, considered separately, would reveal the same type of factors as would be revealed by a study of the whole department.

Secondly, it was decided to place the group to be studied in a separate room. This was done reluctantly, because it meant a change in the workers' environment. The alternative of allowing the workers to remain where they were was unfeasible. In the first place, it would have been extremely difficult for an observer to keep adequate records of behavior without making a nuisance of himself. The ordinary shop was not so arranged that an outsider could mingle readily with the workers or sit at a desk near them. In the second place, it was felt that the group studied might feel uneasy in the presence of acquaintances not included in the study. They might feel obliged to do or refrain from doing certain things in order to keep in good standing with the remainder of the group. Such problems would not arise if the group to be studied were segregated.

Thirdly, in order to assess the effect of placing the group in a separate room, base period studies were to be made before either the workers or their immediate supervisors knew anything about the study.

Fourthly, nothing was to be said or done in selecting the group to be studied, in explaining the study to them, or in removing them from the department which might alter their status in any way.

Fifthly, no records were to be taken which might tend to make the workers apprehensive or too consciously aware that they were being studied. For example, they were unaccustomed to having their output recorded at short consecutive time intervals. It was decided at the outset, therefore, not to take such readings. To do so might arouse many apprehensions which would be difficult to allay. Similarly, records of such things as diet and hours of sleep were not to be taken because of the antagonism which such personal inquiry might arouse.

The investigating work itself was functionally divided between an observer and an interviewer. This was done in the belief that the types of material to be obtained by the two people were quite different and, furthermore, that both types of material could not be obtained equally well by one person.

The observer was stationed with the group in the role of a disinterested spectator. His function was to keep necessary records of performance as well as records of events and conversations which he considered significant. The role of a disinterested spectator was a difficult one to maintain. In order to obtain the confidence of the group, the observer had to establish friendly relations with everyone in it. This inevitably meant that he became a part of the situation he was studying. To keep his own feelings and prejudices from coloring the material recorded and to keep his own personality from affecting the situation under observation required a high degree of personal insight and objectivity.

It was decided beforehand that the observer should adhere to certain general rules: (1) He should not give orders or answer any questions which necessitated the assumption of authority. (2) He should not enter voluntarily into any argument. If forced to do so, he should be as noncommittal as possible. (3) He should not force himself into a conversation or appear to be either anxious to overhear what was going on or overinterested in the group's behavior. (4) He should never violate confidences or give any information to supervisors, whatever their rank. (5) He should not by his manner of speech or behavior set himself off from the group. It was recognized, of course, that rules like these could only help the observer to define his role; what measure of success he was to achieve depended upon his own ability and personality.

Apart from the observer's relations with the group, there was the question of what constituted a significant event. The observer had to make some selection of material to record, but what should he select? Of course, common sense determined part of the selection; for example, a heated argument between two operators or a clash between an operator and a supervisor would be noted by anyone. But the question goes much deeper. The point is that observation, if it is to be at all scientific, must be guided by a working hypothesis which enables the observer to make active discriminations in the complex interplay of factors before him. Without such guidance he is likely to miss much of significance and become lost in a welter of irrelevancies. It may be well, therefore, to state what the investigators agreed upon as being important for the observer to look for and record.[2]

2. The investigators were fortunate in having the counsel of William Lloyd Warner, at that time Assistant Professor of Social Anthropology at Harvard University and now Professor of Anthropology and Sociology at the University of Chicago, who had become interested in the research program about the middle of 1930. The general methodological concepts employed throughout this study were chiefly derived from Mr. Warner; however, he should not in any sense be held responsible for their detailed application to this industrial situation. Mr. Warner frequently discussed the investigators'

First of all, the observer had to have clearly in mind what the situation was demanding of the supervisors and employees. In other words, he had to know the formal and technical organization of the department. The formal and technical organization provided an object of reference to which observations of performance and behavior could be related. Every item which indicated a similarity or difference between the actual situation and the way it was supposed to be was to be recorded.

Secondly, he was to look for evidences of any informal organization which the employees in their face-to-face relations consciously or unconsciously formed. To this end he was to watch for (a) recurrent verbal utterances or overt acts which were indicative of the relations between two or more people; (b) manifestations of the kind and extent of a person's participation in the immediate group situation; (c) evidences of the existence of a group solidarity (the importance of crises in bringing out the group organization was stressed); (d) if there was such a group solidarity, to what occupational groups it extended and how it was expressed.

Thirdly, should the observer detect evidences of an informal organization, he should attempt to understand the functions it fulfilled for the employees and how it was related to the formal company organization. It was assumed here that every group organization fulfills functions both for the people participating in it and for the larger structure of which the group is a part. Sometimes these functions are explicitly stated, but more frequently they are not. For the most part, they can be assessed only after a careful, objective study of the group and its relation to other organizations.

It may be well to add a few words regarding the attitude required of a person doing the kind of observational work being discussed. He must above all else refrain from evaluational judgments. His function is to observe and to describe. Whether or not the conduct of those he is observing is right or wrong is entirely irrelevant to his function. The reason for this is that, as soon as one becomes involved in questions of right or wrong, attention is diverted from the only significant areas, personal and social, in which an explanation of a given action can be found. The observer's attitude toward the situation he is studying should be exactly the same as that of the interviewer toward the interviewee or of the doctor toward his patient. Instead of asking, "Is this man's conduct such that it should be stopped?" he should be asking such questions as, "Why does he act this way? What do his actions indicate his position in the group to be? How do his actions affect the interpersonal relations of others in the group?"

problems with them and called their attention to the similarity between the problems confronting them and those confronting the anthropological field worker. He also directed their attention to the works of such people as Durkheim, Malinowski, Radcliffe-Brown, and Georg Simmel, from which a wealth of background material was obtained. . . .

Such questions provide fruitful leads for further research; they lead the investigator directly to a consideration of the personal and social contexts to which the actions are related, whereas evaluational judgments merely lead to a statement of the observer's own sentiments and to the formulation of irrelevant questions.

The interviewer, as contrasted with the observer, was to remain an outsider to the group as much as possible. Although he was to be in daily touch with the observer, he was not to enter the observation room unless it was necessary. It was felt that if the interviewer was an outsider the workers would feel more like telling him about themselves, their work, and occurrences in the observation room. In other words, the mere fact of talking to an outsider gave point to their relating certain events and experiences in the immediate work situation which they might otherwise pass over as being common knowledge. The interviews were to be held by appointment and conducted in privacy.

The function of the interviewer, as contrasted with that of the observer, who was to describe the actual verbal and overt behavior of the operators, was to gain some insight into their attitudes, thoughts, and feelings. He was to look for the values and significances for them of their situation. In addition, the interviewer was to learn what he could about each person's personal history, family situation, and social life outside the plant. . . .

The method of study developed can be summarized by visualizing a simple diagram consisting of three concentric circles: the innermost of which represents the department; the second, the company as a whole; and the outermost, the total community. The workers to be studied participated in all three areas. Their active participation in the department and, to a certain extent, in the larger company structure was subject to direct observation. Their participation in the wider community and their subjective attitudes, beliefs, and feelings toward their immediate surroundings in the plant could not, however, be observed. Such material had to be elicited from the individual and the best available technique was the personal interview. The functions of the observer and interviewer, therefore, were complementary. Their attention was fixed upon the same group, and one simply attempted to get information which the other, because of his relation with the group, either could not get as well or could not get at all.

INTERLOCKING METHODS OF ORGANIZATIONAL STUDY

Ralph M. Stogdill

The studies are aimed at discovering general principles concerning administrative leadership, as well as practical applications. The practical objectives have been stated as follows: (1) to determine the value of various methods of appraising leadership performance, (2) to develop facts and methods for use in the selection, assignment and transfer of persons in positions of leadership, and (3) to derive basic principles and methods which may be applied by Naval officers in evaluating the leadership requirements of various group situations. Although these objectives are stated in practical terms, the task is not conceived as one of problem solving, but as one in basic research. . . .

The following methods have been employed in the Navy project:

1. *Interview with commissioned officers.* This includes questions pertaining to the history and aims of the organization and its various subdivisions, the responsibilities of the executive, and his methods of communications and working with staff.

2. *A study of organization charts and manuals.* These sources provide data as to the formal structure of the organization, its goals, functions, and responsibilities.

3. *Sociometric Methods.* The executive's list of the persons with whom he spends the most time in getting work done permits the charting of informal organization. The test-retest correlation with a two-year interval for one sample is .9.

4. *Time expenditure logs and check lists.* These check lists require the executive to estimate or log the time he spends in various kinds of work performance. The test-retest correlations with a two-year interval range from .0 to .9 for self-estimates of various kinds of work performance.

5. *RAD Scales.* These rating scales require the executive to estimate the level of his own authority, responsibility, and the authority he delegates to others. Split-half reliabilities of these scales range from .6 to .8.

6. *Leader Behavior Descriptions.* Scales which can be used for self-descriptions or for descriptions by others. The behaviors to be described are Communications, Production, Representation, Domination, Recognition,

Reprinted in part from "Studies in Naval Leadership: Part II," in *Groups, Leadership and Men;* Research in Human Relations (Harold Guetzkow, ed.) by permission of the publisher. (Copyright, 1951, by Carnegie Press, Pittsburgh, Pennsylvania.)

Initiation, Systematization, Membership, and Integration. Split-half reliabilities range from .6 to .9.

7. *Rating Scales.* Morale ballots, estimates of group opinion forms, decision-making scales, and other devices.

8. *Production records.* Performance records, reenlistment records, disciplinary records, and other records indicative of performance and morale.

These methods have been employed in the study of a rather wide variety of Naval organizations. Approximately twenty ships and twenty shore establishments have been studied.

LEVELS OF ANALYSIS. The first organizations studied served the purpose primarily of testing and revising methods. Nevertheless, they yielded information which has been subjected to several levels of analysis. First, it is possible to construct a profile of the responses of a single individual. Second, it is possible to obtain a profile of the average of the responses of several individuals in the same professional specialty, thus yielding some idea as to what variables are specific to various technical and professional positions. In the same way it is possible to obtain a profile of the average responses of individuals in different echelons in the organization, thus yielding an index of variables that are characteristic of performance at different administrative levels. Third, it is possible to compare the average scores of all members of the organization with average scores of all members of another organization on the same variable. This level of analysis permits us to determine what aspects of performance are specific to a particular organization. Fourth, it is possible to compare the responses of an individual with those of his superiors and subordinates. This permits us to study relationships at a very simple level. Fifth, through the use of sociometric charts it is possible to study the working relationships among all members of an organization. Sixth, through the correlation of each variable with every other variable it is possible to gain some conception of an organization as a constellation of interacting variables, and to isolate some of the factors which appear to describe the organization as a going concern.

I should like to present briefly some of the results that have been obtained at each of these levels of analysis. First, the construction of a profile of a single individual is useful primarily as source material for other levels of analysis. The second level involves the construction of an average profile for the members of a given professional specialty, or level of organization. For example, the work profile of personnel officers shows time spent in Personnel Activities, Planning, Coordination, and Interpretation; while public information officers are shown to spend time in Public Relations, Planning, and Evaluation. If we inspect the profiles of the members of an organization when classified as to echelon, we find that top level administrators spend major proportions of their time in Planning and Public Relations. Second echelon administrators spend large proportions of their time in Evaluation and Planning. Third echelon administrators spend major portions of their time in Planning and Coordination, while fourth echelon administrators spend more of their time in Planning, Evaluation, Supervision, and Interpretation than in other responsibilities. It can be observed that work becomes more diversified at the fourth echelon in the organization hierarchy. Analysis reveals increasing diversification of function at successively lower echelons, but not to a statistically significant degree.

The third level of analysis, which permits a determination of the factors that are common to all the organizations studied and those that are unique for specific organizations, yields a large body of information. These results may be illustrated by describing the findings from an analysis of data from four Naval and four business organizations. This analysis, done by Mr. E. A. Fleishman, indicates that there are no significant differences among the eight organizations in average amount of time spent by administrators and executives in Inspection, Interpretation, Research, Personnel Activities, and acting as Professional Consultant. Significant differences are observed among Naval organizations, among business organizations, and between Naval and business organizations in Coordination and Reading and Answering Mail. Naval and business organizations differ significantly in the average amounts of time spent with Assistants and with Outside Persons, as well as in Thinking and Examining Reports. Naval officers differ significantly from business executives in self-estimates of level of Responsibility and Delegation of Authority to subordinates, but no significant differences are found between Naval officers and business executives in self-estimates as to level of Authority.

The fourth level of analysis permits us to determine certain relationships between the performance of superiors and subordinates. It is observed, for example, that persons who describe themselves as delegating more authority to their subordinates have subordinates who in turn describe themselves as possessing a higher degree of responsibility and authority and who delegate more to their assistants than do their associates whose superiors do not delegate so freely. The superiors who tend to delegate more also tend to receive a larger number of nominations as work partners than do those who delegate less freely.

The fifth level of analysis permits us to chart the working relationships among all members of the organization. When the sociometric chart is superimposed upon the formal organization chart, discrepancies between formal organization and informal organization become readily apparent. It has been found in all Naval as well as business organizations studied, that some discrepancies appear. Reference to interview data, however, reveals that most of these discrepancies are related to the demands of short-term objectives and work requirements. There are, of course, some instances in which discrepancies appear to be related to personal factors. Those persons who are revealed as having the greatest number of working relationships within the organization are usually those who are at the focal point of activities necessary for the attainment of the immediate primary objectives of the organization. Those individuals who bypass one or two superiors in order to work with an individual who is in a still higher echelon, are found to be technical specialists such as public information officers, public works officers, and legal officers who possess technical information that cannot be readily transmitted through their immediate superiors.

The sixth level of analysis permits us to study an organization as a complex of selected variables in interaction. The basic method is that of constructing a table of intercorrelations among all the variables. Cluster analysis and factor analysis are probably the most efficient methods for isolating the combinations of variables that describe the operations of an organization as revealed through a table of intercorrelations. Using factor analysis, it is possible to rotate the factors in such a manner as to determine which are common to all the organizations for which data on the same variables are available. Such a factor analysis was performed by Dr. Robert H. Wherry on tables of intercorrelations obtained from a study of three Naval organizations. The following factors were found in common in the three organizations: (1) high level administration, (2) high level policy making, (3) methods planning, and (4) personnel functions. Two other factors, each specific to a single organization, were found. These were (1) technical consulting and (2) investigation-report writing. These are not characteristics of persons, but of organizational functioning as measured by the performances of persons.

The Relation of Estimated Time to Logged Time. A large portion of the data we collect consists of self-descriptions, self-estimates, self-perceptions. One of the troublesome questions we always have in mind is whether administrators can with any high degree of accuracy estimate the way they spend their time. If we are to place reliance upon our data it is necessary to have an answer to this question. In order to obtain data on this point, a restudy was made in 1949 of a Naval Air Station that had been previously studied in 1947. Mr. Charles F. Elton assisted in the study. Forty officers were asked to keep daily work logs. The logs could be simply executed by checking the beginning and end of a task on a chart subdivided into one-minute intervals, and by entering on the chart a code letter to indicate the kind of work performed. Because of emergency conditions caused by heavy snowstorms and interruption of operating schedules, it was possible to keep the log for only a period of three days. At the end of this period, the logs were collected and forms were distributed requiring the officer to estimate the amount of time spent in various kinds of work performance during the period over which the log was kept. Analysis of the results indicates that there is a fairly high correspondence between logged time and estimated time in such performances as Writing Reports, Reading Mail, Talking with Other Persons, Operating Machines, and Attending Meetings. The correlations between logged time and estimated time on these variables range from .4 to .8. However, the correlation between logged time and estimated time for Thinking is .3 and for Planning .o. Some of the correlations are lowered by the fact that very small amounts of time were logged or estimated for the performances in question. These tentative results suggest that self-estimates of objectively observable kinds of work performance have some correspondence with logged time in the same performances. . . .

JOB VERSUS MAN. One of the questions in which we have been very much interested may be stated somewhat as follows: Does an administrator develop certain patterns of work performance which he carries into a new position, no matter what its nature, or is his pattern of work performance determined by the requirements of the job? Our restudy of a Naval Air Station after a lapse of two years, permitted us to acquire tentative information on this question. In the restudy we found a number of officers who occupied the same position as two years previously. We found that a number of officers had been transferred to different positions within the organization. A number of positions were occupied by officers who had not been on the station two years previously. This enabled us to study Same Man in Same Position; Same Man in Different Position; Different Men in Same Position. It was possible to construct three tables of intercorrelation, correlating data found in 1947 with those obtained in 1949. The variables that appeared to be characteristic of the *man* rather than the position are Delegation practices, time spent in Public Relations, Evaluation, Reading and Answering Mail, Reading technical publications, and time spent with Outside Persons. Variables that appeared to be characteristics of the *position* rather than of the man are Level in the organization structure, Military Rank, time spent in Personal Contacts, time spent with Assistants, time spent with Superiors, time spent in Supervision, Coordination, and Writing Reports, as well as number of nominations received for working partner. That these results are not entirely unrealistic is indicated by the fact that Military Rank for Same Man—Same Position is correlated .9 even though a two year period elapsed between the data collections. The correlation for Level in the organization is .8. Both of these correlation coefficients dropped to .o for Same Man—Different Position, but were raised to .9 and .6 for Different Man in Same Position. The very fact that these findings reveal a characteristic condition of an organization, namely that the same position is likely to remain approximately at the same echelon level over a period of time and is likely to be filled by a person of the same military rank, suggests that the other results obtained may have some validity also.

In addition to obtaining general information, we feel that our methods should be tested to determine what practical applications they may have. As one step in this direction, we designed what might be called a clinical prediction study, in which we shall attempt to follow up officers who have been transferred to new positions. The plan requires us to study an officer in his present position immediately before his transfer to a new position. Then, before he arrives in his new position, we shall study the present occupant of that position. On the basis of the information accumulated from the transferee, his superiors and his subordinates, and from the occupant of the job to which he is to be transferred and that person's superiors and subordinates, we shall make a prediction as to what changes will occur after he has become established in his new position. The prediction is then to be checked by a follow-up study six or eight months later of the officer in his new position. All data including interview data, observations, and impressions, in addition to the quantitative data, will be utilized in making a recorded prediction on each of the variables for which quantitative data are obtained for an individual. In addition, the reason will be written out, justifying the prediction on each variable. These predictions, which are made by several researchers, are then to be sealed and put away until after the follow-up data have been collected. We have just completed a pilot study in which we interviewed ten officers who are to be transferred, as well as their superiors and subordinates and other members of their organizations. We have also interviewed the officers whom they are to replace and other members of their organizations. The data have been transferred to special forms devised by Dr. David Bakan in order to facilitate the recordings of our predictions, but since we have just returned from this field trip, it has not been possible as yet to record our predictions. The trial study indicates that it is at least possible and feasible to collect data for such purposes. It is planned to obtain data on fifty or sixty transferees and on the officers whom they are to replace as the next phase of our data collection program. Whether we succeed in our attempts to predict an officer's future behavior in the new position is perhaps not of as great an importance as that we have made the attempt, and have been willing to subject our methods to a rigorous and realistic type of test.

Since this list of works is intended to supplement the materials in the *Reader*, we do not cite here the fifty-or-so selections included in the book itself. Additional sources, bearing upon specific points under discussion, will be found in many of the selections and in the books and articles listed below. For the student interested in the comparative study of bureaucracy, we have suggested a few descriptive accounts of bureaucracy in societies not touched upon in the *Reader*. It will be noted, however, that no systematic attempt has been made to sample the numerous writings on bureaucracy in the literature of European social science.

1. *Theoretical Conceptions*

Appleby, Paul H., *Big Democracy*, New York: Knopf, 1945.

Arensberg, Conrad M., "Behavior and organization: industrial studies," in John H. Rohrer and Muzafer Sherif, eds., *Social Psychology at the Crossroads*, New York: Harper and Brothers, 1951, 324-352.

Barnard, Chester I., *Organization and Management*, Cambridge: Harvard University Press, 1948.

Bendix, Reinhard, "Bureaucracy: the problem and its setting," *American Sociological Review*, 1947, 12, 493-507.

Dahl, Robert A., "The science of public administration, three problems," *Public Administration Review*, 1947, 7, 1-11.

Fayol, Henri, *Industrial and General Administration*, London: Sir Isaac Pitman & Sons, 1930.

Florence, P. Sargant, *The Logic of Industrial Organization*, London: Routledge, 1933.

Friedrich, Carl J., *Constitutional Government and Democracy*, Boston: Little, Brown, 1941.

Gaus, John M., "A theory of organization in public administration," in John M. Gaus, Leonard D. White, and Marshall E. Dimock, eds., *The Frontiers of Public Administration*, Chicago: University of Chicago Press, 1936.

Gulick, Luther and Urwick, L., *Papers on the Science of Administration*, New York: Institute of Public Administration, 1937.

Laski, Harold J., "Bureaucracy," *Encyclopedia of the Social Sciences*.

Lasswell, H. D., *Politics: Who Gets What, When, How*, New York: McGraw-Hill, 1936.

Lepawsky, Albert, *Administration, The Art and Science of Organization and Management*, New York: Knopf, 1949.

Marx, F. Morstein, "Bureaucracy," in R. V. Peel and J. S. Roucek, eds., *Introduction to Politics*, New York: Thomas Y. Crowell Company, 1941, ch. 19.

Marx, F. Morstein, ed., *Elements of Public Administration*, New York: Prentice-Hall, 1946.

Mayer, J. P., *Max Weber and German Politics: A Study in Political Sociology*, London: Faber and Faber, n.d.

Merton, Robert K., *Social Theory and Social Structure*, Glencoe, Illinois: The Free Press, 1949, pts. 1, 3.

Metcalf, Henry C. and Urwick, L., eds., *Dynamic Administration, The Collected Papers of Mary Parker Follett*, New York: Harper and Brothers, 1940.

Mooney, James D. and Reiley, Alan C., *The Principles of Organization*, New York: Harper and Brothers, 1939.

Moore, Wilbert E., *Industrial Relations and the Social Order*, New York: Macmillan, 1951, rev. ed.

Parsons, Talcott, *Essays in Sociological Theory, Pure and Applied*, Glencoe, Ill.: The Free Press, 1949.

Parsons, Talcott, *The Structure of Social Action*, Glencoe, Ill.: The Free Press, 1949.

Selznick, Philip, "An approach to a theory of bureaucracy," *American Sociological Review*, 1943, 8, 47-54.

Selznick, Philip, "Foundations of the theory of organization," *American Sociological Review*, 1948, 13, 25-35.

Shartle, Carroll L., "Organization structure," in Wayne Dennis, ed., *Current Trends in Industrial Psychology*, Pittsburgh: University of Pittsburgh Press, 1949, 14-31.

Stene, Edwin O., "An approach to a science of administration," *American Political Science Review*, 1940, 34, 1124-1137.

Stogdill, Carroll L., "Leadership, membership and organization," *Psychological Bulletin*, 1950, 47, 1-14.

Tead, Ordway, *The Art of Administration*, New York: McGraw-Hill, 1951.

Truman, David B., *The Governmental Process*, New York: Knopf, 1951.

Urwick, L., *The Elements of Administration*, New York: Harper and Brothers, 1943.

Watson, Goodwin, ed., "Problems of Bureaucracy," *Journal of Social Issues*, 1945, Vol. 1, no. 4.

Whitehead, T. N., *Leadership in a Free Society*, Cambridge: Harvard University Press, 1937.

2. Bases for Growth

Barker, Ernest, *The Development of Public Services in Western Europe, 1660–1930*, New York: Oxford University Press, 1944.

Bartholdy, Albrecht M., "Bureaucracy in a nation's lean years: the German experience," in Leonard D. White, ed., *The New Social Science*, Chicago: University of Chicago Press, 1930, 16-27.

Dickinson, John, "Administrative law and the fear of bureaucracy," *American Bar Journal*, 1928, 14, 513-16, 597-602.

Finer, Herman, *The Theory and Practice of Modern Government*, New York: Henry Holt, 1949, rev. ed.

Herring, E. Pendleton, "Social forces and the reorganization of the federal bureaucracy," *Southwestern Social Science Quarterly*, 1934, 15, 185-200.

Lea, Henry C., *Studies in Church History*, Philadelphia: Henry C. Lea's Son and Company, 1883.

Lefas, Alexandre, *L'Etat et Les Fonctionnaires*, Paris: M. Giard and E. Brière, 1913.

Mannheim, Karl, *Diagnosis of Our Time*, London: Kegan Paul, 1943.

Mannheim, Karl, *Freedom, Power, and Democratic Planning*, New York: Oxford University Press, 1950.

Mannheim, Karl, *Man and Society in an Age of Reconstruction*, New York: Harcourt Brace, 1940.

Marx, F. Morstein, "German bureaucracy in transition," *American Political Science Review*, 1934, 28, 467-480.

Mills, C. Wright, *White Collar: The American Middle Classes*, New York: Oxford University Press, 1951.

Norton, H. L., "Foreign office organization. A comparison of the British, French, German and Italian foreign office organisations with that of the Department of State of the U. S. A.," *Annals* of the American Academy of Political and Social Science, 1929, Vol. 143, Suppl.

Polanyi, Karl, *The Great Transformation*, New York: Farrar and Rinehart, 1944.

Schumpeter, Joseph A., *Capitalism, Socialism, and Democracy*, New York: Harper and Brothers, 1947, 2nd ed.

Skevington, Leonard, "The crisis of the bureaucracy," *Pilot Papers*, 1947, 2, 71-84.

Stein, Lorenz, "Die Lehre von der vollziehenden Gewalt, ihr Recht und ihr Organismus," first part of *Die Verwaltungslehre*, Stuttgart, 1865.

Tout, Thomas Frederick, *The Place of the Reign of Edward II in English History*, Manchester: University Press, 1936, 2nd ed.

Weber, Alfred, "Der Beamte," in *Ideen zur Staats- und Kultursoziologie*, Karlsruhe: G. Braun, 1927.

3. Bureaucracy and Power Relations

Power Environment

Appleby, Paul H., "Civilian control of a Department of National Defense," in Jerome G. Kerwin, ed., *Civil-Military Relationships in American Life*, Chicago: University of Chicago Press, 1948, 62-90.

Arnold, Thurman, *The Symbols of Government*, New Haven: Yale University Press, 1935.

Bendix, Reinhard, "Socialism and the theory of bureaucracy," *The Canadian Journal of Economics and Political Science*, 1950, 16, 501-514.

Blaisdell, Donald D., "Economic power and political pressures," in U. S. Temporary National Economic Committee, *Investigation of Concentration of Economic Power*, Monograph No. 26, 1940.

Brady, Robert A., *Business as a System of Power*, New York: Columbia University Press, 1943.

Cahen-Salvador, Jean, *La Représentation des Intérêts et les Services Publics*, Paris: Sirey, 1935.

Chardon, Henri, *L'Administration de la France: Les Fonctionnaires*, Paris: Perrin et Cie., 1908.

Cole, Taylor, "Italy's Fascist bureaucracy," *American Political Science Review*, 1938, 32, 194-209.

Committee on Public Administration Cases, *The Battle of Blue Earth County*, Washington, D. C., 1949, mimeo.

Committee on Public Administration Cases, *Casebook*, Harold Stein, ed., to be published January, 1952.

Committee on Public Administration Cases, *The Foreign Service Act of 1946*, Washington, D. C., 1949, mimeo.

Committee on Public Administration Cases, *The Sale of the Tankers*, Washington, D. C., 1950, mimeo.

Committee on Public Administration Cases, *The Transfer of the Children's Bureau*, Washington, D. C., 1949, mimeo.

Dimock, M., *Free Enterprise and the Administrative Process*, Tuscaloosa, Ala.: University of Alabama Press, 1951.

Dorn, Walter L., "The Prussian bureaucracy in the 18th century," *Political Science Quarterly*, 1931, 46, 403-23; 1932, 47, 75-94, 259-73.

Ferrero, Guglielmo, *The Principles of Power* (trans. by Theodore Jaeckel), New York: G. P. Putnam's Sons, 1942.

Garceau, Oliver, *The Political Life of the American Medical Association*, Cambridge: Harvard University Press, 1941.

Golden, Clinton S. and Ruttenberg, Harold J., *The Dynamics of Industrial Democracy*, New York: Harper and Brothers, 1942.

Goldhamer, H. and Shils, E. A., "Types of power and status," *American Journal of Sociology*, 1939, 45, 171-182.

Gordon, Lincoln, *The Public Corporation in Great Britain*, New York: Oxford University Press, 1938.

Greaves, H. R. G., *The Civil Service in the Changing State*, London, Harrap, 1947.

Herring, E. Pendleton, *Public Administration and the Public Interest*, New York: McGraw-Hill, 1936.

Hyneman, Charles S., *Bureaucracy in a Democracy*, New York: Harper and Brothers, 1950.

Kosok, Paul, *Modern Germany: A Study in Conflicting Loyalties*, Chicago: University of Chicago Press, 1933, ch. 8.

Lasswell, H. D. and Kaplan, Abraham, *Power and Society: A Framework for Political Inquiry*, New Haven: Yale University Press, 1950.

Latham, Earl, "Giantism and basing-points: a political analysis," *Yale Law Journal*, 1949, 58, 383-399.

Leiserson, Avery, *Administrative Regulation: A Study in the Representation of Interests*, Chicago: University of Chicago Press, 1942.

Lindsell, W. G., *Military Organization and Administration*, Aldershot: Gale and Polden, 1925.

Lippincott, Benjamin E., ed., *Government Control of the Economic Order*, Minneapolis: University of Minnesota Press, 1935.

MacIver, Robert M., *Leviathan and the People*, University, La.: University of Louisiana Press, 1939.

MacIver, Robert M., *The Web of Government*, New York: Macmillan, 1947.

Marx, F. Morstein, "Bureaucracy and dictatorship," *Review of Politics*, 1941, 3, 110-117.

Mason, Alphens T., "Business organized as power: the new *imperium in imperio*," *American Political Science Review*, 1950, 45, 323-342.

Millett, John D., *The British Unemployment Assistance Board*, New York: McGraw-Hill, 1940.

Pritchett, C. H., *TVA: A Study in Public Administration*, Chapel Hill: University of North Carolina Press, 1943.

Rademacher, Arnold, *Die Kirche als Gemeinschaft und Gesellschaft; eine Studie zur Soziologie der Kirche*, Augsburg: Literar-Institut Haas und Grabherr, 1931.

Renner, Karl, *Demokratie und Bureaukratie*, Wien, Universum, 1946.

Sayre, Wallace C., "Political neutrality," in F. Morstein Marx, ed., *Public Management in the New Democracy*, New York: Harper and Brothers, 1940, 202-218.

Selznick, Philip, "The iron law of bureaucracy," *Modern Review*, 1949, 3, 157-165.

Sprout, Harold, "Trends in the traditional relation between military and civilian," *Proceedings*, American Philosophical Society, 1948, 92, 264-270.

Vagts, Alfred, *A History of Militarism*, New York: W. W. Norton and Company, 1937, 269-97, 350-90.

Warner, W. Lloyd and Low, J. O., *The Social System of the Modern Factory*, New Haven: Yale University Press, 1947.

Ownership, Management and Power

Arnold, Thurman W., *The Folklore of Capitalism*, New Haven: Yale University Press, 1937.

Burnham, James, *The Managerial Revolution*, New York: John Day, 1941.

Drucker, Peter F., *Concept of the Corporation*, New York: John Day, 1946.

Gablentz, O. H. von der, "Industriebürokratie," *Schmollers Jahrbuch*, 1926, 50, 539-572.

Marx, F. Morstein, "The bureaucratic state: some remarks on Mosca's Ruling Class," *Review of Politics*, 1939, 1, 457-72.

Mosca, Gaetano, *The Ruling Class*, New York: McGraw-Hill, 1939.

Spitz, David, *Patterns of Anti-Democratic Thought*, New York: Macmillan, 1949.

Sweezy, Paul M., "The illusion of the 'managerial revolution,'" *Science and Society*, 1942, 6, 1-23.

Veblen, Thorstein, *Absentee Ownership and Business Enterprise in Recent Times*, New York: Viking, 1915.

Veblen, Thorstein, *The Engineers and the Price System*, New York: Viking Press, 1933.

4. The Structure of Bureaucracy

Authority and Decision-Making

Black, Duncan, "The elasticity of committee decisions with an altering size of majority," *Econometrica*, 1948, 16, 262-270.

Black, Duncan, "On the rationale of group decision-making," *Journal of Political Economy*, 1948, 56, 23-34.

Bryce, James, "Obedience," *Studies in History and Jurisprudence*, New York: Oxford University Press, 1901, 463-502.

Chardon, Henri, *Le Pouvoir Administratif*, Paris: Perrin et Cie., 1911.

Cole, Taylor, *The Canadian Bureaucracy: A Study of Canadian Civil Servants and Other Public Employees, 1939–1947*, Durham, N. C.: Duke University Press, 1949.

Committee on Public Administration Cases, *The Disposal of the Aluminum Plants*, Washington, D. C., 1948, mimeo.

Committee on Public Administration Cases, *The Latin American Proceeding*, Washington, D. C., 1949.

Committee on Public Administration Cases, *Smith and the OPA: A Regional Administrator Resigns*, Washington, D. C., 1949.

Demeter, K., *Das Deutsche Heer und Seine Offiziere*, Berlin: Verlag von Reimar Hobling, 1935.

Doucet, Robert, "La bureaucratie et les bureaucrates," *Journal des Economistes*, 1919, 6 ser., 61, 209-227.

Duguit, Léon, "La question de la coexistence de la responsabilité de l'état et de la responsabilité personnelle des fonctionnaires," *Revue du Droit Public et de la Science Politique*, 1923, 40, 23-40.

Finer, Herman, "Administrative responsibility in democratic government," *Public Administration Review*, 1941, 1, 335-350.

Friedrich, Carl J., "Public policy and the nature of administrative responsibility," in C. J. Friedrich and E. S. Mason, eds., *Public Policy*, Cambridge: Harvard University Press, 1940, 3-24.

Gibbon, I. G., "The official and his authority," *Public Administration*, 1926, 4, 81-94.

Gladden, E. N., *Civil Service Staff Relationships*, London: William Hodge, 1943.

Katona, George, *Psychological Analysis of Economic Behavior*, New York: McGraw-Hill, 1951. Part 3, "Business Behavior."

Laski, H. J., *The Limitations of the Expert*, Fabian Tract No. 235, London, 1931.

Lasswell, H. D., "The relation of ideological intelligence to public policy," *Ethics*, 1942, 53, 25-34.

Leigh, Robert D., "Politicians vs. bureaucrats," *Harper's Magazine*, January 1945, 97-105.

Leighton, Alexander, *Human Relations in a Changing World: Observations on the Use of the Social Sciences*, New York: Dutton, 1949.

Levitan, David M., "The responsibility of administrative officials in a democratic society," *Political Science Quarterly*, 1946, 61, 562-598.

Leys, Wayne A. R., "Ethics and administrative discretion," *Public Administration Review*, 1943, 3, 10-23.

Macmahon, Arthur W., Millett, John D., and Ogden, Gladys, *The Administration of Federal Work Relief*, Chicago: Public Administration Service, 1941.

McCamy, James L., "Analysis of the process of decision-making," *Public Administration Review*, 1947, 7, 41-48.

Merton, Robert K., "The role of applied social science in the formation of policy: a research memorandum," *Philosophy of Science*, 1949, 16, 161-181.

Merton, Robert K., "Role of the intellectual in public bureaucracy," *Social Forces*, 1945, 23, 405-415.

Millspaugh, Arthur C., *Crime Control by the National Government*, Washington: The Brookings Institute, 1937, ch. 11.

Morgan, A. E., "Vitality and formalism in government," *Social Forces*, 1934–35, 13, 1-6.

Page, Charles H., "Bureaucracy and higher education," *The Journal of General Education*, 1951, 5, 91-100.

Selvin, Hanan C., "The interplay of social policy and social research in housing," *Journal of Social Issues*, 1951, Vol. 7, nos. 1-2, 172-185.

Shister, Joseph, "The locus of union control in collective bargaining," *Quarterly Journal of Economics*, 1946, 60, 513-545.

Shister, Joseph, "Trade union government: a formal analysis," *Quarterly Journal of Economics*, 1945, 60, 78-112.

Social Science Research Council, Committee on Public Administration, *Case Reports in Public Administration*, 1940.

South, E. B., "Some psychological aspects of committee work," *Journal of Applied Psychology*, 1927, 2, 348-368, 437-464.

Speier, Hans, "'The American Soldier' and the sociology of military organization," in R. K. Merton and P. F. Lazarsfeld, eds., *Continuities in Social Research*, Glencoe, Ill.: The Free Press, 1950.

Stewart, Donald D., *Local Board: A Study of the Place of Volunteer Participation in a Bureaucratic Organization*, Columbia University, Department of Sociology, unpublished Ph.D. dissertation, 1950.

Status Systems and Gradations of Prestige

Anon., "Informal social organization in the army," *American Journal of Sociology*, 1946, 51, 365-370.

Arensberg, Conrad M. and MacGregor, D., "Determination of morale in an industrial company," *Applied Anthropology*, 1942, 1, 12-34.

Blau, Peter M., *The Dynamics of Bureaucratic Structure: A Study of Interpersonal Relations in Two Government Agencies*, Columbia University, Department of Sociology, forthcoming Ph.D. dissertation.

Chapple, Eliot D., "Organization problems in industry," *Applied Anthropology*, 1941, 2-9.

Dicks, Henry V., *Psychological Foundations of the 'Wehrmacht,'* London, War Office, 1944.

Firey, Walter, "Informal organization and the theory of schism," *American Sociological Review*, 1948, 13, 15-24.

Freeman, Felton D., "The army as a social structure," *Social Forces*, 1948, 27, 78-83.

Gardner, B. B., "The factory as a social system," in W. F. Whyte, ed., *Industry and Society*, New York: McGraw-Hill, 1946.

Gardner, B. B. and Whyte, W. F., "The man in the middle: position and problems of the foreman," *Applied Anthropology*, 1945, 4, 1-28.

Gouldner, Alvin, *Bureaucracy and Industry*, Columbia University, Department of Sociology, forthcoming Ph.D. dissertation.

Homans, George, *The Human Group*, New York: Harcourt Brace, 1950.

Lewis, R., "Officer-enlisted men's relationships," *American Journal of Sociology*, 1947, 52, 410-419.

Mayo, Elton, *The Social Problems of an Industrial Civilization*, Boston: Harvard University Graduate School of Business Administration, 1945.

Merton, Robert K., "Patterns of influence: a study of interpersonal influence and of communications behavior in a local community," in P. F. Lazarsfeld and F. N. Stanton, eds., *Communications Research, 1948-1949*, New York: Harper and Brothers, 1949, 180-219.

Myers, Richard R., "Interpersonal relations in the building industry," *Applied Anthropology*, 1946, 1-7.

Page, Charles H., "Bureaucracy's other face," *Social Forces*, 1946, 25, 88-94.

Roethlisberger, F. J., "The foreman: master and victim of double talk," *Harvard Business Review*, 1945, 23, 283-298.

Shils, E. A., "Primary groups in the American army," in R. K. Merton and P. F. Lazarsfeld, eds., *Continuities in Social Research*, Glencoe, Ill.: The Free Press, 1950.

Shils, E. A., "The study of the primary group," in Daniel Lerner and H. D. Lasswell, eds., *The Policy Sciences*, Palo Alto: Stanford University Press, 1951.

Shils, E. A. and Janowitz, Morris, "Cohesion and disintegration of the Wehrmacht in World War II," *Public Opinion Quarterly*, 1948, 12, 280-315,

Spindler, C. Dearborn, "The military—a systematic analysis," *Social Forces*, 1948, 27, 83-88.

Whyte, William Foote, "Small groups and large organizations," in John H. Rohrer and Muzafer Sherif, eds., *Social Psychology at the Crossroads*, New York: Harper and Brothers, 1951, 297-312.

Wilson, Logan, *The Academic Man*, New York: Oxford University Press, 1942.

Wray, Donald E., "Marginal man of industry—the foreman," *American Journal of Sociology*, 1949, 54, 298-301.

Conflicts of Authority

Bennett, Vincent M., Jr., "Modern constitutional development: a challenge to administration," *Public Administration Review*, 1944, 4, 159-161.

Chamberlin, Neil W., *The Union Challenge to Management Control*, New York: Harper and Brothers, 1948.

Committee on Public Administration Cases, *The Air Coordinating Committee's Search and Rescue Program*, Washington, D. C., 1949, mimeo.

Committee on Public Administration Cases, *The Consumers' Counsel and the National Bituminous Coal Commission*, Washington, D. C., 1949, mimeo.

Committee on Public Administration Cases, *The Enactment of the FBI Retirement Bill*, Washington, D. C., 1949, mimeo.

Committee on Public Administration Cases, *The Feasibility Dispute: Determination of War Production Objectives for 1942 and 1943*, Washington, D. C., 1950, mimeo.

Committee on Public Administration Cases, *Gotham in the Air Age*, Washington, D. C., 1950, mimeo.

Howe, Irving and Widick, B. J., *The U.A.W. and Walter Reuther*, New York: Random House, 1949.

Muste, A. J., "Factional fights in trade unions," in J. B. S. Hardman, ed., *American Labor Dynamics*, New York: Harcourt, Brace, 1928.

The President's Committee on Administrative Management, *Administrative Management in the Government of the United States*, Washington: Government Printing Office, 1937.

Rogers, Lindsay, "Civilian control of military policy," *Foreign Affairs*, 1940, 18, 280-291.

Wallace, Schuyler C., *Federal Departmentalization, A Critique of Theories of Organization*, New York: Columbia University Press, 1941.

5. Recruitment and Advancement

Bendix, Reinhard, *Higher Civil Servants in American Society*, Boulder, Colorado: University of Colorado Press, 1949.

Corson, John J., "A case study in the selection of administrative personnel," *Public Personnel Review*, 1940, 1, 36-42.

Herring, E. Pendleton, *Federal Commissioners, A Study of Their Careers and Qualifications*, Cambridge: Harvard University Press, 1936.

Macmahon, Arthur W., "Senatorial confirmation," *Public Administration Review*, 1943, 3, 281-296.

Mills, C. Wright, "American business elite: a collective portrait based on the *Dictionary of American Biography*," *Journal of Economic History*, 1945 supplement to Vol. 5, 20-44.

Nightingale, R. T., *The Personnel of the British Foreign Office and Diplomatic Service, 1851–1921*, Fabian Tract No. 232, London, 1930.

Oxenfeldt, Alfred R., *New Firms and Free Enterprise*, Washington: American Council on Public Affairs, 1943, ch. 6.

P.E.P. (Political and Economic Planning, London), "Recruiting civil servants," *Planning, a Broadsheet*, No. 266, May 1947.

Rabany, C., "Les types sociaux—le fonctionnaire," *Revue Générale d'Administration*, 1907, 5-28.

Sayre, Wallace S., "The triumph of techniques over purpose," *Public Administration Review*, 1948, 4, 134-137.

Strong, Jr., Edward K., "The interests of forest service men," *Educational Psychology Measurement*, 1945, 5, 157-173.

Strong, Jr., Edward K., "Interests of senior and junior public administrators," *Journal of Applied Psychology*, 1946, 30, 55-71.

Swart, K. W., *Sale of Offices in the Seventeenth Century*, The Hague: Martinus Nijhoff, 1949.

Taussig, F. W. and Joslyn, C. S., *American Business Leaders*, New York: Macmillan, 1932.

Wallas, Graham, *Human Nature in Politics*, New York: Knopf, 1920, pt. II, ch. 3.

Warnotte, Daniel, "Bureaucratie et le fonctionnaire," *Revue de l'Institut de Sociologie*, 1937, 17, 219-260.

Warren, R. L., "The Naval Reserve officer: a study in assimilation," *American Sociological Review*, 1946, 11, 202-11.

White, Leonard D., Bland, Charles H., Sharp, Walter R., and Marx, F. Morstein, *Civil Service Abroad: Great Britain, Canada, France, Germany*, New York: McGraw-Hill, 1935.

White, Leonard D., *Further Contributions to the Prestige Value of Public Employment*, Chicago: University of Chicago Press, 1932.

White, Leonard D., *The Prestige Value of Public Employment*, Chicago: University of Chicago Press, 1929.

6. The Bureaucrat

Beard, Miriam, *A History of the Business Man*, New York: Macmillan, 1938.

Clemens, Severus, *Der Beruf des Diplomaten*, Berlin: Deutsche Verlagsgesellschaft für Politik und Geschichte, 1926.

Finer, Herman, "The administrative class: past and future," *Public Administration Review*, 1942, 2, 259-265.

Fisher, Richard, *The American Executive*, Hoover Institute Studies, Ser. B, Elite Studies, No. 5, forthcoming.

Fisher, Richard, and Summers, Thomas, *The British Executive*, Hoover Institute Studies, Ser. B, Elite Studies, No. 6, forthcoming.

Fisher, Richard, and de Messières, Claude, *The French Executive*, Hoover Institute Studies, Ser. B, Elite Studies, No. 7, forthcoming.

Glover, John D. and Hower, Ralph M., eds., *The Administrator*, Chicago: Richard D. Irwin, 1949.

Gouldner, Alvin, ed., *Studies in Leadership*, New York: Harper and Brothers, 1950.

Hardman, J. B. S. and Neufeld, Maurice F., eds., *The House of Labor: Internal Operations of American Unions*, New York: Prentice-Hall, 1951.

Henry, William E., "The business executive: the psychodynamics of a social role," *American Journal of Sociology*, 1949, 54, 286-291.

Hiller, E. T., "Social structure in relation to the person," *Social Forces*, 1937, 16, 34-44.

Hughes, Everett C., "Institutional office and the person," *American Journal of Sociology*, 1937, 43, 404-413.

Hughes, Everett C., "Personality types and the division of labor," *American Journal of Sociology*, 1928, 33, 754-768.

Jenkins, W. O., "Review of leadership studies with particular reference to military problems," *Psychological Bulletin*, January 1947, 54-79.

Knight, Max, *The German Executive*, Hoover Institute Studies, Ser. B, Elite Studies, No. 4, forthcoming.

Lasswell, H. D., *Power and Personality*, New York: Norton, 1948.

Lasswell, H. D. and Almond, G., "Aggressive behavior by clients toward public relief administrators: a configurative analysis," *American Political Science Review*, 1934, 28, 643-655.

Lasswell, H. D., *Psychopathology and Politics*, Chicago: University of Chicago Press, 1930.

Lederer, Emil, *The Problem of the Modern Salaried Employee: Its Theoretical and Statistical Basis*. A translation for the Works Progress Administration and the Department of Social Science, Columbia University, 1937, mimeo.

Leighton, Alexander, *The Governing of Men*, Princeton: Princeton University Press, 1945.

Lerner, Daniel, *et al.*, *The Nazi Elite*, with an introduction by Franz L. Neumann, Hoover Institute studies, ser. B: Elite studies, No. 3, August, 1951.

Levitan, D. M., "Political ends and administrative means," *Public Administration Review*, 1943, 3, 353-359.

Lowenthal, Leo and Guterman, Norbert, *The Prophets of Deceit*, New York: Harper and Brothers, 1949.

Lyel, P. G., "Some psychological factors in public administration," *Journal of Public Administration*, 1930, 8, 131-147.

Mills, C. Wright, *The New Men of Power: America's Labor Leaders*, New York: Harcourt, Brace, 1948.

Neumann, Sigmund, "Leadership: institutional and personal," *Journal of Politics*, 1941, 3, 33-53.

Pigors, Paul, *Leadership or Domination*, New York: Houghton Mifflin, 1935.

Reismann, Leonard, "A study of role conceptions in bureaucracy," *Social Forces*, 1949, 27, 305-10.

Robson, William Alexander, ed., *The British Civil Servant*, London: G. Allen and Unwin, 1937.

Schueller, George K., *The Politburo*, with an introduction by Harold H. Fisher, Hoover Institute studies, ser. B: Elite studies, No. 2, August, 1951.

Shartle, Carroll L., "Leadership and executive performance," *Personnel*, 1949, 25, 370-380.

Shartle, Carroll L., "Studies in naval leadership, part I," in Harold Guetzkow, ed., *Groups, Leadership and Men: Research in Human Relations*, Pittsburgh: Carnegie Press, 1951.

Speier, Hans, *The Salaried Employee in German Society*. A translation of *Die*

Angestellten in der Deutschen Gesellschaft, for the Works Progress Administration and the Department of Social Science, Columbia University, New York, 1939, mimeo.

Speier, Hans, "The salaried employee in modern society," *Social Research,* 1934, 1, 111-133.

Staïnov, P., *Le Fonctionnaire,* Paris: Bibliothèque de l'Institut International de Droit Public, 1933.

Stewart, Donald D., "The place of volunteer participation in a bureaucratic organization," *Social Forces,* 1951, 29, 311-17.

Stogdill, Ralph M., "Personal factors associated with leadership: a survey of the literature," *Journal of Psychology,* 1948, 25, 35-71.

Strong, Jr., Edward K., "Differences in interests among public administrators," *Journal of Applied Psychology,* 1947, 31, 18-38.

Strong, Jr., Edward K., "Interests of public administrators," *Public Personnel Review,* 1945, 6, 166-173.

Walker, E. Ronald, *The Australian Economy in War and Reconstruction,* New York: Oxford University Press, 1947.

7. Social Pathologies of Bureaucracy

Allen, C. K., *Bureaucracy Triumphant,* London, 1931.

Beck, James M., *Our Wonderland of Bureaucracy,* New York: Macmillan, 1932.

Carr, Cecil Thomas, "Bureaucracy," *Columbia University Quarterly,* April 1941, 33, 105-120.

Clark, John M., *Alternative to Serfdom,* New York: Knopf, 1948.

Committee on Public Administration Cases, *The Development of Self-Insurance Plans in the Treasury Department, 1918–1937,* Washington, D. C., 1949, mimeo.

Crider, John H., *The Bureaucrat,* Philadelphia and New York: Lippincott, 1944.

Finer, Hermann, "Critics of 'bureaucracy,'" *Political Science Quarterly,* 1945, 60, 100-112.

Hayek, Friedrich von, *Road to Serfdom,* Chicago: University of Chicago Press, 1944.

Juran, J. M., *Bureaucracy: A Challenge to Better Management,* New York: Harper and Brothers, 1944.

Mises, Ludwig von, *Bureaucracy,* New Haven: Yale University Press, 1944.

Niles, Mary C., *Middle Management,* New York: Harper and Brothers, 1941.

Sullivan, Lawrence, *The Dead Hand of Bureaucracy,* Indianapolis: Bobbs-Merrill, 1940.

8. Field Methods

Anderson, William and Gaus, John M., *Research in Public Administration,* Chicago: Public Administration Service, 1945.

Bales, Robert F., *Interaction Process Analysis,* Cambridge: Addison-Wesley Press, 1950.

Bingham, Walter V. D. and Bruce, V. Moore, *How to Interview,* New York: Harper and Brothers, 3rd ed., 1941.

Chapple, Eliot D., with the collaboration of Conrad M. Arensberg, "Measuring human relations: an introduction to the study of the interaction of individuals," *Genetic Psychology Monographs,* 1940, 22, No. 1.

Chapple, E. D. and Donald, Gordon, "A method for evaluating supervisory personnel," *Harvard Business Review,* 1946, 24, 197-214.

Gardner, Burleigh B. and Whyte, William F., "Methods for the study of human relations in industry," *American Sociological Review*, 1946, 11, 506-512.

Glaser, Comstock, *Administrative Procedure, A Practical Handbook for the Administrative Analyst*, Washington: American Council on Public Affairs, 1941.

Gordon, Joel, "Operating statistics as a tool of management," *Public Administration Review*, 1944, 4, 189-196.

Gottschalk, Louis, Kluckhohn, Clyde, and Angell, Robert C., *The Use of Personal Documents in History, Anthropology, and Sociology*, New York: Social Science Research Council, 1945.

Hyman, Herbert, "Interviewing as a scientific procedure," in Daniel Lerner and H. D. Lasswell, eds., *The Policy Sciences*, Palo Alto: Stanford University Press, 1951.

Jahoda, Marie, Deutsch, Morton, and Cook, Stuart W., *Research Methods in Social Relations*, New York: The Dryden Press, 1951.

Jennings, Helen Hall, *Leadership and Isolation: A Study of Personality in Inter-Personal Relations*, New York: Longmans, Green, 1950, 2d ed.

Kendall, Patricia L. and Lazarsfeld, Paul F., "Problems of survey analysis," in R. K. Merton and P. F. Lazarsfeld, eds., *Continuities in Social Research*, Glencoe, Ill.: The Free Press, 1950.

Lazarsfeld, Paul F., "Use of panels in social research," *Proceedings, American Philosophical Society*, 1948, 92, 405-410.

Lazarsfeld, Paul F. and Barton, Allen H., "Qualitative measurement in the social sciences: classification, typologies and indices," in Daniel Lerner and H. D. Lasswell, eds., *The Policy Sciences*, Palo Alto: Stanford University Press, 1951.

Lazarsfeld, Paul F. and Rosenberg, Morris, eds., *Selected Readings in Social Research Methodology*, Glencoe, Ill.: The Free Press, to be published in 1952.

Likert, Rensis, "The sample interview survey," in Wayne Dennis, ed., *Current Trends in Social Psychology*, Pittsburgh: University of Pittsburgh Press, 1947, 196-225.

McNemar, Quinn, "Opinion-attitude methodology," *Psychological Bulletin*, 1946, 43, 289-374. (Includes extensive bibliography.)

Merton, Robert K., "Selected problems of field work in the planned community," *American Sociological Review*, 1947, 12, 304-312.

Moreno, J. L., with the collaboration of Helen Hall Jennings, *Who Shall Survive? A New Approach to the Problem of Human Interrelations*, Nervous and Mental Disease Monograph Series No. 58, Washington, D. C.: Nervous and Mental Disease Publishing Company, 1934.

The OSS Assessment Staff, *The Assessment of Men*, New York: 1948.

Parten, Mildred B., *Surveys, Polls, and Samples*, New York: Harper and Brothers, 1950.

Ridley, Clarence E. and Simon, Herbert A., *Measuring Municipal Activities*, Chicago: International City Managers Association, 1938.

Rogers, Carl R., "Nondirective method as a technique in social research," *American Journal of Sociology*, 1945, 50, 279-283.

Rogers, Maria, "Problems of human relations in industry," *Sociometry*, 1946, 9, 350-371.

Stein, Harold, "Preparation of case studies: the problem of abundance," *American Political Science Review*, 1951, 45, 479-487.

Steinzor, Bernard, "The development and evaluation of a measure of social interaction," *Human Relations*, 1949, 2, 103-122.

Stogdill, Ralph M., "The sociometry of working relationships in formal organizations," *Sociometry*, 1949, 12, 276-286.

Stogdill, Ralph M. and Shartle, Carroll L., "Methods for determining patterns of leadership behavior in relation to organization structure and objectives," *Journal of Applied Psychology*, 1948, 32, 286-291.

United Nations Educational, Scientific, and Cultural Organization, *Contemporary Political Science: A Survey of Methods, Research, and Teaching*, Publication No. 426 of the UNESCO, Paris, 1950.

Waldo, Dwight, *The Administrative State, A Study of the Political Theory of American Public Administration*, New York: Ronald, 1948.

Waldo, Dwight, "Organizational analysis: some notes on methods and criteria," *Public Administration Review*, 1947, 7, 236-244.

Webb, Sidney and Beatrice, *Methods of Social Study*, London: Longmans, Green, 1932.

Whyte, William F., "Challenge to political scientists," *American Political Science Review*, 1943, 37, 692-697.

9. Comparative Bureaucracy

Ch'ien, Tuan-shêng, *The Government and Politics of China*, Cambridge: Harvard University Press, 1950.

Eberhard, Wolfram, *A History of China*, (trans. E. W. Dickes), Berkeley and Los Angeles: University of California Press, 1950.

Eberhard, Wolfram, "Some sociological remarks on the system of provincial administration during the period of the five dynasties," *Studia Serica*, 1949, 7, 1-18.

Kracke, E. A., Jr., "Family vs. merit in Chinese civil service examinations under the Empire," *Harvard Journal of Asiatic Studies*, 1947, 10, 103-123.

Latourette, Kenneth Scott, *The Chinese: Their History and Culture*, New York: Macmillan, 1946, ch. 14.

Rotours, Robert des, *Traité des Fonctionnaires et Traité de l'Armée*, traduits de la *Nouvelle Histoire des T'Ang*, chs. 46-50, 2 vols., Leyden: E. J. Brill, 1947.

Vinacke, Harold M., *A History of the Far East in Modern Times*, New York: F. S. Crofts & Co., 1933, ch. 1.

Weber, Max, *Religion of China*, (trans. by H. H. Gerth), Glencoe, Ill.: The Free Press, 1951.

Wittfogel, Karl A. and Chia-Sheng, Feng, *History of Chinese Society, Liao (907–1125)*, American Philosophical Society, Philadelphia. New York: Macmillan, 1949.

Wittfogel, Karl A., *Wirtschaft und Gesellschaft Chinas*, Leipzig: Hirschfeld, 1931. Section on "der Staat als übergreifendes Organ der agrikolen Produktion in China."

Hirschfeld, Otto, *Die kaiserliche Verwaltungsbeamten bis auf Diokletian*, 2nd ed., Berlin: Weidmann, 1905.

Homo, Léon, *Roman Political Institutions from City to State*, London: Kegan Paul, Trench, Trubner, 1929, esp. Book 4 (includes extensive bibliography).

Jolliffe, Richard O., *Phases of Corruption in Roman Administration in the Last Half-Century of the Roman Republic*, Menasha, Wis.: George Banta, 1919.

Mattingly, Harold, *The Imperial Civil Service of Rome*, Cambridge: The University Press, 1910.

Pflaum, Hans Georg, *Essai sur Les Procurateurs Equestres sous Le Haut-Empire Romain*, Paris: Librairie d'Amérique et d'Orient Adrien Maisonneuve, 1950.

Rostovtzeff, M., *The Social and Economic History of the Roman Empire*, Oxford: Clarendon Press, 1926.

Schiller, A. Arthur, "Bureaucracy and the Roman law," *Seminar*, Annual Extraordinary Number of *The Jurist*, 1947, 5, 26-48.

Schiller, A. Arthur, "The jurists and the praefects of Rome," *Revue Internationale des Droits de L'Antiquité*, 1949, 2, 319-359.

Ashby, Eric, *Scientist in Russia*, London, 1947.

Batsell, Walter, *Soviet Rule in Russia*, New York, 1929.

Bettelheim, C., *La Planification Soviétique*, Paris, n.d.

Bienstock, Gregory, Schwartz, Solomon M., and Yugow, Aaron, *Management in Russian Industry and Agriculture*, London: Oxford University Press, 1944.

Curtiss, J. S., *Church and State in Russia, 1900–1917*, New York: Columbia University Press, 1940.

Moore, Jr., Barrington, "The influence of ideas on politics as shown in the collectivization of agriculture in Russia," *American Political Science Review*, 1947, 41, 733-743.

Moore, Jr., Barrington, *Soviet Politics: the Dilemma of Power*, Cambridge: Harvard University Press, 1950.

Nemzer, Louis, "The Kremlin's professional staff: the apparatus of the Central Committee, Communist Party of the Soviet Union," *American Political Science Review*, 1950, 44, 64-85.

Vucinich, Alexander, "The structure of factory control in the Soviet Union," *American Sociological Review*, 1950, 15, 179-186.

10. Some Literary Portraits of Bureaucracy

Balzac, Honoré de, *The Government Clerks*.

Courteline, Georges, *Messieurs les Rondes-de-Cuir*, Paris: Flammarion, 1927.

Dickens, Charles, *Bleak House*.

Dickens, Charles, *Little Dorrit*.

Gogol, Nikolai, *The Government Inspector*, (trans. D. J. Campbell), London: Sylvan Press, 1947.

Kafka, Franz, *The Castle*, New York: Knopf, 1941.

Kafka, Franz, *The Trial*, New York: Knopf, 1950.

Riemkasten, Felix, *Der Bonze*, Berlin: Brunnen-Verlag, 1930.

Shanks, Edward, *The Old Indispensables*, London: M. Secker, 1919.

Trollope, Anthony, *Autobiography*, New York: Oxford University Press, 1923.

Trollope, Anthony, *The Three Clerks*, New York: Oxford University Press, 1929.

Wolfe, Humbert, *Dialogues and Monologues*, New York: Knopf, 1929, ch. on "Public servants in fiction," 137-172.